J. Ranade Workstation Series

To order, or to receive additional information on these or any other McGraw-Hill titles, please call 1-800-822-8158 in the United States. In other countries, please contact your local McGraw-Hill representative.

BC15XXA

AIX/6000
System Guide

Frank Cervone

McGraw-Hill

New York   San Francisco   Washington, D.C.   Auckland   Bogotá
Caracas   Lisbon   London   Madrid   Mexico City   Milan
Montreal   New Delhi   San Juan   Singapore
Sydney   Tokyo   Toronto

Library of Congress Cataloging-in-Publication Data

Cervone, Frank
 AIX/6000 system guide / Frank Cervone.
   p. cm. -- (J. Ranade workstation series)
 Includes index
 ISBN 0-07-024129-5 (pbk.)
 1. AIX (Computer file) 2. Operating systems (Computers) 3. IBM
RS/6000 Workstation. I. Title. II. Series.
QA76.76.063C4 1995
005.4'469—dc20   95-23306
                    CIP

McGraw-Hill

A Division of The McGraw·Hill Companies

 3 4 5 6 7 8 9 0 AGM/AGM 9 0 0 9 8 7

ISBN 0-07-024129-5

*The sponsoring editor for this book was Jerry Papke, the editing
supervisor was David E. Fogarty, and the production supervisor was
Pamela A. Pelton. It was set in Century Schoolbook by Ron Painter of
McGraw-Hill's Professional Book Group composition unit.*

Printed and bound by Quebecor/Martinsburg.

This book is printed on acid-free paper.

To Nonnie

Contents

Part 1   AIX Overview

Part 2   Basic Operating System Usage

Preface

Most people do not read the prefaces to books for one simple reason—they are interminably boring.[1] And this preface will be no exception. Just kidding.

All that most people want from a preface is a brief explanation of what the book is about and why they should buy it; not an eight-page autobiography complete with the philosophical musings of the author. So, here it goes:

Buy this book because it explains, in a simple and straightforward manner, the vast majority of things you will need to know in order to run or use AIX. Pretty simple, no?

This book contains three parts which are divided into fourteen chapters. Part 1 is an overview of AIX which

Explains the RS/6000 in general terms (Chapter 1)

Details specifics about using AIX for the first time (Chapter 2)

Presents an overview of the architecture of AIX (Chapter 3)

Part 2 details the commands and functions of AIX in separate chapters devoted to

Starting and stopping AIX (Chapter 4)

Files and directories (Chapter 5)

File systems and logical volumes (Chapter 6)

Processes, queues, and jobs (Chapter 7)

Printing (Chapter 8)

Users, groups, and system security (Chapter 9)

Hardware management (Chapter 10)

Networking (Chapter 11)

---

[1]The prefaces, not the people.

Part 3 discusses vi (Chapter 12), the Korn shell (Chapter 13), and miscellaneous user commands (Chapter 14). The appendixes discuss some basic problem-solving techniques and tools, error log identifiers, and LED indicators.

This book is comprehensive in the subject areas which are treated so that the users, whether novice or advanced, should find it a useful addition to their bookshelf.

Now, what is not covered? I have not discussed any of the games that come with AIX.[2] Really, you don't care about this, do you? I thought not.[3]

On a more serious note, this book does not discuss application developmnt in the UNIX environment. For that, I recommend the book *UNIX Developer's Tool Kit* by Kevin Leininger (McGraw-Hill, 1993). For a detailed discussion of networking, I recommend *TCP/IP: Architecture, Protocols, and Implementation* by Sidnie Feit (McGraw-Hill, 1993). On the Korn shell, *KornShell Programming Tutorial* by Barry Rosenberg (Hewlett-Packard, 1991).

This book does not explicitly discuss SMIT, which is the menu-driven sysem interface tool. Quite honestly, SMIT is very easy to use and really does not need much explanation. I thought it more useful to discuss what SMIT was actually doing behind the scenes.

In any case, whether you have bought or borrowed this book, I hope you enjoy it and find it useful as you explore the AIX operating system.

Frank Cervone

---

[2]These include arithmetic, back, bj, craps, fish, fortune, hangman, moo, quiz, ttt, and wump. Oops, I guess this means I did.

[3]But, of course, since they are part of the system, it wouldn't be a bad idea to make sure they work.

Acknowledgments

Special thanks must go to

Jay Ranade, Jerry Papke, and Dave Fogarty for their patience and suggestions, especially when this went way over deadline

Bob Miller and Rocky Woodson, for general support

Steve Cooper, for everything

Jeff Graubart-Cervone, who, regardless of the circumstances, has been and remains a very good friend

Trademarks

AIX, AIXwindows, MVS, System/370, System/390, ES/9000, POWER Architecture, InfoExplorer, Netview, SNA, and VTAM are trademarks of International Business Machines, Incorporated.

Digital, DEC, DEC VT100, DEC VT200, and Alpha OSF/1 are trademarks of the Digital Equipment Corporation.

Ethernet is a trademark of Xerox Corporation.

IEEE and POSIX are trademarks of the Institute of Electrical and Electronic Engineers.

INed is a trademark of INTERACTIVE Systems Corporation.

ISO is a trademark of the International Organization for Standardization.

Motif, OSF/Motif, OSF, and OSF/1 are trademarks of the Open Software Foundation.

NCS and Network Computing System are trademarks of Hewlett-Packard Company.

NFS, Network File System, SunOS, and Solaris are trademarks of Sun Microsystems, Inc.

System V and UNIX are trademarks of UNIX Systems Labs, Inc.

X11 and X Window System are trademarks of the Massachusetts Institute of Technology.

X/Open is a trademark of the X/Open Corporation.

Wyse is a trademark of WYSE Corporation.

AIX/6000
System Guide

AIX Overview

Introduction
to the RS/6000

The RS/6000 along with its companion operating system, AIX/6000, is IBM's solution for open-systems RISC-based computing.

Although one product line, the physical packaging of the RS/6000 is divided into four "types," desktop (200-series), workstation (300-series), deskside (500-series), and rack-mounted (900-series).

1.1 Hardware

The IBM RS/6000 is based on the RISC (reduced instruction set computing) model as opposed to CISC (complex instruction set computing) model. In its most pure form, RISC-based computing implements a very limited number of instructions. Complex instructions are coded in the application based on sequences of the basic functions defined. Although the hardware architecture is relatively simple, application coding can be complex. With the limited number of instructions, all of them can be, and usually are, hardwired into the processor. Typically, most instructions are executed in one machine cycle (clock tick).

CISC-based computing employs a large instruction set that defines most operations which can be performed on the hardware. This simplifies application coding but complicates the hardware architecture. The volume of instructions usually prevents all of them from being wired into the hardware, so an additional layer, referred to as microcode, is introduced. This microcode, which is typically stored in nonvolatile storage in the machine, provides the interface for implementing the more complex machine instructions on the actual hardware. The Intel 80x86 processor is an example of a CISC processor.

The external differences between the two approaches, however, have become blurred. Although the RS/6000 is a RISC-based machine, it has more instructions that the original System/360 mainframe, which is considered by most to be a CISC-based machine. Indeed, the number of instructions on the RISC 6000 processor approaches the number on the CISC 80x86 processors. The differences between the two, while interesting, are for the most part not particularly meaningful in everyday use. Both are means to the same end—getting the work done.

1.1.1 POWER architecture

All IBM RS/6000 machines use the same RISC architecture which is referred to as "the *POWER* architecture" (Performance Optimization with Enhanced RISC). The POWER architecture is a superscalar architecture; that is, multiple instructions are issued and executed simultaneously. Instead of the traditional, single execution unit, the POWER architecture (Fig. 1.1) uses three separate execution units: a branch processor, a floating-point processor, and a fixed-point processor. In addition, instruction pipelining is used to keep all of the processors as busy as possible. Pipelines are similar to assembly lines; while the first stage is decoding an instruction, the second stage is moving data into storage. Additionally, the third stage is executing an instruction while the fourth stage moves its result to the desired storage location (Fig. 1.2). Using these two techniques, it is possible for up to four instruction operations to occur within the same machine cycle: a fixed-point calculation, a floating-point operation, a branch, and a condition code operation.

Each processor in the POWER architecture can set a condition code based on the last operation performed. To prevent contention and increase the degree of parallel activity, condition codes are implemented in eight independent fields. By using multiple condition codes, which are separately defined for each processor, interlocks are avoided and better throughput is achieved.

The POWER architecture implements several instructions not usually found in RISC-based machines. For example, the floating-point processor implements add, subtract, multiply, and divide instructions. Unique to the POWER architecture, the multiply-add instruction allows a double precision floating-point add and double precision floating-point multiply to complete within the same clock cycle.

Additional non–floating-point instructions include the load-and-update and store-and-update instructions which allow data to be moved while an address register is updated. Five string manipulation instructions are provided: load string indexed, load string immediate, store string indexed, store string immediate, and load string and compare byte indexed. None of these instructions have restrictions on how the data is aligned.

1.1.2 Memory implementation

The POWER architecture currently supports up to 4 Gbytes (gigabytes) of main storage. Up to 16 million 256 Mbyte (megabyte) segments are available, resulting in a total virtual storage size of 256 Tbytes (terabytes).

Two caches are implemented: one for data and the other for instructions. During each machine cycle, up to four instructions may be fetched from the in-

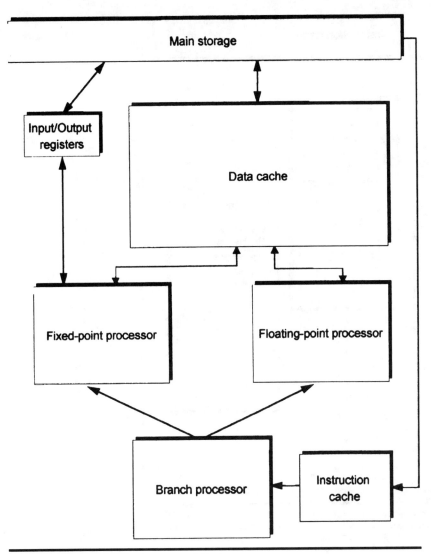

Figure 1.1 POWER RISC processor architecture.

struction cache. These are in turn fed into an instruction buffer which is used by the branch processor to look ahead for upcoming branches. The data cache, which is 32K on smaller machines and 64K in larger ones, has both store-back and reload buffers. These allow the CPU to continue, using data in registers or the cache, while memory is being accessed. Furthermore, the store-back cache defers updating main storage until the data in the cache must be replaced.

Memory interleaving is used to access two different storage cards concurrently. The four-way interleaving on the RS/6000 allows access to two words of memory from two cards, for a total of four 32-bit words, during each machine cycle.

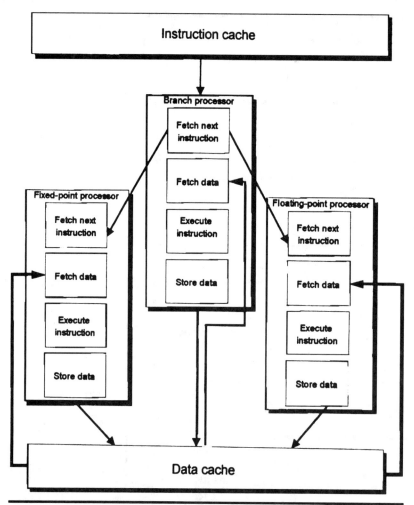

Figure 1.2 Pipelined processors enhance POWER RISC performance. All three processors (branch, fixed-point, and floating point) execute concurrently. Given an optimally designed program, each phase in every processor will continually have an operation ready to execute.

To optimize the implementation of the large virtual storage size, virtual storage address translation is performed in separate instruction and data *translation look-aside buffers* (TLBs). The 128-entry data TLB contains information on page protection and data locking in addition to address translation. It is double-linked to the 32-entry instruction TLB, which helps to alleviate thrashing. By using an inverted page table, a significant amount of real storage can be reclaimed that is typically occupied by page translation tables. Instead of using traditional page tables, which map all of the virtual storage in a segment to a real address, the inverted page table maps real storage only to allocated virtual storage.

Finally, an extensive range of registers is provided: thirty-two 32-bit general purpose registers, thirty-two 64-bit floating point registers, sixteen segment registers, six floating-point rename registers, and two floating-point divide registers.

1.1.3 Devices

The RS/6000 supports a wide variety of input/output (I/O) devices. The I/O system architecture is based upon the IBM PC's Micro Channel Architecture but with some additions. Streaming Data Transfer (SDT) Mode has been added (burst mode in System/370 parlance) which increases the capacity of the I/O bus from 20 Mbytes to 40 Mbytes. In addition to data and address parity checking, synchronous exception handling is supported. This allows exceptions to be signalled during the machine cycle in which they are detected.

For interaction with the user, IBM ASCII terminals (3151, 3161, 3163, 3164) and several non-IBM ASCII terminals are supported by AIX. This includes terminals by Digital Equipment Corporation (DEC VT100, VT220, VT320, and VT330) and Wyse (WYSE 30, 50, 60, and 3500). Several types of graphics adapters are available: grayscale, color, 8-bit 3-dimensional, and 24-bit 3-dimensional. These facilitate the connection of monochrome (8503, 8507, 8508) and color graphics displays (5081-16, 6091-19, 6091-23, 8512, 8513, 8514). Support for the X-windows environment is provided by two Xstation models, the 120 and 130.

Printed output is supported on dot-matrix, laser, and color plotters.

Internal 3.5-in diskette drives are supported on all RS/6000 models. 5.25-in diskette drives are supported internally on rack-mounted systems, and externally on all others.

CD-ROM drives capable of holding up to 600M of information are available either internally, on the 500 and 900 series machines, or externally.

Fixed disks are available in a wide of range of storage sizes—from 160 Mbytes to 2 Gbytes. Externally attached units are available which allow the easy transfer of data from one system to another.

Three types of tape devices are supported on the 900-series: 8 mm, $\frac{1}{4}$-in, and $\frac{1}{2}$-in 9-track. The 8 mm (holding up to 2.3 Gbytes) and $\frac{1}{4}$-in (up to 150 Mbytes) formats are supported on all models of the RS/6000.

Communication adapters include 8-, 16-, and 64-port asynchronous controllers for ASCII terminals, SCSI device adapters for connecting disks and tape, and Ethernet and token-ring adapters for connecting to local area networks. Connection to wide area networks is available through the 4-Port Multiprotocol Adapter or the X.25 Interface Co-Processor. The 3270 Connection Adapter allows the RS/6000 to connect to a System/390 mainframe as a single 3270-type terminal. The Block Multiplexor Channel Adapter allows the the RS/6000 to connect to a S/390 mainframe channel in Block Multiplexor Mode. Finally, the FDDI Adapter allows the RS/6000 to connect to *Fiber Distributed Data Interface* (FDDI) networks.

To facilitate the use of the RS/6000 as a workstation, a three-button mouse and input tablet are available. A digitizer (the 5084) provides large-scale digitizing functions.

1.2   Software

AIX/6000[1] is just one of the members of IBM's UNIX-based operating system family. Companion versions of AIX are currently available for IBM-compatible personal computers via AIX PC/2, the IBM RT with AIX/RT,[2] PowerPC machines with AIX Lite, and on IBM-compatible mainframes with AIX/ESA[3] (or its predecessor AIX/370). Even though all of these operating systems share the same name, they are not 100 percent compatible; AIX/ESA and AIX/6000 are very closely related, but AIX PC/2 and AIX/RT are no more related to the other AIXs than any other UNIX-based operating system. However, before going into the story of AIX and its predecessors, a quick UNIX history lesson is in order.

1.2.1   A brief history of UNIX

The UNIX operating system was developed as a direct result of the failure of another operating system development project. The Multics project was undertaken by the Massachusetts Institute of Technology (MIT), General Electric (later, Honeywell) and Bell Labs (AT&T) in the early 1960s to create the first operating system written almost exclusively in a high-level language. In addition, the primary interface to the system was to be interactive instead of batch-oriented. At the time Multics was developed, the only high-level language that could even come close to doing what was necessary was PL/I. Unfortunately, the PL/I compilers of the time did not generate very efficient code, which resulted in an operating system that performed very poorly. In addition, the development of the operating system proved to be more complicated than initially envisioned.

Even though Multics was quite advanced for its time, the inherent performance problems and frequent project delays in the initial versions soured the management of AT&T on the operating system and they withdrew their funding and personnel from the project.

One of the developers from AT&T, Ken Thompson, had developed a game on Multics called *Space Travel*. With the loss of the Multics system, it was impossible to run the program. So, using an unwanted Digital Equipment Corporation (DEC) PDP-7, he began implementing the program on the new machine. However, the operating system of the PDP-7 was very primitive and lacked many of the programming niceties that had been available under Multics. To solve these and other problems with the system, Thompson soon ended up writ-

---

[1]The PowerPCs run the same version of AIX as do the RS/6000's.

[2]This machine is no longer manufactured.

[3]IBM has announced plans for multiprocessing versions of AIX; for tightly coupled processors as AIX/SMP and for loosely coupled processors as AIX/Cluster, both due in June 1995. A system for embedded systems, AIX Runtime is due in January 1996.

ing a small, but programmer-friendly operating system for the machine. But the lack of good high-level programming languages necessitated that the operating system be written in PDP-7 assembler language.

In order to continually enhance and develop the operating system, it was necessary to find a more practical use for the operating system other than running game programs. It just so happened, that in 1970, the patent department at AT&T needed a text processing system. This was the opportunity for which Thompson had been waiting. With a real application in hand, Thompson received approval to port the operating system to a larger machine, the PDP-11/20.

One of the first problems the developer faced were the differences in the assembler languages between the two machines. Although the transfer of the operating system code to the PDP-11/20 was performed in assembler language, Thompson developed a language which was to be used for any further enhancements to the system, *Basic Combined Programming Language* (BCPL). After several improvements, it became known as simply B.

Another developer at AT&T, Dennis Ritchie, assisted Thompson in his conversion of the operating system to the PDP-11/20. During the process, Ritchie noticed several flaws in the basic design of B and soon developed a new high-level language, C. The creation of C was a major step in the development of UNIX. The advent of C allowed the developers to rewrite the operating system[4] in an efficient, high-level language. With this independence from machine-dependent assembler languages, it was possible to move the operating system from one platform to another with relative ease.

During the early 1970s, UNIX become quite popular within AT&T. But, because of the 1956 Consent Decree from the U.S. Department of Justice which barred AT&T from entering the computer system market, AT&T could not resell the operating system. In order to make some money from the operating system, in 1974, AT&T started to license UNIX to universities for a nominal fee.

The institution received a tape with the UNIX source code and instructions on how to set up the system. Installation and resolving problems with the software was the responsibility of the user. With this setup, two things occurred. First, a loyal following of users developed who shared enhancements and modifications to the system. Second, a plethora of varieties appeared. To further complicate matters, in 1977, AT&T began licensing the UNIX source code to hardware manufacturers, who also added their own enhancements and modifications to the base UNIX system.

Of the many varieties of UNIX to arise during this period, the most popular was the version produced by the University of California at Berkeley. This was due in great part to the work Dennis Ritchie performed while he took a sabbatical there. During his stay, he restructured the file system and rewrote the virtual memory manager. The Berkeley version became known as the Berkeley Software Distribution, or simply bsd.

---

[4]Except for a very small portion of the kernel.

With the divestiture of AT&T in 1984 and their entry into the computer system marketplace, AT&T began actively marketing its own version of UNIX, System V. However, the initial versions of System V did not offer many of the additional features the bsd implementations did, such as demand-paged memory. This, combined with an unsuccessful venture into computer hardware, caused AT&T's initial computer marketing efforts to falter.

Because of this and other market pressures, AT&T teamed up with Sun Microsystems to create a new unified version of UNIX. This resulted in a version (System V, Release 3.2) which consolidated AT&T's System V, Berkeley's 4.2 bsd, and Xenix.[5] The following release, System V Release 4 (SVR4), completed the consolidation of AT&T and Sun versions of UNIX (Fig. 1.3). This partnership was named UNIX International.

In response to this partnership, several of the other UNIX hardware and software vendors (IBM, Digital Equipment, and Hewlett-Packard) formed their own partnership, the Open Software Foundation (OSF). The goal of this group was to produce a UNIX that was vendor independent, i.e., not under AT&T control.

The underlying structure of the OSF-based operating systems is the Mach kernel which was developed at Carnegie-Mellon University. The Mach kernel is not inherently tied to UNIX. It provides basic operating system services which are presented to a user via an operating system shell which can, but does not have to, be UNIX. This distinct kernel-and-shell implementation prevents the user from directly interacting with the kernel. These concepts are the logical extension of the UNIX shell implementation, discussed in Chapter 2.

For the most part, the initial significance of the individual groups has diminished somewhat, although both continue their work. Because of vendors' increased acceptance of open system standards (Table 1.1), the primary goals of the groups (particularly OSF) have been obtained. Most current UNIX implementations (Table 1.2) incorporate the best of both System V and bsd functionality with proprietary extensions. Furthermore, the OSF group has provided the UNIX world with a standard graphical interface, Motif, and definition of a distributed computing environment (DCE).

In 1992, AT&T exited the operating system business by selling its UNIX development arm, UNIX Systems Laboratories (which had been spun off from Bell Labs in 1991), to Novell. What this will mean to the UNIX world at large remains to be seen.

1.2.2   A brief history of AIX

IBM's adventures in UNIX-based computing can be traced back to 1983 when the IBM RT PC was announced. This reduced instruction set computer (RISC), which included a UNIX-variant operating system called PC/IX, was greeted with almost universal disdain. In addition to being prone to hardware failure, the operating system was not particularly robust. Although it was based on AT&T's System V Release 2 (SVR2), it was not a complete implementation.

---

[5]A version of UNIX developed by Microsoft to run on PCs.

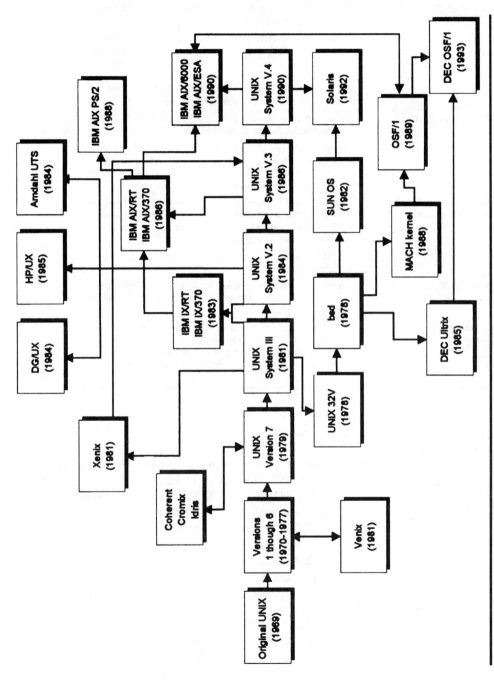

Figure 1.3 UNIX family tree. The lineages of the various UNIX versions can get quite complex.

TABLE 1.1   Open Systems Standards

Federal Information Processing Standard (FIPS) 151-1	Based on POSIX, this US Government standard includes further definitions of those areas left open in the POSIX standard.
International Standards Organization (ISO) Code Sets	Standardized definitions of how characters will be represented through the ASCII code set in various languages. Some of these sets include ISO 8859-1 (Latin 1, used for most European-based languages), ISO 8859-7 (Greek), ISO 8859-9 (Turkish), ISO 8859-6 (Arabic), ISO 8859-8 (Hebrew).
Network File System (NFS)	The de facto standard developed by SUN Systems for distributed file system access.
Open Software Foundation	A non-profit organization of several vendors and user-organizations that defines specifications and develops software to make available an open, portable application environment.
Portable Operating System for Computer Environments (POSIX) 1003.1	This standard, developed by the IEEE, defines a standard application interface to operating system services for input/output, file system access, and process management.
System V Interface Definition (SVID)	A USL specification of source-code level user and program interfaces.
Transmission Control Protocol/ Internet Protocol (TCP/IP)	A communications protocol suite which has become the standard for connecting computers and networks of differing architectures.
X/Open Portability Guide (XPG3) Issue 3	This interface definition simplifies the process of creating applications that recognize the local operating environment and apply the appropriate date, currency, language, and sort order of the country or locale.

Even worse were the many proprietary extensions that did not follow industry standards.

A companion operating system was released for those customers who wanted a mainframe-based UNIX-solution, IX/370. In addition to sharing the same lack of functionality that PC/IX had, IX/370 was totally dependent on a Virtual Machine (VM) operating system host. IX/370 could not directly control the machine; it needed VM to manage the hardware.

By the late 1980s, the IX operating system had developed an incredibly bad reputation. To rectify this, IBM renamed the operating system when the next major revision was made. This "new" operating system, AIX, was available initially on three platforms: RT (AIX/RT), IBM PS/2 (AIX PS/2), and 370-architecture machines (AIX/370).

When a new RISC machine, the RS/6000, was announced in 1989, AIX/6000 was the *only* operating system available for that platform.

Although they share the same moniker, two separate lineages have developed within this operating system family. As with IX, all of the AIX systems were initially based on SVR2. However, as the operating systems have been enhanced, AIX/370 to AIX/ESA and AIX/6000 v.3.1 to AIX/6000 v.3.2, they have

TABLE 1.2   UNIX Implementations

OS name	Vendor	Based on
A/UX	Apple	System V Release 2.2
AIX	IBM	System V Release 4
Coherent	Mark Williams	
Dynix	Sequent	
ESIX System V	ESIX	System V Release 3.2
HP/UX	Hewlett-Packard	System V Release 3.0
ix/386	Interactive	System V Release 3.2
LynxOS	Lynx	
Mach	Carnegie-Mellon	
MORE/bsd	Mt. Xinu	4.3 bsd
OSF/1	DEC	AIX/Mach
OSx	Pyramid	
PC UNIX	UHC	System V, Xenix, 4.3 bsd
QNX	Quantum	
Solaris	SunSoft	System V Release 4
SunOS	Sun	4.3 bsd
System V/386	SCO	System V, Xenix
Topix	Sequoia	
Ultrix	DEC	4.2 bsd
Unixware	Novell	System V Release 4
UTS	Amdahl	System V Release 3
Xenix	SCO	System V

been reengineered to conform more closely to industry standards, major bsd enhancements, and, as it has developed, the OSF system architecture.

Currently, only AIX/ESA is totally based on the OSF model. AIX/6000 is completely compatible with the OSF model, but is not based on its kernel. AIX PS/2 is still based on SVR2, and will probably remain so.

1.2.3   Related program products for AIX/6000

In addition to the standard operating system components (which IBM refers to as *Basic Operating System,* BOS) and the "standard" UNIX utilities (vi, sed, awk, NFS, UUCP, etc.), a number of related program products are available which extend the functionality of the system.

InfoExplorer is a hypertext documentation system. IBM can provide *all* of the RS/6000 and AIX/6000 documentation on-line through this program. Users can use InfoExplorer, in conjunction with InfoCrafter, to create local hypertext databases.

The High Availability Network File System (HANFS) provides for greater stability by using RS/6000 systems to back each other up, in the event of one system's failure.

To provide enhanced connectivity to Systems Network Architecture (SNA) networks, two products, AIX 3270 Host Connection Program/6000 (HCON) and AIX SNA Services/6000, are available. SNA services provide support for terminals (LU2), printers (LU1 and LU3), and Advanced Program-to-Program communication (APPC) with LU6.2. The RS/6000 appears to the host machine as a regular 3174-type controller (PU2) or as a peer system (PU2.1). HCON allows an ASCII terminal connected to the RS/6000 to emulate a 3270-type terminal. This program can be used to provide 3270-functionality to Transmission Control Protocol/Internet Protocol (TCP/IP) clients. RS/6000 users in conjunction with AIX SNA Services. AIX Network Management/6000 can be used with these two products to gather data at the RS/6000 and pass it to the mainframe NetView management system. (See Fig. 1.4.)

The RS/6000 can also function as a server for PC-based LANs with NetWare for AIX/6000. The AIX AS/400 Connection Program facilitates the interchange of data between an AS/400 and the RS/6000.

AIXwindows Environment/6000 provides the windowing services which graphics workstations attached to the system use. The AIX Xstation Manager/6000 facilitates management activities for an Xstation environment.

Several programming languages are supported in addition to the C compiler supplied with the operating system: C++, RS/6000 Assembler, AIX XL Pascal, AIX XL Fortran, AIX Ada, and AIX VS COBOL.

To facilitate "downsizing" of mainframe applications, CICS/6000 and DB2/6000 are available.

In addition to the wide variety of program products IBM has produced for the RS/6000 (Table 1.3), many third-party products are available for the RS/6000. It is currently estimated that there are over 8,000 applications available for the RS/6000. Many of these are detailed in the latest IBM *RS/6000 Application Directory,* which is available from your IBM representative.

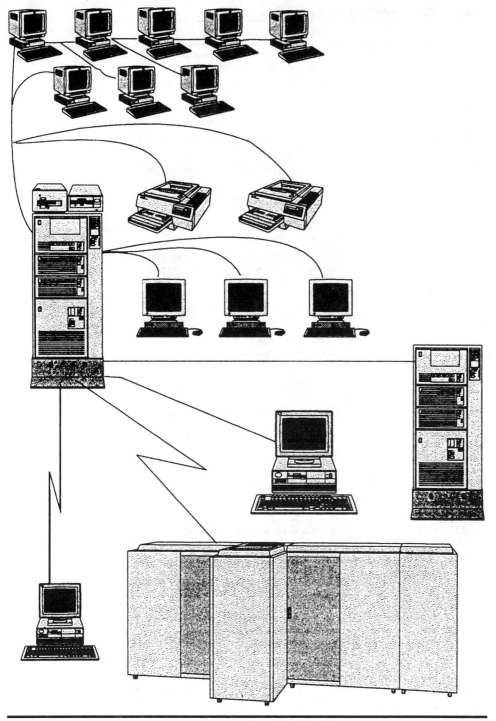

Figure 1.4   The networking capabilities of the RS/6000, including TCP/IP and SNA networking protocols and extensive hardware options, allow for easy connectivity within larger networks.

TABLE 1.3   AIX/6000 Component Parts and Optional Products

Component Parts	
BOS—Basic Operating System	The basic operating system components: basic UNIX commands, vi editor, smit
NSF—Network Support Facilities	Includes TCP/IP (Transmission Control Protocol/Internet Protocol), NFS (Network File Systems), NCS (Network Computing Systems), SNMP (Simple Network Management Protocol)
NFS Encryption Feature (US Only)	Enables the receipt and transmission of secured messages of a network
InfoExplorer	The online hypertext documentation system
HANFS—High Availability Network File System	Provides for greater network file system support by distributing the work of multiple systems
BOS Extensions 1	Includes extended commands, mail, Basic Networking Utilities (uucp), C Shell, CGI device drivers, Remote Customer Services
BOS Extensions 2	Includes accounting services, asynchronous terminal emulation, Ethernet Data Link Controls, SDLC Data Linke Control, Token-ring Data Link Control, IEEE 802.3 Data Link Control, X. 25 QLLC Data Link Control, X. 25 Application, AIX/DOS Utilities, games
DOS Server	Allows PC-DOS clients to use AIX/6000 as a file server
INed	An enhanced text editor
GNU Emacs Editor	Another enhanced editor, well known for its extensibility
TFS—Text Formatting System	troff, Writer's Tools, Formatting Services, laser printer fonts
BOSM—Base Operating System Messages	Available in several languages including English, German, Spanish, French, Italian, Dutch, Norwegian, Swedish, and Japanese
XL C Compiler	The optimizing C compiler for AIX/6000
Base Application Development Toolkit	Include the Application Development Toolkit, X-development Environment (xde), Base profiling support

Optional Products	
AIX 3270 Host Connection Program/6000 (HCON)	Provides SNA (and non-SNA) connectivity for RS/6000 users in conjunction with AIX SNA Services
AIX SNA Services	Provides SNA network control for the RS/6000; essentially AIX/VTAM.
AIX 3278/79 Emulation/6000	Allows a RS/6000 Workstation to emulate a 3278 or 3279 terminal
AIX Network Management/600	Provides for the management of RS/6000 network data and the interchange of collected data with other management products
CALLPath DirectTalk/6000	Connects a telephone PBX to the RS/6000 as a voice server
NetWare for AIX/6000	Allows an RS/6000 to serve as a NetWare server
AIX AS/400 Connection Program	Facilitates the interchange of data between an AS/400 and the RS/6000

TABLE 1.3   AIX/6000 Component Parts and Optional Products (*Continued*)

AIXwindows Environment/6000	Provides X-windows services
C++, Assembler, AIX XL Pascal, AIX XL Fortran, AIX Ada, AIX VS COBOL	Additional programming languages for those who do not wish to use C
AIX Personal Computer Simulator/6000	Allows real-mode PC-DOS programs to run on the RS/6000
AIX Xstation Manager/6000	Facilitates the management activities in an X-station environment
AIX InfoCrafter/6000	Provides the facilities for creating InfoExplorer-based hypertext databases
CICS/6000	The popular mainframe-teleprocessing monitor transported to the RS/6000 environment
DB/2 for AIX/6000	The heretofore mainframe-based relational database management system as implemented on the RS/6000

Chapter

2

Introduction
to AIX/6000

In this chapter, the reader is introduced to the AIX operating system. Starting with a discussion of some architectural issues, this chapter guides the user through an interactive session, introducing some of the more common AIX commands.

2.1   The Kernel

The base of the AIX operating system, as with all UNIX-based operating systems, is the *kernel*. The kernel provides the interface between user programs and the hardware of the system. It facilitates the transfer of data from hardware devices to programs (and vice versa) and concurrent execution of programs, among other things. The kernel uses two methods to communicate with programs: *system calls* and *interrupts*. System calls are well-defined interfaces which are invoked by user programs to send and receive information from the kernel. Interrupts are the equivalent hardware mechanism for transferring information.

The two basic system models within the AIX system are *files* and *processes*. Unlike other operating systems which have many different types of objects, everything within the AIX system is implemented as either a file or a process. By keeping the implementation of the operating system simple, it is easier to maintain the operating system and transport it to other types of hardware. Simplification also allows for shifting the burden of supporting hardware-specific information to modules distinct from the operating system itself. These additional modules can then be inserted or removed from the system as needed.

2.2   Files

From the perspective of AIX, everything on the system, except a running program, is a file of one type or another. But what is a "file"? In the most generic sense, a *file* is a sequence of organized data bytes which reside in some type of storage medium which may be temporary, but more commonly is stable, i.e., disk or tape. To implement all of the objects on the system, AIX defines seven types of files: ordinary disk files, directories, block special files, character special files, pipes[1], symbolic links, and sockets. Note that AIX does not define a file type as an access method as most operating systems do,[2] but according to functional types.

2.2.1   Ordinary files

Ordinary files are used for programs, documents, and program source code; in fact, for most of the items that are typically thought of when a file is discussed. Unlike other operating systems, AIX does not have a preconceived notion about the contents of a file or its organization. Although AIX itself views all ordinary files as a simple sequence of bytes, AIX does not impose a logical structure on the user of these ordinary files. It is up to the individual user program to determine and define how the file is used. For example, unlike PC-DOS, where executable program file names are suffixed with a .EXE, AIX does not assume[3] that a file is an executable program just because it ends with a .EXE suffix. An AIX executable program typically does not have *any* suffix.

In order to facilitate the use of files, user programs typically draw a distinction between those files which contain *binary* information, and those which contain *ASCII* information. In simplest terms, ASCII files can be processed by a text editor with meaningful results, whereas binary files cannot.

Because AIX does not have any method for accessing data from a file except sequentially, user programs that need to access data in a nonsequential manner must implement nonsequential access methods on their own. Although this may seem to be a problem, in fact it is not. Recognizing that most people do not want to devise access methods for every application, most programming languages supported by AIX have libraries that implement the two common nonsequential access methods, indexed and random. So, even though the program uses an indexed file, the operating system does not know (or care) that the file is indexed.

2.2.2   Directories

Directories are the next most common type of file on an AIX system. A directory is simply an ordinary file that points to other files and the information about those files. This definition, however, belies the importance of directories. The entire system of file management in AIX is built on a hierarchical directory structure.

---

[1]Sometimes pipe files are referred to as first-in-first-out or FIFO files.

[2]The most obvious, and famous, are the IBM-mainframe operating systems—MVS and VSE—which implement file types as several distinct access methods and hardware devices as discrete families of objects.

[3]In fact, there is no way for it to know.

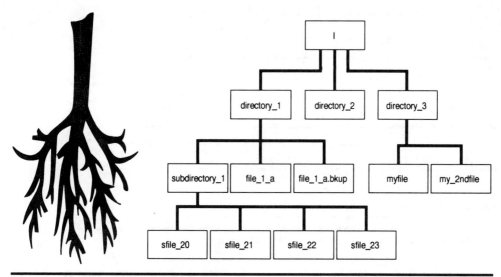

Figure 2.1   Bearing a striking resemblance to an upside-down tree, the AIX file system is usually described as being an *inverted tree*.

This structure can be visualized as an upside-down tree (Fig. 2.1). At the top of the file structure is the *root* directory (/); all files in the system eventually can be traced back to the root directory. As the root directory does not actually have a name, it is represented only by the directory name separator character (/) when referenced in file names.

Each directory in the file structure points to files, and possibly, other directories. And so it is with the root directory. Within the root directory, several *subdirectories* can be found. The subdirectories, in turn, point to other directories and files. For the moment, the most important pointer in the root directory is to the /u subdirectory. On most AIX systems, the /u subdirectory contains the pointers to the directories of the individual users on the system.[4] These directories (Fig. 2.2) are referred to as a user's *home directory*. The purpose and uses of the other directories are explored in Chapter 5.

2.2.3   Special files, pipes, symbolic links, and sockets

Special files are used for communicating with the devices on the system. All I/O performed to a device is performed by the kernel as if it were writing to a regular, sequential file. The special file is not a real file, such as a disk file, but a path to the device. Devices are grouped into two major categories, represented by two different types of special files: *block* and *character*. Block devices perform I/O by means of blocks of data—tape and disk drives, for example.

---

[4]On some systems, the home directories of the users may be in the /usr directory, but this is uncommon.

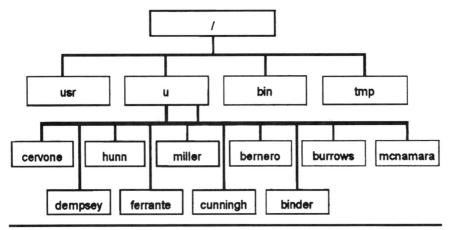

Figure 2.2   The u directory is the parent of all user HOME directories.

Character devices are usually associated with user input and output—terminals and modems, for example.

Pipes are transient files used for redirecting the output of one program to the input of another program. Pipe files are similar to ordinary files but they do differ from ordinary files in some significant ways. Pipe files are transparent to the user; they can never be explicitly referenced as pipe files cannot be given a file name. Additionally, a pipe file can *never* be stored on a stable storage medium (tape or disk). Pipes exist only in memory until they have been processed by the receiving program.

A *named pipe* is a pipe explicitly created by an application program to communicate with another program. These pipes are not normally visible to the user, and need not be of any concern.

A *symbolic link* is a file that contains a path name, either relative or absolute, to another file. This makes it possible for a file to reside in more than one directory at once.

Sockets are used as a connection mechanism between applications to exchange data quickly. As such, sockets are used primarily, although not exclusively, with network applications. Although socket files are visible as directory entries, they can be used only by processes directly involved in the socket connection.

2.2.4   File and directory naming conventions

For compatibility with other UNIX-based operating systems, file names are typically restricted to 14 characters. AIX, however, allows for file names up to 255 characters long. When a file to be used is not in the current working directory of the user, the file name must be preceded by the directory path name. Although there are multiple ways of specifying the directory path name, the entire length of the file *and* directory path name cannot be longer than 1023 bytes.

In general, a file name can contain *any* ASCII character that can be generated on the keyboard. This means that a file name can contain special charac-

TABLE 2.1   Special Characters to be Avoided in File Names

Dollar sign	$	Asterisk	*
Semicolon	;	Left bracket	[
Backslash	\	Right bracket	]
Ampersand	&	OR symbol	|
Exclamation point	!		

ters, which is usually forbidden in other operating systems. One must be careful, though. The command interpreter (or *shell*) interprets the characters in Table 2.1 as wild-card operators or special characters; it is best to avoid using them in file names.

Just as with files, directory names are typically restricted to 14 characters for compatibility reasons. AIX allows for a directory name to be up to 255 characters, but the entire path name cannot be more than 1023 bytes.

The forward slash (/) is used to delimit the various components in a file name. For example, cervone/first_file refers to the file named first_file in the directory cervone; cervone/projects/status.doc refers to the file status.doc in directory projects which is a subdirectory of the cervone directory.

The forward slash also determines whether an *absolute* or *relative* directory reference is being used. In an absolute directory reference, the complete path to the file is specified; the current working directory is irrelevant to the search for the file. Absolute references always begin with a forward slash. In a relative reference, which *never* begin with a slash, AIX assumes that directory references are related to the current working directory. In most cases, the relative reference points to a file which is in a subdirectory of the current working directory, although this does not have to be the case.

To facilitate upward or lateral movement in the directory hierarchy, AIX provides two "shorthand" methods of indicating directory names. The first method is not particularly useful in most cases; a single dot (.) in a path name represents the current working directory. Since the current working directory is assumed if no other specification is made, the dot is usually used only for clarity. Of more interest is the double dot (..) which represents the parent directory of the current working directory. With the double dot, it is possible to transverse up the directory tree instead of downward.

With relative file names the "name" of the file changes depending on the current working directory. Returning to the file name example mentioned, the absolute name of the file is /u/cervone/projects/status.doc. The relative name, however, varies. If the current working directory is /u/cervone/projects, the name is simply status.doc, or, less commonly, ./status.doc. If the current directory is /u, though, the name would have to be specified more fully—cervone/project/status.doc. What if the current working directory were /u/cervone/doc? The path to status.doc would take a different form; as both doc and projects are subdirectories of the cervone directory, an upward reference from the current working directory could be used: ../projects/status.doc. Figure 2.3 demonstrates how the relative path name can change depending where the current working directory is.

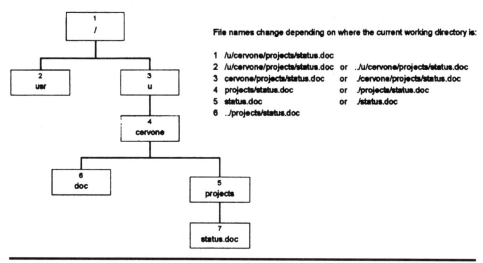

Figure 2.3   Relative path names.

2.3   Processes

Executing programs are referred to as *processes* in AIX. This program can be an operating system command, a shell (the user interface to the operating system) or an application program, it makes no difference to AIX; they are all processes.

Processes exist within a parent-child hierarchy that is not that much different from that used in other operating systems. While a process may have multiple subprocesses (or children), a process has only one parent process. Each process is assigned a unique process identification number (PID) when it is started. Even if multiple instances of a program are started, each has a unique PID.

Each process on the system is also assigned a priority by the scheduler. This priority is determined by the operating system based on several factors including the type of process (computation or I/O bound), the requesting user, and overall system load. This priority is dynamically modified by the operating system as is necessary. A user cannot raise the priority of its processes to the detriment of others; only a user with root authority (a superuser) may raise the priority of a process. The priority of a process is changed by the nice and renice commands. In fact, the priority of an AIX process is usually called the *nice value*.

Most processes are *foreground processes*. Foreground processes are able to interact with the user via the user's terminal. By default, all processes are run in the foreground. However, there are many instances where it is not necessary for a process to interact with the user. In these cases, the user can start a process in the *background*. A process in the foreground can be sent to the background after it has started, and alternatively, processes in the background can be brought to the foreground, if necessary.

There are some tasks that must run in the system which are not necessarily tied to any particular user. Examples of this are the processes that handle login processing, manage the print queues, and control the communications network traffic scheduling. In AIX, and all UNIX-based operating systems, these processes are called *daemons*. Daemons are started when the system is booted, and do not stop, under normal circumstances, until the system is shut down.

Zombie processes are processes that have stopped performing any useful function, but have not been completely removed from the system. In most cases, this is a temporary state. However, it is possible that a process will not leave the zombie state, and completely terminate, until its parent terminates. This may be intentional if the child process is restartable; there is less overhead in restarting a process than in recreating it. However, for the most part, zombie processes that last for more than a few minutes are the result of a programming error; usually these processes can be terminated only by shutting down the system.

2.4 Shells

Users communicate with the operating system through a *shell*. Unlike most other operating systems, the command interface between the user and the AIX operating system is not built into AIX. Instead, programs separate from the base operating system are used to retrieve information from the user's terminal and translate it into a form the operating system can understand. The shell concept is one of the great advantages of UNIX-based operating systems as it allows every user on the system to choose the shell which best meets their needs (see Table 2.2). And the shell itself is very flexible in allowing for customization and reconfiguration. In fact, new shells can be created for special applications, if needed.

When a user is added to the system, one of the attributes the system administrator must define is which shell program will be invoked when the user logs on. This then becomes the user's *default shell*. After signing on to the system, the user can switch to another shell, either temporarily or permanently.

The shell is able to accept commands from the user whenever the shell *command prompt* is displayed. The default prompt in most cases is the dollar sign ($), but the user can change this. When the shell receives a command, which is signalled by the user pressing the enter key on the terminal, the

TABLE 2.2   Shells supplied with AIX

Korn shell—ksh	The default login shell for most users. This shell is a superset of the Bourne shell and incorporates many of the features of the C shell.
Bourne shell—bsh	The original shell used with bsd versions of UNIX. Supplanted for the most part by the Korn shell.
Restricted shell—rsh	A limited version of the Bourne shell. Useful for restricting access to many AIX commands.
C shell—csh	A shell developed with the C programmer in mind. It provides a C-like programming language for constructing scripts.
Trusted shell—tsh	The trusted shell is provided as a means of ensuring that only *trusted* commands (see Chapter 7) are issued by the user.
Remote shell—rsh	The remote shell is (infrequently) used for logging in to a remote system.

shell attempts to evaluate the input and carry out the request. Depending on the command, the shell writes the output or an error message to the terminal. Typically, input to a shell is processed interactively from a terminal, but it can be processed also from a batch file or *shell script.*

Shell scripts provide a mechanism for grouping long or complex sequences of commands into a single "command." In addition, shell scripts are also used for creating *batch jobs:* long-running, multistep tasks that do not require user interaction. To facilitate the use of shell scripts, each shell implements a programming language which is used to control and adjust the sequence of command execution within a script based on the outcome of prior commands.

But in addition to processing input, the shell processes the output of commands. Because terminal input and output are directed through the shell, it is possible for the shell to manipulate these data streams or *redirect* them which is discussed in the next section.

2.5   Input and Output

Input and output on AIX is based on a rather simple premise: a command reads input from *standard input,* writes output to *standard output* and sends all error messages to *standard error.* To further simplify things, all three files are directed, by default, to the user's terminal.

All AIX commands follow this model.[5] Because of this, the shell is able to redirect input and output from the terminal to files, or, less commonly, to other devices. This standardization also facilitates the redirection of one command's output to another command's input or *piping.*

Four symbols are used to indicate redirection: ($<$) to redirect standard input, ($>$) to redirect standard output, ($>>$) to append standard output to an existing file, and ($|$) which pipes data from standard output to standard input.

The less than symbol ($<$) is used to read input from a file. Although most commands that expect a "real" file as input allow for the specification of the file's name as part of the command, some do not. The wc command is an example of a command that reads its input from standard input only. Considering that this command counts the number of lines, words, and characters in a file, it is obvious that redirection is necessary for almost all uses of wc. The command

```
wc < input.data
```

causes the shell to pass the file input.data to the wc command as standard input.

Output redirection is similar. Normally, commands write output to standard output. If this output must be saved for later use, it is necessary to redirect it to a file. The ls command, which is used to list the contents of a directory, is a good example. As would be expected, the directory information from the command is directed to standard output; therefore, it is displayed on

---

[5]Strictly speaking, this is not true. There are a few esoteric commands that do not follow this standard. They will be noted, as appropriate.

the user's terminal. To save the directory information in a file named directo-ry.out for later use, the user would issue the command

```
ls > directory.out
```

The output redirection operation creates a new file; an existing file with the same name is deleted. To keep the existing information in the directory.out file and simply append the new information to the existing file, the command is slightly different

```
ls >> directory.out
```

With this redirection operator, the original file is kept, and the new data is added at the end of the original file. If the file to which standard output is being redirected does not exist, it is created.

Redirecting the output of one command to the input of another is accom-plished with the OR symbol (|). To direct the output of a directory listing into the word count program, the following command could be issued

```
ls | wc
```

The result of this command would be a display of the number of lines, words, and characters in the directory listing.

Pipes flow from left to right with all of the commands in the pipe running concurrently. Pipe processes wait when there is no input to be read from an active prior process or when the following process in the pipe is full. As each command in the pipe runs as a separate process, each command has its own process ID. There is no inherent limit on the complexity of a pipe command and long-running pipe commands may be executed in the background if that is more convenient for the user.

As stated earlier, when a command starts, three files are opened, *stdin* (standard input), *stdout* (standard output), and *stderr* (standard error). In ad-dition to standard names, these three files are also assigned to a standard *file descriptor* within the command program. A file descriptor is a number that is associated with each open file in a program. The following file descriptors are associated with the standard files:

0 is used for standard input (the keyboard)

1 is used for standard output (the terminal)

2 is used for standard error (the terminal)

By default, the redirector operator for input (<) assumes that file descriptor 0 is to used. Likewise, the output redirectors (> and >>) assume file descriptor 1 is to be used. Specifying a file descriptor before the redirection operator al-lows redirection to take place for the file referred to by the file descriptor number. This is how standard error is redirected. For example,

```
ls >ls.out 2>ls.errors
```

directs the output of the ls command to ls.out, and any error messages from the command to the file ls.errors. If a command directs output to several different files, each file can be independently redirected as the user sees fit. As an example, assume that a user-written application program, yourcmd, writes three different output files, which are associated with file descriptors 4, 5, and 6. Redirecting the output of this command could be accomplished as follows:

```
yourcmd 2>err.log 4>trans.log 5>oob.data 6>misc.data
```

In this example, standard error is directed to err.log, the data file 4 to trans.log, data file 5 to oob.data[6] and data file 6 to misc.data. If any output is written to standard output, that data would appear on the terminal as if standard output *was not* redirected.

2.6 Logging In, Logging Out, and User Profiles

To use the RS/6000 (and AIX), the user must sign on. After the terminal has connected to the RS/6000, AIX displays the login prompt as demonstrated in Fig. 2.4. The users enter their user identification (*user id*) and press the enter key. Unlike other systems, the user id is entered in lower case letters; entering the user id in all upper case letters causes an error message to be issued by AIX[7] Assuming the user id is not in all upper case letters, most users are then prompted to enter their password (terminated by pressing enter).[8] Note

---

[6]When something is out of balance, there is always oob data.

[7]This is the only sign on error that explicitly identifies the user id as being incorrect. It is also the only error that causes a message to be issued before the password, if required, is entered.

[8]Users who are required to use passwords must change their password the first time they log into the system.

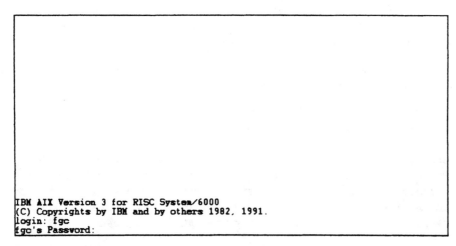

```
IBM AIX Version 3 for RISC System/6000
(C) Copyrights by IBM and by others 1982, 1991.
login: fgc
fgc's Password:
```

Figure 2.4 The AIX login screen.

that the password is never displayed when the user types it in. If both pieces of information are entered correctly, sign on processing continues. Otherwise, access is denied.

In most circumstances, each user of the system has a unique user id and password. When a user successfully logs on, the default shell (as defined by the AIX system administrator) is started and system shell information is processed. Afterward, the shell is directed to the user's default or *home* directory. In the home directory, the shell may find a hidden shell script called the *profile* file[9] which is executed before the shell turns control over to the user.

The profile shell script contains commands that customize the AIX environment for the individual user; commands that make it simpler for the user to perform the functions necessary to get the job done. Examples of commands in a shell file include setting up the *search path* for finding commands, checking to see if any electronic mail has arrived, and customizing the shell prompt to make it more meaningful.

Figure 2.5 shows the default profile for a Korn shell user. The first line of the profile defines the directory search sequence for programs and commands and sets a *shell variable* to this search sequence. The second line uses the shell variable in a *shell directive*. Shell directives are commands to the shell itself, not to AIX, to perform a particular operation. The export directive used in line two tells the Korn shell to make the variable PATH available to all programs running in the shell. The last three lines check for mail; if there is mail for the user, the predefined shell variable $MAILMSG[10] is displayed on the user's terminal. At this point, the shell prompt is displayed and control is passed to the user.

One of the great advantages of AIX is the flexibility afforded in defining how user ids may be used. If it is desired, a single user id can be simultaneously shared by several people. Or, a single user can logon concurrently to separate user accounts from the same terminal, as long as two different shells are used. Finally, if the RS/6000 is connected to a larger network of other AIX or UNIX-based machines, a user can use a *remote login* to gain concurrent access to the other systems. This topic is discussed further in Chapter 11, Networking and Communications.

Users can terminate the shell with which they are working by entering the command exit. If the shell happened to be the user's primary shell, this com-

---

[9] The actual name of the file is .profile. Any file name that begins with a dot is hidden from directory displays unless special options are used.

[10] This variable was set in the system shell profile. See Chapter 14 for more details.

```
PATH=/bin:/usr/bin:/etc:/usr/ucb:$HOME/bin:/usr/local/bin:.
export PATH
if [ -s "$MAIL" ]        # This is at Shell startup. In normal
then echo "$MAILMSG"     # operation, the Shell checks
fi                       # periodically.
```

Figure 2.5 The default Korn shell profile.

mand causes the user to be logged off. To explicitly logoff AIX, the user can enter `logoff`.

2.7   Commands

As with any system, there are some basic commands that are important for a user to know. Without these commands, it is very difficult to use the system in a meaningful way.

Some commands consist of only the command name itself. Other commands use *flags* to indicate specifics of the action to be taken. Flags are most often entered on the command line as the second operand(s) in the command, before the names of files and other such information.

With almost all AIX commands, unless specifically stated otherwise, commands *must* be entered in lowercase. Using uppercase letters results in error messages stating that the command cannot be found.

2.7.1   news

The `news` command is often placed in the user's .profile file. Executing the command `news` displays the news items in the `/usr/news` directory that have not already been displayed by the user.

2.7.2   mail

Closely related to news is `mail`. The mail command provides a way for users of the system to send and receive messages from users on local or remote systems. This section is only a brief overview of mail; the mail command is more fully discussed in Chapter 11.

Upon entering the mail program, the user is presented with the first message in the mailbox. The first line of all mail items is the *postmark* which contains information about the sender. The text of the message follows the postmark. After the message text has been fully displayed, the user is prompted with a question mark (?).

In response to the question mark prompt, the user may enter another question mark to get help. To display the next message, the user presses the enter key and to delete the message, the user enters d. When all messages have been displayed, the mail program automatically terminates; however, the user can terminate mail by entering q at a prompt.

2.7.3   ls—Display a directory

The `ls` command is used to view the names of files in a directory. In its simplest form, it displays only a list of the actual file names or subdirectories

```
$ ls
Mail      info      data.out
$
```

If the directory is empty (or contains only hidden files) the directory listing
is null

```
$  ls
$
```

By using the -l flag, the user can obtain more detailed information on the
files and directories

```
$  ls -l
total 56
drwxr-xr-x     4  fgc      staff      512 Jul 09 09:05 .
drwxr-xr-x    28  bin      bin        512 Jun 22 09:24 ..
drwx--x--x     2  fgc      staff      512 Apr 29 10:04 Mail
drwxrwxr-x     3  fgc      staff      512 Mar 31 16:06 info
-rw-rw-r--     1  fgc      staff        0 Jul 09 09:05 data.out
$
```

The first column of information details the *permissions* for the files, "fgc" is
the *owner* of the file, and the file is associated with the *group* "staff." The fifth
column indicates the number of bytes the file occupies, and is followed by the
data and time of last update and the file or directory name.

Finally, *all* of the files in the directory are displayed if the -s flag is used,
either singly

```
$  ls -s
.             ..          .mh_profile    .profile      .sh_history
Mail      info        data.out
$
```

or in combination with the -l flag

```
$  ls -ls
total 56
drwxr-xr-x     4  fgc      staff       512 Jul 09 09:05 .
drwxr-xr-x    28  bin      bin         512 Jun 22 09:24 ..
-rw-rw-r--     1  fgc      staff        11 Apr 29 10:04 .mh_profile
-rwxr-----     1  fgc      staff       346 Apr 29 16:28 .profile
-rw-------     1  fgc      staff      3120 Jul 09 09:05 .sh_history
drwx--x--x     2  fgc      staff       512 Apr 29 10:04 Mail
drwxrwxr-x     3  fgc      staff       512 Mar 31 16:06 info
-rw-rw-r--     1  fgc      staff         0 Jul 09 09:05 data.out
$
```

Directories other than the current working directory can be displayed by
entering the name of the directory after any flags

```
$  ls -ls /usr/news
total 34
drwxr-xr-x     4  fgc      staff      512 Jul 09 09:05 .
drwxr-xr-x    28  bin      bin        512 Jun 22 09:24 ..
-rw-r--r--     1  root     adm        211 Jun 23 11:14 newempl
-rw-r--r--     1  fgc      staff      346 Jun 25 17:38 picnic
$
```

2.7.4 `cat`—Display a file

The `cat` command is derived from the word *concatenate* because the actual purpose of the `cat` command is to concatenate files. However, because of the way the command works, a side effect[11] of the command can be used to display files. To display the contents of the .profile file, the user would enter:

```
cat .profile
```

This would be followed by a display on the terminal of the contents of the .profile file. Because the display is continuous, large files cannot be conveniently viewed by using this method. For larger files, the `pg` command should be used.

2.7.5 `pg`—Display a file in full-screen mode

The `pg` (pager) command allows the user to page through the contents of a file or files in full-screen mode. Pager has a variety of commands to control the display of information; these are outlined in Table 2.3. The pager commands are entered at the bottom of the screen, after the colon (:) prompt.

To display a single file, the user enters the name of the file after the `pg` command, for example

```
pg .profile
```

To display multiple files, multiple file names are used

```
pg file_one file_two file_three
```

---

[11]Many commands in AIX have side effects. Unlike the common definition of the term, a side effect in AIX does not imply a pejorative meaning. Furthermore, side effects of commands are not usually accidental; they are simply not the primary purpose of the command.

TABLE 2.3   Pager Commands

l	Display one more line at the bottom of the screen
-l	Display one more line at the top of the screen
xl	Begin the screen display at line x
(enter key)	Display the next screen
n	Move to screen n
+n	Move forward n screens
-n	Move backward n screens
d	Scroll forward by one-half of a screen
.	Redisplay the current screen
f	Skip the next screen
$	Go to the last screen
h	Help
n	Go to the next file
p	Go to the previous file
q	Quit

In order to use full screen mode, the correct terminal type must be defined to the shell.

2.7.6 `echo $TERM` and `export TERM`—Terminal settings

In most cases when a user logs in to AIX, the shell can determine the type of terminal being used and stores this information in the shell variable TERM. For most commands and applications, the terminal type is not important. However, the terminal type is critical for commands that operate in full-screen mode; it is the only way for the command to know what control characters should be used to format full-screen displays.

The user can display the value of a shell variable by using the shell directive echo. To display the terminal type, the user would enter:

```
echo $TERM
```

The output of the directive would be the value of the TERM variable; i.e., the current terminal type. For example, a user at a VT-220 type terminal would see:

```
$ echo $TERM
vt220
$
```

If the shell cannot determine the terminal type, it will set the value of TERM to dumb. In that case, the user would see the following:

```
$ echo $TERM
dumb
$
```

The user can change the value of TERM if it is not correct. To change the value of any shell variable, the user must assign a new value to it, and issue the export shell directive. For the TERM variable, the new value assigned must be a valid terminal type (see Table 2.4). Although any value can be assigned to TERM, commands that rely on the TERM variable do not execute correctly if the TERM variable is not a valid terminal name. Assuming that the

TABLE 2.4 Predefined Terminal Types

TERM value	Terminal name
dumb	Unknown terminal type
ibm3151	IBM 3151
ibm3151-25	IBM 3151 in 25 line mode
ibm3161	IBM 3161 or IBM 3163
ibm3162	IBM 3162
tty	Generic ASCII terminal
vt100	DEC VT-100
vt220	DEC VT-220
wyse50	WYSE WYSE-50
wyse60	WYSE WYSE-60

shell did not correctly determine that a VT-220 was being used, the user could set the terminal type to VT-220 with the following directive

```
export TERM = vt220
```

2.7.7 who and whoami—Locating users

The who command displays the names of the users on the system. The output of the command lists the user name, what terminal the user is on, and when the user logged into the system. On large systems with many users, it may be best to pipe the output of who into the pager

```
who | pg
```

Otherwise, the user display scrolls off the screen.

The whoami command displays the name of the logged-on user. This can be helpful when the user is switching between several sessions and wants to check what user id is being used.

2.7.8 passwd—Changing passwords

The passwd command is used to change passwords. When the users enters the command, they are prompted to enter their old password. After successfully entering the old password, the user is prompted to enter a new password. subsequently, the user is prompted to reenter the new password. During this process, there is no display of the information being entered; this is why the user is prompted to enter the new password twice. If the second new password does not match the first new password, the prompting for the new password is restarted.

Passwords should be chosen with care. It should be easy for the user to remember, but difficult for others to guess. This means that the names of family members or pets are not good choices for passwords. In addition, many obvious words such as sex, love, money, guest, god, pass, genius, and fred[12] are not good either. In general, passwords should be at least six characters long and contain one digit or nonalphabetic character.

2.7.9 cp and mv—Copy and move files

The cp command is used to copy a file to another file. After the execution of the command, two copies of the file exist: the original, and the new one. The mv command moves a file; after execution only the new file exists, the original file is deleted.

The format of the cp command is straightforward

```
cp old_file_name new_file_name
```

---

[12]For some reason, "fred" is one of the most common passwords used in England.

If the new file name already exists, the user is prompted as to whether the old file should be overlaid with the new file or not.

The mv command is usually used with the -i flag:

```
mv -i old_file_name new_file_name
```

The reason for this is that without the -i flag, the mv command overlays existing files. The -i flag forces the mv command to prompt the user as to whether the existing files should be overlaid or not.

2.7.10 vi—The editor

Like most other UNIX-based operating systems, AIX comes with several text editors. But most of these are line editors; that is, they do not use the full-screen of the terminal for displaying and manipulating text. The only full-screen editor that is *always* supplied with AIX and other UNIX-based operating systems is vi, the visual editor (Chapter 15). (Chapter 12)

Quite honestly, vi is not very easy to use.[13] However, once it has been mastered, a user's vi skills are transferable to any other UNIX system. None of the other full-screen editors, such as emacs, which are available for AIX or UNIX are any better in the user-interface department.

---

[13] It has been suggested that the name vi did not come from visual, but instead from vile.

3

AIX/6000
Architecture

This chapter provides an introduction to the architecture of the AIX operating system. While in most respects AIX is similar to other UNIX-based operating systems, in many areas it has expanded upon the functionality typically provided by most UNIX implementations.

3.1 Overview

In order to understand the architectural organization upon which UNIX-based operating systems such as AIX are built, it is important to remember that the original UNIX system was designed as a reaction to a very large and cumbersome operating system, MULTICS. The overriding factor in all design decisions was a desire to keep things small and efficient, sometimes at the expense of clarity and usability.

UNIX was designed with programmers, not application users, in mind. This is most evident in the implementation of the user command interface. Until UNIX, operating systems were built with the interface between the user and operating system incorporated directly into the operating system. While this is efficient, it provides for no flexibility on the user's part for extending (or limiting) the command interface. By implementing the command interface as a program which was separate and distinct from the operating system, UNIX extended to the user the ability to modify the user-machine interface as much as desired. In fact, this makes it feasible to even create command interfaces or *shells* that simulate other, non-UNIX based, operating systems.

As seen in Fig. 3.1, AIX is a layered operating system; each layer depends upon a lower layer for services, and provides the higher layer with enhanced services. Most descriptions of the operating system divide AIX into five components

the kernel (or the base operating system)

the user command interface (the shells)

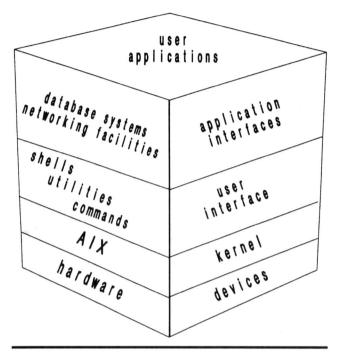

Figure 3.1   AIX functional architecture.

the commands and utilities

the system services

the programming interface

This book is primarily concerned with the first four items and the user's interaction with them. Although the last item, the programming interface, is primarily the domain of programmers, it will be referenced as appropriate and needed.

Before delving into the specifics of the kernel, a quick discussion of the other items is in order.

As previously discussed, shell programs implement the user command interface in AIX. First-time users often find the user interface of UNIX-based operating systems to be extremely unfriendly and cryptic. For the nonprogrammer, this is, for the most part, true. Because of this, several different interfaces are available, each geared to slightly different audiences: the C shell is popular with C programmers whereas the Korn shell is more popular with general users of the system. In addition, public domain shells are available for those users who desire different functionality, and many third-party vendors supply shells which are specifically designed for use with their products. For users of graphics workstations, a shell that is designed to work with graphics terminals using windows is available.

The commands and utilities of AIX provide operating system functionality that is not provided by the kernel directly; for example, the commands to copy files, stop a task, or print a report. AIX commands and utilities are implemented in two ways: as built-in shell functions or as distinct programs. Commands built into a shell are available only as part of that specific shell, whereas programs can be invoked from any shell. While part of the AIX distribution, these commands and utilities are not part of the kernel.

AIX system services provide several different areas of functionality: system administration, system configuration, file system maintenance, networking services, etc. These are implemented as separate programs or subsystems.

The programming interface provides the mechanism for user programs to access system functions. By calling the routines defined in the *run-time library,* the user program can request services of the kernel which include management of system resources such as memory, disk storage, and peripherals. The run-time library maps the system calls in the program to the kernel routines that perform the specified function.

3.2   Kernel Overview

The kernel is referred to as the *base operating system* because all other functions of AIX ultimately depend on it. In the nomenclature of other operating systems, the kernel performs the same function as a nucleus or supervisor does. Regardless of name, it provides the services that user and utility programs depend upon to function.

The kernel is the lowest level of the AIX operating system structure, and as such, provides the layer which interfaces directly with the hardware. The kernel manages and schedules processes, allocates and deallocates memory, starts and stops devices, checks and resets device status codes, and reads and writes data from or to devices.

However, the kernel itself has several layers as demonstrated by Fig. 3.2. In addition to the hardware layer, there is the kernel services layer which provides the support for mapping user level system calls to kernel level actions. User level system calls include requests for general input/output services, file system access, terminal handling, process creation and termination, and transmission and receipt of data. This level also handles switching a process from user mode to kernel mode so protected kernel mode functions can be performed.

The highest layer of the kernel consists of the user processes. This is where shells, commands, utility and application programs run. This level has no direct access to kernel routines or functions; all access to kernel functions must be transmitted through the kernel services layer.

In addition to this layering of services, the kernel divides the physical memory of the system into two distinct areas or *spaces:* user space and kernel space.

User space occupies all of the physical memory that is not used by kernel processes and data. All user processes are loaded into this storage area. The storage in the user space is protected; it is not possible for one user process to interfere with another. The only processes that can access an individual user space, except for the user process itself, are kernel processes. While in user space, a process runs in *user mode.*

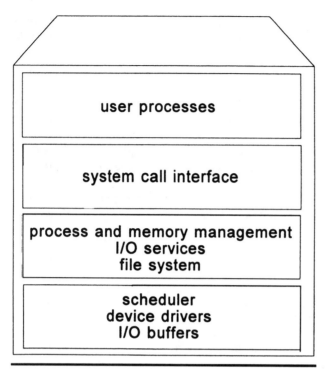

Figure 3.2 Kernel architecture.

Kernel space is the part of physical memory where the kernel resides and kernel processes execute. Kernel space is *privileged,* it cannot be accessed by a user process except through system calls. A user process enters *kernel mode* when it executes a system call that invokes kernel code on behalf of the user process. User processes also enter kernel mode when I/O completes. Upon completion of an input or output operation, the I/O device sends a completion signal or *hardware interrupt* to the kernel *device handler* which is responsible for translating the I/O stream into and from the format the device understands. Each type of device on the system has its own device handler. System error conditions, as opposed to application error conditions, are trapped by the kernel. The user process enters kernel mode to allow the kernel to either correct the condition, signal the application of the error, or, in severe cases, terminate the process.

As the user space and kernel space are in different address spaces, a mechanism must exist to transfer data between the two areas when a system call is made. For the most part, this transfer is performed through the process *u area*. The u area of a process contains the control information for the process. The exact contents of the u area are listed in Table 3.1.

The kernel is not a monolithic, static structure. It is made up of a number of separate parts or *modules,* each of which provides a unique service or facility. This facet of the UNIX architecture is exploited by AIX, which among the UNIX-based operating systems, is unique in its use of a kernel that dynamically modifies itself depending on the operating environment. If kernel mod-

TABLE 3.1   The u Area

```
struct user {
      /* swappable process context */
      struct mstsave     u_save;          /* machine state save area */
      struct proc *u_procp;               /* pointer to proc structure */
      /* system call state */
      short        u_errcnt;              /* syscall error count */
      char               u_error;          /* return error code */
      char               u_pad;
      label_t            *u_kjmpbuf;       /* top of kernel exception longjmp */
                                          /* buffer stack, or NULL */
      long               u_iorb;           /* I/O request block - not used */
      /* signal management */
      struct sigcontext *u_sigctx;        /* signal context structure */
      sigset_t           u_oldmask;        /* mask from before sigpause */
      int                u_code;           /* ``code'' for syscall handler */
      char               *u_sigsp;         /* special signal stack */
      void               (*u_signal[NSIG])(int); /* disposition of sigs */
      sigset_t           u_sigmask[NSIG];  /* sig's to be blocked */
      char               u_sigflags[NSIG]; /* sig action flags */
      /* user-mode address space mapping */
      adspace_t    u_adspace;             /* user-mode address space */
      struct segstate u_segst[NSEGS];     /* info on use of each segment */
      /* auditing stuff */
      int    u_auditstatus;               /* auditing RESUME or SUSPEND */
      struct auddata {                    /* audit relevant data */
            ushort   svcnum;              /* name index from audit_klookup */
            ushort   argcnt;              /* number of arguments stored */
            int    args[10];              /* Parameters for this call */
            char  *audbuf;                /* buffer for misc audit record */
            int    bufsiz;                /* allocated size of pathname buffer */
            int    buflen;                /* actual length of pathname(s) */
            ushort         bufcnt;        /* number of pathnames stored */
            ulong status;                 /* audit status bitmap */
      } u_audsvc;
      long         u_pad1[1];             /* spare word */
      /* address map (mmap) */
      char         *u_map;
      /* current exec file information */
      union execunion {                   /* file header union */
            struct xcoffhdr u_xcoffhdr;   /* xcoff header */
            char u_exshell[SHSIZE];       /* #! + name of interpreter */
      } u_exh;
      char         u_comm[MAXCOMLEN + 1]; /* basename of exec file */
      short        u_lock;                /* process/text locking flags */
      char         u_sep;                 /* flag for I and D separation */
      char         u_intflg;              /* catch intr from sys */
      /* user identification and authorization */
      struct ucred      *u_cred;          /* user credentials (uid, gid, etc) */
            uinfo_t      u_uinf;          /* usrinfo() buffer */
            int          u_compatibility; /* compatibility/user mode bit masks */
      /* per-process timer management */
      struct       t     u_timer;         /* user timer array and active list */
      struct sem_undo   *u_semundo;       /* semaphore undo struct pointer */
      /* accounting and profiling data */
      time_t             u_start;
      time_t             u_ticks;
      struct profdata { /* profile arguments */
            short *pr_base;               /* buffer base */
            unsigned   pr_size;           /* buffer size */
            unsigned   pr_off;            /* pc offset */
            unsigned   pr_scale;          /* pc scaling */
      } u_prof;
```

TABLE 3.1   The u Area (*Continued*)

```
        short u_acflag;                       /* accounting flag */
        struct rusage       u_ru;             /* this process resource usage value */
        struct rusage       u_cru;            /* accumulated children's resources */
#define u_utime     u_ru.ru_utime.tv_sec      /* this process user time */
#define u_stime     u_ru.ru_stime.tv_sec      /* this process system time */
#define u_cutime    u_cru.ru_utime.tv_sec     /* sum of children's utimes */
#define u_cstime    u_cru.ru_stime.tv_sec     /* sum of children's stimes */
        /* resource limits and counters */
        unsigned    u_tsize;                          /* text size (bytes) */
        struct rlimit       u_rlimit[RLIM_NLIMITS];   /* resource limits */
#define u_ssize     u_rlimit[RLIMIT_STACK].rlim_cur   /* current stacksize */
#define u_limit     u_rlimit[RLIMIT_FSIZE].rlim_cur   /* max file size */
#define u_minflt    u_ru.ru_minflt                    /* minimum page fault count */
#define u_majflt    u_ru.ru_majflt                    /* major page fault count */
#define u_ior               u_ru.ru_inblock           /* block read count */
#define u_iow               u_ru.ru_oublock           /* block write count */
        long        u_ioch;                           /* I/O character count */
        /* controlling tty info */
        pid_t       *u_ttysid;                /* ptr to session leader id in tty */
        pid_t       *u_ttyp;                  /* ptr to controlling tty pgrp field */
        dev_t       u_ttyd;                   /* controlling tty dev */
        off_t       u_ttympx;                 /* mpx value for controlling tty */
        unsigned    *u_ttys;                  /* pointer to t_state in tty struct */
        int         u_ttyid;                  /* tty id */
        int         (*u_ttyf)();              /* tty query function pointer */
        void        *u_loginfo;               /* loginfo pointer */
        struct upfbuf       *u_message;       /* uprintf buffer pointer */
        int         u_dsize;                  /* current break value */
        int         u_sdsize;                 /* data size from shared lib */
        struct pinprof *u_pprof;              /* pinned user profiling buffer - struct
                                              pinprof defined in mon.h */
        struct xmem *u_dp;                    /* memory descriptor for pinned prof
                                              buffer */
        /* file system state */
        struct vnode        *u_cdir;          /* current directory of process */
        struct vnode        *u_rdir;          /* root directory of process */
        ushort              u_vfs;
        struct vnode        *u_pdir;          /* vnode of parent of dirp */
        pid_t       u_epid;                   /* proc id for file locks */
        int         u_sysid;                  /* system id for file locks */
        char        *u_lastname;              /* lastname component */
        short       u_cmask;                  /* mask for file creation */
        long        u_ioctlrv;                /* return value for PSE ioctl's */
        long        _u_fsspace[7];            /* more spare room */
        long        u_loader[64];             /* loader area */
        short       u_maxofile;               /* maximum u_ofile index in use */
        struct ufd {
            struct file *       fp;
            int             flags;
        } u_ufd[OPEN_MAX];                    /* User's file descriptor table */
};
```

ules are no longer needed, they are removed from the kernel space; if new or additional kernel modules are needed during the course of the run, they are loaded dynamically into kernel space.

3.3 Memory Management

The POWER architecture, as currently implemented, can support up to 4

Gbytes of real storage on a machine. However, current hardware cannot support more than 512 Mbytes. Access to this memory is performed via segments, called *pages,* that are 4 Kbytes in size.[1] Every page of memory is assigned a *page number* by which it is addressed. AIX constructs a *memory free list* that indicates whether or not a particular page of real storage is used, and if used, by whom.

Real storage is used in AIX for supporting processes in *virtual storage.* Virtual storage is a concept which allows the operating system to load more programs into real storage than actually fit. On an AIX system, many programs run at the same time. These programs support the multiple users and the many processes that perform functions for the system overall. At any one time, only a portion of each of these programs is actually being used; the rest of the program is dormant. There is no reason for the dormant routines of these programs to reside in memory unless they are needed. Virtual storage allows the operating system to write out those portions of the program not currently needed to a special file on disk, the *paging space,* where the pages are stored until needed. This process of writing a program out to disk is referred to as *paging out.* As long as a page is not modified, it is only necessary to write it to the paging file once, regardless of the number of times the page is actually removed from real storage. However, once a page has been modified, it must be written to the paging file if removed from physical memory.

The opposite process occurs when the operating system detects that a portion of the program not currently in real storage is needed (a *page fault*); it *pages in* the necessary portion of the program from disk (Fig. 3.3).

This paging architecture, *demand paging,* differs from the original UNIX implementations which used *swapping.* Conceptually, swapping is not much different from paging; however, instead of transferring a single page, multiple pages are transferred. Originally, UNIX systems did not implement virtual storage and the only way to provide for multiple, concurrent users was to take a user's *entire* storage space[2] and write it out to disk, while, at the same time, bringing into storage another user's processing space. Most recent UNIX systems only use swapping when the paging rate reaches a critical point. In these situations, the operating system swaps out entire processes until the overall system paging rate returns to a reasonable level. Gradually, these swapped out processes are reintroduced into the system.

Demand paging relies on the ability of the operating system to determine how often, or if, a page in real storage has been referenced. Obviously, pages that have not been used recently are the best choice to be paged out when paging is necessary. In traditional UNIX systems, a software mechanism is used to determine the age of pages in real storage. This process, the *pagedaemon,* periodically scans all real storage and maintains tables which track which pages are being used and by whom. Software processes are necessary as some computer architectures do not have a way to indicate this informa-

---

[1] Most UNIX-based operating systems implement a 1 Kbyte page size.
[2] Excluding the kernel and shared storage pages.

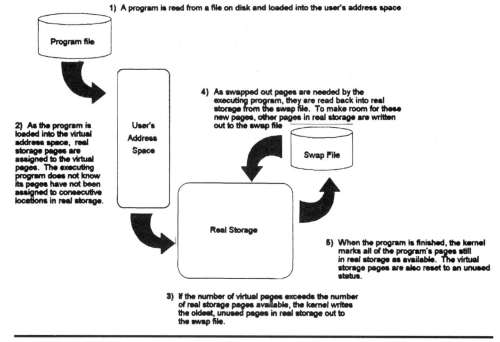

1) A program is read from a file on disk and loaded into the user's address space

Program file

2) As the program is loaded into the virtual address space, real storage pages are assigned to the virtual pages. The executing program does not know its pages have not been assigned to consecutive locations in real storage.

User's Address Space

4) As swapped out pages are needed by the executing program, they are read back into real storage from the swap file. To make room for these new pages, other pages in real storage are written out to the swap file

Swap File

Real Storage

5) When the program is finished, the kernel marks all of the program's pages still in real storage as available. The virtual storage pages are also reset to an unused status.

3) If the number of virtual pages exceeds the number of real storage pages available, the kernel writes the oldest, unused pages in real storage out to the swap file.

Figure 3.3 Paging.

tion in the hardware. This is not the case with the POWER architecture hardware; page use information is available directly from the hardware, therefore the *pagedaemon* process is not necessary in AIX.

Virtual storage also allows the operating system to present an application program with a linear memory space. This *address space* always starts at the same location and is unique to each process (Fig. 3.4). For all practical purposes, the user process does not know that the storage it "sees" is not real. Each process on the system believes that it has exclusive access to 256 Mbytes of real storage. The user process accesses data and instructions via the *virtual address-es* of the address space (Fig. 3.5). When the user process accesses these virtual addresses, the operating system must translate them to the real address where the information is actually loaded. This is performed via *page tables* (Fig. 3.6).

In a traditional virtual memory operating system, a separate table is constructed in real storage for each virtual address space used on the system. Each of these tables can occupy quite a bit of storage, and when many virtual storages are active, these tables can occupy an inordinate amount of real storage. Additionally, the size of these tables increases as the size of the real storage increases. As AIX can implement up to 16 million 256-Mbyte address spaces, another approach using *inverted page* tables was taken.[3] The inverted

---

[3] If another approach had not been tried, real storage would be totally occupied with page tables and no storage would be available for the application programs.

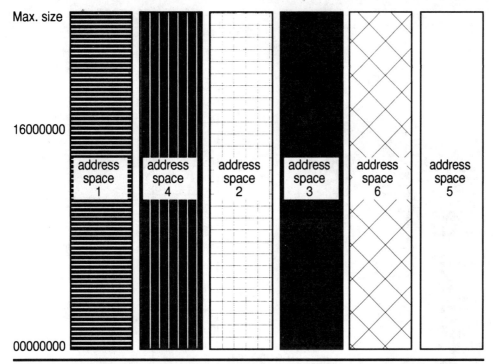

Figure 3.4 Every address space is unique, although each address space starts at the same location and uses similar address locations.

page table is constructed to represent the available real storage and points back to the virtual storage. With this architecture, only one entry is required in the table for each real storage page, which dramatically cuts down the amount of real storage needed for the page table. The normal page translation tables are necessary, but they are no longer required to be locked in real storage. As can be seen from Fig. 3.7, there is more page translation overhead involved using this scheme, but the real storage savings offset the disadvantages.

Within the virtual address space of each process, memory is divided into several sections: text, data, stack, and optionally, shared. The text area is where the program code is loaded. The data area contains all of the static data areas used by the program. Even if data definitions are interspersed throughout the program source code, the compilation and link editing processes move all data definitions to the data area (Fig. 3.8). The stack area has two primary uses. The stack area is foremost for storing information when transferring control between programs or parts of programs, and it is used as an area for creating dynamic data structures. The shared area is used for sharing data between processes allowing each sharing process access to the data as if it were its own.

In AIX, the text segment of a process's virtual storage cannot be modified. In addition to providing for greater code reliability, this permits the operating system to skip the page out process for all text segments of programs, which

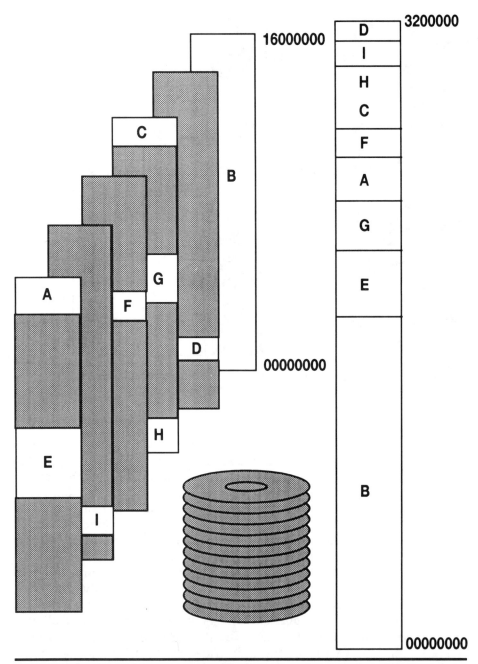

Figure 3.5 Virtual-to-real storage mapping. The linear virtual storage of an address space can be distributed throughout real storage and the swap file.

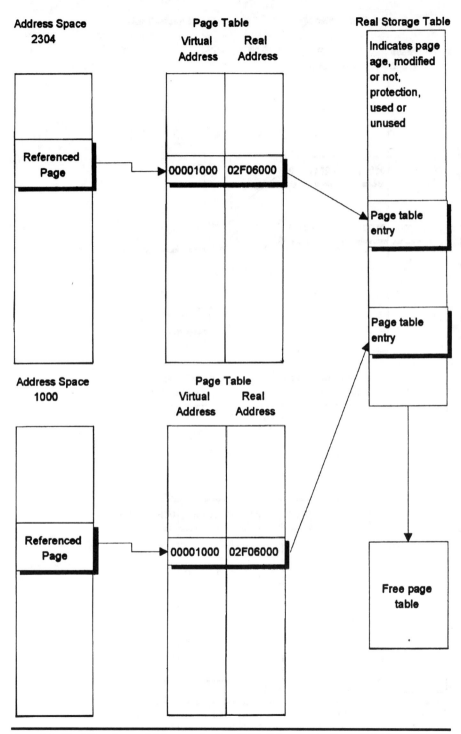

Figure 3.6 Traditional page table organization. With this organization, all tables must be in real storage at all times.

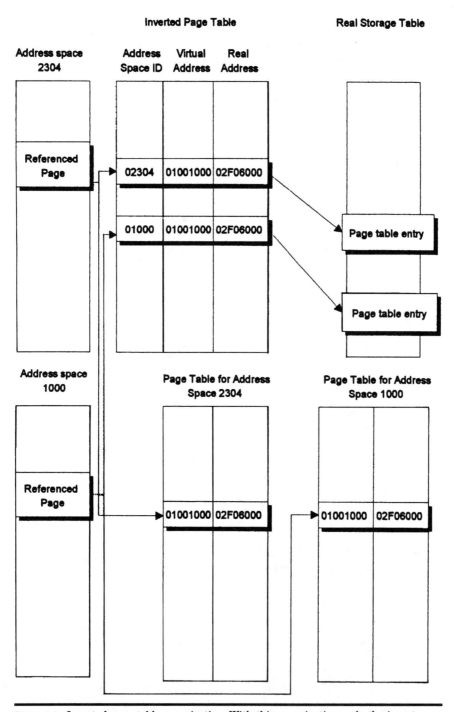

Figure 3.7 Inverted page table organization. With this organization, only the inverted page table is locked in real storage; the traditional page tables are pageable.

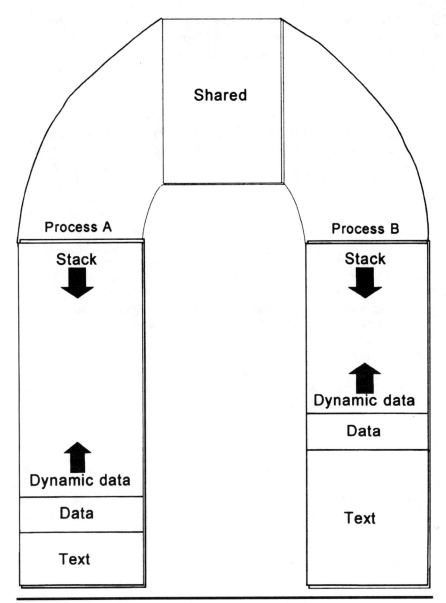

Figure 3.8 Process structure.

can result in better performance on systems that are deficient in available real storage.

3.4 Process Management

Every process on the system competes with every other process for the resources of the system; the most noticeable resources being execution time, storage, and input/output services.

AIX divides the time of the system processing units among the executing processes by *time-slicing*. Each process is allotted a maximum amount of time in which to run. During the period of time the process is running, it is said to be *in control* of the system. If the maximum time limit is reached, the kernel stops the current process and schedules another process to run. Processes which have been stopped are referred to as *sleeping*.

In many cases, a process never uses its entire allotment of time as it "voluntarily" gives up control. This occurs whenever an input or output operation occurs. Although this surrender is not really voluntary, it is perfectly reasonable. In general, when a process is waiting for an input or output operation to complete, it cannot perform any other additional instructions until the I/O is complete. It is not reasonable for the processors to lie idle while a process is waiting for an input or output operation to complete. Therefore, the kernel gives control of the processors to another process as soon as an I/O is initiated.

But in addition to voluntarily giving up control, processes may involuntarily give up control of the processor. Every process of the system is scheduled by the kernel based on a priority and the ability of the process to run. When the scheduler selects a process to run, it always selects the highest priority process on the system not waiting for an external event, like I/O. Unlike other UNIX-based operating systems, AIX provides for process preemption; the kernel can preempt a running process to serve another, higher priority process. In fact, even kernel processes are preemptible. Because of this capability, AIX can provide *real-time* execution facilities whereas many other UNIX-variants cannot.

The scheduling of processes is performed by the highest-priority kernel process, the *swapper,* sometimes also referred to as *process 0* since it always runs under process ID zero. Every process on the system is created as a child of process 1, init, by means of the fork (or vfork) system call (Table 3.2).

The *fork* system call tells the kernel to create a child process for the requesting process. The child process is created by duplicating the parent process; the image of the parent process is copied into the new address space. Although the kernel assigns a new process id to the child, the child address space shares many of the parent's facilities; in particular, when the *fork* system call is used,

---

TABLE 3.2   Process Initialization Overview

Allocate a new *proc(ess)* structure
Copy parent proc structure to child *proc* structure
Set up new information (process ID, CPU time, etc.)
Set up file structures (*inodes*) for sharing
Set up shared memory for child process
Split into two processes
Allocate real storage for child process
Copy *text, data,* and *stack* regions from parent
Copy *user* structure from parent
Access new program and read in headers
Check memory requirements
Detach old regions
Attach new regions

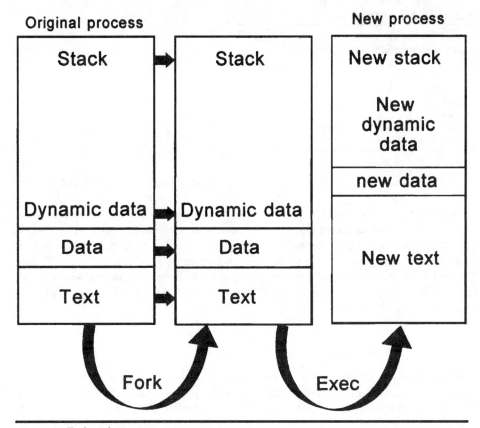

Figure 3.9 Fork and exec process.

the two address spaces share text areas and file descriptors.[4] Furthermore, although the data and stack areas are not shared, the *fork* system call does copy the information from the parent to the child when the child process is created.

The *exec* system call is then used to load the new program into the child process (Fig. 3.9). Without the exec system call, the child process would execute the same program as the parent.

There is quite a bit of overhead in performing all of this information copying from the parent to the child. In the vast majority of cases, this overhead is unjustified as a new program will be loaded into the child process. To circumvent this problem, the *vfork* system call is used. This system call, which is a relatively new addition to the world of UNIX, only creates a new process; it does not copy information from parent to child. It is assumed that a *vfork* call is followed by an *exec* call to load a program into the address space.

---

[4]The child process even has the same file location pointers.

TABLE 3.3   Process Termination Overview

Release all memory used by process except *user* structure
Reduce all file reference counts, close if necessary
Detach from shared memory areas
Change process state to *zombie*
Mark *exit* status in process table entry
Release *user* structure
Signal parent process
Attach remaining child processes to *init* process
Switch control to another process

A process can either terminate itself normally or be abnormally terminated via the *kill* system call.[5] A process cannot terminate until the kernel has "cleaned up" all of resources the process has used. While the process is waiting for the kernel to clean up, the process is in a *zombie* or *defunct* state. In general, processes pass through this state quickly (Table 3.3). However, in unusual circumstances zombie processes can exist for long periods of time. The most common cause of long-running zombie processes is system or application failure. In these cases, the zombie process can be terminated only by shutting down the system.

3.5   Interprocess Communication

AIX provides several mechanisms for interprocess communication: pipes, signals, shared memory, message queues, semaphores, and sockets. A user of the system can directly manipulate or influence the first two via commands. The other four mechanisms can be accessed only by systems calls from application programs.

A pipe, as discussed earlier, is actually a type of file, albeit a special type of file. Implemented in a *first-in-first-out* (FIFO) manner, pipes are primarily used to pass data from one program to another. At any given time, only two processes may use a pipe: one to read the pipe, and the other one to write to it. Even though pipes are implemented as files, they are not associated with any directory. Furthermore, pipes are transient; once data has been read from the pipe it can never be reread, and once the processes using the pipe terminate, the pipe can never be used again.

Signals are a system call used to notify a process of an event, although in some cases signals are used to inform the process that it needs to take some type of action. In either case, it is up to the process being signalled to determine what, if any, action occurs. Users most commonly send signals to processes via shell commands; most often these signals are used to terminate or restart processes.

Shared memory provides processes with a means of sharing large amounts of data. This is accomplished by creating a separate, shared memory address space

---

[5] For more details on *kill,* see Chapter 6.

which is equally accessible to all concerned processes. There are no inherent rules as to whom may read or write data, or how the data is organized. This is arranged and managed by the application programs using the shared memory.

Message queues are a more formal way of organizing data that is passed between processes. Although there are no AIX-imposed rules on who may read or write the message queue, by its nature it is organized in a first-in-first-out manner.

Semaphores are very much like signals. The primary difference between the two is that semaphores are not predefined by the operating system, whereas signals are.

Sockets are used to provide addressable endpoints for communication. They facilitate communication, based on a defined protocol, between processes and are used extensively to implement client/server functionality.

In the client/server environment, the server side creates a socket, assigns an address to the socket, and listens for activity. The client connects to the server using the defined socket address. If more than one client can connect to the socket, the server negotiates with the client to move to another socket where client/server communication can take place. This leaves the original socket free to receive more incoming clients.

Some servers services are commonly implemented, particularly in regard to networking. To facilitate intersystem connectivity, these services are routinely assigned to the same socket address regardless of the host system. This type of socket address is called a *well-known address.*[6]

3.6   Logical and Physical Volumes

The file system is the kernel subsystem responsible for storing the data of the system. It is, for the most part, the most visible part of the operating system to the user. Although the user-level presentation of the file system on AIX differs very little from other UNIX-implementations, the underlying structure is very different.

To begin with, file systems on locally-mounted magnetic media (fixed disk drives) are implemented via a *journaled file system.* Journaling techniques, similar to those used in database systems, are automatically performed for AIX file systems. This helps prevent damage to the file systems in the event of a system abend.

An abstraction layer is imposed upon the physical hardware representation. Every file system exists within a *logical volume* which is part of a *volume group* which consists of one or more *physical volumes* (the actual disk drives). Figure 3.10 demonstrates this mirrored hierarchy.

A volume group is a system-wide, logical entity consisting of 1 to 32 physical volumes which may or may not be of the same size or type (Fig. 3.11). An AIX system can have up to 255 volume groups; the default number of volume groups

---

[6]A common example is the TELNET server, which is routinely assigned to address 23.

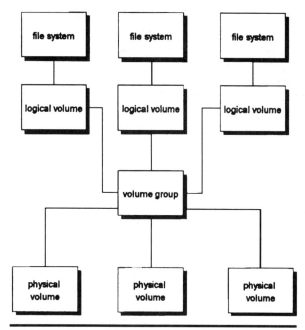

Figure 3.10   Storage hierarchy.

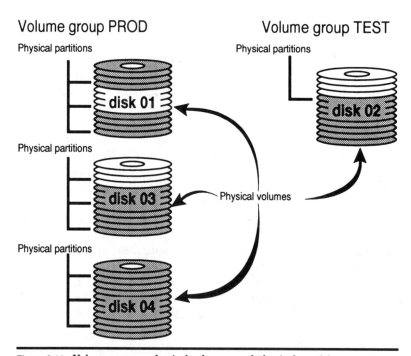

Figure 3.11   Volume groups, physical volumes, and physical partitions.

is one. The primary purpose of a volume group is to define a structure for the physical volumes upon which a logical volume resides. After initial installation of the operating system, a single volume group will exist. This root volume group, rootvg, contains all the logical volumes required to start the system.

Each physical volume is divided into *physical partitions*—equal-size segments of space on the disk which are the actual physical units of disk space allocation. Physical partition size is defined at the volume group level and can be any power of two from 1 to 256 Mbytes. The size of the physical partitions on a disk are defined automatically when the disk is added to a volume group. There is no inherent limit on the maximum number of physical partitions on a single disk drive, but the maximum number of physical partitions within the volume group is specified when it is defined[7] and is limited to either a maximum of 256 physical partitions or 4 Gbytes of storage, whichever is reached first.

Logical volumes are the instruments by which multiple physical partitions are presented to the file system as if they were one contiguous space (Fig. 3.12). A logical volume, in turn, consists of one to three *logical partitions*. The secondary and tertiary logical partitions, if present in the logical volume, are

---

[7] While this can subsequently be increased, it cannot be decreased.

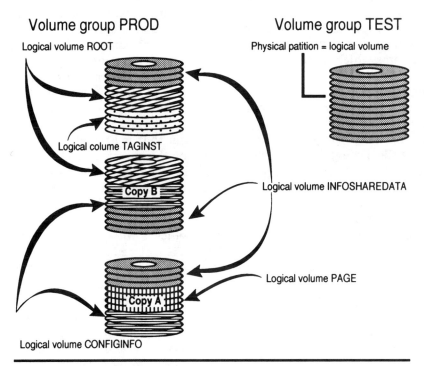

Volume group PROD

Logical volume ROOT

Logical colume TAGINST

Copy B

Logical volume CONFIGINFO

Copy A

Volume group TEST

Physical patition = logical volume

Logical volume INFOSHAREDATA

Logical volume PAGE

Figure 3.12   Logical volumes. Logical volumes can reside on one or more physical partitions. A physical partition may contain unique data or be a mirror-image of the data of the primary physical partition.

used to implement storage mirroring of the primary logical partition; all of the logical partitions within a logical volume, under normal circumstances, contain the same data.

Volume groups, and by association their constituent physical volumes, are made available or unavailable to the system through a vary on/vary off process. In normal operation, volume groups are varied on during system startup and are left available until system shutdown. This is necessary as data in the volume group cannot be accessed until the volume group is varied on. During vary on processing the *logical volume manager* (LVM) reads control information from the physical volumes, the most significant being the *volume group descriptor area* (VGDA) which describes all the logical and physical volumes that belong to the volume group and the *volume group status area* (VGSA) which contains information on the synchronization level and availability of all the physical partitions. These two data areas are used to determine whether or not all of the data in the volume group is accessible and current. This is done by insuring that a majority or *quorum* of the VGDAs and VGSAs can be read. If a majority of the VGDAs or VGSAs cannot be read, the volume group is not varied on and recovery action must be taken.

3.7 File Systems

As discussed earlier, an AIX file system is a hierarchical structure of files and directories. In most operating systems that implement a hierarchical file system, a single structure is shared by all users of the system. UNIX-based operating systems are unique in that they can implement several distinct file systems which can be combined in different ways depending on the needs of the individual user. To the user, the file system hierarchy appears as one single, unified entity. In actuality, the file system hierarchy for the user is a collection of separate file systems, related to each other by the *mounting* process.

On an AIX system, there is only one file system that is absolutely necessary: the *root* file system. This file system contains the operating system programs needed to start and manage AIX. To allow the system to reference this file system, the root directory (/) is automatically mounted when the system is started. When the system starts, it inserts the root file system into the top of the directory tree structure.

The mounting process is the mechanism by which a file system is made available to users. It becomes available because it is inserted into the directory structure (Fig. 3.13). The inserted file system appears to the user as if it were a subdirectory of another directory. Usually, a file system is inserted into the directory structure at an unused point, but this is not mandatory. Mounting a file system over an existing directory precludes access to the original directory until the newly mounted file system is unmounted (Fig. 3.14). Additionally, a single file system can be mounted at several different points. This facility would allow, for example, a file system to be inserted into a user's private directory structure (Fig. 3.15).

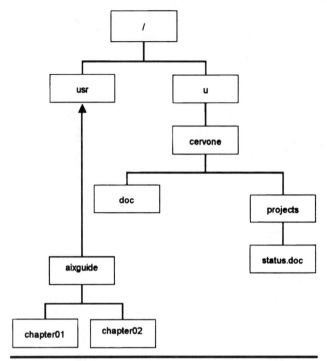

Figure 3.13 Mounting a file system. In this figure, the
/aixguide file system is mounted under the usr subdirectory; the full path name is /usr/aixguide.

Examination of the AIX file tree demonstrates the use of mount points.
Looking at the subdirectories of the root, it is not intuitively obvious that all
of the subdirectories are not integral parts of the root file system, but the
/home, /usr, /tmp, and /var directories are actually distinct file systems.

In actuality, the directories just referred to as file systems are not, in fact,
file systems, but *mount point* names. A mount point name is the external name
of a file system which is presented to the user. The operating system uses a different name to refer to the file system; this internal system name is in actuality the name of the file system. The mount point name can be changed by
unmounting the file system and remounting it with a different name. The
internal system name can be changed only by recreating the file system.

This is demonstrated in Table 3.4. When the command to mount a file system is given, AIX loads the internal name as the name of the mount point.
For example, the command to mount the usr file system is

```
mount /dev/hd2 /usr
```

which mounts file system /dev/hd2 as /usr.

Also invisible to the general user is the mapping between a file system and
a logical volume. Each file system on AIX is created within a specific logical

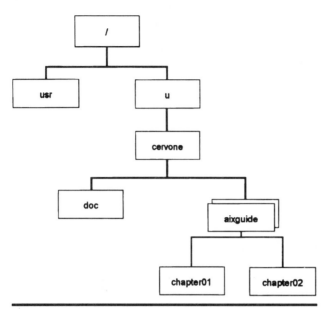

Figure 3.14 Mounting a file system over an existing object. In this figure, the /aixguide file system is mounted over the /projects subdirectory. The projects subdirectory will be inaccessible until the aixguide file system is unmounted. The full path name to the /aixguide file system is /u/cervone/aixguide.

volume. As demonstrated in Fig. 3.12, the use of logical volumes allows a file system to span multiple volumes. In most UNIX-based systems, a file system must reside entirely, and only, on one volume. When the file system becomes larger than the physical disk drive, it must be divided. Logical volumes in AIX help alleviate this problem.

AIX supports three types of file systems, each designed for different media and needs. To the general user of the system, there is little (if any) difference in the usage of the different file system types. As previously discussed, the *journaled file system* (JFS) is the native file system for disk devices. The *network file system* (NFS) is an industry-standard mechanism for accessing and sharing files which reside on remote systems as if they were locally mounted. The *CD-ROM file system* allows CD-ROMs to be loaded and accessed as if they were part of the regular file system.

3.7.1 The AIX file tree

The organization of the AIX file tree is similar to that found in other UNIX-based operating systems (Fig. 3.16). There are, in fact, several distinct journaled file systems[8] within AIX, each with a specific purpose. Some significant

---

[8]From this point on, unless noted otherwise, references to the AIX file system are specifically referring to a journaled file system.

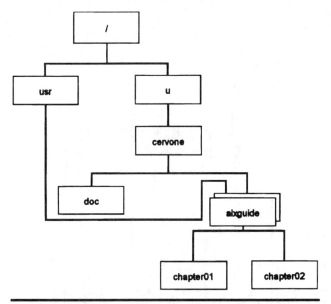

Figure 3.15 Mounting a file system multiple times. In this figure, the /aixguide file system is mounted over the /projects subdirectory and underneath the usr subdirectory; therefore, it is accessible through either path name: /u/cervone/aixguide or /usr/aixguide.

TABLE 3.4   File System and Mount Point Names

File system name	Mount point
/dev/hd1	/home
/dev/hd2	/usr
/dev/hd3	/tmp
/dev/hd4	/
/dev/hd9	/var

variations exist between the AIX file tree and those of other UNIX-based operating systems. This is primarily because AIX follows an OSF file model; it does not conform to the bsd or System V models. To facilitate conversion from other systems,[9] Table 3.5 delineates some of the more noticeable differences in the file directories of AIX and other implementations.

Within each file system in the file tree, functionality is delineated by placing specific functions within subdirectories. To avoid duplication among the file systems and to provide more convenient and flexible access to functions, some subdirectories do not contain data at all, but instead are *links* to other directories. This permits the file system to contain multiple references to a

---

[9]And other texts which follow either the System V or bsd conventions.

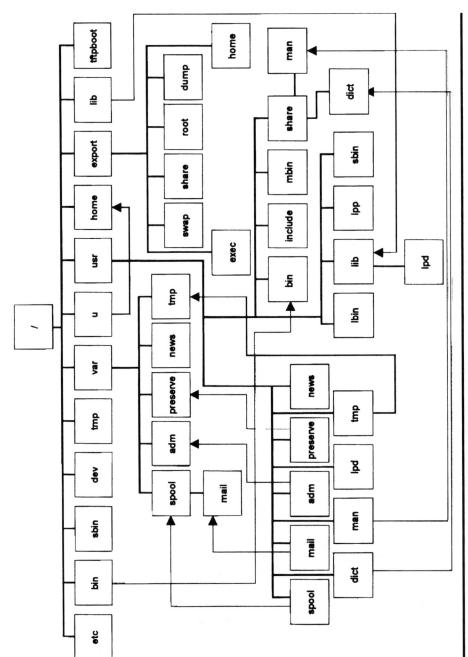

Figure 3.16 The root file tree. The bold lines indicate directory paths; the light lines indicate links.

TABLE 3.5   Divergent AIX Directories

UNIX directory name	AIX directory linked to
/bin	/usr/bin
/lib	/usr/lib
/unix	/usr/lib/boot/unix
/usr/adm	/var/adm
/usr/dict	/usr/share/dict
/usr/man	/usr/share/man
/usr/news	/var/news
/usr/pub	/usr/share
/usr/src	none†
/usr/spool	/var/spool
/usr/sys	empty‡
/usr/tmp	/var/tmp
/usr/userid	/u/userid§

†This directory (and its subdirectories) does not exist in AIX.
‡Although this directory exists in AIX, it does not contain any members.
§The older UNIX convention of placing individual user directories directly into the /usr file system is not followed in AIX. Instead the user's directory is created under the /u directory, which points to the /home file system.

TABLE 3.6   The Root File System

Directory name	Use
/bin	Link to /usr/bin
/dev	Special files for local system devices; printers, disks, tapes, and terminals
/etc	Configuration files and links to system administration programs in other directories
/export	Directories and files on the server for client use
/home	Mount point for a file system containing user home directories
/lib	Link to /usr/lib
/sbin	External commands used during the boot process
/tftpboot	Contains boot images and information for diskless clients
/tmp	Mount point for file system that contains system-generated temporary files
/u	Link to the /home directory
/usr	Mount point for the usr file system
/var	Mount point for the var file system

single file. When a reference is made to a file through a directory that is actually a link, the operating system substitutes the real directory for the link. This substitution is transparent to the user.

The root file system is at the top of the hierarchy. It contains files and directories that are essential for system operation; this includes device drivers, the kernel, and the mount points for other file systems. Within the root file system there are several directory entries. The uses of these directories are listed in Table 3.6.

Architecture dependent files which can be shared and which are not essential for system operation are located in the /usr file system.[10] This read-only file system contains programs, libraries, and data which can be used by any RS/6000 machine. On a standalone or server system, /usr is a separately mounted file system. On client machines, a directory on the remote RS/6000 server is mounted in read-only mode as the /usr file system. The subdirectories of the /usr file system are described in Table 3.7.

The /usr/share directory in /usr is usually treated as if it were a separate file system although it is not. This is because, unlike the rest of the /usr file system, it is can be used by any AIX system, regardless of the underlying architecture. This directory contains only text files (Table 3.8).

The /var file system contains files that are variable; typically these files are specific to applications and users and tend to grow—mail and spool files, for example. Table 3.9 describes the subdirectories that are created when the system is installed.

---

[10]Just because they are not essential does not mean that they are frivolous. It simply means they are not essential to start and run the system in a limited-functionality mode.

TABLE 3.7   The /usr File System

Directory name	Use
/usr/adm	Link to /var/adm
/usr/bin	Ordinary command and shell scripts
/usr/dict	Link to /usr/share/dict
/usr/include	Include (header) files for program development
/usr/lbin	Programs that perform backend processing for commands
/usr/lib	Program development libraries
/usr/lpd	Link to /usr/lib/lpd
/usr/lpp	Optionally installed IBM program products
/usr/mail	Link to /var/spool/mail
/usr/man	Link to /usr/share/man
/usr/mbin	National Language Support (NLS) versions of commands in /usr/sbin
/usr/news	Link to /var/news
/usr/preserve	Link to /var/preserve
/usr/sbin	System administration utilities
/usr/share	Text files that can be shared among machines with different architectures
/usr/spool	Link to /var/spool
/usr/tmp	Link to /var/tmp

TABLE 3.8   The /usr/share File System

Directory name	Use
/usr/share/dict	Spelling dictionary and indexes
/usr/share/info	InfoExplorer database files
/usr/share/lib	Architecture-independent data files such as *terminfo, macros,* and *learn*
/usr/share/lpp	Information on optionally installed IBM program products
/usr/share/man	Manual pages, if they have been loaded

TABLE 3.9   The /var File System

Directory name	Use
/var/adm	System logging and accounting files
/var/news	System news files
/var/preserve	Preserved data from interrupted edit sessions
/var/spool	Files being processed by programs which utilize spooling, i.e., electronic mail, printing, job queueing
/var/tmp	Temporary files†

†This directory is infrequently used. Its function has been taken over, for the most part, by the /tmp file system.

TABLE 3.10   The /export Directory

Directory name	Use
/export/root	Mounted as the client's root file system
/export/exec†	Contains versions of the /usr file system which are mounted as the client's usr file system.
/export/share	Mounted as the client's /usr/share directory
/export/home	Contains individual directories for each client which are mounted as the client's home file system
/export/swap	Contains separate directories for each client which are mounted if the client does not have its own local swapping space
/export/dump	Contains separate directories for each client which does not have local dump space

†This directory is also known as the *Share Product Object Tree* (SPOT). Different versions of the operating system are stored as SPOTs in this directory. The default location is *RISCAIX*.

The /home file system is used for storing user-specific directories. When AIX is installed, this file system has no subdirectories. Subdirectories are created only when users are added to the system or applications are installed.

Finally, on systems which are hosts for remote clients, an /export directory contains server files that are exported to the clients. The major subdirectories of /export are discussed in Table 3.10.

3.7.2   File organization

As discussed in Section 2.2, AIX defines seven types of files: ordinary disk files, directories, block special files, character special files, pipes, symbolic links, and sockets. AIX does not define a file type as an access method as most operating systems do but according to functional types.

Ordinary disk files in a file system are uniquely identified and numbered in an *inode* structure. The inode structure is a 128-byte control block that contains complete information about a file (size, last access, etc.) including the pointers to the locations on disk where the data actually resides. Table 3.11 describes the major fields of the inode, most of which are self-explanatory.

The last fields of the inode point to the actual data of the file. Files of 32,768 bytes or less are completely addressed by the inode in the eight address pointers, each of which points to a 4,096-byte block of data.

TABLE 3.11   Inode Fields

Field name	Purpose
i_mode	Describes the file type and general access permissions
i_size	Size of the file in bytes
i_uid	Access permissions for the user
i_gid	Access permissions for the group
i_nblocks	Number of blocks allocated
i_mtime	Time of last modification
i_atime	Time of last access
i_ctime	Time of last inode modification
i_nlinks	Number of hard links
i_rdaddr	Array of eight fields pointing to the real disk addresses of the first eight blocks of the file
i_rindirect	Real disk address of the indirect block, if present

Larger files contain the *i_rindirect* field which points to an *indirect block*. Depending on the size of the file this can be either a *single indirect block* or a *doubly indirect block*. The single indirect block contains 1,024 disk addresses which provides a total addressability of up to 4 Mbytes. For files larger than 4 Mbytes, AIX uses the *i_rindirect* field to point to a doubly indirect block which contains 512 disk addresses; these in turn, point to single indirect blocks. This provides for files with up to four Gbytes of data (Fig. 3.17).

Note that in the inode structure, the file name is not represented in any of the inode fields. This is because files on AIX are not identified by name, but by inode number.[11] The directory entry of a file links a file name to an inode number. Because the inode is not inherently related to a specific file name, they can be assigned to multiple file names.[12]

The other six types of files on the system are also represented by inodes; however, the internal structure of these inodes varies from that used by ordinary files.

3.8   Input and Output

UNIX-based operating systems handle input and output differently from most other operating systems. Typically, operating systems divide input and output functions into two distinct subsystems: device-level I/O and file-level I/O. In UNIX-based operating systems, devices are not viewed by the I/O system as being any different from files; devices are accessed through the same routines that are used for file I/O. Every device on the system is associated with a *special file* which is used to communicate with the device. This I/O implementation allows for the creation of special files that manage system resources other than real I/O devices, such as memory or virtual terminals.

---

[11] To determine the inode number of a file, use the ls -i command.
[12] This is what the ln command does.

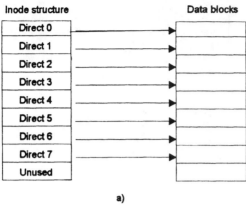

a)

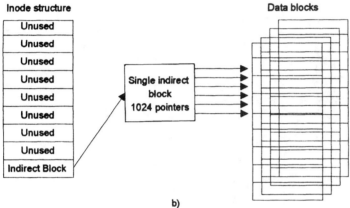

b)

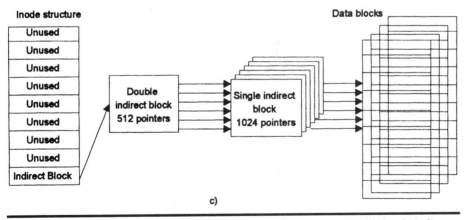

c)

Figure 3.17 Inodes. (a) Direct pointers for file less than or equal to 32K. (b) Single indirect pointers for files greater than 32K but less than or equal to 4 Mbytes. (c) Doubly indirect for files greater than 4 Mbytes but less than or equal to 4 Gbyte files.

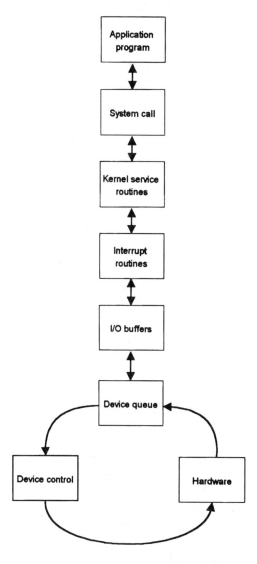

Figure 3.18 I/O Path from application program to physical device.

As discussed in Chap. 2, the special file is not actually a file on disk, but instead is a path to a device. Associated with each special file is a *device driver*. Device drivers are programs that serve as the interface between the kernel and a device (Fig. 3.18). Unlike other operating systems, the AIX kernel does not contain any code which allows it to control physical devices. All instructions to control and access devices are sent to the special file and to the driver. It is the responsibility of the device driver to interpret the command sent to the device and to translate it into the appropriate commands. Because of this separation of function, great flexibility in adding devices to an AIX system is possible. In other operating systems, adding new devices requires the regeneration of the operating system.

Devices are divided into two types: block and character. Block devices, such as tape or disk drives, generally perform I/O with blocks of data. Almost all other devices are character devices, which perform I/O via a stream of bytes. Examples of character devices include terminals, printers, and modems. Block devices often have a character driver, in addition to the block driver, for special purpose, low-level I/O functions.

3.9 Networking

By far, the most common networking protocol used with AIX is *Transmission Control Protocol/Internnet Protocol* (TCP/IP). This protocol was developed under the auspices of the *Advanced Research Projects Agency* of the *U.S. Department of Defense* (DARPA) to facilitate host-to-host interconnection between dissimilar systems. In addition to being independent of hardware and operating system considerations, TCP/IP is also designed to be media- and data-link independent (Table 3.12). Because of these design points, TCP/IP is very flexible and can be easily implemented by users. As a nonproprietary protocol, it has been widely supported by a number of vendors.

TCP/IP supports two types of application communication: connection-oriented and *connectionless*. The TCP part of TCP/IP provides for connection oriented, reliable, peer-to-peer communications. Examples of this type of application communication are file transfers and terminal sessions.

Connectionless communication is used for data transfers which do not require the reliability and continuity provided by TCP. An example of this type of communication would be where a client application sends an asynchronous request for data to a server application. At some later point, the server replies to the client application. This communication protocol, called *User Datagram Protocol* (UDP), is very fast compared to TCP, but is far less reliable. It does not provide for error notification or message sequencing; that is, the entire communication from one application to another must fit in one transmission unit.

TCP/IP also includes several basic network support functions: file transfer (via the *File Transfer Protocol,* or FTP), terminal access (via TELNET), and electronic mail (via the *Simple Mail Transfer Protocol* or SMTP). In addition to these basic applications, the *network file system* (NFS) is implemented via TCP/IP.

TABLE 3.12 TCP/IP Network Functions and their Relationship to ISO Layers

ISO Layer	Network Function
Application	FTP, TELNET, rlogin, NFS, applications using sockets
Presentation	Library routines, stream modules
Session	Sockets, Remote procedure calls
Transport	TCP
Network	IP
Data Link & Physical	Ethernet, Token-Ring, x.25

NFS allows a user of one system to access the files on another system as if they were mounted on the user's local system. The end-user and application programs on the local system are completely shielded from the network interfacing activity necessary to access the remote files. In addition to providing client services, NFS provides the services on the server machine necessary to share files with other systems.

The *High Availability Network File System* (HANFS) is an AIX extension to NFS which facilitates the distribution of data over several systems. This is primarily to ensure that access to data is not interrupted in the event of a system outage.

The Internet Protocol (IP) part of TCP/IP provides the addressing and data segmentation and numbering functions for messages to be routed through the network. Fig. 3.19 demonstrates the relationship between the various components of TCP/IP.

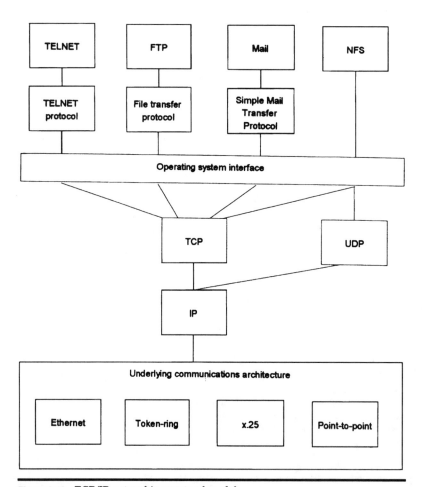

Figure 3.19   TCP/IP networking protocol model.

In addition to TCP/IP, AIX supports connection to a SNA-based network through AIX/6000 SNA Services. For sites running IBM mainframe-based networks, SNA Services allows the AIX system to participate in the network. This could be as a bridge between SNA and TCP/IP, or more typically, to allow the AIX user to connect to the mainframe system through the RS/60000. This participation is in conjunction with another program product, AIX/6000 Host Connection Program, which allows an AIX terminal-device to connect to the SNA network as if it were a native 3270-type device. SNA Services provide support for LU types 0, 1, 2, 3, and 6.2 and PU types 2 and 2.1 on the AIX machine.

And finally, AIX also provides support for the *Basic Networking Utilities* (BNU), sometimes referred to as uucp in deference to the utilities' most famous command. Although used quite extensively in the past for UNIX-to-UNIX connectivity and communications, this networking facility has been superceded, for the most part, by the superior facilities of TCP/IP.[13]

---

[13] Minor editorializing every now and then never hurt anyone.

Basic Operating System Usage

4

Starting and
Stopping the System

This chapter discusses the procedures for starting and stopping the AIX operating system under normal and abnormal conditions.

4.1 Booting

The process of loading and initializing the AIX operating system is referred to as *booting*. This is a corruption of the original term, *bootstrapping,* which was derived from the analogy of the computer "pulling itself up by its bootstraps." People with a mainframe background sometimes refer to the initialization process as an *initial program load* (IPL), which is a far more accurate description of what actually transpires.

The boot process, under normal circumstances, is generally uneventful (Table 4.1). However, the boot process and its associated processes and information are very critical to the system. An error during the initialization process can result in an unstable or completely unusable system.

In addition to correctly functioning hardware, the operating system needs two items to start successfully. The first is a *boot image* which is the first

TABLE 4.1 Boot Process Steps

The RS/6000 main hardware unit is initialized
The boot image is loaded
The kernel is initialized
Control is passed to the kernel
The kernel configures itself based on the tape and disk drives on the system
Task 1 (the paging task) is started
The init command is run and the inittab is processed
The console and terminals are configured
The system enters multiuser mode

program loaded into the machine. The boot image contains hardware configuration information and controls the loading of the kernel. In addition to the boot image, AIX must be able to access the root (/) and usr (/usr) file systems. If either of these file systems is unavailable or corrupted, AIX does not start.

AIX differentiates between three types of system boots

Normal—when a machine loads the boot image from a locally attached disk

Standalone—when a machine loads the boot image from a maintenance diskette or tape

Network—when a machine loads the boot image from another system attached to the network

This chapter discusses the first two types of boot; the third is addressed in the chapter on diskless workstations (Chapter 12).

4.2   Normal System Initialization

During a normal system initialization, AIX does not require any operator intervention to start the hardware and software on the system. AIX locates all of the information it needs to start the system in files on local disks.

The actual initialization process can be divided into three steps

ROS kernel initialization

Base device configuration

System boot

4.2.1   ROS Kernel Initialization

After the machine has been turned on (or reset), the *read-only storage* (ROS) kernel begins with a hardware check to ensure there are no problems with the *system motherboard*. The central processor and memory of the system are located on the system motherboard. After the motherboard test, control is passed to read-only storage which performs the *power-on self-test* (POST). Assuming the POST test is successful, the next step checks the *user boot list*. The user boot list is a table of valid boot devices which is stored in *nonvolatile random access memory* (NVRAM).[1]

Starting with the first device in the boot list, ROS reads the first record of the device selected. If the record is determined to be a valid boot record, it is placed in the *initial program load* (IPL) control block and control passes to the next step. If it is not a valid boot record, the next device in the boot list is selected and this step is repeated until a valid boot record is found, or the boot device list is exhausted. If the boot device list is exhausted before a valid

---

[1]The system maintains a default boot list in ROS which is used if the list in NVRAM has been deleted or corrupted.

boot record is found, an error number is displayed on the hardware LED[2] and the initialization process stops.

When a valid boot image is finally located, it is loaded into central storage based upon the loading information in the boot record. The boot image contains the AIX kernel and a RAM file system. The RAM file system consists of the files used by the kernel before the root file system is mounted.[3]

At this point, control is passed to the second phase, base device configuration.

4.2.2   Base device configuration

After the boot image has been loaded, control is passed to the kernel. The first order of business for the kernel is to configure the hardware of the system. Therefore, the kernel first calls the *object data manager* (ODM) to determine what devices are attached to the system. It then issues the cfgmgr command (from the RAM file system) to dynamically configure all of the devices found.[4] The *root volume group* (rootvg) is varied online after all of the disks in the root file system have been configured. Control then passes to the final phase of system initialization.

4.2.3   System boot

After the root volume group has been mounted, the paging manager is started and the remaining, active file systems are mounted.

When all of the file systems have been successfully mounted, the kernel issues the init command which processes the inittab file. The inittab contains commands to run programs or shell scripts, and is discussed in detail in Section 4.3. The entries in the inittab are used to start AIX subsystems or daemons, such as TCP/IP, print spoolers, and database managers. After the information in the inittab has been processed, the console and terminals are configured and the system enters multiuser mode.

Finally, all of the locally attached terminals are sent the AIX login prompt which invites users to begin working with the system.

4.3   Starting Processes Automatically During Initialization

The inittab is used during system initialization to run processes that are not part of the basic boot procedure. The processes that are described in inittab include some entries which are necessary and should never be deleted, but mainly concern subsystems and daemons which are unique to the particular system. For example, the basic boot process does not do anything regarding networking facilities; these are started via the inittab.

---

[2]Appendix A is a listing of some of the most common LED code numbers and their meanings.

[3]For example, the RAM file system contains a program file for the mount command.

[4]Only minimal configuration is performed for terminal devices. They are actually configured in a subsequent step.

```
init:2:initdefault:
brc::sysinit:/sbin/rc.boot 3 >/dev/console 2>&1 # Phase 3 of system bo
powerfail::powerfail:/etc/rc.powerfail >/dev/console 2>&1   # d51225
rc:2:wait:/etc/rc > /dev/console 2>&1   # Multi-User checks
fbcheck:2:wait:/usr/lib/dwm/fbcheck >/dev/console 2>&1 # run /etc/firs
srcmstr:2:respawn:/etc/srcmstr            # System Resource Controller
rctcpip:2:wait:/etc/rc.tcpip > /dev/console 2>&1 # Start TCP/IP daemon
rcnfs:2:wait:/etc/rc.nfs > /dev/console 2>&1 # Start NFS Daemons
cons:0123456789:respawn:/etc/getty /dev/console
piobe:2:wait:/bin/rm -f /usr/lpd/pio/flags/*  # Clean up printer flags
cron:2:respawn:/etc/cron
qdaemon:2:wait:/bin/startsrc -sqdaemon
writesrv:2:wait:/bin/startsrc -swritesrv
uprintfd:2:respawn:/etc/uprintfd
rcncs:2:wait:sh /etc/rc.ncs
tty1:2:off:/etc/getty /dev/tty1
lpd:2:once:startsrc -s lpd
```

Figure 4.1   /etc/inittab.

But in addition to use during system initialization, the inittab is used by the init process to determine what action should be performed when one of the entries in the table terminates.

Figure 4.1 illustrates a typical inittab. By convention, the inittab is located in the /etc file system; therefore, the path to the inittab is /etc/inittab. Each line of the inittab is a separate entry that consists of four fields: entry name, system run level, action, and command.

The first field, entry name, is the only mandatory one. Each entry name within the inittab must be unique to a 14-character identifier. The second field controls when the command in the fourth field is processed. The numbers in the second field indicate the system run level during which the command should be processed. As can be seen in Table 4.2, there are many system run levels in AIX, but run level 2 is the most common as it is the default. The system run level field may be blank depending on what is coded in the action field. For the most part, the values coded in the action field (Fig. 4.1) are possible during any system run level; therefore, it is necessary to specify what initialization states are applicable for the entry. Some actions, however, are related to a specific time during initialization, *powerfail* and *sysint* for example. For these actions, system run level is not applicable, and is ignored

TABLE 4.2   System Run Levels

Run Level	Use
0	Reserved for future use by IBM
1	Reserved for future use by IBM
2	Multiuser mode
3-9	User-definable
a,b,c	Used to define states which are run in conjunction with other run levels
Q,q	Used to have init reprocess the /etc/inittab file

if coded.[5] For most user entries, though, the two most common actions are *once* and *respawn*. *Once* is used to start the subject process during system initialization. If the subject process stops at a later point in time, the `init` process does not restart it. *Respawn* is used to have `init` restart the subject process whenever `init` detects it is not running .

In normal system operation, the inittab is read only during the boot process. Processing of the entries by the ongoing `init` process is based on the entries in the table at the time of the boot. To change the inittab, without rebooting the system, the root user (or person with root user authority) issues the `telinit` command[6] with the q option

```
$ telinit q
$
```

This command instructs `init` to reread inittab and process the entries which apply in the current initialization state and have *changed* since the last time the inittab was read.

4.3.1   Modifying the `inittab`

Modification of the inittab in AIX is performed with four commands

`mkitab`	to add entries
`chitab`	to change entries
`rmitab`	to remove entries
`lsitab`	to display entries

4.3.1.1   Displaying entries in the `inittab`. The `lsitab` command lists entries in the inittab. To list all of the records in the inittab, the user enters

---

[5]Lines 2 and 3 of Fig. 4.1 demonstrate this.
[6]A contraction of tell init.

TABLE 4.3   inittab Action Field Values

Value	Meaning	Wait for process to complete
boot	Run the first time the inittab is processed	No
bootwait	Run the first time the inittab is processed	Yes
initdefault	Set the initial run-level	N/A
off	Terminate the process if it is running	N/A
once	Start the process once	No
ondemand	Same effect as respawn	No
powerfail	Execute when the `init` process receives a power failure signal	No
powerwait	Execute when `init` process receives a power failure signal	Yes
respawn	Start the process if it is not running	No
sysinit	Execute before enabling the console	Yes
wait	Start the process once	Yes

```
lsitab -a
```

which displays every entry in the /etc/inittab file. A specific entry can be displayed by coding the entry name after the lsitab command

```
lsitab entryname
```

For example

```
$ lsitab powerfail
powerfail::powerfail:/etc/rc.powerfail >/dev/console 2>&1
$
```

4.3.1.2 Adding entries to the inittab.   Entries are added to the inittab with the mkitab command. The format of the command is:

```
mkitab 'entryname:run level:action:command'
```

As an example, to add a one-time entry for a Korn shell script named tagsh for run level 2, the following command would be issued:

```
mkitab 'tag:2:once:ksh tagsh >/dev/console 2>&1'
```

The command field indicates that the Korn shell should be invoked (ksh) for the tagsh shell. The standard output is redirected to the console device (>/dev/console). Standard Error is redirected to the device the standard output is using (2>&1).

4.3.1.3 Changing entries in inittab.   An entry in the inittab is changed by using the chitab command. The user enters the entry name and the new run level, action, and command. Even if only one field is changed, all four must be specified. For example, to change the above entry for the tag to use the Bourne shell and run at levels 2 and 3, the command would be

```
chitab 'tag:23:once:sh tagsh >/dev/console 2>&1'
```

4.3.1.4 Deleting entries from inittab.   Entries in the inittab are deleted by specifying the rmitab command with the entry identifier. Using the tag as an example again, to remove it from the inittab, enter the command

```
rmitab tag
```

4.3.2 Run control (rc) scripts

Several entries in the inittab are not direct commands, but instead, shell scripts. These are used primarily to start subsystems, TCP/IP, SNA, and print queues, for example. Those shell scripts which begin with the *rc* prefix are referred to as *run control shell scripts*. AIX uses run control shell scripts during initialization to perform actions which cannot be succinctly stated or controlled with the facilities of the inittab. Run control scripts that are "routinely" modified for local site use are stored in the /etc subdirectory. Some of the more common rc shell scripts are */etc/rc.sna* which controls *Systems Network Architecture* (SNA) services startup, */etc/rc.tcpip* for TCP/IP startup, */etc/rc.nfs* for *Network File System* (NFS) startup, and */etc/rc.hcon* for *Host Connection Program* (HCON) startup.

4.4   Shutting Down the System

Terminating the running AIX system is the prerogative of the root user. System shutdown is very simple: the root user enters the shutdown command. This shell script invokes several other commands to ensure that an orderly termination of the system is achieved. The first thing the shutdown procedure does is to send a message to all users that the machine is coming down in one minute. These messages are broadcast to all users with the wall command. The shutdown procedure then waits for 60 seconds before sending another message to all remaining users. This second message is simply a directive to log off immediately.

At this point, the shutdown process sends messages to all running daemons (subsystems) telling them to terminate. When all requested subsystems have terminated, the system kills all other remaining processes. After these remaining processes have been killed, all nonroot volume group file systems are unmounted and the sync command is repeatedly issued. This is to ensure that all data destined for disk drives on the root volume group have been completely flushed from the disk buffers and committed.

At this point, the operating system has terminated, so the kernel displays a message, "Halt completed," on the console. Then the hardware may be turned off.

The shutdown command offers several options to terminate the system. These are outlined in Table 4.4. The most commonly used options are -F which tells shutdown to skip the one-minute delay before starting the shutdown process, -r

TABLE 4.4   shutdown **Command Options**

Option	Meaning
-c	Inhibits the file system check upon restart
-d	Brings the system down from distributed mode to multiuser mode (i.e., terminate server services)
-F	Performs a fast shutdown; bypasses sending messages to users and the one minute wait period for users to logoff
-h	Halts the system completely (same as -v, this is the default)
-i	Perform an interactive shutdown; guides the operator through the shutdown tasks instead of having AIX automatically perform them
-k	Goes through shutdown processing but does not actually stop the system
-m	Brings the system down to singleuser (maintenance) mode
-r	Restarts the system after shutdown is complete
-v	Halts the system completely
+x	Extends the waiting period during which users can log off to x minutes

which instructs the kernel to automatically reboot the system after shutdown, and -m which puts the system into singleuser mode for maintenance.

4.5   Standalone System Initialization

The standalone system initialization procedure is used only for special purposes, such as installing new or updated AIX software, performing diagnostic checks, or recovering from catastrophic system failure.

The standalone initialization process is similar to the normal initialization process. First, a hardware check is performed to ensure there are no problems with the system motherboard. After the motherboard test, the power-on self-test is performed. When the POST test is complete, the first device in the boot list is checked to see if it is mounted.[7] If so, the first record of the selected device is read. If the record read is a valid boot record, it is placed in the *initial program load* (IPL) control block and processing continues. If the record is not a valid boot record, the next device in the boot list is selected; this step is repeated until a valid boot record is found, or the boot device list is exhausted. If the boot device list is exhausted before a valid boot record is found, an error number is displayed on the hardware LED and the initialization process stops.

When a valid boot image is finally located, it is loaded into central storage based upon the loading information in the boot record. The boot image contains an AIX kernel and a RAM file system. After the boot image has been loaded, control is passed to the kernel which configures the hardware of the system. The kernel issues the cfgmgr command to dynamically configure all of the devices found, including all of the disk drives that are to contain the root volume group. Unlike a normal system initialization, the root volume group is *not* varied online since it may not even exist. Networking facilities, if available, are configured and started at this point. Control is then passed to the installation, maintenance, diagnostic, or restore program to be used.

4.6   Performing a Standalone Boot

Unlike a normal system initialization, a standalone boot requires several actions on the part of the operator. Before starting, the operator should ensure that the system is turned off. After placing the mode switch in the SECURE position, the operator turns the system on, and waits until the 200-message appears in the hardware LED. Then the operator places the boot diskette or boot tape in the applicable device. The mode switch is then positioned to the SERVICE mode, and the operator presses the yellow reset button twice in quick succession. While the system is booting, it displays several message indicators on the hardware LED. The meaning of most of these indicators is discussed in Appendix A. They are used to inform the operator on the status of the system.

---

[7]Tape drives are placed before disk drives in the boot list. This ensures that a standalone boot tape, if present, is read instead of the mounted disks.

```
┌─────────────────────────────────────────────────────────────────────┐
│              AIX 3.2 INSTALLATION AND MAINTENANCE                     │
│                                                                       │
│                                                                       │
│ Select the number of the task you want to perform.                   │
│                                                                       │
│   1   Install AIX.                                                    │
│   2   Install a system that was created with the SMIT "Backup         │
│       the system" function or the "mksysb" command.                   │
│   3   Install this system for use with a "/user" server.             │
│   4   Start a limited function maintenance shell.                     │
│                                                                       │
│                                                                       │
│ Type the number for your selection, then press "Enter":  ■            │
│                                                                       │
└─────────────────────────────────────────────────────────────────────┘
```

Figure 4.2 The AIX standalone boot "Installation and Maintenance" menu. Option 2 is used to restore the system from a standalone backup tape, and option 4 is used for performing diagnostics.

If the system is booted from a diskette, a c07 message displays in the hardware LED after the diskette has been loaded; the operator must then place the display diskette in the drive. If the system is configured with graphics adapters, there may be two display diskettes. The operator should insert the *BOS Display Extensions* diskette first. The system prompts for the second *BOS Display* diskette by issuing the c07 message again. Note that the diskette drive does not stop spinning when the c07 message is displayed, so the operator should not wait for the drive to stop before changing diskettes.

The system configures all of the display devices attached to the system; therefore, the operator must indicate which terminal is to be used as the primary console. This is done by responding to the prompt to identify the primary console by entering a 1 at the terminal, which will be used as the primary console.

If the boot device is on diskette, the system prompts the operator again, this time to insert the *BOS Installation/Maintenance* diskette.

After the BOS installation code is loaded, the system displays a menu, similar to that shown in Fig. 4.2, which allows the user to choose which function should be performed. At this point, the system has completed the standalone initialization.

4.7   Additional Restart and Stop Commands

The following commands are not commonly used. It is preferable to use the shutdown command to perform a system shutdown.

4.7.1   halt / fasthalt—Stop the processor

The halt command flushes the disk buffers on the system[8] and then stops the

---

[8] By calling sync.

processor. It does not terminate any process normally or ensure that all pending I/O is completed. Use of the halt or fasthalt commands can cause file system damage. The halt command is recommended only for those situations where a normal shutdown cannot be performed: when processes will not stop and are preventing shutdown from proceeding normally.

The halt command has four flags: -l inhibits logging of the shutdown in the accounting file, -n skips the flush of the disk buffers, -q causes an immediate halt, and -y allows the system to be halted from a dial-up terminal.

The fasthalt command is identical to the halt command; it is provided for bsd compatibility only.

4.7.2 fastboot / reboot—Restart the system

The reboot command flushes the disk buffers on the system and then restarts the processor. It does not terminate any processes other than those of the invoking user nor ensure that all pending I/O is complete. The reboot command is normally used only when the system is in maintenance mode. When other users are on the system, the shutdown command should be used.

The halt command has three flags: -l inhibits logging of the reboot in the accounting file, -n skips the flush of the disk buffers, and -q causes an immediate halt. Use of the -n flag can result in file system corruption.

The fastboot command is identical to the reboot command; it is provided for bsd compatibility only.

Files and Directories

In Chapters 2 and 3, the AIX file system was introduced and discussed from an architectural perspective. This chapter builds upon those discussions by introducing the AIX commands which create, manipulate, maintain, and destroy files and directories.

5.1 File-Naming Conventions

Before proceeding further, a quick review of AIX file-naming conventions is in order

File names may be no longer than 255 characters

The combined length of the complete directory path and file name may be no more than 1023 characters

Alphabetic and numeric characters, in addition to the underscore, are permitted

Several nonalphanumeric characters should be avoided as they have special meaning to the operating system; these include / \ " ' * ; - ? [] ( ) ! ~ $ { } < > # @ & |

AIX is case-sensitive; therefore MYFILE, myfile, MyFile, and Myfile are the names of four distinct, unrelated files

File names which are preceded by a dot (.) are considered to be *hidden* files. They are not displayed in regular file directory listings

File names should be meaningful

5.2 Creating Files

Files are the direct result of a program creating output. Most commonly, files are created as output from an application program such as a general ledger pro-

TABLE 5.1   cat **Command Flags**

Flag	Meaning
-b	If the -n flag has been specified, omit line numbers when displaying blank lines.
-e	If the -v flag has been specified, display a dollar sign ($) at the end of every line.
-n	Precede every output line displayed with a line number, starting at 1.
-q	Suppress error messages if an input file cannot be found.
-s	Same as -q flag
-S	Replace multiple, consecutive blank lines with one blank line.
-t	If the -v flag has been specified, display tab characters as ^I.
-u	Do not buffer output.
-v	Display nonprintable characters as visible characters.
-	Use standard input as the input file.

gram, a FORTRAN compiler, or a database result set. Files which contain textual data are typically created directly by users with a *text editor*. Text editors allow a user to create, modify, and save files. In AIX, vi (discussed in Chapter 15) is the most commonly used editor for composing and maintaining text files.

Files can also be created with operating system commands.

5.2.1   cat—Concatenate files

The cat command (Table 5.1) is used to concatenate files. It reads the file name(s) specified on the command line and writes the files(s) to standard output. The original input file is not modified. By far, the most frequently use of cat is to display a file at a terminal screen. The command

```
cat input.file
```

entered at the user's terminal would display the file input.file. By specifying

```
cat -S input.file
```

the user could suppress the display of multiple blank lines.

Redirecting the standard output of the cat command creates a regular file on disk. Therefore,

```
cat input.file > new.input.file
```

creates a new file, new.input.file, which contains the same information as the original, input.file.

A more realistic usage is the case where a user must consolidate several documents into a final comprehensive one. This is accomplished by

```
cat chapter1 chapter2 chapter3 chapter4 > finaldoc
```

The output file, finaldoc, has the contents of each of the input files. If it were necessary later to add a fifth chapter to the finaldoc file, the command

```
cat chapter1 chapter2 chapter3 chapter4 chapter5 > finaldoc
```

is used. But a far better method is to use the append operator

```
cat chapter5 >> finaldoc
```

By using the append operator ($>>$) the original output file is retained, and the new information is appended at the end.

The cat command uses information from standard input when the minus sign (-) is used as a part of the input file group. Consider the command

```
ls -al /tmp | cat ls.command.explanation - > section5.3
```

This command writes the file ls.command.explanation out to the file named Section 5.3; it then concatentates the standard output of the ls command,[1] which has been piped to the standard input of the cat command, to the file section (Section 5.3).

5.2.2 csplit—Split files by context

This command is the counterpart to cat. The csplit command (Table 5.2) takes an input file and splits it out into a maximum of 99 other files. The division of the input file is based on a recurring pattern found within the input text. The input file is not modified.

All of the output files share a common name prefix. The default prefix name is *xx* but this can be overridden by using the -f prefixname flag to explicitly name the segments. The segments of the file receive information as follows:

Segment 00 receives all data from the beginning of the file to the line immediately preceding the first split pattern

Segment 01 receives the data from the line referenced by the first split pattern to the line immediately preceding the second split pattern

Segment N-1 receives the data from the line referenced by the preceding split pattern up to the line immediately preceding the last split pattern

Segment N receives the data from the line referenced by the last split pattern to the end of the input file

---

[1]The ls command is discussed in Section 5.13.3.

TABLE 5.2 csplit **Command Flags**

Flag	Meaning
-fprefix	Specifies the *prefix* variable for the output file segments. The default value is -fxx.
-k	Specifies that, in the event of an error, the already created segments should be retained.
-s	Suppresses the display of character counts in the segments.

TABLE 5.3 `csplit` **Pattern Definitions**

Pattern	Meaning
/pattern/	Creates a file segment which includes that part of the input file from the current line up to, but not including, the *pattern*.
%pattern%	Sets the current line pointer to the next line found which contains the *pattern*.
pattern+number	Moves the current line pointer forward the indicated number of lines after the immediately preceding pattern has been found; for example %Chapter%+5.
pattern-number	Moves the current line pointer backward the indicated number of lines after the immediately preceding pattern has been found; for example /Chapter/-10.
linenumber	Creates a file segment which includes that part of the input file from the current line for the *linenumber* number of lines.
{number}	Is used in conjunction with the other commands to repeat the command *number* times. If used with a pattern, the pattern is reused *number* times. If used with *linenumber,* the input file is split from the current line for the number of lines specified by *linenumber*.

NOTE: Patterns must be enclosed in quotation marks if spaces or other characters special to the shell are used within the pattern. A pattern *may not* contain new-line characters.

As demonstrated by Table 5.3, division of the segments can be further influenced by the definition of the split pattern.

The *split pattern* is a regular expression[2] that in most cases is enclosed within quotes. Whenever the split pattern contains space characters or characters with special meaning to the shell[3] it must be enclosed within quotes.

Returning to the example in Section 5.2.1, the master document, finaldoc, can be split into separate files with the following command

```
csplit finaldoc "/^ Chapter *[k.0-7]k./" {7}
```

In this example, the input file, finaldoc, is searched for the split pattern defined as lines containing only the word *Chapter* followed by a number from 0 through 7. The {7} after the split pattern indicates that the maximum number of output files to be created by the split is seven.

5.2.3 mv/ move—**Move or rename files and directories**

The mv or move (Table 5.4) commands move files or directories from one directory to another. The commands are used also to rename files. Once a file has been moved, the original file is no longer available. The two commands are functionally equivalent; usage of one over the other is simply a matter of preference.

The behavior of the move commands is slightly different depending on whether a file or directory is being moved, and whether the file or directory is being moved to a new file system.

---

[2]Regular expressions are discussed in Chapter 14—Shells.
[3]See Section 5.1 for a list of these characters.

TABLE 5.4   mv (move) **Command Syntax**

Move file(s) to another directory while retaining the original file names

```
{mv | move} [-f] [-i] [-] originalfile [...] newdirectory
```

Move a directory (or directories) to another directory retaining the original directory and file name(s)

```
{mv | move} [-f] [-i] [-] originaldirectory [...] newdirectory
```

Move and rename a file

```
{mv | move} [-f] [-i] [-] originalfile newfile
```

Move and rename a directory

```
{mv | move} [-f] [-i] [-] originaldirectory newdirectory
```

When a file is moved from one directory to another, the name of the file in the new directory is the same as the name of the file in the old directory. When the move is within the same file system, all links of the file are retained. If the file is moved to a different file system, any links are discarded.

When a directory is moved to an existing directory, the directory and all of the objects underneath it are added to the new directory. If the directory is moved within its existing file system, all of the links of the directory and its subsidiary objects are retained. If the directory is moved to a different file system, all links of the directory and its objects are discarded (Fig. 5.1).

The move commands do not, by default, prompt the user for authorization to overwrite an existing file when a duplicate file name is detected. The user is prompted for confirmation only if the move commands are invoked with the -i flag.

Renaming a file is straightforward. The user supplies the name of the file to be renamed, and the new name. For example, the command

```
mv original.file new.file
```

renames the file original.file to new.file. Because the -i flag was not used, the contents of file new.file—if it currently exists—are replaced by the contents of the original file.

To move a directory and its contents, the command format is identical

```
mv original.directory new.directory
```

The end result is that new.directory contains all of the objects of original.directory. If new.directory is an existing directory, any preexisting objects in it are overlayed if similarly named objects exist in original.directory. If new.directory did not previously exist, the original.directory directory is simply renamed.

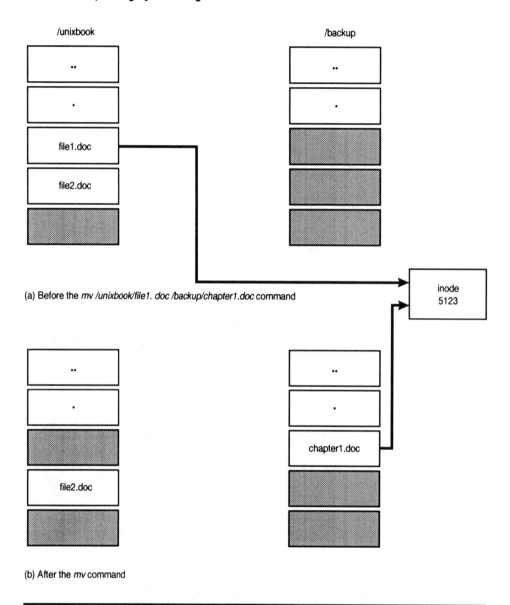

(a) Before the *mv /unixbook/file1. doc /backup/chapter1.doc* command

(b) After the *mv* command

Figure 5.1 Moving files. When a file is moved, the data within the file itself is not moved; the directory is changed. In this example, the file *file1.doc* is moved from the */unixbook* directory to the */backup* directory as *chapter1.doc*. The only information which actually changes are the pointers within the directories.

Perhaps the most confusing aspect to the move commands, at least initially, is the vague syntax between files and directories. Moving a file from one directory to another, and giving the file a new name is not too obtuse.

```
mv original.file new.directory/new.file
```

This command takes the file original.file in the current directory and puts it in the subdirectory new.directory as new.file. But what does the following command do?

```
mv original.file new.directory
```

Understanding of this particular command is aided somewhat by the names of the objects, but the significance of this example is that the objects in the command are not equivalent; they are not the same type of object. The first is a file and the second is a directory. The command must first resolve the unstated elements; in this case, the directory of the input file and the name of the output file. With these elements in place, the file original.file is moved from the current directory, which was assumed since no explicit directory was stated, to the subdirectory new.directory; the name original.file is kept since no explicit file name was stated.

Multiple files can be moved in one command execution. The user specifies multiple file names after the move command, terminating the command with the name of the directory into which the files should go. The command

```
mv chapter1 chapter2 chapter3 chapter4 unixbook
```

would move the files chapter1, chapter2, chapter3, and chapter4 from the current directory into the subdirectory named unixbook. A more concise command can be achieved by using wildcard characters

```
mv chapter* unixbook
```

This command would move all files beginning with chapter to the unixbook subdirectory. Wildcard characters can also be used to help clarify the intent of a command. Although the command

```
mv . /u/horizon
```

would move the contents of the current directory to the /u/horizon directory, the following command is more clear

```
mv ./* /u/horizon
```

Note however, that the two commands are not exactly equivalent. If the /u/horizon directory did not previously exist, the first command would rename the current directory to /u/horizon, but the second command would only transfer the contents of the current directory to /u/horizon. The current directory would remain after processing of the second move command, even though the directory would be empty. In the case where /u/horizon did exist, the first command would move the current directory and all of its contents into the /u/horizon directory. However, the second command would, again, transfer only the contents of the current directory to /u/horizon and leave the current directory intact, but empty.

5.2.4   cp/ copy—**Copy files and directories**

The cp and copy commands (Table 5.5) create a distinct copy of a file or directory. Unlike the move commands, the copy commands do not, in any way, affect the input source; therefore, after a copy operation two separate instances of the object exist, the original and the new copy. The two copy commands (cp and copy) are functionally equivalent; usage of one over the other is simply a matter of preference.

When a file is copied from one directory to another, the name of the file in the new directory is the same as the name of the file in the old directory. Any links to the file being copied continue to point to the original file. Copied files which contain links to files continue to point to the original destination file.

When a directory is copied to another directory, the original directory and all of the objects underneath it are added to the new directory (Figure 5.2).

Like the move commands, the copy commands do not prompt the user for authorization to overwrite an existing file when a duplicate file name is detected during a move operation. The user is prompted only for confirmation if the copy commands are invoked with the -i flag.

Copying a file is simple. The user supplies the name of the file to be copied and the new file name. For example, the command

```
cp original.file new.file
```

copies original.file to new.file. Because the -i flag was not used, the contents of new.file, if it currently exists, are replaced by the contents of original.file.

Copying a file from one directory to another is straightforward. To copy a file named original.file in the current directory to the directory new.directory, the user would enter the command

```
cp original.file new.directory
```

TABLE 5.5   cp (copy) **Command Flags**

Flag	Meaning
-h	Forces the command to follow symbolic links, typically used with the -R flag.
-i	Causes the command to prompt the user before overwriting an existing file. A response of **y** (or the local equivalent) overwrites the existing file.
-p	Sets the modification time and permissions of the copied files or directories to those of the original file or directory.
-r	If used with a directory, copies the file hierarchy to the destination. This recursive function copies the directory, regular and special files in the directory, every subdirectory, and every regular and special file in every subdirectory. Symbolic links are followed.
-R	If used with a directory, copies the file hierarchy to the destination. This recursive function copies only regular files and directories. Symbolic links and special files are recreated; therefore, only the directory, regular files in the directory, subdirectories and regular files within them are copied. This flag is preferred over the -r flag.
–	Indicates that the following parameters are file names.

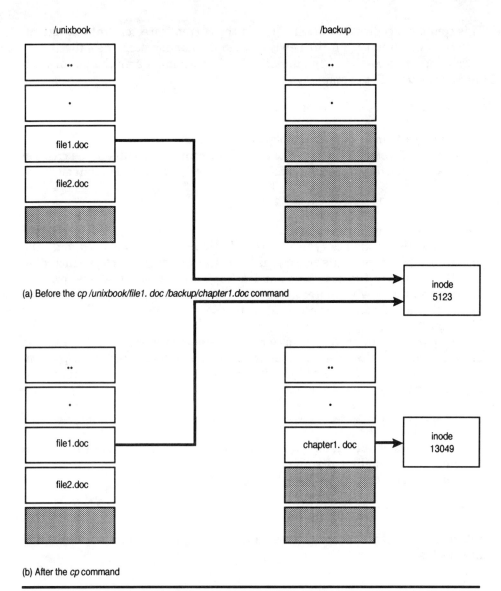

/unixbook   /backup

(a) Before the *cp /unixbook/file1. doc /backup/chapter1.doc* command

inode
5123

inode
13049

(b) After the *cp* command

Figure 5.2 Copying files. When a file is copied, the data within the file itself is moved; the original directory and data remain unchanged. In this example, the file *file1.doc* is copied from the */unixbook* directory to the */backup* directory as *chapter1.doc*. While the original information remains, a new directory entry is created in */backup* and a new physical file is created. The new file has a different i-node than the original file.

After execution, the directory new.directory contains a copy of the file named original.file. To copy, with a new name, the file original.file to the destination directory, the user must specify the name of the file to be copied, the destination directory, and the new file name

```
cp original.file new.directory/new.file
```

This command copies also original.file in the current directory into the subdirectory new.directory, but the newly created file has the name new.file.

Copying the contents of one directory to another mandates the use of wildcard characters. For example

```
cp original.directory/* new.directory
```

copies every file in original.directory to new.directory.

Copying a directory, as opposed to copying its contents, results in the creation of a new subdirectory under the receiving directory. That is, the command

```
cp -R original.directory new.directory
```

creates a directory original.directory under new.directory. When copying directories, the -R flag is typically used. If the -R flag is not used, only the directory itself (none of its objects) is copied to the new directory. Including this flag instructs the copy command to copy all the objects of the original directory to the newly created directory. That is, all files and subdirectories in the original directory are copied to the new directory in addition to the directory itself.

Multiple files can be copied in one copy command execution. As with the move commands, the user specifies multiple file names after the copy command, terminating the command with the name of the directory into which the files should go. The command

```
cp chapter1 chapter2 chapter3 chapter4 unixbook
```

copies the files chapter1, chapter2, chapter3, and chapter4 from the current directory to the subdirectory named unixbook.

Wildcard characters could have been used instead

```
cp chapter* unixbook
```

resulting in a command that copies any file, beginning with chapter, to the unixbook subdirectory.

5.2.5 tee—Display and copy a file

The tee command reads standard input and concurrently writes it to standard output and to the file named on the command line. This command is useful for situations where a user needs to see information, but also has to save the information in a file. For example, the command

```
ls -al /tmp | tee tmp.directory
```

displays the directory for the /tmp file system and stores it in the file named tmp.directory. This saves the user from invoking the command twice, i.e.,

```
ls -al /tmp
ls -al /tmp > tmp.directory
```

The tee command uses only two flags: -a to append the information to the output file, as opposed to overwriting the output file, and -i which directs tee to ignore interrupts.

5.2.6 touch—Change the access and modification times of a file

The touch command changes the access and modification time of the files specified as the operand of the command. The touch command is discussed in this section because its execution creates the specified file if the file does not already exist.[4]

To update the access and modification times of a file named chapter5.doc, and its corresponding index, chapter5.idx, the command

```
touch chapter5.doc chapter5.idx
```

is used. Because none of the optional flags are specified, the full function of the command is assumed. That is, the files, if they already exist, are modified so that the access and modification times are set to the current time and date. If either of the files does not exist, an empty file with the applicable name is created using the current time and date as the access and modification times.

To inhibit the creation of a file that does not already exist, the -c flag must be used. If this command is modified to

```
touch -c chapter5.doc chapter5.idx
```

only the preexisting files named chapter5.doc and chapter5.idx are modified; no new files are created.

The -a flag can be used to change only the access time; alternatively, the -m flag is used to change only the modification time.

The two remaining flags are used to set the access and modification times to a value other than the current date and time. The -r flag is used to set the access and modification times in reference to another file. For example, the command

```
touch -r chapter4.doc chapter5.doc
```

sets the access and modification times of chapter5.doc to be the same as those for chapter4.doc. The -t flag allows for an explicit specification of the time and date to be set. The format of the time operand is YYYYMMDDhhmmss where YYYY is the year, MM is the month, DD is the day, hh is the hour (in

---

[4]Unless this is specifically overridden by using the -c flag.

24-hour format), mm is the minute, ss is the second. To set the access time of the file chapter5.idx to December 5, 1993 at 1:30 PM, the command is

```
touch -a -t 19931205133000 chapter5.idx
```

Similarly, to set the modification time to September 20, 1994 at 9:03 AM, the command is

```
touch -m -t 19940920090300 chapter5.idx
```

5.2.7 `split`—Split a file into pieces

Related to the `csplit` command, but far less functionally rich, the `split` command reads the specified file and writes it to a set of output files. The names of the output files are constructed by combining a prefix (the default is x, the maximum length is twelve characters) with an incremental suffix which starts at aa and ends at zz. Because of this convention, the maximum number of output files is 676. The format of the command is

```
split [increment_number] input_file [prefix]
```

where the increment_number determines the number of lines in each segment except for the last, input_file names the file to be split, and prefix specifies the prefix for the output files. Issuing the command

```
split complete_book
```

results in the file complete_book divided into 1000-line segments, with the first segment named xaa. Subsequent segments are named xab, xac,...until xzz, at which point split processing terminates, and the rest of the input file is appended to this last segment.

To divide the file into 5000-line segments with a prefix of segment, the following command is used

```
split 5000 complete_book segment
```

The result is 5000-line segments, starting with a file named segmentaa.

5.3 Displaying Files

There are several ways in AIX to display the contents of a file. As one would expect, there are also several ways to display the contents of a directory. In this section, each command is reviewed but only the more common (or functionally rich) commands are given extensive treatment.

5.3.1 `cat`—Display a file

As discussed in Section 5.2.1, the `cat` command can be used to display the contents of a file on a display terminal. However, except for small files, the

TABLE 5.6   pg **Command Flags**

Flag	Meaning
-c	On those terminals which support the function, this flag forces the command to clear the screen and locate the cursor at the home position before each page is displayed.
-e	Does not pause the display at the end of each file if used with multiple input files. Can result in the end of one file being displayed with the beginning of another.
-f	Inhibits the automatic splitting of lines which are longer than the screen width.
-n	Continues processing as soon as a valid pg command is entered. In normal operation, the command must be terminated with a new-line character which is typically the enter key.
-p*string*	Allows the user to specify a custom command prompt. Within the *string* the variable %dmay be used to display the current page number within the prompt. If the string contains spaces, it must be enclosed within quotation marks.
-s	For terminals which support it, highlights all messages and prompts.
+*linenumber*	Starts processing at the specified line number.
-*number*	Specifies the number of lines in the display window. The default is one less than the number of lines supported by the terminal.
+/*pattern*/	Starts processing at the first line which contains the specified pattern.

use of cat is limited, in that there is no convenient way to stop the display of information from scrolling off the screen. Far more frequently, the pg command is used to display a file.

5.3.2   pg—Display a file, one screen at a time

The pg command (Table 5.6) is used to display a file in full-screen mode at a display terminal. The specified input file(s) are read and displayed one screen at a time on the standard output device. After a screen of information is displayed, a pg command prompt is issued. At this point, the user may enter a pg command (Table 5.7) to modify the order of information displayed or search for a particular character string. Alternatively, the user may press the enter key to display the next page of information.

The pg command uses the value of the TERM environment variable[5] to determine the terminal type. If this variable is not set, the pg command assumes a default, dumb terminal type. If the TERM variable is incorrectly set, the results of the pg command are unpredictable.

5.3.3   more/ page—Display a file, one screen at a time

To provide compatibility with both major variants of UNIX (SVR4 and bsd 4.3), AIX provides the display commands of both. This results in three differ-

---

[5]Environment variables are discussed in Chapter 14—Shells.

TABLE 5.7   pg **Subcommands**

Subcommand	Meaning
new-line (enter)	Displays the next page.
page	Displays page number *page*.
+*number*	Advances *number* pages.
-*number*	Pages back *number* of pages.
l	Scrolls forward one line.
*number*l	Displays the page beginning with line number l.
+*number*l	Scrolls forward *number* lines.
-*number*l	Scrolls backward *number* lines.
d	Scrolls half a screen forward.
-d	Scrolls half a screen backward.
. (dot)	Redisplays the current page.
$	Displays the last page of the file.
[*number*]n	Skips to the next file entered on the command line. If specified with *number*, the *number* of files are skipped before starting the display of the next file.
[*number*]p	Skips to the previous file. If specified with *number*, the *number* of files are skipped before the display is restarted.
[*number*]w	Displays the next window/screen of information. If specified with *number*, the window/screen is resized to the *number* of lines.
s *file*	Saves the input of the current file to the specified file.
h	Displays a summary of available subcommands.
q	Terminates pg command processing.
Q	Terminates pg command processing.
!*command*	Sends the specified *command* to the shell for processing.
ctrl-c	Interrupts processing, returns to command mode.
ctrl-\	Quits and Produces a dump.
[*number*]/*pattern*/	Searches forward for the first occurrence of the specified *pattern*. If *number* is specified, the *number* occurrence of the pattern is searched for.
[*number*]?*pattern*?	Searches backward for the first occurrence of the specified *pattern*. If *number* is specified, the *number* occurrence of the pattern is searched for. {*number*]~*pattern*~ See [*number*]?*pattern*?.

NOTE: With the three pattern commands, the default action is to make the line where the pattern is found the first line of the screen display. This can be changed for the current and all subsequent searches by appending an m, b, or t to the command. In this case, the found pattern line is displayed in the middle of the screen if m is used, at the bottom if b is used, and reset to the top if t is used.

ent commands to display a file on a terminal, one screen at a time. With one exception, the more and page commands (Tables 5.8 and 5.9) are identical. The two are different in that the page command always clears the screen before displaying a new page; more simply scrolls the screen up.

The primary differences between more and pg are the different subcommands used:

more   indicates the percentage of the file displayed

more   uses the space bar to advance by a screen—the enter key only advances the display by a line

TABLE 5.8 more/page **Command Flags**

Flag	Meaning
-c	Does not scroll; display information a screen at a time.
-d	Prompts the user to continue, quit, or obtain help.
-f	Counts logical lines as opposed to screen lines.
-l	Ignores the form feed character (ctrl-L). If not specified, the more command pauses whenever a form feed is encountered, as though a full screen of information had been displayed.
-n*number*	Sets the number of lines on the screen.
-p	Inhibits scrolling and clears the screen before each page is displayed.
-s	Combines multiple blank lines into one for display purposes.
-u	Prevents more from using extended characters to display underlined characters.
-v	Inhibits the display of nonprintable characters.
-w	Keeps the current file open even after reaching end-of-file. This is used to view output from a pipe or the output of a file which is being appended to.
-z	Displays control characters: backspace (ctrl-*H*) as ^H, return (ctrl-*M*) as ^M, and tab (ctrl-*I*) as ^I.
+number	Starts the display at line number *number*.
+g	Starts the display at the end of the file.
+/*pattern*	Starts the display two lines before the line containing the specified pattern.

pg	allows for more complex searching
pg	allows multiple files to be displayed with one command invocation

5.3.4 head—Display the beginning of a file

The head command is used to display the beginning lines or bytes of a file or files. By default, the first 10 lines of the input file(s) are displayed; however, the -n flag can be used to specify a different number.[6] Using the command

```
head first.data.file
```

would display the first 10 lines of first.data.file on the standard output device; typically the user's terminal. The command

```
head -n1 *.data.file > head.data
```

writes the first line of every file with suffix .data.file in the current directory and outputs the file named head.data.

5.3.5 tail—Display the end of a file

The tail command is used to display the last lines or bytes of a file. Although there are several flags which can be used with the command (Table 5.10), only two are common. The command

---

[6]This is the only flag the head command has.

TABLE 5.9   `more/page` **Subcommands**

Subcommand	Meaning
(spacebar)	Displays the next screen.
number(spacebar)	Advances *number* of lines when the spacebar is pressed.
`ctrl-D`	Displays the next 11 lines.
*number*d	Displays 11 more lines. If *number* is specified, the number of lines to scroll forward is determined by *number*.
*number*z	Sets the screen size to *number* lines. If no *number* is specified, display advances one screen.
*number*s	Skips the *number* of lines before displaying the next screen of information. If no *number* is specified, the display advances a line at a time.
*number*f	Skips forward the *number* of screens before displaying the next screen of information.
*number*b	Skips backward the *number* of screens before displaying the next screen of information.
*number*ctrl-B	See *number*b.
q	Exits from more.
Q	Exits from more.
=	Displays the current line number.
v	Invokes the *vi* editor at the current line.
h	Displays a list of the available subcommands.
number/*pattern*	Searches for the *number* occurrence of the specified *pattern*.
*number*n	Searches for the *number* occurrence of the last pattern entered.
' (apostrophe)	Goes to the location where the last search started. If no search has been previously performed, goes to the beginning of the file.
!*command*	Invokes the specified shell *command*. An exclamation point (!) in the *command* is replaced by the last entered shell command. A percent sign (%) in the *command* is replaced by the current file name. To use either punctuation mark in the command sequence as the character itself, precede the character by a backslash, \! or \%.
number:n	Skips to the *number* file following in the command line. If *number* is not valid, more skips to the last file.
number:p	Skips to the *number* previous file in the command line.
:f	Displays the current file name and line number.
:q	Same as q.
:Q	Same as Q.
. (dot)	Repeats the prior command.

```
tail head.data
```

displays the last 10 lines of the file named head.data. The command

```
tail -20 head.data
```

demonstrates the use of the count flag, which in t his case is used to instruct `tail` to display the last 20 lines of head.data. When the `-f` flag is used, the tail command follows the growth of the subject file. After the initial display of the last lines of the file, the tail command waits for new lines to be added to the subject file which are then displayed on the standard output device.

TABLE 5.10 `tail` **command Flags**

Flag	Meaning
`-c` *number*	Starts processing the file at byte *number*.
`-f`	Follows the file. If the input file is a regular or FIFO file, `tail` does not terminate when end-of-file is detected; instead, waits for additional information from the input file as it becomes available. This allows a file to be monitored as it grows.
`-r`	Display the input file in reverse order; last line to first line.
`-m` *number*	Starts processing the file at byte *number*. This flag ensures that consistent results are obtained regardless of whether a single- or double-byte character set is being used.
`-n` *number*	Starts processing the file at line *number*.
`-b` *number*	Starts processing the file at 512-byte block *number*.
`-k` *number*	Starts processing the file at 1-kbyte block *number*.

The tail command is most frequently used to monitor the output of a program in execution to determine where in the processing cycle the program actually is.

5.3.6 `bfs`—Scan a file

Essentially, `bfs` is a read-only editor. It is used to scan a file for character strings or patterns, but it cannot modify the input file. Four types of searches are possible; the search type is indicated by the characters used to delimit the search pattern

`/pattern/`	indicates a forward, wraparound search
`?pattern?`	indicates a backward, wraparound search
`>pattern>`	indicates a forward, to end-of-file search
`<pattern<`	indicates a backward, to beginning-of-file search

The subcommands of `bfs` are described in Table 5.11.

5.3.7 `look`—Find a line in a sorted file

The `look` command searches a sorted file for a string and writes every line which begins with the string to standard output. Two flags are used with the command. The first, -d, indicates that dictionary order is to be used. This means that only letters, digits, tabs, and spaces are considered when the comparison is made. The second flag, -f, indicates that the search should be case insensitive; that is, lowercase and uppercase letters are considered equivalent. If the -f flag is used, the input files must have been sorted with the -f option. To search for all lines in the files grocery.shopping.list and hardware.shopping.list which begin with a *b*, the user would enter

```
look b grocery.shopping.list hardware.shopping.list
```

If no file name is entered, the system dictionary (/usr/share/dict/words) is

TABLE 5.11 `bfs` **Subcommands**

Subcommand	Meaning
`e file`	Read in a different file named *file*.
`(1,$)g/pattern/subcommandlist`	Run the *subcommandlist* against every line within the specified range which contains *pattern*. If no range is specified, the default action is to process the entire file. This can be explicitly indicated by coding (1,$).
`(1,$)v/pattern/subcommandlist`	Run the *subcommandlist* against every line within the specified range which *does not* contain *pattern*. If no range is specified, the entire file is processed. This is the default (1,$).
`(start,end)n`	Displays the indicated lines, from *start* to *end*. Each line is preceded by its line number; the current line is set to the line indicated by *end*.
`(start,end)p`	Displays the indicated lines, from *start* to *end*; the current line is set to the line indicated by *end*.
`q`	exit `bfs`.
`(1,$)w file`	Write the indicated lines to the specified *file*. If no line numbers are given, the default (1,$) is assumed, which writes line 1 to the end-of-file to the new file.
`=`	Display the current line number.
`$ =`	Display the line number of the last line in the file.
`! command`	Execute the indicated AIX command. The percent sign (%) is used within the command to insert the name of the current file into the command. The exclamation point (!) is used to represent the last command executed. For example, !! is used to repeat the last executed command.

searched. Therefore, to find all of the words that begin with *ch* in the system dictionary, the command would be

```
look ch
```

5.3.8 `strings`—Display the printable characters within a file

The `strings` command looks within a file for ASCII character strings of at least four bytes, and when found, prints the string on standard output. This command can be useful when the contents of a file or the parameters of a command are not known.

The `strings` command has three flags. A single minus sign is used to search everywhere in an executable file; the default is for the `strings` command to search only the data storage part. When the -o flag is used, the command displays the offset of each each string within the file. And finally, the -n flag is used to change the minimum size of the character string.

The final operand of the `strings` command is the name of the file (or a list of files) to be searched. As an example of command usage, the following command

```
strings - -2 /usr/bin/pg
```

TABLE 5.12   rm **command Flags**

Flag	Meaning
-e	Displays a message after each file is deleted
-f	Suppresses prompting before removing a write-protected file
-i	Prompts the user before each file is deleted
-r	Recursively processes directories and their contents; facilitates deleting a directory and its contents
-R	Same as -r
—	Indicates the following parameter is a file name

would search the entire pg executable file (not just the data segment part) for all ASCII strings in the file which have two or more characters.

5.4   Removing Files

When files are no longer useful or needed, they must be removed from the system. In AIX, there are three commands which are related to file removal: rm, del, and delete.

5.4.1   rm / delete—Remove a file or directory

The rm command (Table 5.12) is used to remove an entry for a file from a directory. If there are no links to the specified file when the rm command is issued, the file is deleted. If there are links to the file, only the entry name in the directory is removed.

Therefore, to delete a file named old.data, the user would enter

```
rm old.data
```

After execution of the command, access to the file via the name old.data is impossible. If there were no links to old.data, the file was also physically deleted.

The -i flag provides for interactive prompting during the deletion process. This is particularly useful when using wildcards in the rm command. For instance, the command

```
rm -i /u/tmp/*
```

prompts the user to confirm the deletion of ea ch file within the /u/tmp directory. If the user enters a response other than "y," the file is not deleted and processing continues with the next file in the /u/tmp directory. If there are any subdirectories in the /u/tmp directory, they are *not* processed. This form of the command processes only regular files.

Therefore, in addition to the -i flag, the -R flag is necessary to recursively remove directory entries. This is essential when a directory and all of its entries, including the subdirectories, are to be deleted. But care must be taken, as the -R flag deletes the directory itself, in addition to all of its objects.

Going back to the prior example, if it is necessary to delete subdirectories in /u/tmp in addition to files, the following command must be used

```
rm -iR /u/tmp
```

This command prompts the user to confirm the deletion of each entry regardless of whether it is a file or subdirectory. If all of the entries are deleted, the system then prompts the user to confirm the deletion of the /u/tmp directory. If the user decides not to delete the /u/tmp directory, any response other than "y" prevents its deletion.

The delete command is functionally equivalent to the rm command.

5.4.2 del—Delete files with confirmation

The del command is a limited function, a more verbose version of the rm command. It *always* requests confirmation before deleting files; however, the confirmation is, by default, for a group of files instead on an individual file basis. Furthermore, depressing the enter key is the same as answering "y." That is, the command

```
del /u/tmp/*
```

deletes all of the files in the /u/tmp directory with a single confirmation of "y" and/or pressing the enter key. To prevent deletion, a character other than "y" must be keyed before hitting the enter key. The user can request individual file confirmation by using the dash (-) flag.[7] That is

```
del - /u/tmp/*
```

prompts the user before deleting each file in the directory, exactly as the rm -i format command would do.[8]

It is important to note that the del command does not process directory entries; therefore, subdirectories within a directory are not deleted by the del command. Additionally, the del command ignores file protection; it allows the owner of a file to delete it even if the file is write-protected.

5.5 Linking Files

The ln (Table 5.13) command in AIX is most commonly thought of as a facility to assign an additional name (or names) to a file. And, although it does do that, that definition misses the underlying point. All file names in AIX are links; links are simply a logical connection between the internal representation of a file on disk and a name for that file. AIX refers to files by their i-node number; the file names are provided solely for the convenience of the human user. It is

---

[7]This is the only flag of the del command.
[8]The actual wording of the prompt is different, but the net effect is the same.

TABLE 5.13 ln **Command Flags**

Flag	Meaning
-f	Replaces any destination path that already exists. If this flag is not used, and a link already exists, an error message is produced, and processing continues with any remaining files.
-s	Creates a symbolic link. The symbolic link contains the name of the file to which it is linked; it is that file which is actually used when the link is referenced. When creating a symbolic link, absolute path names must be used, or unpredictable results may occur. Using a symbolic link does not guarantee that the referenced file exists.

this independence between physical and logical representation of files that allows multiple logical names to represent the same physical file (Figure 5.3).

In practice, there are two types of links. A *hard* link allows direct access to the data of a file. Because it is a direct pointer to the i-node of the file, a hard link ensures the existence of a file. A file exists as long as there is at least on e hard link to its i-node. When multiple hard links exist for a file, the i-node of the file is not released, thereby deleting the file, until the last hard link is removed with either the rm, del, or delete command. Because they are direct pointers to the i-node of a file, hard links can be created only within a file system.

Soft links are used to provide access to data in another file system. A soft or *symbolic link* is a regular file which contains only a path name. When a process encounters the symbolic link, AIX appends the path name in the symbolic link to the search path the process is using and the search continues. Symbolic links do not protect a file from being deleted; therefore, they cannot guarantee its existence either.

Links are commonly used to isolate the user from the specifics of the file system hierarchy. A good example of this is with the installation of software packages. When a new release is installed, users do not want to have to change their procedures to specify a new path to the software. And it is also necessary to keep a back-level of the software available, just in case there is a need to return to the prior version. The solution is to use symbolic links. Assuming the software was installed in individual directories, such as

/home/infoshare.1100   for version 1.1
/home/infoshare.1200   for version 1.2
/home/infoshare.2000   for version 2.0

the system administrator needs only to change the symbolic link (/usr/local/infoshare) to point the user to the correct version; providing, of course, the user uses the symbolic link and not the hard link. To set the version to 1.2, the administrator would enter

```
ln -s /usr/local/infoshare /home/infoshare.1200
```

When version 2.0 is fully tested and ready to go into production, the users can be migrated simply by changing the link

```
rm /usr/local/infoshare
ln -s /usr/local/infoshare /home/infoshare.2000
```

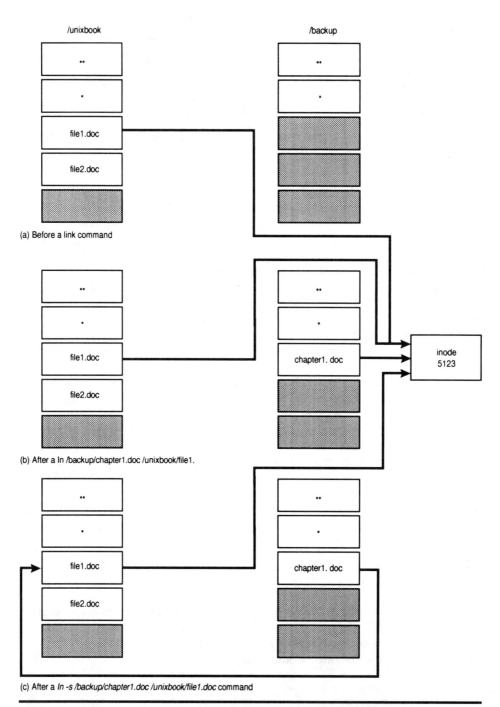

Figure 5.3 Linking files. When a file is linked, the data within the file itself is not modified. Only the directory entries change. In example b, the file in directory /backup named *chapter1.doc* is linked to the file in the /unixbook directory named /file1.doc. After the link, both files point to the same i-node; the data in the files is identical. In example c, the file in directory /backup named *chapter1.doc* is only a pointer to the *file1.doc* file in the /unixbook directory. When /backup/chapter1.doc is accessed, it is used as a directory path to the "real" file /unixbook/file1.doc.

This example demonstrates that when an existing link is changed, the administrator must first remove the current link. Only then may the new symbolic link be set.

For users with root authority, two additional commmands are available, `link` and `unlink`. These commands are typically used only to deal with unusual problems, such as moving an entire directory to another part of the directory tree, or creating self-contained directory systems where neither access nor escape is permitted. Because these commands do no error checking, the user must ensure that the desired action occurred as the result of the command. The following guidelines should be observed when using the link and unlink commands with directories:

ensure the directory links to itself via the dot (.) link

ensure the directory links to its parent via the double dot (..) link

ensure the directory has no more than one link to itself or its parent

ensure the directory is accessible from the root of its file system

To switch the file current.chapter from chapter4.doc to chapter5.doc, the following command sequence would be used:

```
unlink current.chapter
link chapter5.doc current.chapter
```

Neither command, link or unlink, has any optional flags.

5.6   File Ownership and Access

Every file in an AIX system has an owner, usually the user who created the file. In addition, a file is also owned by the group it is assigned to. Access to a file is controlled at two levels: by user and by type of access. User access is defined at three levels: the rights of the owner, the rights of the members of the owning group, and everyone else. File access is defined as read, write, and execute permission. By default, when a file is created the owner has read, write, and execute permission; the group ownership is set to the owner's default group which, like everyone else, only has read and execute permission.[9]

5.6.1   chown—Change the owner of a file or directory

The owner or owning group of a file can be changed with the chown command. This is frequently used when one user takes over the responsibilities of another. For example, to transfer the file birthday.list from user fgc, belonging to group profsrvc, to user jpg, belonging to group sysdev, user fgc would enter the command

```
chown jpg birthday.list
```

---

[9]This default can be changed in the user's profile if tighter security controls are necessary.

This transfers ownership of the file to user jpg, but it does not transfer file access rights to the group, sysdev. The group owner is still profsrvc. To transfer group rights from profsvcs to sysdev, user jpg must enter the command

```
chown :sysdev birthday.list
```

Of course, user fgc could have avoided this by specifying both the new owner and group in the initial command

```
chown jpg:sysdev birthday.list
```

The chown command can also be used to change the ownership of directories. When it is used for this purpose, the flags of the chown command, -f and -R, are also usually used. The -R flag instructs the command to recursively descend the directory tree and change the ownership of every file encountered. Note, that if a symbolic link is encountered, the ownership of the symbolic link is *not* changed, but the ownership of the object of the symbolic link *is*. The -f flag suppresses the display of error messages when a file cannot be changed.

Returning to our prior example, user jpg is now tired of maintaining the birthday.list, and all of the other miscellaneous files in the /u/misc/personnel directory and desires to return all of these to user fgc. Assuming user fgc agrees,[10] user jpg can transfer the entire directory with the command

```
chown -R fgc:profsvcs /u/misc/personnel
```

This command ensures that all of the miscellaneous personnel files were made the property of fgc, and would transfer group ownership to fgc's group.

5.6.2   chgrp—Change the group owner of a file or directory

There is a separate command for changing group ownership, chgrp. It does not provide any additional functionality over chown; because of this, chgrp is not as commonly used. However, had user jpg chosen to only transfer ownership of the directory to user fgc,[11] user fgc could change the group by using the command

```
chgrp -R profsvcs /u/misc/personnel
```

5.6.3   chmod—Change access mode

Files can be either read, written, or executed. These three access modes are represented symbolically by the letters r, w, and x (Table 5.14).

For a particular file, a user can display the access modes of the file with the ls -l *filename* command. The first ten characters of the display show the file

---

[10]Actually, user fgc does not have to agree to this file transfer. User jpg can transfer them to user fgc regardless of fgc's feelings on the issue. It is unlikely, however, that the transfer will result in productive work if user fgc does not agree beforehand.

[11]With the command chown :-R fgc /u/misc/personnel.

TABLE 5.14   Access Modes

Mode	Meaning
-	No access.
r	Read access.
s	Set user-id or set group-id permission for executing user to that of the file.
S	Set user-id or set group-id permission has been specified, but the owner and group owner do not have execute permission.
t	Link permission for directories, save text attribute for files; restricts delete permission to the owner.
T	Link permission for a directories or the save text attribute for a files has been specified, but the owner and group owner do not have execute permission.
w	Write access.
X	Execute permission if the specified file is a directory, ignored otherwise.
x	Execute permission; search permission for directories.

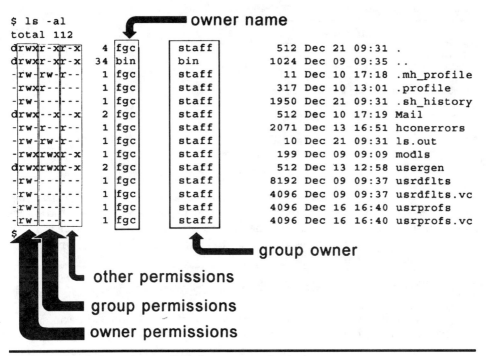

```
$ ls -al
total 112
drwxr-xr-x    4 fgc    staff     512 Dec 21 09:31 .
drwxr-xr-x   34 bin    bin      1024 Dec 09 09:35 ..
-rw-rw-r--    1 fgc    staff      11 Dec 10 17:18 .mh_profile
-rwxr-----    1 fgc    staff     317 Dec 10 13:01 .profile
-rw-------    1 fgc    staff    1950 Dec 21 09:31 .sh_history
drwx--x--x    2 fgc    staff     512 Dec 10 17:19 Mail
-rw-r--r--    1 fgc    staff    2071 Dec 13 16:51 hconerrors
-rw-rw-r--    1 fgc    staff      10 Dec 21 09:31 ls.out
-rwxrwxr-x    1 fgc    staff     199 Dec 09 09:09 modls
drwxrwxr-x    2 fgc    staff     512 Dec 13 12:58 usergen
-rw-------    1 fgc    staff    8192 Dec 09 09:37 usrdflts
-rw-------    1 fgc    staff    4096 Dec 09 09:37 usrdflts.vc
-rw-------    1 fgc    staff    4096 Dec 16 16:40 usrprofs
-rw-------    1 fgc    staff    4096 Dec 16 16:40 usrprofs.vc
$
```

owner name

group owner

other permissions

group permissions

owner permissions

Figure 5.4   Permission and owner fields in ls command output.

type and the access modes for the three groups (owner, group, other). The third and fourth columns list who the owner and owner group are (Fig. 5.4).

Within the access mode column, the first character of the column indicates the AIX file type of the entry. Although there are several possible indicators (Table 5.15), the most common are the dash (-) indicating a regular file, and a d indicating a directory. The remaining characters in the column represent the three access groups and their permissions. Characters two through four

TABLE 5.15   File Type Codes

Code	Meaning
-	Ordinary file
b	Block special file
B	Remote block special file
c	Character special file
C	Remote character special file
d	Directory
D	Remote directory
F	Remote ordinary file
L	Remote symbolic link
l	Symbolic link
p	FIFO (first-in-first-out) special file
P	Remote FIFO special file
s	Local socket

TABLE 5.16   Numeric Access Modes

Mode	Meaning
0	No access
1	Execute permission; search permission for directories
2	Write access
3	Execute/search permission and write access
4	Read access
5	Execute/search permission and read access
6	Read and write access
7	Execute/search permission and read and write access

indicate the read, write, and execute permissions for the owner of the file. Characters five through seven represent the owner group, and characters eight through ten represent all other users of the system. An access mode entry with a dash (-) indicates that the particular type of access is prohibited. It can be seen that the entry

```
-rwxr-----   1 fgc      profsvcs    346 Apr 29 16:28 .profile
```

is a regular file where the owner has read, write, and execute permissions, the group profsvcs has read access only, and everyone else has no access.

Internally, AIX represents the three access group permissions as numeric values: read is represented as 4, write as 2, and execute as 1 (Table 5.16). The previous example would be represented numerically as 740

$4 + 2 + 1 = 7$ for the owner (read, write, execute)

4 for the group (read only)

0 for everyone else (no access)

The AIX command to change access permissions, chmod, allows the user to specify permissions with either symbolic letters or with the numeric codes.

TABLE 5.17   Absolute Permission Mode

Mode	Meaning
4000	Set user-id on execution
2000	Set group-id on execution
1000	Set link permission for a directory; save text attribute for a file
0400	Owner read permission
0200	Owner write permission
0100	Owner execute and search permission
0040	Group read permission
0020	Group write permission
0010	Group execute and search permission
0004	All other users read permission
0002	All other users write permission
0001	All other users execute and search permission

The chmod command uses the same two flags as the chown and chgrp commands; however, there is a subtle difference in the way the -R flag behaves with chmod. This flag instructs the chmod command to recursively descend the directory tree and change the ownership of every file encountered. But, unlike chmod and chgrp, when a symbolic link is encountered, the ownership of the symbolic link is changed but the ownership of the object to which the symbolic link points is not. As with the other two commands, the -f flag suppresses the display of error messages when a file cannot be changed.

Using the numeric or *absolute* mode of chmod is relatively easy.[12] After calculating the access mode (Table 5.17), the user enters a command in the format

```
chmod [-f][-R] value filename
```

To give universal access to the .profile file, the command would be

```
chmod 777 .profile
```

This, of course, would be highly irregular. More likely, the owner of this profile would want to prohibit any outside access, and would probably also want to protect against inadvertent erasure; therefore, the following command would be more likely

```
chmod 500 .profile
```

This could also have been performed with the symbolic parameters (Table 5.18). The syntax of symbolic mode is more complex, but it is far more flexible than absolute mode. Repeating the previous example, to give universal access to the .profile file, the command in symbolic mode would be

```
chmod uso=rwx .profile
```

---

[12]Absolute or numeric mode should never be used for a file with an ACL; see Chapter 9 for further details.

TABLE 5.18 Symbolic Mode

Symbol	Meaning
	First Parameter Group—User Indicator
u	File owner.
g	Group owner.
o	All others.
a	User, group, and all others. Equivalent to ugo.
	Second Parameter—Action
-	Remove specified permission.
+	Add specified permission.
=	Clear the specified permission and set it as indicated. If a third parameter(s) does not follow the = , all permissions are removed from the selected field.
	Third Parameter Group—Permissions
r	Read permission.
w	Write permission.
x	Execute permission.
X	Execute/search permission if the file is a directory.
s	Set user-id or group-id on execution.
t	Link permission for a directory or save text attribute for a file. The save text attribute gives delete permission to the owner of the file only.

or

```
chmod a=rwx .profile
```

The first example explicitly names the three types (uso= for user, group, other) where the second uses the global identifier for all (a=).

To restrict access to the owner, who, in turn, has only read and execute access, the command could be

```
chmod u=rx,go= .profile
```

or

```
chmod u-w,go=rwx .profile
```

The first of these examples explicitly gives read and execute permission to the owner (u=rw), and no permissions to the group or others (go=). The second example removes write access from the owner (u-w), and all access permissions from the group and others (go-rwx). Although both examples reach the same end result, the path is not quite the same.

With both formats of the command, it is possible to perform a function called *set user id on execution* for an executable file. This allows a program to run with the privileges of the owner,[13] even when it is invoked by another user. Use

---

[13]This is referred to as the effective ID.

of this facility allows a program and its data to be used with full function by any user, and at the same time prohibits access to the data except through the program. For example, assume that a database manager named dbdrvr was owned by sys. This program accesses the files dbindex, dbinvert, dbmain, dbancill. To allow user fgc to run the program, but not access the individual data files outside of the program, the following commands could be used by user sys

```
chmod u=rw,go= dbindex dbinvert dbmain dbancill
chmod ugo = x,u+s dbdrvr
```

The first command changes the access mode of the four files to read/write fo r the owner only (u=rw), all other users have no rights at all (go=). The second command gives all users the ability to execute the program (ugo=x) but with an effective ID of the owner (u+s). Because the users run the program with the effective ID of the owner, they have all of the access privileges of owner when the program is running. The effective ID lasts only for the duration of the program's execution; once the program ends, access rights revert to those of the real user.

The same functionality exists with the group owner. The function *set group id on execution* allows a program to run with the privileges of the group (as opposed to the owner) even when the command is invoked by a user who is not part of the group. The g flag is used to set the group id on execution.

5.6.4 umask—Define default file creation characteristics

The umask is not actually an AIX command but a shell environment characteristic. It is used to override the default file creation characteristics of the system for a specific user. All files created by a user get their file permission and access characteristics from the umask, regardless of whether it is explicitly or implicitly set.

Because of its far-reaching effects, the umask is normally set during login processing. The syntax of the command is simply umask [mask]. When the umask command is issued with no mask, the current umask setting is displayed on standard output. When the mask is specified, it must be a three-digit octal number. The mask is subtracted from the default file creation permission (777) to generate the desired access permission. For example, if the desired access permission is 744 (read/write/execute access for the owner and read/execute for the group and others) then the umask would be 033, because 777 − 033 = 744. Therefore, if the desired file permission characteristic was to ensure that no one but the owner had access to newly created files the umask would be 077 (777 − 077 = 700).

The system default umask is set in either the /etc/profile file or the /etc/environment file.

5.7   File Information

The commands cksum, sum, wc, and file provide information about a file. Typically they are not used as individual commands, but as part of a shell script.

5.7.1 `cksum`—Display the checksum and byte count of a file

The `cksum` command is most commonly used to compare a file to its trusted copy to ensure that no information has been lost or changed. Perhaps the most common use of this command is to ensure that a file has been transferred correctly over a network. First, the cksum command is run against the file on the host system. After the file has been transferred, the command is run against the transferred file and the result is compared with the output from the cksum of the file on the host system. It the two outputs are identical, it is assumed that the file has been transferred intact. The algorithm used by `cksum` is not cryptographically secure, but in actual practice it is extremely unlikely that an unintentionally damaged file will produce the same CRC as the trusted file.

When executed, the `cksum` command reads each file specified, and in turn, writes an information line to standard output about each file. The information line displays the 32-bit CRC (*cyclical redundancy check*) checksum, the byte count, and file name.

The `cksum` command has no optional flags.

5.7.2 `sum`—Display the checksum and block count of a file

The `sum` command operates in the same manner as the cksum command, however, the algorithm used by sum is different from that used by cksum. Therefore, the output of sum does not correspond to that of cksum. As with the `cksum` command, the `sum` command is most commonly used to compare a suspect file to its trusted copy to ensure that no information has been lost or changed. The `sum` command is run against both copies of the file and the results are compared. If the two outputs are identical, it is assumed that the file has been transferred intact.

The algorithm used by `sum` allows for two different ways of computing the checksum. Although neither is cryptographically secure, in practice it is unlikely that an unintentionally damaged file will produce the same checksum as the trusted file.

When executed, the `sum` command reads each file specified, and in turn, writes an information line to standard output about each file. The information line displays the checksum, the number of 1024K blocks in the file, and the file name. For example

```
$ sum s*
25477       2 smit.log
39346       1 smit.script
14500      62 snaprof
$
```

The `sum` command has three flags which influence how the checksum algorithm works. The `-r` flag is the default, which uses a byte-by-byte method for computing the checksum. Specifying `-o` instructs the algorithm to use a word-by-word method for computing the checksum. The `-i` flag is used with binary files to exclude the header information of the file from the checksum computation. If the input file is not a binary file, this flag is ignored.

Using the preceding example with the -o flag demonstrates how the two options significantly affect the output results

```
$ sum -o s*
39966       2 smit.log
2961        1 smit.script
41581      62 snaprof
$
```

5.7.3 wc—Compute the number of lines, word, and bytes in a file

The wc command counts the number of lines, words, and bytes in the specified files. When executed, the wc command reads each file specified and writes an information line to standard output about each file. In addition, a summation line is written which contains the totals for all of the files read. If no flags are used, the information lines display the line, word, and byte counts of the file and the file name.

```
$ wc s*
52 178 1394 smit.log
4 10 51 smit.script
3258 6965 63225 snaprof
3314 7153 64670 total
$
```

When flags are used, the order of the flags determines the order of the output fields. The flags are -1 to count lines, -w to count words, -c to count bytes, and -k to count characters.

```
$ wc -w s*
178 smit.log
10 smit.script
6965 snaprof
7153 total
$
```

When the -k flag is used, the -c flag counts characters instead of bytes. Furthermore, when the -k flag is used in conjunction with other flags, the -c flag *must* be specified if characters are to be counted.

```
$ wc -cw s*
1394 178 smit.log
51 10 smit.script
63225 6965 snaprof
64670 7153 total
$
```

5.7.4 file—Display the type of a file

The file command reads the specified files and performs tests on each to determine the type of the file. When a classification has been determined, an information line is written to standard output.

The file command uses a database of information to determine the type of

```
#       Basically, the fields of this file are as follows:
#              1 byte offset,
#              2 value type,
#              3 optional relational operator ("=" by default) and
#                value to match (numeric or string constant),
#              4 string to be printed.
#
#       Numeric values may be decimal, octal, or hexadecimal.
#     Strings can be entered as hex values by preceding them with
#     '0x'.
#       Also, the last string may have one printf format specification.
#
#       The '>' in occasional column 1's is magic: it forces file to
#       continue scanning and matching additional lines. The first line
#       afterwards not so marked terminates the search.
#
0     short      070707          cpio archive
0     string     070707          ASCII cpio archive
0     short      017436          packed text
0     string     <aiaff>         archive
0     string     Rast            RST format font raster
0     short      0x01df          executable (RISC System/6000 V3.1) or object module
>12   long       >0              not stripped
0     short      0x0103          executable (RT Version 2) or obj module
>2    byte       0x50            pure
>28   long       >0              not stripped
>6    short      >0              version %ld
0     short      0x0104          shared library
0     short      0x0105          ctab data
0     short      0xfe04          structured file
0     string     0xabcdef        message catalog
0     short      0x1f9d          compressed data
>2    byte       &0x80>0         block compressed
>2    byte       &0x1f>0         %d bit
```

Figure 5.5 The magic file (/etc./magic).

a file. This file, /etc/magic (Fig. 5.5), contains constant information which appears in each given file type. The file command applies this information to the subject files to identify the file type.

If a file appears to be an ASCII text file, the file command scans the first 512 bytes of the file to determine the language. If a file does not appear to be ASCII text, the file command attempts to differentiate truly binary files from text files which contain extended characters. When an object module or executable is encountered, the version stamp is also displayed on the information line.

The -m flag allows a different database other than the /etc/magic file to be used as the type database. The -c flag indicates that instead of performing file typing, the specified file should be checked for format errors based on its type.

The -f parameter indicates that a file of file names is to be used as the input. Each file in the list is fed into the file command. For example, to determine the file type of every file in the /tmp directory, the following command could be used

```
ls /tmp >directory.list | file -f directory.list
```

The output of the /tmp directory listing is created as a file (directory.list)

```
$ file -c
level  off type opcode       mask     value   string
   0     0   1       0  ffffffff       71c7   cpio archive
   0     0   3       0                070707   ASCII cpio archive
   0     0   1       0  ffffffff       1f1e   packed text
   0     0   3       0              <aiaff>    archive
   0     0   3       0                  Rast   RST format font raster
   0     0   1       0  ffffffff        1df   executable (RISC System/6000 V3.1) or object module
   1    12   2       1  ffffffff          0   not stripped
   0     0   1       0  ffffffff        103   executable (RT Version 2) or obj module
   1     2   0       0  ffffffff         50   pure
   1    28   2       1  ffffffff          0   not stripped
   1     6   1      11  ffffffff          0   - version $ld
   0     0   1       0  ffffffff        104   shared library
   0     0   1       0  ffffffff        105   ctab data
   0     0   1       0  ffffffff       fe04   structured file
   0     0   3       0              0xabcdef   message catalog
   0     0   1       0  ffffffff       1f9d   compressed data
   1     2   0       1        80          0   block compressed
   1     2   0      11        1f          0   $d bit
$
$ (file .*;file *)
.:                          directory
..:                         directory
.old_profile:               commands text
.profile:                   commands text
ac:                         symbolic link to /usr/sbin/acct/ac
cksum.out:                  ascii text
compress.out:               ascii text
file.out:                   [nt]roff, tbl, or eqn input text
smit.log:                   ascii text
smit.script:                ascii text
snaprof.Z:                  compressed data block compressed 16 bit
snasize.pck:                ascii text
unpack.out:                 empty
usergen:                    directory
$
```

Figure 5.6 File command usage example.

which is then used as the input list for the file command. Figure 5.6 shows some examples of file command usage.

5.7.5 istat—Display information about a file

The istat command can be used to display detailed information about a file in an easy to understand format. This command uses no flags; therefore the syntax is simply

```
istat filename
```

As an example, the information for the file /tmp/FTAG.82736 displays as follows:

```
$ istat /tmp/FTAG.82736
Inode 934 on device 08/4 File
Protection: rw-r--r--
Owner: 26(tag) Group: 16(notis)
```

```
Link count: 1 Length 554240 bytes
Last updated: Tue Apr 05 01:07:36 1994
Last modified: Wed Apr 06 12:11:47 1994
Last accessed: Wed Apr 06 12:11:50 1994
$
```

5.8   Compacting Files

AIX provides two sets of compaction commands. Both sets of commands are used to reduce the amount of disk storage a file occupies. Compaction is frequently used before transferring large files from one system to another simply because a compacted file takes less time to transfer than an uncompacted one. Compaction is also a good way to reduce the amount of disk space infrequently accessed files occupy. The one drawback to compacting a file is that the only commands that can be used on a compacted file are the movement commands such as mv, cp, etc. All other commands expect an uncompacted file. Therefore, once a file has been compacted, it cannot be directly used again until it has been uncompacted.

The differences between the two compaction methods is primarily due to the different algorithms used to compact the file. The pack, unpack, and pcat commands use Huffman encoding where the compress, uncompress, and zcat commands use an adaptive Lempel-Zev algorithm. In general, the adaptive Lempel-Zev algorithm produces a more compact file in less time than Huffman encoding does.

5.8.1   pack—Compact a file using Huffman encoding

The pack command takes the specified input file, compacts it, and creates a packed file of the same name with a .z suffix. For a text file, a compaction ratio of 25 to 40 percent is common. This new file has the same owner, access modes, and access and modification dates as the original input file.

The input file name cannot be more than 253 characters to allow for the naming of the output file with the .z suffix. If the pack command is successful, the original file is deleted. It can be recreated by using the unpack command.

If the pack command cannot create a smaller file as the result of compaction, it terminates with a message reporting that compaction was unsuccessful, as demonstrated in the following example

```
$ ls -al *.out
-rw-rw-r--   1 fgc      staff       512 Dec 08 09:15 cksum.out
-rw-rw-r--   1 fgc      staff       523 Dec 09 09:05 diff.out
-rw-rw-r--   1 fgc      staff      1014 Dec 09 09:34 diff3.out
-rw-rw-r--   1 fgc      staff       934 Dec 10 12:05 ls.out
$ pack *.out
pack: cksum.out: no saving
     - file unchanged
pack: diff.out: no saving
     - file unchanged
pack: diff3.out: no saving
     - file unchanged
pack: ls.out: no saving
     - file unchanged
$
```

In general, any file of three blocks or less does not pack successfully. Other reasons for unsuccessful execution of the pack command are: the input file is already packed, the input file name is longer than 253 bytes, the input file has links, the input file is a directory, the input or output file cannot be opened, an output file of the same name (inputfilename.z) already exists, or any I/O error occurs.

Whenever the pack command fails, the original file is left undisturbed. The original file is deleted only when the pack command executes successfully and exits with a return code of zero. A return code of greater than zero indicates the number of files which could not be compacted.

```
$ ls -al snaprof*
-rw-rw-r--  123 fgc      staff       63225 Nov 18 11:24 snaprof
$ pack snaprof
pack: snaprof: 36.9% Compression
$ ls -al snaprof*
-rw-rw-r--   78 fgc      staff       39895 Dec 06 09:37 snaprof.z
$
```

Pack uses only two flags. The first, - (the minus sign), is used in conjunction with a file name as a toggle to display statistics about the file. The first use of the flag turns on statistic reporting, the second use turns the statistics off, the third turns it on again, and so forth. The other flag, -f, is used to force compaction and is most frequently used when compressing an entire directory. A directory does not compact if all of the files in the directory do not benefit from compaction. This flag forces the entire directory to be compacted, even if some individual files are not smaller after compaction.

5.8.2 unpack—Uncompact a file processed with pack

The unpack command is the counterpart of pack; it takes a file processed by pack and transforms it back into its original form. Because the input file must be a file processed by pack, the file name can be entered with or without the .z suffix. That is, either unpack chapter.one or unpack chapter.one.z unpacks the file named chapter.one.z and, if successful, replaces it by a file named chapter.one. The newly created file has the same owner, access modes, and access and modification dates as the original input file.

A return code from unpack greater than zero indicates the number of files which could not be unpacked. This can be caused by a number of reasons: the input file is not packed, the input file name is longer than 253 bytes excluding the .z suffix, the input or output file cannot be opened, an output file with the same unpacked name already exists, or any I/O error occurs.

If the unpack command fails, the original file is left undisturbed. The original file is deleted only when the unpack command executes successfully and exits with a return code of zero.

Unlike pack, unpack allows processing of an input file with links. However, because of the links, the input file cannot be deleted and a warning message is issued. The other files linked to the original input file remain in packed format.

The unpack command has no optional flags.

5.8.3   `pcat`—Unpack a file to standard output

The `pcat` command performs the exact function as `unpack`; it takes a file processed by `pack` and transforms it back into its original form. The difference between `pcat` and `unpack` is that `pcat` writes the uncompacted file to standard output. It does not create a new disk file,[14] therefore, the original file is not removed.

The input file must be processed by `pack`. This being the case, the file name can be entered with or without the pack .z suffix. Either `pcat chapter.one` or `pcat chapter.one.z` unpacks the file named chapter.one.z.

The `pcat` command has no optional flags.

5.8.4   `compress`—Compact a file using adaptive Lempel-Zev encoding

The `compress` command reads the input file specified, compacts it, and creates a compressed file of the same name with a .Z[15] suffix. Typically, the compaction ratio is from 50 to 75 percent. The new, compressed file has the same owner, access modes, and access and modification dates as the original input file. If the `compress` command is successful, the input file is deleted. It can be recreated by using the `uncompress` command.

If the `compress` command cannot create a smaller file as the result of compaction, it terminates with a message reporting that compaction was unsuccessful. Other reasons for unsuccessful execution of the `compress` command are: the input file is not a regular file, the input file name is too long and the .Z suffix cannot be appended to it, the output file already exists and the -f (or -F) flag was not specified, the input or output file cannot be opened, or an I/O error occurs.

Whenever the `compress` command fails, the original file is left undisturbed. The original file is deleted only when the `compress` command executes successfully and exits with a return code of zero.

`Compress` has several flags. The first two, -f and -F, perform exactly the same function; they force compression to occur. By forcing compaction to occur, two distinct actions are involved: an existing, compressed file is overwritten and the file is compressed even if the compaction ratio is 0 percent.

The -b `number_of_bits` flag indicates the maximum number of bits to use when replacing common substrings in the file. By default this is set to the maximum value of 16. The minimum number of bits is nine. When compacting the data in the file, the algorithm uses the 9-bit codes (257 through 512) to replace as many substrings within the file as possible. If the number of bits has been set to greater than nine, the algorithm then uses the 10-bit codes, increasing through the codes until the number specified by the -b flag is reached. There is no real benefit to limiting the number of bits to less than 16 as this limits the

---

[14]Unless standard output has been redirected to a disk file.

[15]Note that the pack command produces a file with a lower-case z suffix while the compress produces a file with an upper-case Z suffix.

number of strings that can be replaced. The only exception to this is for small files that contain excessive redundant information. Once the available codes have been exhausted, the algorithm periodically checks the compaction ratio. If it is increasing or remaining steady, the existing compaction code table is retained. Otherwise, the code table is discarded and rebuilt which allows the algorithm to adapt to the remaining portions of the file.

The -q flag suppresses the display of compaction statistics, and the -v flag requests these statistics. The -V flag displays version information and compile options of the files. Both -v and -V information is written to standard error, not standard output. This is because the -c flag allows the compacted output file to be directed to standard output. When this option is used, the original uncompressed file is not deleted, even upon successful execution of the compress command.

The -n flag is provided for backward compatibility. It excludes the compressed file header from the compressed file.

The last flag, -d, makes the compress command function as if it were the uncompress command.

Using our prior example of file snaprof, it is readily apparent that the compress command results in a smaller output file.

```
$ ls -al snaprof*
-rw-rw-r--  123 fgc     staff     63225 Dec 06 09:43 snaprof
$ compress -v -V snaprof
Options: BITS = 16
snaprof: Compression: 71.42%
— replaced with snaprof.Z
$ ls -al snaprof*
-rw-rw-r--   36 fgc     staff     18026 Dec 06 09:44 snaprof.Z
$
```

5.8.5 uncompress

The uncompress command is the counterpart of compress; it takes a file processed by compress and transforms it back into its original form.

Uncompress uses many of the same flags as compress, although their functions differ slightly. For example, the -f flag forces decompression to occur by overwriting an existing, uncompressed file if it already exists. The -F flag is equivalent to the -f flag. The -q flag suppresses the display of the compressed file's statistics, and the -v flag requests these statistics. The -v flag displays version information and compile options of the files being decompressed. Both -v and -V information is written to standard error, not standard output. This is because the -c flag allows the uncompacted output file to be directed to standard output.[16] When this option is used, the original compressed file is not deleted, even on successful execution of the uncompress command. Finally, the -n flag is provided for backward compatibility. It excludes the file header from the uncompressed file.

---

[16]This is the exact function as the zcat command.

To uncompress a file named chapter5.Z and display all of the file statistics and information, the command would be

```
uncompress -v -V chapter5.doc.Z
```

This would create a new, uncompressed file named chapter5.doc if it did not already exist. To replace an existing file, the user would have to enter

```
uncompress -V -V -f chapter5.doc.z
```

to create the uncompressed file. The newly created file has the same owner, access modes, and access and modification dates as the original, compressed input file.

If the return code from uncompress is greater than zero, some type of error occurred: the input file was not created by compress, the input or output file cannot be opened, an output file with the same unpacked name already exists and the -f flag was not specified, or an I/O error occurred.

As with all of the other compaction commands, if the uncompress command fails, the original file is left undisturbed. The original file is deleted only when the uncompress command executes successfully and exits with a return code of zero.

5.8.6 zcat—Uncompress a file to standard output

The zcat command performs the exact same function as uncompresss. That is, it takes a file processed by pack and transforms it back into its original form. But, the difference between zcat and uncompress is that zcat writes only the uncompacted file to standard output. It does not create a new disk file,[17] therefore, the original file is not removed.

Although the zcat command supports the -f and -F flags as described in Section 5.8.5, they are rarely used. The only flag ever used with any type of frequency is -n which excludes the file header from the uncompressed file.

To borrow the previous example, to uncompress a file named chapter5.Z and display it at the terminal device, the command would be

```
zcat chapter5.doc.Z | pg
```

We pipe the output to pg so as to not have the information from the file scroll off the screen in an uncontrolled manner.

5.9 File Comparisons

In AIX there are several commands available which allow for files to be compared against each other. As would be expected, these commands locate inconsistencies between the compared files and report on the differences found.

---

[17]Again, as with pcat, unless standard output has been redirected to a disk file.

For all of the commands in this section (cmp, diff, diff3, bdiff, sdiff, and comp), a minus sign (-) may be used as a file name to indicate that the input should be read from standard input.

5.9.1   cmp—Compare two files

The cmp command is the simplest of the comparison commands. It compares the contents of two files[18] and writes the result to standard output. If the two files are the same, no output is produced; if the two files differ, the output consists of the byte and line number at which the first difference is detected. If the -1 flag is used, the output displays the byte number of the difference and the differing bytes in octal. The -s flag suppresses any display; the result of the command is known only by the return code

0 indicates the files are identical

1 indicates the the files differ

2 indicates that an error occurred

Once the first difference is found, the command terminates.

5.9.2   diff—Compare text files

The diff command compares text files and reports on the differences. It can also be used to compare the contents of directories. In this case, the command takes the names of two directories and compares the text files in the two directories which are common. Common subdirectories, files that appear in only one directory, and binary files that differ are listed.

In most cases, though, the diff command is used to compare regular text files. When run against text files, whether directly or indirectly through directory comparisons, the output of the diff command is a listing of what lines must be changed in the files to make them equivalent. When differences are detected, a line is written to the output in the format: line numbers affected in the first file, and action (*a* for add, *d* for delete, *c* for change) and the affected lines in the second file. Following this is a display of the text of the affected lines in the first file. These lines are preceded by a (<) less than sign. Then the affected lines of the second file are displayed; these are preceded by a (>) greater than sign.

There are several flags which can be used with diff. These are discussed in Table 5.19.

The following example shows the result of a diff command processed against the current .profile file and the most recent backup copy.

```
$ cat .profile
PATH=/bin:/usr/bin:/etc:/usr/ucb:$HOME/bin:/usr/local/bin:.
```

---

[18]Standard input can be used as one of the input files by coding a minus sign (-) as one of the file names.

TABLE 5.19   `diff` **Command Flags**

Flag	Meaning
-b	Ignores leading spaces and tabs; compare strings of spaces as equal.
-C *lines*	Produces a comparison with a context area equal to the number of *lines* specified. This flag marks all differing lines with an introductory line of 12 asterisks (************). Those lines which have been removed from the first file are indicated by a leading minus (-), those lines added to the second file are indicated by a leading plus (+), and lines which are not equivalent between the two files are indicated by an exclamation point (!).
-c [*lines*]	This flag is similar to the -C flag, except that the number of context lines does not have to be explicitly given. If it is omitted, the default context area is taken to be three.
-D [*string*]	Writes to standard output a merged version of the two input files. This is primarily used with C programs. The merged output file contains C pre-processor directives which produce the first input file if the *string* is not defined, but produce the second input file if the *string* is defined.
-e	Produces output which can be used by the ed editor to create the second input file from the first file. When used while comparing directories, extra commands are included which produce a shell script to convert the common files between the directories from their state in the first directory to their state in the second directory.
-f	Produces output which indicates what must be done to make the first input file equivalent to the second file. This output is not usable by ed.
-h	Can be used only with the -b flag; all others are ignored. This flag instructs diff to use an alternate comparison method which can be faster when run against long files having short, well-defined, and nonoverlapping changed sections.
-i	Ignores case when performing comparisons.
-l	Long output format. Prepares the difference output in a more formal report structure.
-n	Produces output in the format expected by the *Revision Control System* (RCS).
-r	When used with a directory, this flag causes the diff command to recursively apply the comparison to common subdirectories.
-s	Reports on files which are equivalent and would not otherwise be reported.
-S [*file*]	When used with directory comparisons, instructs diff to ignore files whose names collate before the specified *file*. This flag does not work with subdirectories that are entered as a result of the specification of the -r flag.
-t	Expand tabs in the output lines. This flag helps to preserve the original indentation of the source file.
-w	Ignores all space and tab characters.

```
export PATH
if [-s "$MAIL"]          # Th is is at Shell startup. In normal
then echo "$MAILMSG"     # operation, the Shell checks
fi                       # periodically.
PS1='$PWD>'
ENV=$HOME/.kshrc
LESS=b20CeMQ
umask 002
export LESS
export ENV
echo ""
/usr/games/fortune
$
```

```
$ cat .old_profile
PATH=/bin:/usr/bin:/etc:/usr/ucb:$HOME/bin:/usr/local/bin:.
export PATH
if [-s "$MAIL"]        # This is at Shell startup. In normal
then echo "$MAILMSG"   # operation, the Shell checks
fi                     # periodically.
PS1='! $PWD>'
ENV=$H OME/.kshrc
LESS=b20CeMQ
umask 002
export LESS
export ENV
echo ""
/usr/games/fortune
$


$ diff .profile .old_profile
6c6
< PS1='! $PWD>'
---
> PS1='$PWD>'
$
```

5.9.3 diff3—Compare three files

The diff3 command allows for the comparison of three files at the same time. The output of the command is not the same as the diff command. The information directed to standard output includes the lines of text that are different flagged with one of the following indicators:

====	all three files are different
====1	file 1 is different
====2	file 2 is different
====3	file 3 is different

Also directed to standard output is an edit script with the changes needed to convert a portion of one file to match the contents of another. The edit script produces two types of information; the first describes text that is to be added. A line in the format

    file:linenumber a

indicates that text must be added after the *linenumber* in *file*. The file indicator is either 1, 2, or 3 as applicable. A line in the format

    file:startline[,endline] c

indicates that the text is to be changed. If the beginning and ending lines are the same, the ending line is not displayed.

There are five flags for diff3, each of which controls what is written to the edit script on standard output. The -3 flag produces an edit script which incorporates only the changes flagged by ====3. The -e flag produces an edit script to incorporate into file 1 the changes flagged by ==== and ====3. The -x flag produces an edit script for only those lines flagged with a ====.

The -E and -X flags are similar to -e and -x but treat the overlapping changes (flagged by ====) in a different way. When the edit script is produced, these lines are bracketed by <<<<<< and >>>>>>> lines. This helps to aid visual identification of the lines.

Using our prior example of the .profile files, if we add the second oldest backup copy to the comparison, the diff3 command yields quite different results compared to those of the diff command.

```
$ cat old_profile.backup
.PATH=/bin:/usr/bin:/etc:/usr/ucb:$HOME/bin:/usr/local/bin:.
export PATH
if [-s "$MAIL"]          # This is at Shell startup. In normal
then echo "$MAILMSG"     # operation, the Shell checks
fi                       # periodically.
ENV=$HOME/.kshrc
LESS=b20CeMQ
export LESS
export ENV
echo ""
export TERM
umask 002
$

$ diff3 .old_profile.backup .old_profile .profile
====
1:5a
2:6c
  PS1='! $PWD>'
3:6c
  PS1='$PWD>'
====1
1:7a
2:9c
3:9c
  umask 002]
====1
1:11,12c
  export TERM
  umask 002
2:13c
3:13c
  /usr/games/fortune
$
```

5.9.4 bdiff—diff **for very large files**

In most cases, the diff command is more than sufficient for performing file comparisons. However, for some extremely large files, diff cannot function correctly. In these cases, bdiff must be used. Essentially, the bdiff command is a preprocessor for diff. The first order of processing for bdiff is to skip over the common, beginning portions of the two files. Then bdiff breaks the large files into smaller segments and calls diff to work on the corresponding segments. By default, bdiff uses 3500 line segments. In some cases, even this is too much for diff, so the syntax of the command allows for an overriding specification of the segment limit

```
bdiff file1 file2 [segment_limit] [-s]
```

The -s flag suppresses the error messages that the bdiff command might issue. It does not suppress the error messages issued by the called diff command.

5.9.5 sdiff—Compare two files and display the differences in side-by-side format

The sdiff command is another diff preprocessor. It is used to generate the results of a diff comparison in a side-by-side format. Unless the -s flag is used, each line of the two input files is displayed on the output. If the -l flag is used, it suppresses the display of the line from file 2 if the two lines are identical. The -s flag suppresses the display of any identical lines.

In the output, if the two lines (one from each file) are separated by spaces, they are equal. If the two lines are separated by a less than sign (<) then the line exists only in the first file; a greater than sign > indicates the line exists only in the second file. A vertical bar (|) indicates that the two lines are different.

An important note is that sdiff invokes diff with a -b flag; therefore, trailing spaces and tabs are ignored in the comparisons, and spaces and strings of spaces are treated as equal for comparison purposes.

The -w line_size flag can be used to set the width of the output line. The default number of characters is 130.

5.9.6 comm—Select or reject lines common to two sorted files

The comm command reads the two sorted input files specified and produces a report on the commonality and differences of the two files. The report consists of three columns. The first column lists only those lines found in the first file, the second file lists the lines found only in the second file, and the third column lists the common lines.

The flags of this command indicate which column of output should be suppressed. For example, the command

```
comm daily.routine weekly.routine
```

produces a report where the first column indicates daily tasks, the second column lists weekly tasks, and the third column lists those tasks common to both lists. The command

```
comm -12 daily.routine weekly.routine
```

produces a report of only those items which are common to both lists, where the command

```
comm -13 daily.routine weekly.routine
```

produces a report of those items unique to the weekly.routine file.

5.10 Manipulating the Contents of Files

In addition to tools like awk and sed, AIX provides several different commands which modify the contents of a file. Most of these commands are fairly primitive; they perform one and only one function. Most commonly, they are used as functions within a shell script.

5.10.1 `tab`—Change spaces to tabs

The `tab` command reads the input file and replaces all spaces in the file with tabs.[19] If a disk file was used as input, this file is replaced; if standard input was used, the output is directed to standard output. The only flag for the `tab` command is `-e` which limits the replacement of space characters to the first characters of the line up to the first nonspace character. The format of the command is

```
tab [-e] [file_name]
```

For most purposes, the `unexpand` command (Section 5.10.4) is more appropriate.

5.10.2 `untab`—Change tabs to spaces

The `untab` command reverses the action of the tab command; it takes the input file and changes every tab character into a space character. If the input is from standard input, the output is directed to standard output, otherwise the input file is replaced by the output file. There are no flags with the `untab` command

```
untab [file_name]
```

For most purposes, the `expand` command (Section 5.10.3) is more appropriate.

5.10.3 `expand`—Change tabs to spaces

The `expand` command, like the `untab` command, translates tab characters into space characters. However, the `expand` command always directs its output to standard output, so the input file is never changed as a result of its execution. Furthermore, the `expand` command allows the user to determine the width of the tab stops, either as a relative value (such as every eight characters) or absolutely (at 8, 24, 44, 72, etc.).

To replace all of the tabs in a file named example.tab with a space character, the command is

```
expand example.tab
```

To replace the tabs in the same file with 3 spaces for each tab, the command is

```
expand -3 example.tab
```

To set the first three tabs to absolute columns 5, 15, and 25, enter the command

```
expand -5,15,25 example.tab
```

---

[19]The tab stops are set at eight and cannot be changed.

5.10.4 `unexpand`—Replace spaces with tabs

The `unexpand` command replaces spaces in the input file with tabs and writes the output to standard output. Unlike the `tab` command, the default action of `unexpand` is to replace only leading spaces. Spaces embedded in the lines are not replaced by tabs unless the -a flag is specified.

To convert the previously used file, example.tab, back to its original form, the command `unexpand -a example.tab` is used.

5.10.5 `rev`—Reverse the characters on each line in a file

The `rev` command reads the specified file and writes a reverse image of each line to standard output. That is, input file column 1 becomes output file column 80, input file column 2 becomes output file column 79, etc. Assuming that the file fruit.dat contained the following lines

```
apples
dates
pumpkin
```

the following command

```
rev fruit.dat > rev.fruit
```

creates a file, named rev.fruit, with the following lines

```
selppa
setad
nikpmup
```

This highly useful command has no flags.

5.10.6 `fold`—Fold lines for printing on a different carriage size

The `fold` command is used to display or print output with a large line size on a device with a smaller line size. For example, most standard report output uses 132 columns. When this is displayed at a 80-column terminal device, it generally does not look very good. In many cases, the `fold` command can be used to format this larger output so that it looks better when printed on the smaller device.

The three flags of the command control various formatting issues. The -w flag allows the user to specify a maximum line width different from the default of 80. The -b flag tells the `fold` command to count width by number of bytes rather than by number of characters. The -s flag causes the lines to be broken at the rightmost blank within the defined width. The default action is to make each line as long as possible within the defined width.

5.11 Joining, Merging, and Translating Files

The commands in this section, `cut`, `join`, and `paste` are used to combine and separate the data in a file as opposed to commands such as `split` which work on a file indifferent to the data contained within.

5.11.1   cut—Extract selected bytes, characters, or fields from a file

Perhaps the most simple and useful command on the AIX system for parsing, the cut command facilitates the extraction of information from each line of a file. This processing can be by bytes with the -b flag, by characters with the -c flag, or by fields with the -f flag; one of these flags must be used.

For each of the flags, a list parameter must be specified. The list parameter is either a comma-separated or minus-separated list of increasing numbers. A comma-separated list indicates individual values whereas a minus-separated list indicates a range. For example

```
cut -b1,3,6 data.file >data.out.file
```

extricates bytes 1,3, and 6 from each line of data.file, but

```
cut -b1-6 data.file >data.out.file
```

extracts bytes 1 through 6 inclusive. If the last number of a minus-separated list is not specified, it indicates that the range extends to the end-of-line, wherever that may be, i.e., -b40- indicates that all characters starting at position 40 to the end-of-line are included.

When the -b flag is used, the -n flag can also be used to indicate that multibyte characters should not be split. If the last byte of the multibyte character falls within the cut range, the character is included, otherwise it is excluded.

The cut command is most commonly used to extract fields of information from a file. The additional flag -d must be used when field cutting is performed to indicate what the field separator character is, and the -s flag may be used to suppress lines which do not contain the delimiter character. When using the -d flag to indicate the delimiter character, use quotation marks around characters which have special meaning to the shell.

Figure 5.7 demonstrates some uses of the cut command.

5.11.2   paste—Merge the lines of several files or subsequent lines of one file

The paste command merges the contents of several files into standard output—the inverse action of the cut command. Merging is done on a line-by-line basis. The input files are simply treated as columns of the new file to be created. By default, each line of the input files is joined to each other by a tab character.

The delimiter can be modified by specifying the -d flag. In addition to regular characters, the following special characters can be used

\n	new line
\t	tab
\\	backslash
\0	empty string, not a null character

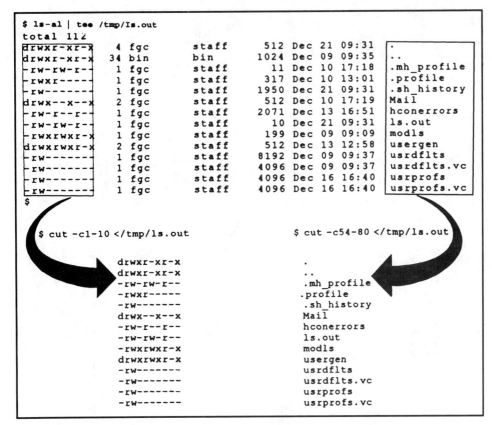

Figure 5.7   cut command.

Quotation marks must be used around characters which have special meaning to the shell.

Unlike the cut command, the paste command supports alternating delimiter characters. If more than one character is specified, the characters are repeated in order until the end of the output. The lines from the last file always end with a newline character.

The -s command is used to concatentate subsequent lines of the files. When used this way, the paste command joins the first and second lines and creates the first line of the output file. Next, the third and fourth lines of the first input file are joined and written as the second line of the output, and so on, until end-of-file is reached on the first file. At this point, a new line is forced in the output, and the second file is processed in the same manner as the first. When end-of-file is reached on the second file, a new line is forced, and the file is closed.

Examples of the paste command are demonstrated in Fig. 5.8

5.11.3   join—Join the data fields of two files

The join command is used to merge two sorted files. The join command uses the join field in the input files as the key field. For each key field matched in

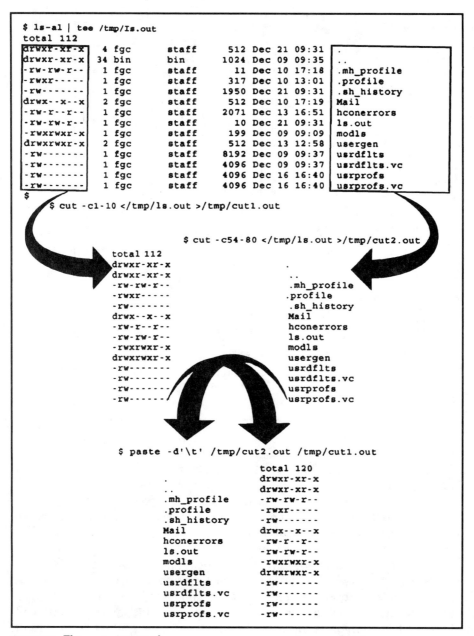

Figure 5.8   The paste command.

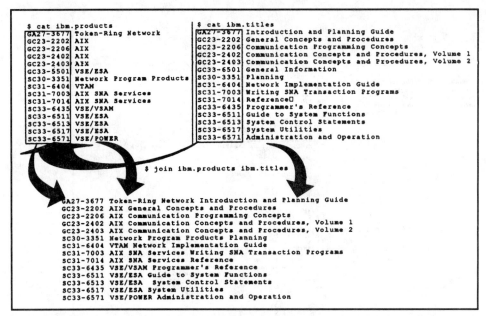

Figure 5.9 The `join` command. In this example, the file ibm.products is joined to ibm.titles (join ibm.products ibm.titles). Because no matching field is explicitly coded, the first field of the first file is used as the control. Only those lines which have matching keys in the first field of both files are printed. Because no output field definitions are used, all of the fields from the first file are displayed after the key value, followed by all of the fields from the second file.

both input files, one line of output is produced (Fig. 5.9). Each output line contains the key field, the remaining portion of the line from the first input file, and the remaining portion of the line from the second input file. Standard input can be used as one of the input files by coding a - (minus sign) as the name of one of the input files.

Unlike the `cut` and `paste` commands, the `join` command assumes default delimiter characters (the space, tab, and new line characters) unless otherwise directed. Furthermore, leading delimiters are discarded and consecutive ones are treated as one instance of a delimiter. The `-t` flag is used to specify a delimiter character other than the default characters.

Join processing is controlled by the flags `-1` *fieldnumber* and `-2` *fieldnumber*. Each flag takes as an operand the number of field which is to be used as the join field. The `-1` flag indicates that the controlling field is found in the first file; the `-2` flag indicates that it is found in the second file. The default is to use the first field in the first file.

Output is constructed by using the `-o` flag which takes as its operands a list of fields to be included in the output. The format of each entry within the list is *filenumber.fieldnumber*.

The flag `-a` *filenumber* is used to request that in addition to the regular output, an output line be produced for each line in the file indicated by the filenumber which does not have a matching join field in the other input file. Figure 5.10 outlines a shell script which shows how applying this flag to both

```
sort -t, -k2 -k1 -k3,4n ibm.info
```

Phase 1

The input file is in random order. The sort command instructs that the field delimiter is a comma (-t,) and the major sort field is the second field (-k2). The first minor sort field is the first (-k1). The most minor key field is the third, which is a four digit numeric field (-k3,4n)

```
AIX,GC23,2403,Communication Concepts and Procedures,Volume 2
VSE/ESA,SC33,6513,System Control Statements
Network,SC30,3351,Program Products Planning
VSE/ESA,SC33,6517,System Utilities □□
VTAM□SC31,6404,Network Implementation Guide
Token-Ring,GA27,3677,Network Introduction and Planning Guide
AIX,GC23,2402,Communication Concepts and Procedures ,Volume 1
VSE/POWER,SC33,6571,Administration and Operation □□□
AIX,GC23,2202,General Concepts and Procedures
VSE/ESA,SC33,6511, Guide to System Functions
AIX,SC31,7003,SNA Services Writing SNA Transaction Programs
AIX,SC31,7014,SNA Services Reference
VSE/VSAM,SC33,6435,Programmer's Reference
AIX,GC23,2206,Communication Programming Concepts
□
```

Phase 2

The first pass of the sort orders the file in key sequence by field number 2.

```
Token-Ring,GA27,3677,Network Introduction and Planning Guide
AIX,GC23,2403,Communication Concepts and Procedures,Volume 2
AIX,GC23,2402,Communication Concepts and Procedures ,Volume 1
AIX,GC23,2202,General Concepts and Procedures
AIX,GC23,2206,Communication Programming Concepts
Network,SC30,3351,Program Products Planning
VTAM,SC31,6404,Network Implementation Guide
AIX,SC31,7003,SNA Services Writing SNA Transaction Programs
AIX,SC31,7014,SNA Services Reference
VSE/ESA,SC33,6513,System Control Statements
VSE/ESA,SC33,6517,System Utilities □□
VSE/POWER,SC33,6571,Administration and Operation □□□
VSE/ESA,SC33,6511, Guide to System Functions
VSE/VSAM,SC33,6435,Programmer's Reference
```

Phase 3

In this phase, the data in field one is sorted within the constraints of the already sorted major field. Major movement of records does not occur, just those which are not in collating sequence within the major groups.

```
Token-Ring,GA27,3677,Network Introduction and Planning Guide
AIX,GC23,2403,Communication Concepts and Procedures,Volume 2
AIX,GC23,2402,Communication Concepts and Procedures ,Volume 1
AIX,GC23,2202,General Concepts and Procedures
AIX,GC23,2206,Communication Programming Concepts
Network,SC30,3351,Program Products Planning
AIX,SC31,7003,SNA Services Writing SNA Transaction Programs
AIX,SC31,7014,SNA Services Reference
VTAM,SC31,6404,Network Implementation Guide
VSE/ESA,SC33,6513,System Control Statements
VSE/ESA,SC33,6517,System Utilities □□
VSE/ESA,SC33,6511, Guide to System Functions
VSE/POWER,SC33,6571,Administration and Operation □□□
VSE/VSAM,SC33,6435,Programmer's Reference
```

Phase 4

Again, in this phase, major movement of records does not occur. The major and first minor fields have already been sorted. The only record movement that occurs is for those records which are out of order in the second minor control field and are also in a group of the major and first minor control field.

As this is the last sort key, when this phase is complete, the sorted data is output to standard output

```
Token-Ring,GA27,3677,Network Introduction and Planning Guide
AIX,GC23,2202,General Concepts and Procedures
AIX,GC23,2206,Communication Programming Concepts
AIX,GC23,2402,Communication Concepts and Procedures ,Volume 1
AIX,GC23,2403,Communication Concepts and Procedures,Volume 2
Network,SC30,3351,Program Products Planning
AIX,SC31,7003,SNA Services Writing SNA Transaction Programs
AIX,SC31,7014,SNA Services Reference
VTAM,SC31,6404,Network Implementation Guide
VSE/ESA,SC33,6511, Guide to System Functions
VSE/ESA,SC33,6513,System Control Statements
VSE/ESA,SC33,6517,System Utilities □□
VSE/POWER,SC33,6571,Administration and Operation □□□
VSE/VSAM,SC33,6435,Programmer's Reference
```

.**Figure 5.10** Sort processing.

files and using diff on the results can produce a listing of the unmatched keys in the two files.

The -v *filenumber* flag is similar to the -a flag. It is used to suppress regular output while producing output lines for each line in the file indicated by the filenumber which does not have a matching join field in the other input file.

Finally, the -e flag is used to replace with a string empty output fields. This is frequently used in conjunction with the -a or -v flags to indicate that an error has occurred.

5.11.4 tr—Translate characters

The tr command is a filter. It translates or deletes characters from the standard input file and writes the modified output to standard output. The format of the command is

```
tr [-d] [-s] [-A] [-c] string1 string2
```

If no flag is used, the tr command translates one set of characters represented by string1 into another represented by string2. When the -d flag is used, the tr command deletes string1 characters as they are read from standard input. The -s flag is used to remove all but the first in a sequence of repeated characters. In this context, string1 represents those characters which should be processed when the input is originally read from standard input, and string2 represents those characters which should be processed immediately before output is written to standard output.

The syntax for specifying the strings is quite rich. The simplest instance is a range of characters; the range is indicated by beginning and ending characters enclosed within brackets. For example

```
tr '[a-v]' '[A-V]' <input.txt >out.doc
```

translates all characters from a to v into the corresponding upper case letter. A number of repetitions of a character can be indicated by [C*number] where *C* indicates the character and *number* indicates the repetitions.

```
tr -d [a*7] <input.txt >out.doc
```

deletes all instances of seven a's (aaaaaaa) from the output. An abbreviated form with no number can be used when coding string2 to indicate the repetition factor is the same as string1.

Various classes of characters can be indicated with class notation

```
[:classname:]
```

where the classnames are

alnum	alphanumeric characters
alpha	alphabetic characters

`blank`	blank class of characters
`cntrl`	control characters
`digit`	numeric characters
`lower`	lowercase alphabetic characters
`print`	all printable characters
`punct`	punctuation characters
`space`	space class of characters
`upper`	uppercase alphabetic characters

Classes can make specification simpler

```
tr '[:lower:]' '[:upper:]' <input.txt >out.doc
```

is clearer in stating its purpose than

```
tr '[a-z]' '[A-Z]' <input.txt >out.doc
```

although both are equally valid.

Certain control characters can be explicitly coded

`\a`	alert
`\b`	backspace
`\f`	form feed
`\n`	new line
`\r`	carriage return
`\t`	tab
`\v`	vertical tab
`\\`	backslash character
`\[`	left bracket
`\-`	minus sign
`\0`	null character
`\octal`	any three digit octal value

This allows for simpler manipulation of files with unusual or difficult sequences. For example, to compress each instance of multiple blank lines to a single blank line, the command would be

```
tr -s '\n' <input.txt >out.doc
```

Another common use is to filter out nonprinting characters before output is sent to a printer

```
tr -c '[:print:][:cntrl:]' '[?*]' <input.txt >out.doc
```

This command replaces every instance of a nonprinting character, except valid control characters, with a question mark.

Finally, the `-A` flag tells `tr` to ignore the current locale collating sequence, and instead, use a byte-by-byte direct ASCII collating sequence.

5.12   Sorting Data

As UNIX-based operating systems move into the traditional domain of main-frame operating systems, many of the concerns of high data volume environments are being more seriously addressed by the UNIX-operating systems. Nowhere is this change more evident than in the growth and enhancements that have gone into the sort command. Although the AIX sort still does not totally compare to the functionality of sorts available on platforms such as MVS or VSE, the sort command in AIX is fully capable of supporting the processing needs of most AIX computing environments.

5.12.1   The sort command

As is true for every other data manipulation command on AIX, the sort command uses a line of data within a file as the medium of information. The sort command sorts the lines within a file (or files) and writes the result to standard output unless specifically directed to an output file with the -o flag. Multiple files are sorted at the same time by concatenation; the sort command simply treats all of the input files as if they were one large file. When no flags are specified on the sort command line, it sorts the entire line of the input file based on the current locale collation sequence.

5.12.2   Sort keys

In AIX, a sort key is simply a portion of the line identified as a field. Within a field, a byte may be identified which signifies the beginning of a subfield. By default, a space, a tab, or a sequence of spaces is used as the field delimiter. All three are treated as a single field delimiter. For nontext files this is usually not sufficient, therefore, the -t flag can be used to identify a different delimiter character.

The AIX sort command supports more than one sort key. In fact, up to ten sort keys can be specified per sort. The sort command first orders all records based on the first key specifications (Figure 5.10). Records which have duplicate first sort keys are then subordered based on the specifications of the second sort key, and so on, until all records have been sorted or all of the sort keys have been processed. If after all sort keys have been processed there are still records which have duplicate keys, the duplicate records are placed in order by using the entire record as a sort key.

The syntax for specifying a sort key is quite flexible; the format is

    -k [field][.column][mod][,fieldEnd][.columnEnd][mod]

If only *field* is coded, the sort key begins at column one of the indicated field and continues until the delimiter character is encountered within the line.[20]

---

[20]The astute will have observed that this allows for variable length sort keys. This is something no mainframe sort can do.

When *column* is specified along with *field,* the sort key begins at the indicated column within the field. If *column* is specified without a field, the column indicates an absolute value at which the sort key begins within the line. The mod variable allows for several characteristics of the key to be modified (Section 5.12.3). If the fieldEnd value is coded, it determines when the sort key ends. Since the fieldEnd value can be in a different field than the beginning one, a sort key may include more than one data field. If no endColumn is coded, the sort key ends the first time the delimiter value is detected after the columnEnd field, otherwise it ends at the specified column within the endColumn field. And, as with column, if endColumn is specified without a field, then endColumn indicates an absolute value at which the sort key ends.

Within a field, blank characters within a default field separator are considered a part of the following field. Leading blanks, however, are not counted as part of the first field, and delimiter characters as defined by the -t flag are never counted as part of a field.

5.12.3   Sort key modifiers

Several flags are available to modify the behavior of sort keys. When a flag is specified before the sort key definitions, it applies to all sort keys subsequently defined. Once a sort key has been defined, the flags may only be used as modifiers for individual keys.

The -b flag is used to ignore leading spaces and tabs when locating the first or last column of a field. The -d flag forces the key to be sorted in dictionary order; that is, only letters, digits, and spaces are considered when making comparisons. Any other characters within the key are simply ignored. Closely related is the -i flag, which causes all nonprinting characters to be ignored when making comparisons. Upper and lowercase letters can be forced to compare equal by using the -f flag.

Numeric sort fields are typically indicated by the -n flag. This flag forces the key to be sorted in arithmetic value. The field may contain leading blanks, a plus or minus sign, decimal digits, thousands-separator characters, and a radix (or decimal) point. Nonnumeric characters are not rejected out-of-hand, but cause unpredictable results.

Collating order is usually determined by the collatin g sequence of the current locale. To force a sort to conform to the ASCII collation order, the -A flag must be specified.

Regardless of collating sequence, the majority of sorts are in ascending sequence. Most sort implementations also allow for descending sorts. The sort command implements a descending sort via the -r (or reverse) flag. Unlike many sort implementations, ascending and descending combinations of sort keys can be mixed within one invocation of sort.

5.12.4   Sort Output and Performance

As stated earlier, the default output destination is standard output. To explicitly name a file, the -o *filename* flag can be used to specify a filename for the output.

The -u flag is used to remove duplicate keys from the output. This flag suppresses all but the first instance of a line in a set of lines which sort equally on all keys.

Affecting both output and performance is the -T flag. This flag allows the user to specify the directory into which all temporary sortwork files should be placed. By default, the sortwork files, if necessary, are placed into the current directory. By directing the sortwork files to a low-volume file system, overall performance can be increased.

The biggest performance boost, however, is by specifying the -y flag for those sorts which involve a number of files or lines. The -y flag has three options. Alone, it tells the sort command to use as much virtual storage as possible for sorting the records before using sortwork files for temporary storage. The -y0 flag tells the sort command to use only the minimal amount of storage. Except for very small sorts, this ensures that sortwork files will be used. The final option is to code a value with the flag to specify an exact amount of storage, such as -y256 to indicate that the sort should use 256K for the sort work area. While sorting a small file in -y space is wasteful, sorting a large file in -y0 space can cripple a system. A good rule of thumb is to allocate an amount of storage equal to the size of the file to be sorted.

5.13 Directories

Although directories are nothing more than AIX files, they have special properties. In order to administer directories, some additional commands are provided for directory functions. In this section, the discussion is limited to those commands which are unique to directories. Several commands have already been discussed (chgrp, chmod, cp, delete, mv, and rm) which work on both regular files and directories. As the full functionality of these commands has already been discussed, they are not treated in this section.

5.13.1 pwd—Display the current directory

One of the simpler commands, pwd, writes the full path name of the current working directory to standard output. The root directory is represented by the first /. The last directory named is the current directory.

As an example, consider the user named fgc who created a unixbook directory and was currently working in it. If the pwd command were to be issued, the dialog would be as follows

```
$ pwd
/home/fgc/unixbook
$
```

For more information on directory naming conventions, refer to Section 2.2.4. The pwd command takes no operands and has no flags.

5.13.2 cd—Change the current directory

The cd command facilitates moving from one directory to another. To successfully switch to a new directory, the user must have, at least, execute/search permission in the new directory.

Fully qualified path names, in addition to relative path names, can be used with the cd command. A fully qualified path name, provided the user has adequate permissions, becomes the current directory after command execution.

For a relative path name, the shell searches for the directory relative to one of the path names in the change directory shell variable.[21] If it is found in one of the paths, that path, as resolved to a fully qualified name, becomes the current directory.

Executing the cd command with no operands switches the users to their home directory.[22] In addition, the dot dot (..) shorthand for the parent directory may also be used to traverse up the path.

Consider the following cases:

cd	changes the current directory to the user's home directory
cd ..	changes the current directory to the next higher level in the current directory path[23]
cd unixbook	searches the paths in the current search sequence for a subdirectory named unixbook; if found, it becomes the current working directory
cd /usr/local/data	changes the current working directory to the fully qualified path of /usr/local/data

5.13.3   li, ls, and di—Display the contents of a directory

The ls, li and di commands are all used to display the contents of a directory. Of the three commands, ls is probably the most commonly used.

The ls command displays the contents of the specified directory on standard output. If no directory is specified, the current directory is displayed. If no flags are used, this display consists of four columns which simply list the names of the files in the directory. This information is displayed, by default, in alphabetic sequence. No other additional information about the files is displayed. Furthermore, entries for files beginning with a dot (.) are not displayed unless the -a or -A flag is used.[24]

When more complete information on a file is requested via the -e or -l flag, the first column of the output displays the file type. The entries in this column are interpreted using the values in Table 5.15.

The subsequent nine characters are divided into three sets of three characters each where the first set represents the owner's rights, the next set of three characters represents the group owner's rights, and the last set represents the rights of all other users.

---

[21]This is the $CDPATH variable in the Korn and Bourne shells, and the $cdpath variable in the C Shell.

[22]MS-DOS users take note! This is represented by the Korn (or Bourne) shell variable $HOME or by the C Shell variable $home.

[23]Unless the current directory is the root directory (/), in which case the command has no effect at all.

[24]When executed by a user with root authority, the -A flag is always assumed.

The three characters in each set represent the read (r), write (w), execute/search (x), or null (-) permissions of the entry.[25] Note that the x permission represents execute permission for a file, but search permission for directories. For files which have set user id on execute or set group id on execute permission, the s character is used instead of the x character.

When the -e flag is used, an additional, 11th column is used. A minus sign (-) indicates that no extended security information exists for the entry. A plus sign (+) indicates the entry has extended security information—the file may have extended ACL, TCB, or TP attributes. This access control list (ACL) can be displayed only by using the aclget command. The value of the TCB and TP attributes can be displayed only by using the chtcb command.

By using the optional flags (Table 5.20), it is possible to format the output in more usable formats

One entry per line with the -l or e flags

Multiple columns by using either the -C or -x flag

In a comma-separated series with the -m flag

Figure 5.11 demonstrates some examples of ls command and flag usage.

The li command also lists the contents of a directory, but it is designed to be more flexible in how the output is presented to the user. The li command can process archived files; when the -R flag is specified the command lists the files in the archive.

Unlike the ls command, li lists regular files before directories, and the file and directory names are in collating order.[26] If control characters are present in a file name, the control character is displayed in expanded form, that is control-Z would be displayed as \^Z.

When the -l p flag is used, the first 10 columns of the display correspond to the information displayed by the ls -l command. If the -e flag is used, a twelfth column is added. The 11th character of the field, regardless of whether -l p or -e is specified, is normally empty. However, if the entry is a directory with link permission, or a regular file with the save text attribute, a t is displayed. When the -e flag is used, the 12th column corresponds to the 11th column of a ls -e command.

Unlike the ls command, the li flags are grouped into functional areas: include field (-I), exclude field (-E), restriction (-O), recursion (-R), and sort order (-S). Each flag takes one or several variables which indicate what fields are to be acted on. These fields are documented in Table 5.21. The only field included by default is the name (n) field. If more than one field is used, the li command lists the output one entry to a line.

Some combinations of flags do not work well together, for example, li -vRa

---

[25]This is similar to the prior discussion in chmod.

[26]This is not necessarily the same as alphabetic order. Alphabetic order ignores nonprinting and control characters.

TABLE 5.20   ls **Command Flags**

Flag	Meaning
-A	Lists all entries, except private files and the parent directory.
-a	Lists all entries, including private files and the parent directory.
-b	Displays nonprinting characters in octal notation. See also -q.
-c	Must be used with either the -l or -t flag. This flag instructs ls to use the time of last modification of the i-node of a linked file, as opposed to the time of the last modification of the linked file itself.
-C	Sorts the output in a vertical, multicolumn format. This is the default when ls is run from a terminal.
-d	Displays information for the specified directory only. Typically, used in conjunction with -l.
-e	Displays the mode, number of links, owner, group, size in bytes, time of last modification, and name of each file. For special files, the size field is replaced by the major and minor device numbers. For symbolic links, the symbolic link is followed, and the path of the linked-to file is preceded by a -> sign.
-f	Displays the name in each slot of the directory named. By default, the -a flag is turned on, and the -l, -t, -s, and -r flags are turned off.
-F	Indicates file type by suffixing special characters to the file name as follows: slash (/) after each directory name, asterisk (*) after executables, equal (=) after sockets, pipe (I) after FIFO special files, and at sign (@) after symbolic links.
-g	Same as the -l flag except that no owner information is displayed.
-i	Displays the i-node of each file in the first column of the report.
-L	For symbolic links, lists the file or directory contents that the link references, that is, symbolic links are followed. This is the default action.
-l	Displays the mode, number of links, owner, group, size in bytes, time of last modification, and name for each file. For special files, the size field is replaced by the major and minor device numbers. For symbolic links, the symbolic link is *not* followed; the path of the linked-to file is preceded by a -> sign.
-m	Creates the output display as a series of comma-separated fields.
-n	Displays the same information as the -l flag, except the user and group names are replaced by the user and group ids (i.e., user and group numbers).
-N	For symbolic links, lists the file or directory contents of the link, *not* that of the file the link references. That is, symbolic links are *not* followed. This is the opposite action of the -L flag.
-o	Displays the same information as the -l flag, except the group owner is not displayed.
-p	Suffixes a slash (/) to the name of any directory listed.
-q	Displays a nonprinting character in a file name as a question mark (?). See also -b.
-r	Reverses the order of display. This results in a descending alphabetic or oldest first display, depending on the other flags used.
-R	Recursively lists all subdirectories.
-s	Displays the size of files in kilobytes.
-t	Sorts by time of last modification instead of by name.
-u	Uses the time of last access instead of the time of last modification. Useful only in conjunction with the -l or -t flags.
-x	Sorts output horizontally in multicolumn format.
-1	Forces output to one-entry-per-line format.

```
$ ls -alF
total 232
drwxr-xr-x    4 fgc      staff        1024 Dec 21 10:30 ./
drwxr-xr-x   34 bin      bin          1024 Dec 09 09:35 ../
-rw-rw-r--    1 fgc      staff          11 Dec 10 17:18 .mh_profile
-rwxr-----    1 fgc      staff         317 Dec 10 13:01 .profile*
-rw-------    1 fgc      staff        3646 Dec 21 10:30 .sh_history
drwx--x--x    2 fgc      staff         512 Dec 10 17:19 Mail/
-rw-r--r--    1 fgc      staff        2071 Dec 13 16:51 hconerrors
                                   .
                                   .
                                   .

$ ls -ail
total 240
15394 drwxr-xr-x    4 fgc      staff        1024 Dec 21 10:30 .
    2 drwxr-xr-x   34 bin      bin          1024 Dec 09 09:35 ..
15639 -rw-rw-r--    1 fgc      staff          11 Dec 10 17:18 .mh_profile
15395 -rwxr-----    1 fgc      staff         317 Dec 10 13:01 .profile
15636 -rw-------    1 fgc      staff        3698 Dec 21 10:30 .sh_history
23555 drwx--x--x    2 fgc      staff         512 Dec 10 17:19 Mail
15638 -rw-r--r--    1 fgc      staff        2071 Dec 13 16:51 hconerrors
                                   .
                                   .
                                   .

$ ls -an
total 240
drwxr-xr-x    4 214      1            1024 Dec 21 10:33 .
drwxr-xr-x   34 2        2            1024 Dec 09 09:35 ..
-rw-rw-r--    1 214      1              11 Dec 10 17:18 .mh_profile
-rwxr-----    1 214      1             317 Dec 10 13:01 .profile
-rw-------    1 214      1            3886 Dec 21 10:33 .sh_history
drwx--x--x    2 214      1             512 Dec 10 17:19 Mail
-rw-rw-r--    1 214      1           37397 Dec 21 10:33 diffls
                                   .
                                   .
                                   .

$ ls -alt
total 240
drwxr-xr-x    4 fgc      staff        1024 Dec 21 10:34 .
-rw-rw-r--    1 fgc      staff           0 Dec 21 10:34 lsalt.out
-rw-------    1 fgc      staff        3934 Dec 21 10:34 .sh_history
-rw-rw-r--    1 fgc      staff        2219 Dec 21 10:33 lsan.out
-rw-rw-r--    1 fgc      staff       37397 Dec 21 10:33 diffls
-rw-rw-r--    1 fgc      staff       21265 Dec 21 10:32 lsalLetc.out
-rw-rw-r--    1 fgc      staff       26410 Dec 21 10:32 lsaletc.out
                                   .
                                   .
                                   .
```

Figure 5.11 Example ls commands.

TABLE 5.21   li **Command Flags**

Flag	Meaning
	Miscellaneous Flags
-a	Lists all entries, including hidden files (those beginning with a period (.).
-d	Lists only the name, not the contents, of any directory encountered.
-e	Displays the mode, number of links, owner, group, size in bytes, time of last modification, and name of each file.
-f	Interprets each file parameter specified on the command line as a directory and lists the names found in each slot of the directory file(s).
-l	Shorthand way of getting a -Icglmop listing.
-L	Follows symbolic links.
-n	Suppresses interpretation of control characters in file names.
-s	Suffixes the name of certain files with a special character to indicate the file type. Subdirectories are suffixed with a slash (*filename/*), executables with an asterisk (*filename**), special files with a question mark (*filename?*), and symbolic links with an at-sign (*filename@*). The type indicators do *not* affect the sort order.
-v	Prefixes and suffixes the names of certain files with special characters to indicate the file type. Subdirectories are surrounded by brackets ([*filename*]), executables are surrounded by angle brackets (<*filename*>), special files are surrounded by asterisks (**filename**), and symbolic links are surrounded by at-signs (@*filename*@). These characters are applied before any sorting is performed; therefore, they affect the sort order. The result is that these four file types are grouped by type, and all other file types appear separately as they normally would.
-x	Displays every available field; shorthand for -labcfglimoprsu.
-number	Defines the maximum number of columns to be the value of *number*.
	Include and Exclude Flags
-I[hiplogcsmaunrfb]	Includes the indicated fields. If no fields are indicated, all fields are included.
-E[hiplogcsmaunrfb]	Excludes the indicated fields. If no field is indicated, all fields are excluded.
	Fields
h	Headers.
i	i-node number.
p	Protections.
l	Link count.
r	Node where entry resides.
o	Owner name or UID.
f	Raw UID of owner.
g	Group name or GID.
b	Raw GID of group.
c	Character count.
s	Physical disk size in 512-byte blocks.
m	Last modified time.

TABLE 5.21   `li` **Command Flags**   *(Continued)*

Flag	Meaning
	Fields *(Continued)*
a	Last access time.
u	Last updated (i-node modified) time.
n	Name.
	Restriction Flag
`-O[abcdfpx]`	Restricts the listing to certain file types
	Types
a	Archives.
b	Block devices.
c	Character devices.
d	Directories.
f	Regular files.
p	FIFO (pipe) files.
x	Executables (files with an execute permission bit set).
	Recursion Flag
`-R[`*number*`]apq`	Determines the maximum level of recursion while processing directory hierarchies. If no specific limit is set with *number,* recursion occurs until the lowest level is reached. Typically, the display is indented as each level is processed. Using any of the subflags (a, p, or q) suppresses this indentation. The a subflag indicates that the full path name of each file should be displayed. The p subflag indicates that the relative path name should be displayed. The q flag requests that the contents of archive files be listed.
	Sort Flag
`-S[acmnrsux]`	Determines the order in which the directory listing is displayed. The default order is, by name, `-Sn`. If another order is desired, subflags may be used.
	Subflags
a	Access time, latest to earliest
c	Character count, largest to smallest
m	Modified time, latest to earliest
n	Name, ascending
r	Reverses the order of the sort
s	Size in 512-byte blocks, smallest to largest
u	Updated time, latest to earliest
x	Performs no sort

looks peculiar, and `li -RSx` and `li -Sx *` become unintelligible if subdirectories are found.

The `di` command is equivalent to the `li` command with the `-I` flag and `almops` variables.

5.13.4   `du`—Display the number of blocks in a directory or file

The `du` command is used to produce a listing of the number of blocks used in a file or directory. If a specific file or directory is not used in the command invocation, the current directory is used by default.

For each entry found, or requested via flags, a separate line is produced on standard output listing the number of blocks and the entry name. When the command is used with a directory, all subdirectories of the named directory are searched recursively as well as the top-level directory.

The `-a` flag is used to generate individual file statistics when a directory listing is requested. Otherwise, the listing contains only a summary for the entire directory.

The `-k` flag is used to count the number of blocks in 1K increments, rather than the default of 512-byte blocks.

The `-r` flag causes the command to report the names of files or directories which cannot, for whatever reason, be read. When this flag is not used, inaccessible files or directories are bypassed.

Finally, the `-s` flag is used to force the command to report only summary information, regardless of the number of files or subdirectories found.

5.13.5   `dircmp`—Compare two directories and their contents

The `dircmp` command actually performs two functions. The first function is always performed; it compares the list of files in one directory with that of another. The second function of the command comes into play only when files with identical names are found in the two directories. When this occurs, the contents of the identically named files are compared with each other.

The output of the command is in several parts. The first section identifies the files found in the first directory, those found in the second directory, and those found in both directories. For those files found in both directories, the listing denotes whether the contents of the two files are identical.

Two flags are used with the `dircmp` command. The `-d` flag is used to produce a comparison listing, in `diff` format, of those files found in the two directories. The `-s` flag is used to prevent the command from listing the names of files found in both directories; in effect, producing a listing of the differing files in the directories.

For example, to compare the contents of one directory named current.chapter to another named current.chapter.backup, the user enters

```
dircmp current.chapter current.chapter.backup
```

The resulting output lists the common and differing files between the two directories. The common files would be flagged as to whether the contents were the same or not. If the user wanted to see what differences, if any, existed between the files, the -d flag is required

```
dircmp -d current.chapter current.chapter.backup
```

Alternatively, to display *only* the differing files, the -s flag is necessary

```
dircmp -s current.chapter current.chapter.backup
```

5.13.6 mkdir—Make a directory

The mkdir command is used to create a new directory. Users may create a new directory only if they have write permission to the parent of the new directory.

Two flags are commonly used with the mkdir command. The first flag, -m, allows the numeric permission bit string for the new directory to be set while creating the directory. The meaning of the permission bit string is documented under the chmod command. The second flag, -p, automatically creates any intermediate pathnames which do not exist. If -p is not specified, the parent directory of the new directory must already exist.

The usefulness of this flag can be demonstrated by the example of the subdirectories of /usr/local. When AIX is first installed, the directory /usr/local is not created, but many software products use it as a directory under which they place local information. Therefore, when the first product is installed which expects to use /usr/local as a base for creating further subdirectories, it fails. Instead of having to explicitly create this directory and its subsequent subdirectory with a command sequence such as

```
mkdir /usr/local
mkdir /usr/local/tag
```

the -p flag can be used instead

```
mkdir -p /usr/local/tag
```

In this case, if /usr/local does not already exist, it is automatically created. In the unlikely event /usr did not exist, it too would be created.

5.13.7 mvdir—Move a directory

Technically, the mvdir command is obsolete. Functionally, it has been replaced by the mv command; however, the command is still available and frequently used.

The syntax of the command is very simple

```
mvdir current_directory new_directory_location
```

If the new_directory_location does not exist, the current directory is simply renamed to the new_directory_location name. Otherwise, the current directory is moved and becomes a subdirectory of the new_directory_location.

The mvdir command has no flags.

5.13.8   rmdir—Delete a directory

The rmdir command is used to delete an empty directory from the file system structure. In addition to requiring that the directory be empty, the user must have write permission to the parent directory of the directory to be deleted. Therefore, to delete a directory with rmdir, the user must first delete all files in the directory, and then use the rmdir command

```
rm baddir/* baddir/.*27
rmdir baddir
```

The one flag of this command, -p, removes all of the directories in the path name specified. The restrictions mentioned must be observed with the -p flag: every directory in the path must be empty and the user must have write access to all directories in the path, including the parent directory of the highest level directory to be deleted. The command

```
rmdir -p /usr/local/tag/tag.1100
```

first attempts to delete /usr/local/tag/tag.1100. If successful, it then attempts to remove /usr/local/tag. Again, if successful /usr/local is the next to go, and finally, /usr if it were empty and the user had write permission to the directory.

The ramifications of this flag can be quite extensive. Use with the utmost care.

5.13.9   whereis—Locate system files in system directories

Whereis is a useful tool for locating where AIX system files are located. Oftentimes, there may be more than one version of a file with the same name in the search path and this command helps track down some of those situations. It is not a substitute for the find command (see Section 5.13.10) because it searches only specific system directories for the file(s).

The various flags of the whereis command are discussed in Table 5.22; however, at its simplest, the command searches for any instance of the file named. That is

```
whereis pg
```

searches for the pg command in the standard system directories which are: /lib, /etc, /usr/lib, /usr/bin, /usr/ucb, /usr/lpp, /usr/share/doc (and its subdirectories), /usr/share/man (and its subdirectories), and finally in the current working directory.

A more complex use is to find commands which do not have documentation. As in the following example, this is accomplished with the -u switch:

---

[27]Note that the user must explicitly delete any file names that begin with a dot (.). The "regular" rm * does not delete these files.

TABLE 5.22 whereis **Command Flags**

Flag	Meaning
	Type Flags (a maximum of two may be used)
-b	Searches for files with a binary section.
-m	Searches for files with a manual section.
-s	Searches for files with a source section.
-u	Searches for unusual files. Unusual files are those which do not contain an entry of the requested type.
	Search Flags (if used, the last entry must be followed by -f)
-B	like -b, but adds a search directory for the binary section.
-M	like -m, but adds a search directory for the manual section.
-S	like -s, but adds a search directory for the source section.
-f	terminates the list of -B, -M, and -S directory entries.

```
whereis -u -M /usr/share/man/ -S /usr/bin -f *
```

Here the user is requesting a list of all files in the current directory that are not documented in the /usr/share/man directory with matching source in the /usr/bin directory.

5.13.10 find—Locate a file

The find command allows the user to search directory structures to locate files. The format of the command is

```
find dir-path expression-list
```

where dir-path contains one or more path names upon which the search is performed and expression-list contains a set of commands upon which the search and output results are based. Note that in addition to the directories in the dir-path, all subdirectories in the dir-path are searched as well.

The power of the find command is exploited in the use of the expression list. Expression list terms are detailed in Table 5.23; however, some of the more commonly used terms are

-print	Print the results of the search (the default is to not print the results)
-name *filename*	Filename being the name of the desired file(s)
-user *user*	User being the name of the user owning the file(s)
-group *group*	Group being the name of the group owning the file(s)
-type *type*	Type being the specific file type to search for
-atime +-n	Access time being + or - *n* days ago
-mtime +-n	Modification time being + or - *n* days ago
-nouser	Indicates that the file owner must not be in the /etc/passwd file
-ls	Requests that full file information be printed for each file matching the search criteria
-exec *operation*	Performs the following operation on all files satisfying the search criteria

TABLE 5.23   Find Command Expression Terms

Note: in the following terms, n is a decimal integer that can be specified as $+n$ indicating more than n; $-n$ indicating less than n; or n indicating exactly n.

Term	Meaning
\(*expression*\)	True if the entire expression within the parenthesis is true.
-cpio *device*	Writes the current file to the specified device in cpio format.
-depth	Is always true. Forces the descent of the directory hierarchy so all entries in a directory are affected before the directory itself is affected.
-exec *command*	True if the specified command runs and completes with a zero (0) return code. The command must be terminated by a quoted or escaped semicolon (";" or \;). A pair of curly braces ({}) can be used as a command parameter to use the currently processed entry as the object of the command.
-fstype *type*	True if the file belongs to a file system of the specified type. Type may be either jfs (journaled file system) or nfs (network file system).
-group *group*	True if the file belongs to the specified group.
-nogroup	True if the file belongs to a group not defined in the /etc/group file.
-inum *n*	True if the file has an i-node matching the value of n.
-links *n*	True if the file has the specified number of links.
-ls	Is always true. Prints the current path name along with its associated statistics. The output of this term is exactly the same as the ls -gilds command, even though the formatting is done directly by the find command. The statistics include i-node number, size in kilobytes (1024 bytes), protection mode, number of hard links, user group, size in bytes, and modification time.
-name *name*	True if the file name matches *name*. Pattern-matching characters may be used. Wildcard characters may be used as long as they are enclosed within quotes.
-newer *file*	True if the file has been modified more recently than *file*.
-ok *command*	Is the same as the -exec term, except find prompts the user whether it should execute the command or not. The specified command must be terminated by a quoted or escaped semicolon (";" or \;). A pair of curly braces ({}) can be used as a command parameter to use the currently processed entry as the object of the command.
-perm *permission*	True if the permission code of the file matches the specified *permission*. If the higher order permission bits are to be tested (set userid or set group-id), the *permission* must be preceded by the minus (-) sign.
-print	Is always true. It causes the currently processed result of the specified search to be printed.
-prune	Is always true. This term stops the descent of the current path name if it is a directory. It is ignored when the -depth flag is specified.
-size *n*	True if the file is n blocks long (512 bytes per block). If a c is appended to the n, then the value is taken to be the number of bytes, not blocks.
-atime *n*	True if the file has been accessed in n days.
-ctime *n*	True if the file i-node has been changed in n days.
-mtime *n*	True if the file has been modified in n days.
-type *type*	True if the file type matches the specified *type*.

TABLE 5.23 Find **Command Expression Terms (*Continued*)**

	Valid types
b	Block special file.
c	Character special file.
d	Directory.
f	Plain file.
l	Symbolic link.
p	FIFO, named pipe.
S	Socket.
-user *user*	True if the file belongs to the specified user.
-nouser	True if the file belongs to a user not in the /etc/passwd file.
-xdev	Always true. This is used to prevent the find command from traversing a file system different from the one specified in the dir-path parameter.

Three boolean operators are used in conjunction with the expression terms. -a is used for logical AND, -o is used for logical OR, and ! (exclamation point) is used to negate an operator.

The best way to understand the find command is through examples. The command

```
find / -name horizon -print
```

searches the entire filesystem (since the search started at the root (/)) for a file named horizon and prints the result. The search is limited to the current directory by using the command

```
find . -name horizon -print
```

or to a specific part of the tree (the /u/horizon directory and its children) by the command

```
find /u/horizon -name horizon -print
```

or several directories (test and production) with

```
find /u/test_horizon /u/prod_horizon -name horizon -print
```

To search for all files on the system which are not owned by a current, valid user, the command is

```
find / -nouser -print
```

Any of the found files may or may not have a valid group owner. The list is expanded by explicitly including those files which do not have a valid group owner

```
find / \(-nouser -o -nogroup\) -print
```

This list contains files with invalid user owners, files with invalid group owners, or both. The backslashes before the parenthesis (which group the logical condition) are necessary to prevent the shell from interpreting the parentheses as special characters. To limit the search to only those files which have both an invalid user and group, the operator changes from OR (-o) to AND (-a)

```
find / \(-nouser -a -nogroup\) -print
```

Limiting the search to those files with an invalid user, but excluding those files owned by a valid group, involves negation of the nogroup operator

```
find / \(-nouser -a ! -nogroup\) -print
```

A common use of the find command is to perform a specific operation on a group of files. One of the most used command sequences is

```
find / \(-name core -o -name junk \) -print -exec rm {} \;
```

This command searches the whole filesystem, prints the result and removes all files (via the -exec rm) named *core* or *junk*. The curly braces are used in the rm to indicate the current file being acted upon by the expression.

Another example of a global operation is

```
find. -exec -name "*.exe" -exec chmod ug + x {}\; -print
```

This command finds all files in the current directory suffixed with a .exe extension and modifies them to ensure that the user and group owners have execute permission.

File Systems, Logical Volumes, and Physical Volumes

In Chapter 3, the AIX file systems were introduced and explained in relationship to the physical and logical volumes on the system. This chapter details the mechanics of defining and using file systems, logical volumes, physical volumes, and volume groups. In addition, backup and restore options are discussed.

6.1 Physical Volumes

The terms disk drive and physical volume are synonymous in an AIX context. As could be extrapolated from the discussion in Chapter 3, physical volumes are not directly used in most AIX system management tasks. In fact, the only significant task directly related to physical volumes is their definition.

There are two ways of defining physical volumes in AIX. The first method uses the system configuration command (cfgmgr) to automatically add the disk drive devices to the system. The second method uses explicit definitions to add the disks to the system. The second method is normally used only if automatic definition is not possible.

6.1.1 cfgmgr—Automatically add and configure devices

The cfgmgr command is used to add, configure, and make available devices on the system. By making use of the device configuration database, it can, in most cases, automatically add new devices to the system without any external intervention.

The cfgmgr always runs during the system boot process. This is a two-phase process. The first phase configures all of the devices necessary for base initialization of the machine. The second phase is called after phase one completes successfully to configure the rest of the devices attached to the system.

If devices are added to the system after the initial boot is complete, the cfgmgr can be invoked again to **configure the newly added devices**. When invoked after initial boot processing, the cfgmgr performs only phase two processing. Therefore, to add a newly attached disk drive to the system, the user need only enter the command

```
cfgmgr -v
```

to do so. The -v flag is not necessary; it instructs cfgmgr to produce extended status messages on standard output.

If cfgmgr is not able to add a device to the system, the mkdev command (Chapter 10) must be used. If the device is not available when the mkdev command is issued, the chdev command (Chapter 10) must be used to bring the device up when it becomes available.

6.1.2 lspv—Display information about a physical volume

lspv is used to display information about the physical volumes on the system. If a specific physical volume is not named, information about every disk device on the system is displayed.

When a specific drive is requested, the following information is displayed (see Fig. 6.1)

Physical volume. The name of the disk drive

Volume group. The volume group the disk drive belongs to

PVstate. The state of the physical volume which may be active, missing, removed, or varied off

VGstate. The state of the volume group which is either inactive, active/complete (all physical volumes are online), or active/partial (some physical volumes are offline)

Allocatable. The allocation permission of the physical volume

Logical volumes. The number of logical volumes on the physical volume

```
PHYSICAL VOLUME:      hdisk0              VOLUME GROUP:       rootvg
PV IDENTIFIER:        000007229401c115    VG IDENTIFIER       00002870ddb1c466
PV STATE:             active
STALE PARTITIONS:     0                   ALLOCATABLE:        yes
PP SIZE:              4 megabyte(s)       LOGICAL VOLUMES:    7
TOTAL PPs:            95 (380 megabytes)  VG DESCRIPTORS:     1
FREE PPs:             0 (0 megabytes)
USED PPs:             95 (380 megabytes)
FREE DISTRIBUTION:    00..00..00..00..00
USED DISTRIBUTION:    19..19..19..19..19
```

Figure 6.1 lspv command.

Stale PPs. The number of physical partitions on the physical volume that are not current

VG descriptors. The number of volume group descriptors on the physical volume

PP size. The size of the physical partitions on the volume

Total PPs. The total number of physical partitions on the volume

Free PPs. The number of free physical partitions on the volume

Used PPs. The number of used physical partitions on the volume

Free distribution. The number of free partitions available in each volume section

Used distribution. The number of used partitions in each volume section

Additional information about the physical volume can be displayed with three flags. The flags are mutually exclusive.

The -l flag displays the following information for each logical volume on the physical volume (Fig. 6.2)

LVname. The name of the logical volume

LPs. The number of logical partitions within the logical volume that are located on the physical volume

PPs. The number of physical partitions within the logical volume that are located on the physical volume

Distribution. The number of physical partitions of the logical volume that are allocated in each volume section

Mount point. The name of the file system mount point for the logical volume, if mounted

The -M flag displays the following fields for each logical volume on the physical volume (Fig. 6.3)

PVname. The name of the physical volume

PPnum. The physical partition number

```
hdisk0:
LV NAME                 LPs   PPs   DISTRIBUTION          MOUNT POINT
hd5                     2     2     02..00..00..00..00    /blv
hd7                     2     2     02..00..00..00..00    /mnt
hd2                     78    78    15..10..15..19..19    /usr
hd6                     8     8     00..08..00..00..00    N/A
hd4                     2     2     00..01..01..00..00    /
hd8                     1     1     00..00..01..00..00    N/A
hd3                     2     2     00..00..02..00..00    /tmp
```

Figure 6.2 lspv -l command.

```
hdisk0:1   hd5:1
hdisk0:2   hd5:2
hdisk0:3   hd7:1
hdisk0:4   hd7:2
hdisk0:5   hd2:54
hdisk0:6   hd2:55
hdisk0:7   hd2:56
hdisk0:8   hd2:57
hdisk0:9   hd2:58
hdisk0:10  hd2:59
hdisk0:11  hd2:60
hdisk0:12  hd2:61
hdisk0:13  hd2:62
       .
       .
       .
hdisk0:86  hd2:44
hdisk0:87  hd2:45
hdisk0:88  hd2:46
hdisk0:89  hd2:47
hdisk0:90  hd2:48
hdisk0:91  hd2:49
hdisk0:92  hd2:50
hdisk0:93  hd2:51
hdisk0:94  hd2:52
hdisk0:95  hd2:53
```

Figure 6.3 `lspv -M` command.

```
hdisk0:
```

PP RANGE	STATE	REGION	LV NAME	TYPE	MOUNT POINT
1-2	used	outer edge	hd5	boot	/blv
3-4	used	outer edge	hd7	sysdump	/mnt
5-19	used	outer edge	hd2	jfs	/usr
20-27	used	outer middle	hd6	paging	N/A
28-34	used	outer middle	hd2	jfs	/usr
35-35	used	outer middle	hd4	jfs	/
36-38	used	outer middle	hd2	jfs	/usr
39-39	used	center	hd8	jfslog	N/A
40-40	used	center	hd4	jfs	/
41-55	used	center	hd2	jfs	/usr
56-57	used	center	hd3	jfs	/tmp
58-76	used	inner middle	hd2	jfs	/usr
77-95	used	inner edge	hd2	jfs	/usr

Figure 6.4 `lspv -p` command.

LVname. The name of the logical volume with which this physical partition is associated

LPnum. The logical partition number

Copynum. The mirror number

PPstate. If the physical partition is not current, this field contains "stale."

The -p flag lists the following fields for each physical partition on the physical volume (Fig. 6.4)

Range. The range of consecutive physical partitions contained within a single region of the volume

State. The state of the physical partitions: free, used, or stale

Region. The volume region in which the physical partition is located

LVname. The name of the logical volume with which the physical partition is associated

Type. The type of logical volume with which the physical partition is associated

Mount point. The name of the file system mount point for the logical volume, if mounted

6.1.3 chpv—Change the characteristics of a physical volume

The state of a physical volume is changed with the chpv command. The two variables that may be changed are overall availability with the -v flag (with the operands a for available and r for removed), and additional allocation with the -a flag (and its operands y for yes and n for no).

To make disk01 available for use, the command

```
chpv -v a hdisk0
```

is appropriate. To inhibit further allocation of physical partitions, the command

```
chpv -a n hdisk0
```

is used.

Under normal circumstances, physical volumes are available for use and allocatable, that is, in a state as if the command

```
chpv -a y -v a diskname
```

had been issued.

6.1.4 migratepv—Move the used physical partitions of a physical volume to another physical volume

If it is necessary to move the allocated space of a physical volume to another disk drive, the migratepv command is used. The command moves the allocated physical partitions and their associated data from the source physical volume to one or more other physical volumes. The transfer may be limited to one or more specific physical volumes; if no names are supplied, all physical volumes within the volume group are considered available targets for transfer.

Transfer of physical partitions may take place only between physical volumes in the same volume group. The allocation of the new physical partitions is controlled by the allocation definitions at the logical volume level, regardless of whether only a logical volume is being moved or the entire physical volume.

The migratepv command, without the -l flag, moves all the physical partitions of the source physical volume to the destination physical volume(s). For instance, the command

```
migratepv disk01 disk03
```

moves all of the allocated physical partitions on disk01 to disk03. To move the physical partitions to any available space within the applicable volume group, the command is

```
migratepv disk01
```

If the user wants to move only the physical volumes associated with a particular logical volume, the -l flag is required

```
migratepv -l infosharedata disk01 disk03 disk04
```

This command moves all physical partitions on disk01 associated with the infosharedata logical volume to physical volumes disk03 and disk04.]

It is important to note that if the source volume contains the boot logical volume, the destination physical volume must contain two contiguous physical partitions and enough space to build the new boot image. The -l flag should be used when migrating the boot logical volume. After a successful migration of the boot logical volume, the bosboot command should be run to indicate the boot device has changed.

Finally, because of the way the migratepv command works, the command should not be used on any physical volume that contains any part of the primary dump logical volume. Although the migratepv command executes, all subsequent system dumps fail.

6.2   Volume Groups

As discussed in Chapter 3, a volume group is a collection of physical volumes which are treated as a single entity. The first step in using a volume group is creating it.

6.2.1   mkvg—Define a volume group

The mkvg command creates a new volume group using the physical volumes specified as operands of the command. A specific physical volume belongs to only one volume group. The syntax of the command is straightforward. For example, the command to create the PROD volume group in Fig. 6.5 is

```
mkvg -y PROD disk01 disk03 disk04
```

This command creates a volume group named PROD using the physical drives named disk01, disk03, and disk04. As no additional flags of the mkvg com-

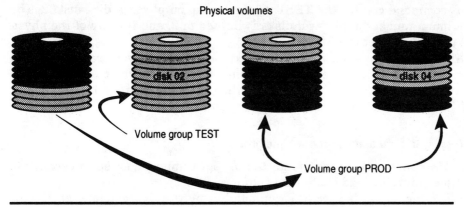

Physical volumes

Volume group TEST

Volume group PROD

Figure 6.5 Creating the PROD volume group from physical volumes disk01, disk03, and disk04. The test volume group contains a single physical volume—disk02.

TABLE 6.1 `mkvg` **Command Flags**

Flag	Meaning
-d *MaxPhyVol*	Used to define the maximum number of physical volumes which are in the volume group. The default is 32, the maximum is 255.
-f	Forces the volume group to be created on the physical volume (for instance, if the device is not in the available state). This option fails if used on a physical volume which is already part of a volume group.
-i	Reads the name of the new volume group from standard input.
-m *MaxPvSize*	Specifies the maximum number of physical partitions on the physical volume. If this flag is not specified, then 1016 physical partitions are assumed by default. See the -s flag for more information.
-n	Suppresses the automatic activation of the volume group at system boot time. The default value automatically activates the volume group.
-s *size*	Sets the size of physical partitions. The default value is 4 Mbytes; valid values are 1, 2, 4, 8, 16, 32, 64, 128, and 256 Mbytes. This, combined with the -m value, determines the maximum amount of storage which can be used, regardless of the amount of real physical storage available.
-v	Specifies the major number of the volume group. Normally, this is not specified and the system-supplied value is taken.
-y *vgname*	Allows the user to specify a name for the volume group. This name, which must be unique within the system, can range from 1 to 15 characters. If no name is given, the system generates one and displays it on standard output.

mand are used (see Table 6.1), the size of the physical partitions is set to the default of 4 Mbytes, the maximum number of physical partitions on the drive is set to the default maximum of 1016, and the default maximum number of volumes is taken (32).

To create the test volume group, explicit values are set as it is not very large

```
mkvg -y TEST -d 2 -s 1 disk02
```

This command creates the TEST volume group on physical disk disk02. The maximum number of physical disks is limited to 2, and the size of the physical partitions is set to 1 Mbyte.

Although volumes may be added (extendvg) or removed (reducevg) from the volume group after definition, the only values which can be changed after definition are related to whether and when the volume group is varied on or off. These are changed with the chvg command.

6.2.2 lsvg—Display information about a volume group

The lsvg command is very similar to the lspv command, except it pertains to volume groups instead of physical volumes.

When the -o flag is used, the command displays only the names of the currently active volume groups. No detailed information is displayed.

If no flags are specified, the following information is displayed (see Fig. 6.6)

Volume group. The name of the volume group.

Volume group state. The state of the volume group which is either inactive, active/complete (all physical volumes are online), or active/partial (some physical volumes are offline).

Permission. The access permission which is either read-only or read-write.

Max LVs. The maximum number of logical volumes allowed in the volume group.

LVs. The number of logical volumes in the volume group.

Open LVs. The number of open logical volumes in the volume group.

Total PVs. The number of physical volumes within the volume group.

Stale PVs. The number of stale physical volumes in the volume group.

Active PVs. The number of active physical volumes in the volume group.

VG identifier. The volume group identifier.

PP size. The size of the physical partitions.

Total PPs. The total number of physical partitions in the volume group.

Free PPs. The number of unallocated physical partitions in the volume group.

```
VOLUME GROUP:    rootvg       VG IDENTIFIER:   00002870ddb1c466
VG STATE:        active       PP SIZE:         4 megabyte(s)
VG PERMISSION:   read/write   TOTAL PPs:       600 (2400 megabytes
MAX LVs:         256          FREE PPs:        116 (464 megabytes)
LVs:             11           USED PPs:        484 (1936 megabytes
OPEN LVs:        10           QUORUM:          2
TOTAL PVs:       3            VG DESCRIPTORS:  3
STALE PVs:       0            STALE PPs        0
ACTIVE PVs:      3            AUTO ON:         yes
```

Figure 6.6 lsvg command.

Alloc PPs. The number of physical partitions in the volume group allocated to logical volumes.

Quorum. The number of physical volumes needed for a majority.

VGDS. The number of volume group descriptor areas in the volume group.

Auto-on. Automatic activation at system startup—yes or no.

If a specific volume group is named, then only information on that volume group is displayed; otherwise, this detailed information is displayed for all volume groups on the system.

Additional information on volume groups can be displayed using three additional flags. These flags are mutually exclusive.

The -l flag displays the following information for each logical volume within the group specified (Fig. 6.7)

LV. The name of the logical volume within the volume group

Type. The logical volume type

LPs. The number of logical partitions within the logical volume

PPs. The number of physical partitions used by the logical volume

PVs. The number of physical volumes used by the logical volume

Logical volume state. The state of the logical volume which can be either opened/stale (in use, but not in sync), opened/syncd (in use and in sync), or closed (not in use)

Mount point. The name of the file system mount point for the logical volume, if mounted

The -M flag displays the following fields for each physical volume used by a logical volume within the volume group (Fig. 6.8)

PVname. The name of the physical volume

PPnum. The physical partition number

```
rootvg:
LV NAME              TYPE      LPs    PPs   PVs  LV STATE        MOUNT POINT
hd6                  paging    8      8     1    open/syncd      N/A
hd61                 paging    8      8     1    open/syncd      N/A
hd5                  boot      2      2     1    closed/syncd    /blv
hd7                  sysdump   2      2     1    open/syncd      /mnt
hd8                  jfslog    1      1     1    open/syncd      N/A
hd4                  jfs       2      2     1    open/syncd      /
hd2                  jfs       257    257   3    open/syncd      /usr
hd9var               jfs       2      2     1    open/syncd      /var
hd3                  jfs       7      7     3    open/syncd      /tmp
hd1                  jfs       65     65    2    open/syncd      /home
lv00                 jfs       130    130   1    open/syncd      /infowork
```

Figure 6.7 lsvg -l command.

```
rootvg
hdisk0:1    hd5:1
hdisk0:2    hd5:2
hdisk0:3    hd7:1
hdisk0:4    hd7:2
hdisk0:5    hd2:54
      .
      .
      .
hdisk0:91  hd2:49
hdisk0:92  hd2:50
hdisk0:93  hd2:51
hdisk0:94  hd2:52
hdisk0:95  hd2:53
hdisk1:1    hd2:148
hdisk1:2    hd2:149
hdisk1:3    hd2:150
hdisk1:4    hd2:151
hdisk1:5    hd2:152
      .
      .
      .
hdisk1:247      lv00:100
hdisk1:248      lv00:101
hdisk1:249      lv00:102
hdisk1:250      lv00:103
hdisk2:1    hd1:40
hdisk2:2    hd1:41
hdisk2:3    hd1:42
hdisk2:4    hd1:43
hdisk2:5    hd1:44
      .
      .
      .
hdisk2:212      hd2:254
hdisk2:213      hd2:255
hdisk2:214      hd2:256
hdisk2:215      hd2:257
hdisk2:216-255
```

Figure 6.8 lsvg -M command.

LVname. The name of the logical volume with which this physical partition is associated

LPnum. The logical partition number

Copynum. The mirror number if the volume group is mirrored

PPstate. If the physical partition is not current this field contains "stale".

The -p flag lists the following fields for each physical volume within the volume group specified (Fig. 6.9)

Physical volume. The name of the physical volume

PV State. The state of the physical volume

Total PPs. The number of physical partitions on the physical volume

```
rootvg:
PV_NAME          PV STATE   TOTAL PPs   FREE PPs   FREE DISTRIBUTION
hdisk0           active     95          0          00..00..00..00..00
hdisk1           active     250         0          00..00..00..00..00
hdisk2           active     255         116        25..51..00..00..40
```

Figure 6.9 lsvg -p command.

Free PPs. The number of unallocated physical partitions on the volume

Distribution. The number of physical partitions within each section of the physical volume

6.2.2.1 lsvgfs—List the file systems in a volume group. The lsvgfs command displays, for a given volume group, the names of the file systems defined in the volume group. Each name is printed on a separate line. The syntax of the command is

```
lsvgfs volumegroup
```

6.2.3   chvg—Change the activation status of a volume group

The chvg command is used to change the activation status of a volume group. The command has two flags. The -a flag takes as its operand y if the volume group is to be made active when the system starts up. If the operand is n the volume group is changed so that it does not automatically become active when the system starts.

The -Q flag sets the action to occur when the volume group looses its quorum of physical volumes. The default action (-Q y) is for the volume group to be varied off-line when the quorum is lost. This can be modified, with -Q n, such that the volume group is not varied off until every physical volume becomes unavailable. Under normal circumstances, a volume group should be made available unless the quorum can be satisfied.

6.2.4   extendvg—Add physical volumes to a volume group

Extendvg is used to add physical volumes to a volume group. The command syntax is

```
extendvg [-f] volumegroupname newphysicalvolume
```

Therefore, the command

```
extendvg PROD disk05
```

adds physical disk disk05 to volume group PROD. The -f flag has the same use and meaning as it does with the mkvg command.

It is important to note that depending on what was specified when the volume group was initially created not all of the newly added volume may be usable. Recall that the maximum size of the volume group is determined by the maximum number of physical partitions and the size of the physical partitions. If the newly added disk has more storage than the maximum allowed for the volume group, the extra space is not be used by the volume group. And, since a physical volume may belong only to a single volume group, the extra space cannot be used anywhere else.

6.2.5 `reducevg`—Remove physical volumes from a volume group

The counterpart of `extendvg` is `reducevg`. This command removes physical volumes from a volume group. When all of the physical volumes of a volume group have been deleted, the volume group itself is automatically deleted from the system.

Before a physical volume can be removed from a volume group, all of the logical volumes (and their partitions) on the physical volume must be removed. This can be accomplished with the `rmlv` command (see Sec. 6.3.8) which is the preferred method as this ensures that the logical volume and its partitions are in a consistent state. Alternatively, the `reducevg` command allows for the use of a `-d` flag which can be used to delete the existing logical volumes (and associated partitions) on the physical volume. Normally, user confirmation of the deletion is requested; the `-f` flag suppresses such confirmation and deletion is automatic. The use of the `-d` flag does not ensure consistency of the logical volume before deletion. That is, if a logical volume resides on several physical volumes, using the `-d` flag jeopardizes the consistency of the logical volume as only part may have been deleted. As an example, the command

```
reducevg PROD disk05
```

removes the physical volume disk05 from volume group PROD only if there are no logical volumes currently on disk05. To force the removal of the disk from the volume group, the command

```
reducevg -d PROD disk05
```

is used. But, as stated before, this could leave any logical volumes which had data on disk05 in an unusable state.

6.2.6 `redefinevg`—Synchronize the logical and physical volumes in a volume group

Although the system normally keeps the device configuration database and the logical volume manager information synchronized, occasionally inconsistencies can occur. The `redefinevg` command is used to resolve such inconsistencies. It determines which physical volumes belong to the specified volume group and verifies (and reenters if necessary) this information in the device configuration database. Redefinevg determines which physical volumes belong to a given volume group by comparing the volume group ids.

The redefinevg command determines the volume group id to be compared based on one of two flags. One of the flags must be specified; there is no default. The -i flag explicitly indicates which volume group id number is to be used, whereas the -d flag extrapolates the volume group id from an existing device.

The following two commands:

```
redefinevg -d hdisk0 rootvg
```

and

```
redefinevg -i 1 rootvg
```

accomplish the same thing. In the first example, the volume group id is extrapolated from that of physical device hdisk0. In the second example, the volume group id is explicitly stated as being 1. Both commands search all of the physical drives on the system and ensure that all drives found with the specified volume group id are correctly defined in the device configuration database.

If the command is incorrect, that is, if hdisk0 did not belong to volume group rootvg, the command fails. Likewise, in the second command, if the rootvg volume group does not have a volume group id of 1, the command fails.

6.2.7   syncvg—Synchronize mirrored partitions

AIX supports, at the logical volume level, mirroring. Mirroring is the process where the operating system transparently makes duplicate (or triplicate) copies of data to facilitate recovery in the event of a system problem. The syncvg command is used to resynchronize the noncurrent physical partitions of a volume group used for mirroring.

Normally, when a volume group is brought online,[1] the physical partition copies within a volume group are synchronized automatically, so the syncvg command is not usually explicitly invoked. However, it is possible during the course of system operation for the copies to become unsynchronized often because of a device failure.

The level for which resynchronization takes place is denoted by the use of a flag: -l for a logical volume, -p for a physical volume, and -v for an entire volume group. The command

```
syncvg -v PROD
```

resynchronizes all of the copies on the PROD volume group whereas

```
syncvg -p disk01
```

---

[1]With the varyonvg command.

resynchronizes only the copies of the physical volume disk01, and

```
syncvg -l infosharedata
```

resynchronizes all copies in a logical volume named infosharedata, regardless of the physical volume on which the copies were actually located.

Two other flags are available. If used, either or both must precede the -l, -p, or -v flag. When the -f flag is used, the system searches for a good physical copy of each partition and propagates the partition to all other copies whether it is necessary or not. The normal action of the command is to update only those copies which are known to be unsynchronized. It is necessary to use this flag when the logical volume does not have mirror write consistency recovery.[2]

The -i flag instructs the syncvg command to read the names from standard input. This is useful when using the command as part of a shell script or to process a group of volume groups, physical volumes, or logical volumes in a batch.

6.2.8   varyonvg—Activate a volume group

The varyonvg command is used primarily during system startup to activate volume groups. It may also be used during the normal course of system operation to bring new volume groups on-line; for instance, after a successful importvg command has been processed. During activation, physical partitions used for mirroring[3] are automatically synchronized if they are not current.

Most of the flags for the varyonvg command are used to override consistency checking. This allows the user to bring the volume group on-line when errors occur, but be aware that doing so may, and probably will, corrupt data.

The command at its simplest is

```
varyonvg volumegroup
```

where volumegroup is the name of the applicable volume group. The -f flag forces the volume group to be made active even if the device configuration database does not match the actual physical volumes. The -n flag suppresses the synchronization of stale mirrored partitions. Again, neither of these flags should be used except in extraordinary circumstances.

The -p flag ensures that all physical volumes are present and available before the volume group is activated. Finally, the -s flag makes the volume group available in system management mode. This enables the system administrator to issue logical volume commands (to repair an error for example) but prevents the logical volumes from being used for regular input and output operations. So, to bring up the PROD volume group in system administrator mode, ensuring that all physical volumes are present, requires the command

```
varyonvg -p -s PROD
```

---

[2]See the mklv command for a discussion of this topic.
[3]See the syncvg command for further details.

6.2.9 `varyoffvg`—Deactivate a volume group

Before a volume group can be deactivated with the `varyoffvg` command, all of the logical volumes in the volume group must be closed; that is, all file systems must be unmounted.

Volume groups with paging space defined cannot be varied off while the paging space is active. To deactivate a paging space, it must be changed such that it is not automatically activated at system startup;[4] then the system must be rebooted.

The `varyoffvg` command has only one flag: `-s`. This flag puts the volume group in system management mode after the volume group has been deactivated. As with the `-s` flag of the `varyonvg` command, this mode enables the system administrator to issue logical volume commands to correct errors but prevents the logical volumes from being used for regular input and output operations.

6.2.10 `exportvg`—Export a volume group and its data from the system

The `exportvg` command exports the definition of a deactivated volume group from the system. After execution of the command, the volume group is inaccessible from the system. No data is deleted from the physical volumes; therefore once exported, the volume group can be imported to another system[5] or reimported to the same system. The primary use of the `exportvg` command is to transfer portable volumes from system to system.

The syntax of the command, which does not have any flags is

```
exportvg volumegroup
```

Note that the volume group must be deactivated with a `varyoffvg` command before it can be exported.

6.2.11 `importvg`—Import a volume group and its data into the system

A previously exported volume can be made known to the system with the `importvg` command. The syntax of the command is

```
importvg [-f] [-V vgnumber] [-y name] physicalvolume
```

where the physicalvolume specifies one of the physical volumes of the volume group; the remaining physical volumes are identified by the `importvg` command and automatically included in the import process. The `-y` command is used to give the volume group a user-defined name. If not specified, the system generates a name. The `-v` flag is used to specify an explicit volume group number; normally the system automatically assigns this number.

---

[4]For more information, see the chps command.
[5]With the `importvg` command.

Before a new volume group can be used, it must be varied on with the varyonvg command.

When a volume group with file systems already on it is imported into a system, the /etc/filesystems file is updated with the values for the new file systems and their associated mount points. If a logical volume of the same name already exists on the system, the name of the new logical volume is changed and a message is sent to standard error which indicates the new logical volume name. Before the newly imported file systems can be used, the fsck command must be run.

6.2.12 reorgvg—Reorganize the physical partition allocation of a volume group

This command reorders the placement of the physical partitions allocated to a volume group. Before a logical volume within the volume group can be reorganized, it must be set to a relocatable status with the chlv -r command.

The only flag used with the reorgvg command is -i. This allows the reorgvg command to read the names of physical volumes from standard input. When this is done, only the physical volume whose name has been read is selected for reorganization. Otherwise, the syntax of the command is

```
reorgvg [-i] volumegroup [logicalvolume...]
```

If logical volume names are specified, the reorganization is performed giving highest preference to the logical reorganization of the first-named logical volume, decreasing in importance until the last logical volume named. For example

```
reorgvg PROD infosharedata
```

reorganizes the infosharedata logical volume on volume group PROD. The command

```
echo "disk01 disk03" | reorgvg -i PROD infosharedata
```

reorganizes only the infosharedata logical volume data on physical volumes disk01 and disk03.

6.3 Logical Volumes

As discussed in Chapter 3, logical volumes are a level of abstraction not normally found in UNIX-based systems. On traditional UNIX systems, file systems are mounted directly on a physical volume. In addition to limiting the file system to a single disk drive, this arrangement limits the overall flexibility of the system. The logical volume concept allows a file system to span several physical volumes and provides for much greater flexibility in configuring the system. Furthermore, it provides for automatic mirroring of data which can aid in error recovery efforts.

The first step in creating a logical volume is to make the logical volume with the `mklv` command.[6]

6.3.1 `mklv`—Create a logical volume

The `mklv` command creates a new logical volume in the specified volume group. Each logical volume supports a single file system. The characteristics of the logical volume are defined via the flags of the `mklv` command (see Table 6.2). The syntax of the command is

```
mklv [flags] volumegroup partitions [physicalvolumes]
```

Volumegroup names the volume group which contains the new logical volume. Partitions specify the number of partitions to allocate initially. If specified, physicalvolumes limit the allocation of the partitions to the indicated physical devices.

Although a logical volume may span several physical volumes, the maximum size of a logical volume is 2 Gbytes. The default allocation policy is to try to use a minimum number of physical volumes per logical volume; however, if not specifically limited to particular physical volumes, the entire volume group is considered a valid target during the allocation of the partitions for the logical volume.

Logical volumes may be mirrored. With this function, the operating system automatically creates a second (or third) copy of all data in the logical volume. The duplicate copy can be used to recover from a failure on the primary logical volume. Additional copies of the logical volume are kept in synchronization with the original by the operating system without (under normal circumstances) user intervention. The only restriction for using mirrored logical volumes is that the primary dump device and paging spaces may not be on mirrored logical volumes.

The following are two examples of creating new logical volumes. The statement

```
mklv -Y infosharedata PROD 32
```

creates a new logical volume with the prefix infosharedata on volume group PROD. The initial allocation would be 32[7] partitions.

```
mklv -c 2 -e x -a c -y tempdata PROD 4 disk03 disk04
```

is a command that creates a mirrored logical volume (-c 2) named tempdata in volume group PROD on physical volumes disk03 and disk04. The physical partitions are allocated from the center of the physical volume (-a c) (Fig. 6.10) and the maximum number of physical volumes are used (-e x).

---

[6]This, of course, assumes that the physical volumes and target volume group have already been defined.

[7]The number of logical and physical partitions is equal since this logical volume is not mirrored.

TABLE 6.2 `mklv` **Flags**

Flag	Meaning
-a *position*	Indicates which section of the physical disk is to be used for partition allocation. The indicators are m (outer middle, the default), c (center), e (outer edge), ie (inner edge), and im (inner middle).
-b *badblocks*	Indicates if bad-blocks should be relocated. The default for *bad-blocks* is y for yes; n prevents bad-block relocation from occurring (not recommended).
-c *#copies*	The default value, 1, indicates that no mirroring is to occur for this logical volume. 2 creates one duplicate copy, 3 creates two duplicate copies.
-d *schedule*	Defines how mirrored writes should occur. The default value, p, indicates that all writes should occur in parallel. The value s causes the writes to the copies to be performed sequentially; this can significantly slow down application performance.
-e *range*	Determines the allocation policy. The default value, m, allocates partitions across the minimum number of physical volumes. The value x sets the allocation policy to use the maximum number of physical volumes; in many cases this option leads to better overall system performance.
-i	Indicates that the physical volume names should be read from standard input.
-L	Sets the logical volume label. The default is none. If the logical volume is a journaled file system (see below), then this field is used by the system to store the mount point of the file system.
-m *mapfile*	Is used when the user wants to allocate the logical volume on specific physical partitions. The *mapfile* parameter names the file which contains the physical partition definitions (ppd file). The ppd file consists of one or more lines in the format: *PVname:PPnum1[-PPnum2*. Each line defines a physical volume (PVname), the starting physical partition number (PPnum1), and optionally, an ending physical partition number (PPnum2).
-r *relocate*	Sets the reorganization relocation flag. A *relocate* value of y (the default) allows the logical volume to be relocated during a reorgvg command. A value of n prevents relocation during reorganization; this value should be used only if explicitly required by the application using the logical volume (a database management system, for example).
-s *strict*	Determines the allocation policy when mirrored copies are created. The default value of y indicates that copies of a physical partition may not reside on the same physical drive. A value of n allows all of the mirrored copies to reside on the same physical drive.
-t *type*	Sets the logical volume type. The default type is jfs which is a regular journaled file system. The other types are jfslog (for keeping the log of a jfs), copy (for mirror copies) and paging. Logical volumes of these last two types may not be mirrored.
-u *maximum*	Determines the maximum number of physical volumes to be used for new allocation. The default is the total number of physical volumes in the volume group.
-v *verify*	The default value of n indicates that writes to the physical volume should not be verified. A value of y causes every write operation to be verified before processing continues; this can cause severe performance degradation.

TABLE 6.2 `mklv` **Flags** *(Continued)*

Flag	Meaning
`-w consistency`	Is used to ensure that mirrored copies are kept synchronized by the operating system during normal I/O operations. If the value n is used, the operating system does not perform this checking; the user must then periodically run the `syncvg` command with the `-f` flag to synchronize the logical volume.
`-x partitions`	Sets the maximum number of logical partitions that can be allocated to the logical volume. If mirroring is not used, then there is a one-to-one correspondence between physical and logical partitions. If single-image mirroring is used, there is a two-to-one correspondence between physical and logical partitions; dual-image mirroring results in a three-to-one correspondence. The default value is 128.
`-y LVname`	Lets the user give the logical volume a name, as opposed to having the system generate a name. The name may be from one to fifteen characters long.
`-Y prefix`	Lets the user give the logical volume a prefix to which the system then appends a two-digit number. The prefix name may not be more than 13 characters long.

6.3.2 `lslv`—Display information about a logical volume

`lslv` is used for displaying the characteristics and status of logical volumes. With optional flags, the logical volume allocation map of the physical partitions may also be displayed. If a specific logical volume is not named, information of all logical volumes on the system is displayed. If no flags are specified, the following information is displayed (Fig. 6.11):

Logical volume. The name of the logical volume

Volume group. The name of the volume group to which the logical volume belongs

Logical volume identifier. The identifier of the logical volume

Permission. The access permission of the logical volume, either read/write or read-only

Volume group state. The current state of the owning volume group; either inactive, active/complete (all physical volumes are online), or active/partial (some physical volumes are offline)

Logical volume state. The state of the logical volume which can be either opened/stale (in use, but not in synchronization), opened/syncd (in use and in synchronization), or closed (not in use)

Type. The logical volume type

Write verify. The current write verify state; either yes or no

Mirror write consistency. The current mirror write consistency value, either yes or no

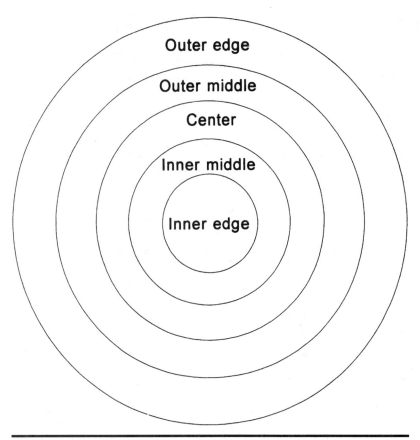

Figure 6.10 Physical volume sections. Partitions are allocated on the physical volume in sections. This allows the partitions of a logical volume to be clustered on the disk based on expected use patterns.

```
LOGICAL VOLUME:       lv00                 VOLUME GROUP:     rootvg
LV IDENTIFIER:        00002870ddb1c466.11  PERMISSION:       read/write
VG STATE:             active/complete      LV STATE:         opened/syncd
TYPE:                 jfs                  WRITE VERIFY:     off
MAX LPs:              130                  PP SIZE:          4 megabyte(s)
COPIES:               1                    SCHED POLICY:     parallel
LPs:                  130                  PPs:              130
STALE PPs:            0                    BB POLICY:        relocatable
INTER-POLICY:         minimum              RELOCATABLE:      yes
INTRA-POLICY:         middle               UPPER BOUND       3
MOUNT POINT:          /infowork            LABEL:            /infowork
MIRROR WRITE CONSISTENCY: on
EACH LP COPY ON A SEPARATE PV ?: yes
```

Figure 6.11 lslv command.

Max LPs. The maximum number of logical partitions allowed in the logical volume

PP size. The size of the physical partitions

Copies. The number of mirror copies of the logical volume

Schedule policy. Indicates whether the scheduling policy is sequential or parallel

LPs. The number of logical partitions in the logical volume

PPs. The number of physical partitions in the logical volume

Stale partitions. The number of physical partitions which are unsynchronized

Bad blocks. Indicates the current bad-block relocation policy

Interpolicy. Indicates the physical volume allocation policy: either minimum or maximum

Allocation. Indicates what the actual current allocation state is: either strict or nonstrict

Intrapolicy. Indicates from which region on the physical volume the physical partitions are allocated

In band. Indicates the number of physical partitions which are actually in the region named in the intrapolicy field

Upper bound. The maximum number of physical volumes which can be used in this logical volume

Relocatable. Indicates whether the partitions can be relocated during a reorganization

Mount point. The file system mount point of the logical volume, if mounted

Strict. Indicates what the allocation policy was defined as (see *allocation* for the actual state)

Label. Specifies the label field of the logical volume

PV distribution. Displays the distribution of the logical volume within the volume group including the physical volumes used, and the number of logical and physical partitions on each physical volume

Additional information can be displayed through the use of optional flags. The -1 flag displays the following information for each physical volume in the logical volume (Fig. 6.12):

PV. The name of the physical volume

Copies. The number of nonmirrored, single-copy, and double-copy logical partitions on the physical volume

```
lv00:/infowork
PV                    COPIES           IN BAND       DISTRIBUTION
hdisk1                130:000:000      20%           000:027:003:050:050
```

Figure 6.12 `lslv -l` command.

In band. The percentage of physical partitions that are allocated in their defined region

Distribution. The number of physical partitions allocated within the five regions of the physical volume: inside edge, inside middle, center, outside middle, outside edge

The -m flag displays the following fields for each logical partition (Fig. 6.13)

LPs. Logical partition number

PP1. The physical partition number allocated to the primary logical partition

PP2. The physical partition number allocated to the first copy of the logical partition

PP3. The physical partition number allocated to the second copy of the logical partition

PV1. The physical volume name where the primary physical partition of the logical partition is located

PV2. The physical volume name of the volume where the first copy of the logical partition is located

PV3. The physical volume name of the volume where the second copy of the logical partition is located

The -p flag takes a physical volume name as an argument. This is to request a display of the logical volume allocation map for a the specified

```
lv00:/infowork
LP     PP1  PV1              PP2   PV2                 PP3   PV3
0001   0148 hdisk1
0002   0149 hdisk1
0003   0150 hdisk1
0004   0151 hdisk1
0005   0152 hdisk1
        .
        .
        .
0126   0081 hdisk1
0127   0082 hdisk1
0128   0083 hdisk1
0129   0084 hdisk1
0130   0085 hdisk1
```

Figure 6.13 `lslv -m` command.

physical volume. If used in conjunction with a logical volume name, any partition allocated to the indicated logical volume is listed by logical partition number. Physical partitions outside of the logical volume are used, free, or stale. For example, the command

```
lslv -p disk03 infosharedata
```

displays information about physical volume disk03 with an allocation map indicating the number of each logical partition allocated to the logical volume infosharedata.

6.3.3 chlv—Change the characteristics of a logical volume

The chlv command changes the characteristics of a logical volume. This includes allocation policies, bad-block relocation, scheduling, logical volume name, read-write permission, reorganization policy, volume type, write-verify status, and write consistency status. To change the number of mirrored copies, the mklvcopy command (to increase) or rmlvcopy (to decrease) must be used. Table 6.3 describes the flags of the chlv command, which are, for the most part, identical to their mklv equivalents.

To change the name of a logical volume, the syntax of the command is

```
chlv -n NewLVname OldLVName
```

To change any other characteristic of the logical volume, use the syntax

```
chlv flag operand [flag operand ...] LVname
```

6.3.4 mklvcopy—Define or increase mirroring for a logical volume

The mklvcopy command is used to either add or increase the level of mirroring for an existing logical volume. Unless the -k flag is used, the new copy level does not go into effect until a syncvg or varyonvg for the volume group is processed. As indicated in Table 6.4, the flags of the mklvcopy command are similar to those of the mklv command. The syntax of the mklvcopy command is the same as that of the mklv command.

6.3.5 rmlvcopy—Decrease or remove mirroring from a logical volume

The logical counterpart to mklvcopy is rmlvcopy which decreases or entirely removes mirroring from a logical volume. The syntax of the command is

```
rmlvcopy LVname #ofcopies [PVname]
```

The user must supply the name of the logical volume from which the copies are to be removed. If a physical volume is used with the command, then

TABLE 6.3 `chlv` **Flags**

Flag	Meaning
-a *position*	Indicates which section of the physical disk is to be used for future partition allocation. The indicators are **m** (outer middle, the default), **c** (center), **e** (outer edge), **ie** (inner edge), and **im** (inner middle). This change affects only new partitions which are allocated.
-b *badblocks*	Indicates if bad-blocks should be relocated. The default for *bad-blocks* is **y** for yes; **n** prevents bad-block relocation from occurring (not recommended).
-d *schedule*	Defines how mirrored writes should occur. The default value, **p**, indicates that all writes should occur in parallel. The value **s** causes sequential writes to the copies; this can significantly slow down application performance.
-e *range*	Determines the allocation policy. The default value, **m**, allocates partitions across the minimum number of physical volumes. The value, **x**, sets the allocation policy to use the maximum number of physical volumes; in many cases this option leads to better overall system performance.
-L	Sets the logical volume label. The default is none. If the logical volume is a journaled file system (see -t *type*), then this field is used by the system to store the mount point.
-n *NewLVname*	This flag may not be used in conjunction with others. The *NewLVname* indicates to which name the current logical volume name should be changed. The maximum length is 15 characters.
-p *permission*	A value of **w** (the default) sets the access permission to read/write. A value of **r** sets the permission to read-only.
-r *relocate*	Sets the reorganization relocation flag. A *relocate* value of **y** (the default) allows the logical volume to be relocated during a reorgvg command. A value of **n** prevents relocation during reorganization; this value should be used only if explicitly required by the application using the logical volume (a database management system, for example).
-s *strict*	Determines the allocation policy when mirrored copies are created. The default value of **y** indicates that copies of a physical partition may not reside on the same physical drive. A value of **n** allows all of the mirrored copies to reside on the same physical drive.
-t *type*	Sets the logical volume type. The default type is `jfs` which is a regular journaled file system. The other types are `jfslog` (for keeping the log of a jfs), `copy` (for mirror copies) and `paging`. Logical volumes of these last two types may not be mirrored.
-u *maximum*	Determines the maximum number of physical volumes to be used for new allocation. The default is the total number of physical volumes in the volume group.
-v *verify*	The default value of **n** indicates that writes to the physical volume should not be verified. A value of **y** causes every write operation to be verified before processing continues; this can cause severe performance degradation.
-w *consistency*	Is used to ensure that mirrored copies are kept in synchronization by the operating system during normal I/O operations. If the value **n** is used, the operating system does not perform this checking; the user must then periodically run the syncvg command with the -f flag to synchronize the logical volume.

TABLE 6.3 `chlv` **Flags** (*Continued*)

Flag	Meaning
-x *partitions*	Sets the maximum number of logical partitions that can be allocated to the logical volume. If mirroring is not being used, then there is a one-to-one correspondence between physical and logical partitions. If single-image mirroring is used, there is a two-to-one correspondence between physical and logical partitions; dual-image mirroring results in a three-to-one correspondence. The default value is 128.

TABLE 6.4 `mklvcopy` **Flags**

Flag	Meaning
-a *position*	Indicates which section of the physical disk is to be used for partition allocation. The indicators are m (outer middle, the default), c (center), e (outer edge), ie (inner edge), and im (inner middle).
-e *range*	Determines the allocation policy. The default value, m, allocates partitions across the minimum number of physical volumes. The value x sets the allocation policy to use the maximum number of physical volumes; in many cases this option leads to better overall system performance.
-m *mapfile*	Is used when the user wants to allocate the logical volume on specific physical partitions. The *mapfile* parameter names the file which contains the physical partition definitions (ppd file). The ppd file consists of one or more lines in the format: *PVname:PPnum1[-PPnum2]*. Each line defines a physical volume (PVname), the starting physical partition number (PPnum1), and optionally, an ending physical partition number (PPnum2).
-s *strict*	Determines the allocation policy when mirrored copies are created. The default value of y indicates that copies of a physical partition may not reside on the same physical drive. A value of n allows all of the mirrored copies to reside on the same physical drive.
-u *maximum*	Determines the maximum number of physical volumes to be used for new allocation. The default is the total number of physical volumes in the volume group.

only the mirror partitions on that physical volume are removed. Under normal circumstances, this is not done; the entire mirror copy should be removed.

6.3.6   `cplv`—Copy a logical volume to another logical volume

A logical volume and its contents may be copied to another logical volume (either new or existing) with the `cplv` command. The command does not check the sizes of the source and destination volumes to ensure that the copy completes successfully; therefore, it is imperative for the user to ensure that the destination logical volume is at least as large as the source. Failure to do so results in a corrupted file system on the new volume because data (including the superblock) is missing.

The cplv command uses several flags; some are valid only when creating a new logical volume, the others are valid only when copying to an existing logical volume.

When creating a new logical volume, the syntax allows for the specification of a different volume group for the new logical volume (with the -v flag) and for naming the new volume absolutely (-y flag) or with a prefix (-Y). That is, the command

```
cplv -v PRODHOLD -Y infosharedata infosharedata
```

copies the data in the infosharedata logical volume to a new logical volume with a name beginning with the prefix infosharedata in the PRODHOLD volume group.

When copying from one logical volume to a preexisting logical volume, the -v, -Y, and -y flags are not used. Instead, the -e flag is used to identify the destination logical volume. Any data on the destination logical volume is destroyed when the copy is performed. To help ensure that a primary logical volume copy is not inadvertently destroyed, the existing destination logical volume must have a logical volume type of copy. The -f flag may be used in conjunction with the -e flag to suppress user confirmation of the copy operation.

6.3.7 extendlv—Increase the physical size of a logical volume

extendlv is very similar to the mklv command, except that only the -a, -e, -s, and -u flags are valid and it is used only to increase the number of logical partitions in a logical volume. By definition, a corresponding increase of physical partitions occurs.

The syntax of the extendlv command is the same as the mklv command

```
extendlv [flags] Logicalvolume partitions [physicalvolumes]
```

The use of the flags affects only the new partitions allocated as a result of the command; they do not permanently change the characteristics of the logical volume as a whole.

In the command, the user specifies the number of additional logical partitions to add to the logical volume. Based on the level of mirroring used, the system adds physical partitions, as appropriate, to the logical volume.

Expansion can be limited to a particular physical volume by specifying a physical volume name. If this is not done, all physical volumes within the volume group of the logical volume are considered valid targets for expansion.

The -m flag may be used with a map file which is in the same format as for the mklv command. The syntax of the command is then slightly different

```
extendlv -m mapfile logicalvolume partitions
```

6.3.8 rmlv—Remove a logical volume from a volume group

The rmlv command is used to remove a logical volume. If the logical volume contains a file system, it must be unmounted with umount and removed with rmfs before the logical volume can be removed.[8] As would be expected, this command destroys all the data in the affected logical volume.

This command has only two flags, which are both optional. The -f flag suppresses user confirmation of the operation. The -p flag allows the user to specify that only the partitions on the specified physical volume should be deleted. This option allows the user to remove a physical volume from a logical volume without removing the logical volume itself.

The syntax of the command, therefore, is

```
rmlv [-f] [-p physicalvolume] logicalvolume
```

6.3.9 synclvodm—Synchronize the device configuration database with the logical volume manager and the physical disk drives of the volume group

Normally, the device configuration database remains in synchronization with the logical volume manager which in turn remains in synchronization with the physical volumes of the volume group. If, for some reason, this consistency is upset, the synclvodm command can be used to resynchronize. The command can be used to resynchronize the entire volume group and all of its constituent logical volumes by using the syntax

```
synclvodm volumegroup
```

or for just a single logical volume with the syntax

```
synclvodm volumegroup logicalvolume
```

The only flag for this command is -v which produces a detailed status report at each step of the synchronization process.

6.4 File Systems

Once the physical and logical volume functions have been performed (Fig. 6.14), file systems can be created and used. To create a file system the crfs command is used.

---

[8]Actually, the rmlv command is not usually used to delete the logical volume if the logical volume had a file system mounted on it, the rmfs command removes the logical volume automatically as part of its processing.

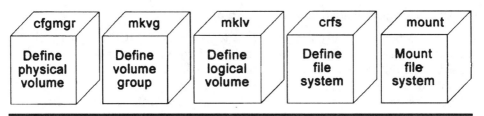

Figure 6.14 The steps necessary to create and use a file system.

6.4.1 `crfs`—Create a new file system

The command to create a file system in AIX is `crfs`.[9] The file system must be created within an existing volume group. If an existing logical volume is not specified in the command syntax, AIX automatically creates one in the volume group based on the characteristics specified for the file system.

The flags of the `crfs` command are detailed in Table 6.5 and consistent regardless of the file system type. The only flag that is file-system-type dependent is the `-a` flag. The attributes of a file system are defined in the /etc/vfs (Fig. 6.15) file.[10] For a given file system type, only those attributes defined for the file system type in the /etc/vfs file may be changed. As an example, in the journaled file system,[11] the `size` attribute is used to allocate physical space in 512-byte blocks. The `-a` flag, also used with the `LogName=` attribute, defines where the log for the journaled file system is kept.

Once the file system is created, an entry is made in /etc/filesystems defining the file system.

As an example, the following command creates a new file system named horizon in the PROD logical volume with an initial physical size of 32768 512-byte blocks[12]

```
crfs -v jfs -g PROD -m /horizon -a size=32768
```

6.4.2 `lsfs`—List information about a file system

The `lsfs` command is used to display the characteristics of the defined file systems. This information includes the mount point, automatic mounts, permissions, and size (Fig. 6.16). With the use of optional flags, specific file systems, file system types, or mount groups can be viewed.

---

[9]An additional command, mkfs, is provided for compatibility with other types of UNIX. It does not enable the range of functions that the crfs command does and is not considered any further in this text. For more information on mkfs and its associated commands, mkproto and proto, see the *AIX Version 3.2 Commands Reference* (vol. 3, 1993).

[10]The /etc/vfs file, or its individual entries, may be viewed with the `lsvfs` command. To list file types, enter the command `lsvfs  -a`; to view a specific type, such as paging, enter `lsvfs paging`.

[11]By far, the most common type of file system.

[12]Which works out to 16 Mbytes.

TABLE 6.5 `crfs` **Flags**

Flag	Meaning
-a *attribute=value*	The use of this flag is dependent on file system type. For each type of file system, different attributes may be set. These attributes are defined in the /etc/vfs file (Fig. 6.15).
-A	If specified with yes, the file system is automatically mounted at system startup. Use *no* to suppress automatic mounting.
-d *device*	Specifies the name of the device or logical volume (depending on file system type) upon which the file system is created. This presupposes that the logical volume already exists.
-g *VolumeGroup*	Specifies the name of the volume group upon which the file system should be created. If used without the -d flag, the system creates a new logical volume (with a default system name) for the file system.
-i *LogSize*	For journaled file systems without an existing log, this flag is used to specify the number of logical partitions to be used for the log file.
-m *mountpoint*	Is used to define the directory name where the file system is made available.
-n *nodename*	If the new file system is to be created on a remote machine using the *network file system* (nfs), this parameter identifies the name of the remote machine; otherwise this flag is not used.
-p	Is used to set the file permissions for the file system which is either ro for read only or rw for read/write.
-t	Is used to enable or disable accounting for the file system; with yes, accounting is enabled, with no, it is disabled.
-u *mountgroup*	Specifies the name of the mount group of the file system. For further information, see the mount command.
-v *fstype*	Indicates the file system type; the default is jfs (journaled file system)

The four flags of the `lsfs` command are

-c	Which indicates the output should be in colon delimited format
-i	Which indicates the output should be in list format
-u *Mountgroup*	Which requests a report on all file systems within the indicated mountgroup
-v *fstype*	Which requests a report on all file systems of the indicated file system type

For example, to display information on all file systems, the command used is

```
lsfs
```

To limit this to just file systems of the jfs type, the command is

```
lsfs -v jfs
```

To view a specific file system, such as /usr, the command is

```
lsfs /usr
```

```
# @(#)vfs  @(#)77   1.20  com/cfg/etc/vfs, bos, bos320 6/7/91 07:47:30
#
# COMPONENT_NAME: CFGETC
#
# FUNCTIONS:
#
# ORIGINS: 27
#
# (C) COPYRIGHT International Business Machines Corp. 1985, 1989
# All Rights Reserved
# Licensed Materials - Property of IBM
#
# US Government Users Restricted Rights - Use, duplication or
# disclosure restricted by GSA ADP Schedule Contract with IBM Corp.
#
# this file describes the known virtual file system implementations.
# format: (the name and vfs_number should match what is in <sys/vmount.h>)
#
# The standard helper directory is /etc/helpers
#
# name      vfs_number mount_helper filsys_helper
#
# Uncomment the following line to specify the local or remote default vfs.
%defaultvfs    jfs  nfs
#
cdrfs      5   none                          none
jfs        3   none                          /sbin/helpers/v3fshelper
nfs        2   /sbin/helpers/nfsmnthelp none remote
```

Figure 6.15 /etc/vfs file.

```
Name          Nodename   Mount Pt    VFS    Size      Options  Auto Accounting
/dev/hd4      --         /           jfs    16384     --       yes  no
/dev/hd1      --         /home       jfs    532480    --       yes  no
/dev/hd2      --         /usr        jfs    2105344   --       yes  no
/dev/hd9var   --         /var        jfs    16384     --       yes  no
/dev/hd3      --         /tmp        jfs    57344     --       yes  no
/dev/hd7      --         /mnt        jfs    --        --       no   no
/dev/hd5      --         /blv        jfs    --        --       no   no
/dev/lv00     --         /infowork   jfs    1064960   rw       yes  no
/dev/lv99     --         /horizon    jfs    --        rw       yes  no
```

Figure 6.16 `lsfs -v jfs` command.

6.4.3 `df`—Display information about space in a file system

Information about file system space usage is displayed with the `df` command. In its simplest form,[13] the `df` command displays information about all of the currently mounted file systems (Fig. 6.17). If a specific file system or file name is entered, then the display is limited to the requested information.

Two of the flags for `df`, `-i` (display i-node information) and `-l` (display free and used space), are the default values as seen in Fig. 6.17. If the `-M` flag is used, the mount point information is displayed in the second column instead of the last. Verbose mode, which displays all information about the specified file system, is requested with the `-v` flag. Finally, the `-s` flag is used to have

---

[13]That is, with no parameters and no flags.

```
Filesystem      Total KB     free %used    iused %iused Mounted on
/dev/hd4            8192     1744   78%      1046    51% /
/dev/hd9var         8192     4836   40%       140     6% /var
/dev/hd2         1052672   144204   86%     34044    12% /usr
/dev/hd3           28672    16236   43%       148     1% /tmp
/dev/hd1          266240    90692   65%      1849     2% /home
austen:/emma     1572864   895092   43%         -     -  /emma
/dev/lv00         532480   291860   45%        25     0% /infowork
poe:/infodata    1150976   531216   53%         -     -  /infodata
poe:/data3       1150976   139504   87%         -     -  /data3
```

Figure 6.17 df command.

the command actually search the free-block list for the number of unused blocks in the file system, instead of relying on the counts in the superblock of the file system.[14]

6.4.6 dumpfs—Dump file system information

Primarily used for debugging purposes, the dumpfs command prints the superblock, i-node map, and disk map for a file system. The syntax of the command is

    dumpfs filesystem

Fig. 6.18 shows an example of the *dumpfs* command on a file system.

6.4.5 ff—Display statistics of a file system

The ff command writes information about the requested file system to standard output. Exactly what information is written is determined by the flags (Table 6.6) used with the command. The output listing is in i-node order with tabs between each data item. The default information produced by the command, that is, when no flags are specified, is a line for each file consisting of the path name and the i-node number. In general, the find command is more useful than the ff command.

The ff command syntax is

    ff [flags] [-i i-nodelist] filesystem

6.4.6 chfs—Change the attributes of a file system

The chfs command is used to change the attributes of a preexisting file system. The flags of the chfs command are similar to those of the crfs command (Table 6.7). As with the crfs command, the -a flag is file-system-type dependent. For a given file system type, only those attributes defined in the /etc/vfs

---

[14]Using this option can result in a significantly longer command execution time.

```
/tmp:

magic              0x43218765      cpu type          0x0
file system type   0               file system size    57344
block size         4096            allocation group size   2048 (pgs)
file system name   /tmp            volume name         /tmp
log device         0xa0005 ·       log serial number   0x10f
file system state  1               read only         0
last update            Thu Jun 24 09:57:36 1993

Inode Map:
PAGE 0: size=8192, freecnt=8044, agsiz=2048, agcnt=4
totalags=4, lastalloc=113, clsize=8, clmask=0xff
ags: [0]: 1935,     [1]: 2013,      [2-3]: 2048,
tree:    [0]: 0xffff,   [1]: 0x0, [2-5]: 0xffff,
    [6-9]: 0x0,    [10-25]: 0xffff,   [26-41]: 0x0,
    [42]: 0xff,    [43-84]: 0xffff,
maps:    [0-2]: 0xffffffff,  [3]: 0xffff8000,    [4-63]: 0x0,
    [64]: 0xffffffff,   [65]: 0xe0000000,   [66-255]: 0x0,
    [256-447]: 0xffffffff,

Disk Block Map:
PAGE 0: size=7168, freecnt=4097, agsiz=2048, agcnt=4
totalags=4, lastalloc=1037, clsize=8, clmask=0xff
ags: [0]: 26,  [1]: 1127,      [2]: 1984,
    [3]: 960,
tree:    [0]: 0xffff,   [1]: 0x0, [2]: 0xe0,
    [3-4]: 0xffff,  [5]: 0xff00,    [6-11]: 0x0,
    [12]: 0xe000,   [13]: 0xe0e0,   [14]: 0xc0,
    [15]: 0xe0ff,   [16-23]: 0xffff,    [24-49]: 0x0,
    [50-51]: 0xc0e0,    [52-54]: 0x0,   [55]: 0xe000,
    [56]: 0xc0e0,   [57]: 0x8000,   [58-59]: 0x0,
    [60-61]: 0xc0, [62]: 0xe000,   [63]: 0x80,
    [64]: 0xff,    [65-73]: 0xffff,    [74]: 0xff,
    [75-84]: 0xffff,
maps:    [0-31]: 0xffffffff, [32]: 0xfffcfff7,    [33-34]: 0xffffffff,
    [35]: 0xbffcfff1,   [36]: 0xffffffff,   [37]: 0xfc7fffff,
    [38]: 0xfffcf8ff,   [39-51]: 0xffffffff,    [52]: 0xffff8ff,
    [53-56]: 0xffffffff,    [57]: 0xfffcffff,   [58]: 0xffffffff,
    [59]: 0xfff1ffff,   [60]: 0xffffffff,   [61]: 0xfefffff,
    [62-74]: 0xffffffff,    [75]: 0xff97ffff,   [76-77]: 0xffffffff,
    [78]: 0xffffffdc,   [79-80]: 0xffffffff,    [81]: 0xffffff8ff,
    [82-85]: 0xffffffff,    [86]: 0xffffffde,   [87-90]: 0xffffffff,
    [91]: 0xf0000000,  [92-95]: 0x0,  [96]: 0x7fffff,
    [97]: 0xffffffff,   [98]: 0xff800000,   [99-127]: 0x0,
    [128-129]: 0xffffffff,  [130-191]: 0x0,     [192-193]: 0xffffffff,
    [194-223]: 0x0,     [224-447]: 0xffffffff,
```

Figure 6.18 dumpfs /tmp.

file may be changed. Changes to the file system are reflected in the entry in the /etc/filesystems file.

A common use of this command is to expand the size of an existing file system. The following command increases the size of the horizon file system by 8192 512-byte blocks[15]

```
chfs -a size=+8192 /horizon
```

---

[15]That is, 4 Mbytes.

TABLE 6.6 ff **Flags**

Flag	Meaning
-a *number*	Displays the file if it has been accessed within the *number* of days. *number* may be an absolute value, or a relative value of more than (+*number*) or less than (-*number*)
-c *number*	Displays the file if its i-node number has been changed within the indicated *number* of days. *number* may be an absolute value, or a relative value of more than (+*number*) or less than (-*number*)
-i *i-nodenumber[,i-nodenumber...]*	Displays the files associated with the specified i-nodes
-I	Suppresses the display of the i-node number after the path name
-l	Generates a list of all of the path names for files which have more than one link
-m *number*	Displays the file if it has been modified within the *number* of days. *number* may be an absolute value, or a relative value of more than (+*number*) or less than (-*number*)
-n *file*	Displays the file if it has been modified more recently than the *file* specified
-o *options*	Limits the display relative to the indicated specific file system option
-p *prefix*	Adds the given prefix to the path name of each path name. The default is . (dot)
-s	Requests the file size in bytes be displayed for each file
-u	Requests that the owner name be displayed for each file displayed
-V *fstype*	Tells the ff command to assume the file system is of the *fstype*, rather than the actual file system type.

The mount point of the system is changed to /test_horizon with the command

```
chfs -m /test_horizon /horizon
```

6.4.7 mount—Make a file system available for use

In order for a file system to be used, it must be placed at a specific point in the system directory hierarchy.[16] This is performed with the mount command.

In its simplest form, the mount command displays basic information about all of the currently mounted file systems (Fig. 6.19). When used to mount a file system, the simplest form of the command takes a mount point as its parameter; this parameter is looked up in the /etc/filesystems file. The mount command then mounts the file system according to the instructions it found in /etc/filesystems.

---

[16]A detailed discussion of the mounting process can be found in Chapter 3.

TABLE 6.7 chfs **Flags**

Flag	Meaning
-a *attribute = value*	The use of this flag is dependent on file system type. For each type of file system, different attributes may be set. These attributes are defined in the /etc/vfs file (Fig. 6.15).
-A	If specified with *yes,* the file system is automatically mounted at system startup. Use *no* to suppress automatic mounting.
-m *newmountpoint*	Is used to define a new directory name where the file system is made available.
-p	Is used to set the file permissions for the file system which is either ro for read only or rw for read/write.
-t	Is used to enable or disable accounting for the file system; with yes, accounting is enabled, with no, it is disabled.
-u *mountgroup*	Specifies the name of the mount group of the file system. For further information, see the mount command.
r	Requests interactive file renaming during restore processing. If the file is not to be renamed, the current name must be entered, otherwise cpio skips the file.
s	Swaps bytes. This is useful when copying from a system which uses a different byte-ordering system. Data can be lost if there is an odd number of bytes in the file being processed.
S	Swaps half-words. Data can be lost if there is an odd number of half-words in the file being processed.
t	Displays the contents of the archive media.
u	Requests an unconditional copy. An older file of the same name replaces a newer file on the output media.
v	Requests a list of file names. When used with the t flag, the output looks similar to the output of the ls -l command.
6	Processes a file in UNIX Sixth Edition format.

```
 node     mounted          mounted over    vfs     date          options
-------  ---------------   --------------   ------  ------------   ----------------
         /dev/hd4          /                jfs     Mar 28 07:33   rw,log-/dev/hd8
         /dev/hd9var       /var             jfs     Mar 28 07:33   rw,log-/dev/hd8
         /dev/hd2          /usr             jfs     Mar 28 07:33   rw,log-/dev/hd8
         /dev/hd3          /tmp             jfs     Mar 28 07:34   rw,log-/dev/hd8
         /dev/hd1          /home            jfs     Mar 28 07:35   rw,log-/dev/hd8
austen   /emma             /emma            nfs     Mar 28 07:35   rw,soft,bg,intr
         /dev/lv00         /infowork        jfs     Mar 28 07:35   rw,log-/dev/hd8
poe      /infodata         /infodata        nfs     Mar 28 07:35   rw,hard,bg,intr
poe      /data3            /data3           nfs     Mar 28 07:35   rw,hard,bg,intr
```

Figure 6.19 mount command.

Three flags are used to perform more generic mounting tasks. The -a flag is used to mount all of the file systems in /etc/filesystems with the true mount attribute. The all flag is a synonym for -a. The -t *type* flag is used to mount those file systems in /etc/filesystems of the indicated type which are not already mounted.

Several flags are used only under specific circumstances. A mount can be forced by using the -f flag; typically, this is done only during the system initialization process to load the root file system. A file system can be set to read-only status, regardless of the setting in /etc/filesystems, by mounting it with the -r flag. Removable file systems can be created by using the -p flag. They behave in the same way other file systems do as long as files in the file system are opened. As soon as all of the files are closed, including directory references, AIX flushes the buffer of the file system and forgets its structure. The file system must be remounted before it can be used again.

File-system-type-specific options can be communicated to the mount command with the -o flag. Multiple options of the -o flag should be separated only by a comma, not a space. The most common options for a jfs file system are

bg	If the first attempt at mounting is unsuccessful, continue trying in the background
retry=n	Specifies the number of mounting retry attempts (the default is 10000)
rsize=n	Sets the read buffer size to n bytes (the default is 8K)
wsize=n	Sets the write buffer size to n bytes (the default is 8K)
rw	Mounts the file system as read-write
ro	Mounts the file system as read only
nosuid	Prohibits set user id or set group id program execution on the file system
nodev	Prohibits direct *open* of a device from the file system

Users can mount directories only if they belong to the system group and have write access to the mount point where the file system is to be mounted. The real user id is used to determine whether the user has appropriate access; that is, a su command has no influence on the mount command. The root user, however, can issue any mount command.

To mount the previously defined horizon file system, the user enters the following command

```
mount -o rsize=32768 /horizon
```

The -o flag is included to increase the size of the read buffer for the file system to 32K.

6.4.8   umount/ unmount—Remove a file system from use

Both the umount and unmount commands perform the same function: unmount a previously mounted file system, directory, or file. Members of the system user group and the root user can issue any unmount request; other users must have write permission to the directory to be unmounted.

The unmount command takes as its operand either the name of a file system (or file), a specific type of file system (with the -t *type* flag), or all which unmounts all file systems except those with a mount type (in /etc/filesystems) of automatic.

Usually, a file system must be unmounted before maintenance can be performed. Furthermore, all file systems within a logical volume must be unmounted before the logical volume can be deleted.

6.4.9 `rmfs`—Remove a file system and its associated logical volume

The `rmfs` command is somewhat unusual in that it does more than its name implies. In addition to removing a file system, it also removes the logical volume upon which the file system resided.

The syntax of the command is simple

```
rmfs filesystem
```

There are no optional flags.

6.4.10 `sync`/ `update`—Commit file system buffers to disk

When the `sync` command is issued, AIX schedules a flush of the file system buffers in system storage. It does not necessarily guarantee that the buffers are written; therefore, it is usually used twice. The second invocation waits for the flush scheduled by the first invocation to complete. Typical usage is therefore

```
sync;sync
```

During the normal course of system operation, explicitly performing this function is not necessary; AIX handles it automatically. However, after performing some system maintenance functions, and during system shutdown, this function may be invoked to ensure that the file systems are committed.

The `update` command performs the same synchronization function as the `sync` command, except the `update` command does not terminate; it continues to issue the sync command every 30 seconds until the command is killed.

6.4.11 `fsck` and `dfsck`—Check file system consistency

`fsck` is automatically invoked during system startup to ensure that the mounted file systems are consistent and correct. It can be used at other times to perform the same function, and in some cases, perform minor corrections to a file system which has been corrupted.[17] When errors are found, `fsck` displays appropriate information about inconsistencies and prompts the user for permission to correct the error. If the user has write permission for the affected file, `fsck` attempts to correct the error.

In general, the `fsck` command attempts to avoid data loss; however, there are occasions when `fsck` recommends that the entire file be removed. The user may reply "no" in these cases, and attempt manual correction with the `fsdb` command.

When the `fsck` command is invoked without a specific file system parame-

---

[17] Major corrective action to a file system is performed with fsdb. For further information, consult the *AIX Version 3.2 Commands Reference* (vol. 2, 1993) and the *AIX Version 3.2 System User's Guide* (1993).

ter, it checks in the /etc/filesystems file for the default. These file systems are identified by the check=true parameter.

The fsck command checks for several types of errors that may occur in a file system

Incorrectly allocated blocks

Inconsistencies in the link count of a file

Size errors

Inconsistent disk maps

Inconsistent i-node numbers

Unreachable directories

Unreferenced files

In addition to messages issued on standard output and standard error, the exit value indicates the relative success of the command

0   All checked file systems are okay.

2   fsck terminated before all checks and repairs could be completed.

4   The file system was changed; the system must be rebooted as soon as possible.

8   The file system cannot be repaired.

The fsck command, when used with the -p flag, attempts to process file systems concurrently. This can speed up processing when more than one file system must be checked. In addition to this option, the dfsck command can be used to execute two distinct fsck commands at the same time.[18]

The -f flag requests fast file system checking. Fast checking first determines if the file system was cleanly unmounted,[19] if so, the file system is assumed to be correct and no further consistency checking is performed. In the vast majority of cases, the -f flag is used to eliminate unnecessary effort and speed up the checking process.

The -d flag and -i flag are similar in function. While the -d searches for references to a specific disk block, and the -i searches for references to a specific i-node, both, upon finding their indicated target, display the full path name associated with it.

In addition to allowing concurrent processing, the -p[20] flag automatically corrects minor problems found in the file system. This is not as far-reaching as the -y flag which indicates that a yes response should be assumed for all questions asked by fsck. The -y flag should only be used with severely damaged file systems. Its counterpart is the -n flag which assumes a no answer to all questions; therefore, no corrections (even minor) are made.

---

[18]dfsck cannot be used against the root file system.

[19]That is, with no errors.

[20]This flag should always be specified when running fsck during system start-up.

As with many of the other file system commands, the -v flag can be used to override the file system type. If this flag is not used, the file system type from the file system's entry in the /etc/filesystems file is used.

The final flag of fsck is -t *filename*. This flag is primarily used when checking large file systems. Large file systems may cause fsck tables to exceed the storage area of the fsck address space; the -t *filename* is used in this case as a scratchpad area. The scratch file must be located in a file system other than the one being checked.

The syntax of the fsck command is

```
fsck [flags] FileSystem1[- FileSysstem2]
```

If more than one file system name is given as an argument to the command, a dash must be used to separate the names of the file systems.

The syntax of the dfsck command is

```
dfsck [flags] FileSystem1—[flags] FileSystem2]
```

Again, the dash must be used to separate the names of the two file systems.

For example, the command

```
fsck
```

with no flags or parameters checks all of the default file systems—those with a check=true statement in the /etc/filesystems file. The command

```
fsck -p
```

checks the same file systems, but also performs minor corrections automatically.

The dfsck command is used in the following example to check two file systems at the same time. Note that scratch pad files are also specified; this is always a good idea when using the dfsck command

```
dfsck -p -t/tmp/home.fsck /home - -p -t/tmp/usr.fsck /usr
```

6.4.12 skulker—Clean up file systems

Not a command, but a shell script, skulker removes old and unwanted files from file systems. In traditional UNIX-based systems, when the system is booted, the /tmp file system is cleaned. AIX does not work in this manner. During AIX system start-up, no files are automatically deleted. Files are deleted only by specific action on a user's part or as part of the daily processing of the root user, if the skulker facility has been enabled.

As distributed, the skulker shell script purges files in the /tmp directory, files older than a specified age,[21] a.out files, core files, and ed.hup files. The

---

[21] The exact age depends on the type of file.

script (Fig. 6.20) may be modified to fit local needs. All changes to skulker should be tested very carefully; because it is run by root and deletes files, unexpected and extremely undesirable results are possible when coding errors are made. All additional command lines in the skulker script should first be tested manually with the xargs -p command.

To run skulker automatically, uncomment the entry for /etc/skulker in the /var/spool/cron/crontabs/root file.

6.5   Backup and Restore

In AIX there are several commands which can be used to back up and restore files and filesystems; each performs the function from a different perspective. The dd command is primarily a mechanism for transferring information from one device to another. The cpio, tar and pax commands create and process file archives. backup and restore provide for basic file based processing. Finally the mkboot and mksysb commands are used for creating a bootable media.

Before deciding upon a backup format and policy, consider the following items

What type of physical media is available?

What method is most cost and time effective, based on the physical media?

What type of external labelling procedures will be used?

Does the policy allow for recovery from catastrophic errors?

Are backups periodically checked to ensure they are usable?

What type of backup cycle (generation) is desirable, (daily, weekly, monthly, yearly)?

In addition, the following items are always good rules of thumb when performing backups

Always check file systems before backing them up with fsck,

Ensure file systems are not in use during backup; this eliminates possible inconsistencies in the backup,

Always back up the system before making modifications to it.

6.5.1   dd—Convert a file from one format to another

Given no parameters, the dd command reads standard input and copies it to standard output. Names for the input and output files can be specified with the if= and of= flags, respectively.

Generally, a conversion takes place between the input and output. This conversion most often involves the block size and/or format or character-set implementation (ASCII to EBCDIC, or vice versa).

```
#!/bin/bsh
# @(#)28  1.16  com/cmd/cntl/skulker.sh, bos, bos320 5/13/91 23:32:43
#
# COMPONENT_NAME: (CMDCNTL) system control commands
#
# FUNCTIONS:
#
# ORIGINS: 27
#
# (C) COPYRIGHT International Business Machines Corp. 1989
# All Rights Reserved
# Licensed Materials - Property of IBM
#
# US Government Users Restricted Rights - Use, duplication or
# disclosure restricted by GSA ADP Schedule Contract with IBM Corp.
#

date=`date`
uname=`uname -nm`
if msg=`dspmsg skulker.cat 1 '\n%1$s started at %2$s on %3$s\n' $0 "$date" "$uname"`
then :
else msg='echo "\n$0 started at $date on $uname\n"'; fi
eval echo $msg

# Uncomment the NATIVE entry that is appropriate for your system.
# For Distributed environments, '/native' is a path to the local filesystems;
# '/' is sufficient for standalone systems.
# NATIVE=/native/
NATIVE=/

if [ -d ${NATIVE}var/spool/structmail ]
then
   find ${NATIVE}var/spool/structmail -mtime +2 -atime +2 -type f -exec /bin/rm -f {} \;
fi

# get rid of old primary.outputs that got lost
if [ -d ${NATIVE}var/spool/qdaemon ]
then
   find ${NATIVE}var/spool/qdaemon -mtime +4 -type f -exec /bin/rm -f {} \;
fi

# get rid of old qdir files
if [ -d ${NATIVE}usr/lib/lpd/qdir ]
then
   find ${NATIVE}usr/lib/lpd/qdir -mtime +4 -type f -exec /bin/rm -f {} \;
fi

# get rid of files that get left in the mail queues
if [ -d ${NATIVE}var/spool/qftp ]
then
   find ${NATIVE}var/spool/qftp \( -name 'tmp*' -o -name '[0-9]*' \) -mtime +2 -exec
/bin/rm -f {} \;
fi

# Check if regular files are in ${NATIVE}tmp.
# If there are no files in tmp, do not invoke xargs.
# If xargs received no input (except for EOF),
# it would execute its command once.
# In that case, $0 would expand to "sh"
# and find would produce an error message.

expr 0 = `li -naOf ${NATIVE}tmp | \
         grep -v "\`echo '[ \t]'\`"  | wc -l` > /dev/null
case $? in
 1 )
# get rid of all ordinary files in the ${NATIVE}tmp directory older than 24
```

Figure 6.20   skulker shell script.

Table 6.8 outlines the various flags of the dd command. Some examples will clarify command usage. To convert a file named trans.data to an EBCDIC tape (on device rmt0) with 4k blocks, the command is

```
dd if=trans.data of=/dev/rmt0 cbs=4096 conv=ebcdic
```

```
# hours and not accessed or modified in the past 24 hours.
#
#    first line   finds names of all ordinary files in ${NATIVE}tmp
#                 lists them one per line, with control chars not expanded
#    second line  filters out dangerous characters that might terminate
#                 xarg's argument (space and tab).
#    last lines   runs find on groups to find non-current files and rm's them
#                 the "-type f" redundant, unless the egrep list is flakey.
#
        li -naOf ${NATIVE}tmp | \
        grep -v "`echo '[ \t]'`" | \
        xargs -e sh -c \
         '`find ${@:-"$0"} -atime +1 -mtime +1 -type f -exec /bin/rm -f {} \; `'
                 ;;
esac

# clean out ${NATIVE}var/tmp
if [ -d ${NATIVE}var/tmp ]
then
   find ${NATIVE}var/tmp -atime +1 -mtime +1 -type f -exec /bin/rm {} \;
fi

# get rid of news items older than 45 days
if [ -d ${NATIVE}var/news ]
then
   find ${NATIVE}var/news -mtime +45 -type f -exec /bin/rm {} \;
fi

# get rid of *.bak, .*.bak, a.out, core, proof, galley, ...*, ed.hup files
# that are more than a day old.
# proof and galley files must not be owner-writable
#
# Use the -xdev flag to prevent find from traversing a filesystem
# on a different device, this will prevent it from searching nfs
# mounted filesystems.  You may want to add filesystems here
# that you want to be cleaned up.
find $NATIVE ${NATIVE}usr ${NATIVE}var ${NATIVE}tmp ${NATIVE}home \
   \( \( \( -name "*.bak" -o -name core     -o -name a.out -o   \
        -name "...*"  -o -name ".*.bak" -o -name ed.hup \)     \
     -atime +1 -mtime +1 -type f                              \
   \)                                                         \
   -o                                                         \
   \( \( -name proof -o -name galley \)                       \
     -atime +1 -mtime +1 -type f ! -perm -0200                \
   \)                                                         \
   \) -xdev -exec /bin/rm  -f {} \;

# get rid of anything in a .putdir directory more than a day old.
for i in `find $NATIVE ${NATIVE}usr ${NATIVE}var ${NATIVE}tmp \
     ${NATIVE}home -xdev -type d -name ".putdir" -print`
do
     find $i -mtime +1 -type f -exec /bin/rm {} \;
done

date=`date`
if msg=`dspmsg skulker.cat 2 '\n%1$s finished at %2$s on %3$s\n' $0 "$date" "$uname"`
then :
else msg='echo "\n$0 finished at $date on $uname\n"'; fi
eval echo $msg
```

Figure 6.20 *(Continued)*

To copy one tape to another and reblock the output to 32K, the command is

```
dd if=/dev/rmt0 of=/dev/rmt1 obs=32k
```

The dd command can also be used as a filter for other commands, for example

```
cat mixed.case.text | dd conv=ucase
```

displays the file mixed.case.text with all alphabetic characters translated to upper case.

TABLE 6.8   dd **Command Flags**

Flag	Meaning
Primary Options	
cbs = *blocksize*	Is used when either conv = block, conv = unblock, conv = ascii, conv = ebcdic, or conv = ibm is specified. This indicates the conversion block size when fixed-length to variable-length or variable-length to fixed-length block conversions are performed.
count = *inputblocks*	Limits the copy function to the indicated number of blocks from the input file.
files = *inputfiles*	Limits the copy function to the *inputfiles* number of files from the input media. Meaningful only when used with a tape input device.
fskip = *FilestoSkip*	Skips the *FilestoSkip* number of files on the input device before starting the copy operation. Meaningful only when used with a tape input device.
if = *inputfile*	Specifies the name of the input file or device. If not specified, standard input is assumed.
of = *outputfile*	Specifies the name of the output file or device. If not specified, standard output is assumed.
seek = *record*	Skips to record number *record* before starting the copy operation.
skip = *skippedblocks*	Skips the *skippedblocks* number of blocks before beginning the copy operation.
Blocking Factors	
ibs = *blocksize*	Specifies the input block size in bytes. The default is 512 bytes or one physical block. The value of the ibs flag must be a multiple of the physical block size of the input device.
obs = *blocksize*	Specifies the output block size in bytes. The default is 512 bytes or one physical block. The value of the obs flag must be a multiple of the physical block size of the output device.
bs = *blocksize*	Specifies both the input and output block size in bytes, superseding any ibs or obs options. The default is 512 bytes or one physical block. The value of the bs flag must be a multiple of the physical block size of both the input and output devices.
Conversions—All Options Are Prefixed with Conv =	
ascii	Converts EBCDIC input to ASCII output.
ebcdic	Converts ASCII input to EBCDIC output.
ibm	Converts ASCII input to IBM EBCDIC output.
block	Converts variable-length records to fixed-length. The output block size is determined by the cbs flag.
unblock	Converts fixed-length records to variable-length. The output block size is determined by the cbs flag.
lcase	Converts all alphabetic characters to lowercase.
ucase	Converts all alphabetic characters to uppercase.
iblock	Minimizes data loss from read errors on disk drives. When an error does occur, the dd command tries to read a smaller unit of data; if the sector size can be determined, this results in each sector of the block being read individually.
oblock	Performs the same function as iblock except the function is performed on the output file.

TABLE 6.8 dd **Command Flags** (*Continued*)

Flag	Meaning
sync	Pads every short input block to the ibs value.
noerror	Does not stop processing when errors occur.
swab	Swaps every pair of bytes.
notrunc	Suppresses output file truncation. All blocks are written to the output file.

For backup and restore from tape devices, the backup, restore, tar, and cpio commands are preferred over the dd command. These other commands are especially designed for use on tape devices.

6.5.2 cpio—Copy files to and from archive storage and directories

For the most part, the cpio command can be treated as three separate commands. The cpio -o command reads the names of files from standard input and copies these files to standard output. The cpio -i command reads an archive file, created by the cpio -o command, from standard input and extracts files from it. The cpio -p command reads file names from standard input and copies these files into a directory.

6.5.2.1 cpio -o—Create an archive. This option of the command creates an output archive file based upon the file names read from standard input. The maximum length of a file name processed in this way may not be more than 128 characters. This option of the command supports the a, c, v, B, and C flags (Table 6.9).

TABLE 6.9 cpio **Flags**

Flag	Meaning
a	Sets the access time of the new, copied files to the current time.
b	Swaps both bytes and half-words (see s and S). Data can be lost if there is an odd number of bytes or half-words in the file being processed.
B	Performs block I/O using 5120 byte blocks. If using a tape device, then 5120 bytes must be a valid multiple of the physical block size of the device. This parameter, if specified during creation, must also be specified during restoration.
c	Reads and writes header information in ASCII-character format (instead of binary). If used to create the archive, this flag must be used to restore it.
Cvalue	Similar to B except the user specifies the block size as a multiplication factor of 512. For example, -C4 indicates a block size of 2048 (512 * 4 = 2048). The size of the block must be a valid multiple of the physical block size of the device. This parameter, if specified during creation, must also be specified during restoration.
d	Creates directories as necessary.
f	Copies all files except those matching the specified pattern.
l	Links files, rather than copying them, if possible.
m	Makes the modification time of the new copied files the same as the modification time of the original file.

Because cpio reads the names of the files to process from standard input, it is extremely common to see it used as the second operand of a piped command. For example

```
ls -R -1 /usr | cpio -ov >/dev/rmt0
```

results in an output tape on device rmt0 which contains the entire /usr directory structure. Alternatively, the current directory and all of its subdirectories are copied to a backup directory with the command

```
find . -print | cpio -ov >/backup/$PWD.backup 22
```

6.5.2.2 cpio -i—Extract an archive. Using a previously created archive tape, the cpio -i command extracts select files from standard input and copies them into the current directory. If a directory tree structure was saved when the archive was created, the cpio -i command can recreate that tree if the d flag is used.

The cpio -i command determines which files to select for restore based upon a pattern (or patterns) specified on the command line. The pattern follows the standard file name notation of the Korn shell (ksh), with the wildcard characters

* (asterisk)	Indicating one or more characters
? (question mark)	Indicating exactly one character
[x ... y]	Indicating once character in a range

The default pattern is a single asterisk (*), that is, all files.

To restore all of the files with a suffix of .txt from the first example in Sec. 6.5.2.1 to the current directory, the command is

```
cpio -idv "*.txt" </dev/rmt0
```

The quotes around the pattern name are necessary to allow the cpio command to interpret the asterisk. If not provided, the shell interprets the asterisk, resulting in a different command. The -d flag is used to recreate any files in subdirectories; if the subdirectories do not already exist in the current directory structure, they are created.

The command

```
cpio -imv [a-z]*.tx? </dev/rmt0
```

restores into the current directory only those files from the tape which begin with a lowercase *a* through *z* and have a three-character suffix that begins with *tx*.

---

[22] The $PWD in this command is a shell variable which names the current working directory.

The contents of an archive created with the cpio -o command can be viewed (without restoring the actual contents) by using the -t flag. Without the -v flag, only the names of the files in the archive are listed. The command syntax is

```
cpio -itv </dev/devicename
```

The valid flags of the cpio -i command are: b, B, c, C, d, f, m, r, s, S, t, u, v, and 6 (Table 6.9).

6.5.2.3 cpio -p—Copy one directory to another. The cpio -p command is used to transfer the contents of one directory (and its subdirectories) to another directory structure. The directory structure into which the new files are to be placed must already exist.

The command reads the names of the input files from standard input and copies the file to the new directory. As an example, the following commands back up the /home/frank directory to the /backup/frank directory

```
cd /home/frank
find. -print | cpio -pdmv /backup/frank
```

The end result of this command is a directory structure in /backup/frank which is identical to /home/frank.

The valid flags for the cpio -p command are: a, d, 1, m, u, and v.

6.5.3   backup—Back up files and filesystems

Two different backup formats are provided by the backup command; backup by name or backup by i-node. Both types may be used as input to the restore command.

Backing up by name is requested with the -i flag. Standard input is read for the names of the files to be backed up and the resulting files are then copied to the output device. If no output device is explicitly defined, the default is /dev/rfd0 (the diskette drive).

Backing up by i-node provides an incremental backup facility which is not available when backing up by name. There are ten levels within the structure, level 0 being a complete file system backup. A backup at level n includes all files that have been modified since the level $n-1$ backup occurred. If the -u flag (Table 6.10) is used with incremental backups, the system updates the backup database (/etc/dumpdates). This provides a method of tracking backups for each file system.

An interesting anomaly of the backup command is that if the backup media (tape drive, diskette) is not ready when performing a backup by i-node, the command fails. However, when performing a backup by name, the media does not have to be ready; the command prompts the user to ready the media.

It is worth noting that if the output device is an 8 mm tape drive using variable-length blocks (blocksize=0), special measures must be used during restore, as the restore command cannot directly read variable-length blocks.

TABLE 6.10   Backup Flags

Flag	Meaning
-b*number*	Defines a block size to be used. If not specified, a default value appropriate for the output device is used. The *number* parameter is a multiplier for the standard block size, 512. The resulting value must be a valid block size for the physical device being used.
-c	For tape devices only, this indicates that the tape is a cartridge, not a nine-track.
-e *expression*	Indicates, when the -p flag is used, what files should *not* be compressed. Wildcard characters (as discussed in Sec. 6.5.2.2) may be used.
-f*device*	Indicates the output device. This is either the path name of the device (/dev/rmt0, for instance) or a minus sign (-) to indicate standard output. For diskette drives, the backup command allows a range of names to be given (/dev/rfd0-5). Each drive is used, in sequence, before backup halts and requests new volume mounts. All drives used in this manner must be of the same density.
-i	Requests a backup by file name. If relative path names are used, then, when the files are restored, it will be relative to the current directory of the restore. Files backed up with absolute names are restored to their absolute location.
-l*number*	For diskette drives, limits the total number of blocks to be used on the backup medium. The *number* must be an integral value of 18.
-o	Creates by-name backups which are compatible with AIX v. 2.
-p	Indicates that files should be packed before they are copied to the output medium.
-q	Used only with backup by name, this flag indicates that the output device is ready to use. Use of this flag suppresses the initial mount message for the output device.
-u	Used only with backup by inode, this flag logs the backup in the system backup database (/etc/dumpfiles).
-v	Requests detailed status reporting during each phase of the backup process.
-w	Displays the latest backup information for each file system logged in the system backup database.
-*level*	Indicates which increment *level* this backup should be.

The default action of the backup command, if no flags or parameters are specified, is to perform a level-9 backup of the root file system by i-node to the system diskette drive (/dev/rfd0). That is,

```
backup
```

is the same as

```
backup -9 -u -f/dev/rfd0
```

The first incremental backup afterward is

```
backup -1 -u -f/dev/rfd0 /
```

Users can back up to tape their default directory with the command

```
find $HOME -print | backup -ipv -b8 -f/dev/rmt0
```

The `find` command prints the list of all the files in the user's home directory to standard output. `backup` reads this list as input, and copies the files to the tape output device (/dev/rmt0). The files are compressed on the output media (-p). The blocks on the tape are 4096 bytes because the -b8 flag is used. In addition, a detailed status report during execution is produced because the -v flag is used.

Sometimes, the output of the backup command is piped as input to the `dd` command. For instance

```
find $HOME -print | backup -if- b8 | dd of=/dev/rmt0 bs=8b
```

This command sequence is used to take advantage of the conversions and improved I/O performance available with the `dd` command. To restore this archive tape, the `dd` command has to pipe its output to the `restore` command.

If backups are directed to tape, several may be placed on the same physical media. Care must be taken, after the first backup command, to position the tape at the end of the backup file. If all of the backups on the medium are to be performed at the same time, the device name suffix .1 is used to suppress automatic rewind of the tape drive. Therefore, to back up the root and /usr file systems onto the same tape, the command sequence is

```
tctl -f /dev/rmt0 rewind
find / -print | backup -ipv -b8 -f/dev/rmt0.1
find /usr -print | backup -ipv -b8 -f/dev/rmt0.1
tctl -f /dev/rmt0 rewind
```

To place a level-1 incremental backup on the same tape as the original level-0 backup, the command sequence is

```
tctl -f /dev/rmt0 fsf 1
find $HOME -print | backup -ipv -b8 -f/dev/rmt0.1
tctl -f /dev/rmt0 rewind
```

To add further incremental backups to the tape, simply increase the number of files to forward space as appropriate in the first `tctl` command.

Finally, the `backup -W` command is used to display the latest backup information in the system backup database.

6.5.4   `restore`—Restore files and filesystems

`restore` reads the output medium created by the `backup` command and restores files from it (Table 6.11).

When using the `restore` command, the user generally does not need to be concerned about whether the `backup` was created as a by-file or by-i-node backup. However, certain flags require knowledge of the backup format. The

TABLE 6.11   Restore Flags

Flag	Meaning
-b*number*	Defines a block size to be used. If not specified, a default value appropriate for the output device is used. The *number* parameter is a multiplier for the standard block size, 512. The resulting value must be a valid block size for the physical device being used.
-B	Is used to indicate that the input medium is in backup by inode format. This flag or -s or -X must be used when a no-rewind tape device is used for restoring.
-d	By-name and version 2 format backups, indicates that if the file name specified for restoration is a directory, all files in the directory should be restored.
-f*device*	Indicates the input device. This is either the path name of the device (/dev/rmt0, for instance) or a minus sign (-) to indicate standard output. For diskette drives, the restore command allows a range of names to be given (/dev/rfd0-5). Each drive is used, in sequence, before restore halts and requests new volume mounts. All drives used in this manner must be of the same density.
-h	For by-inode backups, restores only the directory, not the files within the directory. This cannot be used in conjunction with the -r or -R flags.
-i	Indicates restore should run in interactive mode. The input media must be in by-inode format. Valid subcommands are:

	ls *directory*	Displays the given directory. Directories indicated by a slash (/) after the name, files to be replaced are indicated by an asterisk (*) before the name.
	cd *directory*	Changes the current directory to the indicated directory.
	pwd	Displays the current directory path name.
	add [*File*]	Indicates the file to restore. If the file is a directory, all of its files and subdirectories are also restored (unless the -h flag has been used). If no *file is specified, the current directory is assumed.*
	delete [File]	Indicates a file not to be restored. If the file is a directory, this also applies to all of its files and subdirectories. If no *file* is specified, the current directory is assumed.
	extract	Restores all selected files.
	setmodes	Causes the restore command to set the owner, mode, and times of all files restored instead of using the values from the backup medium.
	verbose	Turns detailed status report mode on and off.
	help	Displays interactive restore help.
	quit	Terminates the restore command immediately.

Flag	Meaning
-M	For by-name backups, causes the restore command to set the owner, mode, and times of all files restored instead of using the values from the backup medium.
-m	Indicates the backup tape is in by-inode format.
-p	Suppresses tape rewind after restoring an individual file. This flag speeds up processing time when restoring several files individually. In this case, use the output of the restore -T command to order the processing list.
-q	Suppresses the initial prompt to ready the output device.

TABLE 6.11   Restore Flags *(Continued)*

Flag	Meaning
-r	Restores an entire file system. Restores a full backup (level-0) only to an empty file system. Uses the crfs command to create the new file system. To restore an entire file system to an specific incremental level, restore the full backup of the file system to an empty file system, and then restore each level of increment up to the desired level. After each restore pass, run the fsck command on the restored file system.
-R	For a by-inode backup, allows an interrupted restore to be continued. Using the -R flag makes the restore command ask for the beginning volume number when restoring from a multivolume backup set.
-s *skip*	Is used with a no-rewind tape device, to position the tape *skip* number of files forward relative to the current position of the tape. This allows an individual backup file on a multifile volume to be restored.
-t	For by-inode backups, displays the table of contents; for by-name backups, displays the header information of the backed-up files. Cannot be used with the -T flag.
-T	Displays the names of the files on the backup medium. Cannot be used with the -t flag.
-v	Requests detailed status reporting during each phase of the restore process.
-X *volume*	By-name backups, allows the starting volume number to be specified by the operator. Subsequent volumes are used only if files requested for restoration are found on subsequent volumes.
-x	Restores individually named files. If no name is given, all files on the medium are restored. For a by-name backup, the restore command uses whatever name is specified during backup; that is, if the backup is relative to the current directory, so is the restore, if the backup is absolute, the restore is also absolute. By-inode restores are always absolute.
-y	Tells restore to suppress user prompting on media errors. In effect, the command skips all bad blocks.

format of a backup file can be determined with the

```
restore -t -finputdevice
```

command. If the -f flag is not used to indicate the input media, the system diskette drive (/dev/rfd0) is assumed.

There are two modes of operation for the restore command, interactive (requested with the -i flag) and command-mode. Interactive mode may be used only with a backup tape in by-i-node format.

To restore a directory named /home/frank from a backup tape, the command used is

```
restore -xdv -f/dev/rmt0 /home/frank
```

To restore the directory named /var/spool/infoshare from the fourth backup file on the tape, the following commands are used

```
tctl -f /dev/rmt0 rewind
restore -xdv -s4 -f/dev/rmt0.1 /var/spool/infoshare
```

or the initial command is slightly changed to permit the second restore to take place without the intervening tctl

```
restore -xdv -f/dev/rmt0.1 /home/frank
restore -xdv -s3 -f/dev/rmt0.1 /var/spool/infoshare
```

If the output of the backup command is piped to the dd command, then the dd command must be used during the restore process. The dd command pipes its output to the restore command. For example

```
dd if=/dev/rmt0 bs=8b | restore -xf- b8
```

6.5.4.1 Restoring variable-length block tapes. An additional use for dd piping is when the backup command creates a backup tape on an 8-mm tape device using variable-length blocks (block length 0). The restore command cannot read these types of files directly. In this case, some type of piping into the restore command must be used. In the case of by-name backups, the most common pipe technique is to use dd

```
dd if=/dev/rmt0 bs=51200 | restore -xvqf-
```

It is also possible to use the pipe

```
restore -xvqf- </dev/rmt0
```

However, this is not nearly as efficient or timely as the dd pipe.

For by-i-node backups, the commands are almost identical, except that the -m flag must be used

```
dd if=/dev/rmt0 bs=51200 | restore -xvqmf-
```

or

```
restore -xvqmf- </dev/rmt0
```

**6.5.5 tar—Write files to and retrieve files from an
archive medium**

tar format backups are probably the most frequently used method for transfer-ring information from one system to another. The advantage tar has over cpio is that a tar archive can be updated,[23] a cpio archive cannot. The disadvantage is that only the last copy of an archived file can be retrieved from the archive media. Another disadvantage of tar, compared to backup, is that a tar archive cannot span more than one physical volume whereas a backup archive can.

In addition to backing up data, the tar command also stores the ownership

---

[23]Unless the output media is a tape drive, in which case, the archive may not be updated.

data of each file archived. This information is restored when the file itself is restored.[24]

There are five `tar` functions, which are requested via one of the following flags

-c	Creates a new archive and add the specified member
-r	Adds a new member to an existing archive
-t	Lists the files in an archive
-u	Adds a member to an existing archive only if it does not already exist in the archive or if has been updated since last being written to the archive
-x	Retrieves a member from an archive

If the member in a command is a directory, the `tar` command processes all of the files in the directory as well as the directory itself. If no member name is given for the -c, -r, or -u flags, the member name is assumed to be the current working directory. With the -x flag, if no member name is given, the entire archive is assumed.

Note that the `tar` command may create work files during its processing in the /tmp directory. These work files always begin with a tar prefix. If there is not enough room in the /tmp file system when one of these work files is needed, the `tar` command fails.

The optional flags of `tar` are explained in Table 6.12. These are used quite extensively to manipulate the behavior of the `tar` command. For example, to create an archive named franks.backup in the /archive directory of the /home/frank file system, the user codes

```
tar -cf /archive/franks.backup /home/frank
```

It might be desirable, however, to see the names of the files as they are backed up, in which case the following command is more appropriate

```
tar -cvf /archive/franks.backup /home/frank
```

To list the files on the archive tape, the following command is issued

```
tar -tvf /archive/franks.backup
```

To restore the files in the /home/frank directory, the command is

```
tar -xvf /archive/franks.backup /home/frank
```

Often, the output of tar is piped to another program. Output is frequently piped to compress when writing an archive file to get more information onto the output medium. This compressed data is then sent to dd to copy the file to tape. Using the prior example, a possible command sequence is

---

[24]Userid and groupid number greater than 65535 are corrupted when restored to systems which do not support user or group ids greater than these values.

TABLE 6.12   tar **Optional Flags**

Flag	Meaning
-B	Forces the archive block size to 10400 bytes.
-b *number*	Indicates a multiplication factor by which 512 is multiplied to determine the block size. The default and maximum value is 20 (same size as if -B had been used). Valid only when used with the -c flag. See also the -N flag.
-C *directory*	When a file name is preceded by a -C flag, tar performs a chdir to the *directory* name. This is useful when archiving several files from unrelated file systems. When this flag is used multiple times, the result of the previous chdir action must be taken into account.
-d	Allows block files, special character files, and FIFO files to be archived. Normally, these files are skipped during the archive process. Only a user with root authority can restore these files.
-F	Eliminates certain types of files from the archive: SCCS, RCS, core, errs, a.out, and all files ending in .o are skipped.
-f *archive*	Denotes the name of the archive to be used. The default is /dev/rmt0 (a tape drive). If the archive is specified as a minus sign (-), the standard input is read or standard output is written, as appropriate.
-h	Forces the tar command to follow symbolic links. Normally, symbolic links are not included in an archive.
-i	Indicates that checksum errors should be ignored. This flag should be used only to restore data from an already damaged physical medium.
-L *names*	Indicates the name of a file which contains the names of files to be written to an archive. If directory entries are specified in the file, only the directory is copied; the files in the directory must be explicitly requested.
-l	Tells tar to write message to standard output if all of the links to an archived file cannot be resolved. The default is to suppress these messages.
-m	Indicates that modification time should be set to the time of extraction. The default is to preserve the time of the file in the archive.
-N *blocks*	Is used to have tar create blocks larger than 10400 bytes. Because tar can not automatically detect block sizes which are larger than 10400, an archive created with this flag can be accessed correctly only when this flag is specified. The maximum value depends on the type of tape device used.
-p	Indicates that the restored files should be created with the original permissions, not the permissions of the current user as set with umask.
-s	Indicates that a soft link should be created if a hard link fails during restore.
-s *number*	Is used to inform the tar command how long the tape is. The first format is used with the -b flag to specify the number of blocks on the tape. When used without the -b flag, the *number* is taken to be the number of feet on the tape and the default density of the drive is assumed. The final form, *feet@density*, allows both the feet and density to be specified.
-v	Lists information of each file as it is processed.
-w	Confirmation mode. When used, tar displays the action to be taken and the file name, and then waits for the user to confirm the action.
-*device*	Is a shortcut method of specifying another tape device other than the default. A -2 indicates that the default tape drive should be taken to be /dev/rmt2.

```
tar -cf- /home/frank | compress | dd of=/dev/rmt0
```

The tar command reads in the files and subdirectories of /home/frank and writes the tar output to standard output (f flag) which is passed to compress as standard input. The compressed data is then written to the standard output of compress; in turn, it is passed to the standard input of dd which writes the data to the tape drive (of=/dev/rmt0).

Restoring the data is the reverse of the previous process

```
dd if=/dev/rmt0 | uncompress | tar -xf- /home/frank
```

6.6   Backing Up the System

There are two special commands which are used to create a bootable system backup, mkszfile and mksysb.

6.6.1   mkszfile—Prepare for the system backup

This command creates the file system size database (/.fs.size) for the use of the mksysb command. The command may be executed only by the root user. After execution of the mkszfile command, the /.fs.size database contains the latest size, mount point, and name information for every file system in the root (rootvg) volume group. mksysb uses the information in this file to create an installable image of the file system on the backup medium.

Before creating the final installation image, the mksysb command first creates the image in the /tmp file system. If the creation of the image in the /tmp file system fails, the command terminates.

Because of this, the mkszfile command first ensures that the /tmp file system has enough free space to create the installation image. If the command terminates because there is not enough space, extraneous files in the /tmp file system are removed and, if necessary and possible, the /tmp file system is enlarged.[25] Alternatively, the mkszfile command can be reissued with the -f flag. This option does not increase the amount of space in the /tmp file system, but instead changes the entry for the /tmp file system in the /.fs.size file and states that it is bigger than it really is. This is dangerous because the created image may not be restorable; mksysb is unable to restore the installation image if the destination system does not have sufficient physical space to accommodate the larger /tmp file system.

6.6.2   mksysb—Create a bootable backup of the root volume group

After the mkszfile command has completed successfully, the mksysb command creates the installation backup image. The command sequence is

```
mkszfile
mksysb /dev/rmt0
```

when the installation image is to be created on tape, and

---

[25] With the chfs command.

```
mkszfile
mksysb /dev/rfd0
```

when the installation image is to be created on diskette.

The installation image created by mksysb is used to install a new system or restore an existing system. The only caveat when using the image to install a new system is that the IP address of the restored system must be changed before the restored system is attached to the network.

Normally, the mksysb command is used to create a bootable tape. When the system is booted from the tape, a base level of operating system information is restored to the system, then the *Installation and Maintenance* menu appears. This menu allows the operator to continue restoring the system from the mksysb image. This restoration is very similar to a system install, and as it is menu driven, fairly simple. The entire process is documented in the *AIX Version 3.2 Installation Guide* (1993).

If the installable system image is created on diskettes, the operator needs the BOS Boot, Display Extensions, Display, and Installation/Maintenance diskettes, in addition to the installable system image diskettes, to boot the system. If the original diskettes which were created during system installation are not available, they can be recreated. Four formatted, high-density diskettes are needed, one for each of the following commands

```
bosboot -a -d fd0
mkextdskt
mkdispdskt
mkinstdskt
```

6.7   Diskettes

Although file systems can be created on diskettes, this is infrequently done. More often, diskettes are used as a backup medium or to transfer data to and from a PC-DOS/MS-DOS based system.

6.7.1   AIX diskette commands

AIX provides three commands for processing diskettes directly: format, fdformat, and flcopy.

6.7.1.1 format/fdformat—Format diskettes. The format and fdformat commands format diskettes. The format command has three flags. The first, -d *device* names the output device to be formatted; if not specified the default device is /dev/rfd0. The second flag, -f, is used to perform a quick format. In this case, the command does not check for bad-tracks during the formatting process.[26] The final flag, -1, forces a low-density format—that is, a 5.25-in,

---

[26] It is not advisable to use this option.

1.2 Mbyte diskette is formatted for 360K, and a 3.5-in, 1.4 Mbyte diskette is formatted for 720K.

The `fdformat` command has one flag only and takes the opposite approach. Its default is to format at low density unless the flag -h is used, in which case, the format is at high density. Therefore, we have the following commands

```
format -d /dev/rfd0
```

and

```
fdformat /dev/rfd0 -h²⁷
```

6.7.1.2 `flcopy`—Copy one diskette to another.   This command is used to copy one diskette to another. To facilitate this process, the system transfers the contents of the floppy disk to a file in the current directory named floppy. When this is complete, the user is prompted to change diskettes. After the user has responded to the system message to change diskettes, the floppy file is copied to the new diskette.

The -f *device* flag is used to specify a floppy diskette other than the default /dev/rfd0. The -t*number* flag is used to limit the copy to a specific number of tracks. The -r flag skips the second part of the copying process. That is, the contents of the diskette are transferred to the floppy file and then the command terminates. The -h command is used to skip the first part of the copying process, and as such, is the counterpart to -r. The -h flag causes the `flcopy` command to transfer the floppy file in the current directory to the diskette drive.

6.7.2   DOS diskette commands

Five commands are provided for working with DOS diskettes: `dosdir`, `dosread`, `doswrite`, `dosdel`, and `dosformat`. DOS file-naming conventions are used with all of the commands, except for two items: the AIX subdirectory delimiter character (/) must be used in all file names; the backslash (\) and the wildcard characters of * and ? in DOS cannot be used.

6.7.2.1 `dosdir`—Display the DOS file directory.   The `dosdir` command displays directory information from DOS diskettes. If used with no flags or parameters, it displays the names of all the files in the root file system on the diskette, along with a report of available free space.

Several flags enhance the amount of information available. The -a flag is used to display information about all files; this includes the hidden and system files. The -1 flag is used to produce a full directory listing of the files. This information includes creation data, size in bytes, and attributes. The

---

²⁷If a specific device name is used with the fdformat command, the -h flag must follow the device name.

attribute indicators follow the DOS convention: A for archive, D for directory, H for hidden, R for read-only, and S for system. The -e flag writes a list of the clusters assigned to each file.

The -v flag is used to verify the format of a diskette. This allows the user to ensure that the diskette is indeed a DOS-format diskette.

Using -t flag produces a complete display of the directory structure starting at the named directory. Normally, a DOS directory display includes only the current level; subdirectories are not listed except to indicate their presence.

Finally, the -D flag is used to specify a device other than the default DOS device /dev/fd0.

6.7.2.2 dosread—Copy a DOS diskette file to an AIX file. The dosread command copies the requested file to standard output, or to the designated AIX file. If a path is not specified for the AIX file, the DOS file is copied to the root directory.

Therefore, to display a file named stuff.c on a DOS diskette, the command is

```
dosread stuff.c
```

The -a flag is used to replace all CR-LF (carriage return-line feed) sequences in the input file with only a LF in the AIX output file. The DOS end-of-file control-Z character is converted to an end-of-line character. Therefore, to copy the stuff.c file to an AIX file in the /home/frank directory, the command is

```
dosread -a stuff.c /home/frank/stuff.c
```

If a binary file is transferred, the -a flag is not used.

As with the dosdir command, the -v flag is used to verify the format of a diskette which allows the user to ensure that the diskette is indeed a DOS-format diskette. The -D flag is used to specify a device other than the default DOS device /dev/fd0.

6.7.2.3 doswrite—Copy an AIX file to a DOS diskette file. The doswrite command copies the requested file to the designated DOS file. The -a flag performs exactly the opposite function it performed in dosread: it replaces all LF (line feeds) in the input file with the CR-LF (carriage return-line feed) sequence in the DOS output file. A control-Z character is added at the end of the output file. Therefore, to copy the /home/frank/stuff.c file on AIX back to the diskette, the command is

```
doswrite -a /home/frank/stuff.c stuff.c
```

If a binary file is being transferred, the -a flag is not used.

As with the other two DOS commands, the -v flag is used to verify the format of a diskette which allows the user to ensure that the diskette is indeed a

DOS-format diskette. The -D flag is used to specify a device other than the default DOS device /dev/fd0.

6.7.2.4 `dosdel`—Delete a file on a DOS diskette. The `dosdel` command is used to delete a file from the DOS diskette. For example, to delete the stuff.c file on the diskette, the command is

```
dosdel stuff.c
```

As with the other three DOS commands, the -v flag is used to verify the format of a diskette which allows the user to ensure that the diskette is indeed a DOS-format diskette. The -D flag is used to specify a device other than the default DOS device /dev/fd0.

6.7.2.5 `dosformat`—Format a diskette for use with DOS. The `dosformat` command is used to format a diskette so that it can be used with the DOS operating system. A diskette formatted for DOS on AIX should not be used for creating a DOS boot diskette.

The flags of the `dosformat` command are

-V *label*	Allows a volume label of *label* to be placed on the diskette
-D *device*	Allows for the specification of diskette type and density; valid values are
/dev/fd0h	3.5 in, 1.44 Mbytes (the default)
/dev/fd0l	3.5 in, 720 Mbyte
/dev/fd1.15	5.25 in, 1.2 Mbytes
/dev/fd1.9	5.25 in, 360 K
-4	Specifies low density

To format a 3.5 in, 1.44 Mbytes diskette with a volume label of backup, the command is

```
dosformat -V backup
```

To format a low-density, 1.44 Mbytes diskette, either of the two following commands are used

```
dosformat -V backup -D /dev/fd0l
```

or

```
dosformat -V backup -D /dev/fd1 -4
```

Processes
and Subsystems

As discussed in Chapter 2, executing programs are referred to as processes in AIX. Processes may be an operating system command, a shell, or an application program.

Each process exists in a parent-child relationship. A process may have multiple subprocesses (or children), but a process has only one parent process. Each process is assigned a unique *process identification number* (PID) when it is started. Even if multiple instances of a program are started, each has a unique PID.

Each process on the system is also assigned a priority by the scheduler. This priority is determined by the operating system based on several factors including the type of process (computation or I/O bound), the requesting user, and overall system load. This priority is dynamically modified by the operating system as is necessary. Users cannot raise the priority of their processes to the detriment of others; only a user with root authority (a superuser) may raise the priority of a process. The priority of a process is changed by the nice and renice commands. Because of this, the priority of an AIX process is usually called the nice value.

Most processes are foreground processes. Foreground processes are able to interact with the user via the user's terminal. By default, all processes are run in the foreground. However, there are many instances where it is not necessary for a process to interact with the user in which case the user can start a process in the background. A process in the foreground can be sent to the background after it has started, and alternatively, processes in the background can be brought to the foreground, if necessary.

There are some tasks that must run in the system which are not necessarily tied to any particular user. Examples of this are the processes that handle login processing, manage the print queues, and control the communications network traffic scheduling. These processes are called daemons. Daemons are usually started when the system is booted, and do not stop, under normal circumstances, until the system is shut down.

Zombie processes are processes that have stopped performing any useful function, but have not been completely removed from the system. In most cases, this is a temporary state. However, it is possible that a process does not leave the zombie state, and completely terminate, until its parent terminates. This may be intentional if the child process is restartable; there is less overhead in restarting a process than in recreating it. However, for the most part, zombie processes that last for more than a few minutes are the result of a programming error; usually these processes can be terminated only by shutting down the system.

Subsystems are groups of processes that execute on behalf of a common purpose. For example, the network protocols SNA and TCP/IP use several different daemons to perform the many functions involved in managing the network. Although these daemons function can be managed individually, is also necessary to manage them as a group. Subsystems are managed through the *System Resource Controller* (SRC) facility.

7.1   Starting Processes

At a terminal-type device, a process is started by entering the name of the command or program at the system prompt. For example, entering the word

```
myjob
```

at the system prompt starts the command named myjob. Unless otherwise directed through file redirection, the command uses the terminal as standard input, standard output, and standard error. While the process is running, other processes cannot be started at the terminal until the process completes or is halted by the user.

In many cases, it is not necessary for the user to interact with the application. In this case, the process can run in the background. To run a process in the background, the user simply appends an ampersand (&) to the end of the command. When running processes in the background, it is customary to redirect standard input, output, and error. If these are not redirected, the process in the background uses the terminal device just as it would if it were in the foreground. This can cause undesirable results if another process, foreground or background, is also using the terminal. Therefore, to use the prior example as a task in the background, the user codes

```
myjob <myjob.in >myjob.out 2>&1
```

where myjob.in is a file which contains an input data the myjob command needs, and myjob.out is the output file that is created. The 2>&1 is a shorthand method for specifying that standard error should be directed to the same file as standard output.[1]

---

[1]For more information on this, see Chapter 2.

7.1.1 `nice`—Run a process at a different priority

The `nice` command is used as a front end to run a command at a priority different from the default priority of the user. Most often this command is used to start a job in the background at a low priority. Only users with root authority may specify a higher priority.

If an absolute priority value is not specified, the `nice` command sets the priority of the command to be executed at low priority. This simply means that the priority of the command to be executed is always less than the priority of any foreground process associated with the same user.[2]

Absolute priority settings on AIX run from a low of 20, to the highest user settable value of -20. The priorities of 0 and 20 are special. Processes with a priority of 20 run only when no other process can be dispatched. On a very busy system, processes with this priority can be blocked from execution for very long periods of time. Setting a process to the value of 0 indicates that the process should run at the user's default priority level.

Several applications are well suited for low-priority, background processing; these include compiling programs and queueing print output. As an example, if a user desires to print out all of the C programs in a given directory, it would be most appropriate to send this request to the background at low priority with a command like

```
nice -20 (find *.c -print | lp -)&
```

Because both the `find` and the `lp` commands are to be sent to the background, they are enclosed in parentheses. The `nice` command itself does not require this; the value specified for the priority applies to all of the given command string. For example, if the command is executed in the foreground,[3] it is

```
nice -20 find *.c -print | lp -
```

Of course, the parentheses could be left in, if only to make the intent clearer.

The root user may start a process with highest priority by using the -20 value

```
nice —20 wall <shutdown.message
```

7.1.2 `renice`—Change the priority of an executing process

`renice` permits a user to alter the priority of a process once it has started. Users with root authority can change the priority of all processes on the system; the value of the new priority for the process may be either higher or lower. Regular users may change only the priority of their own processes; the

---

[2]This vagueness is because the system is constantly monitoring and changing the priorities of processes as it sees fit. Only processes given an absolute priority value with nice or renice maintain a constant priority level.

[3]This would be very odd, but it could happen.

new priority may be a request to reset it to the standard system priority or a request to lower it.

Three flags are used with the command. All of the processes of a given user can be changed by using the -u *username flag. Similarly, all of the processes of a group id can be changed with the* -g groupid flag. If neither of these two flags is used, the process to be changed must be identified by its process id (the flag -p *processid*). Use the ps command to find the process id associated with the command.

In addition to specifying an absolute value, the renice command allows for a positive relative value. For example, to increase the priority of all processes owned by user bosun by one level, the command is

```
renice +1 -u bosun
```

Alternatively, an absolute value could be used:

```
renice 0 -u bosun
```

As with the nice command, absolute priority settings run from a low of 20, to the highest user-set value of -20; processes with a priority of 20 run only when no other process can be dispatched and 0 is used to set a process to the user's default priority level.

7.2   Stopping a Process

A process running in the foreground can be terminated by pressing the interrupt key which is usually either control-C or control-backspace. Tasks in the background (or those of other users) cannot be stopped in this manner. The kill command is used.

7.2.1   kill—Stop a process

The kill command is used to send a signal to an executing process, usually this signal (Table 7.1) is an indication for the process to terminate itself. The root user can kill any process, regular users may kill only processes they have started.

As with the renice command, identification of the process to be killed is usually done by process id.

The syntax of the kill command is

```
kill [-s [signalname | signalnumber ]] processid ...
```

If no signalname or signalnumber is specified, the default is to use SIGTERM. Processid may be an actual process id or either 0 or -1. If an actual process id is used, the signal is sent to the process and any children it may have. If the process id is -1, all processes with the user id of the sender are sent the signal. If the process id is 0, all processes with the group ID of the sender are sent the signal.

TABLE 7.1 `kill` **Signals**

Name	Number	Meaning
SIGHUP	1	/* hangup, generated when terminal disconnects */
SIGINT	2	/* interrupt, generated from terminal special char */
SIGQUIT	3	/* (*) quit, generated from terminal special char */
SIGILL	4	/* (*) illegal instruction (not reset when caught)*/
SIGTRAP	5	/* (*) trace trap (not reset when caught) */
SIGABRT	6	/* (*) abort process */
SIGEMT	7	/* EMT instruction */
SIGFPE	8	/* (*) floating point exception */
SIGKILL	9	/* kill (cannot be caught or ignored) */
SIGBUS	10	/* (*) bus error (specification exception) */
SIGSEGV	11	/* (*) segmentation violation */
SIGSYS	12	/* (*) bad argument to system call */
SIGPIPE	13	/* write on a pipe with no one to read it */
SIGALRM	14	/* alarm clock timeout */
SIGTERM	15	/* software termination signal */
SIGURG	16	/* (+) urgent condition on I/O channel */
SIGSTOP	17	/* (@) stop (cannot be caught or ignored) */
SIGTSTP	18	/* (@) interactive stop */
SIGCONT	19	/* (!) continue (cannot be caught or ignored) */
SIGCHLD	20	/* (+) sent to parent on child stop or exit */
SIGTTIN	21	/* (@) background read attempted from control terminal*/
SIGTTOU	22	/* (@) background write attempted to control terminal */
SIGIO	23	/* (+) I/O possible, or completed */
SIGXCPU	24	/* cpu time limit exceeded (see setrlimit()) */
SIGXFSZ	25	/* file size limit exceeded (see setrlimit()) */
SIGMSG	27	/* input data is in the HFT ring buffer */
SIGWINCH	28	/* (+) window size changed */
SIGPWR	29	/* (+) power-fail restart */
SIGUSR1	30	/* user-defined signal 1 */
SIGUSR2	31	/* user-defined signal 2 */
SIGPROF	32	/* profiling time alarm (see setitimer) */
SIGDANGER	33	/* system crash imminent; free up some page space */
SIGVTALRM	34	/* virtual time alarm (see setitimer) */
SIGMIGRATE	35	/* migrate process (see TCF)*/
SIGPRE	36	/* programming exception */
SIGVIRT	37	/* AIX virtual time alarm */
SIGGRANT	60	/* HFT monitor mode granted */
SIGRETRACT	61	/* HFT monitor mode should be relinquished */
SIGSOUND	62	/* HFT sound control has completed */
SIGSAK	63	/* secure attention key */

TABLE 7.1   `kill` **Signals (*Continued*)**

Name	Number	Meaning
* additional signal names supplied for compatibility, only		
SIGIOINT	SIGURG	/* printer to backend error signal */
SIGAIO	SIGIO	/* base lan i/o */
SIGPTY	SIGIO	/* pty i/o */
SIGIOT	SIGABRT	/* abort (terminate) process */
SIGCLD	SIGCHLD	/* old death of child signal */
SIGLOST	SIGIOT	/* old BSD signal ?? */

Therefore, to stop a specific process, and allow it to perform normal clean-up, the syntax is

```
kill processid
```

To stop a process unconditionally, the syntax is

```
kill -kill processid
```

To stop all of the processes a user owns, the syntax is

```
kill -kill -1
```

7.2.2   `killall`—Cancel all background processes

The `killall` command is a special form of the `kill` command. Its primary function is to allow a user to unconditionally terminate all of the user's background processes at the same time.

The command `killall` terminates all of the background processes immediately. In effect, all background processes are sent a SIGKILL signal.

The command `killall` - sends a SIGTERM to all background processes and then waits for 30 seconds. Any tasks which still exist after the 30 seconds are then sent a SIGKILL signal.

Finally, a specific signal can be sent to all background processes with the syntax

```
killall -signal
```

where *signal* is any valid signal (Table 7.1)

7.3   Suspending and Restarting Processes

A process can be suspended by pressing the control-Z key. At some later point in time, the process will need to be restarted or terminated. There are several ways to restart a suspended task. If the user is not using the Korn shell, the

```
kill -SIGCONT process id
```

command must be used. The command sends the continue signal to the specified process id. The task then starts executing in the background.

If the user is running the Korn or C shell, suspended tasks can be restarted in the background by issuing the bg command. The bg command works on a LIFO (last-in-first-out) basis; the last suspended task is restarted in the background. If the bg command is issued again, the process suspended prior to the last task is then restarted in the background, and so on. If a specific process id is passed as a parameter to the bg command, that process is restarted in the background.

Korn and C shell users can bring a task back into the foreground by using the fg command. If no process id is specified, the most recently "background-ized" process is brought to the foreground.[4]

7.4 Scheduling Processes

AIX is primarily designed to be an interactive system. However, there are cases when commands need to be run in batch mode at scheduled times. These may either be one-shot or regularly scheduled jobs. Two facilities are available to provide for both functions. The at facilities allow a user to schedule one-shot jobs for later execution, and the cron facilities permit the scheduling of processes on an ongoing basis. Both facilities are controlled by the same daemon: cron.

Both facilities, at and cron, are enabled or disabled at the user level. A user is permitted to use at but not cron or vice versa. This is controlled for each facility by its *allow* or *deny* file. An allow file defines which users are permitted to use the facility; a deny file defines which users are not permitted to use the facility. For each facility, either one or the other file may be used, but not both.[5,6] If neither file is defined, only the root user may use the facility. The structure of the allow and deny files is straightforward: each line of the file contains a user name which is either allowed or denied use of the facility, as applicable for the file type.

In most systems, the cron facility is defined through an allow file (/var/adm/cron/cron.allow) since the number of users allowed to use cron facilities is usually small.[7] The at facility is usually defined by a deny file (/var/adm/cron/at.deny). If no users are denied access, the /var/adm/cron/at.deny must be created; however, it will be empty.[8]

Once the allow or deny file is defined, the facility may be used.

A record of all events scheduled and processed by the at and cron facilities is kept in the file /var/adm/cron/log.

---

[4]Bourne shell users are more or less out of luck if the process needs to be brought to the foreground.

[5]If both files should happen to exist (that is both cron.deny and cron.allow or at.deny and at.allow), the allow file is always used.

[6]If allow files are used, for either at or cron, the following userids must always be present: root, sys, and adm.

[7]If the deny facility is used in cron, the deny file is named /var/adm/cron/cron.deny.

[8]The command touch /var/adm/cron/at.deny can be used to create an empty at deny file.

7.4.1 `batch`—Schedule commands for later execution

A simple command for scheduling job execution at a later time is `batch`. The syntax of the command is

```
batch < file_of_commands_to_be_run
```

`batch` reads from standard input the commands which are to be executed at a later time when the system load permits. When the `batch` command is executed, it retains the shell variables and current directory information for the commands to be queued.

If standard output and standard error are not redirected, the output of the commands are sent to the user as mail.

7.4.2 `at`—Schedule jobs for later execution

Like the `batch` command, the `at` command reads from standard input the names of commands to be executed at a later time. Unlike the `batch` command, the `at` command allows the user to define when the commands will be run. Jobs submitted to `at` retain the shell variables and current directory information at the time of submission. And, if standard output and standard error are not redirected, the output of the commands are sent to the user as mail.

The flags of the `at` command allow for the specification of a particular shell, queue, and time. Normally, the shell for job execution is the same as the shell used for queueing the job. This can be overridden with the -c flag which indicates that the C shell should be used for executing the job; the -k flag which indicates that the Korn shell should be used; the -s flag which indicates that the Bourne shell should be used. The Korn and C shells also have their own queues; -qe is the Korn shell queue, -qf is the C shell queue. The default queue is -qa, the at queue. The `batch` queue is -qb, cron jobs are in -qc, and sync jobs are in -qd.[9]

The -t flag is used to specify the execution date and time. The strict format of the date variable is

```
[[CC]YY]MMDDhhmm[.ss]
```

where

CC	Is the first two digits of the year (19 or 20)
YY	Is the second two digits of the year (00–99)
MM	Is the month (01–12)
DD	Is the day (01–31, as appropriate)
hh	Is the hour (00–23)

---

[9]The queue definitions may be found in the /var/adm/cron/queuedefs files.

mm   Is the minute (00–59)

ss   Is the second (00–59)

So, to schedule myjob at 4:00 pm on Sunday May, 1, 1994 the command is

```
at -t 9405011600 < myjob
```

However, the syntax of at also permits the specification of a time parameter. This is more Englishlike than the time specification. For example, the same request is made in time format as

```
at 4pm May 1, 1994 < myjob
```

When using this syntax, a time and/or date specification can be made. Time specification is made relative to a 24- or 12-hour clock. When using a 12-hour clock, the pm suffix must be used for times after noon. The use of the am suffix for times before noon is optional. The values of noon, midnight, and now may also be used to indicate time. Date indication may be date specific, such as May 1, 1994, day specific, such as today, tomorrow, Monday, Tuesday, etc., or relative, such as +15 minutes or next week. The valid relative identifiers are minute(s), hours(s), days(s), week(s), month(s), and year(s).

Therefore, myjob can be scheduled to run

At 4:00pm today	at 4:00pm < myjob
At this time tomorrow	at tomorrow < myjob
At 4:00pm tomorrow	at 4pm tomorrow < myjob
At this time next week	at next week < myjob
Three months from now	at +3 months < myjob

When the -m flag is used, a message is mailed to the submitting user when the job finishes execution.

Two additional flags are used with the at command. Both of these flags change its function. The first flag, -1, is used to request the status of a job or a job queue. Users can list all of the jobs they have queued for execution by using the

```
at -1
```

command. A specific queue can be viewed by also using the -q flag as defined. The following command is used to view all of the jobs in the Korn shell queue

```
at -1 -qe
```

The -r flag is the other flag which changes the function of the at command. It is used to delete a job from the queue. The syntax of the command is

```
at -r jobnumber
```

Except for the root user, users may delete only jobs which they own.

7.4.3 `atq`—Display the job queue

`atq` displays the user's job queue in order by time of execution. The `-c` flag may be used to change the display order to that of the time of submission. When the `-n` flag is used, only the number of jobs in the queue is displayed. The root user can look at the queue of jobs for a specific user by supplying the name. The syntax of the command is

```
atq [-c] [-n] [user ...]
```

7.4.4 `atrm`—Delete jobs in the job queue

The `atrm` command allows a user to delete a specific or all jobs queued for execution. Users can delete all of their queued jobs with the command

```
atrm -
```

Typically, a user includes the `-i` flag which causes the `atrm` command to prompt for confirmation before deleting a job.

A specific job can be removed by using the syntax

```
atrm jobnumber
```

The root user may also delete all jobs of a specific user with the command

```
atrm userid
```

7.4.5 `crontab`—Maintain `cron` jobs

The `crontab` command is a multifaceted utility that is used to submit, edit, list, and remove commands to be run via `cron`.

The commands a user schedules to be run through `cron` are contained in a file named after the user on the path name /var/spool/cron/crontabs. Therefore, the crontab for user boss is named /var/spool/cron/crontabs/boss.

The cron daemon reads only the crontabs when it starts, which is usually only during system initialization. Therefore, changes made directly to a user's crontab are not picked up by `cron` until the next time the `cron` daemon starts. Changes made via the `crontab` command are signaled immediately to the cron daemon.

Each line in a crontab (Fig. 7.1) contains six fields which indicate

The minute	(0–59)
The hour	(0–23)
The day of the month	(1–31)[10]

---

[10]A day value of 30 or 31 is interpreted as the last day of the month for those months which do not have as many days.

```
# @(#)08  1.15  com/cmd/cntl/cron/root, bos, bos320 9/9/91 06:04:47
#
# COMPONENT_NAME: (CMDCNTL) commands needed for basic system needs
#
# FUNCTIONS:
#
# ORIGINS: 27
#
# (C) COPYRIGHT International Business Machines Corp. 1989,1991
# All Rights Reserved
# Licensed Materials - Property of IBM
#
# US Government Users Restricted Rights - Use, duplication or
# disclosure restricted by GSA ADP Schedule Contract with IBM Corp.
#
0 3 * * * /etc/skulker
#45 2 * * 0 /usr/lib/spell/compress
#45 23 * * * ulimit 5000; /usr/lib/smdemon.cleanu > /dev/null
0 11 * * * /usr/bin/errclear -d S,O 30
0 12 * * * /usr/bin/errclear -d H 90
01 4 * * * /etc/lpp/diagnostics/bin/test_batt 1>/dev/null 2>/dev/null
01 3 * * * /etc/lpp/diagnostics/bin/run_ela 1>/dev/null 2>/dev/null
```

Figure 7.1 crontab.

The month of the year	(1–12)
The day of the week	(0–6 for Sunday–Saturday)
The command to be run	

Each of the first five fields can contain one of the following:

A number in the specified range

An inclusive range indicated by two numbers separated with a dash

A list of individual numbers separated by commas

An asterisk (*) indicating all allowed values

Jobs are scheduled in accordance with the following rules (Table 7.2):

TABLE 7.2 crontab **Job Scheduling**

Month	Day of the month	Day of the week	Command runs
*	*	*	Everyday
*	*	Value	On specified day(s) of the week
Value	*	*	Everyday in specified month(s)
*	Value	*	On specified day(s) of every month
Value	Value	*	On specified day(s) in the specified month(s)
*	Value	Value	On specified days(s) of the week and on specified day(s) of the month
Value	Value	Value	On specified day(s) of the week and specified day(s) in the specified month(s)

If the month, day of the month, and day of the week fields contain an asterisk, the command executes every day.

If the month and the day of the month fields contain values, and day of the week is an asterisk, the command executes on the specified month(s) and day(s) of the month.

If the month and day of the month fields are asterisks, and the day of the week field has a value, then the command executes only on the specified day(s) of the week.

If either the month or day of the month field contains a value and the day of the week contains an asterisk, then the month or day of the month field specifies the day(s) when the command is executed.

If all three fields contain values, then the command is executed every day matched by either the day of the week or by month and day of the month.

The command in the sixth field can be a single command, or a group of commands. If a group of commands is given, they can be enclosed in parentheses to redirect the output of every command to the same place. If the output of a command is not redirected, it is sent to the user as mail.

In a command, a percent sign (%) can be used to delimit the command from data; for example the entry

```
0 9 15,31 * * wall %Good morning !%Remember to turn in your time sheet
```

runs the `wall` command at 9:00 am on the 15th and last day of every month. It displays two messages on every logged-on user's screen: "Good morning!" and "Remember to turn in your time sheet."

An important point, which is often overlooked, is that the default for cron table entries is the Bourne shell. This frequently causes problems because the Korn shell is the default for most users. If a shell other than the Bourne shell is to be used to run a crontab entry, prefix the command with the appropriate shell invocation: `ksh` for the Korn shell or `csh` for the C shell.

Entries in a crontab may be disabled temporarily by placing a pound sign (#) in the first position of the line. All lines prefixed with a pound sign are treated as comments by the `cron` daemon.

7.4.5.1 Using the `crontab` command. The `crontab` command is invoked with one of four flags. The `-l` flag is used to list the user's crontab. The `-v` flag is used to display the status of the user's crontab jobs. The `-r` flag is used to delete the user's crontab; the entire table is erased.

The `-e` flag is used to create an initial crontab or edit the user's existing crontab. The first action the `crontab` undertakes is to invoke the user's default editor on the crontab file. The default editor is `vi`, unless users have changed this in their shell profile. Editing is performed directly on the /var/spool/cron/crontabs/*userid* file. When the user is finished and terminates the editing session, the `crontab` command informs the `cron` daemon of the changes made so that they may go into effect immediately. If the file is edited directly, `cron` is not informed of the changes.

7.4.6   cronadm—List or remove `cron` or `at` jobs

This command may be used only by the root user. Its function is to list or remove all of the jobs a user has scheduled, either by `cron` or by `at`. The command has two different syntaxes, depending on whether it is being used for `cron` or `at`.

7.4.6.1   cronadm cron—List or remove `cron` jobs by user.   Three flags are used with the `cronadm cron` command

`-l`	To list crontab files
`-r`	To remove crontab files
`-v`	To display the status of all crontab jobs

A user name may be specified after each flag, in which case the action applies only to the specified user. Note the implications this has for the `-r` flag; if a user name is not supplied, all crontabs are deleted.[11]

To display the list of all jobs queued via `cron` for user bosun, enter the command

```
cronadm cron -v bosun
```

To delete all of user bosun's crontab jobs, permanently, enter the command

```
cronadm cron -r bosun
```

The `cronadm` command purges all of bosun's jobs from the queue and deletes the /var/spool/cron/crontabs/bosun file.

Individual crontab jobs cannot be deleted; it is all or nothing when deleting crontab jobs.

7.4.6.2   cronadm at—List or remove at jobs by user.   Only two flags are used with the `cronadm at` command

`-l`	To list at jobs, and
`-r`	To remove at jobs.

A user name may be specified after the `-l` to limit the display to a specific user. The `-r` flag, however, requires either a user name or a job number. If a user name is given, all of the at jobs for the user are deleted.

---

[11]Ouch!

To display the list of all jobs queued via at for user bosun, enter the command

```
cronadm at -l bosun
```

To delete all of user bosun's crontab jobs, permanently, enter the command

```
cronadm at -r bosun
```

7.5   Process Status

The ps command is used to display the status of processes on the system. The simplest form of the command is ps which, when issued from a display terminal, displays for the user all of the processes ids and command names associated with the terminal session; that is, all of the user's foreground and background processes. For example

```
$ ps
  PID    TTY TIME CMD
12396 pts/0 0:00 ps
33591 pts/0 0:00 -ksh
$
```

There are many flags associated with the ps command; some are prefixed with a minus (-) sign, some are not. In addition, there are a large number of data fields that can be displayed. Tables 7.3 and 7.4 list the data fields which can be displayed, which flags cause the field to be displayed, and what the field means. Table 7.5 details the flags used with ps.

Because of the flexibility of the ps command, many different combinations of output are possible. For example, to see all of the processes for user bosun, one uses the command ps -f -l -ubosun

```
$ ps -f -l -ubosun
F     S      USER   PID  PPID   C  PRI NI ADDR    SZ     WCHAN    STIME
TTY   TIME CMD
240801 S      bosun 15416  5467    0  60 20 1d8f     88     1fd598 11:34:02
-   0:00 /usr/nh/bin/dispatch /usr/nh/etc/nh
240801 S      bosun 34174  5467    0  60 20 181     116     1fd44c 10:03:40
-   0:00 /usr/nh/bin/dispatch /usr/nh/etc/nh
$
```

or see slightly different information by using ps -ef | grep bosun

```
$ ps -ef | grep bosun
bosun 15416  5467    0  11:34:02           - 0:00 /usr/nh/bin/dispatch
/usr/nh/etc/nh.ini
fgc 32122 33591    1 15:18:30  pts/0  0:00 grep bosun
bosun 34174  5467    0  10:03:40           - 0:00 /usr/nh/bin/dispatch
/usr/nh/etc/nh.ini
$
```

Information about processes running on tty0 and tty1 is displayed with the command ps -t tty/0, tty/1

TABLE 7.3 ps **Fields**

Field	Displayed with Flags	Meaning
%CPU	u, v	CPU percentage since the process started
%MEM	u, v	Percentage of real storage used by the process
ADDR	-1, 1	Segment number of the process stack; for kernel processes this is the address of the preprocess data area
C	-f, -1, 1	Current CPU utilization of the process
CMD	-f	the full command name and parameters
CMD	1, 1	The command name
COMMAND	s, u, v	The command name
F	-1, 1	Process flags (Table 7.4). These values are in octal and are cumulative
LIM	v	Soft limit on memory used; xx if no limit has been set, UNLIM if unlimited
NI	-1, 1	Nice value; the value the process priority was set to
PGIN	v	Number of pages read in from secondary storage per second
PID	(all)	The process ID
PPID	-f, -f, 1	The process ID of the parent process
PRI	-1, 1	Actual process priority; the higher the number the lower the priority
RSS	v	Amount of real storage used by the process in 1K units
S	-1, 1	Process state (see STAT)
SIZE	v	Size in 1K units of the data area of the process
SSIZ	s	The size of the kernel stack
STAT	s, u, v	

	Process state
0	Defunct
S	Sleeping
W	Waiting
R	Running
I	Changing states
Z	Canceled
T	Stopped
K	Available kernel process
X	Acquiring virtual storage

Field	Displayed with Flags	Meaning
STIME	-f, u	Process start time
SZ	-1, 1	Size in 1K units of the process's core image
TIME	(all)	The total execution time
TRS	v	Amount of real storage used by the text area
TSIZ	v	Size of the text area (program)
TTY	(all)	The controlling display terminal of the process
TTY	-	No display is associated with the process
TTY	?	Cannot be determined
TTY	*number*	The TTY number of the display terminal
UID	-1, 1	The user ID (numeric) of the process owner
USER	-f, u	The login name of the process owner
WCHAN	1	The address of the event for which the process is waiting
WCHAN	-1	The event for which the process is waiting

TABLE 7.4   Process Flags

Value	Meaning
00000001	Process is operating in core.
00000002	Process cannot be swapped out.
00000008	Process is running with trace on.
00000010	Process is stopped with trace on.
00000020	Process has stopped after a fork with trace on.
00000040	Process has stopped after an exec with trace on.
00000080	Process has stopped after a load or unload with trace on.
00000100	Process has a fixed priority.
00000200	Process is a kernel process.
00000400	Restoration of the old program mask after a signal has been received.
00000800	Indicates that a signal will end the process's sleep state.
00001000	Process is in user mode.
00002000	Process has outstanding locks.
00004000	Process is a debugging process.
00008000	Process is a debugging process for multiple processes.
00010000	Process is terminating.
00020000	Process is selecting wake up or waiting.
00040000	Process is in an orphaned process group.
00080000	Process' controlling terminal has been released.
00100000	when they stop, child processes do not send SIGHLD to their parent.
00200000	Process has been run.
00400000	Process is using job control.
00800000	Process is free from job control.
01000000	Process is used by the program-check handler.
02000000	Process removed shared memory during termination.
04000000	The process slot is free.
08000000	The process has sent all messages.

```
$ ps -t tty/0, tty/1
   PID    TTY   TIME CMD
12405  tty/0  0:00 ps
33591  tty/0  0:00 ksh
$
```

or with the command `ps t 0; ps t 1`

```
$ ps -t 0; ps -t 1
  PID    TTY   TIME CMD
 4751      0  0:00 tsm
  PID    TTY   TIME CMD
11410      1  0:00 tsm
$
```

Detailed, "system programmer-type" information can be displayed with `ps v`

```
$ ps v
PID    TTY STAT  TIME PGIN  SIZE   RSS   LIM  TSIZ  TRS
%CPU %MEM COMMAND
12415  pts/0 R    0:00    0   120   188 32768    35    48  0.0  1.0 ps v
```

TABLE 7.5   ps Flags

Flag	Meaning
-A	Information about all processes is displayed.
-a	Information about all processes, except the process group leaders (parent processes) and processes not associated with a terminal, is displayed.
-d	Information about all processes, except the process group leaders, is displayed.
-e	Information about all processes, except kernel processes, is displayed.
-f	Generates a full listing.
-F format	Displays information as described by the *format* variable. The format variable is either a list of comma-separated field specifiers or a list of field descriptors separated by commas or spaces and enclosed in double quotes (" "). The string within the double quotes may contain additional characters which may be used to format the output. Each field specifier has a default heading name which can be overridden by appending an equal sign (=) and user-defined header information; the header text can be set to null by not specifying any information after the equal sign. The default size of the field is the size of the header text, either user-defined or the default. The valid field specifiers are

Specifier	Descriptor	Default header meaning
args %a	COMMAND	Full command name and parameters.
comm %c	COMMAND	Command name, no parameters.
etime %t	ELAPSED	Elapsed time since the process started.
gname %G	GROUP	The effective process group name.
nice %n	NI	Scheduling priority value.
pcpu %c	%CPU	Current CPU usage percentage.
pgid %r	PGID	Process group number.
pid %p	PID	Process id.
ppid %P	PPID	Parent process id.
rgname %g	RGROUP	The real process group name.
runame %u	RUSER	The real user name.
time %x	TIME	The cumulative time since the process started.
tty %y	TT	The controlling terminal name.
uname %U	USER	The effective user name.
vsz %z	VSZ	The process's virtual storage size.

Flag	Meaning
-G list	Information about the processes associated with the indicated process group is displayed. The *list* variable is either a list of comma-separated group names, or a list of group names separated by spaces and enclosed in double quotes (" ").
-g list	Same as the -G flag.
-k	Lists kernel processes.
-l	Generates a long listing. Refers to the l flag.
-p list	Information about processes with the process numbers specified in the *list* is displayed. The *list* variable is either a list of comma-separated process numbers or a list of process numbers separated by commas or spaces and enclosed in double quotes (" ").

TABLE 7.5   ps **Flags** (*Continued*)

Flag	Meaning
-t *list*	Information about processes associated with the specified display device is displayed. The *list* variable is either a list of comma-separated display device identifiers or a list of display device identifiers separated by commas or spaces and enclosed in double quotes (" ").
-U *list*	Information about processes associated with the user name (or user number) is displayed. The *list* variable is either a list of comma-separated user names (or user numbers) or a list of user names (or user numbers) separated by commas or spaces and enclosed in double quotes (" ").
-u *list*	Same as the -U flag.
a	Information about processes associated with terminals is displayed.
c	Displays the command name rather than the command parameters.
e	Displays the environment as well as the command parameters (80 character limit).
ew	Same as e, except the display wraps to an additional line.
eww	Same as e, except the display wraps as many times as necessary.
g	Displays all processes.
l	Displays a long listing. This include the fields F, S, UID, PID, PPID, C, PRI, NI, ADR, SZ, PSS, WCHAN, TTY, TIME, and CMD.
n	Displays numeric data instead of textual data for those fields where it is applicable.
s	Displays the size of the kernel stack for each process.
t *TTY*	Displays information on processes associated with tty*TTY* only. For tty0, the flag would be t 0. If specified, this must be the last flag on the command line.
U	Updates the ps internal database file /etc/ps_data if the user has permission to write to the database. Generally, this flag is used only during system startup (in the /etc/rc file). If the internal database is not current, the ps command must read the /etc/passwd file every time a ps command is used.
u	Displays user-oriented output. This includes the fields USER, PID, %CPU, %MEM, SZ, RSS, TTY, STAT, STIME, TIME, and COMMAND.
v	Displays the PGIN, SIZE, RSS, LIM, TSIZ, TRS, %CPU, and %MEM fields.
w	Specifies that 132 rather than 80 columns should be used for output formatting.
ww	Specifies that arbitrarily wide output lines should be used.
x	Display processes not associated with a terminal.

```
33591  pts/0 S     0:00   30   108    360 32768    306  252   0.0  1.0 -ksh
$
```

Or, a user can build a custom display, for example

```
$ ps -ef -F "%u / %U <%p%> %c : %z -> %a"
root /    root <      1> init         248 : /etc/init
root /    root < 1348> srcmstr        192 : /etc/srcmstr
root /    root < 1645> biod           156 : /usr/etc/biod 6
root /    root < 1922> cron           148 : /etc/cron
root /    root < 2830> syncd           56 : /etc/syncd 60
root /    root < 3151> syslogd        128 : /etc/syslogd
root /    root < 3600> errdemon       220 : /usr/lib/errdemon
root /    root < 4178> sendmail       244 : /usr/lib/sendmail -bd -q30m
root /    root < 4751> tsm            240 : /etc/getty /dev/tty0
```

```
root /      root <  4905> tsm          220 : /etc/getty /dev/console
root /      root <  5208> portmap      132 : /usr/etc/portmap
root /      root <  5467> inetd        204 : /etc/inetd
root /      root <  5728> snmpd        388 : /usr/sbin/snmpd
root /      root <  5993> biod         180 : /usr/etc/biod 6
root /      root <  7301> qdaemon      104 : /etc/qdaemon
root /      root <  7538> nfsd         228 : /usr/etc/nfsd 8
root /      root <  7796> nfsd         124 : /usr/etc/nfsd 8
root /      root <  9595> rpc.mountd   140 : /usr/etc/rpc.mountd
root /      root <  9853> rpc.statd    132 : /usr/etc/rpc.statd root /
            root <10111> rpc.lockd     180 : /usr/etc/rpc.lockd
root /      root <10637> uprintfd      44 : /etc/uprintfd
root /      root <10891> writesrv      96 : /etc/writesrv
root /      root <11410> tsm          244 : /etc/getty /dev/tty1
root /      root <11694> lpd          128 : /usr/lpd/lpd
root /      root <11924> pdnsd        188 : /usr/lpp/xlC/browser/pdnsd
fgc /       fgc <12424> ps            200 : ps -ef -F %u /%U <%p> %c %z : %a
root /      root <12730> infod         80 : /usr/lpp/info/bin/infod
root /      root <12965> pd_watchdog  148 : pd_watchdog
root /      root <13483> hcondmn     1104 : /usr/bin/hcondmn
root /      root <14902> telnetd      212 : telnetd
bosun /     bosun <15416> dispatch     88 : /usr/nh/bin/dispatch /usr/nh/etc/nh
root /      root <18971> luxcps       184 : luxcps
root /      root <23063> luxcr        180 : /usr/lpp/sna/bin/luxcr sna
root /      root <23581> luxlns        72 : luxlns
root /      root <24094> luxihd        44 : luxihd
root /      root <24863> luxtracedm    76 : luxtracedm
root /      root <26908> luxlrm        60 : luxlrm
fgc /       fgc <32873> ftpd          376 : ftpd
fgc /       fgc <33591> ksh           108 : -ksh
bosun /     bosun <34174> dispatch    116 : /usr/nh/bin/dispatch /usr/nh/etc/nh
$
```

7.5.1 w—Print summary system activity

The w command displays a summary of current system activity. Depending on the flags used, the information includes a header line that shows the time of day, how long the system has been running, the number of users logged on, and the number of processes that can be run. For each user, a detail is displayed with information about

Who is logged on

What the user is doing

The terminal associated with the process

The time the user logged on

The number of minutes the terminal has been idle

Total system time used by the processes associated with the user

System time of the currently active process

Name and arguments of the current process

Note in the sample display that the login time field can be represented in three different formats

09:34am   Login occurred today

Wed09am	Login occurred within the last seven days, but longer than 24 hours ago
04May94	Login occurred more than a week ago

The flags of the w command are

-h	Suppresses the heading
-l	Prints the summary in long form; this is the default display for the user-detailed information
-s	Prints a summary form; the *tty* name is abbreviated and the login time, system unit times, and command arguments are omitted
-u	Prints only the header line
-w	The default flag, a combination of -l and -u

7.6   Miscellaneous Process Control Commands

The commands in this section, while affecting processes, do not fit into any convenient category. This does not demean their importance or usefulness.

7.6.1   sleep—Suspend execution for a given interval

Most often, the sleep command is found in shell scripts when it is necessary to suspend execution for a certain amount of time. However, it can be used also as part of a command sequence, for instance

```
(wall <shutdown.5min.msg; sleep 240; shutdown)¹²
```

This sends a message to all users telling them that the system will shut down in five minutes, wait (sleep) for 240 seconds, and then start shutdown procedure.
The syntax of the sleep command is

```
sleep number_of_seconds_to_wait
```

The maximum number of seconds is 2,147,483,647, over 67 years.

7.6.2   wait—Synchronize process execution

The wait command pauses execution until the process id given to the command as an argument terminates. If no process id is passed as an argument, the wait command suspends execution until all processes of the invoking shell terminate; this feature is used frequently to suspend execution of a parent process until all of the child processes have terminated.
The syntax of the command is

```
wait [processid ...]
```

---

[12]The observant will notice that the command is waiting only four minutes, not five. This is because the shutdown command automatically sends out a one-minute warning message as long as the -F flag is not used.

7.6.3 nohup—Allows a process to continue executing after the user logs out

The nohup command is used to run processes in the background after the user logs off the system. The syntax of the command is

```
nohup command_and_arguments [&]
```

If nohup is used without the ampersand suffix (&), the command is queued until the user logs out, otherwise, execution of the command begins immediately in the background.

If the output of the command is not redirected to a file, the nohup appends the standard error and standard output files in the nohup.out file in the current directory. If the file does not exist already, nohup tries to create it. If nohup.out cannot be created in the current directory, nohup tries try to append to the existing file or creates a new file in the user's home directory. If this fails, the command is not executed.

If nohup is used to run a shell script, it assumes that the Bourne shell is used. To use the Korn or C shell, insert the name of the appropriate shell between the nohup command and the shell script name

```
nohup ksh a_korn_shell_script
```

7.6.4 lastcomm—Display information about the last commands executed

The lastcomm command is available only if accounting support has been started in the system. The command displays, in reverse chronological order, information about all previously executed commands which are still in the process summary database (/var/adm/pacct).

The command takes three arguments: command name, user name, and terminal. Entering the command

```
lastcomm
```

displays all the information in the process summary database. A specific command can be interrogated by entering

```
lastcomm command_name
```

where command_name is the command for which information is to be displayed.
For each process used, the following information is displayed:

Name of the user who ran the process

Special accounting flags

C	The command ran in PDP-11 compatibility mode
D	The command abended with a dump
F	The command ran after a fork

S	The root user executed the command
X	The command was terminated by a signal

Name of the command under which the process was called

CPU time, in seconds, used by the process

Process start time

7.6.5 `fuser`—Identify what processes are using a file

The `fuser` command lists the number of processes on the local system[13] that are using the file passed to the `fuser` command as a parameter. For example, the command

```
fuser /home/infoshare
```

lists all of the processes that were using the /home/infoshare directory.

The process numbers are written to standard output as a single line. The process ids are separated from each other by a single space. Each process is suffixed by a one-character indicator of how the process is using the file

c	Indicates the file is the current directory of the process
p	Indicates the file is the parent of the process' current directory
r	Indicates the process is using the file as its root directory

If the `-u` flag is used, the process id is followed by the process's user name in parentheses.

The root user may use the `-k` flag which sends a KILL signal to each process using the file. For example, the root user terminates all tasks using the /home directory with the command

```
fuser -k -u /home
```

7.7 Subsystem Control

The *System Resource Controller* (SRC) is the primary mechanism through which subsystems are controlled. Technically, a subsystem is a program (or set of programs) designed to provide independent system functions to be used in conjunction with other related functions (inetd, the network messaging daemon). These related functions (subsystems) are taken together to form a subsystem group (Fig. 7.2), TCP/IP for example. Specific functions within a subsystem are implemented by subservers. Subservers are totally dependent on their parent subsystems: they start when their parent starts and end when their parent ends.

---

[13]NFS use of the file, if any, is not reflected.

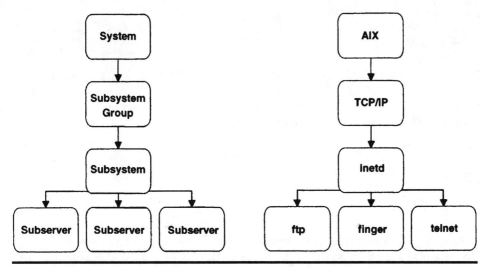

Figure 7.2 The System Resource Controller hierarchy. Left, the conceptual model; right, an implementation (TCP/IP).

Four commands are provided at the user level for interacting with the system resource controller to control SRC resources (subsystems and subservers): lssrc to display information about SRC resources, startsrc and stopsrc to start and stop SRC resources, and refresh to inform a subsystem or subserver that a configuration change has taken place.

7.7.1 lssrc—Display the status of a subsystem or subserver

The status of all subsystems and subservers on a system can be requested with the

```
lssrc -a
```

command. The lssrc command uses additional flags to limit or expand the amount of information returned.

For example, the status of a particular subsystem group can be requested with the -g flag.

```
lssrc -g tcpip
```

displays information on the TCP/IP subsystem group. The status of a particular subsystem can be requested with the -s flag which identifies the subsystem by name, or the -p flag which identifies the subsystem by process id. So, if a user wants to know the status of inetd, which has a process id of 57, either one of these commands would return the desired information

```
lssrc -s inetd
```

or

```
lssrc -p 57
```

A subserver can be displayed with the -t flag; the user must already know the process id of either the subsystem or the subserver. To request information about the ftp daemon (ftpd, a subserver of inetd) which is running as process 923, the user issues the command

```
lssrc -t ftpd -P 923
```

or

```
lssrc -t ftpd -p 57[14]
```

If the -l flag is omitted from subserver or subsystem display request, the SRC displays a short status. The information is based on the status of the subsystem or subserver as the SRC currently knows it. When the -l flag is used, the SRC sends a request to the subsystem or subserver to update the SRC information before the SRC displays the status information.

Remote systems can be checked by using the -h flag. For instance, to check the subsystem status of another machine named *maupin,* the user would enter the command

```
lssrc -h maupin -a
```

Similarly, a specific subsystem group, such as SNA Services, checks with the command

```
lssrc -h maupin -g sna
```

7.7.2 startsrc—Start a subsystem or subserver

Once the status of a subsystem or subserver is known, the next action is often to start or stop it. Subsystems can be started with the startsrc command. Most often, this command is used during system startup, but it may be used at any time to start an inactive subsystem or subserver.

Starting a subsystem group is indicated by the -g flag, a subsystem by the -s flag. An argument to the command may be passed to the program(s) with the -a flag. The argument may not be longer than 1200 characters and should be enclosed in quotation marks. Additionally, environment variables can be set for the process(es) by using the -e flag. The environment variables, like the argument, may not exceed 1200 characters, and the entire string should be enclosed within quotes. Variables within the string are delimited by

---

[14]-P identifies a subserver process id; -p identifies a subsystem process id.

spaces. As an example, starting the TCP/IP subsystem group with a default terminal type of ibm3151, is accomplished with the command

```
startsrc -g tcpip -e "TERM=ibm3151"
```

As with the lssrc command, remote systems can be controlled by using the -h flag. To start SNA services on the remote host *maupin,* the user enters the command

```
startsrc -h maupin -s sna
```

Starting a subserver is more complex as the user must already know the process id of the controlling subsystem. To start a subserver of TCP/IP, ftpd, for instance, the user first has to determine the process id of inetd. This is done with the

```
lssrc -s inetd
```

Armed with the process id of inetd (let us say it is 1246), the user may now start ftpd with the command

```
startsrc -t ftpd -p 1246
```

7.7.3 stopsrc—Stop a subsystem or subserver

Subsystems and subservers are stopped with the stopsrc command. Three types of stop are available for subsystems, normal (no flag), cancel (-c), and force (-f). A forced stop sends a KILL signal to all processes associated with the subsystem or subserver; normal end-of-process clean-up does not take place. A cancel stop allows a subsystem the opportunity to perform normal end-of-process cleanup; if all activity of the subsystem does not end within a predetermined period of time,[15] the SRC sends all of the remaining processes a KILL signal.

Stopping a subsystem group is indicated by the -g flag, a subsystem by the -s flag if termination is by subsystem name, -p if termination is by subsystem process id. The -a flag indicates that all subsystems are to be terminated; this is normally used only during system shutdown or when performing system maintenance. Remote systems can be controlled by using the -h flag. To stop all of the subsystems on remote host *maupin,* the user enters

```
stopsrc -h maupin -a[16]
```

---

[15]This time period is defined individually for each subsystem in the SRC configuration database.

[16]It is assumed that the users on *maupin* have been notified that this action is going to take place.

Stopping a subserver is more complex as the user must know its process id. To stop our previous example, the TCP/IP ftpd daemon, the user first has to determine the process id of ftpd. This is done by looking through the output of

```
lssrc -s inetd
```

or, better yet, the command

```
ps -ef | grep ftpd
```

Once the process id is determined (let us say it is 39483), the subsystem is terminated with the command

```
stopsrc -t ftpd -p 39483
```

Although it is possible, and probably faster, to just kill the subserver with a

```
kill -KILL 39483
```

command, this method does not inform the controlling subserver of what is going on. This can possibly leave the system in an undesirable (read as unusable) state.

7.7.4 refresh—Inform a subsystem that a configuration change has taken place

The refresh command is used to send a refresh message to a subsystem. This is most often used in conjunction with a change in the subsystem configuration, but it may be used at any time a subsystem refresh is desired. The actual action performed by the subsystem when it receives the refresh request is up to the subsystem: it might ignore the request, it might tell its subserver to reread the configuration files, or it might terminate all of its subservers and restart them.

Refreshing a subsystem group is indicated by the -g flag, a subsystem by the -s flag if the refresh is done by subserver name, and -p if the refresh is done by a specific subsystem process id. Remote systems can be controlled by using the -h flag. To refresh SNA Services,[17] the user enters the command

```
refresh -s sna
```

---

[17]Unfortunately, an all too common function.

Printing

Printing tasks on AIX can be separated into two major areas: using the print facilities and defining and maintaining them. Three commands are provided to the user for sending output to the printer: lp, lpr, and qprt. The first two commands are older and were designed to control line printers. The qrpt command is a more recent introduction to the UNIX command set; it allows for greater control of laser printers and plotters than do the other two.

Several additional commands provide services to manage the printers and their output queues: qadm, qcan, qchk, qpri, and qstatus. These are in addition to the original UNIX commands, lpq, lprm, lpstat, lptest, enable, cancel, disable, and splp. The majority of users now prefer the "q" commands, but all of these are common print commands a typical AIX user utilizes.

The remaining printing commands define and maintain the real printers on the system, the virtual printers which allow a real printer to support more than one type of data stream (i.e., text and graphics), the queues into which jobs spool output and from which printers retrieve jobs to print, and the various files which allow a site to customize the banner pages of output and other local modifications.

When a file is printed (Fig. 8.1), AIX sends streams of data to the printer. All of these codes indicate to the printer a specific action to take: print a zero, skip a page, etc. Control codes which make the printer perform a special functions (as opposed to print alphanumeric characters) are in many cases interpreted differently by different printers. However, when a file is sent for printing, it does not actually go directly to the printer. First, the file is placed in a queue until a printer that reads from the queue is available. When a printer for the queue does become available, the queue scheduling daemon (qdaemon) starts up a piobe (printer input/output backend) process. The piobe processes the file and interprets the control codes within the file in the context of the physical device upon which the queue entry is to be printed.

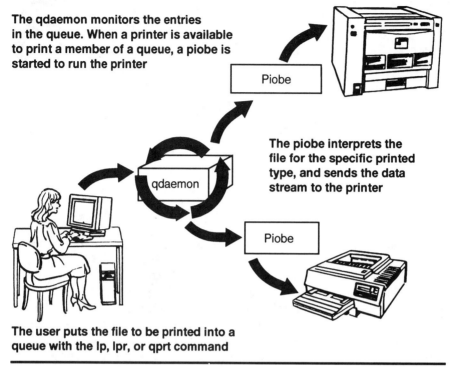

The qdaemon monitors the entries in the queue. When a printer is available to print a member of a queue, a piobe is started to run the printer

The piobe interprets the file for the specific printed type, and sends the data stream to the printer

The user puts the file to be printed into a queue with the lp, lpr, or qprt command

Figure 8.1   The printing process.

8.1   Printing Files

Files may be printed with one of three commands: lp, lpr, or qprt. The first two commands are simpler to use but do not allow for the flexibility qprt does. An additional command is pr which does not spool output to a print queue, but instead acts as a preprocessing formatter for output to be spooled.

8.1.1   pr—Format a file for printing

The pr command writes an unformatted file or files to standard output in a form appropriate for printing. The formatting that is performed includes putting a heading at the top of each page that includes the page number, date, time, and name of the file (Table 8.1).

The output of pr is almost always piped into one of the print-spooling commands. For example, to print the file vacation.list with headings and page numbers, the user enters the command

```
pr vacation.list | lp -c
```

If a more descriptive title is desired, the -h flag is used in the command

```
pr -h "Vacation schedule for 1994" vacation.list | lp -c
```

TABLE 8.1 pr **Flags**

Flag	Meaning
-a	Displays multicolumn output across the page. Valid only with the *-column* flag.
-d	Double-spaces the output.
-e [*character*] [*gap*]	Expands tabs into eight-character positions. The default character is a space. If a *character* is specified, that character is interpreted in the input as a tab character. Specifying a number for *gap* allows the number of character positions to be changed from the default of 8.
-F	Uses a form-feed character to advance to new page. Otherwise, pr uses line feeds to advance to new page.
-f	Same as -F.
-h "header"	When used, the "header" replaces the file name as the page header.
-i [*character*] [*gap*]	Replaces repeating spaces wherever possible by inserting tabs. If a *character* is specified, that character is used as the tab character in the output. Specifying a number for *gap* allows the number of repeating spaces to be changed from the default of 8.
-l	Defines the number of lines per page. The default is 66.
-m	Merges files. Lines from the two files are printed side-by-side (two-up) in columns on the output. Cannot be used with the *-column* flag.
-n [*width*] [*character*]	Provides line numbering. The number of digits in the line number is determined by the *width*. The *character value* is used to separate the line number from the rest of the line. The default *character* is a tab.
-o *offset*	Indents each line by the specified number of character positions. The default value is zero.
-p	Pauses before beginning each page if the output is being displayed on a terminal. Press the enter key to continue.
-r	Does not display error messages if files cannot be opened.
-s *character*	Separates columns by the indicated *character*. The default value is a tab.
-t	Suppresses the display of the header and trailer information.
-w *width*	Sets the number of column positions per line to the *width* size. There is no default width.
-*column*	Sets the number of columns to the value specified as *column*. This option cannot be used with the -m flag and the -e and -i flags are assumed.
+*page*	Starts the output at the indicated page number. The default value is 1.

The column-formatting feature is used to print a list of items on fewer pages

```
pr -4 dictionary.lst | lp -c
```

Two files can be merged and printed side by side with the -m flag

```
pr -m -h "Words and index number" dictionary.lst index.tbl | lp -c
```

For files that are already formatted, or do not have any special formatting requirements, the pr command is not used. Instead the gprt or lp command is used.

8.1.2   lp—Print a file

The lp command queues the indicated file (or standard input if no file is specified) for printing. Several files can be specified at once, and the minus (-) character can be used within a list of files to indicate that the standard input should be included.

If no flags are used, the file is queued to the default printer. If subsequent modifications are made to the file before it is physically printed, these are reflected in the hard copy. The -c flag is used to copy the file immediately to a separate print queue entry; this way, subsequent actions on the file are not reflected in the printed output.

The -d flag is used to queue a file to a specific queue. For example, the command

```
pr vacation.list | lp -q laser_jet
```

ensures that the vacation.list file will print on a laser jet printer.

A user can be notified when a job has finished printing by either the -w or -m flag. The -w flag sends a completion message to the terminal of the user when the file has completed printing; the -m flag sends a mail message to the user after the file has finished printing.

Additional copies of a file can be printed by using the -n *copies* flag.

A title message to be printed on the banner page is specified with the -t flag. Using the prior example

```
pr vacation.list | lp -q laser_jet -n2 -m -t'Vacation'
```

prints two copies of the vacation.list file on the laser jet. To aid identification, the banner page includes the title 'Vacation' and the user is sent a mail message when all of the copies finish printing.

8.1.3   lpr—Print a file

The lpr command is also used to print files. It combines rudimentary functions of the pr command with those of the lp command. Files formatted with pr should not be queued with lpr, use lp or qprt instead.

If no flags are used, lpr simply sends the file to to the default printer. Unlike the lp command, the lpr command automatically makes a copy of the file and places it in the print queue. This way, if the file is modified before printing has taken place, the modifications do not affect the printed output. This function can be suppressed by using the -s flag.

If the printer environment variable is set, lpr uses this PRINTER as the default unless the LPDEST variable is set, in which case LPDEST is used as the default printer. The default can be overridden by specifying the -P *printer* flag.

Formatting of the output occurs only when the -p flag is used. The other formatting flags

-i *indent*	To indent the output *indent* number of spaces
-T *title*	To replace the file name in the header with the value of the *title* variable
-w *width*	To specify a width for the page are valid only when the -p flag is specified.

Output control flags include

-# *number*	To print multiple copies of a file
-C *class*	To print a job class on the burst page
-h	To suppress printing of the burst page
-J *job*	To specify a job name on the burst page
-m	To send the user a mail message when printing is complete
-r	To delete the file after it has been printed
-s	To suppress the automatic copy function

To use the prior example from lp with the lpr command, the command is

```
lpr -P lp2 -#2 -m -T'Vacation' vacation.list
```

assuming that lp2 is a laser printer.

8.1.4 qprt—Print a file

Of the three commands to print a file, the qprt command is by far the most flexible and complex. As with the other two commands, if a specific file is not indicated in the command line, the input is assumed to be coming from standard input.

Many of the flags of the qprt command are not valid with all printers. The flags are discussed in Table 8.2. Although there are many more flags that may be used with the qprt command, most are not frequently used as the printers on the system are usually set up with appropriate default values.

To demonstrate the differences and similarities between the print commands, we return to our prior example from the lpr command; the command using qprt now looks like this

```
qprt -P laser_jet -N2 -fp -n -h'Vacation' vacation.list
```

To print the file on the default printer with default values, enter

```
qprt vacation.list
```

8.2 Controlling Print Facilities

There are several different commands which control printers and print queues. As stated before, some of the commands (the lp series) are older and

TABLE 8.2 `qprt` **Flags**

Flag	Meaning
`-b` *number*	Specifies the number of lines to be left blank to form the bottom margin.
`-B` *value*	Specifies whether burst pages should be printed or not. *Value* is a two-character field; the first character specifies the option for the header pages; the second character specifies the option for the trailer pages.

Valid options	
a	Always print, for each file in the job.
n	Never print.
g	Print only once per job.
`-c`	Specifies that the system should copy each file queued for printing to a special queue file. This prevents any subsequent modifications to the file from affecting the print output. When print is spooled to a remote system, this flag is assumed.
`-C`	Specifies that all messages from or about a print job should be mailed. If the user is logged on, the default is to send a message to the user's terminal.
`-d` *type*	Is used to identify the character control used in the input file. If the printer selected does not support the specified character control code, the `piobe` tries to use a filter to convert the data into a more acceptable format.

Valid types	
a	Extended ASCII.
c	PCL.
d	Diablo 630.
g	HPGL.
p	pass-through (send data to printer unmodified).
s	PostScript.
`-D` *username*	Specifies that the header page should be labeled for delivery to the specified user instead of the submitter.
`-e` *option*	Specifies whether emphasized print is wanted; + for *yes*, ! for *no*.
`-E` *option*	Specifies whether double-high print is wanted; + for *yes*, ! for *no*.
`-fp`	Specifies that the input file should be passed through the `pr` command for formatting.
`-g` *page*	Specifies the page number where printing should begin. This flag is valid only when the `-d a` flag is used.
`-G` *option*	Specifies how pages should be printed on laser printers that cannot print to the edge of the paper; + indicates the whole-page coordinate system, - indicates the print-page coordinate system.
`-h` *text*	Specifies the title text to be passed to the `pr` command when the `-fp` flag is used.
`-H` *name*	Replaces the host name on the header page with the name indicated by the *name* variable.

TABLE 8.2 qprt **Flags (Continued)**

Flag	Meaning
-i *number*	Causes each line to be indented the *number* of spaces.
-I *number*	Specifies a font identifier. This flag overrides the pitch (-p) and type style (-s) flags.
-j *option*	Indicates whether the printer should be initialized before each file is printed: 0 for *no,* 1 for full initialization, and 2 for emulator selection only.
-J *option*	Specifies whether the printer should be restored to its default settings at the end of the print job; + for *yes,* ! for *no.*
-k *name*	Specifies the print color. Consult the printer manual for colors supported by the printer.
-K *option*	Indicates whether condensed print is wanted; + for *yes,* ! for *no.*
-l *number*	Sets the page length to the *number* of lines. The page length includes the top and bottom margins of the paper; if a zero is specified, the output is treated as if it were one continuous page.
-L *option*	Indicates whether lines wider than the page width should be wrapped to a new line or truncated; + for wrapping, - for truncation.
-m *text*	Specifies that the message *text* is to be printed on the console before the job starts printing. The print job does not proceed until the message is acknowledged at the console.
-M *file*	Specifies that the message text to be printed on the console before the job starts printing should be retrieved from the indicated *file.* The print job does not proceed until the message is acknowledged at the console.
-n	Indicates that the user is to be notified when the job finishes printing. If another user id was specified with the -D flag, that user, also, will be notified.
-N *number*	Indicates the number of copies to be printer. The default is one.
-O *value*	Indicates the type of input paper feeding: 1 for manual, 2 for continuous forms, and 3 for sheet feed.
-p *number*	Sets the pitch to *number* characters per inch. Typically, this is either 10 or 12. The pitch is also affected by the setting of the -K and the -W flags.
-P *queue[:queuedevice]*	Specifies the print queue to which the output should be directed. Optionally, a specific device serving the queue can be named. If this flag is not used, and the PRINTER environment variable is set, qprt uses this PRINTER as the default printer unless the LPDEST variable is set, in which case LPDEST is used as the default printer. If neither variable is set, the system default printer is used.
-q *value*	Specifies the print quality: 0 for fast, 1 for draft, 2 for near letter, and 3 for enhanced.
-Q *value*	Specifies a paper size for the print job. This value is printer-dependent. Consult the printer manual for the correct values.
-r	Indicates that the print file should be deleted after it is printed.
-R *priority*	Specifies the priority of the print job. Higher values indicate higher priority, the default is 15, the maximum for a regular user is 20, and 30 for the root user and members of the system group.

TABLE 8.2 qprt **Flags (Continued)**

Flag	Meaning
-s *style*	Specifies a type style name. The values for *style* are printer-dependent. Consult the printer manual for supported type styles.
-S *option*	Indicates whether high-speed printing should be used; + for *yes,* ! for *no.*
-t *number*	Indicates the number of lines to be left blank to form the top margin.
-T *text*	Specifies that the print job title is the text variable. If not specified, the name of the first file in the command is used.
-u *value*	Indicates the paper source; 1 for primary, 2 for alternate, and 3 for envelopes.
-U *option*	Specifies whether unidirectional printing is required: + for *yes,* ! for *no.*
-v *number*	Sets the line density to the number of lines per inch specified by the *number* variable.
-V *option*	Specifies whether vertical printing is wanted: + for *yes,* ! for *no.*
-w *width*	Sets the page width to the indicated number of *width* characters.
-W *option*	Indicates whether double-wide characters are wanted: + for *yes,* ! for *no.*
-x	Indicates how automatic line feed and carriage return are to be handled: 0 no automatic line feed or carriage return, 1 a line feed should be added to every carriage return, and 2 a carriage return should be added to every line feed and vertical tab.
-X *page*	Specifies the code page name. The code page in the user's locale definition is the default.
-y *option*	Indicates whether double-strike printing is wanted: + for *yes,* ! for *no.*
-Y *option*	Specifies whether the print output should be duplexed: 0 *no,* 1 duplex (must be switched manually), 2 duplex-tumble (automatic) option.
-z *option*	Rotates the page output the number of quarter-page turns as specified by *option:* these values are 0 for portrait, 1 for landscape right, 2 for upside-down portrait, and 3 for landscape left.
-Z *option*	Indicates whether a form-feed command should be sent to the printer after each print file: + for *yes,* ! for *no.*

provide only basic functionality. Others are more modern (the q series) and allow greater flexibility in controlling the applicable facility.

8.2.1   enable—Bring a printer on-line

The enable command takes as its argument the name of the printer which is to be brought on-line. The command syntax is

```
enable printer_name
```

Once the printer has been started, jobs waiting in the printer's queue begin printing.

8.2.2 `disable`—Take a printer off-line

When used without the -c flag, the `disable` command stops a printer after all of the current jobs in the queue have finished printing. When the -c flag is used, the printer stops immediately. The syntax of this command is

```
disable [-c] printer_name
```

8.2.3 `cancel`—Remove a job from a print queue

The `cancel` command allows the user to delete a specific print job or all print jobs queued to a printer by the user.

When the argument to the `cancel` command is a print job number, only that job is cancelled; if it is currently printing, it is flushed. If the argument is a printer name, all of the jobs queued to that printer by the user are flushed. The syntax of the command is

```
cancel printer_name | job_number
```

8.2.4 `lprm`—Remove a job from a print queue

The `lprm` command is very similar to the `cancel` command as it removes entries from the print queue just as `cancel` does. However, `lprm` is more flexible in that it allows a user with appropriate permission to delete the entries of another user. The syntax of the command is

```
lprm [-P printer] [jobnumber] [user] [-]
```

To remove a queue member from a specific printer's queue, the user must include the -P flag. To remove a specific job, the jobnumber variable must be specified. All of the entries for a user can be deleted by entering the user's name as the last parameter of the command line without a job number. Additionally, users can delete all of their own entries in a queue by using the minus (-) as the last parameter on the command line.

8.2.5 `qcan`—Remove a job from a print queue

The `qcan` command also allows a user to cancel a specific job or all of the jobs in a designated queue. The root user and members of the print group (printq) may kill any job on the system with the flag -x.

A user may cancel a specific job number by using the -x *job_number* flag where job_number specifies a queued job owned by the user. User may cancel all of their jobs in a particular printer queue by using the -P flag; for example

```
qcan -P laser_jet
```

cancels all of the user's jobs queued to the laser_jet printer queue. Alternatively, the user cancels only those jobs directed to a specific printer in the queue with the syntax

```
qcan -P queue:device
```

8.2.6   lpq—Display the status of a print queue

The lpq command is used to view the status of a print queue. When used with no flags, the command displays information about all of the jobs in the default queue. For each job in the queue, lpq displays

User's name

Job rank (priority)

Job name

Job number

Number of copies

Specific queue device (if applicable)

Job status (running, held, etc.)

Size

Percent printed (if in running status)

If remote print queues are defined, the command also displays information on them; execution time of the lpq command in this environment is significantly longer than in a local environment.

The syntax of the command is

```
lpq [+number] [-l] [-P printer] [jobnumber] [user]
```

To view the queue of a specific printer, the user must include the -P flag. To view information about a specific job, the jobnumber variable must be specified. Information about the specific user can be requested by entering the user's name as the last parameter of the command line.

Long output format is requested with the -l flag. This contains more detail than the normal one-line-per-job display. By using the +number flag the command may be executed continuously until the queue empties. The number variable indicates the number of seconds to wait before refreshing the queue display.

A sample use of the lpq command would be to continuously display the job queue of printer lp3, updating the display every 30 seconds is

```
lpq +30 -P lp3
```

8.2.7 lpstat—Display print queue status

When used with no flags, the lpstat command displays information about all of the print queues on the system, including any remote ones that have been defined. Flags are used to limit the amount and type of information displayed. The -a, -c, -o, -p, -u, and -v flags can be used with a list of item names. The list must be in one of two forms: a comma-delimited group or a quoted group with the individual members inside the quotes delimited by either a space or a comma.

The -a and -c flags both display status and job information on a queue basis. The -p flag is used to display information on a printer basis. The -o flag is used to display the status of a list of print jobs and/or print queues; both types of items (job numbers and queue names) may be intermixed in the list.

The -d flag is used to display information about the system default printer queue. The -r flag is used to request a regular status display for every queue in the system, while the -s flag is used to display a short status, and the -t flag is used to request a long status display of every queue.

The status of print jobs by user can be requested with the -u flag.

And finally, the -v flag generates a list of printer names.

So, to display the status of all print queues on the system, the user enters

```
lpstat
```

or for a full information listing

```
lpstat -t
```

To view the output of certain users, a list of names is passed with the -u flag

```
lpstat -u"frank,gina,swati,paula"
```

This displays only information about jobs that the four specified users had submitted.

8.2.8 qchk—Display print queue status

Print queue status can be displayed with the lpstat or qchk command; the qchk command requires, however, that at least one of its flags be used whenever the command is invoked. To display the status of all of the queues on the system, use the -A flag. To display information about the system default printer queue, use the -q flag. A specific job number can be looked up with the -# flag, the jobs on a particular printer with the -P flag, and the jobs of an individual with the -u flag.

The -L flag requests that a long status (which consists of several lines for each queue entry) be displayed.

Like the lpq command, a continuously refreshed queue display can be requested with the -w flag. The number of seconds to wait before refreshing the display is entered after the -w flag

```
qchk -A -w 30
```

This command displays information about all queues on the system, updating the display every 30 seconds, until all of the queues become empty, at which point the command terminates.

8.2.9   qpri—Change the priority of a print job

The root user and members of the print group (printq) can change the priority of a submitted print job with the qpri command. The syntax of the command is

```
qpri # jobnumber -a priority
```

where *jobnumber* is the job number to be changed and *priority* is the new priority.

8.2.10   lptest—Generate a test pattern for a printer

The lptest command generates a ripple test pattern which is useful in testing output devices. The ripple test pattern generates every printable character in every character position on a line. As there are 96 printable ASCII characters, a full test takes 96 lines to complete.

The lptest command allows the user to specify the line width (the default is 79) and number of lines to be generated (the default is 200). To specify the number of lines, the user must specify the line width. To test four times a 132-character line printer named line_printer, the command is

```
lptest 132 384 | qprt -P line_printer
```

8.2.11   qadm—Control the print queueing system

Members of the print group (printq) and the root user perform system administration functions for the print spooling system with qadm. System administration functions include

Starting and stopping printers

Starting and stopping queues

Starting and stopping the print queueing subsystem

Cancelling jobs

Printers and queues are stopped with the -D or the -K flag. For both flags, the operand is the name of the printer or queue to be stopped. The current job printing, if any, is allowed to complete when the -D flag is used; the current job is flushed when the -K flag is used.

A printer (and its queue) is started with the -U flag. The name of the queue and the printer to be started must be specified as the argument.

All the jobs in a queue can be cancelled at once with the -x flag. The operand is the name of the queue to be cleaned out.

The entire print subsystem can be brought down with the -G flag. All jobs currently processing are allowed to complete. Therefore, to terminate all spooling, the print administrator enters

```
qadm -G
```

To stop a queue named laser_jet after the current job(s) finish printing, the command is

```
qadm -D laser_jet
```

To stop the laser_jet queue printer lp02 immediately, the user enters the command

```
qadm -K laser_jet:lp02
```

To restart the printer, the administrator enters

```
qadm -U laser_jet:lp02
```

8.3 Print Queue Administrator Functions

The commands in this section are concerned with defining, changing, and deleting printers, queues, and the print queueing system as a whole. The process of defining a printer consists of four steps

Defining the physical device

Defining the queue

Defining the physical devices using the queue

Defining the virtual printers for the physical devices

8.3.1 Defining the physical printers

As discussed in Chapter 6, the cfgmgr command is used to add, configure, and make available devices on the system. By making use of the device configuration database, it can, in most cases, automatically add new devices to the system without any external intervention.

Because it always runs during the system boot process, a new device can be added to the system and automatically configured the next time the system is powered up. If a new printer is added to the system after the initial boot is complete, cfgmgr can be invoked to configure the new printer.

If cfgmgr is not able to add a device to the system or adds it incorrectly, the mkdev command (Chapter 10) must be used instead. If the device is not available when the mkdev command is issued, the chdev command (Chapter 10) must be used to bring it up when it becomes available.

8.3.2 mkque—Define a print queue

A print queue is defined with the mkque command. Successful definition of a queue results in an entry in the system queue information file (/etc/qconfig) for the added queue. In addition, the qdaemon is informed of the change; therefore, the queue can be used immediately.

When defining a queue, the major decision is what the name of the queue will be. It is indicated with the -q flag. Attributes of the queue are specified with the -a flag; each attribute is enclosed in quotes and specified with a separate instance of the flag. The valid attributes for a queue are

Acctfile	Defines the accounting file name (default, no accounting)
Discipline	Defines the job selection mechanism
fcfs	For first-come, first-served (default)
sjn	For shortest job next
up	Status of the queue after system startup, either *TRUE* (default) or *FALSE*
feed	Indicates whether feed pages are to be sent to the printer when it becomes idle, doing so makes tearing continuous form paper easier; values are
never	The default, which suppresses the function
1-9	A numeric value which indicates the number of pages to feed
host	Is set to the name of the remote host if this is a remote print queue definition
rq	Is set to the name of the print queue on the remote host where output is to be directed if this is a remote print queue definition

To set up a queue named laser_jet using shortest job next queueing,[1] the command is

```
mkque -q laser_jet -a 'discipline = sjn'
```

To set up a remote print queue, use the mkprtsv command.

A print queue can be made the default system queue by using the -D flag. This adds the new entry to the /etc/qconfig file at the beginning; the first queue named in this file is the system default queue (Fig. 8.2).

8.3.3 mkquedev—Associate a physical device with a queue

Physical printer devices are associated with a print queue through the mkquedev command. The device to be added to the queue is indicated with the -d flag. The queue to which it is associated is indicated with the -q flag, and, as with the mkque command, the attributes of the device are specified with the -a flag; each attribute is enclosed in quotes and specified with a separate instance of the flag. The most common attribute sets for a device are

---

[1]Before defining a remote print queue, the mkprtsv command must be issued.

```
* @(#)33  1.4  com/cmd/que/qconfig.sh, bos, bos320 8/20/90
10:26:02
* PRINTER QUEUEING SYSTEM CONFIGURATION
*
* EXAMPLE of local print queue configuration
laser_jet:
        discipline - sjn
        up - TRUE
        device - lp2

lp2:
        backend - /usr/lpd/piobe
        file - TRUE
        align - false
        header - group

Chicago:
        device - lp1
        up - TRUE
        pserver - Chicago1
        host - Chicago1
        s_statfilter - /usr/lpd/aixshort
        l_statfilter - /usr/lpd/aixlong
        rq - external

lp1:
        backend - /usr/lpd/rembak
```

Figure 8.2   /etc/qconfig file.

align	Should a form feed be sent before starting a job (the default is *TRUE*)
header	Should a header be printed before a job; values are
	Never (the default)
	Always
	Group (only at the beginning when printing multifile jobs)
trailer	Should a trailer be printed after a job; values are
	Never (the default)
	Always
	Group (only at the end when printing multifile jobs)
file	Should the file be copied to the spool area by default (the default value is *FALSE*); setting the value to *TRUE* ensures that the output will not be affected by modifications to the file after it was queued
case	Should lowercase characters be translated to uppercase; either *no* (the default) or *yes*
line	Sets the number of lines per page; the default is 66

A mandatory attribute for all devices is backend =. This is used to define the backend processor for the printer. Unless there is some overriding reason to change the value,[2] this attribute is always set to backend = /usr/lib/lpd/piobe.

------

[2] Such as the manufacturer supplying a special backend for the device.

To add the printer lp2 to the laser_jet queue, the print administrator enters

```
mkquedev -d lp2 -q laser_jet -a 'backend = \
/usr/lib/lpd/piobe' -a 'align=FALSE' -a'file=TRUE' -\
a'header=group'
```

It is the administrator's preference that all output queued for spooling to this device be placed into the spooling area, instead of printing directly from the queued file. In addition, because this is a laser jet-type printer, the align value is set to FALSE. Header pages print on this printer only at the beginning of the job.

8.3.4 `mkvirprt`—Define a virtual printer

For every physical printer at least one virtual printer must be defined. The virtual printer definition defines the data stream(s) a physical device supports. Printers that support only one type of data stream, need only one virtual printer definition. Printers that support multiple data streams must have a virtual printer defined for each data stream type.

The name of the queue device[3] with which the virtual printer is to be associated is defined with the -d flag. The queue with which the virtual print is associated is indicated by the -q flag; the name of the physical device is indicated by the -n flag. The type of data stream this virtual printer interprets is defined by the -s flag. The types of data streams are

asc	Extended ASCII
ps	PostScript
pcl	HP PCL
630	Diablo 630
855	TI 855
gl	HPGL
kji	Kanji

Finally, the type of physical printer must be indicated with the -t flag.[4]

To define a virtual printer for an HP LaserJet 2 physical printer, the print administrator enters

```
mkvirprt -d lp2 -n lp2 -q laser_jet -s pcl -t hplj2
```

8.3.5 `mkprtsv`—Configure remote printing services

If an AIX system is connected to other AIX or UNIX-based systems via a TCP/IP network, remote printing services can be used. An AIX system may

---

[3]Unless explicitly changed in the /etc/qconfig file this is the same as the physical device name.

[4]The types of printers supported on the system, and their code names, can be viewed with the `lsdev -P -c printer | pg` command.

be defined as either a print client of another system, as a host for other systems, or both. When the mkprtsv command is used to configure a client system, it performs the required mkque and mkquedev commands for the remote print queue; when used to define a server, it also calls the ruser command to define the remote users, and startsrc to start the lpd and qdaemon daemons.

8.3.5.1 Configure a client print server. When configuring client information, the -c flag must be used. The following information must be supplied to configure the client print queue:

The name of the local queue from where remote requests are transmitted

The name of the remote server

The name by which the local system refers to the remote printer

The queue information is supplied to the command with the -q flag. The name of the remote server and the printer name are supplied as attributes to flag -a. The attributes of flag -a are for defining the print queue

acctfile	Defines the accounting file name (default, no accounting)	
argname	Specifies the logical printer name for the local users	
discipline	Defines the job selection mechanism	
	fcfs	For first-come, first-served (default)
	sjn	For shortest job next
up	Status of the queue after system startup, either *TRUE* (default) or *FALSE*	
host	The name of the remote host	
rq	The name of the remote queue on which the jobs are printed	
s_statfilter	Used to name the filter used for sending short status requests to the host, supplied filters include	
	/usr/lpd/aixshort	For AIX v3 systems
	/usr/lpd/bsdshort	For bsd hosts
	/usr/lpd/attshort	For System V.3 hosts
	/usr/lpd/aixv2short	For AIX v2 hosts
l_statfilter	Used to name the filter used for long status requests, supplied filters include	
	/usr/lpd/aixlong	(for AIX v3 systems)
	/usr/lpd/bsdlong	(for bsd hosts)
	/usr/lpd/attlong	(for System V.3 hosts)
	/usr/lpd/aixv2long	(for AIX v2 hosts)

The attributes of flag -b are for defining the print device

align	Should a form feed be sent before starting a job (the default is *TRUE*)
header	Should a header be printed before a job; values are
	Never (the default)
	Always
	Group (only at the beginning when printing multifile jobs)
trailer	Should a trailer be printed after a job; values are
	Never (the default)

Always

Group (only at the end when printing multifile jobs)

`feed`   Indicates whether feed pages are to be sent to the printer when it becomes idle, doing so makes tearing continuous form paper easier; values are

Never   The default, which suppresses the function

1-9   A numeric value which indicates the number of pages to feed

A mandatory attribute specified with flag -b is `backend` =. This is used to define the backend processor for the printer. For client-printer definitions, this attribute is always set to `backend` = /usr/lib/lpd/rembak.

If the -s flag is used, the client print server is started after it has been configured.

The command

```
mkprtsv -c -q Chicago -a 'pserver = Chicago1' -a '\
argname = Chicago_prt' -a 'host = Chicago1' -a 'rq = \
external' -b 'backend = /usr/lib/lpd/rembak'
```

sets up a remote print queue named Chicago. The logical printer associated with the remote host is named Chicago_prt; the remote host is named Chicago1. Since it is also an AIX system, the s_statfilter and l_statfilter attributes are not required.

8.3.5.2 Configure a server print server. When configuring the server side, the -s flag must be used. The following information must be supplied to configure the server print queue:

The name of the local queue from where remote requests are printed

The names of the remote hosts allowed to use this server

The printer associated with the print queue

The queue information is supplied to the command with the -q flag. The name of the remote hosts are supplied either as a list with the -h flag or in a file which is specified with the -H flag. The name of the printer associated with the queue is supplied by the -v flag.

The -a flag is used here, for the most part, as it was in the client definition, except that the pserver attribute is not valid for a server. The attributes of flag -b are the same as they were for defining the client, except that the mandatory attribute specified with flag -b (`backend` =) should be set to `backend` = /usr/lib/lpd/piobe.

And as before, if the -s flag is used, the server print server is started after it has been configured.

The command

```
mkprtsv -s -S -q remote -v lp2 -a'discipline = sjn' -b\
'backend = /usr/lib/lpd/piobe' -b 'header = group' -\
h'Pittsburgh1,NewYork1,NewYork2'
```

defines a server print queue named remote which services all remote requests from hosts Pittsburgh1, NewYork1, and NewYork2. Additional hosts can be set up in separate queues or added to this one with the chprtsv command.

8.3.6 lsallq—Display the names of all configured queues

The lsallq command displays the names of all configured queues. If the optional -c flag is used, the names of the queue devices within each queue are also displayed. For example

```
$ lsallq
default
laser_jet
Chicago
$
```

8.3.7 lsallqdev—Display the names of all printers in a queue

The lsallqdev command displays the names of all printers defined for a particular queue. The queue is identified with the -q flag. If the optional -c flag is used, the output is displayed in queuename:printername format. To list all of the devices in the laser_jet queue, use the command

```
lsallqdev -q laser_jet
```

8.3.8 lsque—Display queue configuration information

To display configuration information about a queue, use the lsque command. The queue to be displayed is identified by the -q flag. For example

```
$ lsque -q laser_jet
laser_jet:
     device = lp2
     discipline = sjn
     up = TRUE
$
```

8.3.9 lsquedev—Display configuration information for a queue device

The syntax of this command is

```
lsquedev -q queue_name -d printer_name
```

The output of the command is a display of the configuration information for the device

```
$ lsquedev -q laser_jet -d lp2
lp2:
     FILE = /dev/lp2
     BACKEND = /usr/lib/lpd/piobe
     align = FALSE
     header = group
```

```
                file = TRUE
        $
```

8.3.10   lsvirprt—Display the attributes of a virtual printer

The lsvirprt command is used to display the attribute values of a virtual printer. The syntax of the command is

```
    lsvirprt -q queue -d device [-a attribute]
```

The -q and -d flags are mandatory, the -a flag is optional, but if used must be the last flag on the command line. If it is not specified, all attributes of the virtual printer are displayed. If it is used, it limits the attribute display to only those attributes specified. The attributes for the default values of the qprt command can be specified by entering the applicable qprt flag; for example

```
    lsvirprt -d lp2 -q laser_jet -a w file
```

displays the default page width and the value of the file attribute for the lp2 printer in queue laser_ jet.

8.3.11   lsprtsv—Displays remote print server information

The lsprtsv command displays information on the client and server definitions for remote print services. The -c flag requests a display of the locally customized print server information, and the -p flag displays the predefined (or default) print server information. If the -h flag is used, the command displays a list of all the hosts which have access rights to the local server. A specific logical print queue can be displayed with the -q queue_name flag.
   Some examples of the commands usage include

```
    lsprtsrv -c -h
```

to display the list of hosts which can access the server,

```
    lsprtsrv -c -q Chicago
```

to display configuration information about the remote queue, Chicago.

8.3.12   chque—Change an attribute of a queue

Attributes of a queue may be changed with the chque command. The -q flag identifies the queue, and the -a attribute identifies the attribute to be changed. As an example, to change queue laser_ jet so that it uses first-come, first-served queueing instead of shortest-job-next, the print administrator enters

```
    chque -q laser_jet -a 'discipline=fcfs'
```

8.3.13 chquedev—Change an attribute of a queue device

As the chque command manipulated the queues, the chquedev command changes the devices in the queue. A queue name must be specified with the -q flag, and a device name must be specified with the -d flag. The attribute to be changed is indicated with the -a flag. To change the lp2 printer in the laser_jet queue to print trailers, the print administrator enters the command

```
chquedev -q laser_jet -d lp2 -a'trailer=group'
```

8.3.14 chvirprt—Change the attributes of a virtual printer

The chvirprt command is used to change the attribute values of a virtual printer. The syntax of the command is

```
chvirprt -q queue -d device [-a attribute]
```

All flags are mandatory, but the -a flag may be repeated. The attribute values for qprt command can be specified by using the applicable qprt flag; for example

```
chvirprt -d lp2 -q laser_jet -a w=80 -a'file=FALSE'
```

changes the default page width to 80 characters and sets the file attribute for the lp2 printer in queue laser_jet to false.

8.3.15 chprtsrv—Change the remote print server

Print server configuration changes are made with the chprtsrv command. When the mkprtsv command is used to change a client system, it disables the client spool queue, performs the required chque and chquedev commands, and reenables the client spool queue. When the command is used to change a server, it also calls the ruser command to change the remote users (if necessary), and runs the refresh command to restart the lpd and qdaemon daemons.

The default action when configuring either side is to delay implementing changes until the system is rebooted; this can be explicitly requested with the -d flag. To have changes go into effect immediately, the -i flag must be used.

As with the mkprtsv command, client configuration is indicated by the -c flag and server configuration by the -s flag. In addition, the other flags follow the same format as the mkque command: the affected queue is indicated with the -q flag, the name of the printer is supplied by the -v flag, the -a flag changes the attributes of the print queue, and the -b flag changes the attributes of the print device. Remote hosts may be included with h flags and excluded with x flags; as a list with the -x flag or in a file with the -x flag.

If the print administrator wants to change the remote queue definition to disable the Pittsburgh1 host and add the NewYork3 host, the command

```
chprtsv -s -i -q remote -v lp1 -x'Pittsburgh1' -\
h'NewYork3'
```

suffices. Because of the -i flag, the change takes effect immediately.

8.3.16   rmque—Delete a queue from the system

The rmque command deletes a printer queue from the system. The command syntax is

```
rmque -q queue_name
```

All of the devices in the queue must have been previously deleted with the rmquedev command before this command completes successfully.

8.3.17   rmquedev—Delete a queue device

Queue devices are deleted with the rmquedev command. All of the devices in a queue must be deleted before the queue can be deleted. The syntax of the command is

```
rmquedev -d device_name -q queue_name
```

8.3.18   rmvirprt—Remove a virtual printer

Virtual printers are removed from the system with the rmvirpt command. The syntax of the command is

```
rmvirprt -q queue_name -d device
```

8.3.19   rmprtsv—Remove a remote print server

The rmprtsv command removes part or all of a client or server print server. As with the other print server commands, the -c flag indicates client configuration; -s is used for the server side. When used to change a client system, the rmprtsv command issues the required rmque and rmquedev commands. When the command is used to change a server, it calls the stopsrc command first to disable the lpd and qdaemon daemons. After the rmque and rmquedev commands have been processed, the ruser command is called to remove remote users, if necessary.

8.3.20   Modifying the burst page

The header and trailer burst pages may be modified to support local considerations. The templates for the burst pages are found in the /usr/lib/lpd/pio/burst directory. The format of the file name is *X.yyy* where *X* is either H for the header page or *T* for the trailer page. The last characters indicates the type of data stream, such as ASCII or ps for PostScript, etc.

The variables available to the user are

%D	User to whom output is to be delivered
%H	Name of the machine printing the job
%P	Time the job was printed
%Q	Time the job was queued
%S	User who submitted the job
%T	Job title

Predefined labels for the variable fields can be displayed by using the applicable lowercase letter. In addition, the special label %e can be used to display the message

```
END OF OUTPUT FOR :
```

on the trailer page.

Users, Groups, and Security Considerations

One of the most difficult challenges facing a system administrator is to define a system such that it allows users the maximum amount of flexibility to perform their functions, yet keeps the system safe from unwanted access or modification.

Security measures take two forms, physical and logical. Physical security includes protecting the computer from unauthorized physical tampering, such as switching off the machine. Logical security restricts who may logon to the system and what they may access after they do.

In order to secure the system, the system administrator must properly define the system software, input, output, and storage devices. The administrator must define the user's access rights, and how they are identified or *authenticated*.

On AIX, there are four aspects in configuring system security. These are

Access control. Addresses the integrity, availability, and privacy of the data on the system

Identification and authentication. Determines how users are identified and how that identification is verified

Auditing. Recording and analyzing events that take place on the system

Trusted computing base. Enforces the defined security policies

9.1 Users

User administration primarily involves defining the user, the groups to which they belong, how they are authenticated, and what resource constraints are placed upon the user. Several files are involved in the user security definition process; these are outlined in Table 9.1.

TABLE 9.1   Files Associated with System Security

File name	Usage
/etc/group	The group information file.
/etc/passwd	The primary password information file; passwords are encrypted and stored in the /etc/security/passwd file.
/etc/passwd.dat	If hashed password files are used, the hashed password information file.
/etc/passwd.dir	If hashed password files are used, directory for the hashed password index.
/etc/passwd.pag	If hashed password files are used, the hashed password index.
/etc/security/.ids	Defines the standard and administrative user and group IDs.
/etc/security/audit/config	Defines the audit groups and events on the system.
/etc/security/environ	Defines environmental security information.
/etc/security/failedlogin	Contains information about every unsuccessful login.
/etc/security/groups	Defines the security attributes of groups.
/etc/security/limits	Defines system resource access limits.
/etc/security/login.cfg	Defines default values for password creation and the initial login screen.
/etc/security/passwd	Contains the encrypted user passwords; supplements /etc/passwd.
/etc/security/user	The user information file.
/usr/lib/security/mkuser.default	Defines the default system attributes used to create users by the mkuser command.
/var/adm/sulog	Indicates what users have used the su command to switch to another user id.

AIX predefines several users for specific purposes including

adm	Owns the accounting files
bin	Owns certain system executable files
daemon	Executes system server (daemon) processes
lpd	Owns the system printers
nobody	Used by NFS
operator	Has read access to the entire filesystem; assigned to users who must perform system functions but do not need root authority
root (the superuser)	Has unrestricted access to all system functions
sys	Owns certain system files
uucp	Owns the BNU tools and files

The first step in creating a new user is the mkuser command.

9.1.1 mkuser—Define a new user

New accounts on a system which does not use NIS are defined with the mkuser command.[1] The user name must be a unique string of eight characters or less. As AIX is case sensitive, the user names Frank, FRANK, and frank are considered unique identifiers. The user name may begin with any character except the minus sign (-), the plus sign (+), or the tilde (~); it may not contain a colon (:) or be the keywords ALL or default. It is recommended that the user id not be all uppercase alphabetic characters; AIX really does not like all uppercase user ids.

The minimum amount of information that must be specified is the new user's ID. If no attributes (Table 9.2) are explicitly defined, the mkuser command uses the default values found in the /etc/lib/security/mkuser.default file. To override the default information for a particular attribute, specify the attribute and the new value on the command line. For example, the command

```
mkuser hypotenu
```

creates a new user named hypotenu with default values for all attributes. To override the default remote login attribute, the administrator specifies the value for the rlogin attribute on the command line

```
mkuser rlogin=no hypotenu
```

The only flag with the mkuser command is the -a flag which is used to specify that the new user is an administrator.

The mkuser command does not create password information for the user. The administrator must use the passwd or pwdadm command to assign an initial password. Unless the attribute is auth1=NONE, the account is disabled until the initial password is assigned. Keep in mind that users are required to change this password when they first login to the system.

9.1.2 lsuser—Display user information

The system administrator uses the lsuser command to display information about users defined on the system. Either a specific user name, a comma-separated list of user names, or the keyword ALL may be used to indicate what user information is to be displayed.

Two format display options are available: -c for colon-delimited records (attributes separated by colons) or -f for stanza format (each attribute on a separate line). The colon-delimited format is more appropriate for passing to another command or shell script for parsing, whereas the stanza format is more appropriate for regular use as demonstrated

```
$ lsuser -c fgc
#name:id:pgrp:groups:home:shell:gecos
fgc:214:staff:sysadm,sysgen,staff:/home/fgc:/bin/ksh:Frank Cervone
$ lsuser -f fgc
fgc:
        id=214
```

---

[1]Defining and maintaining users in an NIS (network information service) environment is significantly different than local administration. See Sec. 11.8 for further information.

TABLE 9.2 `mkuser` Attributes

Attribute	Meaning
`admin=`	*yes* if the user is an administrator, *no* if the user is not (only the root user or an administrator can change the value of this attribute).
`admgroups=`	A comma-separated list of group names for which this user is an administrator.
`auditclasses=`	A comma-separated list of audit classes for which this user is audited. ALL indicates the user is audited for all classes.
`auth1=`	Defines the primary authentication method for this user. The value may be a list of comma-separated *Method;Name* pairs where *Method* is the name of an authentication method defined in the /etc/security/login.cfg file, and *Name* is the name of the user to be authenticated. If this field is not specified then the default value of *SYSTEM* is used which indicates that local password authentication is to be used. *NONE* indicates that no authentication is performed.
`auth2=`	Defines the secondary authentication method for this user. The values for auth2 are the same as for auth1 except that the default value for auth2 is *NONE*.
`core=`	The maximum size core dump this user can produce. The value is expressed as a number of 512-byte blocks.
`cpu=`	The maximum CPU time in seconds the user can use. There is no default limit.
`daemon=`	*yes* if the user may initiate programs with `cron` and use the system resource controller commands. *No* if the user may not initiate programs with `cron` nor use the system resource controller commands.
`data=`	The maximum size data segment the user's process can create. The value is expressed as a number of 512-byte blocks. The minimum value is 1272.
`expires=`	*MMDDhhmmyy* which indicates the expiration date of the account in the form: *MM* for month, *DD* for day, *hh* for hour, *mm* for minute, and *yy* for year. If the value is 0, the account does not expire.
`fsize=`	The maximum size file the user may create. The value is expressed as a number of 512-byte blocks. The minimum value is 8192.
`gecos=`	General, descriptive information about the user. This is a string with no embedded colons (:) or semicolons (;).
`groups=`	A comma-separated list of the groups to which the user belongs.
`home=`	The home directory of the user; this must be specified as a full path name.
`id=`	Specifies the user id number for this user. It is best, under most circumstances, to let AIX supply this attribute.
`login=`	*Yes* if the user can log directly into the system; *no* if the user cannot use the login command.
`pgrp=`	Names the principal group of the user.
`rlogin`	*yes* indicates the user can use the `rlogin` or `telnet` command; *no* disables `rlogin` and `telnet` for this user id.
`rss=`	The maximum amount of physical storage the process can allocate. The value is expressed as a number of 512-byte blocks.
`shell=`	The user's default shell. The default is the Korn shell (/usr/bin/ksh). A full path name must be specified.
`stack=`	The maximum size stack segment the user's processes can create. The value is expressed as a number of 512-byte blocks. The minimum allowed value is 49.

TABLE 9.2 `mkuser` **Attributes**

Attribute	Meaning
`su=`	Indicates whether another user can use the `su` command to switch to this account; either *yes* or *no*.
`sugroups=`	Is a comma-separated list of groups which can use the `su` command to switch to this user account. ALL is used to indicate all groups; an exclamation point (!) can be used in front of a group name to exclude that group.
`sysenv=`	A comma-separated list of the protected-environment (system-state) variables for the user.
`tpath=`	Indicates the trusted path status of the user
`always`	Indicates the user may only execute trusted processes.
`notsh`	The user cannot invoke the trusted shell on a trusted path.
`nosak`	The secure attention key is disabled for all processes run by the user.
`on`	The user has normal trusted path characteristics and can invoke a trusted path. This is the default value.
`ttys`	Defines a comma-delimited list of terminals from which this user may login. ALL indicates all terminals, and a terminal may be excluded in the list by coding an exclamation point (!) in front of the terminal name.
`umask`	Defines the permissions a file does *not* have when the user creates it; the value is a three-digit octal number as defined in the `chmod` command.
`usrenv`	A comma-separated list of the unprotected-environment (user-state) variables for the user.

```
        pgrp=staff
        groups=sysadm,sysgen,staff
        home=/home/fgc
        shell=/bin/ksh
        gecos=Frank Cervone
    $
```

The other flag is `-a` which is used to limit the output to a certain group of attributes. The valid attributes are outlined in Table 9.2.

For example, to display information only about the authentication methods for user hypotenu, the command is

```
lsuser -f -a auth1 auth2 hypotenu
```

9.1.3 `chuser`—Change user information

The attributes of a user can be changed with the `chuser` command. The attributes which may be changed are outlined in Table 9.2. The syntax of the command is

```
chuser attribute=value ... username
```

As an example, to add user hypotenu to the group printq in addition to the default group staff and to change the maximum amount of storage hypotenu could allocate to 8 Mbytes, the administrator issues the command

```
chuser groups=staff,printq rss=16384 hypotenu²
```

There are no flags with the chuser command.

9.1.4 rmuser—Remove a user account

User accounts can be deactivated by using the rmuser command. When the command is executed for a specific user, all attributes of the user are removed from the /usr/security/user file, which prevents further logons. The home directory and files owned by the user are not removed. A user is not completely removed from the system until the rmuser -p command is executed. This command deletes all user password and attribute information in the /etc/passwd and /etc/security/passwd files. The command syntax is

```
rmuser [-p] user_name
```

9.1.5 Securing the root user

As the root user id is common to all UNIX systems, it is a great security exposure. This is especially true given the all-encompassing power the account has. If this account is enabled, a computer hacker has already won half of the battle in gaining unauthorized access to a system; the only thing to be guessed at is root's password.

Several measures can be taken to protect the root account. However, before changing the root account make sure there is a way of recovering from an inadvertent error. Trashing the root account, and not having any way of recovering, leaves your system unusable.

That having been said, the most common security precaution is to disable remote logins to the root account. This is accomplished by changing the rlogin= attribute of the root user to no. This prevents anyone at a terminal not directly connected to computer from logging in to the user account. It does not prevent a remote user from using the su command to gain access to the root account.

An additional security measure is to completely disable logins to the root account. This is accomplished by changing both the rlogin= and login= attributes of the root user to no. When this has been done, the system always rejects logins with the root account, even if the correct password is supplied. In order to gain access to the root account, a user must first login with another valid user id and then use the su command to switch to the root account.

The final method of securing the root user is to change its identity. There is nothing magical about the user name root; the significance of the root user is that its user ID number is zero. Any user name can be defined with the user number zero; it inherently becomes a user with root authority. After a user name with an id=0 attribute has been defined, this account may be used

---

²Remember, storage allocation is defined as the number of 512-byte blocks that may be allocated: 16384 512-byte blocks = 8192 1K blocks = 8 Mbytes.

instead of the root account. The root account could then be deleted from the system.

9.1.6   who—Identify users logged on the system

The who command displays information about all of the users currently on the local system. At a minimum, the output of the command details the following information for each user: login name, terminal id, and the date and time of login. Normally, the /etc/utmp file[3] is used for determining who is logged onto the system; however, the /var/adm/wtmp file or the /etc/security/failedlogin files may also be used as input to the who command. Using /var/adm/wtmp as input creates a historical display of logins, logout, system startups and shut-downs; for example

```
$ who /var/adm/wtmp
Name         Line           Time            Hostname
root         pts/0      May 14 10:32     (cheese-wiz.acme.com)
mlb          pts/0      May 14 14:13     (slip50.acme.com)
mlb          pts/0      May 14 20:05     (cheese-wiz.acme.com)
mlb          pts/0      May 14 21:09     (cheese-wiz.acme.com)
mlb          pts/0      May 15 11:03     (local473.acme.com)
sd           pts/1      May 15 11:03     (local473.acme.com)
mlb          ftp67550   May 15 11:44     (local473.acme.com)
jmd          pts/2      May 15 12:22     (slip49.acme.com)
jmd          pts/3      May 15 12:24     (slip49.acme.com)
mlb          ftp40882   May 15 12:36     (local473.acme.com)
jmd          pts/5      May 15 12:37     (slip49.acme.com)
mlb          ftp47360   May 15 13:00     (local473.acme.com)
fgc          pts/0      May 15 13:10     (slip50.acme.com)
$
```

The /etc/security/failedlogin file can be used as input to view information on, as would be expected, failed logins.

There are several flags which can be used with the who command to influence the display of information (Table 9.3). A user can determine who is logged in at a terminal with either the who am i command or the who -m command

```
$ who -m
fgc          pts/0      May 15 13:10     (slip50.acme.com)
$ who am i
fgc          pts/0      May 15 13:10     (slip50.acme.com)
```

All active processes generated by init are displayed with the -p flag

```
$ who -p
srcmstr        .     Apr 12 19:32   old      1446    id=srcmstr
cron           .     Apr 12 19:32   old      4841    id=cron
uprintfd       .     Apr 12 19:32   old      3572    id=uprintf
browser        .     Apr 12 19:32   old     11770    id=browser
```

The status of all processes, current and expired, is displayed with the -a flag

---

[3]The logged-on users database.

TABLE 9.3 who Command Flags

Flag	Meaning
-a	All information; equivalent to using the -AbdHlprTtu flag string.
-b	The most recent system startup time and data information is displayed.
-d	All processes which have terminated without being regenerated by init are displayed. The exit and termination status are displayed for the processes.
-h	Help.
-i	The user name, terminal, login time, line activity, and process ID are displayed.
-l	All login processes are displayed.
-m	Information about the current terminal; equivalent to whoami or who am i
-p	All current active processes generated by init are listed.
-q	A brief listing of all users on the system is displayed.
-r	The current run-level of the process is displayed.
-s	Only the name, terminal, and time fields are displayed; this is the default.
-t	The last change to the system clock via the date command is displayed.
-u	Same as -i.
-w	Same as -T.
-A	All accounting entries in /etc/utmp are displayed.
-H	Prints a header line.
-T	Displays the status of the terminal line:
+	Writable by anyone.
-	Writable by root and the owner only.
?	Line error.

```
$ who -a
Name      ST Line        Time       Activity    PID
Hostname/Exit
          .    system boot Apr 12 19:31
          .    run-level 2 Apr 12 19:31            2    0    S
          .          .     Apr 12 19:32   old      1598 id=rc       term=0 exit=0
          .          .     Apr 12 19:32   old      1444 id=fbcheck  term=0 exit=0
srcmstr   +        .       Apr 12 19:32   old      1446 id=srcmstr
          .          .     Apr 12 19:32   old      3495 id=rcsna    term=0 exit=0
          .          .     Apr 12 19:32   old      3498 id=rctcpip  term=0 exit=0
          .          .     Apr 12 19:32   old      4807 id=rcnfs    term=0 exit=0
          .   + tty0       May 13 18:37   old      19144
          .          .     Apr 12 19:32   old      4840 id=piobe    term=0 exit=0
cron      +        .       Apr 12 19:32   old      4841 id=cron
          .          .     Apr 12 19:32   old      3306 id=qdaemon  term=0 exit=0
          .          .     Apr 12 19:32   old      3309 id=writesr  term=0 exit=0
uprintfd  +        .       Apr 12 19:32   old      3572 id = uprintf
          .          .     Apr 12 19:32   old      3317 id = rcncs  term=0 exit=0
          .          .     Apr 12 19:32   old      3319 id=infod    term=0 exit=0
          .          .     Apr 12 19:32   old      11512 id=lpd     term=0 exit=0
          .          .     Apr 12 19:32   old      11769 id=local   term=0 exit=1
browser   +        .       Apr 12 19:32   old      11770 id=browser
fgc       + pts/0          May 15 13:10    .       32561 (slip50.acme.com)
          .   pts/1        May 15 13:08   old      21385

                           .
                           .
                           .


          .   pts/32       Apr 28 16:35   old      13616 id=pts/32  term=0 exit=0
          .   pts/29       Apr 28 16:43   old      33185 id=pts/29  term=0 exit=1
          $
```

9.2   User Passwords

The default authentication method in AIX is by password verification. Every user is required to login to the system; generally, they are also required to supply a password. In addition to user passwords, groups may have passwords as well; this provides a second layer of protection.

Selecting good passwords is the single most important aspect in ensuring system security. The ideal password is hard to guess, yet easy for the user to remember and type. Bad choices for passwords include

Words found in a dictionary[4]

Names (or any part thereof) associated with the users, their extended family, and pets,

Significant numbers (i.e., telephone, social security, birthdate, current month)

Names or items associated with the user's organization

Based in any other way on attributes of the user

Of course, published password examples, good and bad, are always a bad choice.

Choosing a perfect password is impossible; however choosing a good password can be aided by following these suggestions

If a common word is used, misspell it (pitzaah)

Interleave words (your mama = ymoaumra)

Embed special characters (ymoa$umra)

Mix the case of alphabetic characters (yMoa$umRa)

As a password in AIX may only be eight characters long,[5] it is very important that good password choices be made. To help the user along, the system administrator can define guidelines for password creation in the /etc/security/login.cfg file. These guidelines are enforced whenever a new password is defined for a user or group. The guidelines defined apply to all users on the system; it is not possible to have different criteria for special groups or users.

There are six aspects to a password that may be controlled (Table 9.4). These are the minimum number of weeks that must pass before the password can be changed, the maximum number of weeks that may pass before the password can be changed, the minimum number of alphabetic characters in the password, the minimum number of nonalphabetic characters in the password, the maximum number of times a character may repeat, and the minimum number of characters which differ in the old and new passwords.

---

[4]In addition to the primary language, this would include any secondary languages. In Canada, this would mean French and English. In Holland, this would preclude Dutch, English, French, and German words.

[5]Any additional characters in a password are ignored.

TABLE 9.4 Password Restriction Values

Restriction value	Advised value	Default value	Maximum value
minage	1	0	52
maxage	8	0	52
minaplha	5	0	8
minother	2	0	(8-minalpha)
mindiff	3	0	8
maxrepeats	1	8	8

9.2.1 pwdadm—Set user passwords

The root user or a member of the security group can change or set the initial password of a user or group with the pwdadm command. The -q flag displays password status information for a specific user or group. The information displayed includes when the password was last changed and the password attributes. The password attributes, which can be changed with the -f flag are

NOCHECK   Which specifies that new passwords for this user have to follow the restrictions in the /etc/security/login.cfg file

ADMIN   Which specifies that password information for this user may be changed only by the root user

ADMCHG   Which, when set, forces users to change their password the next time they login

When the command is executed, the users are prompted for a password. If the password is correct, they are allowed to change the user's or group's password. The system automatically sets the ADMCHG attribute, so the users are required to change the password the next time they login.

Users should not change their own password with this command; use passwd instead.

To set user hypotenu's initial password, the security administrator enters

```
pwdadm hypotenu
```

The administrator is prompted to enter a verification password; if this is correct, then the user's initial password can be set. If the administrator queries the status of user hypotenu's password, the result looks like this

```
$ pwdadm -q hyptenu
hypotenu
     lastupdate=
     flags=ADMCHG
$
```

9.2.2 passwd—Change passwords

The passwd command allows regular users to change their or other user's passwords. When the command is invoked with a user name, the password for the indicated user is changed. When the command is invoked with no user name, the invoking user's password is changed.

If changing the password for another user, the passwd command first requires the user to enter the password to be changed. If the user password is not known, the root password works also. Only if a correct password is given is the user allowed to change the other user's password.

The passwd command has two flags. Both cause another program to be invoked after the passwd command has successfully completed: -f invokes the chfn command so the users can change their gecos information, and -s which invokes the chsh command so the users can change their default shell.

Most frequently, the passwd command is used to change the user's own password. This is performed by entering

```
passwd
```

The users are prompted for their old password. The users are then prompted for the new password, and asked to verify it.

A password can be set to null,[6] or no password, by pressing the enter key in response to the prompt for the new password.

9.2.3 mkpasswd—Create the hashed password file

The mkpasswd command is used to generate a hashed password file. Normally, when verifying password information, AIX searches the /etc/passwd and /etc/security/passwd files sequentially. The mkpasswd command generates an indexed list of user information which AIX can read directly; this improves the overall performance of the system. In most cases, the difference between the sequential and indexed searches is not noticeable unless there are more than 100 users defined on the system.

Generating the indexes can be a hassle. Whenever the passwd or pwdadm commands are run, the mkpasswd command also should be run because the hash tables are invalidated by the two aforementioned commands. The problem is that the two commands do not automatically invoke mkpasswd after they have completed processing. One solution is to create a cron table entry which runs the mkpasswd command at predetermined intervals. Another solution is to place a preprocessor shell around the passwd and pwdadm commands which would invoke mkpasswd when the commands are done.

In any case the syntax of the command is fixed as

```
mkpasswd /etc/passwd
```

The optional -v flag is used to display the name of each user as it is processed.

9.3 Groups

Groups may be defined for any purpose. AIX predefines several groups for specific purposes including

---

[6]This is possible only if the system configuration permits it. In any case, it is extremely unadvised to have a null password for any account.

daemon	Members of this group own various parts of the spooling directories (/var/spool).
printq	Print administrators belong to this group.
security	Security administrators belong to this group.
staff	The default user group.
system	Members of this group are allowed to use the su command to become the root user.[7]

The first step in creating a new group is the mkgroup command.

9.3.1 mkgroup—Define a new group

New groups on the system are defined with the mkgroup command. As with user name, the group name must be a unique string of eight characters or less. The group name may begin with any character except the minus sign (-), the plus sign (+), or the tilde (~); it may not contain a colon (:) or be the keywords ALL or default.

Two flags are used with the mkgroup command. The -a flag indicates that the new group is an administrative one. The -A flag indicates that the invoker of the command is the administrator of the new group.

To create a new group, db_admin with the creating user as the administrator, the user enters

```
mkgroup -A db_admin
```

To give the new group an initial password, a security administrator (or the root user) must use the passwd or pwdadm command.

9.3.2 lsgroup—Display group information

The lsgroup command displays information about groups defined on the system. Either a specific group name, a comma-separated list of group names, or the keyword ALL may be used to indicate what group information is to be displayed.

Two format display options are available: -c for colon-delimited records (attributes separated by colons) or -f for stanza format (each attribute on a separate line). The colon-delimited format is more appropriate for passing to another command or shell script for parsing, whereas the stanza format is more appropriate for regular use.

The other flag is -a which is used to limit the output display to a certain group of attributes. The valid group attributes are outlined in Table 9.5.

For example, display information about all of the users on the system the command is

```
lsgroup -f ALL
```

---

[7]If no user other than root belongs to this group, then all users may use su to root.

TABLE 9.5   Group Attributes

Attribute	Meaning
adms=	Indicates the users who can administer the group. This value is a comma-delimited list of names. If the value is left blank, when used with the chgroup command, the list of administrators is removed.
admin=	*no* if the root user and users in the security group can change the attributes of the group (this is the default); *yes* if only the root user can change the attributes of the group.
id=	The id number of the group. This value should never be changed with the chgroup command.
users=	Specifies the names of the users who are members of the group. A user cannot be removed from a group if the group is the user's primary group.

However, to find out who is a member of the group printq, the command is

```
lsgroup -f -a users printq
```

9.3.3 chgroup—Change group information

The attributes of a group are changed with the chgroup command. The attributes which may be changed are outlined in Table 9.5. The syntax of the command is

```
chgroup attribute=value ... group_name
```

As an example, to remove user hypotenu from the group printq which already includes users fgc, jpg, and bosun, the command is

```
chgroup users=fgc,jpg,bosun printq
```

although a simpler way is to use the chgrpmem command.

There are no flags with the chgroup command.

9.3.4 chgrpmem—Change the members of a group

A simpler way of changing the members of a group is to use the chgrpmem command. The syntax of the command allows an administrator to add or remove members from the group without having to specify each member's name in a list. A group may be changed only by its administrator, the security administrator, or the root user. A member is added to a group with the syntax

```
chgrpmem -m + user_name group_name
```

where user_name is the name of the user to be added to group_name.

A member may be deleted from a group only if the member does not use it as its primary group. The command syntax is

```
chgrpmem -m - user_name group_name
```

The entire set of members may be respecified with the syntax

```
chgrpmem -m = user_name_list group_name
```

The user_name_list must be a comma-delimited string consisting of the names of the members who will belong to the group.

The same actions may be performed upon the group administrator(s). In that case, the -m flag is replaced by the -a flag.

To return to the prior example, it would have been much simpler (and safer) to remove user hypotenu from the printq group with the command

```
chgrpmem -m - hypotenu printq
```

9.3.5 rmgroup—Remove a group definition

Group definitions are removed by the rmgroup command. The users in the group are not themselves deleted. A group cannot be removed until all users which use the group as their primary group have been moved to another primary group. The command syntax is

```
rmgroup group_name
```

9.4 Remote Hosts

Several commands rely on foreign host databases to determine what access to local resources is permitted and what access is denied. These databases control who may use ftp (file transfer protocol) facilities, remote print queueing facilities, and remote command execution. Remote printing and command execution privileges are granted to specific host machines not to individual users. Contrast this to file transfer protocol access which is granted to all users unless specifically prohibited.

The primary command for defining remote host information is the ruser command.

9.4.1 ruser—Manipulate the foreign hosts' database

The ruser command has two different syntactical formats depending on its uages. The more common form adds or deletes individual user or host information in the database. Because of the peculiarities of each form, each will be examined individually.

9.4.1.1 Restrict ftp account usage. The ftp database (/etc/ftpusers) is manipulated when the -f flag is used with the ruser command. On the local machine this database is used to restrict the accounts which may be used by remote ftp clients. The -a flag is used to add a user to the restricted list; the -d flag is used to remove a user from the restricted list.

At the very least, the root user account is typically added to this list, because the login restrictions defined by the mkuser command (the rlogin and login attributes) do not affect ftp access. The command to remove remote ftp access from the root user account is

```
ruser -a -f 'root'
```

9.4.1.2 Allow remote command execution.

Normally, whenever users want to execute a command on another machine, they must explicitly sign on to the new machine before performing the function they want to do. This can be inconvenient when users need to run only a single command on the other machine. To circumvent the need for certain users to explicitly sign on, the local host uses the /etc/hosts.equiv database to define "trusted" hosts. These trusted hosts are machines which are assumed to be adequately secured. Whenever a remote user connects to the local system with a rlogin, rsh, or rcp, the /etc/hosts.equiv file is checked to see if the remote host of the user is defined[8] If it is and there is an equivalent user id on the local system, the request for a password is suppressed and the user is connected.[9] It does not matter that the passwords for the user accounts on the machines are different; if these two conditions are met, the connection is made.

A remote host is added to the /etc/hosts.equiv database with the -r flag of the rusers command

```
ruser -a -r 'NewYork1'
```

which defines the host named NewYork1 to be a trusted host. Henceforth, all accounts of the NewYork1 and local system are considered equivalent. A remote host can be deleted with the -d flag

```
ruser -d -r 'NewYork1'
```

ends the host equivalence between NewYork1 and the local system.

9.4.1.3 Allow remote print commands.

The /etc/hosts.lpd command is functionally similar to the /etc/host.equiv database except that it is used for controlling access to print facilities. This allows a user to queue a print request to another machine without having to sign on to the other machine.

The local host uses the /etc/hosts.lpd database to define trusted print hosts. These trusted print hosts are machines from which print queue requests are accepted.

A remote print host is added to the /etc/hosts.lpd database with the -p flag of the rusers command

---

[8]If one of these commands is used and no /etc/hosts.equiv file exists, then account equivalence is checked (see Sec. 9.4.2).

[9]The only exception to this is the root account which cannot be made equivalent with this method.

```
ruser -a -p 'NewYork1'
```

which defines the host named NewYork1 to be a trusted print host. After execution of the command, print requests from NewYork1 are honored.

A remote host can be deleted with the -d flag

```
ruser -d -p 'NewYork1'
```

which ends the ability of users on NewYork1 to queue print requests to the local system.

9.4.1.4 Display information in a ruser database. The ruser command with the -s flag allows a user to display the information in any of the three ruser databases. The -P flag displays the /etc/hosts.lpd database, the -F flag displays the /etc/ftpusers database, and the -R displays the /etc/hosts.equiv database. The command

```
ruser -s -F
```

displays a list of all the accounts restricted from ftp access on the local system.

9.4.1.5 Delete all information in a ruser database

The ruser command with the -X flag deletes all of the information in one of the three ruser databases. The -P flag clears out the /etc/hosts.lpd database, the -F flag deletes the /etc/ftpusers database, and the -R removes the /etc/hosts.equiv database. The command

```
ruser -s -F
```

removes all of the accounts which had been previously restricted from using ftp on the local system.

9.4.2 .rhosts files

In most cases, host level equivalence is not necessarily appropriate or adequate. This may be because users have different account names on different hosts, users share accounts on some machines, or that host-level equivalence is too encompassing.

Account-level equivalence is set up by defining a .rhosts file in the home directory of the applicable account. The entries in the file are similar in format to those of the /etc/hosts.equiv file. Each line contains a host name and optionally a list of user names

```
hostname [username ...]
```

If a list of user names is supplied, then every user account on the named host can log into the account; otherwise, only a similarly named account from the host may login. For example, consider the following file for user fgc (/home/fgc/.rhosts):

```
NewYork1
NewYork2   dfk olf
Chicago2   dfk
NewYork1   djt
Pittsburgh      fgc djt
```

From host NewYork1 and host Pittsburgh, user fgc and djt could login, from host NewYork2 users dfk and olf could login, and only user dfk could login from Chicago2.

When remote access is attempted and a /etc/hosts.equiv file does not exist, then account-level equivalence is always attempted. This is also true for the root user. A password should *always* be required for access to the root account of the system, whatever it is actually called. Therefore, it is critical that a .rhosts file *never* exist in the root directory of the system.

9.5   System Integrity

There are several commands in AIX which are used to check and ensure the integrity of the operating system; these include

pwdck	Verification of password databases
usrck	Verification of user definitions
grpck	Verification of groups and their definitions
sysck	Verification of installed software products
tcbck	Verification of the trusted computing base (TCB)
chtcb	Modifies TCB definitions
watch	Observes actions of a program

9.5.1   User and group integrity checking

User integrity checks are performed with the usrck, pwdck and grpck commands. Although each works on a different aspect of a user definition, they all use the same flags. One of the following four flags must be used whenever any of these commands is invoked:

-n	Reports errors but does not fix them
-p	Fixes errors but does not report what actions have been taken
-y	Both reports on and fixes any errors detected
-t	Reports errors and allows the user to decide whether to fix the error or not

9.5.1.1 usrck—Check user definitions.   User definitions are verified with the usrck command. Either a single user (usrck *userid*), a group of users (usrck *userid1 userid2* ...), or all users (usrck ALL) can be checked with a single execution of the command. For example

```
$ usrck -n ALL
3001-611 User uucp has a nonexistent
         or nonexecutable login shell
$
```

Verification processing starts with a verification of the correctness of the user name—that it is unique and compositionally correct.[10] Each user name is then checked to ensure it is in the appropriate security files: /etc/passwd, /etc/security/user, /etc/security/limits, and /etc/security/passwd. Additionally, all groups in the /etc/group file are checked to ensure there is a definition in the /etc/security/group file. If -y flag is used, any user or group definition missing in one of the security files is created.

After this initial processing, each attribute of the user is checked as outlined in Table 9.6. For most of the attributes, error correction simply involves removing the offending attribute from the user definition. For others, however, the user account is disabled. To reactivate the account, the chuser command must be used to reset the expires attribute to a future date and time.[11]

After checking all user definitions, the usrck command also verifies the consistency of the password databases, except the contents, and advises the user to run mkpasswd if necessary.

If the usrck command finds any errors, the grpck and pwdck commands should be run.

9.5.1.2 grpck—Check group definitions. The grpck command verifies the correctness and consistency of group definitions. Either a single group (grpck *groupid*), a group of groups (grpck *groupid1 groupid2 ...*), or all groups (grpck ALL) can be checked with a single execution of the command.

Four attributes of the group are checked

name	That it is unique and compositionally correct. It may not have leading +, :, -, or ~ signs, embedded colons, nor be the keywords *default*, *, nor ALL.
groupID	That it is unique and consists only of decimal digits.
users	That the users listed exist
adms	That the group administrators defined exist.

Error correction is possible only for the users' and adms' attributes. This error correction consists of removing any invalid users from the attribute. Therefore, the command

```
grpck -y ALL
```

reports on all problems with group names, group IDs, users defined as members of the group, and the administrators of the group. It also removes from the group any users defined as members or administrators which do not actually exist.

---

[10]No leading +, :, -, or ~ signs; no embedded colons; not the keywords default, nor *, nor ALL.
[11]A root account is never disabled by the usrck command.

TABLE 9.6 usrck **Attribute Checks and Actions**

Attribute	Check and actions
admgroups	Verifies that all defined admgroups exist. If error correction was requested, nonexistent groups are removed from the admgroups attribute.
auditclasses	Checks that the user id defined for the indicated audit classes is in the /etc/security/audit/config file. If error correction was requested, nonexistent audit classes are removed from the attribute definition.
auth1	Verifies that the primary authentication method is valid (that is, either NONE, SYSTEM, or defined in /etc/security/login.cfg) and can be executed. If error correction was requested, the user account is disabled if the authentication method is invalid or not executable.
auth2	Verifies that the secondary authentication method is valid (NONE, SYSTEM, or defined in /etc/security/login.cfg) and can be executed. There is no error correction for this attribute.
core	Checks that the value is sensible. If not and error correction was requested, the value is set to 200 blocks, the minimum value.
cpu	Ensures that the maximum cpu time is sensible. If not and error correction was requested, the value is set to 120 seconds, which is the minimum.
data	Verifies that the maximum data segment size is a reasonable value. If not and error correction was requested, the value is set to 128 (64K) which is the minimum value allowed.
expires	Is not checked for validity.
fsize	Checks that the maximum file size is reasonable. If not and error correction was requested, the value is set to 200 blocks which is the minimum.
gecos	Is not checked.
home	Verifies that the home directory is accessible in at least read and search mode. If it is not and error correction was requested, the user account is disabled.
id	Verifies that the value is unique and consists only of decimal digits. If either test fails and error correction was requested, the user account is disabled.
login	Is not checked.
pgrp	Ensures that the primary group exists. If it does not and error correction was requested, the user account is disabled.
rlogin	Is not checked.
rss	Ensures that the value for real storage size is sensible. If not and error correction was requested, the value is set to 128 blocks (64K) which is the minimum value.
shell	Verifies that the user's shell exists and can be executed. If either test fails and error correction was requested, the user account is disabled.
stack	Ensures that the value for the user's stack segment is sensible. If not and error correction was requested, the value is set to 128 blocks (64K) which is the minimum value.
su	Is not checked.
sugroups	Verifies that all defined groups exist. If error correction was requested, nonexistent groups are removed from the sugroups attribute.
sysenv	Is not checked for validity.
tpath	Ensures the shell attribute is a trusted process if tpath=always. If the user's shell is not a trusted process when tpath=always and error correction was requested, the user account is disabled.
ttys	Checks for the existence of the defined ttys in the database. If error correction was requested, all undefined ttys are deleted from the ttys list.
usrenv	Is not checked.

As with the usrck command, grpck verifies the consistency of the password databases and advises the user to run mkpasswd if necessary.

9.5.1.3 pwdck—Check the password databases. pwdck verifies both the consistency and the contents of the password databases. As with usrck, either a single user (pwdck *userid*), a group of users (pwdck *userid1 userid2* ...), or all users (pwdck ALL) can be checked with a single execution of the command.

Within the /etc/passwd file, three checks are performed for each user. The first check is of the entry to ensure that it is a valid account, that it is readable and that it contains at least two colons (::). If error correction was requested, invalid entries are discarded. The second check is that the password field is an exclamation point (!). If error correction was requested, an entry other than an exclamation point is transferred to the password field of the /etc/security/passwd file, and the password field of the /etc/passwd file is replaced by an exclamation point. Finally, the user name is checked to ensure it is a unique string of eight bytes or less. Additionally, the user name must not have leading +, :, -, or ~ signs, embedded colons, or be the keywords *default*, *, or ALL.

After the /etc/passwd file is checked, the /etc/security/passwd file is processed. Each line of the file is checked for readability and that it is part of a valid stanza. If error correction was requested, lines not meeting these requirements are deleted. Then, for each valid user, the three attributes of each user in the /etc/security/password are checked.[12] Unless the user has the attribute flags=NOCHECK or the system does not require passwords,[13] the password attribute is the first checked. If passwords are required, the system verifies only that the password attribute is not blank; if it is blank and error correction has been requested, the password attribute is set to an asterisk (*)[14] and the lastupdate attribute is removed. If passwords are required and the lastupdate attribute is invalid, it is updated to the current time if error correction was requested. If an account is not required to have a password, the lastupdate attribute always is deleted if error correction was requested. Finally, the flags attribute is checked to ensure that only valid values are present. If error correction has been requested, all values other than ADMIN, ADMCHG, and NOCHECK are deleted.

The last file checked is the /etc/security/user file which is used to define how users are authenticated. Each user found in the /etc/passwd file is checked to ensure that a usable authentication stanza exists for the user in the /etc/security/file. When error correction is requested, stanzas are created or modified whenever an error is detected for a user—if no stanza exists for a user, it is created; if the auth1 attribute is not defined, it is set to SYSTEM; if the auth2 attribute is not defined, it is set to NONE.

Finally, pwdck verifies the consistency of the password databases which consist of ensuring that the /etc/passwd.dir and /etc/passwd.pag files are

---

[12]Entries which do not correspond to valid accounts are removed from the file.

[13]This is possible only if the minother and minalpha attributes in /etc/security/login.cfg are both set to zero.

[14]This action disables the account.

newer than the /etc/passwd and /etc/security/passwd files. If they are not, the user is advised to run mkpasswd.

The following demonstrates the results of a pwdck -n ALL on one system:

```
$ pwdck -n ALL
The user "markting" has an invalid lastupdate attribute.
The user "termpac" has an invalid lastupdate attribute.
$
```

The user should note that the /etc/passwd and /etc/security/passwd files are locked by pwdck during update processing. If these files are locked by another process when pwdck tries to access them, pwdck spins for a few minutes waiting for the lock to be released. If the lock is not released within this period of time, the pwdck command terminates.

9.5.2 Trusted computing base

The trusted computing base (TCB) is responsible for enforcing the security policies of the system. Although primarily thought of as a software mechanism, it also includes the hardware components of the system.

The software portion of the TCB consists of the kernel (as it exists on disk and the executing image in central storage), the system configuration files (such as /etc/security/login.cfg), and all programs which run with access rights or privileges that allow the program to alter the kernel or the system configuration files. This includes programs which run with root user privileges or sysadm group privilege, any program used exclusively by the root user or sysadm group, and any program that must be run by an administrator while on the trusted path. These programs are considered trusted for two reasons: they have been proven to do only what they are supposed to do (either by the vendor or the local site) and they run with root (i.e., unrestricted) access rights.

9.5.2.1 tcbck—Check the trusted computing base. The tcbck command is used to determine the status of the TCB. System integrity is in jeopardy when the programs and files of the TCB have incorrect values or attributes. The tcbck command audits the TCB files by comparing the information in the /etc/security/sysck.cfg file with the actual state of the files on the system.

Normally, the tcbck command should be used during system initialization to check the state of the trusted files. This can be done by adding the following command to the /etc/rc file:

```
tcbck -p ALL
```

The ALL parameter instructs the command to check all files in the /etc/security/sysck.cfg database to ensure that the files are correct and the -p flag instructs tcbck to fix any errors detected. When the tree parameter is used, every file in the root file system is checked to ensure that no system integrity exposures are lurking—this includes the following checks:

Programs that set uid to root, but are not listed in tcbck database

Files linked to a file in the tcbck database, but not listed themselves in the tcbck database

Files with the TCB attribute but not in the tcbck database

Device special files not in the tcbck database

Files owned by root but with the setuid attribute set

Executable files in the sysadm group with the setgid attribute

One of four flags must be used when the tcbck command is run in checking mode

-n	Reports errors but does not fix them
-p	Fixes errors but does not report what actions have been taken
-y	Both reports on and fixes any errors detected
-t	Reports errors and allows the user to decide whether to fix the error or not

Note that before using the tcbck command with error correction, ensure that all device files are entered in the /etc/security/sysck.cfg database. Failure to do so leads to an unusable system. This is because the tcbck command deletes any device files it finds that are not in the tcbck database. In addition, the following actions occur when error correction is requested:

The setuid bit is cleared for any file owned by root with the setuid bit on.

The setgid is set off for any file owned by sysadm with the setgid bit on.

The tcb bit is set off for all files with the tcb bit set on but not in the tcbck database

Any link to a file in the tcbck database that is not also described in the tcbck database is deleted

The tcbck command is also used to update attributes (Table 9.7) in the /etc/security/sysck.cfg file. This may be information about a specific file, a file system, or a class of files. With the -a flag, information is added or updated and with the -d flag, information is deleted. Global attributes of the database are modified by specifying the special identifier tcbck as the operand; for example, the command

```
tcbck -a tcbck checksum=/usr/audit/secure_check
```

changes the default checksum program to a user-written program name secure_check in the /usr/audit directory.

In other instances, the command is used to modify file definitions within the tcbck database

```
tcbck -d -f /usr/group/nirvana
```

TABLE 9.7 tcbck **Database Attributes**

Attribute	Meaning
	Attributes for Files, File Systems, Directories, and Classes
acl	The access control list for the file. If the value is blank, the attribute is removed. If no value is specified, a value is computed by the system.
class	The group of the file. This is a user-defined value. If the value is blank, the class attribute is removed.
checksum	The checksum value of the file. If no value is given, the value is computed by the sum -r command. If the value is blank, the checksum attribute is removed.
group	The file group. If no value is given, the system computes a value which may be a group ID or group name. If the value is blank, the attribute is removed.
links	The hard links to the file. If the value is blank, the link attributes are removed.
mode	The file mode. If the value is blank, the mode is removed. If no value is given, the system computes a value.
owner	The file owner. If no value is specified, the system computes a value which may be either a user name or user ID. If the value is blank, the owner attribute is removed.
program	The program which checks the file. If the value is blank, the system removes the attribute otherwise an absolute path name must be specified.
symlinks	The symbolic links to the file. If the value is blank, the attribute is removed.
size	The size of the file in bytes. If no value is given, the system computes a value. If a blank is specified, the attribute is removed.
source	The source of the file. If no value is given, the attribute is removed. If specified, the value must be an absolute path name.
type	The file type which must be one of the following: FILE, DIRECTORY, FIFO, BLK_DEV, CHAR_DEV, MPX_DEV
	Attributes for the Database Itself
checksum	Supplies the name of an alternate checksum method which replaces the default, /usr/bin/sum -r. If the value is blank, the alternate checksum method is removed.
setgids	A comma-separated list of additional administrative groups to be checked for setgid programs. If this value is blank, the attribute is removed.
setuids	A comma-separated list of additional users to be checked for setuid programs. If this value is blank, the attribute is removed.
treeck_novfs	A comma-separated list of file system to be excluded from the verification check of the installed file.
treeck novfs	A comma-separated list of file systems to be excluded from the verification check of the installed file system tree. If the value is blank, the attribute is removed.
treeck_nodir	A comma-separated list of directories to be excluded from the verification check. If the value is blank, the attribute is removed.

This command removes all information about the /usr/group/nirvana file from the `tcbck` database. Alternatively, a new trusted program (/usr/group/tool) is added to the database with the command[15]

```
tcbck -a /usr/group/tool size = 54635
```

This adds the program /usr/group/tool to the trusted computing base; the system always checks to ensure that the size is 54635 bytes.

When the `tcbck` command is used against a particular file, file system, or directory with a fix option, the system resets invalid attributes to their default value. In some cases, additional actions occur

checksum	When an error occurs, the file is disabled by clearing the file's access control list.
links	Any missing links are created.
program	The named program is invoked (an error message is printed if it does not exist).
size	When an error occurs, the file is disabled by clearing the file's access control list.
source	The source file is copied to the destination file.
symlinks	Any missing links are created.
type	When an error occurs, the file is disabled by clearing the file's access control list.

9.5.2.2 `chtcb`—Change the trusted computing base.   The `chtcb` command is used to inquire about and set the TCB attribute bit for specific files. There are three options of the `chtcb` command: `on`, `off`, and `query`. For instance, the command

```
chtcb off /usr/group/nirvana
```

turns the TCB bit off for the file /usr/group/nirvana. The command

```
chtcb on /usr/group/tool
```

sets the TCB bit on for file /usr/group/tool.

All files in the trusted computing base must have the TCB bit set on. Conversely, no files outside the trusted computing base should have the TCB bit set on.

9.5.2.3 `sysck`—Check the system inventory information.   In general, the `sysck` command is not used directly. It is called during software installation and updating to verify that the installation (or update) has proceeded correctly. As such, we will not discuss it any further. For further information consult the *AIX Version 3.2 Commands Reference,* vol. 4.

9.5.2.4 `watch`—Observe the execution of a program.   The `watch` command is used by the root user or a member of the audit group to observe the actions of

---

[15]The chtcb command should also be used for the file to set on the TCB attribute bit. See Sec. 9.5.2.2.

a program to determine whether or not it is trustworthy. The command executes the command specified as the argument and records all auditable events, or just specific events[16] if the -e flag is used. In addition to the main process, all child processes are also observed and recorded and the watch process does not terminate until all observed processes have terminated.

As an example, the command

```
watch -e FILE_open (who | pg)
```

displays on the terminal a list of all file-open events during the execution of the who command as it was piped into pg. Analysis of all events is performed with the command

```
watch (who | pg)
```

The output of the watch command can be directed to a specific file with the -o flag. It is more likely that the prior command was

```
watch -o watch.report (who | pg)
```

to allow analysis after the fact.

9.6 Access Control Lists

In addition to file access permissions, AIX has extended file permission capability via *access control lists* (ACLs). Access control lists allow more than one group or user to own a file or set of files without giving the access to all users of the system.

The display of an ACL follows a standard form. In this example, the file is /home/fgc/generic.profile

```
attributes:
base permissions
      owner(fgc):     rwx
      group(sysgen):  r-x
      others:     r--
extended permissions:
      enabled
      deny  rwx   g:genstaff
      permit     rwx   u:syscntrl, g:sysgen
      permit     r-x   g:sysadm
```

The first line (attributes) indicates any of the three special attributes the file or directory may have: SETUID, SETGID, or SVTX (the sticky bit is set). The second section (base permissions) describes the standard file permissions as set by chown or chmod. The most interesting part is the third section: extended permissions. The first line in this section indicates whether extended access

---

[16]See Sec. 9.8 auditing for a list of what events may be logged.

control list entries are used (enabled) or not (disabled). Every subsequent line is an *access control entry* (ACE) which describes a particular access control instance. The format of each line follows the format

```
operation access-types [[user-info] | [group-info]]
```

Three types of operation are supported

> *deny.* Which denies the specified types of access
>
> *permit.* Which allows the specified types of access
>
> *specify.* Which sets the access to the specified type

The access-types are the standard AIX file modes: r for read, w for write, and x for execute. Finally, the user and/or group to which the rule applies is indicated with a prefix with u:, indicating the user name, and g:, the group name. For each individual group or user, a separate ACL entry is created. When a user and group name or multiple group names are combined in a single ACL entry, the rule applies only to the users which satisfy the user and/or group name requirements.

When a file with an ACL is accessed, the base permissions and all of the applicable extended attributes which match the user and the user's group set[17] are combined in a union operation. The end result is such that if the access is permitted and not denied, it is granted; conflicts in access control statements are resolved in favor of restricting access.

Referring to the prior example, the base permissions allow user fgc full access, group sysgen read and execute access, and all others read access only. In the extended access control list, read and write access is extended to group sysadm, user syscntrl when part of the sysgen group is allowed full access to the file, and all members of the group genstaff are denied all access. Consider the case where user syscntrl has both groups genstaff and sysgen; what access would be permitted? The answer is: none. Because conflicts in ACL entries are always resolved in favor of the more restrictive access, the restrictive entry for group genstaff overrides the explicit permit for syscntrl with group sysgen.

The base permissions of a file with an extended access control list may be changed using the symbolic mode of chmod; however, the numeric mode should never be used as it automatically deletes *all* ACL entries for the file.

9.6.1   aclget—Display an access control list

The aclget command takes as its argument the name of the file for which the access control list is to be displayed. Under most cases, the output of the command is sent to standard output, but this can be overridden with the -o flag. Therefore, to store the ACL for file /home/fgc/example_file in the file /home/fgc/acl_skeleton, the command is

```
aclget -o /home/fgc/acl_skeleton /home/fgc/example_file
```

---

[17]The group set is the combination of all of the groups to which the user belongs.

A simple and quick way of copying an ACL definition from one file to another is to pipe the output of `aclget` into the `aclput` command.

9.6.2   `aclput`—Set the access control list for a file

The `aclput` command reads standard input and stores the information as the ACL for the file named in the command argument. A flag, `-i`, can be used to read the ACL entry statements from a file other than standard input, as in

```
aclput -i /home/fgc/acl_skeleton /home/fgc/new_file
```

which takes the /home/fgc/acl_skeleton ACL file and applies it to the /home/fgc/new_file file.

A more common use is to pipe the output of `aclget` into `aclput`, for example

```
aclget /home/fgc/example_file | aclput /home/fgc/new_file
```

This command takes the ACL of /home/fgc/example_file and copies it to the ACL of /home/fgc/new_file.

9.6.3   `acledit`—Edit an access control list

The `acledit` command is actually a combination of the `aclget` and `aclput` commands, interrupted by an intervening session with an editor. The editor is determined by the environment variable EDITOR.[18]

The current ACL for the file is retrieved and opened for editing by the EDITOR variable editor. Lines may be changed, added, or deleted as necessary. Remember, that if adding extended attributes for the first time, to change the ACE disabled entry to enabled. When finished editing, the user exits the editor in the normal fashion.[19] The user is then prompted as to whether the modified ACL should be applied or not. The user can abort the changes at this time by entering "*n*," otherwise, if no errors are detected, the new ACL is applied. If errors are detected, they are noted in the ACL and the user is placed back into the editing environment.

9.7   The Disk Quota System

The disk quota system is used to control the number and size of files that can be allocated by users or groups. A quota system is maintained for each journaled file system. There are three limits in the quota system

A user's or group's soft limit

A user's or group's hard limit

The quota grace period

---

[18]The EDITOR command must specify a complete path name.
[19]In `vi` this would be `:wq`, not `ZZ` or `:q!`

The soft limit defines the number of 1K blocks or files which serves as the "high-water" warning. The hard limit defines the absolute limits on allocation. The quota grace period allows the user to exceed the soft limit for a (usually) short period of time. During the grace period, users should reduce their allocation so that it falls below the constraints of the soft limit. If the quota period expires and the users have not reduced their allocation below the soft limit, the system uses the soft limit as the hard limit and refuses to allocate additional storage. This condition can be reset only by removing enough files to reduct usage below the soft limit.

User and group quotas are tracked in the quota.user and quota.group files. These files exist in the root directory of every file system using the disk quota system.

Generally, the disk quota system is implemented only when a system has limited disk space or advanced file control mechanisms are needed—in a university for example. For the most part, only those file systems which contain user home directories and files need disk quotas as users should not be permitted to create files in other directories. The major exception to this is the /tmp file system, which, because of its nature, should not have quotas.

9.7.1   Setting up the disk quota system

The initial setup of the disk quota system is a manual process. A user with root authority must edit the /etc/filesystems file to add the quota, userquota, and groupquota attributes.

User quotas are added by inserting the line

```
quota = userquota
```

A group quota is added with

```
quota = groupquota
```

Both can be added with

```
quota = userquota, groupquota
```

Under most circumstances, the disk quota files for a file system reside in its root directory. However, an alternate name may be specified. This is useful when a single user or group quota file is to apply systemwide. This attribute is changed with the userquota and groupquota attributes

```
userquota = /usr/quota.user
groupquota = /usr/quota.group
```

Given the following entry from the /etc/filesystems file for the /home file system:

```
/home
dev  = /dev/hd1
```

```
vfs   = jfs
log   = /dev/hd8
mount      = true
check      = true
options    = rw
```

The entry includes three more lines if the disk quota system is to be enabled for the file system, and alternate quota files are to be used

```
/home
dev  = /dev/hd1
vfs  = jfs
log  = /dev/hd8
mount      = true
check      = true
options    = rw
quota      = userquota, groupquota
userquota = /usr/quota.user
groupquota       = /usr/quota.group
```

Although user limits have yet to be defined, the following lines should be added to the end of the /etc/rc file to start up the disk quota system during system startup:

```
echo 'Enabling the Disk Quota System'
/usr/sbin/quotacheck -a -v >/dev/console
/usr/sbin/quotaon -a -v >/dev/console
```

The first command (quotacheck) checks the consistency of the quota files with actual disk usage. The second command (quotaon) starts the disk quota monitoring.

9.7.2   edquota—Defining user limits

The edquota command is used to create and edit user and group quotas. When the edquota command is invoked, the user quota information is processed and placed into a temporary file which is then edited by the user. As with the acledit command, an editor is invoked as determined by the environment variable EDITOR. For each user or group with a disk quota limit, six fields are displayed

Blocks in use	Number of 1K blocks used
Inodes in use	Number of files used
Block soft limit	Number of 1K blocks allowed during normal operations
Block hard limit	Absolute number of 1K blocks allowed
Inode soft limit	Number of files the user may have during normal operations
Inode hard limit	The absolute number of files the user may have

The limit fields are changed as appropriate to grant the user more or less of the applicable resource. Some special values for the limit fields include a hard limit of 1 which indicates that no allocations are permitted, and a soft limit of

1 with a hard limit of 0 which indicates that allocations are permitted only on a temporary basis.

Three primary flags are used with the `edquota` command

-u	To edit users
-g	To edit groups
-t	To change grace periods

To edit the quota of user fgc, the root user enters

```
edquota -u fgc
```

The root user then sees the six fields discussed. If this is the first time quotas are being established for user fgc, another user can be a prototype with the -p flag. For example

```
edquota -u -p proto_admin fgc
```

copies the quota values of user proto_admin to fgc. These values are then edited just as any other definition.

This prototype usage is also possible for groups

```
edquota -g -p sysadm sysgen
```

Again, the values of the prototype (sysadm) are copied to the group to be modified or defined (sysgen).

The -t is used to change the grace period for groups (with the -g flag) or users (with the -u flag). The default grace period is one week. The special value of one second indicates that no grace period is to be extended. To modify the grace period for groups, the root user enters

```
edquota -t -g
```

and to change the grace for users, they enter

```
edquota -t -u
```

9.7.3 `quotacheck`—Check file system quota consistency

The `quotacheck` command examines a file system (as specified in the command line) or all file systems with quotas in /etc/filesystems (if the -a flag is used) to verify that the quota files are in synchronization with actual usage. If inconsistencies are detected, the quota files are corrected, and when the -v flag is used, reported upon.

By default, both user and groups are checked, however, this can be limited to one or the other with the -u (user) or -g (group) flags.

```
quotacheck -u /home
```

checks only user quotas in the /home file system.

If this command is used on an active file system, false inconsistencies may be reported, therefore, it is normally used only on an inactive file system. The most common usage is at system startup time when all file systems are checked with the command

```
quotacheck -a
```

9.7.4   `quotaon`/ `quotaoff`—Enabling and disabling the disk quota system

Normally executed during system startup, the `quotaon` command enables the disk quota system for one file system if a specific file system name is given or all file systems if the -a flag is used. By default, both user and group quotas are enabled, however, this can be limited to one or the other with the -u (user) or -g (group) flags.

```
quotaon -u /home
```

only turns on user disk quotas in the /home file system.

The `quotaoff` command is used to disable disk quota checking. As with `quotaon`, by default both user and group quotas are disabled, however, this can be limited to one or the other with the -u (user) or -g (group) flags.

```
quotaoff -u /home
```

only turns off user disk quotas in the /home file system. If the -a flag is used, quota checking is disabled for all file systems.

With both commands, the -v flag is used to display messages regarding each file system affected by the command.

9.7.5   `quota`—Check user and group disk usage and quotas

Users may display their disk quotas by using the `quota` command. Regular users may also display the disk quotas of the groups they belong to by using the -g flag with the appropriate group name. The root user has the additional privilege of displaying any user's quotas with the -u flag. In all cases, two other flags may be used: -v to request verbose mode which displays information about all file systems regardless of whether the user owns files in them or not, and -q to request terse mode which displays information only on those file systems where a limit has been exceeded.

A typical user and group display appears similar to the following:

```
$ quota
User quotas for user fgc (uid 43) :
Filesystem      blocks      quota       limit       grace       files       quota       limit
/home           432         800         1000        287         384         512
$ quota -g staff
Group quotas for group staff (gid 4) :
Filesystem      blocks      quota       limit       grace       files       quota       limit
/home           5432        8000        10000       847         2048        3840
$
```

9.7.6 `repquota`—Display file system quotas

`repquota` prints a summary of disk usage and quotas on a file system basis. If the -a flag is used instead of a specific file system name, information on all file systems is displayed. Unless otherwise restricted with the -u (user) or -g (group) flags, information on both user and group quotas is displayed.

The syntax of this command is

```
repquota [-v] [-g | -u] [-a | filesystemname]
```

The -v flag prints a header line before the quota summary for each file system. An example of command usage is

```
$ repquota -u /u
      Block limits      File limits
User      used   soft   hard    grace    used   soft   hard    grace
root --   4320    0       0               829    0       0
bend --     32    16      50                7    0       0
fgc --     636    0       0                95    0       0
jdpo ++     65    16      80                10   5       10
spe +-      23    16      30                 4   5       10
tr4 -+      15    16      30                 8   5       10
$
```

The second column indicates whether the block limit has been exceeded (+-), the file limit has been exceeded (-+), or both have been exceeded (++).

9.8 Auditing

The auditing subsystem of AIX provides the facilities to record security information. It consists of three distinct components: event detection, information collection, and information processing.

Event detection is performed by both the kernel and trusted computing base programs. Auditable events are those occurrences which cause a change in the security state of the system and any attempted or actual violation of system access controls or security policies. Event detection can be performed on either a global level or on a per-process level.

All auditable events are reported to the system audit logger which is responsible for collecting the audit information. The system audit logger constructs the audit record which contains information about the audit event, the responsible user, and the time and status of the event. The system audit logger is also responsible for maintaining the system audit trail. The system audit trail can be written to two modes—BIN or STREAM. In BIN mode, records are written to alternating files which can then be processed at a later time; this method is the traditional journaling concept. STREAM mode writes the audit trail to an in-core buffer; it can be used in real-time. Both methods may be used simultaneously.

9.8.1 Audit system setup overview

Several steps are necessary to set up the auditing system. The first step is to determine which events will be audited. Table 9.8 lists all of the native AIX

TABLE 9.8 audit Events

```
auditpr:
* Kernel proc Events
*    fork()
     PROC_Create = printf "forked child process %d"

*    exit()
     PROC_Delete = printf "exited child process %d"

*    exec()
     PROC_Execute = printf "euid: %d egid: %d epriv: %d name %s"

*    setuidx()
     PROC_RealUID = printf "real uid: %d"
     PROC_AuditID = printf "login uid: %d"
     PROC_RealGID = printf "real gid: %d"

*    usrinfo()
     PROC_Environ = printf "buf: %s"

*    sigaction()
     PROC_SetSignal = printf ""

*    setrlimit()
     PROC_Limits = printf ""

*    nice()
     PROC_SetPri = printf "new priority: %d"

*    setpri()
     PROC_Setpri = printf "new priority: %d"

*    setpriv()
     PROC_Privilege = printf "cmd: %d privset %s"

* File System Events

*    open()
     FILE_Open = printf "flags: %d mode: %o fd: %d filename %s"

*    read()
     FILE_Read = printf "file descriptor = %d"

*    write()
     FILE_Write = printf "file descriptor = %d"

*    close()
     FILE_Close = printf "fd: %d"

*    link()
     FILE_Link = printf "linkname %s filename %s"

*    unlink()
     FILE_Unlink = printf "filename %s"

*    rename()
     FILE_Rename = printf "frompath %s topath: %s"

*    chown()
     FILE_Owner = printf "owner: %d group: %d tflag %d filename %s"

*    chmod()
     FILE_Mode = printf "mode: %o filename %s"
```

TABLE 9.8 audit **Events (*Continued*)**

```
*    chacl()
     FILE_Acl = printf "acl: %d"

*    chpriv()
     FILE_Privilege = printf "pcl: %d"

* SVIPC System Events

*    msgget()
     MSG_Create = printf "key: %d msqid: %d"

*    msgrcv()
     MSG_Read = printf "msqid: %d muid: %d mpid: %d"

*    msgsnd()
     MSG_Write = printf "msqid: %d"

*    msgctl()
     MSG_Delete = printf "msqid: %d"
     MSG_Owner = printf "msqid: %d owner: %d group %d"
     MSG_Mode = printf "msqid: %d mode: %o"

*    semget()
     SEM_Create = printf "key: %d semid: %d"

*    semop()
     SEM_Op = printf "semid: %d"

*    semctl()
     SEM_Delete = printf "semid: %d"
     SEM_Owner = printf "semid: %d owner: %d group %d"
     SEM_Mode = printf "semid: %d mode: %o"

*    shmget()
     SHM_Create = printf "key: %d shmid: %d"

*    shmat()
     SHM_Open = printf "shmid: %d"

*    shmctl()
     SHM_Close = printf "shmid: %d"
     SHM_Owner = printf "shmid: %d owner: %d group %d"
     SHM_Mode = printf "shmid: %d mode: %o"

* TCPIP User Level

     TCPIP_config = printf "%s %s %s %s %s"
     TCPIP_host_id = printf "%s %s %s %s"
     TCPIP_route = printf "%s %s %s %s %s"
     TCPIP_connect = printf "%s %s %s %s %s"
     TCPIP_data_out = printf "%s %s %s %s %s"
     TCPIP_data_in = printf "%s %s %s %s %s"
     TCPIP_access = printf "%s %s %s %s %s"
     TCPIP_set_time = printf "%s %s %s %s"

* TCPIP Kernel Level

     TCPIP_kconfig = /etc/ip_auditpr -e TCPIP_kconfig
     TCPIP_kroute = /etc/ip_auditpr -e TCPIP_kroute
     TCPIP_kconnect = /etc/ip_auditpr -e TCPIP_kconnect
     TCPIP_kdata_out = /etc/ip_auditpr -e TCPIP_kdata_out
     TCPIP_kdata_in = /etc/ip_auditpr -e TCPIP_kdata_in
     TCPIP_kcreate = /etc/ip_auditpr -e TCPIP_kcreate
```

TABLE 9.8 audit **Events** (*Continued*)

```
*  Commands

*     tsm
      USER_Login = printf "%s"

*     sysck
      SYSCK_Check = printf "%s"
      SYSCK_Update = printf "%s"
      SYSCK_Install = printf "%s"

*     usrck
      USER_Check = printf "%s"

*     logout
      USER_Logout = printf "%s"

*     chuser
      USER_Change = printf "%s %s"

*     rmuser
      USER_Remove = printf "%s"

*     mkuser
      USER_Create = printf "%s"

*     setgroups
      USER_SetGroups = printf "%s %s"

*     setsenv
      USER_SetEnv = printf "%s %s"

*     su
      USER_SU = printf "%s"

*     grpck
      GROUP_User = printf "grpck: removed user %s from %s in /etc/group"

*     grpck
      GROUP_Adms = printf "grpck: removed admin user %s from %s in /etc/security/group"

*     chgroup
      GROUP_Change = printf "%s %s"

*     mkgroup
      GROUP_Create = printf "%s"

*     rmgroup
      GROUP_Remove = printf "%s"

*     passwd
      PASSWORD_Change = printf "%s"

*     pwdadm
      PASSWORD_Flags = printf "%s"

*     pwdck
      PASSWORD_Check = printf "User = %s Error/Fix = %s Status = %s"
      PASSWORD_Ckerr = printf "User/File = %s Error = %s Status = %s"

*     startsrc
      SRC_Start = printf "%s"
```

TABLE 9.8 `audit` Events *(Continued)*

```
*    stopsrc
     SRC_Stop = printf "%s"

*    addssys
     SRC_Addssys = printf "%s"

*    chssys
     SRC_Chssys = printf "%s"

*    addserver
     SRC_Addserver = printf "%s"

*    chserver
     SRC_Chserver = printf "%s"

*    rmssys
     SRC_Delssys = printf "%s"

*    rmserver
     SRC_Delserver = printf "%s"

*    enq
     ENQUE_admin = printf "queue = %s device = %s request = %s to: %s op = %s"

*    qdaemon
     ENQUE_exec = printf "queue = %s request = %s host = %s file = %s to: %s op = %s"

*    sendmail
     SENDMAIL_Config = printf "%s"
     SENDMAIL_ToFile = printf "Mail from user %s to file %s"

*    at
     AT_JobAdd = printf "file name = %s User = %s time = %s"
     AT_JobRemove = printf "file name = %s User = %s"

*    cron
     CRON_JobRemove = printf "file name = %s User = %s time = %s"
     CRON_JobAdd = printf "file name = %s User = %s time = %s"

*    nvload
     NVRAM_Config = printf " %s"

*    cfgmgr
     DEV_Configure = printf " device %s"

*    chdev
     DEV_Change = printf " params = %s"

*    mkdev
     DEV_Create = printf "mode: %o dev: %d filename %s"
     DEV_Start = printf " %s "

*    installp
     INSTALLP_Inst = printf "Option Name: %s Level: %s Installation %s"
     INSTALLP_Exec = printf "Option Name: %s Level: %s Executed Program %s"

*    updatep
     UPDATEP_Name = printf " %s "

*    rmdev
     DEV_Stop = printf " device %s"
     DEV_UnConfigure = printf " device %s"
     DEV_Remove = printf " device %s"
```

TABLE 9.8 `audit` **Events** *(Continued)*

---

* `lchangelv, lextendlv, lreducelv`
  `LVM_ChangeLV = printf " %s "`

* `lchangepv`
  `LVM_ChangeVG = printf " %s "`

* `lcreatelv`
  `LVM_CreateLV = printf " %s "`

* `lcreatevg`
  `LVM_CreateVG = printf " %s "`

* `ldeletepv`
  `LVM_DeleteVG = printf " %s "`

* `rmlv`
  `LVM_DeleteLV = printf " %s "`

* `lvaryoffvg`
  `LVM_VaryoffVG = printf " %s "`

* `lvaryonvg`
  `LVM_VaryonVG = printf " %s "`

* `backup, restore`
  `BACKUP_Export = printf " %s "`
  `BACKUP_Priv = printf " %s "`
  `RESTORE_Import = printf " %s "`

* `shell`
  `USER_Shell = printf " %s "`

* `objects (files)`

* `/etc/security/environ`
  `S_ENVIRON_WRITE = printf "%s"`

* `/etc/group`
  `S_GROUP_WRITE = printf "%s"`

* `/etc/security/limits`
  `S_LIMITS_WRITE = printf "%s"`

* `/etc/security/login.cfg`
  `S_LOGIN_WRITE = printf "%s"`

* `/etc/security/passwd`
  `S_PASSWD_READ = printf "%s"`

* `/etc/security/passwd`
  `S_PASSWD_WRITE = printf "%s"`

* `/etc/security/user`
  `S_USER_WRITE = printf "%s"`

* `/etc/security/audit/config`
  `AUD_CONFIG_WR = printf "%s"`

* `mount()`
  `FS_Mount = printf "mount: object %s stub %s"`

* `umount()`
  `FS_Umount = printf "umount: object %s stub %s"`

---

audit events.[20] Once the specific audit events have been determined, they must be grouped into classes. These audit classes are defined in /etc/security/audit/config (Fig. 9.1) in the classes stanza. Typically, at least three audit classes are defined

---

[20]These are also described in the file /etc/security/audit/events. This file should be consulted as your system administrator may have changed the audit events.

```
start:
      binmode = on
      streammode = on

bin:
      trail = /audit/trail
      bin1 = /audit/bin1
      bin2 = /audit/bin2
      binsize = 10240
      cmds = /etc/security/audit/bincmds

stream:
      cmds = /etc/security/audit/streamcmds

classes:
      general =
USER_SU,PASSWORD_Change,FILE_Unlink,FILE_Link,FILE_Rename
      objects =
S_ENVIRON_WRITE,S_GROUP_WRITE,S_LIMITS_WRITE,S_LOGIN_WRITE,S
_PASSWD_READ,S_PASSWD_WRITE,S_USER_WRITE,AUD_CONFIG_WR
      SRC =
SRC_Start,SRC_Stop,SRC_Addssys,SRC_Chssys,SRC_Delssys,SRC_Ad
dserver,SRC_Chserver,SRC_Delserver
      kernel =
PROC_Create,PROC_Delete,PROC_Execute,PROC_RealUID,PROC_Audit
ID,PROC_RealGID,PROC_AuditState,PROC_AuditClass,PROC_Environ
,PROC_SetSignal,PROC_Limits,PROC_SetPri,PROC_Setpri,PROC_Pri
vilege
      files =
FILE_Open,FILE_Read,FILE_Write,FILE_Close,FILE_Link,FILE_Unl
ink,FILE_Rename,FILE_Owner,FILE_Mode,FILE_Acl,FILE_Privilege
,DEV_Create
      svipc =
MSG_Create,MSG_Read,MSG_Write,MSG_Delete,MSG_Owner,MSG_Mode,
SEM_Create,SEM_Op,SEM_Delete,SEM_Owner,SEM_Mode,SHM_Create,S
HM_Open,SHM_Close,SHM_Owner,SHM_Mode
      mail = SENDMAIL_Config, SENDMAIL_ToFile
      cron =
AT_JobAdd,AT_JobRemove,CRON_JobAdd,CRON_JobRemove
      tcpip =
TCPIP_config,TCPIP_host_id,TCPIP_route,TCPIP_connect,TCPIP_d
ata_out,TCPIP_data_in,TCPIP_access,TCPIP_set_time,TCPIP_kcon
fig,TCPIP_kroute,TCPIP_kconnect,TCPIP_kdata_out,TCPIP_kdata_
in,TCPIP_kcreate

users:
      root = general
```

Figure 9.1 An /etc/security/audit/config file.

```
/etc/security/environ:
    w = "S_ENVIRON_WRITE"

/etc/security/group:
    w = "S_GROUP_WRITE"

/etc/security/limits:
    w = "S_LIMITS_WRITE"

/etc/security/login.cfg:
    w = "S_LOGIN_WRITE"

/etc/security/passwd:
    r = "S_PASSWD_READ"
    w = "S_PASSWD_WRITE"

/etc/security/user:
    w = "S_USER_WRITE"

/etc/security/audit/config:
    w = "AUD_CONFIG_WR"
```

Figure 9.2 An /etc/security/audit/objects file.

general   Which includes USER_SU, PASSWORD_Change, FILE_Unlink,
            FILE_Link, and FILE_Rename

system   Which includes USER_Change, GROUP_Change, USER_Create,
            GROUP_Create

init   Which includes login, USER_Logout

The third step is to apply the audit classes to users or files. To define an audit class for a specific user, add a line to the users stanza of the /etc/security/audit/config file. To define an audit class for a file, add a stanza for the file to the /etc/security/audit/objects (Figure 9.2) file.

The fourth step involves configuring the type of data collection. For BIN collection, the start stanza in the /etc/security/audit/config file should be changed to binmode=on. Then the bin stanza of the /etc/security/audit/config file must be changed to initialize BIN collection which defines where the system audit trail is, what the two bin (or journaling) files are and their size, and where the backend commands are located.[21] Finally, the /etc/security/audit/bincmds file must be updated to include the commands that process the audit records. As a start, the following command is recommended:

```
/usr/sbin/auditcat -p -o $trail $bin
```

This command appends audit records to the system audit trail file and formats the records for later use by the auditpr command. The $trail and $bin variables are passed from the auditbin daemon; they denote the name of the system audit trail and the current bin (journal) file, respectively.

---

[21]Typically, the system audit trail and bin files are in their own file system or directory named /audit and the backend commands are in /usr/lib/security/audit/bincmds file.

For STREAM collection, the start stanza in the /etc/security/audit/config file should be changed to streammode=on. Then the stream in stanza of the /etc/security/audit/config file must be changed to initialize STREAM collection. Finally, the /etc/security/audit/streamcmds file must be updated to include the commands that process the audit records. As a start, the following sequence is recommended:

```
/usr/sbin/auditstream | /usr/sbin/auditpr -v \
>/dev/console
```

This command formats the records written to the audit stream and displays them on the system console.

After setting up one or both methods for recording information, the next step is to start the auditing subsystem.

9.8.2 audit—Control the state of the auditing subsystem

The audit command controls system auditing. The command

```
/usr/sbin/audit start
```

is usually issued during the auditing system startup in the /etc/rc file. The audit system configuration is read from the /etc/security/audit/config file. Auditing can also be started manually during regular system operation if it was not enabled at start up.

The audit shutdown command is used to disable the audit subsystem. It is typically used only in the event of a system emergency. All audit buffers and configuration information are flushed and audit files are closed after execution of this command. Generally, if auditing must be terminated for a period of time, the audit off command is used. This command suspends the auditing subsystem, instead of closing it. Auditing can be resumed with either the audit start or the audit on command.

A special option of audit on is panic. When used, the audit system ensures that BIN mode can be started. If BIN mode cannot be started, the system automatically shuts down.

The audit query command is used to display the current status of the audit subsystem.

9.8.3 auditcat—Write audit records to the audit trail

Primarily an internal command, auditcat is used to transfer the audit records from the bin files to the system audit trail. Its primary use in command mode is to recover from a error while writing records to the audit trail. The syntax of the command is

```
auditcat -o OutFile -r InFile
```

where *OutFile* represents the name of the system audit trail (or a temporary substitute) file and *InFile* represents the failing bin file.

9.8.4 `auditstream`—Write audit records to the audit channel

Another primarily internal command, `auditstream` is used to transfer the audit records from wraparound buffer to another command for processing. In most cases, the processing command is `auditpr`. The only flag used with `auditstream` is `-c` which limits the output to a particular type of audit class. For example, the following command might be used to write all authentication events to the system console:

```
auditstream -c authentication | auditpr -v >/dev/console &
```

9.8.5 `auditselect`—Filter audit records for analysis

The `auditselect` command is used in the backend processing of audit records. Records which match the selection criteria are written to standard output. Input records may come from standard input or a BIN or STREAM audit record file if a file name is given. If the `auditselect` command is used in the /usr/lib/security/audit/bincmds file, the $bin variable, as discussed, may be used to denote the input file. The selection criteria may be entered as a string with the `-e` flag or from a file with the `-f` flag.

Regardless of the method of input, a selection criteria expression consists of one or more terms joined by a logical operator. The valid logical operators for joining terms are

`&&`	And	The expression is true only when both sides of the expression are true.
`||`	Or	The expression is true if either side of the expression is true.
`!`	Not	The expression is true if the term is not true

Each term, in turn, consists of three parts: a field, a relational operator, and a value. There are nine fields

event	The name of the audit event.
command	The name of the command which caused the audit event.
result	The status of the audit event: valid values are OK, FAIL, FAIL_PRIV, FAIL_AUTH, FAIL_ACCESS, or FAIL_DAC. FAIL matches all FAIL_ codes.
login	The ID of the login user of the process that generated the event.
real	The ID of the real user of the process that generated the event.
pid	The process ID of the process that generated the event.
ppid	The process ID of the parent of the process that generated the event.
time	The time of day the audit event occurred.
date	The date of the audit event.

The valid relational operators are

`==`	Equal to
`!=`	Not equal to
`<`	less than

> greater than

>= greater than or equal to

<= less than or equal to

Note that the mathematical operators ($<$, $>$, <=, and >=) are not valid with the text fields.

A common, nonbackend use of the `auditselect` command is to route specific STREAM audit records to the console. A common usage is to display a message on the console whenever a login fails. This could be accomplished with the following command:

```
auditstream -c authentication | auditselect -e "event \
== User_Login && result == FAIL" | auditpr -m "A signon \
failed :" -v > /dev/console &
```

Another common use is to display a message whenever a user signs on or switches user ids

```
auditstream | auditselect -e 'event == USER_Login || \
event == USER_SU' | auditpr -m "New user :" -v > \
/dev/console &
```

Another use would be to log a message whenever the root user or a user with root authority logged on

```
auditstream | auditselect -e 'login == 0 || login = \
root' | auditpr -m "root has signed on :" -v > /dev/console \
&
```

9.8.6 `auditpr`—Print audit records

In prior examples, the `auditpr` command has been used extensively to print the selected audit records. The command can also be used to print the system audit trail

```
auditpr -v < /audit/trail
```

which prints all of the records in the system audit trail.

Up to this point, only two of the `auditprt` flags have been used: -m to display a message on the audit record header line, and -v to display the full audit record information. There are several other flags which can be used to make the output look much better.

The -t flag is used to display field header information and takes as its argument a numeric value: 0 to suppress titles, 1 to display a title once at the beginning of a series of records, and 2 to display the title before each record.

The -h flag is used to influence the order of field display. The subflags are

e   For the name of the audit event

l   For the user's login name

R   For audit status

t   For the time the record was written

c   For the command name

r   For the real user name

p   For the process ID

P   For the parent process ID

With the -h flag, the prior examples can be made more readable

```
auditpr -t1 -helrtc < /audit/trail
```

and

```
auditstream -c authentication | auditselect -e "event \
== User_Login && result == FAIL" | auditpr -m "A signon \
failed :" -t2 -hlt > /dev/console &
```

and

```
auditstream | auditselect -e 'event == USER_Login || \
event == USER_SU' | auditpr -m "New user :" -t2 -hltp \ >
/dev/console &
```

and

```
auditstream | auditselect -e 'login == 0 || login = \
root' | auditpr -m "root has signed on :" -t2 -hltrp > \
/dev/console &
```

The final flag of `auditprt` is -r which is used to suppress the translation of a user ID in an audit record into the corresponding user name.

9.8.7 `last`—Display information about logins

Although the `last` command is not related to the audit subsystem physically, it is related logically as it is used primarily as part of the auditing process.[22]

The `last` command displays, in reverse chronological order, all previous logins and logoffs still recorded in the /var/adm/wtmp file. The display can be limited to a specific number of records, a particular user, a particular terminal, or any combination of these. However, if both a user and terminal are given, the results are ORed, not ANDed; that is, the `last` command displays records meeting either criteria, not necessarily both. For example, the command

```
last fgc pts1
```

displays all login and logoff information for user fgc and the pseudo-tty[23] pts1. The special name `reboot` can be used to display information on the time between reboots of the system

```
last reboot
```

---

[22]last and lastlogin are actually part of the accounting subsystem, which must be activated for either of the commands to work.

[23]Pseudo-ttys are used by rlogin and telnet.

## Chapter 10

Hardware Management

Device management in AIX is, for the most part, fairly simple as the system configuration command (cfgmgr) runs during system startup to automatically add devices.

All of the types of devices, relationships between devices, and configuration information are contained in the *object data manager* (ODM) device configuration database. When AIX is installed, this database already has a large amount of predefined device configuration information.[1] The most a user must do, in the majority of cases, is to select the specific type of device for which the system should perform a configuration.

The device configuration database consists of two distinct parts: the predefined information for all possible[2] devices, and the customized database which contains configuration information about all of the defined devices.

As everything on an AIX system is really one type of file or another, it is not surprising to find that every device on the system is, from the perspective of AIX, a file. Devices are accessed and controlled through *special files* which act as a conduit to the device. The special files for every device on the system can be found in the /dev directory. If the file for the device cannot be found in the /dev directory, the device cannot be accessed.

Under most circumstances, devices are accessed by application programs through special device drivers which perform the basic housekeeping functions related to I/O, such as blocking. It is possible for a device to be accessed in *raw mode*. This special mode is in most cases used only by system utilities which read or write directly to and from the /dev file. In raw mode, the program is totally responsible for handling all I/O functions: blocking and deblocking, physical device control, and error correction.

---

[1]All IBM-supported devices are defined, and many third-party products also are included.
[2]At least from IBM's point-of-view.

AIX views the devices on the system in a hierarchical arrangement. Devices within a general device type perform the same function. Within the general device type, however, there are lower, finer differentiations in functionality, such as interfaces (RS-232 serial printers versus parallel printers) or modes of functionality (dot-matrix printers versus laser printers). These lower levels are referred to as *device subclasses*.

Each device on the system is in one of four states

Undefined	The device is unknown to the system.
Defined	The device has been defined, but it cannot currently be used by AIX.[3]
Available	The device has been defined and is available to the operating system.
Stopped	Used primarily with networking devices; the device is unavailable, but remains known to the system.

Each device on the system is identified by a location code. A location code consists of four fields depending on the type of device. The fields are

Drawer	The drawer within the main system unit in which the device controller is located.
Slot	The slot on the device controller where the device driver card is connected.
Connector	If used by the I/O adapter, the specific connection the device uses to communicate with the device driver card.[4]
Port	The specific port (or logical unit number for SCSI devices) for those device drivers which use them.

The values of the first two fields (drawer and slot) are encoded values. A value of 00 for the drawer field indicates that the adapter card is located in the CPU drawer or the main system unit depending on the architecture of the machine. Other values indicate that the card is located in an I/O expansion drawer. The first digit of the slot field indicates the I/O bus which contains the adapter card. This is 0 if the standard I/O bus is used and 1 if the optional I/O bus is used. The second digit indicates the actual slot used on the card.

10.1 General Device Configuration

In general, the configuration command mkdev is used only when cfgmgr cannot correctly determine the characteristics of the device which makes automatic definition impossible. The chdev and rmdev are used subsequent to the mkdev or cfgmgr commands to change the characteristics of a device or remove a device from the system, respectively.

---

[3]It may be disconnected, turned off, or possibly, incorrectly defined.
[4]The majority of device types do not use this field; therefore, it is usually 00.

10.1.1 `cfgmgr`—Automatically add and configure devices

The `cfgmgr` command is used to add, configure, and make available devices on the system. By making use of the device configuration database, it can, in most cases, automatically add new devices to the system without any external intervention.

The `cfgmgr` runs always during the system boot process. This is a two-phase process. The first phase configures all of the devices necessary for base initialization of the machine. The second phase is called after phase one completes successfully to configure the rest of the devices attached to the system.

If devices are added to the system after the initial boot is complete, the `cfgmgr` can be invoked again to configure the newly added devices. When invoked after initial boot processing, the `cfgmgr` performs only phase two processing. Therefore, to add a newly attached disk drive to the system, the user need only enter the command

```
cfgmgr -v
```

to do so. The `-v` flag is not necessary; it instructs `cfgmgr` to produce extended status messages on standard output.

If `cfgmgr` is not able to add a device to the system, the `mkdev` command must be used instead. If the device is not available when the `mkdev` command is issued, the `chdev` command must be used to bring the device up when it becomes available.

Although other flags are available with the `cfgmgr` command, they are used only during system startup. The most interesting of these are the `-f` flag which is used to reset the devices in the database and execute the phase one configuration process which senses the devices and adds them to the configuration database and the `-s` flag (the default after system startup) which is used to run only the phase two configuration. This phase senses only for new devices on the system; existing devices are not changed.

10.1.2 `mkdev`—Add a device to the system

When automatic configuration by the `cfgmgr` command does not work or is insufficient, the `mkdev` command can be used to make a device available. The `mkdev` command also may be used to bring a previously defined device on-line.

When defining a new device, the class (`-c class`), subclass (`-s subclass`), type (`-t type`), connection location (`-w connloc`), and parent adapter (`-p parentname`) flags are used to identify the device to AIX.

After successful definition, the device is made available to the system unless the `-d` or `-s` flag is used. The `-d` flag allows a device to be defined without varying it on-line, where the `-s` flag allows a device to be defined and put into the stopped state.[5]

---

[5]This flag can be used only with devices that support the stopped state.

The -l flag allows the user to define a name for the device if it supports user-defined names. If the flag is not specified or the device does not support user-defined names, AIX generates a system name for the device. When the mkdev command is used with only the -l flag, the mkdev command attempts to make the named device available; it is assumed that the device has already been defined. For example, the command

```
mkdev -l hdisk6
```

attempts to vary on the disk named hdisk6. If the disk is not defined, an error results.

Finally, the -a flag allows for the definition of device-specific attributes, such as the baud rate of a terminal device or the receive queue of an Ethernet card.

Normally, for those products which must be configured with mkdev, the product manufacturer supplies suggested values for the flag setting and the attributes.

10.1.3   chdev—Change the characteristics of a device or the operating system

On occasion, it is necessary to change the characteristics of a device after it has been defined. In these cases, the chdev command is used to perform the modifications.

Unlike the mkdev command, the -l flag is mandatory when usign the chdev command. The class, subclass, or type of a device may not be changed,[6] but the connection location (-w *connloc*) and parent adapter (-p *parentname*) of most devices may be changed. The -a flag is used to change device-specific attributes. The lsattr command (Sec. 10.1.6) is very useful in determining which attributes may be changed.

A very common use of chdev -a is to stop tape drives from retensioning every time a new tape is loaded

```
chdev -l rmt0 -a ret=no
```

Normally, after execution of the chdev command, the device is modified according to the new configuration information. Sometimes this is neither possible nor desirable, such as when the device is currently in use. The -P flag circumvents this problem by applying only the update information to the ODM database; the characteristics of the device do not actually change until the next time the system is restarted.

Additionally, the -T flag is used to implement a temporary change; that is, the device is changed but the change is not applied to the ODM database.

---

[6]In these cases, the device must be deleted and redefined.

TABLE 10.1   Changeable Operating System Attributes

Attribute	Meaning
autorestart	Indicates whether the system should automatically reboot after a system crash. The default value is false. To enable the function, specify true.
iostat	Indicates whether disk I/O history should be gathered. The default value is true. To suppress the function, specify false; note that a specification of false inhibits the functioning of the iostat command.
maxbuf	The maximum number of pages allowed in the block I/O buffer cache for block special files. As regular file system I/O is not processed in this buffer pool, the minimum, default, and recommended value is 20. The maximum value is 131072 if no real storage constraint exists.
maxmbuf	The maxmimum amount of real memory, in kbytes, allowed for allocation to mbufs (which are used for buffering network traffic). The default and minimum value is 2000; the maximum is 524288 if no real storage constraint exists.
maxpout	Indicates the high-water mark for pending write-behind I/Os per file. When this value is greater than zero, its value is used to limit the number of pending write-requests from a process. When a process reaches the maxpout value, it is suspended until the number of pending I/Os for the process goes below the value specified in the minpout attribute.
maxuproc	The maximum number of processes allowed per user. The minimum and default value is 40; the maximum is 131072. An increase takes effect immediately; a decrease only takes effect after a system reboot.
memscrub	Memory scrubbing corrects single-bit ECC errors. Although it executes in the background with the lowest priority, it is a load on the system, which, for the most part, is not necessary. The default value is false; to enable the function specify true.
minpout	Indicates the low-water mark for pending write-behind I/Os per file. The default value is 0. This attribute may be used only in conjunction with maxpout. It must be less than maxpout. This attribute specifies at what point a process suspended for exceeding the maxpout value may be restarted.
primary	Names the primary dump device.
secondary	Names the secondary dump device.

When the system is restarted the change is lost and operation reverts to normal.

Some characteristics of the operating system (Table 10.1) are modifiable through the chdev command. The operating system is known as device sys0 and can be changed like any other device. For example, to change the maximum number of processes per user from the default of 40 to 256, enter

```
chdev -l sys0 -a maxuproc=256
```

10.1.4   lsdev—Display the characteristics of a device or the operating system

The lsdev command is used to display information from both parts of the ODM database. General information about the configured devices on the system is displayed with the -c flag; detailed information is displayed with the lsattr command. Information on all possible devices which may be configured on the system is displayed with the -P flag. Subsets of information may be displayed with the -c *class*, -s *subclass*, -t *type*, -l *name*, and -S *state* flags as appropriate.

The following example displays information on all of the predefined tape devices on a system:

```
$ lsdev -P -c tape -H
class type      subclass description
tape  8mm       scsi     2.3 GB 8mm Tape Drive]
tape  9trk      scsi     1/2-inch 9-Track Tape Drive
tape  150mb     scsi     150 MB 1/4-Inch Tape Drive
tape  ost       scsi     Other SCSI Tape Drive
tape  1200mb-c  scsi     1.2 GB 1/4-Inch Tape Drive
tape  3490e     scsi     3490E Autoloading Tape Drive
tape  4mm2gb    scsi     2.0 GB 4mm Tape Drive
tape  4mm4gb    scsi     4.0 GB 4mm Tape Drive
tape  525mb     scsi     525 MB 1/4-Inch Tape Drive
tape  8mm5gb    scsi     5.0 GB 8mm Tape Drive
$
```

A display of the configured disk drives is requested with the command

```
lsdev -C -c disk
```

Information about the system is displayed with the command

```
lsdev -l sys0
```

Two additional flags may be used. The -H flag is used to display column header in the output display. The -r flag is used to display the range of values for a particular column over the specified set of devices. For example, the command

```
lsdev -P -r class
```

displays a list of all othe supported device classes. The command

```
lsdev -P -c tcpip -r subclass
```

lists the supported subclasses of the tcpip class.

10.1.5 lscfg—Display diagnostic information about devices

The lscfg command displays name, location, and descriptive information about every device found in the system. If the -l flag is used, the display is limited to the indicated device,[7] otherwise information on all devices is displayed. A user displays information about all tape drives with the command

---

[7]The device name may include wildcard characters.

```
lscfg -l rmt*
```

When the -v flag is used, *vital product data* (VPD)[8] is also displayed. The command

```
lscfg -v
```

displays VPD information about every device on the system, whereas

```
lscfg -v -l rmt*
```

limits the display to just tape drives.

10.1.6 lsattr—Display the attributes of a specific device

The various attributes and characteristics of devices on the system are displayed with the lsattr command. Four major subsets of display are available

-D	To display default values
-E	To display effective values
-R	To display the range of legal values
-F	Which allows for a user-defined format[9]

The various suboptions for each type are described in Table 10.2.

---

[8]This information includes the part number, serial number, and engineering change level of the device.
[9]This option, -F, will not be discussed in this text.

TABLE 10.2 lsattr Flags

Flag	Meaning
-a attribute	Restricts the information display to the specified attribute(s).
-c class	Indicates a specific type of device class. Valid only in conjunction with the -R or -D flag.
-D	Displays the attribute names, default values, field descriptions, and user-set values for a specific device.
-E	Displays the attribute names, current values, field descriptions, and user-set values of a specific device.
-f file	Reads the flags from the indicated file.
-H	Displays headers above each column of output.
-h	Displays command help.
-l device	Indicates the device for which attributes are to be displayed.
-R	Displays the legal values for an attribute name.
-s subclass	Indicates a specific type of device subclass. Valid only with the -R or -D flag.
-t type	Indicates a specific device type. Valid only in conjunction with the -R or -D flag.

The following example is a display of the attributes of tape drive rmt0 on one particular system:

```
$ lsattr -l rmt0 -E
mode           yes   Use DEVICE BUFFERS during writes True
block_size     1024  BLOCK size (0 = variable length) True
res_support    no    RESERVE/RELEASE support True
var_block_size 0     BLOCK SIZE for variable length support True
density_set_1  21    DENSITY setting #1 True
density_set_2  20    DENSITY setting #2 True
delay          150   Set delay after a FAILED command True
extfm          yes   Use EXTENDED file marks True
rwtimeout      250   Set timeout for the READ or WRITE command True
$
```

When the effective values for a device are displayed, they are obtained from the configuration database, not from the device itself.[10]

10.1.7   rmdev—Remove a device from the system

The cfgmgr command does not remove devices from the system. If a config-ured device cannot be found when the cfgmgr command is run, the device is left in the defined state. To physically remove a device from the configuration database, the rmdev command must be used.

As with the chdev command, the -l flag is mandatory since it names the device to be removed. If no other flag is used, the device is put into the defined state, that is, unconfigured, which makes it unavailable to the operat-ing system. When the -r flag is used, the device configuration information is also physically removed from the ODM database. Note the difference between the two commands

```
$ rmdev -l rmt4
rmt4 defined
$ rmdev -d -l rmt4
rmt4 deleted
$
```

Without the -r flag, the device can be brought back up by running the chdev command. With the -r flag, the device must be completely redefined and con-figured if it is to be used again.

Devices which support the stopped state can be brought to that state by using the -s flag. The best example of this is TCP/IP

```
$ rmdev -S -l inet0
inet0 stopped
$
```

---

[10]If the device has been reconfigured with the chdev command using the -P or -T flag, the infor-mation may not indicate the current device configuration.

10.2 Magnetic Tapes

Four commands are provided which specifically act upon tape drives or their media. These are

mt or tctl	To control a tape drive
tcopy	To copy one tape to another
tapechk	To verify the integrity of a tape cartridge

10.2.1 mt—Magnetic tape control

The mt command is provided primarily as a migration aid from bsd-type UNIX systems. For tape control functions, the tctl command (Sec. 10.2.2) provides greater functionality.

The format of the mt command is

```
mt [-f drive] subcommand [count]
```

The drive parameter indicates the device upon which the indicated action takes place. This may be either the block device or raw device, i.e., /dev/mt0 or /dev/rmt0. If a particular drive is not specified, the action takes place on the default system drive, which is typically /dev/rmt0.

The subcommand parameter is one of the following actions:

eof	Write an *end-of-file* (EOF) marker at the current position of the tape. If *count* is specified, the indicated number of EOFs are written.
fsf	Move the tape forward by one file. If *count* is specified, the tape is moved forward the indicated number of files.[11]
bsf	Move the tape backward by one file. If *count* is specified, the tape is moved backward the indicated number of files or until the beginning of the tape is reached, whichever occurs first.
fsr	Move the tape forward by one record. If *count* is specified, the tape is moved forward the indicated number of records.
bsr	Move the tape backward by one record. If *count* is specified, the tape is moved backward the indicated number of records or until the beginning of the tape is reached, whichever occurs first.
rewind	Rewind the tape drive.
status	Provide a status display concerning the affected tape drive.
weof	Equivalent to eof.

As an example, to rewind a tape on mt0, the user enters

```
mt -f /dev/mt0 rewind
```

---

[11]Be aware that if this command is used on a 9-track open reel tape, it is possible to fsf past the end of the reel magnetic marker and run the tape off the reel.

10.2.2 `tctl`—Magnetic tape control

The `tctl` command is a superset of the `mt` command. In addition to providing tape positioning commands, the `tctl` command also provides a method of reading or writing data to a tape.

10.2.2.1 `tctl` Positioning commands. The syntax for the positioning commands is

```
tctl -f drive subcommand [count]
```

The drive parameter indicates the device upon which the indicated action takes place. This must be the raw device name, i.e., /dev/rmt0. If a drive is not specified, the value in the TAPE environment variable is used. If this environment variable does not exist, the /dev/rmt0.1 device is used.

The subcommand parameter is one of the following actions:

eof	Write an end-of-file (EOF) marker at the current position of the tape. If *count* is specified, the indicated number of EOFs are written.
fsf	Move the tape forward by one file. If *count* is specified, the tape is moved forward the indicated number of files.[12]
bsf	Move the tape backward by one file. If *count* is specified, the tape is moved backward the indicated number of files or until the beginning of the tape is reached, whichever occurs first.
fsr	Move the tape forward by one record. If *count* is specified, the tape is moved forward the indicated number of records.
bsr	Move the tape backward by one record. If *count* is specified, the tape is moved backward the indicated number of records or until the beginning of the tape is reached, whichever occurs first.
rewind	Rewind the tape drive.
offline	Rewind the tape and take the device offline.
erase	Erase the contents of the tape and rewind it.
retension	Rewind the tape, forward space to the end, and then rewind the tape again.
status	Provide a status display concerning the affected tape drive.
weof	Same as eof.

Note the similarity and differences with the prior example for the `mt` command when rewinding a tape on mt0

```
tctl -f /dev/rmt0 rewind
```

Retensioning the tape is performed with the command

```
tctl -f /dev/rmt0 retension
```

10.2.2.2 `tctl` Input/Output commands. The syntax of the `tctl` command involves five additional flags and two different commands—read and write.

---

[12]See footnote 11.

As before, the -f *device* specifies the name of the device upon which the action is to be taken. This must be the raw device name, i.e., /dev/rmt0. If a drive is not specified, the value in the TAPE environment variable is used. If this environment variable does not exist, the /dev/rmt0.1 device is used.

The -b *blocksize* flag is used to specify a fixed block size to use on the output media. To create a variable-blocked tape, the -n flag is used instead. If neither is used, the default block size of the tape drive is used.

By default, a 32768-byte area is used to buffer the transfer of data to and from the device. For fixed-length blocks, the default buffer is sufficient. It may, however, be expanded or contracted by using the -p *buffersize* flag. This is particularly useful for limiting the maximum physical block size of a variable-blocked tape since the maximum size of a variable-length block is the same as the size of the buffer.

When reading a variable-length tape, it is recommended that the -B flag be used. This causes the buffers to be flushed after every physical read.

The final additional flag is -v which sets verbose mode. Every read or write is logged to standard error when this flag is used.

When used for input or output, the tctl command is always part of a pipe, reading data from standard input when used for writing, and writing data to standard output when used for reading. A common example is the case where a user desires to transfer a file to tape for long term storage

```
cat inputtext | tctl -f /dev/rmt0 -b 1024 write
```

This example takes the standard output of the cat command and transfers it to the standard input of tctl which then writes fixed-blocks of 1024 bytes to the output tape.

This file is restored at a later date with the command

```
tctl -f /dev/rmt0 -b 1024 read > inputtext.restored
```

10.2.3 tcopy—Copy a tape to another tape

The tcopy command provides a data-independent means of copying the contents of one tape to another. This command facilitates the transfer of information from one format to another, for example, 8 mm to 9-track. The only restriction is an assumption that the data on the input tape is terminated by two successive tape marks; therefore, the copy operation terminates when two successive tape marks are found on the input tape or the input tape hits the physical end of the media.[13]

The syntax of the command is

```
tcopy source [destination]
```

---

[13]Which could result in the case of nine-tracks, in the input tape running off the reel.

The source and destination names are the names of the raw tape devices. Therefore, to copy a tape in /dev/rmt0 to the tape in /dev/rmt4, the command is

```
tcopy /dev/rmt0 /dev/rmt4
```

If a destination drive is not supplied, the `tcopy` command prints information about the tape: the size of the records and the files.

10.2.4 `tapechk`—Perform consistency checking on a streaming tape device

Consistency checking of tape media can be performed with the `tapechk` command. On tape devices which support it, the `tapechk` command determines if a tape is good by ensuring that the *cyclical redundancy checks* (CRC) are correct.

The `tapechk` command rewinds the tape before each check that it performs. The first parameter to the command tells `tapechk` how many files to check, the second parameter specifies the number of files to skip before beginning the check. When no parameters are given, only the first physical block of the tape is checked.

Like the `tctl` command, `tapechk` uses the device indicated by the TAPE environment variable. If none has been specified, the default is /dev/rmt0.

The `tapechk` command was primarily designed to check tapes created by the `backup` command. An important consideration is that the `backup` command can archive files either individually or as an entire file system. This data, however, is written to the device as a continuous stream, regardless of the number of files specified. These streams are a single file as far as `tapechk` is concerned.

As an example, to check the fourth thorough seventh files on a tape, starting at the fourth file, the command is

```
tapechk 4 3
```

since it checks four files but skips over the first three.

10.2.5 Tape drive special names

In addition to raw and standard device names, AIX tape device names may be appended with a suffix to indicate special processing or density settings. The default settings for a tape drive are assumed to be tape rewound (but not retensioned) and that high-density tape. This can be changed with the suffixes. Using the device /dev/rmt0 as an example, the following list outlines the functions of the suffixes:

/dev/rmt0	Rewind, no retension, high density,
/dev/rmt0.1	No rewind, no retension, high density
/dev/rmt0.2	Rewind, retension, high density
/dev/rmt0.3	No rewind, retension, high density

/dev/rmt0.4	Rewind, no retension, low density
/dev/rmt0.5	No rewind, no retension, low density
/dev/rmt0.6	Rewind, retension, low density, and /dev/rmt0.7 no rewind, retension, low density

10.3 Terminal Control

There are a number of different commands used to control and configure terminals for use with AIX. The most common and frequently used of these is stty.

10.3.1 stty—Set characteristics of a terminal

The stty command sets, resets, and reports on the characteristics of a terminal (Table 10.3). There are actually two types of stty command. The default is the POSIX standard which is what this discussion covers. The other is the bsd version which is provided solely for back-level bsd compatibility. Since use of this is not recommended, it is not discussed in this book.

The syntax of the command is

```
stty [-a | -g] options
```

The flag -a displays, on standard output, the current state of all options in a (relatively) readable format. The -g flag is used to write the options to standard output in a format which can then be used as input to another stty command.

In general, the system is set up such that the user does not need to resort to stty to set most of the control options for a terminal. Primarily, stty is used to map or remap keys which are not defined for the terminal-type being used. A very common use is to set the backspace key to the erase key

```
stty ^H erase
```

indicating that when control-H (indicated by the ^H) is received, it is processed as if it were the erase key.

When a terminal has "gone berserk," the configuration can be reset with the command sequence

```
Control-J stty sane Control-J
```

The Control-J key is used both before and after the command, instead of the Enter key, because AIX can usually recognize the Control-J key even when the Enter key is unavailable.

10.3.2 tset—Initialize a terminal

The tset command (Table 10.4) is used to set the characteristics of a terminal based upon predefined terminal types. The command performs any terminal-dependent processing necessary to correctly initialize the terminal.

TABLE 10.3 `stty` Options

Option	Counter-option	Effect
Control Modes		
clocal	-clocal	Assumes the line is without (with) modem control.
cread	-cread	Enables (disables) the receiver.
cstopb	-cstopb	Two 1 stop bit characters cs5 cs6 cs7 cs8 byte size - 5, 6, 7, or 8 bits
hup	-hup	Hangs up (does not hang up) when connection is closed
hupcl	-hupcl	Same as hup
parenb	-parenb	Enables (disables) parity generation and detection
parodd	-parodd	Selects odd (even) parity
0		Disconnects phone line immediately
50 75 100 134 134.5 150 200 300 600 1200 1800 2400 9600 19200 19.2 exta 38400 38.4 extb		sets the terminal baud rate to the specified number of bits; 19200, 19.2, and exta are synonymous as are 38400, 38.4, and extb
Input Modes		
brkint	-brkint	Signals (does not signal) INTR (interrupt) on BREAK
icrnl	-icrnl	Maps (does not map) CR (carriage return) to NL (new line) on input
ignbrk	-ignbrk	Ignores (does not ignore) BREAK on input
igncr	-igncr	Ignores (does not ignore) CR on input
ignpar	-ignpar	Ignores (does not ignore) parity errors
inlcr	-inlcr	Maps (does not map) NL to CR on input
inpck	-inpck	Enables (disables) input parity checking
istrip	-istrip	Strips (does not strip) characters to 7 bits
iuclc	-iuclc	Maps (does not map) uppercase characters to lowercase
ixany	-ixany	Allows any character (only Control-Q) to restart output
ixoff	-ixoff	Sends (does not send) START/STOP characters when the input queue is almost empty/full
ixon	-ixon	Enables (disables) START/STOP output control Control-S to stop scrolling, Control-Q to resume
imaxbel	-imaxbel	Echoes the BEL character (discards input) if the input buffer overflows
parmrk	-parmrk	Marks (does not mark) parity errors
Output Modes		
ofill	-ofill	Uses fill characters (uses timing) for delays
ocrnl	-ocrnl	Maps (does not map) CR-NL to NL
olcuc	-olcuc	Maps (does not map) lowercase characters to uppercase

TABLE 10.3 `stty` Options *(Continued)*

Option	Counter-option	Effect
onlcr	-onlcr	Maps (does not map) NL characters to CR-NL characters
onlret	-onlret	On the terminal, NL performs (does not perform) the CR function
onocr	-onocr	Does not (does) output CR characters at column zero
opost	-opost	Processes output (does not process output; all other output options are ignored)
ofdel	-ofdel	Uses DEL (delete) (NUL (null)) characters for fill characters

Local Modes		
echo	-echo	Echoes (does not echo) every character typed
echoctl	-echoctl	Echoes (does not echo) control characters; the control character is specified by adding 100 octal to the code of the control character
echoe	-echoe	Echoes (does not echo) the ERASE character as the backspace-space-backspace character
echok	-echok	Echoes (does not echo) a NL character after a KILL character
echoke	-echoke	Echoes (does not echo) the KILL character by erasing each character on the output line
echonl	-echonl	Echoes (does not echo) the NL character
echoprt	-echoprt	Echoes (does not echo) erased characters backwards delimited by the / and \ characters.
icanon	-icanon	Enables (disables) canonical input (which allows input-line editing with the ERASE and KILL characters)
iexten	-iexten	Specifies that implementation-dependent functions will (will not) be recognized in the input data. This includes the eol2, dsusp, reprint, discard, werase, and inext characters and the imaxbel, echoke, echoprt, and echoctl functions
isig	-isig	Enables (disables) the checking of characters against the special control characters INTR and QUIT
noflsh	-noflsh	Does not clear (does clear) buffers after INTR or QUIT
pending	-pending	Causes any input that is pending after a switch from raw to canonical mode to be reinput the next time a read operation is pending
tostop	-tostop	Signals (does not signal) SIGTOU for background output
xcase	-xcase	Echoes (does not echo) uppercase characters on input and displays uppercase characters on output with a preceding \ character.

TABLE 10.3   stty Options (Continued)

Option	Counter-option	Effect
		Control Assignments
control-character x		Sets the control-character x to the indicated control function - INTR, QUIT, ERASE, KILL, EOF, EOL, EOL2, START, STOP, SUSP, DSUSP, REPRINT, DISCARD, WERASE, INEXT, MIN, or TIME. If c is preceded by a \^, then the value is set to the corresponding control character. \^? is interpreted as DEL and \^- is interpreted as undefined
		Combination Modes
evenp		Enables parenb and cs7
parity		Same as evenp
oddp		Enables parenb, cs7, and parodd
-parity		Disables parenb and set cs8
-evenp		Same as -parity
-oddp		Same as -parity
raw		Enables raw input and output (no INTR, QUIT, ERASE, KILL, EOT, REPRINT, DISCARD, WERASE, LNEXT, or output processing)
-raw		Disables raw input and output
cooked		Same as -raw
lcase		ets xcase, iuclc, and olcuc
-lcase		nsets xcase, iuclc, and olcuc
tabs		Preserves tabs when printing
-tabs		Expands tabs to spaces when printing
ek		Sets ERASE and KILL to Control-H and Control-U, respectively
sane		Resets parameters to reasonable values

When no flags are used, tset reinitializes the terminal based on the terminal type in the configuration database, or for nonhardwired terminals, the TERM environment variable.

The tset command is most often used in login profiles to set the terminal type for the TERM environment variable. When used this way, users can dial or telnet into a system and tell AIX exactly what type of terminal they are using, instead of having to settle for some generic terminal type. To support this functionality, the tset command allows for the specification of multiple terminal types depending on where the terminal is connected, and also allows for a default type with user verification. For example, this command in a Korn shell user's profile

```
export TERM='tset - -Q -m ":?vt100"'
```

TABLE 10.4 `tset` **Flags**

Flag	Meaning
`-e` *C*	Sets the erase character to the character specified by *C*.
`-k` *C*	Sets the line-kill character to the character specified by *C*.
`-i` *C*	Sets the interrupt character to the character specified by *C*.
`-`	Indicates that the terminal type should be output to standard output.
`-s`	Used with the C shell to print the sequence of commands that initialize the TERM environment variable.
`-I`	Suppresses the transmission of the terminal initialization settings.
`-Q`	Suppresses the printing of the `tset` default messages: Erase set to *C* and Kill set to *C*.
`-m` *identifierTestbaudrate:Type*	Specifies which terminal type (*Type*) is used on the port indicated by *identifier*. A missing *identifier* matches all ports. A type preceded by a question mark (?) prompts the user to verify the type. For dial-up lines, a default baud rate is specified with *Testbaudrate*.

prompts the user to enter a terminal type; if none is entered, the default type of vt100 is chosen. In either case, the TERM environment variable is set to the value and it is made known to the user's global environment (via the export directive)

10.3.3 `reset`—Reset a terminal

The `reset` command is a superset of the `tset` command. It is most often used when a program dies and leaves the terminal in an indeterminate or incorrect state. The `reset` command performs the following steps before transferring control to `tset`:

It sets cooked and echo modes on

It turns cbreak and raw mode off

It turns on newline translation

It restores the special characters (erase, kill, interrupt) to the default values

The flags of the `tset` command are valid with the `reset` command.

As an example, to set a vt100 type terminal which is not functioning correct to a reasonable state, the operator enters the command

```
Ctrl-J reset vt100 Ctrl-J
```

The control-J sequence is used because the default carriage-return sequence may not be functioning correctly.

10.3.4   `tty`—What terminal is this?

The `tty` command writes the full path name of the terminal to standard output. For example

```
$ tty
/dev/tty0
$
```

If the `-s` flag is used, the path name is not displayed. This flag is commonly used in conjunction with a test of the return code of the `tty` command to determine whether the device is a terminal or not. The following script demonstrates this use:

```
if tty -s
then
     echo 'Running on a terminal'
else
     echo 'Running on a nonterminal device'
fi
```

10.3.5   `terminfo`—Defining the characteristics of a terminal

Actually, terminfo is not a command but a collection of terminal definition files found under the /usr/lib/terminfo directory. For each terminal type, a separate terminal definition file exists. These files define how a terminal works; they define the command sequence used to perform a function, such as "clear the screen" and they define what sequence is transmitted when an event occurs, such as pressing the F1 key.

As can be seen in Fig. 10.1, a terminfo definition file is quite complicated and hardware specific. The source code for the terminfo files is typically found in the /usr/lib/terminfo directory. In most cases, all of the terminal types for a specific manufacturer are grouped into a single source file; i.e., /usr/lib/terminfo/dec.ti for all Digital Equipment Corporation terminals, /usr/lib/terminfo/wyse.ti for all Wyse terminals, etc. Within the file, each terminal type is defined within a stanza, the first line of the stanza identifying the terminal type and any alternate names which may be used. In our example, entering vt100, vt100-am, or dec vt100 are equivalent.

The remaining lines of the stanza define terminal characteristics and control sequences and how they are supported. In the example, the terminal alarm is run when a control-G is sent (bel=^G); the terminal supports eighty columns (cols#80) and twenty-four lines (lines#24). The terminal screen is cleared when the character sequence escape [H escape [2J$<50> is sent (clear=\E[H\E[2J$<50>).

Before a terminal definition can be used, the source files must be compiled with the `tic` command (Sec. 10.3.6).

```
vt100|vt100-am|dec vt100,
        cr=^M, cud1=^J, ind=^J, bel=^G, cols#80, lines#24,
it#8,
        clear=\E[H\E[2J$<50>, cub1=^H, am,
cup=\E[%i%p1%d;%p2%dH$<5>,
        cuf1=\E[C$<2>, cuu1=\E[A$<2>, el=\E[K$<3>,
ed=\E[J$<50>,
        cud=\E[%p1%dB, cuu=\E[%p1%dA, cub=\E[%p1%dD,
cuf=\E[%p1%dC,
        smso=\E[7m$<2>, rmso=\E[m$<2>, smul=\E[4m$<2>,
rmul=\E[m$<2>,
        bold=\E[1m$<2>, rev=\E[7m$<2>, blink=\E[5m$<2>,
sgr0=\E[m\E(B,
        ill=\E[L,        dll=\E[M,

sgr=\E[%?%p1%t;7%;%?%p2%t;4%;%?%p3%t;7%;%?%p4%t;5%;%?%p6%t;1
%;m
                %?%p9%t\E(0%e\E(B%;,
        rs2=\E>\E[?3l\E[?4l\E[?5l\E[?7h\E[?8h, smkx=\E=,
rmkx=\E>,
        tbc=\E[3g, hts=\EH, home=\E[H,
        kcuu1=\E[A, kcud1=\E[B, kcuf1=\E[C, kcub1=\E[D,
kbs=^H,
        ht=^I, ri=\EM$<5>,
        vt#3, xenl, xon, sc=\E7, rc=\E8,
csr=\E[%i%p1%d;%p2%dr,
        smcup=\E[?7h\E[?1l\E(B\E=,        rmcup=\E[?7h,
        box1=\154\161\153\170\152\155\167\165\166\164\156,
batt1=f1,
        box2=\154\161\153\170\152\155\167\165\166\164\156,
batt2=f1md,
        font0=\E(B,      font1=\E(0,      msgr,
        kf1=\EOP,        kf2=\EOQ,        kf3=\EOR,
kf4=\EOS,
        khome=\E[H,      kich1=\E[2~,     knl=\r,
        ktab=^I,         civis=\E[?25l,   cnorm=\E[?25h,
cvvis=\E[?25h,
        mc5=\E[5i, mc4=\E[4i,

Figure 10.1 - The IBM supplied terminfo definition for a
vt100 terminal
```

Figure 10.1 The IBM supplied terminfo definition for a vt100 terminal.

Table 10.5 lists all of the different terminal attributes or features which can possibly be supported. Of course, which ones are actually supported by a specific terminal is dependent on the manufacturer. Therefore, the information in terminfo files is very hardware specific. Additional information on creating terminfo files for a particular device can be obtained from the device manufacturer or in the book *termcap & terminfo* (O'Reilly & Associates, Inc. 1991).

TABLE 10.5 Supported Terminal Features and Functions

Feature	Meaning
Appl_defined_str	Application defined terminal string.
Auto_left_margin	cub1 wraps from column 0 to last column.
Auto_right_margin	Terminal has automatic margins.
Back_tab	Back tab (P).
Beehive_glitch	Beehive (f1 = escape, f2 = ctrl C).
Bell	Audible signal (bell) (P).
Box_attr_1	Attributes for box_chars_1.
Box_attr_2	Attributes for box_chars_2.
Box_chars_1	Box characters primary set.
Box_chars_2	Box characters alternate set.
Carriage_return	Carriage return (P*).
Ceol_standout_glitch	Standout not erased by overwriting (hp).
Change_scroll_region	Change to lines #1 thru #2 (vt100) (PG).
Clear_all_tabs	Clear all tab stops (P).
Clear_screen	Clear screen (P*).
Clr_eol	Clear to end of line (P).
Clr_eos	Clear to end of display (P*).
Color_bg_0	Background color 0 black.
Color_bg_1	Background color 1 red.
Color_bg_2	Background color 2 green.
Color_bg_3	Background color 3 brown.
Color_bg_4	Background color 4 blue.
Color_bg_5	Background color 5 magenta.
Color_bg_6	Background color 6 cyan.
Color_bg_7	Background color 7 white.
Color_fg_0	Foreground color 0 white.
Color_fg_1	Foreground color 1 red.
Color_fg_2	Foreground color 2 green.
Color_fg_3	Foreground color 3 brown.
Color_fg_4	Foreground color 4 blue.
Color_fg_5	Foreground color 5 magenta.
Color_fg_6	Foreground color 6 cyan.
Color_fg_7	Foreground color 7 black.
Column_address	Set cursor column (PG).
Columns	Number of columns in a line.
Command_character	Term set cmd char in prototype.
Cursor_address	Cursor motion to row #1 col #2 (PG).
Cursor_down	Down one line.
Cursor_home	Home cursor (if no cup).
Cursor_invisible	Make cursor invisible.
Cursor_left	Move cursor left one space.
Cursor_mem_address	Memory relative cursor addressing.
Cursor_normal	Make cursor appear normal (undo vs/vi).
Cursor_right	Nondestructive space (cursor right).
Cursor_to_ll	Last line first column (if no cup).

TABLE 10.5   Supported Terminal Features and Functions (*Continued*)

Feature	Meaning
Cursor_up	Upline (cursor up).
Cursor_visible	Make cursor very visible.
Delete_character	Delete character (P*).
Delete_line	Delete line (P*).
Dis_status_line	Disable status line.
Down_half_line	Half-line down (forward 1/2 linefeed).
Eat_newline_glitch	Newline ignored after 80 cols (Concept).
Enter_alt_charset_mode	Start alternate character set (P).
Enter_blink_mode	Turn on blinking.
Enter_bold_mode	Turn on bold (extra bright) mode.
Enter_bottom_mode	Start bottom mode.
Enter_ca_mode	String to begin programs that use cup.
Enter_delete_mode	Delete mode (enter).
Enter_dim_mode	Turn on half-bright mode.
Enter_insert_mode	Insert mode (enter).
Enter_lvert_mode	Start left vertical line mode.
Enter_protected_mode	Turn on protected mode.
Enter_reverse_mode	Turn on reverse video mode.
Enter_rvert_mode	Start right vertical line mode.
Enter_secure_mode	Turn on blank mode (chars invisible).
Enter_standout_mode	Begin stand out mode.
Enter_topline_mode	Start topline mode.
Enter_underline_mode	Start underscore mode.
Erase_chars	Erase #1 characters (PG).
Erase_overstrike	Can erase overstrikes with a blank.
Exit_alt_charset_mode	End alternate character set (P).
Exit_attribute_mode	Turn off all attributes.
Exit_ca_mode	String to end programs that use cup.
Exit_delete_mode	End delete mode.
Exit_insert_mode	End insert mode.
Exit_standout_mode	End stand out mode.
Exit_underline_mode	End underscore mode.
Flash_screen	Visible bell (may not move cursor).
Font_0	Select font 0.
Font_1	Select font 1.
Font_2	Select font 2.
Font_3	Select font 3.
Font_4	Select font 4.
Font_5	Select font 5.
Font_6	Select font 6.
Font_7	Select font 7.
Form_feed	Hardcopy terminal page eject (P*).
From_status_line	Return from status line.
Generic_type	Generic line type (e.g. dialup switch).

TABLE 10.5 **Supported Terminal Features and Functions** (*Continued*)

Feature	Meaning
Hard_copy	Hardcopy terminal.
Has_meta_key	Has a meta key (shift sets parity bit).
Has_status_line	Has extra "status line."
Init_1string	Terminal initialization string.
Init_2string	Terminal initialization string.
Init_3string	Terminal initialization string.
Init_file	Name of file containing is.
Init_prog	Path name of program for init.
Init_tabs	Tabs initially every # spaces.
Insert_character	Insert character (P).
Insert_line	Add new blank line (P*).
Insert_null_glitch	Insert mode distinguishes nulls.
Insert_padding	Insert pad after character inserted (P*).
Key_a1	Upper left of keypad.
Key_a3	Upper right of keypad.
Key_action	Sent by the action key.
Key_b2	Center of keypad.
Key_back_tab	Backtab key.
Key_backspace	Sent by backspace key.
Key_c1	Lower left of keypad.
Key_c3	Lower right of keypad.
Key_catab	Sent by clear-all-tabs key.
Key_clear	Sent by clear screen or erase key.
Key_command	Command request key.
Key_command_pane	Command pane key.
Key_ctab	Sent by clear-tab key.
Key_dc	Sent by delete character key.
Key_dl	Sent by delete line key.
Key_do	Do request key.
Key_down	Sent by terminal down arrow key.
Key_eic	Sent by rmir or smir in insert mode.
Key_end	End key.
Key_eol	Sent by clear-to-end-of-line key.
Key_eos	Sent by clear-to-end-of-screen key.
Key_f0	Sent by function key f0.
Key_f1	Sent by function key f1.
Key_f10	Sent by function key f10.
Key_f11	Sent by function key f11.
Key_f12	Sent by function key f12.
Key_f13	Sent by function key f13.
Key_f14	Sent by function key f14.
Key_f15	Sent by function key f15.
Key_f16	Sent by function key f16.
Key_f17	Sent by function key f17.

TABLE 10.5   Supported Terminal Features and Functions (*Continued*)

Feature	Meaning
Key_f18	Sent by function key f18.
Key_f19	Sent by function key f19.
Key_f2	Sent by function key f2.
Key_f20	Sent by function key f20.
Key_f21	Sent by function key f21.
Key_f22	Sent by function key f22.
Key_f23	Sent by function key f23.
Key_f24	Sent by function key f24.
Key_f25	Sent by function key f25.
Key_f26	Sent by function key f26.
Key_f27	Sent by function key f27.
Key_f28	Sent by function key f28.
Key_f29	Sent by function key f29.
Key_f3	Sent by function key f3.
Key_f30	Sent by function key f30.
Key_f31	Sent by function key f31.
Key_f32	Sent by function key f32.
Key_f33	Sent by function key f33.
Key_f34	Sent by function key f34.
Key_f35	Sent by function key f35.
Key_f36	Sent by function key f36.
Key_f37	Sent by function key f37.
Key_f38	Sent by function key f38.
Key_f39	Sent by function key f39.
Key_f4	Sent by function key f4.
Key_f40	Sent by function key f40.
Key_f41	Sent by function key f41.
Key_f42	Sent by function key f42.
Key_f43	Sent by function key f43.
Key_f44	Sent by function key f44.
Key_f45	Sent by function key f45.
Key_f46	Sent by function key f46.
Key_f47	Sent by function key f47.
Key_f48	Sent by function key f48.
Key_f49	Sent by function key f49.
Key_f5	Sent by function key f5.
Key_f50	Sent by function key f50.
Key_f51	Sent by function key f51.
Key_f52	Sent by function key f52.
Key_f53	Sent by function key f53.
Key_f54	Sent by function key f54.
Key_f55	Sent by function key f55.
Key_f56	Sent by function key f56.
Key_f57	Sent by function key f57.

TABLE 10.5 Supported Terminal Features and Functions (*Continued*)

Feature	Meaning
Key_f58	Sent by function key f58.
Key_f59	Sent by function key f59.
Key_f6	Sent by function key f6.
Key_f60	Sent by function key f60.
Key_f61	Sent by function key f61.
Key_f62	Sent by function key f62.
Key_f63	Sent by function key f63.
Key_f7	Sent by function key f7.
Key_f8	Sent by function key f8.
Key_f9	Sent by function key f9.
Key_help	Help key.
Key_home	Sent by home key.
Key_ic	Sent by ins char/enter ins mode key.
Key_il	Sent by insert line.
Key_left	Sent by terminal left arrow key.
Key_ll	Sent by home-down key.
Key_newline	Newline key.
Key_next_pane	Next pane key.
Key_npage	Sent by next-page key.
Key_ppage	Sent by previous-page key.
Key_prev_cmd	Previous command key.
Key_prev_pane	Previous pane key.
Key_quit	Quit key.
Key_right	Sent by terminal right arrow key.
Key_scroll_left	Scroll left.
Key_scroll_right	Scroll right.
Key_select	Select key.
Key_sf	Sent by scroll-forward/down key.
Key_sf1	Special function key 1.
Key_sf10	Special function key 10.
Key_sf2	Special function key 2.
Key_sf3	Special function key 3.
Key_sf4	Special function key 4.
Key_sf5	Special function key 5.
Key_sf6	Special function key 6.
Key_sf7	Special function key 7.
Key_sf8	Special function key 8.
Key_sf9	Special function key 9.
Key_smap_in1	Input for special mapped key 1.
Key_smap_in2	Input for special mapped key 2.
Key_smap_in3	Input for special mapped key 3.
Key_smap_in4	Input for special mapped key 4.
Key_smap_in5	Input for special mapped key 5.
Key_smap_in6	Input for special mapped key 6.

TABLE 10.5 Supported Terminal Features and Functions (*Continued*)

Feature	Meaning
Key_smap_in7	Input for special mapped key 7.
Key_smap_in8	Input for special mapped key 8.
Key_smap_in9	Input for special mapped key 9.
Key_smap_out1	Output for mapped key 1.
Key_smap_out2	Output for mapped key 2.
Key_smap_out3	Output for mapped key 3.
Key_smap_out4	Output for mapped key 4.
Key_smap_out5	Output for mapped key 5.
Key_smap_out6	Output for mapped key 6.
Key_smap_out7	Output for mapped key 7.
Key_smap_out8	Output for mapped key 8.
Key_smap_out9	Output for mapped key 9.
Key_sr	Sent by scroll-backward/up key.
Key_stab	Sent by set-tab key.
Key_tab	Tab key.
Key_up	Sent by terminal up arrow key.
Keypad_local	Out of "keypad transmit" mode.
Keypad_xmit	Put terminal in "keypad transmit" mode.
Lab_f0	Labels on function key f0 if not f0.
Lab_f1	Labels on function key f1 if not f1.
Lab_f10	Labels on function key f10 if not f10.
Lab_f2	Labels on function key f2 if not f2.
Lab_f3	Labels on function key f3 if not f3.
Lab_f4	Labels on function key f4 if not f4.
Lab_f5	Labels on function key f5 if not f5.
Lab_f6	Labels on function key f6 if not f6.
Lab_f7	Labels on function key f7 if not f7.
Lab_f8	Labels on function key f8 if not f8.
Lab_f9	Labels on function key f9 if not f9.
Lines	Number of lines on screen or page.
Lines_of_memory	Lines of memory if > lines. 0 = > varies.
Magic_cookie_glitch	Number blank chars left by smso or rmso.
Memory_above	Display may be retained above the screen.
Memory_below	Display may be retained below the screen.
Meta_off	Turn off "meta mode".
Meta_on	Turn on "meta mode" (8th bit).
Move_insert_mode	Safe to move while in insert mode.
Move_standout_mode	Safe to move in standout modes.
Newline	Newline (behaves like cr followed by lf).
Over_strike	Terminal overstrikes.
Pad_char	Pad character (rather than null).
Padding_baud_rate	Lowest baud rate where padding needed.
Parm_dch	Delete #1 chars (PG*).
Parm_delete_line	Delete #1 lines (PG*).

TABLE 10.5   Supported Terminal Features and Functions (*Continued*)

Feature	Meaning
Parm_down_cursor	Move cursor down #1 lines (PG*).
Parm_ich	Insert #1 blank chars (PG*).
Parm_index	Scroll forward #1 lines (PG).
Parm_insert_line	Add #1 new blank lines (PG*).
Parm_left_cursor	Move cursor left #1 spaces (PG).
Parm_right_cursor	Move cursor right #1 spaces (PG*).
Parm_rindex	Scroll backward #1 lines (PG).
Parm_up_cursor	Move cursor up #1 lines (PG*).
Pkey_key	Prog funct key #1 to type string #2.
Pkey_local	Prog funct key #1 to execute string #2.
Pkey_xmit	Prog funct key #1 to xmit string #2.
Print_screen	Print contents of the screen.
Prtr_non	Turn on the printer for #1 bytes.
Prtr_off	Turn off the printer.
Prtr_on	Turn on the printer.
Repeat_char	Repeat char #1 #2 times (PG*).
Reset_1string	Reset terminal completely to sane modes.
Reset_2string	Reset terminal completely to sane modes.
Reset_3string	Reset terminal completely to sane modes.
Reset_file	Name of file containing reset string.
Restore_cursor	Restore cursor to position of last sc.
Row_address	Like hpa but sets row (PG).
Save_cursor	Save cursor position (P).
Scroll_forward	Scroll text up (P).
Scroll_reverse	Scroll text down (P).
Set_attributes	Define the video attributes (PG9).
Set_tab	Set a tab in all rows in current column.
Set_window	Current window is lines #1-#2 cols #3-#4.
Status_line_esc_ok	Escape can be used on the status line.
Tab	Tab to next 8-space hardware tab stop.
Teleray_glitch	Tabs destructive magic so char (t1061).
Tilde_glitch	Hazeltine cannot print ~'s.
To_status_line	Go to status line.
Transparent_underline	Underline character overstrikes.
Underline_char	Underscore one char and move past it.
Up_half_line	Half-line up (reverse 1/2 linefeed).
Virtual_terminal	Virtual terminal number (CB/Unix).
Width_status_line	# columns in status line.
Xon_xoff	Terminal uses xon/xoff handshaking.

10.3.6 `tic`—Compile a terminfo file

As discussed in the prior section, the termnfo source file must be compiled before it is used. The `tic` command performs this function. The syntax of the command is

```
tic [-v number] sourcefile
```

The command takes the source file from the /usr/lib/terminfo file and places the compiled executable for each terminal type into the executable directories. The executable directories are identifiable by their one-character designations: /usr/lib/terminfo/i, /usr/lib/terminfo/v, etc. Within each of these directories are the terminal types which begin with the applicable letter. The distribution of files from the compilation process can be somewhat confusing at first and best demonstrated by an actual case. Assume that the /usr/lib/terminfo/dec.ti file contains the source code for only the following DEC-type terminals: vt100, vt220, and vt340. After the source has been compiled, the output of the compilation goes to the files /usr/lib/terminfo/v/vt100, /usr/lib/terminfo/v/vt220, and /usr/lib/terminfo/v/vt340.

The optional -v flag may be used to display status information on the progress of the compilation. As most `tic` compiles are rather quick, this flag is infrequently used. The specified integer value is used to increase the level of status reporting.

10.3.7 `tput`—Display information from a terminfo file

The `tput` command is used to make available information from a terminfo file to the shell. For example, to display the number of columns available on the current terminal, the user enters the command

```
tput cols
```

The -T flag is used to request information on a specific terminal type. Reusing the prior example, to display the number of columns on a vt220 terminal, the user enters

```
tput -T vt220 cols
```

Commands can be sent to a terminal by requesting the appropriate attribute. The command

```
tput clear
```

sends the clear-screen sequence to the terminal and the command

```
tput bel
```

rings the terminal alarm.

10.3.8   `xinit`—Start the X-Windows interface

A graphical user interface to the system is provided with AIX called AIX windows. It is based on X-windows and OSF/Motif.

To use the graphical interface, either a *high function terminal* (HFT) or Xstation must be used. On an Xstation, the graphical interface is started by default; however, not the OSF/Motif interface. To invoke it, enter the following at the command prompt:

```
mwm&
```

To start the graphical interface on an HFT, enter

```
xinit
```

The AIXwindows environment can be customized by creating an .Xdefaults file in the user's home directory. This file should be based upon the template file provided in /usr/lpp/X11/defaults/Xdefaults.tmpl. Every line in this template file is commented. To change a default value, uncomment the appropriate line and modify the value.

Character-based terminal sessions are invoked from within the AIXwindows interface by entering the `aixterm&` at a command prompt.

10.4   Miscellaneous Configuration Commands

The commands in this section are concerned with customizing the global system environment, such as the default language and time zone, the device serving as the console, and the number of users who may logon at any one time.

10.4.1   `chlicense`—Change the maximum number of concurrent users

When an AIX system is installed, the default number of concurrent users is set to two. The `chlicense` command is used by those sites which have licensed a greater number of AIX users to change the concurrent user setting. The syntax of the command is

```
chlicense -u number
```

where *number* is the maximum number of licensed users. Valid values are 2, 8, 16, 32, 64, and 65; the last value represents an unlimited number of users.

Although the number of users can be increased while the system is running, if the value is decreased, it does not take effect until the next time the system is rebooted.

10.4.2   `lslicense`—Display user licensing information

The number of licensed users can be checked with the `lslicense` command. The output of the command is the license group currently in effect. On a system with 64 licensed users, for example, the command output appears as follows:

```
$ lslicense
32-64
$
```

10.4.3 `chlang`—Change the default system language

The `chlang` command is used to change the global environment variable LANG. The syntax of the command is

```
chlang lang_type
```

where *lang_type* is the language identifier which is the *language_country* as explained in the following paragraph.

During installation of AIX, at least one language must be selected for system use. For each language on the system a locale definition file is placed in the /usr/lib/nls/loc directory. The naming convention for the files is *language_locale.codeset*. For example, the locale file for Dutch, in the Netherlands, is /usr/lib/nls/loc/Nl_NL.IBM-850 if the IBM-850 code set is used, or /usr/lib/nls/loc/nl_NL.ISO8859-1 if the ISO8859-1 code set is used. For Dutch, in Belgium, the locale file is /usr/lib/nls/loc/Nl_BE.IBM-850 if the IBM-850 code set is used, or /usr/lib/nls/loc/nl_BE.ISO8859-1 if the ISO8859-1 code set is used. Note that because the first level qualifiers are different (Nl_BE/nl_BE or Nl_NL/nl_NL), the *lang_type* in the `chlang` command can be truncated to just the *language_locale*. That is

```
chlang nl_NL
```

is accepted for the full term

```
chlang nl_NL.ISO8859-1
```

Currently supported locales are listed in Table 10.6.

10.4.4 `chtz`—Change the default system time zone

Time zones in AIX are expressed as the difference between the local time and coordinated universal time (CUT)[14] in accordance with POSIX and X/Open standards. Therefore, to set the system time in Great Britain, the `chtz` command is

```
chtz CUT
```

and to change it in New York, the command is

```
chtz CUT -5
```

---

[14]Previously known as Greenwich mean time (GMT).

TABLE 10.6   Supported Locales

Country	Language	Code Set	Locale
Belgium	Dutch	IBM-850	Nl_BE
Belgium	Dutch	ISO8859-1	nl_BE
Belgium	French	IBM-850	Fr_BE
Belgium	French	ISO8859-1	fr_BE
Canada	French	IBM-850	Fr_CA
Canada	French	ISO8859-1	fr_CA
Denmark	Danish	IBM-850	Da_DK
Denmark	Danish	ISO8859-1	da_DK
FInland	Finnish	ISO8859-1	fi_FI
Finland	Finnish	IBM-850	Fi_FI
France	French	IBM-850	Fr_FR
France	French	ISO8859-1	fr_FR
Germany	German	IBM-850	De_DE
Germany	German	ISO8859-1	de_DE
Great Britain	English	IBM-850	En_GB
Great Britain	English	ISO8859-1	en_GB
Greece	Greek	ISO8859-7	el_GR
Iceland	Icelandic	IBM-850	Is_IS
Iceland	Icelandic	ISO8859-1	is_IS
Italy	Italian	IBM-850	It_IT
Italy	Italian	ISO8859-1	it_IT
Japan	Japanese	IBM-932	Ja_JP
Japan	Japanese	IBM-euc-JP	ja_JP
Netherlands	Dutch	IBM-850	Nl_NL
Netherlands	Dutch	ISO8859-1	nl_NL
Norway	Norwegian	IBM-850	No_NO
Norway	Norwegian	ISO8859-1	no_NO
Portugal	Portuguese	IBM-850	Pt_PT
Portugal	Portuguese	ISO8859-1	pt_PT
Spain	Spanish	IBM-850	Es_ES
Spain	Spanish	ISO8859-1	es_ES
Sweden	Swedish	IBM-850	Sv_SE
Sweden	Swedish	ISO8859-1	sv_SE
Switzerland	French	IBM-850	Fr_CH
Switzerland	French	ISO8859-1	fr_CH
Switzerland	German	IBM-850	De_CH
Switzerland	German	ISO8859-1	de_CH
Turkey	Turkish	ISO8859-9	tr_TR
United States	English	IBM-850	En_US
United States	English	ISO8859-1	en_US

10.4.5 chcons—Redirect the system console

The chcons command is used to redirect the system console to a different device or file. The redirection does not become effective until the system is rebooted. The name of the new console device must be a fully qualified path name to a device or file.

If the console path name points to a character device, the system starts the login program on the device after the next system initialization. Console login can be suppressed by using the -a login=disable flag in the chcons command

```
chcons -a login=disable /dev/tty0
```

Note that if this is the only terminal device on the system, all logins are completely disabled.[15] Login processing may be explicitly enabled with the -a login=enable flag

```
chcons -a login=enable /dev/tty0
```

If a temporary redirection of the running system's console is desired, the swcons command must be used.

10.4.6 swcons—Temporarily redirect console output

Unlike the chcons command, the swcons command takes effect immediately. It temporarily redirects the output of the system console to a different target device (or file) during system operation. Only informational, error, and intervention messages are redirected; if a user invokes a process from the console terminal, that output is not redirected.

The console remains switched to the alternate device or file until one of the following occurs:

Another swcons command is issued.

The system is rebooted.

An error is detected on the switched device or file.

In the first case, console output is redirected to the new device, or in the last two cases, to the device which served as the console during system startup.

The swcons command takes only the new output device as an argument

```
swcons /tmp/console.log      (redirection to a file)
swcons /dev/tty3             (redirection to another device)
swcons                       (redirection to the original console device)
```

---

[15]This is, of course, extremely undesirable.

10.4.7 `lscons`—Display the name of the current console device

As would be expected, since it is possible to change the console device, it is also necessary to be able to display the name of the current device. This is done with the `lscons` command. The `lscons` command can take one of three flags

`-a`	Displays the full path name of the system console to be used on the next system restart.
`-d`	Displays the full path name of the system console when the current system was started.
`-s`	Returns an exit value :
0	The current device is the console.
1	The current device is not the console.
2	The current device was the console at system start but is not currently.
3	An invalid flag was specified.
4	A system error occurred.

This last flag is used in scripts to test if the process is running on the console, for example

```
if lscons -s
then
     echo "Running on the system console"
else
     echo "Running on a user terminal"
fi
```

10.5 Status Information

This section deals with the information commands bootinfo and pstat.

10.5.1 `bootinfo`—Display various boot information

Information about system startup can be displayed with the `bootinfo` command. Although several flags are available most of the interesting information can be retrieved with just a few. These flags include

`-a`	Displays the characteristics of all the installation disks
`-b`	Displays the name of the boot device
`-i`	Lists the disks of the root volume group
`-m`	Displays the machine model code
`-r`	Displays the amount of real memory in Kbytes
`-t`	Specifies the boot type by returning an integer value:
1	Boot from disk
2	Boot from diskette
4	Boot from tape
5	Boot from the network

When a machine is booted from the network the `-c` flag may be used to display the network boot information:

Client IP address

Server IP address

Gateway IP address

Type of network (1 Ethernet, 0 Token-Ring)

Slot number of the network adapter

802.3 indicator

Bootfile

Vendor tag information

Token-Ring speed (even value = 4 Mbytes, odd value = 16 Mbytes).

10.5.2 pstat—Display system table information

The pstat command is used to display information from the AIX system tables. This command is available only to the root user or members of the system group.

The type of information to be displayed depends on the flag used

-a	Displays entries in the process table
-f	Displays the file table
-i	Displays the inode table and inode data block addresses
-p	Displays the process table
-s	Displays paging space usage
-t	Displays the tty structures
-T	Displays the system variables
-u *procslot*	Displays the user structure of the process in the designated slot

The syntax of the command allows for the inspection of system dump files. For example, examining the paging space usage on the current system entails the use of the command

```
pstat -s
```

However, the status from a dump file is examined with the command

```
pstat -s dumpfile
```

assuming, of course, that the dump file had been named dumpfile.

10.6 Login Processing Enablement

During normal system startup, all ports on the system are enabled for use. There are times, however, when it is necessary to stop or prevent terminal activity. The following commands are used to control the use of terminal ports.

10.6.1 `pdisable`—**Disable terminal ports**

The `pdisable` command stops the specified port, even if a user is currently logged on. When used with no operands, the command displays the names of all ports currently disabled

```
$ pdisable
tty2
tty6
$
```

When the command is used with the -a flag, action is taken. If a specific port is not named, all ports are taken out of service. A specific port is taken out by naming the port

```
pdisable -a tty9
```

10.6.2 `phold`—**Prevent further logins**

Like the `pdisable` command, the `phold` command also stops ports; however only those ports not currently in use are stopped. This allows further logins to be halted. When used with no operands, the command displays the names of all ports currently on hold.

When the command is used with the -a flag, unless a specific port is named, all ports are put on hold

```
phold -a
```

A specific port is taken out by naming the port

```
phold -a tty5
```

10.6.3 `penable`—**Enable/display terminal ports**

The counterpart to `pdisable` is `penable` which enables normal ports.[16] When the -a flag is not used, the command displays a list of the currently enabled terminals. The -a flag must be used to enable a terminal. If a specific terminal is not identified all terminals are enabled—for example

```
penable -a
```

10.6.4 `pdelay`—**Enable/display delayed login ports**

Delayed ports are like normal ports except that the login prompt is not displayed until the user types a character. Using the command

```
pdelay -a
```

---

[16]Normal ports allow users to login. The port cannot be acquired by a running process.

sets all ports as delayed. If a specific terminal is named (i.e., pdelay -a tty0), only that terminal is set to delayed. Without the -a flag, the command reports only on which ports are currently defined as delayed.

10.6.5 pshare—Enable/display shared login ports

Shared login ports are bidirectional; that is, a currently running process can acquire the port. As with the other commands, the -a flag is used to indicate that activation is to take place. If a specific port is not named, all ports are set to shared.

10.6.6 pstart—Enable/display ports in their current state

The pstart command is similar to the prior enabling commands except that it respects the current port setting. That is, when a

```
pstart -a
```

command is issued, all of the terminal ports on the system are enabled but in their current status. The pstart command with no operands is used to display the status of all terminal ports on the system.

10.7 Paging Space Definition

A minimal paging space definition is performed during the installation of AIX. In general, this paging space is not sufficient for normal system use. Allocation of paging space depends upon the amount of real storage available. General guidelines suggest the following ratios:[17]

Amount of real storage, Mbytes	Amount of paging space, Mbytes
16m	64m
32m	128m
64m	256m
128m	384m
256m	512m
512m	512m

The commands for manipulating paging space are: mkps, lsps, chps, rmps, and swapon.

---

[17]Again, these are only general guidelines. Many may not agree with these. Just remember that too little paging space will result in processes being terminated, and too much paging space can lead to thrashing.

10.7.1 swapon—Enable paging spaces

Normally this command is used only during system initialization to enable the paging devices. It can be used subsequently, however, to being additional devices on-line. When used with the -a flag

```
swapon -a
```

it reads the /etc/swapspaces file and brings all devices listed in the file on-line for paging. When used without the flag and with a specific device

```
swapon /dev/paging6
```

the command brings only the specified device online.

Because the command which creates a new paging space (mkps) can also bring that space on-line automatically, it is necessary to bring a paging device on-line only if the device was not activated during system startup.

10.7.2 mkps—Define and activate a paging space

The mkps command adds additional paging spaces to the system. This space can be on a local disk or on another system via the *network file system* (NFS).[18]

When the new paging space is to be created on local disks, the syntax of the command is

```
mkps [-a | -n] -t lv -s partitions volumegroup \
[physicalvolume]
```

The user must identify the volume group upon which the paging space is created along with a number of logical partitions to use. Optionally, the specific physical volumes may be identified.

For both locally created and NFS paging systems, the -a flag is used to indicate that the paging space should not be activated until the next system startup (or swapon command); the -n flag is used to indicate that the paging space should be immediately put on-line and into use.

When the new paging space is to be created on a remote system via NFS, the syntax of the command is

```
mkps [-a | -n] -t nfs servername serverfile
```

where a specific server and file on that server must be specified. Of course, if that system is unavailable, the paging space is not used.

---

[18]Creating paging space via NFS is recommended only for diskless workstations. If the NFS server terminates, the client paging space is lost which causes unpredictable problems for the client.

10.7.3 `lsps`—Display paging space information

The paging space definitions on the system are displayed with the `lsps` command. Two flags are used to control the format of the display of information: `-l` is the default which displays information in text format and `-c` displays the information in colon-separated format.[19]

The content of the information displayed is controlled by the remaining flags. The `-a` flag specifies that all paging spaces are to be displayed, for example

```
$ lsps -a
Page Space     Phy Vol    Vol Grp    Size    % Used    Active    Auto
hdisk6         hdisk0     rootvg     64MB    65        yes       yes
hdisk61        hdisk1     rootvg     64MB    42        yes       yes
hdisk62        hdisk2     rootvg     64MB    0         no        no
$
```

In this example, the system has three paging space, only two of which are currently active.

A specific paging space may be displayed by using the syntax

```
lsps pagingspace
```

as in

```
$ lsps hdisk62
Page Space     Phy Vol    Vol Grp    Size    % Used    Active    Auto
hdisk62        hdisk2     rootvg     64MB    0         no        no
$
```

The specific type of paging space also is delimited with the `-t` flag. When `-t lv` is used, the only paging spaces on logical volumes are displayed; when `-t nfs` is used, only network file system (NFS) paging spaces are displayed.

10.7.4 `chps`—Change a paging space

The `chps` command changes the system restart indicator for a paging space. In addition, the command adds additional partitions to a paging space. The syntax of the command is

```
chps [-s partitions] [-ay | -an] pagingspace
```

Additional partitions are added to the paging space with the `-s` flag. If the `-ay` flag combination is specified, the paging space is marked so that it is used when the system is next restarted (this is the default). If the `-an` flag combination is used, the paging space does not become active until the status is changed. Regardless of which flag or flags are used, the user must identify the affected paging space.

---

[19]This format is provided primarily for use in shell scripts.

10.7.5 `rmps`—Remove a paging space

Inactive paging spaces are removed from the system with the `rmps` command. Execution of the command causes both the paging space and the logical volume upon which the paging space resides to be removed. For an NFS paging space, the device and its definition are removed from the client; the NFS server is not affected, that is, nothing is changed on the server itself.

An active paging space may not be removed. The paging space must first be marked as inactive for the next system restart (see above). Then, after the system is restarted, the inactive paging space is deleted with the `rmps` command.

10.8 Program Product Information

Several commands are provided in AIX to display information about the installed system software. These commands include `oslevel`, `uname`, `lslpp`, `lppchk`, and `lsswconfig`.

10.8.1 `oslevel`—Determine the operating system level

The `oslevel` command was introduced in AIX 3.2.4 to provide a simple way for a user to determine the version, release, and modification level of the installed version of AIX.

The `oslevel` command output is directed to standard output and consists of a single line which indicates the operating system version, as in this example

```
$ oslevel
>3250
$
```

The version number is preceded by either an equal sign, a less than sign, or a greater than sign. An equal sign indicates that all of the system software is at the indicated level and has had no service applied. A less than sign indicates that although the base components of AIX are at the indicated level, not all of the other system software is. A greater sign indicates that additional service packages have been applied beyond the indicated install level. A less than and a greater than sign together indicate that products exist at levels above and below the indicated level.

Several optional flags may be used with the command to display further program product information. The `-e` flag requests a list of all products at the current maintenance level, the `-l` flag lists all products below the current maintenance level, and the `-g` flag list all products above the current maintenance level. The `-s` flag is used in conjunction with the `-g` flag also to list subsystem information.

The `-i` flag is used to identify the level of products which are not upgraded by maintenance fixes. These products are upgraded through a complete replacement process rather than selective component fixes.

If the user enters the `oslevel` command and receives a message indicating that the command cannot be found, a version of AIX at the 3.2.3 or prior level is running. In that case, the lslpp command must be used to display the status of the individual components.

10.8.2 uname—Display operating and machine information

The uname command writes operating system information to standard output. When no flags are specified, the displayed information is only the name of the operating system. The following flags may be used to request additional information:

-a	Displays the version banner (i.e., the -m, -n, -r, -s, and -v flags); not valid with -x or -S
-l	Displays the LAN network number
-m	Displays the machine ID number
-n	Displays the UUCP node name
-r	Displays the operating system release number
-s	Displays the system name; the default
-S name	Sets the UUCP node name
-v	Displays the operating system version number
-x	Displays the version banner, plus the LAN network number (equivalent to -a -l)

Therefore, to display the complete version banner and LAN network number information, the user enters

```
uname -x
```

or

```
uname -a -l
```

10.8.3 lslpp—List information about software products

The lslpp command is used to display information about software products. When the -l flag is used (Table 10.7), only information about the base level of the product is displayed. When the -a or -B flag is used with the -l flag, information is displayed about the base product and the updates to the base product.

The most common use of this command is to display update information about a specific product or fix, for example

```
lslpp -ha bos.obj
```

Here, the -ha flags are used to display the installation and update history for the operating system (bos.obj). In the command

```
lslpp -A bos.obj U423240
```

the user is requesting information about what problems in bos.obj are fixed in update number U423240.

Some of the more common program product names are cross-referenced in Tables 10.8 and 10.9.

TABLE 10.7   lslpp Flags

Flag	Meaning
-A	Displays information about all problems, known as *authorized program analysis report* (APARs), fixed by the specified software product or update
-a	Displays information about the software product and any existing updates. This flag cannot be used with the -f flag.
-B	Limits the inputs to APAR ids. Cannot be used with the -f or -I flags
-c	Displays information as a colon-separated list. Cannot be used with the -J flag
-d	Displays software products or updates that are dependent on the specified product
-f	Displays the names of the files added to the system during the installation of the specified product
-h	Displays the installation and update history of the specified product
-I	Limits the input to software products; individual APAR numbers cannot be used. Cannot be used with the -B flag
-i	Displays product information for the specified product or APAR
-J	Generates output in a form suitable for processing by SMIT
-l	Displays the full name, state, and description of the specified product
-O	Limits information to the specified part of the product; valid suboptions are r for the root portion, s for the /usr/share part, and u for the /usr part
-p	Displays the prerequisite information applicable to the specified product or APAR
-q	Suppresses the display of column headings

10.8.4   lppchk—Verify a software product

The lppchk command verifies that the files in a software product match the information in the *software vital product data* (SWVPD) database. The most common use of the lppchk command is after the installation of a software update or fix package. The command

```
lppchk -v
```

is used to ensure that the various system software components have been installed correctly and consistently. A specific component can be checked by appending the product ID to the command. For example

```
lppchk -v -m 3 sna.sna.obj
```

checks the consistency of SNA Services (sna.sna.obj).

The -v flag is actually a combination of the following individual flags:

-c	Performs checksum verification
-f	Performs file size and existence verification
-l	Verifies symbolic links

The level of information is controlled though the -m flag which takes the following values as operands:

1	Displays error messages only (the default)
2	Displays error messages and warnings
3	Displays error, warning, and informational messages

TABLE 10.8 Products to Product Identifiers

Product	Identifier
3270 Host Connection Program (HCON)	hcon.obj, hconm*.msg
3278 Emulator	em78.obj, em78m*.msg
802.3 Ethernet support	bosext2.dlc8023.obj
Accounting	bosext2.acct.obj
Ada Compiler	ada*.*
Ada Run Time	adarte.obj
ADT Profiling	support bosadt.prof.obj
AIX	bos.obj
AIX data files	bos.data
AIXwindows 3D support	X11_3d.*
AIXwindows Development Library	X11dev.obj
AIXwindows documentation	X11*.info
AIXwindows Fonts	X11fnt.*
AIXwindows messages	X11*.msg
AIXwindows Run Time	X11rte.obj, X11rte.ext.obj
Asynchronous Terminal Emulation	bosext2.ate.obj
Base Application Development Toolkit (ADT, includes sccs, dbx, make, assembler, C, lex, yacc)	bosadt.bosadt.*, bosadt.lib.obj
Base system locales	bsl.*
Base system messages	bsm*
Block Multiplexor Support	370p.obj
BOS Extensions 1	bosext1.*
C shell	bosext1.csh.obj
Data Encryption Standards Library	des.obj
DOS Emulator	pci.obj
DOS Utilities	bosext2.dosutil.obj
ESSL (Engineerng and Scientific Subroutine Library)	essl14
Ethernet support	bosext2.dlcether.obj
FDDI	fddi.obj
games	bosext2.games.obj
HANFS	(High Availability NFS) hanfs.obj
InfoExplorer	bssiEn_US.info
Mail	bosext1.mh.obj
Network Computing System	(NCS) bosnet.ncs.obj
NFS	bosnet.nfs.obj
NROFF/TROFF	txtfmt.*
PC Simulator	pcsim.obj, pcsimm*.msg
QLLC support	bosext2.dlcqllc.obj
SDLC support	bosext2.sdlc.obj
SNA Server	sna.*, snam*.msg
SNMP	bosnet.snmpd.obj
TCP/IP	bosnet.tcpip.obj
Token-Ring support	bosext2.dlctoken.obj
uucp	bosext1.uucp.obj

TABLE 10.8   Products to Product Identifiers (*Continued*)

Product	Identifier
VS COBOL Compiler	`cobolcmp.obj`
VS COBOL Run Time	`cobolrte.obj`
XDE (AIXwindows development environment)	`bosadt.xde.obj`
XL C Compiler	`xlccmp.obj`
XL FORTRAN Compiler	`xlfcmp.obj, xlfcmpm*.msg`
XL FORTRAN Run Time	`xlfrte.obj, xlfrtem*.msg`
XL PASCAL Compiler	`xlpcmp.obj, xlpcmpm*.msg`
XL PASCAL Run Time	`xlprte.obj, xlprtem*.msg`
Xstation manager	`x_st_mgr.obj, x_st_mgrm*.msg`

10.8.5 `lsswconfig`—Display information in the Software Configuration Database

The `lsswconfig` command is used to display the names and attributes of the system configuration files.[20] In its simplest form, the command is used to list all of the system configuration files, e.g.,

```
lsswconfig
```

The configuration files for a specific product may be displayed by entering the name of the product on the command line

```
lsswconfig bos.obj
```

If the -a flag is specified

```
lsswconfig -a bos.obj
```

the attributes of the applicable files are displayed.

Current and prior releases of software may be compared and contrasted with additional flags. The -c flag is used to determine which files can be safely combined with a version of the file from a prior version; the -r flag lists all of the files which can be replaced by a version from a prior version; and the -n flag lists those files which cannot be combined or replaced with a version from the prior release. The -l flag lists the location and name of files in the last and current releases; the -p flag lists the location of the files in the prior release.

The last three flags are used to restrict the display to files from a particular directory: -s for files in the /usr/share filesystem, -u for files in the /usr directory, and -m for files in the root (/) directory.

---

[20]The information is extracted from the /usr/lb/objrepos/swconfig_info and /usr/share/lb/objrepos/swconfig_info files.

TABLE 10.9   Product Identifiers to Product

Identifier	Product
`370p.obj`	Block Multiplexor Support
`ada*.*`	Ada Compiler
`adarte.obj`	Ada Run Time
`bos.data`	AIX data files
`bos.obj`	AIX
`bosadt.bosadt.obj, bosadt.lib.obj`	Base Application Development Toolkit (ADT, includes sccs, dbx, make, assembler, C, lex, yacc
`bosadt.prof.objADT`	Profiling support
`bosadt.xde.obj`	XDE (AIXwindows development environment)
`bosext1.*`	BOS Extensions 1
`bosext1.csh.obj`	C shell
`bosext1.mh.obj`	Mail
`bosext1.uucp.obj`	uucp
`bosext2.acct.obj`	Accounting
`bosext2.ate.obj`	Asynchronous Terminal Emulation
`bosext2.dlc8023.obj 802.3`	Ethernet support
`bosext2.dlcether.obj`	Ethernet support
`bosext2.dlcqllc.obj`	QLLC support
`bosext2.dlctoken.obj`	Token-Ring support
`bosext2.dosutil.obj`	DOS Utilities
`bosext2.games.obj`	games
`bosext2.sdlc.obj`	SDLC support
`bosnet.ncs.obj`	Network Computing System
`bosnet.nfs.obj`	NFS
`bosnet.snmpd.obj`	SNMP
`bosnet.tcpip.obj`	TCP/IP
`bsl.*`	Base system locales
`bsm*`	Base system messages
`bssiEn_US.info`	InfoExplorer
`cobolcmp.obj`	VS COBOL Compiler
`cobolrte.obj`	VS COBOL Run Time
`des.obj`	Data Encryption Standards Library
`em78.obj, em78m*.msg`	3278 Emulator
`essl14`	ESSL (Engineerng and Scientific Subroutine Library)
`fddi.obj`	FDDI
`hanfs.obj`	HANFS (High Availability NFS)
`hcon.obj, hconm*.msg`	3270 Host Connection Program (HCON)
`pci.obj`	DOS Emulator
`pcsim.obj, pcsimm*.msg`	PC Simulator
`sna.*, snam*.msg`	SNA Server
`txtfmt.*`	NROFF/TROFF
`x_st_mgr.obj, x_st_mgrm*.msg`	Xstation manager
`X11*.info`	AIXwindows documentation
`X11*.msg`	AIXwindows messages

TABLE 10.9 **Product Identifiers to Product** (*Continued*)

Identifier	Product
X11_3d.*	AIXwindows 3D support
X11dev.obj	AIXwindows Development Library
X11fnt.*	AIXwindows Fonts
X11rte.obj, X11rte.ext.obj	AIXwindows Run Time
xlccmp.obj	XL C Compiler
xlfcmp.obj, xlfcmpm*.msg	XL FORTRAN Compiler
xlfrte.obj, xlfrtem*.msg	XL FORTRAN Run Time
xlpcmp.obj, xlpcmpm*.msg	XL PASCAL Compiler
xlprte.obj, xlprtem*.msg	XL PASCAL Run Time

Networking
and Communications

In most cases, computer systems today do not exist in isolation, but instead are connected to other computer systems through some type of network. For most AIX systems, these networks are based on the TCP/IP (*Transmission Control Protocol/Internet Protocol*) networking protocol and the Ethernet transport protocol.

TCP/IP resulted from the efforts of the *U.S. Department of Defense Advanced Research Projects Agency* (DARPA) to provide a method for allowing disparate computing systems used by the government and its research partners to communicate with one another. A very visible outcome of this project was the network which became the Internet. Originally limited to those agencies or institutions participating in the DARPA projects, this network has experienced phenomenal growth, having been opened to both commercial and private use. In order to provide some order to the network, the Network Information Center was established to regulate many aspects of the network.

TCP/IP is a collection of protocols (currently over 200) used to handle networking methods, application behavior, and theory. The two most common applications in a TCP/IP network from the user's perspective are ftp, an application and protocol for transferring data from one system to another, and telnet, which is an application and protocol for using remote systems.[1] System applications built upon TCP/IP include NFS, the network file system, and NIS, the network information service.

For those sites which need connectivity to IBM mainframe based systems, AIX also provides *Systems Network Architecture* (SNA) connectivity through SNA Services.

---

[1]The rlogin, rsh, and rcp commands introduced earlier can run under TCP/IP. However, because these earlier commands work only in a UNIX-to-UNIX context, they are quickly being abandoned in many cases in favor of ftp and telnet.

11.1   TCP/IP Basics

Every machine on a TCP/IP network must have an *IP address*. The IP address of a machine is unique within a network. When a machine is connected to the Internet, the address of the machine is assigned according to instructions from the *Network Information Center* (NIC). Even for those machines not directly connected to the Internet, the network administrator usually assigns IP addresses according to NIC requirement.

An IP address is a 32-bit binary number. For convenience, it is expressed as 4 octets in dot notation (referred to as *dotted quad* notation) in high- to low-order precedence. The address consists of two variable-length parts—the network address and the local address. The size of the address components vary to allow for network size differentiation. Five classes of networks are provided for

Class a. Large networks; addresses start with 0 through 126; the first octet identifies the network; up to 16777216 nodes are supported.

Class b. Medium size networks; the first two octets identify the network; addresses start with 128 through 191; up to 65536 nodes are supported.

Class c. Small networks; the first three octets identify the network; addresses start with 192 through 223; up to 256 nodes are supported.

Class d. Used for *multicasting* (broadcasting messages to groups of systems on the Internet); addresses begin with 224 though 239.

Class e. Used for experimental systems; addresses start with 240 through 255.

Addresses which start with 127 are used for local loopback testing; these addresses are never assigned to a real network.

Subnetting is a method of partitioning the local address space so smaller portions of the network may be addressed and administered. In class A and class B networks, the second and third octets may be assigned in a manner which allows them to denote specific smaller networks within the larger network. For example, DePaul University is a class B network whose addresses begin with 140.192. The DePaul network is initially defined via a subnetting of the 140 network addresses from 140.192.0.0 to 140.192.255.255. DePaul may subnet its network via the third octet—140.192.1.0 through 140.192.1.255 on one subnet and 140.192.2.0 through 140.192.2.255 on another, and so forth.[2]

Although not all that common, a complete octet does not need to be used to subnet an address. Organizations may choose their own subnet field size; therefore, a method must be provided for external hosts and routers to recognize the subnet field. This is the *subnet mask,* a 32-bit field which is ORed to the host number (network address + subnet portion of the local address). The result of this ORing is that the host number of the IP address is masked out. Referring back to the previous example, the DePaul network would use a sub-

---

[2]The numbers 0 and 255 should be avoided in network addresses. These numbers are used to represent special cases and functions and could conflict with network broadcasts.

net mask of 255.255.255.0 to use the third octet as a subnet indicator. In a class A network, the subnet mask would be 255.255.0.0 to use the second octet as a subnet indicator.

Some addresses have special meanings. As discussed earlier, all address beginning with 127 are used for local loopback tests. The address 255.255.255.255 is used for sending a message to every host on the local network. It is also possible to send a message to all nodes on a remote network. This is done by setting the local portion of the address to 255. That is, on a class C network, the address 204.43.3.255 represents all nodes on network 204.43.3. Similarly, 131.32.255.255 represents all nodes on the class B network 131.32, and 16.255.255.255 represents all nodes on the class A network 16.

Additionally, the address 0.0.0.0 denotes the current host; specifically, "this host on this network." Other hosts on the network can be referenced by using the host number as the local part of the address—0.0.0.13 represents the host numbered 13 on the network.

As is evident, this addressing scheme, while good for machines and network managers, is tedious and cumbersome for the general user. Therefore, in addition to an IP address, every host must also have a *hostname*. The hostname, which may be up to 14 characters in length, is concatenated with a *domain name* and used as a mnemonic for the *IP address* of the machine. The domain name is a descriptive representation of the network address. For example, the class A network starting with address 6 has a domain name of navy.mil; the class A network beginning with 18 has a domain name of mit.edu; the class B network beginning with 140.192 has a domain name of depaul.edu; and the class C network beginning with 192.101.184 has a domain name of notis.com.

The structure of domain names is hierarchical with every network name falling into a domain which represents a type of service or locale. Unlike an IP address, a domain name reads from lowest level qualifier to highest. For example, in the name gopher.library.depaul.edu, depaul.edu represents the domain name; library denotes a subnet in depaul.edu; and gopher represents a specific node in library.depaul.edu. A list of some of the more common domain types is given in Table 11.1.

Hostnames, however, are not directly used for routing information through the network. The advantage of using hostnames is that it is not necessarily tied to a specific IP address.[3] When a user addresses a machine by the host name of the machine another TCP/IP service takes over to provide address resolution. The *domain name server* (DNS) is used to look up the name of the host and find the IP address of the destination machine. The request is then sent to the appropriate machine by way of the IP address. Although there is extra overhead in using host names instead of actual IP addresses, the level of abstraction provided allows functionality to be moved from one machine to another, transparent to the user. This is particularly useful in disaster recovery to allow one host to take over for another host which has failed.

---

[3]Unless the hostname has been assigned to a "static" route in the /etc/hosts file. See Sec. 11.2 for further information on static routes.

TABLE 11.1   Common Domain Qualifiers

Qualifer	Type
COM	Commercial organizations
EDU	Educational institutions
GOV	U.S. Government agencies
MIL	U.S. Military organizations
NET	Systems performing network services
ORG	Noncommercial organizations
INT	International groups
NATO	North Atlantic Treaty Organization
AU	Australia
BE	Belgium
CA	Canada
CH	Switzerland
CZ	Czech Republic
DE	Germany
DK	Denmark
FI	Finland
FR	France
IN	India
IT	Italy
IS	Israel
HK	Hong Kong
JA	Japan
LU	Luxembourg
NL	Netherlands
NO	Norway
NZ	New Zealand
SE	Sweden
UK	United Kingdom
US	United States locale designation
UY	Uruguay
VE	Venezuela
YU	Yugoslavia

11.1.1   `mktcpip`—Define the TCP/IP networking information

The `mktcpip` command is used to define or update TCP/IP networking information. The new or changed values are written to the configuration database and the /etc/resolv.conf and /etc/hosts files as appropriate. The `mktcpip` command uses several flags for defining the various network options (Table 11.2). In general, the following information must be defined before TCP/IP can function correctly:

The machine's host name

The machine's IP address

The network interface card to be used for TCP/IP

TABLE 11.2 `mktcpip` **Flags**

Flag	Meaning
-a *address*	Sets the IP address of the host. Must be specified in dotted quad notation.
-d *domain*	Defines the domain name. This must match the domain name used by the domain name server
-g *gateway*	Defines the IP address of the machine which provides the gateway to the Internet. Must be specified in dotted quad notation.
-h *hostname*	Sets the name of the host. The host name must be 14 characters or less. On systems which use DNS, the complete host and domain name must be specified.
-i *interface*	Specifies the network interface to be used; typically this is either en0 for an Ethernet adapter or tr0 for a Token-Ring adapter.
-m *subnetmask*	Specifies the subnet mask in dotted quad notation.
-n *nameserveraddr*	Sets the address of the name server used for DNS. Must be entered in dotted quad format.
-r *ringspeed*	For Token-Ring adapters only, specifies the speed of the ring in Mbytes-per-second—either 4 or 16.
-s *starts*	The TCP/IP support daemons.
-t *cabletype*	For Ethernet adapters only; defines the type of cable used—dix for thick cable, bnc for thin cable, or N/A for not applicable (twisted pair).

The subnet mask

The gateway machine address

The domain name server's IP address

The domain name

For example, defining a new host at ACME Software (domain name acme.com, network address 203.243.231) results in a command like

```
mktcpip -h coyote.acme.com -a 203.243.231.10 -i en0 -m \
255.255.255.0 -t N/A -g 203.243.231.1 -n 203.243.231.1 -d \
acme.com -s
```

The new machine's name is coyote, its IP address is 203.243.231.10 and TCP/IP is supported via twisted-pair cable (-t N/A) on the first Ethernet adapter (-i en0). The subnet mask is standard for a class C network (255.255.255.0). The domain name is acme.com and the same machine provides both DNS name resolution and the gateway to the Internet (203.243.231.1). TCP/IP is started if the definition is successful because the -s flag is specified.

11.1.2 Starting TCP/IP

If the -s flag is not specified with the `mktcpip` command, TCP/IP is not started. Normally, once TCP/IP is configured, it starts automatically at system startup. However, TCP/IP can be started at any time with the

```
startsrc -s tcpip
```

command.

11.1.3 ifconfig—Configure the network interface

Although the mktcpip command configures the network interface with default
values which are acceptable in most cases, the ifconfig command allows for
further fine tuning. It is the ifconfig command which is used at system startup to define the network interface. When used after system startup, the
ifconfig command can display or redefine network configuration information.
The syntax of the command is

```
ifconfig interface [address] [parameters...]
```

If only the interface name is given, the command defaults to a display of the
current values for the specified interface. An address is usually specified only
when the following parameter (such as alias) requires it. The various parameters that may be specified are outlined in Table 11.3. For example, to disable the default Ethernet interface, the user enters

```
ifconfig en0 down
```

At this point, changes to the interface can be made, such as

```
ifconfig en0 203.243.231.33 alias
```

to add a second IP address to the interface. The interface is then restored to
normal operation with the

```
ifconfig en0 up
```

command.

11.1.4 hostid—Displaying and modifying the host IP
address

The hostid command is used primarily to display a host identifier. The output of the command is the hexadecimal equivalent of the IP address. For
example, for IP address 192.11.199.3, the following exchange results from the
hostid command:

```
$ hostid
0xc00bc703
$
```

The root user may use this command to reset the IP address of the machine
by specifying a new IP address as the operand of the hostid command

```
$ hostid 192.11.199.10
0xc00bc70a
$
```

TABLE 11.3   `ifconfig` **Parameters**

Parameter	Meaning
`alias`	Establishes an additional network address the network interface can use. This is useful when changing network numbering schemes.
`allcast`	Sets a Token-Ring interface to broadcast to all rings on the network.
`-allcast`	Sets a Token-Ring interface to broadcast only on the local ring.
`arp`	Enables the command to use Address Resolution Protocol for mapping network-level address to link-level addresses. This is the default.
`-arp`	Disables the use of ARP.
`broadcast` *address*	Specifies the address to use when broadcasting to all stations on the network.
`debug`	Enables the driver-dependent debugging code.
`-debug`	Turns the driver-dependent debugger off.
`delete`	Removes the specified network address from the interface.
`detach`	Removes the interface from the network interface list.
`dow n`	Marks an interface as inactive.
`hwloop`	Enables hardware loopback on this interface.
`-hwloop`	Disables hardware loopback on this interface.
`metric` *number*	Sets the routing metric for the interface to the specified number. The default value is zero, which indicates the most favored route—higher values indicate less desirable routes.
`mtu`	Sets the maximum IP packet size for the interface. Applicable values are

Interface type	Default value	Maximum value
Ethernet (en)	1500	1500
802.3 Ethernet (et)	1492	1492
4-mb Token-Ring (tr)	1500	4056
16-mb Token-Ring (tr)	1500	17960
x.25 (xt)	576	1024
SLIP (sl)	1006	4096
Serial Optical (op)	61428	61428
loopback (lo)	1500	1500

Parameter	Meaning
`netmask` *mask*	The subnet mask in dotted quad notation.
`up`	Marks the interface as active.

11.1.5   `hostname`—Displays or sets the local host name

Along the same lines as the `hostid` command, the `hostname` command is used primarily to display the name of the local machine. A user with root authority may use the command to change the name of the machine. For example

```
$ hostname
coyote.acme.com
$ hostname roadrunner
roadrunner.acme.com
$
```

In the first command, the root user displays the current name of the host (coyote at acme.com) and then changes the name of the host to roadrunner by the second command.

11.1.6 host—Locate another system

The host command is used to resolve a host name into an IP address or an IP address into a host name. To display the address of a particular machine, the user enters the name of the machine

```
$ host boombox.micro.umn.edu
boombox.micro.umn.edu is 134.84.132.2
$
```

Alternatively, the IP address can be resolved to a host name

```
$ host 128.109.179.5
ftp.cnidr.org is 128.109.179.5
$
```

11.2 TCP/IP Advanced Configuration and Control

Advanced configuration of TCP/IP centers on the /etc/rc.net, /etc/rc.tcpip, /etc/inetd.conf, /etc/services, /etc/hosts, and /etc/resolv.conf files and those commands which manipulate or use them.

11.2.1 /etc/rc.net file—Configure the network environment

For the most part, the /etc/rc.net file is not typically modified unless the system is set up for x.25 or SLIP (Serial Line Interface Protocol) use.[4] This executable file is used during system startup to enable the network.

As can be seen in Fig. 11.1, the preferred method on configuration is to use the "new" method (section one of the configuration file) which relies on information in the system configuration database.[5] For die-hard bsd fans, the old method is outlined in the second section. The third, and final section, uses the hostid and uname command to set the host name and other identifying information. Finally, the no command[6] is called to override the default buffer setting for the network interface card.

11.2.2 /etc/rc.tcpip file—Configure TCP/IP services

Another system startup executable, the /etc/rc.tcpip file, (Figure 11.2) is used to start the individual servers and services of TCP/IP; the most important

---

[4]Configuration of these services is not discussed in this book. For further information refer to the *AIX Version 3.2 System Management Guide: Communications and Networks* (SC23-2487).

[5]For additional information on the new method configuration commands (defif, chgif, definet, and cfginet) the user is referred to *AIX Version 3.2 Commands Reference* vol. 1 (GC23-2376).

[6]Discussed in Sec. 11.3—TCP/IP Tuning Commands.

```
#!/bin/ksh
# @(#)90      1.18  com/cmd/net/netstart/rc.net, cmdnet, bos320, 9150320k 12/11/91
14:40:04
#
# COMPONENT_NAME: CMDNET         (/etc/rc.net)
#
# ORIGINS: 27
#
# (C) COPYRIGHT International Business Machines Corp. 1985, 1989
# All Rights Reserved
# Licensed Materials - Property of IBM
#
# US Government Users Restricted Rights - Use, duplication or
# disclosure restricted by GSA ADP Schedule Contract with IBM Corp.
#
#################################################################
# rc.net - called by cfgmgr during 2nd boot phase.
#
# Configures and starts TCP/IP interfaces.
# Sets hostname, default gateway and static routes.
# Note: all the stdout should be redirected to a file (e.g. /dev/null),
#      because stdout is used to pass logical name(s) back to the cfgmgr
#      to be configured.  The LOGFILE variable specifies the output file.
# The first section of rc.net configures the network via the new
#      configuration methods.  These configuration methods require that
#      the interface and protocol information be entered in the ODM
#      database (with either SMIT or the high level configuration commands
#      (mkdev, chdev).
# The second section (commented out) is an example of the equivalent
#      traditional commands used to perform the same function.  You may
#      use the traditional commands instead of the configuration methods
#      if you prefer.  These commands do NOT use the ODM database.
# The third section performs miscellaneous commands which are
#      compatible with either of the previous two sections.
#################################################################
#
# Close file descriptor 1 and 2 because the parent may be waiting
# for the file desc. 1 and 2 to be closed.  The reason is that this shell
# script may spawn a child which inherit all the file descriptor from the parent
# and the child process may still be running after this process is terminated.
# The file desc. 1 and 2 are not closed and leave the parent hanging
# waiting for those desc. to be finished.
#LOGFILE=/dev/null       # LOGFILE is where all stdout goes.
LOGFILE=/tmp/rc.net.out # LOGFILE is where all stdout goes.
>$LOGFILE               # truncate LOGFILE.
exec 1<&-               # close descriptor 1
exec 2<&-               # close descriptor 2
exec 1< /dev/null # open descriptor 1
exec 2<   /dev/null   # open descriptor 2

no -d lowclust         # set cluster low water mark
#################################################################
# Part I - Configuration using the data in the ODM database:
# Enable network interface(s):
#################################################################
# This should be done before routes are defined.
# For each network adapter that has already been configured, the
# following commands will define, load and configure a corresponding
# interface.
/usr/lib/methods/defif              >>$LOGFILE 2>&1
/usr/lib/methods/cfgif  $*              >>$LOGFILE 2>&1

#################################################################
#  Special X25 and SLIP handling
#################################################################
# In addition to configuring the network interface, X25 and SLIP
# interfaces require special commands to complete the configuration.
# The x25xlate command bring the x25 translation table into the
# kernel while the slattach changes the tty handling for the tty
# port used by the the SLIP interface.   A separate slattach command is
# executed  for every tty port used by configured SLIP interfaces.

X25HOST=`lsdev -C -c if -s XT -t xt -S available`
if [ ! -z "$X25HOST" ]
then
      x25xlate                  >>$LOGFILE 2>&1
fi

SLIPHOST=`lsdev -C -c if -s SL -t sl -S available | awk '{ print $1 }'`
for i in $SLIPHOST
do
      echo $i                  >>$LOGFILE 2>&1
      TTYPORT=`lsattr -E -l $i -F "value" -a ttyport`
      TTYBAUD=`lsattr -E -l $i -F "value" -a baudrate`
      TTYDIALSTRING=`lsattr -E -l $i -F "value" -a dialstring`
      rm -f /etc/locks/LCK..$TTYPORT
      if [ -z "$TTYBAUD" -a  -z "$TTYDIALSTRING" ]
      then
```

Figure 11.1   The /etc/rc.net file.

```
            FromHOST=`lsattr -E -l $i -F "value" -a netaddr`
            DestHOST=`lsattr -E -l $i -F "value" -a dest`
            SLIPMASK=`lsattr -E -l $i -F "value" -a netmask`
            if [ -z "$SLIPMASK" ]
            then
                    ifconfig $SLIPHOST inet $FromHOST $DestHOST up
            else
                    ifconfig $SLIPHOST inet $FromHOST $DestHOST netmask $SLIPMASK up
            fi
            ( slattach $TTYPORT )                >>$LOGFILE 2>&1
    else
            eval DST=\'$TTYDIALSTRING\'           >>$LOGFILE 2>&1
            ( eval slattach $TTYPORT $TTYBAUD \'$DST\' ) >>$LOGFILE 2>>$LOGFILE
    fi
done

###############################################################
# Configure the Internet protocol kernel extension (netinet):
###############################################################
# The following commands will also set hostname, default gateway,
# and static routes as found in the ODM database for the network.
/usr/lib/methods/definet                     >>$LOGFILE 2>&1
/usr/lib/methods/cfginet                     >>$LOGFILE 2>&1


###############################################################
# Part II - Traditional Configuration.
###############################################################
# An alternative method for bringing up all the default interfaces
# is to specify explicitly which interfaces to configure using the
# ifconfig command.  Ifconfig requires the configuration information
# be specified on the command line.  Ifconfig will not update the
# information kept in the ODM configuration database.
#
# Valid network interfaces are:
# lo=local loopback, en=standard ethernet, et=802.3 ethernet
# sl=serial line IP, tr=802.5 token ring, xt=X.25
#
# e.g., en0 denotes standard ethernet network interface, unit zero.
#
# Below are examples of how you could bring up each interface using
# ifconfig.  Since you can specify either a hostname or a dotted
# decimal address to set the interface address, it is convenient to
# set the hostname at this point and use it for the address of
# an interface, as shown below:
#
#/bin/hostname robo.austin.ibm.com  >>$LOGFILE 2>&1
#
# (Remember that if you have more than one interface,
# you'll want to have a different IP address for each one.
# Below, xx.xx.xx.xx stands for the internet address for the
# given interface.)
#
#/usr/sbin/ifconfig lo0 inet loopback    up >>$LOGFILE 2>&1
#/usr/sbin/ifconfig en0 inet `hostname`  up >>$LOGFILE 2>&1
#/usr/sbin/ifconfig et0 inet xx.xx.xx.xx up >>$LOGFILE 2>&1
#/usr/sbin/ifconfig tr0 inet xx.xx.xx.xx up >>$LOGFILE 2>&1
#/usr/sbin/ifconfig sl0 inet xx.xx.xx.xx up >>$LOGFILE 2>&1
#/usr/sbin/ifconfig xt0 inet xx.xx.xx.xx up >>$LOGFILE 2>&1
#
#
# Now we set any static routes.
#
# /usr/sbin/route add 0 gateway             >>$LOGFILE 2>&1
# /usr/sbin/route add 192.9.201.0 gateway     >>$LOGFILE 2>&1

###############################################################
# Part III - Miscellaneous Commands.
###############################################################
# Set the hostid and uname to `hostname`, where hostname has been
# set via ODM in Part I, or directly in Part II.
# (Note it is not required that hostname, hostid and uname all be
# the same.)
/usr/sbin/hostid `hostname`        >>$LOGFILE 2>&1
/bin/uname -S`hostname|sed 's/\..*$//'`   >>$LOGFILE 2>&1


###############################################################
# The socket default buffer size (initial advertized TCP window) is being
# set to a default value of 16k (16384). This improves the performance
# for ethernet and token ring networks.  Networks with lower bandwidth
# such as SLIP (Serial Line Internet Protocol) and X.25 or higher bandwidth
# such as Serial Optical Link and FDDI would have a different optimum
# buffer size.
# ( OPTIMUM WINDOW = Bandwidth * Round Trip Time )
###############################################################
if [ -f /usr/sbin/no ] ; then
     /usr/sbin/no -o tcp_sendspace=16384
     /usr/sbin/no -o tcp_recvspace=16384
fi
```

Figure 11.1 *(Continued)*

```
#! /bin/bsh
# @(#)95        1.48  com/etc/rc.tcpip, tcpip, tcpip320, 9142320
10/10/91 11:19:40
#
# COMPONENT_NAME: TCPIP rc.tcpip
#
# FUNCTIONS:
#
# ORIGINS: 26  27
#
# (C) COPYRIGHT International Business Machines Corp. 1985, 1989
# All Rights Reserved
# Licensed Materials - Property of IBM
#
# US Government Users Restricted Rights - Use, duplication or
# disclosure restricted by GSA ADP Schedule Contract with IBM Corp.
#
###################################################################
# rc.tcpip -
#     assumes interfaces are brought up by /etc/rc.net
#     starts TCP/IP daemons (sendmail, inetd, etc.)
###################################################################
# start -
#     starts daemons using either src or command-line method
# args:
#     $1: pathname of daemon
#     $2: non-null if we should use src to start the daemon
#     $3: any arguments to pass it
#
start()
{
      # just return if the daemon doesn't exist
      #
      [ -x $1 ] || return 0

      # start the daemon using either src or command-line method
      #
      cmd=`basename $1`
      if [ -n "$2" ] ; then
            startsrc -s $cmd -a "$3"
      else
            $1 $3
            echo "\t$cmd"
      fi
}

# check the bootup_option flag in the configuration database
option=`lsattr -E -l inet0 -a bootup_option -F value`
if [ "$option" = "no" ]
then
###################################################################
#
# Check to see if srcmstr is running; if so, we try to use it;
# otherwise, we start the daemons without src
#
i=3 # make sure init has time to start it
while [ $i != 0 ] ; do
      if [ -n "`ps -e | awk '$NF == "srcmstr" { print $1; exit }'`" ]
then
            src_running=1 # set flag
            break
      fi
      i=`expr $i - 1` # decrement count
done
```

Figure 11.2 The /etc/rc.tcpip file.

```
# If srcmstr is running, ensure that it is active before issuing the
# startsrc commands
#
if [ -n "$src_running" ] ; then
      echo "Checking for srcmstr active...\c"
      i=10  # try ten times to contact it
      while [ $i != 0 ] ; do
              lssrc -s inetd >/dev/null 2>&1 && break  # break out on
success
              sleep 1  # otherwise wait a second and try again
              echo ".\c"
              i=`expr $i - 1`  # decrement count
      done
      if [ $i = 0 ] ; then
              echo "\n\nERROR: srcmstr is not accepting connections.\n"
              exit 1
      fi
      echo "complete"
fi

else
      src_running=""
fi
# Start up the daemons
#
echo "Starting tcpip daemons:"

# Start up syslog daemon (for error and event logging)
start /etc/syslogd "$src_running"

# Start up print daemon
start /usr/lpd/lpd "$src_running"

# Start up routing daemon (only start ONE)
#start /etc/routed "$src_running" -q
start /etc/gated "$src_running"

# Start up the sendmail daemon.
#
# Sendmail will automatically build the configuration and alias
# databases the first time it is invoked.  You may wish to update
# the alias source file /usr/lib/aliases with local information,
# and then rebuild the alias database by issuing the command
# "/usr/lib/sendmail -bi" or "/usr/ucb/newaliases".
#
# When the configuration or alias databases are changed, the
# sendmail daemon can be made to rebuild and reread them by
# issuing the command "kill -1 `cat /etc/sendmail.pid`" or, if
# SRC was used to start the daemon, "refresh -s sendmail".
#
# The "qpi", or queue processing interval, determines how
# frequently the daemon processes the message queue.
#
qpi=30m  # 30 minute interval
#
start /usr/lib/sendmail "$src_running" "-bd -q${qpi}"

# Start up Portmapper
mount | grep ' /usr *nfs' 2>&1 > /dev/null
if [ "$?" -ne 0 ]
then
REMOTE_USR="N"
start /usr/etc/portmap "$src_running"
fi
```

Figure 11.2 (*Continued*).

```
# Start up socket-based daemons
start /etc/inetd "$src_running"

# Start up Domain Name daemon
start /etc/named "$src_running"

# Start up time daemon
start /etc/timed "$src_running"

# Start up rwhod daemon (a time waster)
#start /etc/rwhod "$src_running"

# Start up the Simple Network Management Protocol (SNMP) daemon
start /usr/sbin/snmpd "$src_running"
```

Figure 11.2 (*Continued*).

being inetd which controls the socket-based Internet application services of the network such as ftp and telnet.

The first part of the /etc/rc.tcpip file defines a function start which is used to control the execution of the startsrc command on behalf of the TCP/IP daemons. After this, several different checks are made to determine whether the *system resource controller* (SRC) is available. If it is available, the daemons are started under SRC control; if not, the daemons are started as independent processes.

In the default /etc/rc.tcpip file, several common functions are predefined. To enable a function, a start command is given for the function; to disable a function, a pound sign (#) is placed in front of the start command. If a function is not used on a host, the function should not be enabled. This reduces the total load on the system and also enhances security; this is particularly true for sendmail and rwhod.

An important consideration in the /etc/rc.tcpip file is which dynamic routing daemon will be used. For small networks, the routed daemon, which supports the Routing Information Protocol, may be sufficient. For machines attached to larger networks, the gated daemon[7] is more appropriate; however it must be configured before it may be used.[8] Both may not be used at the same time; doing so leads to unpredictable results.

11.2.3 /etc/inetd.conf and /etc/services—Define inetd services

Working together, the /etc/inetd.conf (Figure 11.3) and /etc/services (Fig. 11.4) files define the available TCP/IP Internet services and how they are invoked. This includes standard services such as ftp (file transfer protocol)

---

[7]The gated daemon supports the Routing Information Protocol (RIP), Hello Protocol (HELLO), Exterior Gateway Protocol (EGP), Border Gateway Protocol (BGP) and Simple Network Management Protocol (SNMP).

[8]This is done in the /etc/gated.conf file. For further information refer to the *AIX Version 3.2 System Management Guide: Communications and Networks* (SC23-2487).

```
# @(#)62    1.17  com/etc/inetd.conf, , tcpip320, 9141320 6/13/91 13:31:13
#
# COMPONENT_NAME: TCPIP inetd.conf
#
# FUNCTIONS:
#
# ORIGINS: 26   27
#
# (C) COPYRIGHT International Business Machines Corp. 1985, 1989
# All Rights Reserved
# Licensed Materials - Property of IBM
#
# US Government Users Restricted Rights - Use, duplication or
# disclosure restricted by GSA ADP Schedule Contract with IBM Corp.
#
#  /etc/inetd.conf
#
#              Internet server configuration database
#
#     Services can be added and deleted by deleting or inserting a
#     comment character (ie. #) at the beginning of a line  If inetd
#     is running under SRC control then the "inetimp" command must
#     be executed to import the information from this file to the
#     InetServ ODM object class, then the "refresh -s inetd" command
#     needs to be executed for inetd to reread the InetServ database.
#
#     NOTE: The TCP/IP servers do not require SRC and may be started
#     by invoking the service directly (i.e. /etc/inetd). If inetd
#     has been invoked directly, after modifying this file, send a
#     hangup signal, SIGHUP to inetd (ie. kill -1 "pid_of_inetd").
#
#     NOTE: The services with socket type of "sunrpc_tcp" and "sunrpc_udp"
#     require that the portmap daemon be running.
#
# service     socket      protocol   wait/    user      server      server program
#  name        type                  nowait             program       arguments
#
#uucp        stream        tcp      nowait    root      /etc/uucpd uucpd
ftp          stream        tcp      nowait    root      /etc/ftpd ftpd
telnet       stream        tcp      nowait    root      /etc/telnetd     telnetd
#shell       stream        tcp      nowait    root      /etc/rshd rshd
#login       stream        tcp      nowait    root      /etc/rlogind     rlogind
#exec        stream        tcp      nowait    root      /etc/rexecd      rexecd
#bootps      dgram         udp      wait      root      /etc/bootpd      bootpd
#finger      stream        tcp      nowait    nobody    /etc/fingerd     fingerd
#tftp        dgram         udp      wait      nobody    /etc/tftpd       tftpd -n
#biff        dgram         udp      wait      root      /etc/comsat      comsat
#talk        dgram         udp      wait      root      /etc/talkd       talkd
ntalk        dgram         udp      wait      root      /etc/talkd       talkd
#rexd        sunrpc_tcp    tcp      wait      root      /usr/etc/rpc.rexd rexd 100017 1
#rstatd      sunrpc_udp    udp      wait      root      /usr/etc/rpc.rstatd rstatd 100001 1-3
#rusersd     sunrpc_udp    udp      wait      root      /usr/etc/rpc.rusersd rusersd 100002 1-2
#rwalld      sunrpc_udp    udp      wait      root      /usr/etc/rpc.rwalld rwalld 100008 1
#sprayd      sunrpc_udp    udp      wait      root      /usr/etc/rpc.sprayd sprayd 100012 1
#pcnfsd      sunrpc_udp    udp      wait      root      /etc/rpc.pcnfsd  pcnfsd 150001 1
echo         stream        tcp      nowait    root      internal
discard      stream        tcp      nowait    root      internal
chargen      stream        tcp      nowait    root      internal
daytime      stream        tcp      nowait    root      internal
time         stream        tcp      nowait    root      internal
echo         dgram         udp      wait      root      internal
discard      dgram         udp      wait      root      internal
chargen      dgram         udp      wait      root      internal
daytime      dgram         udp      wait      root      internal
time         dgram         udp      wait      root      internal
```

Figure 11.3 The /etc/inetd.conf file.

```
# @(#)27      1.14  com/cmd/net/services, bos, bos320 6/11/91 16:24:33
#
# COMPONENT_NAME: (CMDNET) Network commands.
#
# FUNCTIONS:
#
# ORIGINS: 26 27
#
# (C) COPYRIGHT International Business Machines Corp. 1988, 1989
# All Rights Reserved
# Licensed Materials - Property of IBM
#
# US Government Users Restricted Rights - Use, duplication or
# disclosure restricted by GSA ADP Schedule Contract with IBM Corp.
#
#
# Network services, Internet style
#
echo          7/tcp
echo          7/udp
discard       9/tcp       sink null
discard       9/udp       sink null
systat        11/tcp      users
daytime       13/tcp
daytime       13/udp
netstat       15/tcp
qotd          17/tcp      quote
chargen       19/tcp      ttytst source
chargen       19/udp      ttytst source
ftp-data      20/tcp
ftp           21/tcp
telnet        23/tcp
smtp          25/tcp      mail
time          37/tcp      timserver
time          37/udp      timserver
rlp           39/udp      resource    # resource location
nameserver    42/udp      name        # IEN 116
whois         43/tcp      nicname
domain        53/tcp      nameserver  # name-domain server
domain        53/udp      nameserver
mtp           57/tcp                  # deprecated
bootps        67/udp                  # bootp server port
bootpc        68/udp                  # bootp client port
tftp          69/udp
rje           77/tcp      netrjs
finger        79/tcp
link          87/tcp      ttylink
supdup        95/tcp
hostnames     101/tcp     hostname    # usually from sri-nic
iso_tsap      102/tcp
x400          103/tcp
x400-snd      104/tcp
csnet-ns      105/tcp
pop           109/tcp     postoffice
sunrpc        111/tcp
sunrpc        111/udp
auth          113/tcp     authentication
sftp          115/tcp
uucp-path     117/tcp
nntp          119/tcp     readnews untp # USENET News Transfer
Protocol
ntp           123/tcp
NeWS          144/tcp
snmp          161/udp                 # snmp request port
snmp-trap     162/udp                 # snmp monitor trap port
smux          199/tcp                 # snmpd smux port
src           200/udp                 # System Resource controller
#
```

Figure 11.4 The /etc/services file.

and `telnet` in addition to other services such as remote user identification (`finger`) and database services.[9]

The default /etc/inetd.conf file supplied with AIX starts only the more common services. Additional entries may be started by removing the leading pound sign (#) from an entry. For security reasons, as with the /etc/rc.tcpip

[9]For more information on TCP/IP services, see the book *TCP/IP Architecture, Protocols, and Implementation* by Sidnie Feit (McGraw-Hill, 1993).

```
# UNIX specific services
#
exec          512/tcp
biff          512/udp     comsat
login         513/tcp
who           513/udp     whod
shell         514/tcp     cmd          # no passwords used
syslog        514/udp
printer       515/tcp     spooler      # line printer spooler
talk          517/udp
ntalk         518/udp
efs           520/tcp                  # for LucasFilm
route         520/udp     router routed
timed         525/udp     timeserver
tempo         526/tcp     newdate
courier       530/tcp     rpc
conference    531/tcp     chat
netnews       532/tcp     readnews
netwall       533/udp                  # -for emergency broadcasts
uucp          540/tcp     uucpd        # uucp daemon
new-rwho      550/udp
remotefs      556/tcp     rfs_server # Brunhoff remote filesystem
rmonitor      560/udp
monitor       561/udp
instsrv       1234/tcp                 # network install service
ingreslock    1524/tcp
writesrv      2401/tcp                 # temporary port number
```

Figure 11.4 (*Continued*).

file, functions which are not used should not be enabled. A common ploy of hackers is to connect to a service (such as finger) and exploit it. This precaution also applies to the /etc/services file. Ports which are not used should not be enabled. As with the other configuration files, place a pound sign (#) in front of the entries to be disabled.

New ports and services may be added simply by adding new lines in the /etc/inetd.conf and /etc/services files. This is very common in database systems that use ports for communication between the database server and the client.

After the /etc/inetd.conf or /etc/services file has been modified, the inetimp command (Sec. 11.2.6) should be executed.

11.2.4 /etc/hosts—The host definition table

The /etc/hosts file (Fig. 11.5) is used to provide for a static name resolution for a host. This static resolution is mandatory for the host machine. Additional hosts, such as print servers, network gateways, and other frequently referenced hosts may also be defined in this file. Hosts defined in the /etc/hosts file are not subject to the overhead involved in resolving the name of the host into an IP address through the domain name server. However, flexibility in altering network resources is lost by using static references.

In general, it is best to define a minimum number of hosts in the /etc/hosts file and let DNS resolve the majority of the requests.

11.2.5 /etc/resolv.conf—Configuring to use a name server

The /etc/resolv.conf (Fig. 11.6) is used to configure a machine to use another host on the network as a domain name server.[10] The /etc/resolv.conf file con-

---

[10]For information on setting up a machine to be a domain name server, consult *TCP/IP Network Administration* (O'Reilly & Associates) and *AIX Version 3.2 System Management Guide: Communications and Networks* (SC23-2487).

```
# @(#)47     1.1  com/cmd/net/netstart/hosts, bos, bos320 7/24/91
10:00:46
#
# COMPONENT_NAME: TCPIP hosts
#
# FUNCTIONS: loopback
#
# ORIGINS: 26  27
#
# (C) COPYRIGHT International Business Machines Corp. 1985, 1989
# All Rights Reserved
# Licensed Materials - Property of IBM
#
# US Government Users Restricted Rights - Use, duplication or
# disclosure restricted by GSA ADP Schedule Contract with IBM Corp.
#
#  /etc/hosts
#
# This file contains the hostnames and their address for hosts in the
# network.  This file is used to resolve a hostname into an Internet
# address.
#
# At minimum, this file must contain the name and address for each
# device defined for TCP in your /etc/net file.  It may also contain
# entries for well-known (reserved) names such as timeserver
# and printserver as well as any other host name and address.
#
# The format of this file is:
# Internet Address       Hostname    # Comments
# Items are separated by any number of blanks and/or tabs.  A '#'
# indicates the beginning of a comment; characters up to the end of the
# line are not interpreted by routines which search this file.  Blank
# lines are allowed.

# Internet Address       Hostname    # Comments
# 192.9.200.1            net0sample  # ethernet name/address
# 128.100.0.1            token0sample       # token ring name/address
# 10.2.0.2         x25sample   # x.25 name/address
127.0.0.1         loopback localhost       # loopback (lo0) name/address
203.243.231.11    roadrunner
203.243.231.10    coyote
203.243.231.01    gateway
```

Figure 11.5 The /etc/hosts file.

```
nameserver  203.243.231.1
nameserver  203.243.231.10
domain      acme.com
```

Figure 11.6 The /etc/resolv.conf file.

tains two types of entries: nameserver entries which indicate which machines (by IP address) to use for name resolution, and domain entries which define the full name of the domain for which the name server is responsible.

In the example in Fig. 11.6, two nameservers are listed for the acme.com domain. If the first nameserver is not reachable or cannot provide a name resolution, the second nameserver is consulted. If neither nameserver can resolve the name, the name resolution fails.

11.2.6 `inetimp`—Update the configuration database with `/etc/inetd.conf` and `/etc/services` information

The `inetimp` command is used to update the system configuration database with the information in the /etc/inetd.conf and /etc/services files. If should always be used after modifying these two files to keep the system in synchronization.

11.2.7 `setclock`—Display or set the system time from a timer server

When used by a nonroot user, the `setclock` command displays the time based on information from the network time server. If used by the root user, the `setclock` command then sets the time on the local host to that retrieved from the time server. The syntax of the command is

```
setclock [timeserver]
```

If an explicit timeserver host is not named, the network default timeserver is used.

Any host on the network may become a timeserver by enabling the time entries in the /etc/inetd.conf file and port 37 in the /etc/services file.

11.2.8 `securetcpip`—Enable the network security features

Enhanced network security is the end result of running the `securetcpip` command. This is accomplished by disabling all nontrusted commands (`rcp`, `rlogin`, `rlogind`, `rsh`, `rshd`, `tftp`, and `tftpd`) and adding a TCP/IP stanza to the /etc/security/sysck.cfg file. These actions are permanent.

Before executing the `securetcpip` command, the system must be quiesced with the `killall` command by the root user. After the `securetcpip` command has run, shut down and restart the system.

11.3 TCP/IP Tuning and Diagnosis Commands

Several commands are provided for diagnosing problems with and optimizing the performance of TCP/IP.

TABLE 11.4 `iptrace` **Command Flags**

Flag	Meaning
`-a`	Suppresses ARP (Address Resolution Protocol) packets
`-b`	Changes the `-d` and `-s z` flags to bidirectional mode
`-d` *host*	Records packets from the destination *host* which may be either a hostname or IP address
`-i` *interface*	Records packets received on the specified *interface*
`-P` *protocol*	Records packets of the specified *protocol*
`-p` *port*	Records packets using the specified *port*
`-s` *host*	Records packets from the source *host* which may be either a hostname or IP address

11.3.1 `iptrace`—Trace IP packets

The `iptrace` command invokes a daemon to record IP packets. Command flags (Table 11.4) are used to limit the amount and type of information collected. For example, the command

```
iptrace /tmp/all.network.trace
```

records all packets coming into and out of the host on all network interfaces in file /tmp/all.network.trace. The command

```
iptrace -i en0 -p ftp -s coyote /tmp/coyote.ftp.trace
```

traces only the ftp packets received on interface en0 from coyote; the name of the trace file is

```
/tmp/coyote.ftp.trace.
```

To interpret the results of the trace, the `ipreport` command is used. The `iptrace` daemon is terminated with the `kill` command.

11.3.2 `ipreport`—Generate an IP trace report

The `ipreport` command generates a human-readable report from an `iptrace` file. Four flags are used with the command

`-e`	To generate the output in EBCDIC; the default is ASCII
`-r`	To decode remote procedure call (RPC) packets
`-n`	To display the packet number
`-s`	To prefix each line with its protocol specification

The syntax of the command is

```
ipreport [flags] inputfile
```

To format our prior example, the command is

```
ipreport -n /tmp/coyote.ftp.trace
```

11.3.3   `ping`—Determine if another host is up

The `ping` command is used to determine the status of foreign hosts. If the foreign host is operational, it responds to the ping command message (ICMP Echo_Request) with a return message. Unless restricted through command flags, the `ping` command sends one message every second and prints a line of output for every response received. It computes roundtrip message times and packet loss statistics and displays a summary upon command completion. A typical example of `ping` output follows:

```
$ ping -c 5 coyote.acme.com
PING coyote.acme.com: (203.243.231.10): 56 bytes
64 bytes from 203.243.231.10: icmp_seq=0 ttl=255 time=25 ms
64 bytes from 203.243.231.10: icmp_seq=1 ttl=255 time=2 ms
64 bytes from 203.243.231.10: icmp_seq=2 ttl=255 time=3 ms
64 bytes from 203.243.231.10: icmp_seq=3 ttl=255 time=2 ms
64 bytes from 203.243.231.10: icmp_seq=4 ttl=255 time=4 ms
64 bytes from 203.243.231.10: icmp_seq=5 ttl=255 time=2 ms
----coyote.acme.com PING Statistics ----
5 packets transmitted, 5 packets received, 0% packet loss
round-trip min/avg/max = 2/3/4 ms
$
```

Table 11.5 describes the command flags available with `ping`.

11.3.4   `spray`—Test network performance characteristics

The `spray` command is used to send a large number of messages to another host. The end result is a report of how many packets were received by the remote host and what the transfer rate was. The remote host must be running the `sprayd` daemon for the function to complete successfully.[11]

The syntax of the command is

```
spray host [-c count] [-d delay]
```

where the host is either the symbolic name or IP address of the remote host to be sprayed. If a specific number of packets is not defined with the -c flag, the `spray` command sends enough packets to equal 100,000 bytes. Normally, there is no pause when sending out the packets; however the -d flag may be used to specify the number of microseconds the system should pause between each sent packet.

---

[11]Actually, if the root user uses the -i flag, the remote host does not need to be running the sprayd daemon. This is because the -i flag causes ICMP echo packets to be sent instead of the normal RPC (remote procedure call) packets. ICMP echo packets are automatically acknowledged.

TABLE 11.5 `ping` **Flags**

Flag	Meaning
`-c count`	Specifies the number of messages to be sent
`-f`	Specifies flood-pinging. This option, which may only be used by the root user, sends ping messages as fast as possible (up to 100 per second). Command execution is terminated with the INTERRUPT (Ctrl-C) key.
`-i wait`	Indicates the number of seconds to wait before sending each message. The default is one second. Incompatible with the `-f` flag.
`-l preload`	Sends the number of packets specified by *preload* as fast as possible before reverting to normal speed (one per second).
`-n`	Specifies numeric output only. No attempt is made to loop up symbolic names for host addresses.
`-p pattern`	Allows for a specific pattern of padding bytes, up to 16 characters long, to be sent.
`-q`	Indicates quiet mode. Only the beginning and ending summary lines are displayed.
`-r`	Bypasses routing tables and sends directly to the host on the attached network; if the host is not on the directly attached network, an error is returned.
`-R`	Requests the route option. If all hosts and gateways along the route support this option, in addition to the regular information, routing information also is displayed.
`-s PacketSize`	Specifies the number of data bytes to be sent. The default is 56 which translates into 64 when the 8-byte ICMP header is included.
`-v`	Requests verbose output, which lists all ICMP packets that are received in addition to the echo-requests.

11.3.5 `traceroute`—Follow the route to a foreign host

The `traceroute` command sends messages to a foreign host much like `ping`, except that the purpose of `traceroute` is to identify the path a message takes to reach its destination. `traceroute` works by sending three initial messages with a *Time to Live* (TTL) set to 1. This causes the first router to return the messages. The TTL is increased to 2 and three more messages are sent. This causes the second router to return the messages. This process continues, with the TTL increased by one each time, until the destination is reached.

By forcing each router along the path to return the messages (by having the TTL expire), each router on the path identifies itself.

The output of the command reports the round-trip time of each of the three messages. Note in the following example how the first message often takes much longer than the subsequent messages. This is usually explained by the fact that the first message is delayed due to address resolution.

```
$ traceroute boombox.micro.umn.edu
traceroute to boombox.micro.umn.edu (134.84.132.2), 30 hops max, 40 byte
packets
1 gateway.acme.com (203.243.231.1) 3 ms 3 ms 3 ms
2 192.101.184.4 (192.101.184.4) 5 ms 5 ms 5 ms
3 dga-nsi.cic.net (131.103.16.145) 8 ms 8 ms 8 ms
4 dgb-eth0.cic.net (131.103.1.2) 9 ms 8 ms 8 ms
```

```
5 umn-dgb.cic.net (131.103.25.2) 17 ms 26 ms 18 ms
6 tc0+.gw.umn.edu (198.174.96.4) 35 ms 19 ms 26 ms
7 tc1.gw.umn.edu (134.84.254.254) 22 ms 35 ms 19 ms
8 boombox.micro.umn.edu (134.84.132.2) 29 ms 20 ms 29 ms
$
```

11.3.6   no—Configure network options

The no command is used to configure network options; most often the size of the buffer pools. Because the changes made with the no command are not permanent,[12] it is typically invoked during system startup in the

```
/etc/rc.net file.
```

But, the no command is also used to display the current network configuration. When used with the -a flag, it displays the configurable options and their current values. The -d flag is used to set the value of a variable (Table 11.6) to its default value. The -o flag is used to set a variable to a new value.

The following command sets the maximum size of the buffer pools to 4 Mbytes:

```
no -o thewall=4096
```

11.3.7   netstat—Display network statistics

The netstat command is used to display information about the network. Depending on the options specified, the command output can take many different forms. The various fields which result as output from this command are documented in Table 11.7. The flags of netstat are documented in Table 11.8.

The most common use of netstat is to display routing table information, such as

```
$ netstat -r
Routing tables
Destination        Gateway           Flags   Refcnt Use
Interface
Netmasks:
(root node)
(0)0 ff00 0
(0)0 ffff ff00 0
(root node)

Route Tree for Protocol Family 2:
(root node)
default            203.243.231.1     UG      9 23495633 tr0
127                localhost.0.0.127. U      8  1687409 lo0
203.243.231.32     coyote.acme.com   U      13  3358083 tr0
(root node)

Route Tree for Protocol Family 6:
(root node)
(root node)
$
```

---

[12]They are not stored in a configuration file.

TABLE 11.6   no **Variables**

Variable	Meaning
arpt_killc	Specifies the time in minutes before an inactive ARP (Address Resolution Protocol) entry is deleted. The default is 20 minutes.
detach_route	Removes a route associated with an interface when the interface is detached (i.e., iconfig detach). The default value is 1; a value of 0 indicates the route is not detached.
dog_ticks	Sets the timer granularity for the interface watchdog routines. The default value of 60 runs the watchdog routines once per second.
ipforwarding	Specifies whether the system should forward packets. The default value of 1 forward packets; a value of 0 prevents packet forwarding.
ipfragttl	Specifies the time to live for IP fragments. The default value is 60 seconds.
ipqmaxlen	Specifies the maximum number of received packets that can be queued on the IP input queue.
ipsendredirects	Specifies whether the system should send redirect signals. The default value of 1 sends redirects, a value of 0 prevents redirects from being sent.
loop_check_sum	Specifies the checksum on a loopback interface. The default value of 1 activates the checksum; 0 deactivates it.
lowclust	Specifies a low-water mark for the cluster message buffer pool. If the number of free buffers in the pool drops below this value, the pool is expanded so that at least the lowclust number of buffers is available.
lowmbuf	Specifies a low-water mark for the message buffer (mbuf) pool. If the number of free buffers in the pool drops below this value, the pool is expanded so that at least the lowmbuf number of buffers is available.
maxttl	Specifies the time to live for RIP (Routing Information Protocol) packets. The default is 255 seconds.
mb_cl_hiwat	Specifies a high-water mark for the cluster mbuf pool. If the number of free buffers in the pool exceeds this value, the pool is contracted until a maximum of mb_cl_hiwatB buffers are available.
nonlocsrcroute	Allows packets to be addressed outside the local ring. The default value of 1 allows packets to be sent to outside hosts; 0 disallows addressing of outside hosts.
rfc1122addrchk	Performs address validation as specified by NIC RFC1122. The default value of 0 does not perform this address validation; a value of 1 performs it.
sb_max	Specifies the maximum buffer size for a socket. The default is 65536 bytes.
subnetsarelocal	The default value of 1 specifies that addresses which match the local network mask are local; the value of 0 indicates that only addresses matching the local subnetwork are local.
tcp_keepidle	Specifies the length of time to keep a connection active, in half-seconds. The default is 14,400 half-seconds (or 2 hours).
tcp_keepintvl	Specifies the interval, in half-seconds, between packets sent to validate the connection. The default value is 150 half-seconds.
tcp_recvspace	Specifies the default buffer size for receiving data. The default value is 4096, however, a value of 16384 improves the performance of Token-Ring and Standard Ethernet networks.
tcp_sendspace	Specifies the default buffer size for sending data. The default value is 4096, however, a value of 16384 improves the performance of Token-Ring and Standard Ethernet networks.

TABLE 11.6 no **Variables (Continued)**

Variable	Meaning
tcp_ttl	Specifies the time to live for TCP packets. The default is 60 ticks (100 ticks = 1 minute).
thewall	Specifies the maximum amount of memory that may be allocated to the mbuf and cluster mbuf pools. The default is 2048 (2 Mbytes).
udp_recspace	Specifies the default buffer size for receiving UDP data. The default is 41,600 bytes.
udp_sendspace	Specifies the default buffer size for sending UDP data. The default is 41,600 bytes.
udp_ttl	Specifies the time to live for UDP packets. The default is 30 ticks (100 ticks = 1 minute).

The routing table display indicates the available routes in the network and their statuses. Each route consists of a destination (either another host or a network) and a gateway to use for routing requests. The first column indicates the destination, the second column shows the gateway to the destination, and the third column displays the flags (Table 11.7) showing the state of the route. The last two columns indicate the number of users on the route, and the number of packets sent on the route, respectively. In most networks, the route tree is populated only for Protocol Family 2, which is TCP/IP and UDP. Protocol family 6 is the Xerox Networking System (XNS).

The netstat -v displays detail network and error-logging data for the device drivers which are active for an interface. On our example system, only one Token-Ring device is active so our display is as follows:

```
$ netstat -v
TOKEN STATISTICS (tr0) :
Hardware Address: 10:00:5a:a8:72:f5
Transmit Byte Count: 3632264077.0    Receive Byte Count: 2545659796.0
Transmit Frame Count: 25407057.0     Receive Frame Count: 31729556.0
Transmit Error Count: 31             Receive Error Count: 0
Max Netid's in use: 1                Max Transmits queued: 0
Max Receives queued: 0               Max Stat Blks queued: 0
Interrupts lost: 0                   WDT Interrupts lost: 0
Timeout Ints lost: 0                 Status lost: 0
Receive Packets Lost: 0              No Mbuf Errors: 0
No Mbuf Extension Errors: 0          Receive Int Count: 32097146
Transmit Int Count: 25406954         Packets Rejected No NetID: 367652
Packets Accepted Valid NetID: 31729556  Overflow Packets Received: 0
Packets Transmitted and Adapter Errors Detected: 31
$
```

The netstat -i display outputs interface information on Internet interfaces

```
$ netstat -i
Name  Mtu   Network       Address          Ipkts      Ierrs  Opkts     Oerrs
lo0   1536  <Link>                         3307661    0      3307661   0
lo0   1536  127           localhost.0.0.1  3307661    0      3307661   0
tr0   1492  <Link>                         31729439   0      25407828  789
tr0   1492  203.243.231   coyote.acme.com  31729439   0      25407828  789
```

TABLE 11.7 `netstat` **Output Fields**

Field	Description
address	The symbolic version of the network address; if this cannot be determined the numeric version is displayed. An asterisk (*) denotes an unspecified address or port.
coll	Displays the number of input and output collisions occurring on SLIP (Serial Line Interface Protocol) interfaces. Not supported for other protocols.
colls	Sames as coll.
conn	For sockets connected to another socket, the control block address of the socket to which it is connected.
destination	Displays the destination host by symbolic name or address.
errs	Displays the input and output errors for the specified interface.
flags	Displays the state of the route; the valid values are U Up. G Route is to a gateway. D Route was created dynamically. H Host identifier. M Route has been modified by a redirect.
foreign address	Displayed in the form 'xxx.yyy' where x is the host address and y is the port address. If the symbolic address is unknown, the address is printed numerically. An unspecified address or port is displayed as an asterisk (*)
gateway	Displays the address of the outgoing interface to be used in forwarding packets.
Ierrs	Displays input errors on a given interface.
Inode	For sockets associated with an inode in the file system; the address of the inode.
Interface	The network interface used for a route. Valid values include tr Token-Ring en Ethernet et 802.3 Ethernet lo loopback
Ipkts	Number of packets received on an interface.
local address	Displayed in the form 'xxx.yyy' where x is the host address and y is the port address. If the symbolic address for an address is unknown, the address is printed numerically. An unspecified address or port is displayed as an asterisk (*).
mtu	Displays the maximum transmission unit (or packet size) allowed on the interface.
name	Displays the name of the interface.
Nextref	See refs.
Network	Displays the network address.
Oerrs	Displays output errors on a given interface.
Opkts	Displays the number of packets sent on an interface.
Packets	Displays the number of incoming and outgoing packets for a specified interface.
PCB/ADDR	The protocol control block address for an active Internet connection; the two addresses shown are the PCB address and the IP or socket address, depending on the socket type.
Proto	Display the protocol type. Valid values include tcp Transmission Control Protocol. ip Internet Protocol. icmp Internet Message Control Protocol. udp User Datagram Protocol.

TABLE 11.7 `netstat` **Output Fields** (*Continued*)

Field	Description
Recv-Q	The number of bytes in the socket receive buffer.
Refcnt	Displays the current number of active users for a particular route.
Refs	For sockets referencing other sockets, this field displays the address of the other socket. The Nextref field contains the address of the first socket referenced by the initially referenced socket.
SADR/PCB	Displays the socket address and its associated protocol control block address.
Send-Q	The number of bytes in the socket send buffer.
Type	The socket type. Current types include
	Stream socket a connection-based byte stream.
	Datagram socket a connectionless-based message.
	Raw socket provides access to Internet network protocols.
Use	Displays a count of the number of packets sent using a given route.
(state)	Displays the internal state of a protocol.

TABLE 11.8 `netstat` **Flags**

Flag	Meaning
-A	Shows the address of protocol control blocks associated with sockets.
-a	Shows the state of all sockets.
-I *interface*	Displays a running count of statistics regarding the specified interface, such as lo, tr, or en. If this flag is used, an *interval* must be specified.
Interval	Specifies the frequency, in seconds, in which the report redisplays output. The initial report is always for the time elapsed since system initialization.
-i	Displays statistics regarding configured interfaces.
-m	Shows statistics records by the network memory management routines (mbufs).
-n	Shows network addresses in numeric form.
-p *protocol*	Shows statistics about the specified protocol: tcp, ip, udp, or icmp.
-r	Shows the routing tables. When used with the -s flag, routing statistics are provided along with the output generated by the -s flag.
-s	Shows the statistics for each protocol.
-u	Displays information about UNIX domain sockets.
-v	Shows statistics for Ethernet, Token-Ring, x.25, and 802.3 Ethernet adapters.

The display shows the name of the interface, the maximum size of a packet, the network to which it is attached, the address of the network, the number of packets received, the number of input packet errors, the number of output packets, and the number of output errors. The coll column is not meaningful for the example for the Token-Ring adapter.

The final `netstat` command is with the -s flag. This command displays statistics for each protocol: ip, icmp, tcp, and upd as demonstrated in Figure 11.7.

```
udp:
       0 incomplete headers
       0 bad data length fields
       0 bad checksums
       100 socket buffer overflows
tcp:
       21879814 packets sent
              8253074 data packets (1617998017 bytes)
              12612 data packets (4594340 bytes) retransmitted
              1025454 URG only packets
              2 URG only packets
              30084 window probe packets
              1150873 window update packets
              11407715 control packets
       27897824 packets received
              6251764 acks (for 1617383155 bytes)
              58545 duplicate acks
              0 acks for unsent data
              7917946 packets (1601153295 bytes) received in-sequence
              28280 completely duplicate packets (1911809 bytes)
              456 packets with some dup. data (4585 bytes duped)
              68641 out-of-order packets (24571272 bytes)
              1271 packets (31923 bytes) of data after window
              1063 window probes
              2429498 window update packets
              1045 packets received after close
              1 discarded for bad checksum
              0 discarded for bad header offset fields
              0 discarded because packet too short
       11345334 connection requests
       27480 connection accepts
       52128 connections established (including accepts)
       11377339 connections closed (including 2607 drops)
       11321674 embryonic connections dropped
       5501692 segments updated rtt (of 16831291 attempts)
       21423 retransmit timeouts
              248 connections dropped by rexmit timeout
       30114 persist timeouts
       7843 keepalive timeouts
              999 keepalive probes sent
              4934 connections dropped by keepalive
icmp:
       1043 calls to icmp_error
       0 errors not generated 'cuz old message was icmp
       Output histogram:
              echo reply: 651
              destination unreachable: 728
       0 messages with bad code fields
       0 messages < minimum length
       0 bad checksums
       6 messages with bad length
       Input histogram:
              echo reply: 211
              destination unreachable: 3657
              source quench: 804
              routing redirect: 1074
              echo: 651
              time exceeded: 1521
              parameter problem: 1
       651 message responses generated
```

Figure 11.7   The netstat output.

11.4   TCP/IP Applications

Several applications are part of TCP/IP. They include a remote terminal facility (telnet), a file transfer program (ftp), a two-way messaging system (talk), and two facilities for checking remote systems (ruptime and rwho).

```
ip:
    35016489 total packets received
    0 bad header checksums
    2 with size smaller than minimum
    0 with data size < data length
    0 with header length < data size
    0 with data length < header length
    146986 fragments received
    0 fragments dropped (dup or out of space)
    52 fragments dropped after timeout
    1 packet forwarded
    0 packets not forwardable
    0 redirects sent
```

Figure 11.7 (*Continued*).

11.4.1 `telnet`, `tn`, and `tn3270`—Connect to a remote host

The `telnet` command connects a terminal or workstation on the local host to a remote host, such as some type of ASCII terminal, using the TELNET protocol. The `tn` command is functionally equivalent to the `telnet` command. The `tn3270` command differs from the `telnet` command in that it connects a terminal or workstation on the local host to a remote host, such as an IBM 3270-type terminal.

The syntax of the command is

```
[telnet | tn | tn3270 [[-d] [-n TraceFile] [-e \
TerminalType] [Host [Port]]
```

where the `-d` flag is used to turn on debugging mode, the `-e` flag is used to specify a nonnegotiable terminal type, and the `-n` flag is used to log network trace information. If the `-e` flag is not used, the local and remote systems negotiate the type of terminal to use based upon the user's TERM environment variable. If a specific host is not entered, the command enters command mode. Command mode is indicated by a telnet>, tn>, or tn3270> prompt.[13]

In command mode, subcommands are used to manage the session with the remote system (Table 11.9). Some of these subcommands return the user to the remote session when they complete. For others, the user must explicitly press the enter key to return to the remote session.

When the telnet command is invoked with a host name, it performs an open subcommand for the designated host with any specified arguments and then enters input mode.

Typically, `telnet` is invoked with only a host name, such as

```
telnet roadrunner
```

or

---

[13]Command mode may also be entered from input mode by pressing Ctrl-] in `telnet`, Ctrl-T in `tn`, or Ctrl-C in `tn3270`.

TABLE 11.9 `telnet` **Subcommands**

Note: Each subcommand should be preceded by the appropriate escape key sequence (Ctrl-], Ctrl-t, or Ctrl-c).

Subcommand	Meaning
`? [Subcommand]`	Requests help on telnet subcommands. Without arguments, the ? subcommand prints a help summary. If a Subcommand variable is specified, help information is displayed for the subcommand.
`close`	Closes the TELNET connection and returns to telnet command mode when the open subcommand is used to establish the connection. When the telnet command is invoked and a host is specified, the close subcommand closes the TELNET connection and exits the telnet program.
`display [Argument]`	Displays all of the set and toggle values if no Argument variable is specified; otherwise, lists only those values that match the Argument variable.
`emulate TerminalType`	Overrides terminal-type negotiation with the specified terminal type. All output received from the remote host is processed by the specified emulator. The initial terminal type to emulate can be specified through the EMULATE environment variable or the -e flag to the telnet command. Possible choices are:
	`?` Prints help information.
	`3270` Emulates a 3270 terminal.
	`none` Specifies no emulation.
	`vt100` Emulates a DEC VT100 terminal.
`mode Type`	Specifies the current input mode. When the Type variable has a value of *line,* the mode is line-by-line. When the Type variable has a value of *character,* the mode is character-at-a-time. Permission is requested from the remote host before entering the requested mode, and if the remote host supports it, it is entered.
`open Host [Port]`	Opens a connection to the specified host. The Host specification can be either a host name or an Internet address in dotted-decimal form. If no Port variable is specified, the `telnet` subcommand attempts to contact a TELNET server at the default port (23).
`quit`	Closes a TELNET connection and exits the telnet program. A Ctrl-D in command mode also closes the connection and exits.
`send Arguments`	Sends one or more arguments (special character sequences) to the remote host. Multiple arguments are separated by spaces. The following arguments can be used:
	`?` Prints help information for the `send` subcommand.
	`ao` Sends the TELNET AO (Abort Output) sequence, which causes the remote host to flush all output from the remote system to the local terminal.
	`ayt` Sends the TELNET AYT (Are You There) sequence, to which the remote system can respond.
	`brk` Sends the TELNET BRK (Break) sequence, which causes the remote system to perform a kill operation.
	`ec` Sends the TELNET EC (Erase Character) sequence, which causes the remote host to erase the last character entered.
	`el` Sends the TELNET EL (Erase Line) sequence, which causes the remote system to erase the line currently being entered.
	`escape` Sends the current telnet escape character. The default escape sequence is Ctrl-] for the telnet command, Ctrl-T for the tn command, or Ctrl-C for the tn3270 command.
	`ga` Sends the TELNET GA (go ahead) sequence, which provides the remote system with a mechanism to signal the local system to return control to the user.

TABLE 11.9 `telnet` **Subcommands** (*Continued*)

Subcommand		Meaning
send Arguments (*Cont.*)	ip	Sends the TELNET IP (interrupt process) sequence, which causes the remote system to cancel the currently running process.
	nop	Sends the TELNET NOP (no operation) sequence.
	sak	Sends the TELNET SAK (secure attention key) sequence, which causes the remote system to invoke the trusted shell. If the SAK is not supported, then an error message is displayed that reads: Remote side does not support SAK.
	synch	Sends the TELNET SYNC sequence, which causes the remote system to discard all previously typed input that has not yet been read. This sequence is sent as TCP/IP urgent data.
set VariableValue		Sets the specified TELNET variable to the specified value. The special value off turns off the function associated with the variable entered. The display subcommand can be used to query the current setting of each variable. The variables that can be specified are:
	echo	Toggles between local echo of entered characters and suppressing local echo. Local echo is used for normal processing, while suppressing the echo is convenient for entering text that should not be displayed on the screen, such as passwords. This variable can be used only in line-by-line mode.
	eof	Defines the character for the `telnet` command. When the telnet command is in line-by-line mode, entering the eof character as the first character on a line sends the character to the remote host. The initial value for the eof character is the local terminal End-Of-File character.
	erase	Defines the erase character for the `telnet` command. When the `telnet` command is in character-at-a-time mode and localchars has a value of true, typing the *erase* character sends the TELNET EC sequence to the remote host. The initial value for the *erase* character is the local terminal ERASE character.
	escape	Specifies the telnet escape character, which puts the `telnet` command into command mode when connected to a remote host. This character can also be specified in octal in the TNESC environment variable
	flushoutput	Defines the flush character for the `telnet` command. When *localchars* has a value of true, typing the *flushoutput* character sends the TELNET AO sequence to the remote host. The initial value for the flush character is Ctrl-O. If the remote host is running AIX, the *flushoutput* variable, unlike the other special characters defined by the `set` subcommand, works only in *localchars* mode since it has no `termio` equivalent.
	interrupt	Defines the interrupt character for the `telnet` command. When *localchars* has a value of true, typing the interrupt character sends the TELNET IP sequence to the remote host. The initial value for the interrupt character is the local terminal interrupt (INTR) character.

TABLE 11.9   `telnet` **Subcommands** (*Continued*)

Subcommand		Meaning
`set VariableValue` (*Cont.*)	`kill`	Defines the kill character for the `telnet` command. When the `telnet` command is in character-at-a-time mode and *localchars* has a value of true, typing the kill character sends the TELNET EL sequence to the remote host. The initial value for the kill character is the local terminal KILL character.
	`quit`	Defines the quit character for the `telnet` command. When *localchars* has a value of true, typing the quit character sends the TELNET BRK sequence to the remote host. The initial value for the quit character is the local terminal QUIT character.
	`sak`	Defines the Secure Attention Key (SAK) for the `telnet` command. When the sak character is entered, the remote system is asked to create a trusted shell. If the remote host does not support the SAK, this sequence has no effect.
`status`		Shows the status of the `telnet` command, including the current mode and the currently connected remote host.
`toggle Arguments`		Toggles one or more arguments that control how the `telnet` command responds to events. Possible values are *true* and *false*. Multiple arguments are separated by spaces. The display subcommand can be used to query the current setting of each argument. The following arguments can be used:
	`?`	Displays valid arguments to toggle.
	`autoflush`	If *autoflush* and *localchars* both have a value of *true* and the AO, INTR, and QUIT characters are recognized and transformed into TELNET sequences, the `telnet` command does not display any data on the user's terminal until the remote system acknowledges (with a TELNET timing-mark option) that it has processed those TELNET sequences. The initial value of *autoflush* is true if the terminal has not done an `stty noflsh`, and false if it has.
	`autosynch`	If *autosynch* and *localchars* are both *true*, then typing the INTR or QUIT character sends that character's TELNET sequence, followed by the TELNET SYNC sequence. This procedure causes the remote host to discard all previously typed input until both of the TELNET sequences have been read and acted upon. The initial value of this toggle is false.
	`crmod`	Toggles carriage return mode. When set to true, most carriage return characters received from the remote host are mapped into a carriage return followed by a line feed. This mode does not affect the characters typed by the user, only those received from the remote host. This mode is useful when the remote host sends only a carriage return and not a line feed. The initial value of this toggle is false.
	`debug`	Toggles debugging at the socket level. The initial value of this toggle is false.

TABLE 11.9 `telnet` **Subcommands (***Continued***)**

Subcommand		Meaning
`toggle Arguments` (*Cont.*)	`lineterm`	Toggles the default end-of-line terminator to CR-LF (ASCII carriage-return line-feed). A telnet client running on an ASCII host should have the user configurable option to send either the CR-NUL or CR-LF terminator when the user presses the end-of-line key. The initial value of this toggle is false.
	`localchars`	Determines the handling of TELNET special characters. When this value is true, the ERASE, FLUSH, INTERRUPT, KILL, and QUIT characters are recognized locally and transformed into the appropriate TELNET control sequences (EC, AO, IP, BRK, and EL, respectively). When this value is false, these special characters are sent to the remote host as literal characters. The initial value of *localchars* is true in line-by-line mode and false in character-at-a-time mode.
	`options`	Toggles the display of internal TELNET Protocol processing options, such as terminal negotiation and local or remote echo of characters. The initial value of this toggle is false, indicating that the current options should not be displayed.
	`netdata`	Toggles the display of all network data (in hexadecimal format). The data is written to standard output unless a Trace File value is specified with the `-n` flag on the `telnet` command line. The initial value of this toggle is false.
`z`		Suspends the TELNET process. To return, use the `fg` built-in command or the `csh` or `ksh` command. Note: The `z` subcommand has the same effect as a Ctrl-Z key sequence for any other process. It suspends Telnet execution and returns you to your original login shell.

```
telnet gopher.acme.com
```

If the command is correct, the user typically sees a display like the following

```
$ telnet roadrunner
Trying . . .
Connected to roadrunner
Escape character is '\^]'.


AIX telnet (host3)
IBM AIX Version 3
login:
```

At this point, users enter their login ID (and password when prompted) for the remote system.

Logging out of the remote system, in most cases, terminates the `telnet` session. In any case, the session may be terminated at any time by pressing the escape sequence and entering `quit` at the command prompt.

11.4.2   `ftp`—The file transfer program

The `ftp` command transfers files between a local and a remote host using the *File Transfer Protocol* (FTP). The advantage of FTP is that files may be transferred between dissimilar systems. FTP does not preserve file attributes such as the protection mode or modification times of a file. Furthermore, `ftp` makes very few assumptions about the structure of a file system and therefore does not provide or allow functions such as recursively copying subdirectories.

The `ftp` command runs in an interactive mode. That is, subcommands are issued after initial command invocation to perform the actual file transfer and other operations. The syntax of the `ftp` command is

```
ftp [-d] [-g] [-i] [-n] [-v] [HostName]
```

where

`-d`	Requests debugging logging via the `syslogd` daemon.[14]
`-g`	Disables the expansion of metacharacters in file names.[15]
`-i`	Turns off interactive prompting during multiple file transfers.
`-n`	Prevents automatic login on the initial connection, otherwise the command searches for a $HOME/.netrc entry that describes the login and initialization process for the remote host.
`-v`	Displays all the responses from the remote server and provides status displays; this is the default display.

The host name is either the symbolic name or the IP address of the machine from which the files are retrieved.

After successful startup, the ftp> prompt appears. At this point, the user enters subcommands (Table 11.10) to perform various file transfer actions, such as

Listing remote directories

Changing the current local directory

Changing the remote local directory

Transferring multiple files in a single request

Creating and removing directories

Escaping to the local system to perform shell commands

Fig. 11.8 demonstrates a sample `ftp` session.

When the user specifies a host name, the `ftp` command tries to immediately establish a connection to the specified host. If the connection is successful,

---

[14]In order for the -d flag to work, one of the following entries must exist in the /etc/syslog.conf file: user.info FileName or user.debug FileName. If one of these entries is not in the file, no messages are logged. After changing the /etc/syslog.conf file, run the refresh -s syslogd command to inform the syslogd daemon of the changes to the configuration file.

[15]Interpreting metacharacters is sometimes called globbing. See the glob subcommand for further information.

TABLE 11.10 `sftp` **Subcommands**

Subcommand	Meaning
`![Command [Parameters]]`	Invokes an interactive shell on the local host. A command, with one or more optional parameters, may be specified.
`$Macro [Parameters]`	Executes the specified macro, previously defined with the `macdef` subcommand. Parameters are not expanded.
`?[Subcommand]`	Displays a help message describing the subcommand. If the user does not specify a Subcommand parameter, a list of known subcommands is displayed.
`account [Password]`	Sends a supplemental password that a remote host may require before granting access to its resources. If the password is not supplied with the command, the user is prompted for the password. The password is not displayed on the screen.
`append LocalFile [RemoteFile]`	Appends a local file to a file on the remote host. If the remote file name is not specified, the local file name is used, altered by any setting made with the `ntrans` subcommand or the `nmap` subcommand. The `append` subcommand uses the current values for `form`, `mode`, `struct`, and `type` subcommands while appending the file.
`ascii`	Same as the `type ascii` subcommand.
`bell`	Sounds a bell after the completion of each file transfer.
`binary`	Same as the `type binary` subcommand.
`block`	Same as the mode `block` subcommand.
`bye`	Ends the file-transfer session and exits the `ftp` command. Same as the `quit` subcommand.
`carriage-control`	Same as the form carriage-control subcommand.
`case`	Sets a toggle for the case of file names. When the `case` subcommand is on, remote file names that are displayed in all capital letters are changed from uppercase to lowercase when written in the local directory. The default is *off*.
`cd RemoteDirectory`	Changes the working directory on the remote host to the specified directory.
`cdup`	Changes the working directory on the remote host to the parent of the current directory.
`close`	Ends the file-transfer session, but does not exit the `ftp` command. Defined macros are erased. Same as the `disconnect` subcommand.
`cr`	Strips the carriage return character from a carriage return/linefeed sequence when receiving records during ASCII-type file transfers. Records on non-AIX remote hosts may have single linefeeds embedded. To distinguish these embedded linefeeds from record delimiters, set the `cr` subcommand to *off*. The `cr` subcommand toggles between on and off.
`delete RemoteFile`	Deletes the specified remote file.
`debug [0 | 1]`	Toggles debug on and off. Specify *debug* or *debug 1* to print each command sent to the remote host and save the restart control file. Specify *debug* again, or *debug 0*, to stop the debug record keeping. The Ctrl-C key sequence also saves the restart control file. Specifying the `debug` subcommand sends debugging information about `ftp` command operations to the syslogd daemon. If the `debug` subcommand is used, one of the following entries must be made in the /etc/syslog.conf file: user.info File name or user.debug File name. After changing the /etc/syslog.conf file,

TABLE 11.10 `sftp` **Subcommands** *(Continued)*

Subcommand	Meaning
`debug [0	1]` *(Cont.)*	the `refresh -s syslogd` command must be run to inform the syslogd daemon of the changes to its configuration file. Further information about debug levels may be found in the /etc/syslog.conf file.
`dir [RemoteDirectory][LocalFile]`	Writes a listing of the contents of the specified remote directory (RemoteDirectory) to the specified local file (LocalFile). If the *RemoteDirectory* parameter is not specified, the `dir` subcommand lists the contents of the current remote directory. If the *LocalFile* parameter is not specified or is a - (hyphen), the `dir` subcommand displays the listing on the local terminal.
`disconnect`	Ends the file-transfer session, but does not exit the `ftp` command. Defined macros are erased. Same as the `close` subcommand.
`ebcdic`	Same as the type `ebcdic` subcommand.
`exp_cmd`	Toggles between conventional and experimental protocol commands. The default is *off*.
`file`	Same as the `struct` file subcommand.
`form [carriage-control` `	non-print	telnet]`	Specifies the form of the file transfer. The `form` subcommand modifies the `type` subcommand to send the file transfer in the indicated form. Valid arguments are: carriage-control — Sets the form of the file transfer to carriage-control. non-print — Sets the form of the file transfer to non-print. telnet — Sets the form of the file transfer to Telnet.
`get RemoteFile [LocalFile]`	Copies the remote file to the local host. If *LocalFile* is not specified, the remote file name is used locally and is altered by any settings made by the `case`, `ntrans`, and `nmap` subcommands. The `ftp` command uses the current settings for the `type`, `form`, `mode`, and `struct` subcommands while transferring the file.
`glob`	Toggles file name expansion (globbing) for the `mdelete`, `mget`, and `mput` subcommands. If globbing is disabled, file name parameters for these subcommands are not expanded. When globbing is enabled and a pattern-matching character is used in a subcommand that expects a single file name (i.e., the `append`, `cd`, `delete`, `get`, `mkdir`, `put`, `rename`, and `rmdir` subcommands), results may be different than expected. Globbing for the `mput` subcommand is done locally. For the `mdelete` and `mget` subcommands, each file name is expanded separately at the remote machine; the lists are not merged. The expansion of a directory name may be different from the expansion of a file name, depending on the remote host and the ftp server. To preview the expansion of a directory name, use the `mls` subcommand: `mls RemoteFile`
`hash`	Toggles hash sign (#) printing. When the `hash` subcommand is on, the `ftp` command displays one (hash sign) for each data block (1024 bytes) transferred.
`help [Subcommand]`	Displays help information. See the `?` subcommand.
`image`	Same as the type image subcommand.

TABLE 11.10   `sftp` **Subcommands** (*Continued*)

Subcommand	Meaning
`lcd [Directory]`	Changes the working directory on the local host. If users do not specify a directory, the `ftp` command uses their home directory.
`local M`	Same as the type local M subcommand.
`ls [RemoteDirectory] [LocalFile]`	Writes an abbreviated file listing of a remote directory to a local file. If the *RemoteDirectory* parameter is not specified, the `ftp` command lists the current remote directory. If the *LocalFile* parameter is not specified or is a - (hyphen), the `ftp` command displays the listing on the local terminal.
`macdef Macro`	Defines a subcommand macro. Subsequent lines up to a null line (two consecutive linefeeds) are saved as the text of the macro. Up to 16 macros, containing at most 4096 characters for all macros, can be defined. Macros remain defined until either redefined or a `close` subcommand is executed. The $ (dollar sign) and \ (backslash) are special characters in ftp macros. A $ symbol followed by one or more numbers is replaced by the corresponding macro parameter on the invocation line (see the $ subcommand). A $ symbol followed by the letter *i* indicates that the macro is to loop, with the *$i* character combination being replaced by consecutive parameters on each pass. The first macro parameter is used on the first pass, the second parameter is used on the second pass, and so on. A \ symbol prevents special treatment of the next character. Use the \ symbol to turn off the special meanings of the $ and \. (backslash period) symbols.
`mdelete RemoteFiles`	Expands the files specified by the *RemoteFiles* parameter at the remote host and deletes the remote files.
`mdir [RemoteDirectories LocalFile]`	Expands the directories specified by the *RemoteDirectories* parameter at the remote host and writes a listing of the contents of those directories to the file specified in the *LocalFile* parameter. If the *RemoteDirectories* parameter contains a pattern-matching character, the `mdir` subcommand prompts for a local file if none is specified. If the *RemoteDirectories* parameter is a list of remote directories separated by blanks, the last argument in the list must be either a local file name or a - (hyphen). If the *LocalFile* parameter is a - (hyphen), the `mdir` subcommand displays the listing on the local terminal. If interactive prompting is on (see the `prompt` subcommand), the `ftp` command prompts the user to verify that the last parameter is a local file and not a remote directory.
`mget RemoteFiles`	Expands *RemoteFiles* at the remote host and copies the indicated remote files to the current directory on the local host. See the `glob` subcommand for more information on file name expansion. The remote file names are used locally and are altered by any settings made by the `case`, `ntrans`, and `nmap` subcommands. The `ftp` command uses the current settings for the `form`, `mode`, `struct`, and `type` subcommands while transferring the files.
`mkdir [RemoteDirectory]`	Creates the directory specified in the *RemoteDirectory* parameter on the remote host.
`mls [RemoteDirectories LocalFile]`	Expands the directories specified in the *RemoteDirectories* parameter at the remote host and writes an abbreviated file listing of the indicated remote directories to a local file. If the *RemoteDirectories* parameter contains a pattern-matching

TABLE 11.10 sftp **Subcommands** *(Continued)*

Subcommand	Meaning
mls *[RemoteDirectories LocalFile]* *(Cont.)*	character, the mls subcommand prompts for a local file if none is specified. If the *RemoteDirectories* parameter is a list of remote directories separated by blanks, the last argument in the list must be either a local file name or a - (hyphen). If the *LocalFile* parameter is - (hyphen), the mls subcommand displays the listing on the local terminal. If interactive prompting is on (see the prompt subcommand), the ftp command prompts the user to verify that the last parameter is a local file and not a remote directory.
mode [stream | block]	Sets file-transfer mode. If an argument is not supplied, the default is stream. Block Sets the file-transfer mode to block. Stream Sets the file-transfer mode to stream.
modtime *[File name]*	Shows the last modification time of the specified file on the remote machine. If the *File name* parameter is not specified, the ftp command prompts for a file name.
mput *[LocalFiles]*	Expands the files specified in the *LocalFiles* parameter at the local host and copies the indicated local files to the remote host. See the glob subcommand for more information on file name expansion. The local file names are used at the remote host and are altered by any settings made by the ntrans and nmap subcommands. The ftp command uses the current settings for the type, form, mode, and struct subcommands while transferring the files.
nlist *[RemoteDirectory][LocalFile]*	Writes a listing of the contents of the specified remote directory (*RemoteDirectory*) to the specified local file (*LocalFile*). If the *RemoteDirectory* parameter is not specified, the nlist subcommand lists the contents of the current remote directory. If the *LocalFile* parameter is not specified or is a - (hyphen), the nlist subcommand displays the listing on the local terminal.
nmap *[InPattern OutPattern]*	Sets or unsets the file name mapping mechanism. If no parameters are specified, file name mapping is turned off. If parameters are specified, source file names are mapped for the mget and mput subcommands and for the get and put subcommands when the destination file name is not specified. This subcommand is useful when the local and remote hosts use different file-naming conventions or practices. Mapping follows the pattern set by the *InPattern* and *OutPattern* parameters. The *InPattern* parameter specifies the template for incoming file names, which may have been processed already according to the case and ntrans settings. The template variables *$1* through *$9* can be included in the *InPattern* parameter. All characters in the *InPattern* parameter other than the $ (dollar sign) and the \$ (backslash, dollar sign) define the values of the template variables. For example, if the *InPattern* parameter is *$1.$2* and the remote file name is *mydata.dat,* the value of *$1* is *mydata* and the value of *$2* is *dat.* The *OutPattern* parameter determines the resulting file name. The variables *$1* through *$9* are replaced by their values as derived from the *InPattern* parameter, and the variable *$0* is replaced by the original file name. Additionally, the sequence [*Sequence1,Sequence2*] is replaced by the value of Sequence1, if Sequence1 is not null; otherwise, it is replaced by the value of

TABLE 11.10   sftp **Subcommands (*Continued*)**

Subcommand	Meaning
nmap [*InPattern OutPattern*] (Cont.)	Sequence2. For example, the subcommand nmap *$1.$2.$3* [*$1,$2*].[*$2,file*] yields myfile.data from myfile.data or myfile.data.old, myfile.file from myfile, and myfile.myfile from .myfile. Use the \ (backslash) symbol to prevent the special meanings of the $ (dollar sign), [(left bracket),] (right bracket), and , (comma) in the *OutPattern* parameter.
non-print	Same as the form non-print subcommand.
ntrans [*InCharacters* [*OutCharacters*]]	Sets or unsets the file name character translation mechanism. If no parameters are specified, character translation is turned off. If parameters are specified, characters in source file names are translated for mget and mput subcommands and for get and put subcommands when the destination file name is not specified. This subcommand is useful when the local and remote hosts use different file-naming conventions or practices. Character translation follows the pattern set by the *InCharacters* and *OutCharacters* parameter. Characters in a source file name matching characters in the *InCharacters* parameter are replaced by the corresponding characters in the *OutCharacters* parameter. If the string specified by the *InCharacters* parameter is longer than the string specified by the *OutCharacters* parameter, the characters in the *InCharacters* parameter are deleted if they have no corresponding character in the *OutCharacters* parameter.
open *HostName* [Port]	Establishes a connection to the FTP server at the host specified by the *HostName* parameter. If the optional port number is specified, the ftp command attempts to connect to a server at that port. If the automatic login feature is set (that is, the -n flag was not specified on the command line), the ftp command attempts to automatically log in the user to the FTP server. A $HOME/.netrc file with the correct information in it and the correct permissions set must be located in the user's home directory.
prompt	Toggles interactive prompting. If interactive prompting is *on* (the default), the ftp command prompts for verification before retrieving, sending, or deleting multiple files during the mget, mput, and mdelete subcommands. Otherwise, the ftp command acts accordingly on all files specified.
proxy [*Subcommand*]	Executes an ftp command on a secondary control connection. This subcommand allows the ftp command to simultaneously connect to two remote FTP servers for transferring files between them. The first proxy subcommand should open to establish the secondary control connection. Enter the proxy ? subcommand to see the other ftp subcommands that are executable on the secondary connection. The following subcommands behave differently when prefaced by the proxy subcommand:
	open Does not define new macros during the automatic login process.
	close Does not erase existing macro definitions.
	get and mget Transfer files from the host on the primary connection to the host on the secondary connection.

TABLE 11.10 sftp **Subcommands** *(Continued)*

Subcommand		Meaning
proxy [*Subcommand*] (*Cont.*)	put, mput, and append	Transfer files from the host on the secondary connection to the host on the primary connection.
	restart	Can be handled by the proxy command.
	status	Displays accurate information.
	File transfers require that the FTP server on the secondary connection support the PASV (passive) instruction.	
put *LocalFile* [*RemoteFile*]	Stores a local file on the remote host. If *RemoteFile* parameter is not specified, the ftp command uses the local file name to name the remote file, and the remote file name is altered by any settings made by the ntrans and nmap subcommands. The ftp command uses the current settings for the type, form, mode, and struct subcommands while transferring the files.	
pwd	Displays the name of the current directory on the remote host.	
quit	Closes the connection and exits the ftp command. Same as the bye subcommand.	
quote *String*	Sends the string specified by the *String* parameter verbatim to the remote host.	
record	Same as the struct record subcommand.	
recv *RemoteFile* [*LocalFile*]	Copies the remote file to the local host. Same as the get subcommand.	
reinitialize	Reinitializes an FTP session by flushing all I/O and allowing transfers to complete. Resets all defaults as if a user had just logged in.	
remotehelp [*Subcommand*]	*Requests help from the remote FTP server.*	
rename *FromName* *ToName*	Renames a file on the remote host.	
reset	Clears the reply queue. This subcommand resynchronizes the command parsing.	
restart get | put | append	Restarts a file transfer at the point where the last checkpoint was made. To run successfully, the subcommand must be the same as the aborted subcommand, including structure, type, and form. One of the valid arguments (get, put, or append) must be used.	
rmdir *RemoteDirectory*	Removes the remote directory specified by the *RemoteDirectory* parameter at the remote host.	
runique	Toggles creating unique file names for local destination files during get and mget subcommands. If *unique local file names* is off (the default), local files are overwritten. Otherwise, if a local file has the same name as that specified for a local destination file, the ftp command modifies the specified name of the local destination file with .1. If a local file is already using the new name, the ftp command appends the postfix .2 to the specified name. If a local file is already using this second name, the ftp command continues incrementing the postfix until it either finds a unique file name or reaches .99 without finding one. If a unique file name cannot be found, the command the transfer does not take place. The runique subcommand does not affect local file names generated from a shell command.	
send *LocalFile* [*RemoteFile*]	Stores a local file on the remote host. Same as the put subcommand.	

TABLE 11.10 sftp **Subcommands** (*Continued*)

Subcommand	Meaning
sendport	Toggles the use of FTP PORT instructions. By default, the ftp command uses a PORT instruction when establishing a connection for each data transfer. When the use of PORT instructions is disabled, the ftp command does not use them for data transfers. The PORT instruction is useful when dealing with FTP servers that ignore these instructions while incorrectly indicating that they have been accepted.
site *Args*	Displays or sets the idle time-out period, displays or sets the file-creation umask, or changes the permissions of a file, using the chmod command. Possible values for the *Args* parameter are umask and chmod.
status	Displays the current status of the ftp command as well as the status of the subcommands.
stream	Same as the mode stream subcommand.
struct [file | record]	Sets the data transfer structure type. Valid arguments are *file* and *record*.
sunique	Toggles creating unique file names for remote destination files during put and mput subcommands. If *unique remote file names* is *off* (the default), the ftp command overwrites remote files. Otherwise, if a remote file has the same name as that specified for a remote destination file, the remote FTP server modifies the name of the remote destination file. Note that the remote server must support the STOU instruction.
system	Shows the type of operating system running on the remote machine.
telnet	Same as the form telnet subcommand.
tenex	Same as the type tenex subcommand.
trace	Toggles packet tracing.
type [ascii | binary | ebcdic | image | local M | tenex]	Sets the file-transfer type. If an argument is not specified, the current type is printed. The default type is *ascii*; other types include

	binary	Sets the file-transfer type to binary image; binary or image must be used to transfer executable files correctly.
	ebcdic	Sets the file-transfer type to EBCDIC.
	image	Sets the file-transfer type to binary image; binary or image must be used to transfer executable files correctly.
	local M	Sets the file-transfer type to local; the *M* parameter defines the decimal number of bits per machine word—there is no default.
	tenex	Sets the file-transfer type to that needed for TENEX machines.

Subcommand	Meaning
user *User* [Password] [Account]	Identifies the local user (User) to the remote FTP server. If the *Password* or *Account* parameters are not specified and the remote server requires it, the ftp command prompts for it locally. If the *Account* parameter is required, the ftp command sends it to the remote server after the remote login process completes. Unless automatic login is disabled by specifying the -n flag on the command line, this process is done automatically for the initial connection to the remote server. A .netrc file must be in the user's home directory in order to issue an automatic login.

TABLE 11.10   `sftp` Subcommands (*Continued*)

Subcommand	Meaning
verbose	Toggles verbose mode. When verbose mode is *on* (the default), the `ftp` command displays all responses from the remote FTP server. Additionally, the `ftp` command displays statistics on all file transfers when they complete.

```
$ ftp coyote
Connected to coyote.acme.com.
220 coyote.acme.com FTP server (Version 4.1 Sat Nov 23 12:52:09 CST
1991) ready.
Name (coyote:fgc): anonymous
331 Password required for anonymous.
Password:
230 User anonymous logged in.
257 "/pub" is current directory.
ftp> status
Connected to coyote.acme.com.
No proxy connection.
Mode: stream; Type: ascii; Form: non-print; Structure: file
Verbose: on; Bell: off; Prompting: on; Globbing: on
Store unique: off; Receive unique: off
Case: off; CR stripping: on
Ntrans: off
Nmap: off
Hash mark printing: off; Use of PORT cmds: on
ftp> pwd
257 "/pub" is current directory.
ftp> dir
200 PORT command successful.
150 Opening data connection for /usr/bin/ls (203.241.231.10,2310)
total 32
drwxr-xr-x    2 gopherd       32 Feb 23 17:55 Win3
Drwxr-xr-x   26 gopherd     4000 May 30 17:18 AIX
drwxr-xr-x    2 gopherd       32 Feb 23 17:55 forsale
drwxr-xr-x    2 gopherd      256 Feb 23 17:55 pubserv
226 Transfer complete.
ftp> quit
221 Goodbye.
$
```

Figure 11.8   Sample ftp session.

ftp searches for a local $HOME/.netrc file in the user's current or home directory. If the file exists, it is searched for an entry that can initiate the login process and command macro definitions for the remote host. If the $HOME/.netrc file or automatic login entry does not exist or if the system has been secured with the securetcpip command, ftp prompts the user for a user name and password regardless of whether the HostName parameter is specified on the command line.

If ftp finds a $HOME/.netrc automatic login entry for the specified host, it uses the information in that entry to logon to the remote host and load any command macros defined in the entry. If the required password is not listed in the automatic login entry, the user is prompted for a password before the ftp> prompt is displayed.

If `ftp` completes the automatic login successfully, the init macro is run if it is defined in the automatic login entry. If the init macro does not exist or does not contain a quit or bye subcommand, `ftp` displays the ftp> prompt and waits for a subcommand.

If the user executes the `ftp` command but does not specify a hostname, `ftp` immediately displays the ftp> prompt and waits for a subcommand. To connect to a remote host, enter the open subcommand. After connection to the remote host, `ftp` prompts for the login name and password before displaying the ftp> prompt again.

The command interpreter handles file-name parameters according to the following rules: if a - (hyphen) is specified for the parameter, standard input is used for read operations and standard output is used for write operations; if the preceding check does not apply and file-name expansion is enabled, the interpreter expands the file name according to the rules of the C shell.

11.4.3   `finger`—Locate a user on another system

The `finger` or `f` command is used to display information about logged on users. For the command to work, the destination system must be running the `fingerd` daemon.[16] The format of the output display varies depending on the options requested. The default format displays the following information:

Login name

Full user name

Terminal name

Write status [An * (asterisk) before the terminal name indicates that write permission is denied.]

Idle time [Idle time in minutes if it is a single integer, hours and minutes if a : (colon) is present, or days and hours if a "d" is present.]

Login time

Site-specific information.

The longer format is used by `finger` when a list of user names is given. This may be either account names or user's first and last names. This format is multiline, and includes all the information above, along with

The user's $HOME directory

The user's login shell

---

[16]Since the `finger` command can expose quite a bit of information about a system and its users, it is very common for the `fingerd` daemon to be disabled, which in turn, disables `finger` requests.

TABLE 11.11 finger **Flags**

Flag	Meaning
-b	Gives a brief long-form listing
-f	Suppresses printing of header line on output
-h	Suppresses printing of .project files on long and brief long-formats
-i	Gives a quick listing with idle times
-l	Gives a long-form listing
-m	Assumes that the *User* parameter specifies a user ID, not a user login name
-p	Suppresses printing of .plan files on long and brief long-formats
-q	Gives a quick listing
-s	Gives a short-format list
-w	Gives a narrow short-format list

The contents of the .plan file in the user's $HOME directory

The contents of the .project file in the user's $HOME directory

The syntax of the command is

```
[finger | f] [flags] [user | User@host | @host]
```

where the flags are documented in Table 11.11 and the host name is either

user	For a specific user on the local system
user@host	For a specific user on a remote system
>Host	For all logged in users on a remote system

For example, to get information about all users logged in to host coyote, the command is

```
finger @coyote
```

However, to get information about user guggenheim on coyote, the command is

```
finger guggenheim@coyote
```

11.4.4   talk—Engage in a two-way conversation with another user

The talk command allows one user to converse with another. The users may be on the same or different hosts[17] to have an interactive conversation. For both users, a send window and a receive window are opened on the users' display. Each user is then able to type into the send window while the talk command displays what the other user is typing.

A conversation is initiated when a user executes the talk command and specifies another user's login ID. If the other user is on a remote host, the name

---

[17]Both systems must be running the talkd daemon for this to work.

of the host must also be specified in one of the following ways: User@Host (pre-ferred), Host!User, Host.User, or Host:User

When the conversation is initiated, a message is sent to the remote user, inviting it. Once this invitation is received, the `talk` command displays two windows on the local user's terminal and displays progress messages until the remote user responds to the invitation.

To have the conversation, the remote user must also execute the `talk` and specify the requesting user's account name and host name, if appropriate. When the remote user accepts the invitation, `talk` displays two windows on each user's terminal, as described. To end the conversation, either user can press the Interrupt (Ctrl-C) key sequence; the connection is closed.

The `talk` command requires binding to a valid address. To use `talk` on a standalone machine, the host name must be bound to the loop-back address (127.0.0.1) in order for the `talk` command to work. For example, two users (fgc and jpg) on a standalone machine could initiate a conversation, by entering

```
talk fgc@loopback
```

To which user fgc responds

```
talk jpg@loopback
```

`talk` command invitations may be disabled with the `mesg n` command.

11.4.5   `rwho`—Find out who's logged on to the local network

The `rwho` command shows which users are logged on to hosts on the local net-work. Execution of the command results in a display of the user name, host name, and start date and time of each session for everyone on the local net-work who is currently logged on to a host running the `rwhod` daemon.

If a workstation is inactive for at least 3 min, `rwho` reports, in the last col-umn, the idle time as a number of minutes. After one hour of inactivity, a user is not included unless the -a flag is specified.

Status information is broadcast once every 3 min by each host running the `rwhod` daemon. Activity that takes place between broadcasts is not reflected until the next broadcast.

The following example is typical of a `rwho` report:

```
$ rwho
fgc      coyote:pts5        Aug 20 16:34 :45
fgc      fred:console       Aug 21 12:41 :34
fgc      roadrunner:pts2    Aug 21 13:21
fgc      roadrunner:pts3    Aug 21 14:01 :23
jpg      roadrunner:pts0    Aug 21 12:02 :41
jpg      roadrunner:pts8    Aug 20 05:27 :29
jpg      barney:console     Aug 21 13:00
gopher   coyote:console     Aug 21 10:57 :35
tester   coyote:pts6        Aug 21 19:04
$
```

11.4.6 `ruptime`—Display the status of each host on the network

Closely related to rwho, the `ruptime` command displays the status of each host that is on a local network and is running the rwhod daemon. The status information is provided in packet broadcasts once every 3 min by each participating network host. As with rwho, any activity that takes place between broadcasts is not reflected until the next broadcast. A host is considered down when no status information has been received for 11 min.

The output of the `ruptime` command consists of a line for each host reporting: hostname, status, time, number of users, and load average. The load average represents load averages over 5-, 10-, and 15-min intervals prior to a server's transmission. The load averages are multiplied by 10 to represent the value in decimal format. Unless overridden by the -l, -t, or -u flags, the status lines are sorted by host name.

The `ruptime` command uses five flags to format output. These flags include

-a	Includes all users. Without this flag, users whose sessions are idle one hour or more are not included.
-l	Sorts the list by the load average.
-r	Reverses the sort order.
-t	Sorts the list by the uptime.
-u	Sorts the list by the number of users.

11.5 BNU (uucp)

The Basic Networking Utilities (BNU) are the AIX version of the UNIX-to-UNIX communication program (uucp) originally developed by AT&T to facilitate intersystem communication between UNIX-based computers. This facility was subsequently enhanced and expanded as part of the Berkeley Software Distribution (bsd).

Before the widespread use of TCP/IP and the Internet, uucp was used extensively in UNIX-based environments. A functionally rich system, it allowed files, mail, and news to be transferred from one system to another, most often over dial-up telephone lines. Transfers could be scheduled at off-hours to take advantage of low phone rates or system utilization.

With the advent of TCP/IP and the Internet, however, the use of uucp is declining rapidly. For further information on uucp the reader is referred to *Using UUCP and Usenet* (O'Reilly & Associates, Inc., 1987).

11.6 mail

The mail program allows a user to create and send mail to other users on the local or a remote network. The mail command is used to read incoming mail, send mail, and customize the user's mail environment.

A mail message is typically a text file, created in an editor like vi. But, a mail message could also be a *system message* which is sent to all users on the local system. Or it could be *secret mail* which can be read only by the recipients if they enter the correct decryption password. Finally, a mail message could be a *vacation message*. When mail is received by the system for a user on vacation, it automatically sends a message back to the originator stating this. Users on vacation may forward their message to another destination.

Each user has a system mailbox and a personal mailbox. The system mailbox is located in the /var/spool/mail subdirectory. For example, the mailbox for user fgc is the directory /var/spool/mail/fgc. The system mailbox contains the mail messages the user has received but not yet processed (read, deleted, or saved).[18] The personal mailbox of a user is located in their home directory in the mbox file. For example, the personal mailbox of user fgc is in /home/fgc/mbox. When users read their mail, the system transfers any mail which has not be deleted or saved into the personal mailboxes. The messages remain there until they are explicitly saved or deleted.

Configuring the mail subsystem is one of the most complex tasks a system administrator can perform. In this section, the focus is on the user interface of mail; for further information on configuring the mail subsystem consult *AIX Version 3.2 System Management Guide: Communications and Networks* (GC23-2487) and *sendmail* (O'Reilly and Associates, Inc., 1993).

11.6.1 Sending mail

The simplest way to send mail is to invoke the `mail` command with the address of the message recipient.

```
$ mail jpg@notis.com
Subj: Test message
Hi there!  This is just a test mail message.  Please respond to let me know
you received it.

Thanks.

Frank
^D
cc: fcervone@wppost.depaul.edu
$
```

The `mail` program first prompts the user for a subject line with the "Subj:" prompt. After entering the subject information and pressing the enter key, input mode is entered. Message input is terminated by entering a Cntl-D.

After the Cntl-D is processed, a "cc:" prompt is displayed to allow for entering a list of other users to whom the mail will be sent. The list is terminated (or simply ignored) by pressing the enter key.

For very short messages, this method is fine. However, for longer, more complex messages, or if the typist is error-prone this method is not particu-

---

[18]By default, when users have read, deleted, or saved all the mail in their system mailbox, the mailbox is deleted. This peculiar behavior is circumvented by setting the permissions on the /usr/mail directory to 775.

larly user-friendly. When mistakes are made during typing, special command sequences must be used to correct the errors. For most people, it is simpler and easier to use a standard text editor, such as vi, to compose the message.[19] This is done in one of two ways: by invoking vi from inside the mail command (explained in the following paragraphs) or by creating a file in advance with vi and using input redirection to the mail command. If the message text from Fig. 11.8 were in a file named message.text, the following interaction would have taken place instead:

```
$ mail jpg@notis.com  < message.text
Subj: Test message
cc: fcervone@wppost.depaul.edu
$
```

As can be seen, the user is still prompted for the subject and the cc recipients, but the text is read from the message.text file.

While inside the mail command in input mode, several escape commands are provided to manipulate and display mail data. These commands, which may be invoked at the beginning of any line, are outlined in Table 11.12. For example, the user may invoke the ~s command to change the subject before sending a message

```
$ mail jpg@notis.com
Subj: Test message
```

---

[19]Not, of course, that vi is necessarily simple. But, at least, the user needs to remember only one set of arcane commands.

TABLE 11.12 mail **Input-Escape Commands**

Command	Meaning
~! *command*	Start a shell, run the command, and return.
~?	Display escape command help.
~| *command*	Pipe the message to standard input of command, and replace the message with the standard output of the command.
~b *addrlist*	Add the user addresses specified to the Bcc: list.
~c *addrlist*	Add the user addresses specified to the Cc: list.
~d	Append the contents of the dead.letter file to the current message.
~f *numlist*	Append the contents of the messages numbered in numlist.
~h	Add to the To:, Subject:, Cc:, and Bcc: lists.
~m *numlist*	Append and indent the contents of the messages numbered in numlist.
~p	Display the contents of the message buffer.
~q	Quit without sending the message.
~r *filename*	Append the contents of *filename* to the current message.
~s *subject*	Set the Subject: line to the string specified by *subject*.
~t *addrlist*	Add the user addresses specified to the To: list.
~v	Start vi to edit the message.
~w *filename*	Write the message contents to *filename*.

```
Hi there!  This is just a test mail message. Please respond to let me know
you received it.

Thanks.

Frank
~s An important test message: Please read
^D
cc: fcervone@wppost.depaul.edu
$
```

Additional recipients (Cc:) could be added with the ~c command

```
$ mail jpg@notis.com
Subj: Test message
Hi there!  This is just a test mail message. Please respond to let me know
you received it.

Thanks.
Frank

~c fred@slate.com, george@spacely.com
^D
cc: fred@slate.com, george@spacely.com,
fcervone@wppost.depaul.com
$
```

In this example, the two recipients added with the ~c command automatically appeared when the cc: prompt was displayed; only the additional recipient (fcervone@wppost.depaul.edu) had to be added.

11.6.2 Receiving mail

Receiving mail is extremely simple; the user enters the mail command with no operands. After an initial display of all of the outstanding messages, the user hits enter (at the & prompt) to display each message in sequence.

The initial display lists the following information about each message:

The message status; several values are possible:

M	Message stored in the personal mailbox
>	Current message
N	Message is new
P	Message preserved in the system mailbox
R	Message has been read
U	Message is unread
*	Message has been saved

The message number

The sender of the message

The date the message was received

TABLE 11.13 `mail` **Receive Escape Commands**

Command	Meaning
`! ` *command*	Start a shell, run the command, and return.
`?`	Display escape command help.
`a`	Display list of aliases and their addresses.
`cd [`*dir*`]`	Change to the home directory or new directory *dir*.
`d [`*msglist*	Delete the current message or the message in *msglist*.
`e [`*num]*	Edit current message or message number *num*.
`f [`*msglist*`]`	Display message headings [of the specified message numbers].
`h [`*num*`]`	Display headings of group containing message or group containing message *num*.
`m [`*addrlist*`]`	Create a new message to address in *addrlist*.
`n`	Display next message.
`pre [`*msglist*`]`	Keep message(s) in system mailbox.
`q`	Quit—apply mailbox commands entered so far.
`R [`*msglist*`]`	Reply to senders of messages in *msglist*.
`r [`*msglist*`]`	Reply to senders and recipients of messages in *msglist*.
`s [`*msglist*`] ` *file*	Append message(s) with headings to *file*.
`t [`*msglist*`]`	Display current message or the message in message list.
`u [`*msglist*`]`	Undelete the current message or the message in *msglist*.
`w [`*msglist*`] ` *file*	Append message(s) without headings to *file*.
`x`	Quit—restore mailbox to state before this session.

The number of lines and characters in the message

The subject of the message

As with the send option, several escape commands are provided during the receive operation; these are documented in Table 11.13

11.6.3 User customization of mail

The default user profile (the .profile file in the user's home directory immediately after account creation) sets up the shell to check periodically for incoming mail. The two environment variables in the process are MAILMSG and MAILCHECK. MAILMSG is used to define the message that is displayed when new mail arrives. The MAILCHECK variable sets the checking interval in seconds. For example, the following two commands in a user's .profile command change the default message and checking interval:

```
export MAILMSG="Incoming messages..... read your mail"
export MAILCHECK=600 # Check for new msgs every 10 minutes
```

Before a `mail` session is started, the `mail` command checks the .mailrc file in the user's home directory. This file is used to issue commands to set the mail environment. Although there are many commands, the most often used are the `alias`, `ignore`, and `set` commands.

The `alias` command is used to set up distribution lists. The format of the command is

```
alias groupname member1 [member2 ... memberN]
```

For example, the statement

```
alias review fcervone jpg@notis.com bob@epa.gov
```

allows the user to address mail, review it, and have it be sent to the three users who are part of the group.

The `ignore` command is used to suppress the display of information in the message header. When mail passes through several systems, extraneous fields are added to the header. This command is used to keep those fields from displaying, thus reducing clutter on the screen. There are many header fields, the most common are: To, From, Date, cc, bcc, Message-Id, Reply-To, Sender, In-Reply-To, References, Keywords, Subject, Comments, Encrypted, Return-Path, Status, Via, Resent-To, Resent-From, Resent-cc, Resent-bcc, Resent-Date, Resent-Sender, Resent-Message-Id, and Resent-Reply-To. Most often, the Message-Id, Received, Status, Via, Return-Path, and Resent-Message-Id fields are suppressed

```
ignore Message-Id Received Resent-Message-Id
ignore Via Status Return-Path
```

The `set` and `unset` commands toggle and set values to change the default operation of the `mail` program. The various options are discussed in Table 11.14.

11.6.4   Setting up vacation mail

When a user is going to be out of the office for an extended period of time, a mail account may be set up to automatically inform senders of mail that the user is away. The first step in this process is for the user to create a vacation message file (named .vacation.msg) in the home directory. After this, the user enters the

```
vacation -I
```

command, creating a .vacation.pag and a .vacation.dir file. The process is completed by the user creating, if it does not already exist, a .forward file. This file, in the user's home directory, contains one line in the format

```
userid, "|vacation userid"
```

So, for user fgc, the .forward file contains the line,

```
fgc, "|vacation fgc"
```

Now, when the user receives a message, the system forwards to the sender the message in the .vacation.msg file. This message is forwarded to a sender

TABLE 11.14 `mail set` and `unset` **Command Options**

Option	Meaning
append	Adds messages saved in the personal mailbox to the end, rather than to the beginning of the file
ask	Prompts the user for a subject line for each new message
askcc	Prompts the user for cc: recipients for each new message
autoprint	Causes the delete commands to delete the current message and print the next message
crt=	Sets the maximum number of lines on the terminal
dot	Allows a single period as the first character of a line to be interpreted as the end-of-message character
folder=	Defines the path where new folders are created
hold	Keeps messages read but not deleted in the system, rather than the personal, mailbox
ignore	Ignores interrupts from the terminal and prints them as the @ "at" character
ignoreeof	Disables the use of Cntl-D (^D) as the end-of-message character
metoo	Allows messages to be sent to the sender if an alias includes the sender
quiet	Suppresses the line containing the name and version number of the mailer at `mail` command startup
record=	Defines the path into which a copy of all outgoing messages will be saved
screen=	Number of lines to display from a list at one time
VISUAL=	Sets the name of the editor to be used with the mail program. Possible choices include `vi`, `e`, and `ined`.

only once a week, regardless of the number of messages actually sent.

The user may cancel the vacation message by entering the following commands from the user's home directory:

```
delete .forward
delete .vacation.*
```

11.7 NFS

The *network file system* (NFS) is a distributed file system which allows disparate and dissimilar systems to share disk space over a TCP/IP network.

NFS servers export their data to NFS clients. Exporting a file system or directory makes the object available to other machines on the network. Access to directories may be restricted to specific clients.

This section discusses only the basics of using NFS. Further information can be found in *AIX Version 3.2 System Management Guide: Communications and Networks* (SC23-2487) and *Managing NFS and NIS* (O'Reilly and Associates, Inc., 1993).

11.7.1 Configuring the NFS server

Before an NFS client can be defined, an NFS server must exist. If this NFS server is an AIX-based machine, configuration consists of two steps: modifying the /etc/exports files and starting NFS.

The /etc/exports file defines all of the directories that a server exports to its clients. If a directory on the server is not defined in /etc/exports, it may not be mounted by a client. The syntax of the entries in the /etc/exports file is

```
directory -options[,option]
```

where *directory* is the full path name of the local mount point. The options specify the characteristics of the exported directory which are

ro	Exports the directory with read-only permission; (the default is read-write permission)
rw=*HostName[:HostName...]*	Exports the directory with read-write permission to the hosts specified by *client* and read-only to all others
anon=*UID*	Sets the UID to the specified user ID if a request comes from a root user; the default value is -2; setting the value to -1 disables anonymous access
root=*HostName[:HostName...]*	Allows root access only to the root users from the specified HostNames; the default is no root access
access=*HostName[:HostName]*	Gives mount access to each host listed; the default allows any machine to mount the directory
secure	Requires clients to use the secure NFS protocol when accessing the directory

As an example, for a server to export the /tmp directory to any other client but with root access from the roadrunner host only and to allow access to the /var directory from the host named coyote only, the entries in the /etc/exports file are

```
/tmp      -rw,root=roadrunner
/var      -access=coyote
```

Once the /etc/exports file has been defined, the mknfs command is run with the -B flag. When NFS is started in this way, it first places an entry in the /etc/inittab file; this starts NFS whenever the system is booted. Additionally, the mknfs command runs the /etc/rc.nfs script to start all the NFS required daemons.

A directory may be unexported (that is, made unavailable to remote hosts) with the exportfs -u command. The syntax of the command is

```
exportfs -u dirname
```

where *dirname* is the name of the local directory to unexport. To remove the export permanently, remove the applicable entry from the /etc/exports file.

11.7.2 Configuring the NFS client

Configuring an NFS client is more involved. First, the /etc/vfs file must be modified. Using a text editor, the following two lines must be uncommented:[20]

---

[20]That is, the first pound sign (#) character must be removed.

```
#%defaultvfs jfs nfs
#nfs 2 /sbin/helpers/nfsmnthelp none remote
```

Note that these two lines are not in the same place in the file. Second, NFS must be started. As with the server, the mknfs command is run with the -B flag.[21] When NFS is started in this way, it first places an entry in the /etc/inittab file which starts NFS whenever the system is booted. Additionally, the mknfs command runs the /etc/rc.nfs script to start all the NFS required daemons.

The third step defines which and how the remote file systems are mounted. Explicit mounts are performed with the mount command. This type of mount must be performed each time the system is rebooted and last until an umount command or the system is shutdown. The syntax of the mount command when mounting remote file systems is

```
mount servername:/remote/directory /local/directory
```

The names of the remote and local directories may or may not be the same.

Predefined mounts are used to activate a remote file system on system startup. Predefined mounts can be defined in one of two different ways. The first, and simplest way, is to add the appropriate mount command, as defined, to the end of the /etc/rc.nfs command file. Alternatively, and perhaps more correct, is to add the remote file system entry to the /etc/filesystems command file.[22]

Finally, automatic mounts allow remote file systems to be mounted on demand; that is, no mount of the file system takes place until a user explicitly references it. Automatic mounting is relatively simple to set up. First, the /etc/mount.map file is created. This file consists of single-line entries for each remote file system to be loaded. The format of the entries is

```
localdir  options    server:remotedir
```

where *localdir* is the name of the lowest level in the directory where the remote directory from the server will be mounted. Options are -ro for read-only and -rw for read-write. Our example file /etc/mount.map file mounts host coyote's /home/fgc and /tmp/workspace directories on the local system as /coyote/userdir/fgc and /coyote/tmp/workspace, respectively

```
$ cat /etc/mount.map
userdir/fgc     -ro  coyote:/home/fgc
tmp/workspace   -rw  coyote:/tmp/workspace
$
```

The highest level of the local directory structure is defined in the automount command.[23] This command starts the automount daemon which processes the

---

[21]Of course, if NFS had already been started on the machine for server functions, there is no reason to start it again.

[22]See Sec. 6.4 for more information on the /etc/filesystems command file.

[23]The automount command is in the /usr/sbin directory.

automount requests. The `automount` daemon is often placed at the end of the /etc/rc.nfs file, but also can be invoked from the command line. The syntax of the command is

```
automount /localdir mountfile
```

where *localdir* represents the highest level qualifier for the directory structure on the local system, and *mountfile* is the name of the mount.map file.

As can be seen, all automounted file systems must belong to the same directory structure. Furthermore, the automount daemon is single-threaded, so requests to systems which are down must wait for timeout before another automount request can be started.

The `automount` daemon is stopped by issuing a `kill` command with the `automount` daemon process id. Never issue a `kill -9` for the `automount` daemon as this prevents it from performing the necessary cleanup tasks it must do.

11.7.3 `showmount`—Display a list of NFS clients

On an NFS server, the `showmount` command is used to display the status of the exported directories and their associated clients. With the `-a` flag, the command displays a list of all remote mounts listing the name of the host and the name of the local directory mounted. The `-d` displays a list of all the directories which have been remotely mounted. The last flag, `-e`, displays a list of all directories which may be exported. With all flags, a specific host may be named. By default, this is the local host; however, by naming a remote host, a client can determine whether a host is up. For example, on host roadrunner, the command

```
showmount -a
```

displays a list of all the remote mounts the roadrunner is servicing. But, the command

```
showmount -a coyote
```

requests a display of all the remote mounts the host coyote is servicing. By definition, this tests whether coyote is up.

11.8 NIS

The Network Information Service, formerly known as the yellow pages, is an extension of NFS used to distribute system information between networked hosts. A NIS server is a host which provides resources and mapping information for other computers on the network. The NIS master server is the host which maintains the authoritative maps of information for a domain. All changes to NIS are made to the master server which in turn propagates these to the slave servers. Slave servers are other hosts on the network which are used to balance processing load and provide for system integrity and backup.

A master server should always have at least one slave server. Hosts which are not master or slave servers are NIS clients.

NIS clients do not maintain NIS mapping information. NIS client hosts make inquiries to NIS servers for server and user account information. No distinction is made on the part of the client between a slave and the master server.

NIS is a distributed database system. The information which is shared is the same information as in the /etc/passwd, /etc/group, and /etc/hosts files on a standalone system. NIS is used to reduce the effort of maintaining a large number of systems. It provides for user and group IDs which are global throughout the domain. Because all of the hosts in the network share the same information, a user need only remember one password to gain access to any authorized system in the domain. When used with NFS, a user's directories and files can be made available on every system within the domain.

NIS configuration can be very complex. This section discusses the basics of using NIS. Further information can be found in *AIX Version 3.2 System Management Guide: Communications and Networks* (SC23-2487) and *Managing NFS and NIS* (O'Reilly and Associates, Inc., 1993).

11.8.1 Configuring a NIS master server

The first step toward creating a NIS system is to consolidate the information from the /etc/passwd, /etc/group, and /etc/hosts files on all of the hosts in the domain into the appropriate files on the master server. After this, the NIS administrators must add the NIS directory path (/usr/etc/yp) to their default path. This is done by adding the following line to each administrator's .profile file:

```
PATH=$PATH:/usr/etc/yp
```

With these two steps complete, the name of the domain must be defined for the master server. The chypdom command[24] performs this function. The syntax of the command is

```
chypdom -B domainname
```

Although the *domainname* may be any name, a recommended practice is to make it the same as the TCP/IP domain name. For example, to define the domain name for the master server on the acme.com network, the command is

```
chypdom -B acme
```

After the chypdom command runs, the master server is configured with the mkmaster command.

---

[24]This command is also located in the /usr/sbin directory.

The syntax of the mkmaster command[25] is

```
mkmaster -s slavehosts -O -p -u -B
```

where *slavehost* represents the name (or list of names) of the slave servers. For example, the following command issued on the host named gateway on the acme.com network, makes coyote a slave server and starts all the necessary NIS daemons on the gateway machine

```
mkmaster -s coyote -O -p -u -B
```

After one slave is defined, the NIS administrator must issue the following command to enable NIS map propagation and to start password resolution on the master server

```
chmaster -s coyote -O -P -U -B
```

11.8.2   Configuring a NIS slave server

Creating an NIS slave server is, at first, similar to creating the master server. The NIS administrators must add the NIS directory path (/usr/etc/yp) to their default path on the slave server. This is done by adding the following line to each administrator's .profile file:

```
PATH=$PATH:/usr/etc/yp
```

The name of the domain must be defined for the slave server with the chypdom command. The domain name must match the name as defined on the master server. So, for the slave server coyote, the command is

```
chypdom -B acme
```

just as it was for the master server gateway.

After the chypdom command runs, the slave server is configured with the mkslave command.

The syntax of the mkslave command[26] is

```
mkslave -O mastername
```

where *mastername* is the name of the master server. For slave coyote, the command is

```
mkslave -O gateway
```

At this point, the administrator must go back to the master server and use the chmaster command to start map propagation and password resolution.

---

[25]Again, this command is located in the /usr/sbin directory.
[26]Again, this command is located in the /usr/sbin directory.

11.8.3 Configuring a NIS client

Creating a NIS client is similar to creating a server. The first two steps are exactly the same. The NIS administrators must add the NIS directory path (/usr/etc/yp) to their default path on the client by adding the following line to each administrator's .profile file:

```
PATH=$PATH:/usr/etc/yp
```

As with the servers, the name of the domain must be defined for the client, also with the chypdom command. The domain name must match the name as defined on the master server. So, for the client roadrunner, the command is

```
chypdom -B acme
```

just as it is for the master server gateway.

After the chypdom command runs, the client is configured with the mkclient command.

The mkclient command[27] takes no parameters and needs none of the optional flags to configure the client correctly. Therefore, the command is simply

```
mkclient
```

At this point, the client machine stops using its local /etc/passwd, /etc/hosts, and /etc/groups files and uses those of the domain.

11.8.4 Adding users in a NIS environment

Once NIS is running, new users may be added only on the master server machine. Although the mkuser command is used still, the subsequent actions are different. After the new user has been created with the mkuser command, the administrator must switch to the /var/yp directory and compile the password file with the make passwd command. The yppush command is then used to force the propagation of the password file to the slave servers; otherwise, the password file is not sent out until the next time the system performs an automatic propagation.[28] Therefore, the command sequence is

```
$ cd /var/yp
$ make passwd
$ yppush
```

11.9 SNA Services

Interconnectivity between IBM-compatible mainframes and UNIX-based machines has traditionally depended on the availability of TCP/IP on the mainframe, as opposed to SNA on the UNIX-based machine. Because SNA is

---

[27]Again, this command is located in the /usr/sbin directory.
[28]This could be several minutes later than a forced propagation.

an IBM proprietary protocol, and UNIX-based systems include TCP/IP networking capabilities, this is not a totally unexpected situation. However, for those networks where TCP/IP is not the native, most common, or preferred network protocol, this can be an untenable situation. In those cases, it would probably be cheaper and more convenient to put the burden of network protocol translation on the UNIX-based machine. AIX SNA Services/6000 provides such functionality to users of the IBM RS/6000 family of computers.

Essentially, AIX SNA Services/6000 is VTAM[29] for AIX/6000. Although the definition of network resources in VTAM is quite different from their definition in SNA Services, the underlying function is the same. SNA Services provides support for the most common logical unit types: LU0 (user-defined), LU1 (printers), LU2 (terminals), LU3 (printers), and LU6.2 (programs). In conjunction with the AIX Host Connection Program/6000, this allows TCP/IP terminals and printers connected to the RS/6000 to appear as 3270-type devices to the mainframe host. With LU6.2 support, application programs on the RS/6000 can converse with applications on the mainframe via advanced program-to-program communication (APPC).

Depending on the level of networking functionality needed, the RS/6000 can connect to the mainframe as a PU2 or PU2.1. Therefore, the RS/6000 can appear to the mainframe as if it were a 3174-type controller, or as a peer system which hosts independent type 6.2 LUs.

Three very important concepts in SNA Services are *profiles, attachments,* and *connections*. Profiles are the AIX SNA Services equivalent of VTAM source statement definitions. All resources of the network are described in one (or more) profiles. An attachment defines the physical characteristics of the communications environment and is described in a profile which contains information on the communications adapter, the data link control, the transmission media, and even the electrical interface. There are several type of attachment interfaces available: Token-ring, standard Ethernet, SDLC (EIA232D, EIA422A, and Smartmodem), IEEE 802.3 Ethernet, and X.25.

A connection defines a LU-LU session. In the connection profile, the user describes the LU names of the local and remote partner, the name of the attachment over which communication occurs, and the session characteristics. Connection definitions are unique to SNA Services; VTAM, for example, does not have this.

A connection profile always points to at least an attachment profile and a local LU profile. For LU6.2 nodes, several other profiles also are needed: the RTPN List and RTPN profiles (available remote programs and their characteristics), the Mode List and Mode profiles (equivalent to a MODETAB in VTAM), the Transaction Program List and Profile (the programs that control LU6.2 conversations on the RS/6000 and their characteristics), and the Conversation Security Access lists and profiles.

---

[29]Virtual telecommunication access method—the program product which provides networking services under IBM's mainframe operating systems—MVS/ESA, VM/ESA, and VSE/ESA.

An attachment profile is linked to other profiles that "flesh out" the attachment description. These include the control point (PU) profile, the logical link profile, the LU address registration profile, and the physical link profile.

Separate from the aforementioned profiles is the SNA Node profile. This "master" profile describes the overall environment in which SNA Services run. Although it does not provide all of the same functionality, it is equivalent to the ATCSTR*xx* member in VTAM.

Defining resources for SNA Services is simplified through the use of the AIX system maintenance tool, SMIT. Although a user could code the resource definitions by hand, SMIT provides a menu-driven interface which automatically generates the required definitions based upon information supplied by the user. In addition to eliminating tedious coding effort, SMIT is programmed to ensure that all of the dependent information in related profiles is kept in synchronization with whatever changes are made.

11.9.1 Configuring the node profile

Configuring the SNA Node profile starts by entering

```
smit sna
```

at the AIX terminal. Note that AIX is case sensitive, therefore, the command *must* be entered in all lowercase letters. After a few seconds, the *SNA Services* menu should appear. Proceed down the menu hierarchy by selecting

Configure SNA profiles

Advanced SNA configuration

Nodes

Systems Network Architecture

Add a profile

Although a choice of names is offered by the *Add a profile* menu, a profile named *sna* must always be present and is the name that should be used. This profile describes the current characteristics of the SNA Services operating environment.

The first three fields (*Total active open CONNECTIONS, Total SESSIONS,* and *Total CONVERSATIONS*) describe, respectively, the maximum number of LU-LU sessions, the total number of all sessions (LU-LU, SSCP-LU, and CP-CP), and the maximum number of conversations. For all of these fields, the recommended *minimum* is twice the number of LUs active at any time. For example, a SNA Services system containing a single PU with 254 LUs, could use 512 as an appropriate number for all three fields. Specifying a number greater than what is needed wastes resources; defining too little prevents successful initialization of network resources.

The *SERVER synonym name* allows the user to specify an alternate name for this profile. This alternate name can be used when issuing the command to start, stop, or list resources of SNA Services. Other than that, it has no use.

The *RESTART* action determines what AIX does if an abnormal termination of SNA Services occurs. The field has two possible values: once or respawn. If *respawn* is chosen, AIX attempts to restart SNA Services in the event of an abnormal termination. Specifying once inhibits a restart attempt.

Perform ERROR LOGGING determines whether SNA Services record internal errors for problem determination. These errors are recorded alternatively in /var/sna/snalog.1 and /var/sna/snalog.2. The recommended setting is *yes*. *No* prevents all internal logging until this value is changed to *yes* and SNA Services is restarted.

The *Standard Input file/device, Standard Output file/device,* and *Standard ERROR file/device* are normally set to /dev/console. This causes all input and output messages to be directed to the RS/6000 console. By selecting a different file name (or device) messages can be directed to another destination. If Standard Output and Standard Error are redirected to a file, they should be directed to separate files, or information may be lost.

After filling in this information, press enter (or send). In a few seconds, the system should respond with *OK* in the command status indicator.

11.9.2   Configuring the node profile

Before starting SNA Services, the Control Point must be defined. To do this, return to the *Node* menu and select the following menu path:

> *Control Point*
>
> *Add a profile*

A meaningful name should be selected for the *PROFILE* name as this is referenced in other profiles. The *XID node ID* is the concatenation of the *IDBLK* and *IDNUM* on the VTAM PU definition. For an RS/6000, the default *IDBLK* type is 071. The *IDNUM* is a user-defined five-digit hexadecimal field that should be chosen so the value does not conflict with other devices on the network. Optionally, the *NETWORK name* and *CONTROL POINT* name fields can be defined. These correspond to the *NETID* and *SSCPNAME* in the start options of the host VTAM system.

After filling in this information, press enter (or send). In a few seconds, the system should respond with *OK* in the command status indicator. At this point, SNA Services can be started even though no resources have been defined yet.

11.9.3   Starting SNA Services

To start SNA Services, return (via the F3 key) to the top of the menu hierarchy (the *SNA Services menu*) and traverse through the menu selections:

> *Control SNA Services*
>
> *Start SNA Resources*
>
> *Start SNA*

If SNA is already active, the system responds with message 0513-029.

11.9.4 Defining an attachment

At this point, further definition of the RS/6000 network diverges depending upon the type of attachment used between the host and the RS/6000. Although the basic procedures are the same for all types of attachment, the individual parameters differ. In the following discussion, a Token-Ring installation is used as the example. It is assumed that the Token-Ring adapter card has been defined to AIX (with smit devices) and activated.

To define the attachment, return to the *SNA Services* menu and traverse through the menu selections

Configure SNA Profiles

Advanced SNA Configuration

Physical Units

Token-Ring

Token-Ring Attachment

Add a Profile

Except for a few cases, the default values provided by the profile are acceptable for most uses. As before, a meaningful name should be selected for the *PROFILE name* as this is referenced by other profiles. Provide the name of the previously defined control point in the *CONTROL POINT profile name* field. As the attachment has two link aspects, logical and physical, both must be defined and pointed to by the *LOGICAL LINK profile name* and *PHYSICAL LINK profile name* fields, respectively. These profiles have not been defined yet; this is done later. For most applications, the *STOP ATTACHMENT on inactivity* field should be set to *no*. However, if *yes* is specified, a value must be provided in the *Inactivity TIMEOUT field*; this specifies the number of minutes to wait before stopping the attachment due to inactivity. *LU address registration* is used only in conjunction with LU6.2 application programs on the RS/6000 that use generic SNA services. The default is *no*.

The *CALL type* field determines whether or not the RS/6000 can initiate a connection with the host. The default value, *call*, allows the RS/6000 to initiate a connection or responds to a request from the host to initiate one. Setting the value to *Listen* prevents the RS/6000 from initiating the connection. In this case, only the host can initiate the connection. In conjunction with listen, specifying *yes* for *AUTO-LISTEN* allows the host to restart a failed attachment. Setting *AUTO-LISTEN* to *no* makes manual intervention necessary in the event of an attachment failure. If *listen* is specified, the *MINIMUM SAP Address* and *MAXIMUM SAP Address* from which a connection is accepted can be defined.

When *call* is specified for the *CALL type*, the type of *ACCESS ROUTING* must be specified. The default method, *link_address*, must be used for communication with a VTAM host. This uses the MACADDR from the PU definition on the host (or LOCADDR from the LINE if the Token-Ring card is connected via an NCP) and SAPADDR to correlate the two sides of the attachment. For attachments between RS/6000s, instead of addresses, names can be used by selecting *link_name*. In this case, the *REMOTE LINK name* is the remote RS/6000 uses as its *LOCAL LINK* in its Token-Ring Physical Link Profile.

11.9.5   Defining a Token-Ring logical link

Defining the Token-Ring Logical Link is very simple in most cases. Return to the *Token Ring* menu and select

> *Token Ring Data Link Control*
>
> *Token Ring Logical Link*
>
> *Add a Profile*

Except in unusual circumstances, the default values provided by the profile are acceptable. Therefore, just select a meaningful name for the *PROFILE* name and hit enter.

The information in the Token-Ring Logical Link Profile is primarily concerned with data pacing and acknowledgment. The *TRANSMIT Window Count* and *RECEIVE Window Count* are equivalent to VTAM PACING values while the *DYNAMIC Window Increment* is used to control network congestion. If the receive buffers at a data bridge are full, the local data transmission window drops to 1. The dynamic window increment is used in this case to specify the number of acknowledged, consecutive packets to be sent before the transmit window is raised. This allows the network traffic to be increased gradually after the congestion period. The *RETRANSMIT count* determines the number of times a remote station can be unsuccessfully polled before it is marked as not working; this is equivalent to the VTAM *RETRIES* parameter. The *RESPONSE timeout* field is used to determine how long to wait before retransmitting.

The *RING ACCESS priority* is a value from 0 to 3 that determines the priority of the frames sent. It is roughly equivalent to a VTAM class-of-service value. Under most circumstances, it should be left at the default, zero.

DROP LINK on inactivity is used in conjunction with the *INACTIVITY timeout* to specify if and when inactivity should terminate the data link. The *ACKNOWLEDGE timeout* field is used to specify the time delay between receiving data and sending the acknowledgment of receipt to the host.

FORCE DISCONNECT timeout indicates the number of seconds SNA Services should wait for a disconnect to complete after a disconnect request for the link has been received. Depending on actual network hardware, a disconnect can take quite a bit of time. This parameter defines what the reasonable amount of time for a disconnect is. If the link is still connected after this period, a disconnect is forced.

When communicating with a VTAM host, it is usually best to let the *DEFINITION of maximum I-FIELD* size default to *system_defined*. This permits the two partners to negotiate the information-field size during connection startup. If, however, there are restrictions in the network, the *user_defined* option can be selected. In that case, the size of the information-field must be specified in the max. *I-FIELD SIZE*.

The final two options in the Token-Ring Logical Link profile are related to problem diagnosis. Setting the *TRACE Link?* field to *yes* causes SNA Services to save link trace information; setting it to *no* inhibits the gathering of this information. Typically, tracing is used only if there is a problem with the link. Once the trace is on, either *short* summary information can be collected, or more detailed *long information* can be saved.

11.9.6 Defining a Token-Ring physical link

Defining the Token-Ring Physical Link is also relatively straightforward. Return to the *Token-Ring Data Link Control* menu and select

> *Token-Ring Physical Link*
>
> *Add a Profile*

In addition to selecting a name for the *PROFILE name,* enter the name of the Token-Ring device used for attachment in the *DATALINK device name.* If the *link_name* method of Token-Ring Attachment is selected, the *LOCAL LINK* name must be defined. This name is used by the partner RS/6000 as the *REMOTE LINK name* in its Token-Ring Attachment profile. This name must be unique within the network. The other values in the profile (*Maximum number of LOGICAL LINKS* and *Local SAP Address*) can be unchanged, in most situations.

11.9.7 Defining terminal and printer devices

In versions of AIX prior to 3.2.2, defining 3270-type devices (LU1, LU2, and LU3) was very cumbersome. Each individual unit had to be defined individually. With AIX 3.2.2, a quick configuration capability was added to SMIT; it allows all of the LUs on an attachment to be defined together, at the same time. To access the quick configuration screen, return to the *Configure SNA Profiles* screen and select *Quickly Configure a 3270 Communication Connection.*

At this point, the system asks for the name of the new configuration. Next, the system asks if the connection is to be configured to an existing attachment. The most common answer is *yes,* in which case, the system asks for the attachment name. After entering the attachment name, the system responds with the *Quickly Configure a 3270 Communications Connection : Information* screen. Many of the fields on this screen (*Quick configuration NAME, ATTACHMENT,* and *Link ADDRESS*) are not changeable; they can be changed only by modifying the attachment profile. Although the *SSCP ID* and *XID Node ID* fields can be set here, the default values from the attachment profile should be used.

It is important to remember that unless the *UPDATE all existing profiles using above values?* is set to *yes,* existing LU and connection profiles with the same name *will not* be updated. This should not be significant for a new connection, but it is an often overlooked item when the connection is modified.

At the bottom of the screen, individual lines are defined for each possible LU address. Each address should be set such that its definition matches the definition on the host. There are five possible values: *LU1 SCS Printer, LU2 Display, LU3 3270 Printer, Not Available,* and *Not Defined. Not available* is used to prevent overwriting of LU6.2 information. *Not defined* is used for LU addresses that are not implemented.

When the definition is completed, two new profiles are created: a connection profile and a local LU profile. In addition, links to the attachment profile, the logical link profile, the physical link profile, and the control point profile are created.

11.9.8   Defining LU6.2 connections

LU6.2 connections can also be defined with the quick configuration facility. To perform a quick LU6.2 configuration, return to the *Configure SNA Profiles* screen and select *Quickly Configure a LU6.2 Connection.* As with the quick-3270 configuration, the system asks for the name of the new configuration. Then, the system asks if the connection is to be configured to an existing attachment. As before, the most common answer is *yes,* and the system asks for the attachment name. After entering the attachment name, the system responds with the *Quickly Configure a LU6.2 Connection : Information screen.*

On this screen, the *Quick Configuration Name* and *Attachment* fields are not changeable. For LU6.2 connections, the *Fully qualified LOCAL LU* name must be entered. This consists of the network name and the LU name as defined in the corresponding LU definition on the host; the format of the name is NETNAME.LUNAME. For independent LU6.2 connections, the *Local LU Address* is set to 0; for dependent LU6.2 connections, set the *Local LU Address* to the appropriate address number and enter the correct *XID node ID.* Session characteristics are defined by the *MODE name;* if the mode name does not exist, the system creates one based on defaults. These characteristics *must* match the LOGMODE specified on the host for the partner LU.

As LU6.2 sessions are actually conversations between programs, it is necessary to define what program the RS/6000 will be using to converse with the host. This program is named in the *Local Transaction Program (TP) name (full path).* The full path of the program name must be entered, regardless of its location. Quick configuration creates a TPN profile for the program, if one does not exist. Whether these defaults are acceptable or not should be discussed in the LU6.2 program's documentation.

The *Fully qualified REMOTE LU name* defines the remote (host) partner for the LU6.2 conversation. This is typically the name of the CICS or IMS region with which the program will be conversing. As with the local LU address, the format of the name is NETNAME.LUNAME. The *Remote Transaction Program (RTP) Name* is used only if the remote transaction program name is not supplied by the source transaction program. Because SNA Services *requires* that a RTP name be defined in all cases, an obviously false name, such as 'NONE' or 'DUMMY' may be used.

Finally, it is usually best to leave the *Link ADDRESS* as it is defined in the attachment.

Having completed the definition, at least two (and usually more) new profiles are created. A connection profile and a local LU profile are always created. Usually, mode list, mode, RTPN list, RTPN, TPN list, and TPN profiles are also created. In addition, the links to the attachment profile, the logical link profile, the physical link profile, and the control point profile are created.

11.9.9   Starting the connection and attachment

Now that the attachment and connection have been defined, they can be started. To start the attachment, return (via the F3 key) to the top of the menu hierarchy (the *SNA Services* menu) and traverse through the menu selections

> *Control SNA Services*
>
> *Start SNA Resources*
>
> *Start an SNA Attachment*

Enter the name of the attachment to be started and press enter (or send). Assuming the definitions on the host and in SNA Services are correct, and the hardware is properly installed, the system responds with a message indicating that the attachment has started.

The connection must then be started. Follow the same described procedure, but use the connection instead.

In order to start automatically SNA Services, the attachment, and the connection when the RS/6000 is booted, the /etc/rc.sna file must be modified. Edit the file and remove the pound sign (#) from the line that reads *startsrc -s sna*. Add the following line to start the attachment. Replace the ???? with the actual attachment name.

```
startsrc -t'attachment' -o'????'
```

11.10   HCON (3270/Host Connection)

With SNA Services active, it is now possible to start using the RS/6000 as a gateway to the mainframe. Even though communication is now possible, there is no application using this facility. The primary reason for implementing SNA Services on the RS/6000, in most cases, is to provide mainframe connectivity to AIX users through their AIX terminal. The 3270 Host Connection Program/6000 provides the emulation services AIX users on non-3270 terminals need to connect to the mainframe.

As supplied by IBM, HCON allows users of VT100, VT220, WYSE 50, WYSE 60, 3151, 3161, 3162, 3163, and 3164 terminals to emulate either a 3278 or 3279 terminal. Through utilities, the system administrator can define emulations for other types of terminals if needed. Furthermore, 3286 and 3287 printer sessions can be emulated; the output can be printed on local, ASCII printers, or stored in a file. Although HCON is used primarily with SNA services (and therefore, with SNA sessions), it also supports SNA or non-SNA DFT terminal emulation sessions through the RS/6000 3270 Connection Adapter, and SNA-like sessions through the RS/6000 Host Interface Adapter, or through a direct TCP/IP connection between the RS/6000 and the host.

HCON allows each user to define up to 26 unique session profiles. A user can invoke as many of these sessions concurrently as is necessary or desired. This allows connection to a single host multiple times (for concurrent TSO and CICS sessions), multiple hosts (CICS in Chicago and IMS in New York), or as multiple devices (terminal and printer).

11.10.1 Preconfiguration work

Before configuring HCON, a new mode table (or additions to the existing mode table) must be created on the host. HCON is very particular about log-mode settings for the terminals it controls. Fig. 11.6 is an example of a default HCON MODETAB for SNA-terminals and printers. It is advised that initial testing of HCON be done with this table.

11.10.2 Defining HCON users

Before using the HCON emulator, users must be registered with HCON by an AIX user with root authority. After being registered, at least one session profile must be created for the user.

To register an HCON user, the system administrator enters

```
smit hcon
```

at the AIX terminal. Note that AIX is case-sensitive, therefore, the command *must* be entered in all lowercase letters. After a few seconds, the *AIX 3270 Host Connection Program/6000 (HCON)* menu appears. Proceed down the menu hierarchy by selecting

> *HCON Administrator Functions*
>
> *Add HCON User*

Enter the AIX userid and press enter (or send). In a few seconds, a message appears stating that the user is now registered.

To create a default profile for a user, return to the *AIX 3270 Host Connection Program/6000 (HCON)* menu, select *HCON User Functions,* and then select *Add an HCON Session.* As the connection being defined is through SNA Services, the *Add SNA Display Session* menu item should be chosen. Enter the

HCON user name and press enter (or send) to display the *Add SNA Display Session* panel.

Each session for a user is assigned a one-character alphabetic name. When the *Add SNA Display Session* panel is first entered, the *SESSION name* field is set to the next available session identifier. Although this field can be changed, it is usually not necessary to do so. The *Session USE* field is for operator information only. Up to 20 characters of information can be entered which are displayed in the status line of the terminal emulator screen whenever the session is active.

Perhaps the most significant field on this screen is the *SNA logical connection prefix* or profile. This field determines which SNA connection this session uses. If a fully qualified name is used, the user is assigned to the same connection, and, therefore, the same logical unit, each time the session is invoked. If the connection is in use by another HCON session when the users try to start their session, the session request is denied. If a generic connection name is used (that is, a connection profile name ending with an asterisk), the session is assigned to a range of profiles (and LUs). HCON selects an available connection from this range; if no connection within the range is available, the session is denied. For example, using a fully qualified name, such as *terminal_FE,* causes a session to always (and only) use the 'terminal_FE' connection profile. If it is already in use, the session request fails. However, if a generic specification, such as *terminal** is specified, this session uses any connection starting with 'terminal.' Only if *all* of the 'terminal' sessions are busy is the session request denied.

A wide variety of languages are supported in AIX. This support is extended to HCON via the *LANGUAGE* parameter. The default AIX system language is used for HCON messages in the defined session unless the *LANGUAGE* parameter is otherwise changed. Default keyboard mapping and screen color files are used unless the *KEYBOARD table* and *COLOR table fields* are changed. Both of these tables can be customized, or new files created, with the *hconutil* program. Different keyboard and color files for each session can be used, if desired.

Unless disabled by remapping, the default keyboard tables include keys for saving or printing the current screen. The save key captures the current screen and adds it to the file defined by *File used by SAVES key*. The replace key replaces the file defined by *File used by REPLS key* with the current screen image. The file name for both assumes that the highest level qualifier is the $HOME environment variable, which points to the HCON user's home directory. If the print key is available on the user's keyboard map, the screen image is directed to the printer named in *Local printer used by PRINT key* when the user presses it.

If the HCON host file transfer capabilities are used in the session being defined, it is important to specify the correct *Host TYPE*. The value of this field is irrelevant for terminal or printer emulation, but the file transfer program and the application program interface rely on this information. The *Host LOGIN ID* is used by the file transfer program and the automatic login facility (discussed later) to identify the user to the host system. The user id may be up to eight characters long.

The *AUTOLOG Node ID* is used to specify an automatic login profile that is used by this session; creating the automatic login profile is relatively simple. *AUTOLOG trace* specifies whether the automatic login procedure should be monitored during processing. This monitoring allows the user to see, in the event of an unsuccessful automatic login, where a failure occurred. The *AUTOLOG Timeout* determines the number of seconds the automatic login facility waits for the host system to send a login prompt before abandoning the automatic login.

The file transfer program on the host must be identified to the RS/6000 file transfer program. The default host file transfer program, *IND$FILE,* is automatically selected for *Host File TRANSFER program.* This is acceptable for all supported languages except Danish, Finnish, Norwegian, and Swedish, which use INDÄFILE; and Chinese, Korean, and Japanese, which use APVUFILE. The *File Transfer DIRECTION* field is used to indicate the most common direction of file transfer (from the RS/6000's perspective). The default is *down*; that is, to the RS/6000. The *File Transfer WAIT Period (minutes)* determines the length of time the background file transfer task on the RS/6000 waits for another file transfer before terminating. If the user performs many file transfers, setting this value higher may improve the overall transfer rate. The savings are primarily due to the avoidance of repetitive logons and logoffs on the host. The default value, zero, indicates that the background task should terminate as soon as the file transfer is complete. Setting the value to *999* indicates that the process should not stop until the HCON session is terminated. The *File Transfer RECOVERY time* value determines for how long, once a file transfer has been successfully initiated, the background task should attempt recovery of sessions that fail. The default, zero, prevents any attempt at recovery. *Maximum I/O buffer size (bytes)* is used by the file transfer program to define the maximum data transfer packet size. The default is acceptable for most applications.

After all the applicable information has been coded, press enter (or send) to define the session. At this point, the user is ready to start up an emulator session. However, the HCON server must be started first.

11.10.3 Starting HCON

Like SNA Services, HCON is an AIX subsystem, and as such it must be started before the emulator program can be used. To start HCON, return to the *AIX 3270 Host Connection Program/6000 (HCON)* menu and select the *HCON Control* item. On the *HCON Control* menu, select *Start the hcondmn subsystem.* In a few seconds, message 0513-059 should appear stating that the system has started. To ensure that the HCON daemon starts whenever the RS/6000 is booted, edit the /etc/rc.hcon file and remove the pound (#) sign at the beginning of the line

```
startsrc -s hcon
```

11.10.4 Using HCON

The user invokes the emulator by entering e789 ? at the AIX terminal. In place of the question mark, the user must specify the session identifier(s) that should be started. A common reason for having two sessions is to start a concurrent terminal and printer emulation sessions. After the emulator session contacts the SNA connection, users see a status line if they are using a twenty-five line terminal. On twenty-four line VT100 and VT220 terminals, the status line can be toggled in and out of the twenty-fourth line by pressing Ctrl-X. Once the SNA connection is established, the terminal functions as any other 3270-type terminal (or printer) does and the users can begin their host application. To exit from the emulator, users press Ctrl-D. A confirmation prompt is issued; pressing any key combination but Ctrl-D returns users to the emulator.

11.10.5 hconutil—The HCON customization utility

The hconutil program is used to customized screen colors, keyboard mapping, configure automatic logon profiles, and perform explicit file transfers. It is a menu-driven program and is fairly simple to use. Unless specifically directed otherwise, customization activities are directed to files that are local to the user who is doing the customizing. However, local changes can be implemented if the session profile is changed to point to the local file instead of to the global system file.

Color customization allows the user to change the background and foreground colors of the terminal status line. In addition, the user can change the way in which 3270 standard attributes display. The system default color table can be modified by invoking the utility with the following command line (be sure to back up the file first):

```
hconutil -c /usr/lib/hcon/e789_ctbl -C /usr/lib/hcon/e789_ctbl
```

The keyboard remapping function allows for the definition of key combinations on non-3270 type terminals to perform the same functions as the keys found on 3270-type terminals. Also, it can be used to remove certain functions from a HCON users' session. For example, by default, an HCON user can escape to the shell while in the emulator. It may be desirable to prevent some AIX users from doing so; hconutil can be used to nullify the key combination that permits this action. As with other customization functions, the default action is to modify only the user's local keyboard table. To change the global system keyboard table enter the following command line (again, be sure to back up the file first):

```
hconutil -c /usr/lib/hcon/e789_ktbl -C /usr/lib/hcon/e789_ktbl
```

It is important to note that global system changes go into effect immediately, and are used the next time the emulator is started.

An automatic logon profile is defined by using the hconutil or genprof command. First, the user records all of the events performed during a login on an AUTOLOG form; this can be found in file /usr/lib/hcon/logform. These are then entered on the *hconutil* or *genprof* screen and saved to a file in the user's home directory.

The automatic login profile can be tested by using the tlog command. To do this, the user starts the regular emulator program, e789, and suspends it by exiting to the shell, typically by pressing Ctrl-Z. In the secondary shell, the user issues the tlog command with the same session identifier operand as was used to start the preceding emulator session. Once testing is complete, the profile can be update by using the file name as the operand for the *AUTOLOG Node ID* for one or more of the user's sessions.

File transfer in hconutil is totally menu-driven. The user indicates which session is to be used for the file transfer, and then supplies standard file transfer information: source and destination file names, transfer direction, translation, replace (yes/no), append (yes/no), record type, logical record length, and code set. Because each type of host session is different, the user *must* specify the correct type of host session: CMS, TSO, VSE, or CICS.

Defining a new terminal type is not quite as simple as some of the preceding functions. Using one of the existing terminal information files as a basis (ibm.ti.H, dec.ti.H, or wyse.ti.H in directory /usr/lib/hcon/terminfo), the user creates a new *terminfo* file. The recommended naming convention is to use the terminal name with the mandatory .H suffix. Therefore, the recommended name for an ADM11 terminal file is adm11.H. Before invoking the terminal information compiler, the user must set the *TERMINFO* environment variable by entering

```
export TERMINFO=/usr/lib/hcon/terminfo.
```

The terminal definition is created by issuing the tic command. All of the terminal definitions (new and existing) are recompiled. The new definition can be used only if the *TERM* environment variable is set to the new terminal name. So, in our example, the user issues the following command

```
export TERM=adm11
```

the ADM11 terminal definition. In some cases, it may be necessary to also create a new keyboard mapping file for the terminal.

User Interface Topics

12

vi

The AIX operating system ships with three different text editors: vi, ed, and Ined. ed was the first UNIX editor. It is a line-based editor, much like Edlin for MS-DOS. The commands for ed are very obscure and the only error message is "?." Nowadays, it is used only under situations of extreme duress, such as when vi does not work for some reason. The vi full-screen editor was developed using the ex editor as its basis.[1] vi is common to all versions of UNIX; where there is a UNIX system, vi is available. Because of this universal availability, vi is the best choice if a person is to learn just one editor. The Ined editor was developed by Interactive Systems Corporation specifically for AIX. Although it is very powerful, it is not available on many other platforms, save AIX. The gnu emacs editor[2] is very popular with programmers. This popularity is based primarily on the powerful scripting language in emacs which essentially allows the editor to function as a programming language. But gnu emacs is not routinely shipped with UNIX systems; it must be installed separately, and it is extremely user-unfriendly.[3]

12.1   An Introduction to vi

The vi editor has three modes of operation. When in command mode, keystrokes are interpreted as editor subcommands to be carried out immediately. The subcommands are not displayed on the screen, only the results of the actions are displayed. Text input mode is fairly self-explanatory. This mode interprets keystrokes as text to be added to the file. Last-line mode does not have anything to do with the last line of the input text; this mode refers to the fact that the command is displayed on the last line of the screen before the command is executed.

---

[1] ex is the bsd implementation of the ed editor.
[2] Which is available as freeware.
[3] Not that vi wins any awards in this area.

The escape key is used to switch between command and text input mode. When in command mode,[4] if a command beginning with a colon (:), slash (/), question mark (?), or exclamation point (!) is entered, the mode switches to last-line mode; pressing the enter key after typing in the last-line command switches back to command mode.

When the vi editor is first started, it is in command mode. The user enters a subcommand (a, A, i, I, o, or O, explained below) to switch to text input mode.

vi is started by specifying the name of the file (or files) to be edited, for example

```
vi myfile
```

When more than one file name are specified on the command line, the editor edits each file sequentially (not concurrently) in the order specified.

vi uses command-line flags to perform file preprocessing. The most common flags are -R, to set the file to read-only mode, and -r, to recover a file after an editor or system crash.

The maximum size file that may be edited with vi is 64 Mbytes. Because all file operations are buffered,[5] the /tmp file system must have free space available to hold the entire file being edited. If there is not enough space, the user receives an error message[6] and vi terminates. In addition, vi has other restrictions

The maximum size of a line of text in the input file is 2048 characters.

A maximum of 128 characters may be used as the object of a find or replace operation.

A maximum of 128 characters may be used in shell command.

A file may contain a maximum of 1,048,560 lines.

The general syntax of vi subcommands follows the form:

```
[namedbuffer][operator][number] object
```

where the namedbuffer is the name of a temporary text storage area; the operator is a vi subcommand or action; the number indicates either the extent or the number of repetitions of the subcommand; and object specifies what to act upon. This may be a text object or a text position.

Many subcommands can take a number as a prefix to indicate a repetition factor. For instance, the subcommand

```
2u
```

---

[4]If there is ever a doubt as to which mode vi is currently in, pressing the esc key twice always returns the user to command mode.

[5]That is, the file is not directly edited, a copy of the file is edited.

[6]0602-103 file too large to place in /tmp.

will undo the last two changes, where the subcommand

   7y

places the next seven lines, starting at the current cursor position, in the yank buffer.

12.2   Movement within a File

Depending on the type of terminal a user has, the arrow keys may not function for cursor movement. To circumvent this problem, cursor movement can be performed in command mode by entering

h	To move one character to the left
l	To move one character to the right
j	To move the cursor down one line
k	To move the cursor up one line

In addition, Ctrl-H moves the cursor one character to the left, Ctrl-J moves the cursor down one line, and Ctrl-P moves the cursor up one line.

12.2.1   Advanced cursor positioning commands

In addition to the basic positioning commands, positioning within a line by characters, words, sentences, and paragraphs is possible in command mode with the following subcommands:

^	Move to the first nonblank character.
0	Move to the beginning of the line.
$	Move to the end of the line.
fx	Move to the next x character.
Fx	Move to the last x character.
tx	Move to one column before the next x character.
Tx	Move to one column after the next x character.
;	Repeat the last f, F, t, or T subcommand.
,	Repeat the last f, F, t, or T subcommand in the opposite direction.
number|	Move the cursor to column 1.
w	Move to the beginning of the next word.
b	Move to the beginning of the previous word.
e	Move to the end of the current word.
(	Move to the beginning of the previous sentence.
)	Move to the beginning of the next sentence.
{	Move to the beginning of the previous paragraph.
}	Move to the beginning of the next paragraph.

12.2.2   Screen positioning commands

Screen positioning commands cause the screen display to change based on the action requested. These commands include

H	Move to the top line of the screen.
L	Move to the last line of the screen.
M	Move to the middle line of the screen.
+	Move to the next line at its first nonblank character.
−	Move to the previous line at its first nonblank character.
(enter)	Move the cursor to the next line at its first nonblank character.
z	Redraw the screen with the current line at the top of the screen.
z-	Redraw the screen with the current line at the bottom of the screen.
z.	Redraw the screen with the current line at the center of the screen.
/pattern/z-	Redraw the screen and place the first line containing the character string *pattern* at the bottom.
z+	Scroll up one screen.
z^	Scroll down one screen.
Ctrl-U	Scroll up one-half screen.
Ctrl-D	Scroll down one-half screen.
Ctrl-F	Scroll forward one screen.
Ctrl-B	Scroll back one screen.
Ctrl-E	Scroll down one line.
Ctrl-Y	Scroll up one line.
Ctrl-L	Refresh the screen.

12.2.3   Searching for a pattern

Searching for patterns in vi can be simple or complex. Searching is permitted in both forward or backward directions for a specific line or a pattern within a line. When the pattern or line is found, the current line, or a given number of lines before or after it can be changed to the found line.

Patterns may be either a literal string, such as "extern," or a regular expression.

A search command may be terminated, before it is complete, by pressing the escape key.

Searching for a specific line number or pattern is done with the following subcommands:

xG	Goes to a specific line and makes it the current line; if no *x* value is given, the last line of the file becomes the current line.
/pattern	Performs a forward search for the specified pattern and makes the line containing the pattern the current line.
/pattern/-Number	Performs a forward search for the specified pattern and designates as the current line the one found *number* of lines before the one containing the pattern.
/pattern/+Number	Performs a forward search for the specified pattern and designates as the current line the one found *number* of lines after the one containing the pattern.
?pattern	Performs a backward search for the specified pattern and makes the line containing the pattern the current line.
?pattern?-Number	Performs a backward search for the specified pattern and designates as the current line the one found *number* of lines before the one containing the pattern.
?pattern?+Number	Performs a backward search for the specified pattern and designates as the current line the one found *number* of lines after the one containing the pattern.

n	Repeats the preceding search, in the same direction.
N	Repeats the preceding search, but in the opposite direction.
%	Searches for the matching limiter.

The special command % searches for a matching delimiter. When the cursor is on a delimiter (one of the following characters: ()[]{}), entering the % subcommand positions the cursor to the matching delimiter of the character.

Several characters have a special meaning when used in a pattern as part of a regular expression. These characters are

^	To match at the beginning of a line
$	To match at the end of a line
.	To match any character
\>	To match at the end of a word
\<	To match at the beginning of a word
[ ]	To match any character within the brackets

For example, the pattern

```
/but
```

finds the next occurrence of *but* while the pattern

```
/^but
```

finds the next line which starts with *but,* and the pattern

```
/bu[mt]
```

finds the next line that starts with either *bum* or *but.*

12.3   Editing Text

Editing text may be performed in input mode and in command mode. When the escape key is pressed from input mode, the user enters command mode. The user enters input mode as the result of entering a command mode subcommand.

12.3.1   Entering text input mode

The add, insert, overwrite, and some change commands move the user from command mode into text input mode. The specific subcommands are

a *text*	Inserts the optionally specified text after the current cursor position; subsequent text input is added after the current cursor position
A *text*	Inserts the optionally specified text at the end of the current line; subsequent text input is added to the end of the line
i *text*	Inserts the optionally specified text into the line before the current cursor position; subsequent text input is inserted into the line at the current cursor position
I *text*	Inserts the optionally specified text into the line before the first nonblank character; subsequent text input is inserted into the line at the current cursor position

o	Adds a blank line immediately after the current line; subsequent text input begins at the first position of the inserted line
O	Adds a blank line immediately before the current line; subsequent text input begins at the first position of the inserted line
C	Changes the line from the current cursor position to the end of the line
c$	Same as C
cc	Changes the entire line
cw	Changes a word

12.3.2 Changing text while in input mode

A select group of subcommands may be used to edit text without leaving text input mode. These subcommands generally have different meanings in command mode. The user should exercise caution when using them lest undesired actions occur.

The text input commands are

Ctrl-H	Erase the last character
Ctrl-W	Erase the last word
\	Quotes the erase and kill characters[7]
Esc	Ends text input and changes to command mode
Ctrl-?	Interrupts and ends insert or Ctrl-D processing
Ctrl-D	Goes back to the previous autoindent stop
^Ctrl-D	Ends autoindent for this line only
0Ctrl-D	Moves the cursor to the left margin
Ctrl-V	Allows for the input of any character

12.3.3 Changing text from command mode

Several commands are available in command mode to manipulate text. Many of these commands allow for the prefixing of a number or a range. In the case of a number, the command is executed the specified number of times. For a range, the command is executed on the lines which fall within its domain. The range 1,$ indicates that the entire file is to be processed.

The commands for changing text in command mode are

cw text	Changes the current word to *text*
D	Deletes from the current cursor position to the end of line
dd	Deletes the current line
dw	Deletes the current word
dG	Deletes to the end of file
dL	Deletes to the end of screen
d)	Deletes to the end of sentence
d}	Deletes to the end of paragraph
d2}	Deletes to the end of next paragraph
xdd	Deletes the next x lines

---

[7]This is used to place the erase and kill characters into the text.

J	Joins the current and next line
rx	Replaces the current character with x
Rtext	Overwrites from the current cursor position with *text*
s	Substitutes characters (changes places)[8]
S	Substitutes lines
u	Undoes a previous change
x	Deletes the character at the cursor position
X	Deletes the character before the cursor position
<<	Shifts the current line to the left
<L	Shifts all lines from the current line to the end of the screen to the left
>	Shifts the current line to the right
>L	Shifts all lines from the current line to the end of the screen to the right
~	Changes the letter at the cursor position to the opposite case

To change more than a few characters of text, the last line mode substitute command is used. The syntax of the command is

```
:[begin,end]s/original_text/substitute_text
```

For example, the command

```
:s/dog/cat
```

changes the next occurrence of dog to cat, while the command

```
:1,$s/dog/cat
```

changes all occurrences within the file of dog to cat. The command

```
:.,.+10s/dog/cat
```

changes every occurrence of dog to cat starting at the current line (.) and for the next ten lines (.+10).

12.3.4   Moving and copying text

The yank, delete, and push commands are used to move and copy text. The action of the yank and delete commands transfers the affected data to an internal buffer. This data is only transferred to the new location when a push command is issued. If yanks or deletes are followed in succession, only the most recently yanked or deleted data is retrieved in a subsequent push.[9] These commands are all used while in command mode.

These commands are

---

[8]This and the S command are not the same as the last-line substitute command.
[9]See Sec. 12.3.5 for further information.

Y	To copy the current line
yw	To copy the current word
yy	To copy the current line
xyy	To copy the next x lines
yG	To copy from the current line to the end of file
y)	To copy to the end of sentence
y}	To copy to the end of paragraph
yL	To copy to end of the screen
D	To delete from the current cursor position to the end of the line
dd	To delete the current line
dw	To delete the current word
dG	To delete to the end of file
dL	To delete to the end of the screen
d)	To delete to the end of sentence
d}	To delete to the end of paragraph
d2}	To delete to the end of the next paragraph
xdd	To delete the next x lines
p	To place the yanked or deleted data before the current position
P	To place the yanked or deleted data after the current position

12.3.5 Restoring (undoing) and repeating changes

Undoing changes is performed with the undo command. The u command undoes the last change where the U command restores the current line if the cursor has not left the line since the last change.

The command "xp allows for old deleted or yanked information to be retrieved. When the command is issued, the last xth delete is pushed into the text. For example, the command

```
"5p
```

retrieves the line (or group of lines) deleted 5 times ago and places it into the text after the current position.

Finally, a dot (period (.)) repeats the last change command or increments the counter in a "xp command. So, if the user entered

after the prior command, the sixth last deleted line or group of lines would be retrieved from the delete buffer and placed into the text at the current position.

12.4 Operations on Files

All of the subcommands associated with operations on files are last line commands.

12.4.1 Saving files

The :w subcommand is used to write the contents of the edit buffer to a file. If no file name is specified, the contents of the buffer are written out to the original file. If a new file name is used, as in :w *newfilename,* the edit buffer contents are written to the file *newfilename.* If any existing file name is used, the w! *existingfilename* command is used to overwrite the contents of the existing file.

The :wq subcommand is similar to the :w subcommand except that after the contents of the edit buffer are written to the file, vi terminates.

The :q subcommand may be used to discard the contents of the edit buffer. If the contents of the edit buffer are different from those of the existing file, a warning message is displayed requesting user confirmation. Replying *y* causes the edit buffer to be discarded and vi to terminate. The :q! subcommand is used to unconditionally discard the contents of the edit buffer and terminate vi.

Alternatively, the :e! command may be used to discard all of the changes in the edit buffer and reedit the original file.

12.4.2 Opening a second editing session

Additionally, the e: subcommand starts a second editing session. When used with a file name, :e *filename,* the file is opened in a second session. When a plus sign is inserted before the filename, the command edits the specified file starting at the bottom (:e + *filename*). Or, a plus sign and a number can be used to start editing at a specific line number (:e + *Number filename*). The :e # subcommand is used to switch between the two editing sessions.[10]

12.4.3 Inserting files

Files may be inserted into the current file with the :r *filename* subcommand. This subcommand reads the designated file into the edit buffer by adding or inserting new lines below the current line.

Closely related, the :r! command runs the specified AIX command and places the standard output into the current file by adding or inserting new lines below the current line. For example, the subcommand

```
:r! ls -al
```

places the output of the ls -al command in the current file.

12.4.4 Editing multiple files in sequence

When a list of files is used on the vi command line, the :n subcommand is used to close the current file and switch to the next file. A new list of files

---

[10]Ctrl-A may also be used to switch between the two editing sessions.

may be specified by listing the names of the new files after the :n subcommand, i.e., :n *newfile1 newfile2 newfile3*.

12.4.5   File statistical information

Finally, Ctrl-G is used to show file statistical information. When Ctrl-G is pressed, the current file name, current line number, number of lines in the file, and relative position of the current line are displayed.

12.5   Exiting to the Shell

Two subcommands allow the user to run AIX commands from within vi. The first, :sh, starts another instance of the shell. This allows the user to run more than one command. Pressing Ctrl-D closes the shell and returns the user to vi.

The subcommand, :! *command,* runs the specified command and immediately returns back to the editor. The subcommand, :!!, repeats the last :! command.

12.6   Customizing the vi Environment

With the set subcommand, the user may customize many of the operational characteristics of the vi editor. These changes may be made only for the current session or saved for use whenever vi is used again.

12.6.1   The set subcommand

The set subcommand turns vi options on and off. Most options may be abbreviated on the command line. The user may spell out the entire option on the subcommand line or use the abbreviation option; either way, the same action is performed.

For all of the options the default setting is *off.* Once an option has been turned on by entering the name of the option as the operand of the set command, the option is turned off again by prefixing it with *no.* For example, to ignore the distinction between upper and lower case letters in a search, the user enters

```
:set ignorecase
```

or

```
:set ic
```

This option is set off with a subsequent command of

```
:set noignorecase
```

or

```
:set noic
```

All of the options are discussed in Table 12.1.

TABLE 12.1   vi set Subcommands

Subcommand	Abbreviation	Meaning
autoindent	ai	In text input mode, automatically indents to the indentation of the previous line by using the spacing between tab stops as specified by the shiftwidth option. The default setting is *noai*. Ctrl-D is used to back up to the previous tab stop.
autoprin	ap	Prints the current line after a command that changes the editing buffer. This is the default. When used with a group of commands, this option applies only to the last command and does not apply to global commands.
autowrite	aw	Writes the edit buffer to the file automatically before the :n, :ta, Ctrl-A, and ! subcommands. The default is *noaw*.
beautifying text	bf	Prevents the user from entering control characters while entering *ext* in command mode. The default is *nobf*.
closepunct=	cp=	Defines a list of closing punctuation which should not be split when using wrapping text mode (wraptype option); for example :set cp=.,;]).
directory=	dir=	Allows the user to set the path for the editing buffer; the default is *dir=/var/tmp*.
edcompatible	ed	Allows certain compatibilities with the ed line editor; retains the *g* (global) and *c* (confirm) suffixes during multiple substitutions and causes the *r* (read) suffix to work like the *r* subcommand. The default is *noed*.
exrc		If not set (noexrc); ignores any local .exrc file. The default is *exrc*.
hardtabs=	ht=	Sets the number of spaces which equal a table stop. The default is *ht=8*.
ignorecase	ic	Ignores the distinction between uppercase and lowercase characters while searching for regular expressions. The default is *noic*.
linelimit=	ll=	Sets the maximum number of lines. This set command may be used only in an .exrc file or EXINIT environment variable.
lisp		Removes the special meaning of the (), {}, and [[]] characters and enables the = (formatted print) operator for s-expressions. These actions enable the editing of LISP programs. The default is *nolisp*.
list		Displays text with tabs and the end of marked lines. Tabs are displayed as ^{I} and the end of lines as $. The default is *nolist*.
modeline		Runs an editor command line if one is found within the first or last five lines of the file. The command may be anywhere within the line; however, in order for the editor to recognize a command line, it must contain a space or tab followed by the ex: or vi: string. The command is ended by a second colon (:). The default is *nomodeline*.
number	nu	Displays lines prefixed with their line numbers. The default is *nonu*.
optimize	opt	Speeds up the operation of terminals that lack cursor addressing. The default is *noopt*.

TABLE 12.1 `vi set` Subcommands *(Continued)*

Subcommand	Abbreviation	Meaning
prompt		Prompts for a new editor command when in command mode by printing a colon (:). The default is *on*.
readonly	ro	Sets the editor to read-only mode. The default is *noreadonly*.
redraw		Simulates a smart workstation on a dumb workstation. The default is *nore*.
report=	re=	Sets the number of times a command may be repeated before a message is displayed. The default is *report*=5.
scroll=	scr=	Sets the number of lines to be scrolled when the user scrolls up or down.
shell=	sh=	Defines the shell for the ! or :! subcommand. The default is the user's login shell.
shiftwidth=	sw=	Sets the distance for the software tab stops used by the autoindent option, the shift commands (> and <), and the text input commands (Ctrl-D and Ctrl-T). This applies only to the indentation at the beginning of a line. The default is *sw*=8.
showmatch	sm	Shows the matching opening parenthesis or bracket as the close parenthesis or bracket is typed. The default is *nosm*.
showmode	smd	Displays a message to indicate when the editor is in input mode. The default is *nosmd*.
slowopen	slow	Postpones updating the display screen during inserts. The default is *noslow*.
sourceany		Restricts editing to files owned only by the user when set to *no*. The default is *on*.
tabstop=	ts=	Sets the distance between tab stops in a displayed file. The default is *ts*=8.
term=		Sets the type of workstation being used. The default is term=$TERM where $TERM is the value of the TERM shell environment variable.
terse		Allows the `vi` editor to display the short form of messages. The default is *noterse*.
warn		Displays a warning message before the ! or :! subcommand executes a shell command if the current edit buffer has not been saved to a file. This is the default.
window=	wi=	Sets the number of lines displayed in one window of text. The default is a full screen minus one line for locally attached terminals.
wrapmargin=	wm=	Sets the margin for automatic word wrapping from one line to the next. The default is *wm*=0. A value of zero turns off word wrapping.
wrapscan	ws	Allows string searches to wrap from the end of the editing buffer to the beginning. This is the default.
wraptype=	wt=	Indicates the method used to wrap words at the end of a line. There are four possible values: *general* allows wraps on word breaks as white space between two characters. *word* allows wraps on words.

TABLE 12.1   vi set Subcommands (*Continued*)

Subcommand	Abbreviation	Meaning
wraptype= (*Cont.*)	wt=	*rigid* allows wraps on column and before closing punctuation. *flexible* allows wraps on column but one character of punctuation can extend past the margin. The default value for *wraptype* is general.
writeany=	wa=	Turns off the checks usually made before a write subcommand (such as, does the file already exist). The default is *nowa*.

12.6.2   Making permanent changes

The options of vi can be made permanent in three ways. The user may put the set subcommand in the EXINIT environment variable in the .profile file. For example, to set *ignorecase* on all of the time, the user enters the following line in the .profile file:

```
export EXINIT='set ignorecase'
```

The vi option may also be made permanent by creating a .exrc file in the user's home directory; this is referred to as the $HOME/.exrc file. This file would consist only of vi set subcommands. For example, the following file sets *ignorecase* and *showmode* on for this user every time vi is invoked.

```
$ cat /home/fgc/.exrc
set showmode
set ignorecase
$
```

In addition, a local .exrc file may exist. This is an .exrc file in a nonhome directory. An .exrc file of this type is used only when editing in the directory in which the .exrc file is located.

By default, vi first looks for the EXINIT environment variable and executes the command found there. If the EXINIT variable does not exist, vi then checks for the .exrc file in the user's home directory. Therefore, both the EXINIT and $HOME/.exrc file cannot be used together. However, the local .exrc file is always executed, whether or not the EXINIT or $HOME/.exrc files is used.

12.7   Exiting from vi

As discussed, the q! subcommand discards the contents of the edit buffer and terminates vi immediately. The subcommand :wq writes the contents of the edit buffer to the file before vi is terminated. Additionally, the command ZZ(note this is *not* a last line command) writes the contents of the edit buffer to the file and terminates vi.

The Korn Shell

In AIX, three basic shell programs are provided

The Korn Shell

The Bourne Shell

The C Shell[1]

The shell programs function as command interpreters for the user. Unlike most other operating systems, the command interface between the user and the AIX operating system is not built into AIX. Instead, programs separate from the base operating system are used to retrieve information from the user's terminal and translate it into a form the operating system can understand. Included in every shell program is a programming language used for creating script files.

The Korn shell is the default shell script on AIX. When a user is added to the system, one of the attributes the system administrator must define which shell program is invoked when the user logs on. This becomes the user's *default shell*. If another shell is not explicitly selected, AIX automatically makes the Korn shell the user's default shell. After signing on to the system, the user can switch to another shell, either temporarily or permanently.

The Korn shell is a superset of the Bourne shell which was the original UNIX shell. The syntax of the Korn and Bourne shells are similar, but not exactly the same. Therefore, not all Bourne shells scripts run unmodified under the Korn shell. The C shell was developed subsequent to the Bourne shell (but before the Korn shell) as a tool for programmers who were used to working with C programming language. The C shell very closely resembles C. Complex pattern matching is simpler in the C shell than in the Korn shell; however the C shell does not support functions, select statements, and coprocesses as the Korn shell does.

---

[1]The other shells, such as the Trusted shell and the Restricted shell, are variations of one of the three basic shells.

Regardless of the shell used, it is able to accept commands from the user whenever the shell *command prompt* is displayed. The default prompt in most cases is the dollar sign ($), but the user can change this. When the shell receives a command, which is signalled by the user pressing the enter key on the terminal, the shell attempts to evaluate the input and carry out the request. Depending on the command, the shell writes the output or an error message to the terminal. Typically, input to a shell is processed interactively from a terminal, but it can also be processed from a batch file or *shell script*.

Shell scripts provide a mechanism for grouping long or complex sequences of commands into a single "command." In addition, shell scripts are used also for creating *batch jobs:* long-running, multistep tasks that do not require user interaction. To facilitate the use of shell scripts, each shell implements a programming language which is used to control and adjust the sequence of command execution within a script based on the outcome of prior commands.

But, in addition to processing input, the shell processes the output of commands. Because terminal input and output are directed through the shell, it is possible for the shell to manipulate these data streams or *redirect* them, as discussed in the next section.

In addition to providing the standard shell services, such as input/output redirection, variable substitution, and filename generation, the Korn shell provides arithmetic functions, command history, coprocessing, and inline editing.

While in the Korn shell, the user may set on command line editing. This provides a way of retrieving previously entered commands and reusing or modifying them for another execution. This feature is set on by entering

```
set -o vi
```

at the command prompt. Once the vi editor is enabled, hitting the escape key at the command prompt moves the user into command mode.

13.1   Input and Output Redirection

Input and output on AIX is based on a rather simple premise: a command reads input from *standard input,* writes output to *standard output* and sends all error messages to *standard error.* To further simplify things, all three files are directed, by default, to the user's terminal.

All AIX commands follow this model.[2] Because of this, the shell is able to redirect input and output from the terminal to files, or, less commonly, to other devices. This standardization also facilitates the redirection of one command's output to another command's input or *piping.*

Four symbols are used to indicate redirection, < to redirect standard input, > to redirect standard output, >> to append standard output to an existing file, and | to pipe data from standard output to standard input.

---

[2]Strictly speaking, this is not true. There are a few esoteric commands that do not follow this standard. They will be noted, as appropriate.

The less than symbol (<) is used to read input from a file. Although most commands that expect a "real" file as input allow for the specification of the file's name as part of the command, some do not. The wc command is an example of a command that reads its input from standard input only. Considering that this command counts the number of lines, words, and characters in a file, it is obvious that redirection is necessary for almost all uses of wc. The command

```
wc < input.data
```

causes the shell to pass the file input.data to the wc command as standard input.

Output redirection is similar. Normally, commands write output to standard output. If this output must be saved for later use, it is necessary to redirect it to a file. The ls command, which is used to list the contents of a directory, is a good example. As would be expected, the directory information from the command is directed to standard output; therefore, it is displayed on the user's terminal. To save for later use the directory information in a file named directory.out, the user issues the command

```
ls > directory.out
```

The output redirection operation creates a new file; an existing file with the same name is deleted. To keep the existing information in the directory.out file and simply append the new information to the existing file, the command is slightly different

```
ls >> directory.out
```

With this redirection operator, the original file is kept, and the new data is added at the end of the original file. If the file to which standard output is being redirected does not exist, it is created.

Redirecting the output of one command to the input of another is accomplished with the OR symbol (|). To direct the output of a directory listing into the word count program, the following command could be issued:

```
ls | wc
```

The result of this command is a display of the number of lines, words, and characters in the directory listing.

Pipes flow from left to right with all of the commands in the pipe running concurrently. Pipe processes wait when there is no input to be read from an active prior process or when the following process in the pipe is full. As each command in the pipe runs as a separate process, each one has its own process id. There is no inherent limit on the complexity of a pipe command and long-running pipe commands may be executed in the background if that is more convenient for the user.

As stated earlier, when a command starts, three files are opened, *stdin* (standard input), *stdout* (standard output), and *stderr* (standard error). In addition to standard names, these three files are also assigned to a standard *file descriptor* within the command program. A file descriptor is a number that is associated with each open file in a program. The following file descriptors are associated with the standard files:

0	Is used for standard input (the keyboard)
1	Is used for standard output (the terminal)
2	Is used for standard error (the terminal)

By default, the redirector operator for input, ($<$), assumes that file descriptor 0 is to be used. Likewise, the output redirectors, ($>$ and $>>$), assume file descriptor 1 is to be used. Specifying a file descriptor before the redirection operator allows redirection to take place for the file referred to by the file descriptor number. This is how standard error is redirected. For example

```
ls >ls.out 2>ls.errors
```

directs the output of the ls command to ls.out, and any error messages from the command to the file ls.errors. If a command directs output to several different files, each file can be independently redirected. As an example, assume that a user-written application program, yourcmd, writes three different output files, which are associated with file descriptors 4, 5, and 6. Redirecting the output of this command is accomplished as follows:

```
yourcmd 2>err.log 4>trans.log 5>oob.data 6>misc.data
```

In this example, standard error is directed to err.log, data file 4 to trans.log, data file 5 to oob.data,[3] and data file 6 to misc.data. If any output is written to standard output, that data appears on the terminal as if standard output *was not* redirected.

13.2 Types of Processing

Like every other executing programs on the system, shells are also *processes*. The command shell is a *foreground* processes because it is able to interact with the user via the terminal.

When the user enters a command in response to the shell prompt, the shell interprets any wildcard characters in the command, and *forks* and makes a copy of itself in storage. The command then runs in this second copy of the shell as a *child* process. Unless otherwise directed through file redirection, the command uses the terminal as standard input, standard output, and standard error. While the process is running, other processes cannot be started at the terminal until the first one completes or is halted by the user. The

---

[3]When something is out of balance, there is always oob data.

shell may have multiple subprocesses or children since each of the child processes may start its own children, but each started processes has only one parent process.

In many cases, it is not necessary for the user to interact with the application. In this case, the process can run in the background. To run a process in the background, the user simply appends an ampersand (&) to the end of the command. When running processes in the background, it is customary to redirect standard input, output, and error. If these are not redirected, the process in the background uses the terminal device just as it would if it were in the foreground. This can cause undesirable results if another process, foreground or background, is also using the terminal. A process is sent to the background by adding an ampersand (&) to the end of the command line

```
somecommand &
```

13.2.1 Coprocessing

Coprocesses are different from both the typical parent-child process relationship and command piping. Coprocesses are atomic operations which send data between two processes at the shell level. That is, instead of the two processes operating independently with the first sending input indirectly through a pipe to the second, the two processes work in tandem with the first directly connected to the second, passing data directly to the coprocess. The coprocess is started by appending |& to the applicable command. This is demonstrated in the following example.

Consider coprocessA which contains the following commands:

```
1a    echo "CoProcess A has started"
2a    ./coprocessB |&
3a    read -p parm1 parm2 parm3 parm4
4a    echo "First Input from CoProcess B => $parm1 $parm2 $parm3 $parm4
5a    print -p "Input Data of CoProcessB"
6a    read -p parm1 parm2 parm3 parm4
7a    echo "Second Input from CoProcess B => $parm1 $parm2 $parm3 $parm4
```

Then consider the following script, coprocessB

```
1b    echo "CoProcess B has started"
2b    read parm1 parm2 parm3 parm4
3b    echo $parm1 $parm2 $parm3 $parm4
```

Running coprocessA results in the following output:

```
$ coprocessA
CoProcessA has started
First Input from CoProcessB => CoProcessB has started
Second Input from CoProcessB => Input Data of CoProcessB
$
```

Examining what happened, the following sequence of events emerges
statement 1a executes and produces the initial message.
statement 2a starts coprocessB.

statement 1b runs and passes output back to statement 3a.
statement 4a executes and produces the second message.
statement 5a passes input data to statement 2b.
statement 3b passes the input from 2b back to 6a.
statement 7a prints the third message based on input received from statement 6a.

13.3 Metacharacter Substitution

Metacharacters are symbols used to represent one or more other characters; a popular alternative name for metacharacters is *wildcard character*. Metacharacters are used to specify a pattern to be used by a command.

The simplest metacharacter is the question mark (?). It is used to match exactly one character, the value of which may be any single ASCII value. For instance, the pattern

```
for?
```

matches any four-character string whose first three characters are for: fora, forZ, for1, for@ and so forth. The pattern

```
a??le
```

matches any five-character string which begins with an *a* and ends in *le* : apple, aPPle,[4] abole. Finally, the pattern

```
?????
```

matches any five-character string (match, table, force).

Brackets are used in patterns to denote a specific subset of ASCII values which are to be matched against. For instance, the pattern

```
for[ekt]
```

matches only the four-character strings fore, fork, and fort. This facility is often used to separate out specific sets

[AEIOU]	matches only an uppercase vowel
[aeiouAEIOU]	matches an uppercase or lowercase vowel
[0-9][0-9][0-9]	matches any three-digit number
[a-z][a-z][0-9]	matches any three-character string beginning with two lowercase letters and ending in an integer

The exclamation point (!) is used for negation. Therefore, the pattern

---

[4]Note that apple and aPPle are different strings.

```
for[!ekt]
```

matches any four-character string beginning with *for except* for, fore, fork, and fort.

The backlash slash (\) is used within patterns to signify that the following character is to be interpreted literally. This allows the special metacharacters, such as ? and !, to be used in patterns. For instance, the pattern

```
ar[\?\!]
```

matches any three-character string beginning with *ar* and ending with a question mark or exclamation point. Similarly, the pattern

```
??[\?\!]
```

matches any three-character string ending in an exclamation point or question mark.

The Korn shell uses the asterisk (*) to represent a match for one, many, or no characters. For example, the pattern

```
*
```

matches everything, except when used to represent a file name.

The pattern

```
for*
```

matches any string beginning with *for*; this would include the strings for, fort, fork, forklift, fortunecookie, etc. The pattern

```
*.bak
```

matches any string ending with the character string .bak. Similarly, the pattern f*r*t matches any string beginning with an *f*, ending with a *t*, and containing an *r* in the middle. Examples include fort, feret, fairmarket, flowright.

Two anomalies occur when the asterisk is used with file names. First, wildcards do not match "dot files," that is, filenames beginning with a dot. To match the dot files, the pattern .* must be used. To match *all* files, the pattern *.* must be used. The same type of behavior occurs when used with a pathname containing the slash (/) character. In order for the slash portion of the path to be matched, it must be explicitly included as part of the pattern. That is, * does not match fgc/myfile, however, */* does.

The OR (|) symbol in combination with parentheses is used within a pattern to select a match based on more than one pattern.

The parentheses are preceded by another metacharacter which indicates the type of match to be performed. When combined with the question mark, as in

```
for?(k|t|ce|mation)
```

the match domain includes fork, fort, force, and formation explicitly, plus *for* and any other four-character string beginning with for,[5] implicitly.

When combined with the at sign (@), the match must be **exact** on one of the specified patterns. The pattern

```
for@(k|t|ce|mation)
```

matches only fork, fort, force, and formation. The pattern

```
@(chicago|new york|san francisco|pittsburgh)
```

effectively defines an enumerated type, matching only chicago, new york, san francisco, or pittsburgh.

When combined with an asterisk (*), the match is for zero or more of the specified patterns in any order or combination. The pattern

```
for*(k|t|ce|mation)
```

matches for, fork, fort, force, formation, forkt, fortk, forcet, formationktce; all possible combinations of *for* and the endings *k, t, ce,* and *mation.* An interesting use is the pattern

```
*([0-9])
```

which matches a null string or any unsigned integer: 0, 234, 23938239861234685455, for example.

Finally, the exclamation (!) may be used to indicate that the match is for anything but the specified patterns. The pattern

```
!(*.bak)
```

matches any string that does not end in .bak. The pattern

```
master!(.bak|.tmp|._*)
```

matches any string beginning with master but not ending in .bak, .tmp. or an underscore followed any or no characters.

Table 13.1 summarizes the use of metacharacters.

13.3.1 Tilde substitution

The tilde character (~), strictly speaking, is not part of the metacharacters. However, it is used as a shorthand method, when specifying file names, for denoting the high-level qualification of a user's home directory. Depending on how AIX is set up, the home directory of user fgc could be /u/fgc, /usr/fgc, or /home/fgc. The command

---

[5]In contrast with its standalone use, in this case the question mark matches the null string.

TABLE 13.1 Metacharacter Patterns

Metacharacter pattern	Pattern matched	Null string matched ?
?	Any one character	No
[char1char2...charN]	Any one character from the list	No
[!char1char2...charN]	Any one character outside of the list	No
[char1-charN]	Any one character from char1 to charN inclusive	No
[!char1-charN]	Any one character other than from char1 to charN inclusive	No
*	Any character or group of characters	Yes
?(pattern1|pattern2...|patternN)	Zero or one of the specified patterns	Yes
@(pattern1|pattern2...|patternN)	Exactly one of the specified patterns	No
*(pattern1|pattern2...|patternN)	Zero, one, or more of the specified patterns in any combination	Yes
+(pattern1|pattern2...|patternN)	One or more of the specified patterns in any combination	No
!(pattern1|pattern2...|patternN)	Any pattern except for those specified	No

```
cd ~fgc
```

changes the current directory to user fgc's home directory, regardless of how the high-level qualification is actually set up. The command

```
cd ~/bin
```

changes the current directory to the bin subdirectory of user fgc's home directory. Assuming the high-level qualification is /u, the current directory is now

```
/u/fgc/bin.
```

This works because of the special action the shell takes when it encounters an unquoted tilde. When this occurs, the shell scans the first word it finds, up to a slash (/), to see if it matches a user name in the /etc/passwd file. If it does, the tilde character is replaced by the name of the user's login directory. If it does not, the shell does not perform any replacement.

However, if the unquoted tilde is the only character in the word, the tilde is replaced by the value of the $HOME variable (see Sec. 13.4.2). If the tilde is suffixed with a plus sign (~+), these characters are replaced by the value of the $PWD environment variable. If the tilde is suffixed with a minus sign (+−), the characters are replaced by the value of the $OLDPWD environment variable.

13.4 Variables

A great deal of the flexibility of the Korn shell comes from its ability to create, store, and operate upon variables. Variables may be local to a particular instance of a shell or global to a shell and its child processes. Variables may be passed between shell scripts, used as operands of commands, or defined to control processing options.

Declaring and assigning variables is most often done at the time they are needed. This is primarily to reduce the overhead in maintaining variable values. Variable assignment at the command prompt is performed by specifying the name of the variable, an equal sign, and the variable value. No spaces are used between the operands. If the variable value contains spaces, quotes must be used to contain the information. The statement

```
user=fgc
```

assigns the value fgc to the variable user. References to the value of variables is done subsequently by prefixing the variable name with a dollar sign ($), as seen in this example

```
$ print $user

cpla:$ user=fgc
$ print $user
fgc
$ print user
user
$
```

Note the error in the last command. The variable *user* is not used. Since *user,* and not *$user,* is the operand, the print command simply printed its literal value.

Variables may be concatenated. Observe how this works in the following example:

```
$ userdir=/fgc
$ maindir=/home
$ print $maindir$userdir
/home/fgc
$ print $maindir $userdir
/home /fgc
$
```

When the variables *$maindir* and *$userdir* are placed directly next to each other, the output form is concatentated with no intervening space. When the variable definitions are separated, so, too, is the output.

By default all variables are considered string variables. To define an integer variable, the variable definition statement must be prefixed with the integer **keyword**

```
integer count=0
```

Constants are defined with the typeset -r statement

```
typeset -r user=fgc
```

which defines the user variable with the value of fgc; this value could not be changed by subsequent assignment statements.

One-dimensional array variables may be defined but are difficult to use and are generally avoided. A variable may not be explicitly declared as an array; it is created the first time a value is assigned to it. Furthermore, the size of an array may not be explicitly defined. Every array holds up to 1024 values, the first cell being number zero. As with all variables, by default, all array variables are considered string arrays unless explicitly defined otherwise. This definition can be done only by first declaring a variable as an integer (or constant) and then using the variable as an array.

Setting the values for array slots is performed in a manner similar to most programming languages: alphabet[0]=a, alphabet[1]=b, alphabet[2]=c and so forth. Referencing the array is a different matter. Curly brackets ({}) are required when using an array index; note the difference when the curly brackets are not used

```
$ print ${alphabet[25]}
z
$ print $alphabet[25]
alphabet[25]
$
```

13.4.1 System variables

The Korn shell predefines several variables used to define and determine the user's operating environment. Table 13.2 lists all of the predefined variables. The user may display the current environment variables and their value by using the set command.

13.4.1.1 path—variable. The PATH variable defines for the shell the search path to be used when the shell is trying to locate a command. The format of the path variable is

```
path:2ndpath:3rdpath:Npath
```

where path is either the name of a directory or a period (.) which denotes the current directory.

Since the PATH variable is like all other environment variables, it may be concatenated with other variables or constants to reassign its value. This feature is often used to add directories to the search path

```
PATH=$PATH:/newdirectory
```

which assigns the current value of PATH plus the constant :/newdirectory,[6] thus resetting its value.

---

[6]The colon (:) is necessary as the delimiter character.

TABLE 13.2   Korn Shell Predefined Environment Variables

Variable	Meaning	Automatically set (Yes, No, Defaults)
CDPATH	Indicates the search path for the `cd` command.	N
COLUMNS	Defines the width of the terminal for shell edit mode commands.	N
EDITOR	Defines the command line editor to be used.	N
ENV	When this parameter is set, parameter substitution is performed on the value to generate the path name of the script which executes when the shell is invoked.	N
ERRNO	Contains the value set by the most recently failed subroutine.	Y
FCEDIT	Specifies the default editor name for the `fc` command.	N
FPATH	Defines the function search path; this path is searched when a function with the `-u` flag is referenced.	N
HISTFILE	Defines the name of the file to be used for storing the shell command history.	N
HISTSIZE	Defines the number of shell commands to be retained in the shell history file; the default is 128.	N
HOME	Contains the name of the user's home directory; initialized during login processing.	Y
IFS	Specifies the field separators (normally, space, tab and new-line) used to separate command words that result from command or parameter substitution.	D
LANG	Provides a default value for all of the LC_* variables.	Y
LC_ALL	Overrides the value of the LANG and LC_* variables.	N
LC_COLLATE	Contains the name of the collating sequence table.	N
LC_CTYPE	Defines the character classification, case conversion, and other character attributes.	N
LC_MESSAGES	Defines the language in which messages should be displayed.	N
LINENO	Contains the line number of the current line within the currently executing script or function.	Y
LINES	Determines the column length used by list printing commands.	N
MAIL	Specifies the path name used by the mail system to detect the arrival of new mail.	N
MAILCHECK	Defines the interval, in seconds, the shell uses for checking for new mail messages; the default value is 600 s.	D
OLDPWD	Contains the name of the previous working directory.	Y
OPTARG	Specifies the value of the last option argument processed by the `getopts` command.	Y
OPTIND	Specifies the inde of the last option argument processed by the `getopts` command.	Y

TABLE 13.2   Korn Shell Predefined Environment Variables *(Continued)*

Variable	Meaning	Automatically set (Yes, No, Defaults)
PATH	Defines the search path used by the shell for finding commands.	D
PID	Displays the current process number.	Y
PPID	Identifies the process number of the parent of the shell.	Y
PS1	Defines the string to be used as the primary system prompt; the default value is a dollar sign ($).	D
PS2	Specifies the value of the secondary prompt string; the default is a greater than sign (>).	D
PS3	Specifies the value of the selection prompt string used within a select loop; the default is #?.	D
PS4	Defines the symbol(s) used to prefix the lines of an execution trace; the default is a plus sign (+).	D
PWD	Contains the value of the current working directory.	Y
RANDOM	Generates a random integer between 0 and 32767.	Y
REPLY	Set by the select and read statements when no arguments are supplied.	Y
SECONDS	Indicates the number of seconds since the shell was invoked.	Y
SHELL	Specifies the path name of the shell.	N
TMOUT	Defines the number of seconds an inactive shell waits before terminating itself. Actually, the shell waits another 60 s after the timeout period has expired. The default value of 0 indicates no time out.	D
VISUAL	Defines the command editor to be used by the shell; this value override the value of EDIT.	N

Common PATH variable errors include

Omitting the current directory

Omitting a needed directory

Concatenating the directories in the incorrect sequence

13.4.1.2 cdpath—variable.   The CDPATH variable sets the search path for the cd command. This allows the user to enter a relative path name that is not in the current path. Consider a CDPATH variable with the value

```
.:/u/fgc/bin:/usr
```

If the user enters the command

```
cd myapp
```

the shell searches the current directory (.), /u/fgc/bin, and finally, /usr, for the myapp subdirectory.

13.4.1.3 `ps1`—variable.   Users may change their command prompt by reset-ting the value of the PS1 variable. The default command prompt is a dollar sign ($) which is not very informative. To provide users with a better sense of where they are, the value of another shell variable is often assigned to PS1. For instance, a common substitution is

```
PS1=$PWD>
```

which changes the command prompt to a display of the current directory fol-lowed by the greater than sign. Note the following example:

```
$ print $PWD
/u/fgc
$ PS1=$PWD>
/u/fgc>
```

Any valid environment variable and constant combination may be used to make the command prompt more useful. To expand the previous example, the following statement is used to make the command prompt display both the current process ID and current working directory:

```
/u/fgc> PS1=$PID $PWD>
102 /u/fgc>
```

13.4.1.4 `export`—Making variables available globally.   By default, all vari-ables are local to the shell in which they are created. To make a variable available to child processes (commands and shells), the `export` directive must be used. The syntax of this directive is

```
export variable[=value]
```

Note that a variable may be set to a value and made global at the same time. For example, the following statements:

```
PATH=$PATH:.
export PATH
```

are the same as

```
export PATH=$PATH:.
```

13.4.2   `.profile` file

To use the RS/6000 (and AIX), the user must sign on. When users successful-ly logs on, their default shell (as defined by the AIX system administrator) is started and system shell information is processed. Afterward, the shell is directed to the users' default or *home* directory as defined in the $HOME variable. When the Korn shell is used, it may find in the users' home directo-ry a hidden shell script, the .profile file, which is executed before the shell turns control over to the users.

```
PATH=/bin:/usr/bin:/etc:/usr/ucb:$HOME/bin:/usr/local/bin:.
export PATH
if [ -s "$MAIL" ]        # This is at Shell startup. In normal
then echo "$MAILMSG"     # operation, the Shell checks
fi                       # periodically.
```

Figure 13.1 The default Korn Shell profile.

The profile shell script contains commands that customize the AIX environment for the individual user; commands that make it simpler for the users to
perform the functions necessary to get their job done. Examples of commands
in a shell file include setting up the *search path* (via the PATH environment
variable) for finding commands, checking to see if any electronic mail has
arrived, and customizing the shell prompt to make it more meaningful.

Figure 13.1 shows the default profile for a Korn shell user. The first line of the
profile defines the directory search sequence for programs and commands by setting the PATH environment variable to the appropriate search sequence. The second line uses the PATH shell variable in a *shell directive*. Shell directives are commands to the shell itself, not AIX, to perform a particular operation. The export
directive used in line 2 tells the Korn shell to make the variable PATH available
to all running programs. The last three lines check for mail; if there is mail for the
user, the predefined shell variable $MAILMSG is displayed on the user's termi-
nal. At this point, the shell prompt is displayed and control is passed to the user.

The .profile file may be customized to perform any type of processing for
the user. A common addition is to change the default command prompt, as
discussed in Sec. 13.4.1.3.

13.4.3 The $env file

The environment file, if used, is a companion to the .profile file. Typically, the
environment file is used to define aliases and functions (see Sec. 13.5) local to
the user. The environment file can be used only if the $ENV environment
variable is set in the .profile file to contain the name of the environment file.
Most often the environment file is named .environ or .kshrc.

13.4.4 Command substitution

Command substitution is similar to variable substitution except that instead
of returning the contents of a variable, the result of a command is returned.

The preferred syntax[7] encloses the commands whose results are to be
returned within parentheses, with a leading dollar sign, i.e., $(*command*) as
in the following example:

```
$ print $(date)
Sun Sep 11 13:30:54 CDT 1994
```

---

[7]The older form used by the Bourne shell which involved enclosing the command within grave
accents (backward quotes) is also supported.

13.5 Aliases

The Korn shell allows the user to rename and join commands via the `alias` facility. Aliases are defined with the `alias` command. The following command defines the command `showfiles` as an alias for `ls`:

```
alias showfiles=ls
```

Commands may be joined together by enclosing them within parentheses. For example, the following defines a new sorted `who` command:

```
alias swho="who | sort"
```

Aliases may be used as if they were regular commands; alias interpretation is recursive. That is, an alias may make reference to another alias.

The constituent parts of an `alias` command may be displayed using the alias as the operand

```
$ alias swho
swho="who | sort"
$
```

If no operand is given, a display of all current aliases is displayed.

Alias may be exported to child processes by defining them with the -x flag

```
alias -x swho="who | sort"
```

Another flag of `alias`, -t the track flag , may be used to enhance the performance of commands and aliases. When the -t flag is used, the shell stores the full directory path of each command. This circumvents the need for the shell to look through the search path each time the command is used. To use this for an individual command, the syntax is

```
alias -t command
```

For example

```
alias -t who
```

creates the alias

```
alias who=/bin/who
```

This option may be turned on for all commands with the

```
set -o trackall
```

directive.

Finally, an alias may be removed with the `unalias` command. An example is the statement

```
unalias swho
```

which removes the swho alias from the shell's list of known aliases.

13.6   Positional Parameters

Positional parameters are used to pass command line arguments to functions or commands within a shell script. Consider a command line

```
doit -al
```

entered to start the doit shell script with the parameter -al. In this example, -al is the first (and only) positional parameter. In the command doit -a -l, the -a is the first positional parameter and -l is the second.

Access to positional parameters and information about them in a shell script is accessed through the positional parameters

$0	Contains the name of the command
$1 through $9	Contain the values of the first nine arguments on the command line
$*	Is a space-separated array of all of the arguments
$#	Is the number of arguments on the command line
$$	Is the process id of the command
$?	Is the exit status of the previous command

The exit status is normally zero if the preceding command terminated successfully. Nonzero values generally indicate some type of error.

13.7   Functions

Shell functions provide a mechanism for more complex aliasing and for creating macros. The function keyword is used to define shell functions. These functions are read and stored in the environment space of the shell. From the user's perspective, functions are executed in the same manner as commands. Unlike commands, functions execute in the same process as their caller; this means they share files and variables with the caller, use the same working directory, and are subject to the same traps. Traps which are not caught or ignored by the function cause the function to terminate; this allows the caller to handle the trap.

Functions may be defined on the fly, in the .profile file, or in the $ENV file. The following dialog demonstrates a simple function using positional parameters:

```
$ function chpermission
> {
>    cd $1
>    chmod $2 *
>    cd $OLDPWD
>    return
> }
$
```

This function changes to the directory indicated by parameter 1, changes the permission bits to the number given as parameter 2, changes the working directory back to the original directory, and then exits.

13.8   Constructing Shell Scripts

The Korn shell contains several very powerful, high-level language constructs which may be used to create complex algorithms. Although it is beyond the scope of this book to teach Korn shell programming, an introduction to the basic concepts is in order.

Almost all Korn shell scripts start with the line

```
#!/bin/ksh
```

in order to guarantee that the shell executes under the control of a Korn shell regardless of what the current shell is.

13.8.1   Testing conditions

In the Korn shell, the preferred syntax for conditional testing is

```
[[{expression}]]
```

where *expression* denotes a valid combination of operators, variables, and literal values. Note in the following comparisons that the brackets are separated on both sides by a blank space. This is *very* important. Failing to code the comparison in this way leads to erroneous interpretation of the statement by the shell.

13.8.1.1   Integer comparisons.   Comparison of integer values is performed with the following operators:

-eq	The values are equal.
-ne	The values are not equal.
-gt	The first value is greater than the second.
-ge	The first value is greater than or equal to the second.
-lt	The first value is less than the second.
-le	The first value is less than or equal to the second.

For example, the statement

```
[$1 -eq $2]
```

tests to see if the positional variable $1 is equal to the positional variable $2. If they are not, the $? positional variable contains a nonzero value.

13.8.1.2   String comparisons.   Comparison of string values is performed with a different set of operators

=	The strings on both sides are equal.
! =	The two strings do not match.
<	The two strings are in ASCII order (lower string first).
>	The two strings are not in ASCII order.

Individual strings may be tested with two operators

-z	The string is zero length.
-n	The string is not zero length.

The statement,

```
[[$1 = $2]]
```

returns a nonzero value in $? if the values of $1 and $2 are not equal.

13.8.1.3 File comparisons. Several operators are used to determine information about files and their status:

-r	The read permission is set.
-w	The write permission is set.
-x	The execute permission is set.
-u	The setuid bit is set.
-g	The setgid bit is set.
-k	The sticky bit is set.
-f	The entry is a file.
-d	The entry is a directory.
-b	The entry is a block special file.
-c	The entry is a character special file.
-p	The entry is a pipe.
-t	The entry is a terminal.
-s	The size of the entry is greater than 0 bytes.
-ef	The two files are links.
-ot	The entry is older than.
-nt	The entry is newer than.
-O	The entry is owned by the user running the process.
-G	The entry is owned by the group running the process.
-L	The entry is a symbolic link.
-S	The entry is a socket.

The statement

```
[[-f $filename]]
```

returns a nonzero value in $? if the name of entry in the filename variable is not a file. Most likely, the comparison

```
[[-z $filename]]
```

is used beforehand to test and make sure a filename is supplied.

13.8.1.4 Compound test operators. Individual tests may be joined together into more complex tests with the compound test operators. Three compound test operators are used

!	Not
&&	Logical AND
| |	Logical OR

For example, the following command tests if the filename variable has a value and if it names a file:

```
[[! -z $filename && -f $filename]]
```

If both conditions are not true, the entire statement is not true.

Precedence of operations works from the left to the right; there is no way to hierarchically group conditional testing otherwise.

13.8.2 Conditional execution

Six different logic constructs are available in the Korn shell.

13.8.2.1 if—Statements.   if statements are used in much the same manner as they are in most other programming languages. The syntax of the statement follows the form

```
if [[ condition ]]
then
     do something
fi
```

for simple conditional checks, and

```
if [[ condition ]]
then
     do something
elsif [[another_condition]]
then
     do something else
else
     do some default thing
fi
```

for more complex situations. In this construction, the elsif / then construct may be repeated as often as logically necessary.

Taking a prior example and making it an if statement leads to the following code segment:

```
if [[ -z $filename ]]
     then print Invalid file name entered
elsif [[ -f $filename ]]
     then print $filename is a file
else
     print $filename is not a file
fi
```

13.8.2.2 `case`—Statements.   `case` statements are used for branching based on a single variable. The syntax of case statement is best demonstrated by example

```
case $count in
[0-9])    print "Count is a numeral"
          ;;
[a-z])    print "Count is a lower-case letter"
          ;;
[A-Z])    print "Count is an upper-case letter"
          ;;
*)        print "Count is a special character or null"
          ;;
esac
```

Each case of the variable is listed along with the action or actions to be taken in the particular case. The default action is indicated by the catchall case *).

13.8.2.3 `while` and `until`—Statements.   Both `while` and `until` statements are used for executing loops. Both commands follow the same basic syntax

```
while [ condition ]
      do
              commands
      done
```
and
```
until [ condition ]
      do
              commands
      done
```

`While` is often used to control the reading of an input file. When reading from an input file, the syntax is

```
while read variables
    do
            commands
    done < filename
```

If only one variable is used in the `while read`, it contains the entire input line read. If multiple variables are used, each variable is filled by parsing the input line for the space and tab key and using those as the field separator characters. Frequently, an extraneous variable is defined to catch any over-flow or unexpected input from the command line; failure to account for all input data from the line causes the `while` loop to abort. The user may often see code like the following

```
while read var1 var2 var3 junk
    do
            command1
            command2
            command3
    done < filename
```

13.8.2.4 `for`—Statements.   The `for` statement is used to process items in a list. Each item in the list is set equal to the controlling variable and then processed against the commands between the do and done statements of the for command. The list of items may be generated in several ways; some of the most common are

Manually   For item in item1 item2 item3

Filename generation   For file in *

Positional parameters   For var in $*

The syntax of the command is

```
for variable in {list of items}
do
      commands
done
```

The following example changes the permissions of each file in a directory:

```
for file in *
do
      chmod 644 $file
done
```

13.8.2.5 select—**Statements.**   The select statement generates a numbered pick list based on the list of items. The user selects the number corresponding to the item and the select sets a variable to the item and performs the commands between the do and done statements, much like the for command. And, as with the for statement, the list of items may be generated in several ways; the most common being

Manually   Select item in item1 item2 item3

Filename generation   Select file in *

Positional parameters   Select var in $*

The syntax of the command is

```
for variable in { list of items}
do
      commands
done
```

The following example allows the user to change the permissions on a particular file. The user is presented with a numbered list of files from which to choose

```
PS3="Please choose a file :"
select file in *
do
      chmod 644 $file
done
```

After entering the appropriate number, the select statement would set the $file variable to the correct file name and run the command(s) between the do and done statements. Note that the environment variable PS3 was set before entering the loop. This was done to make the prompt more userfriendly than the system default.

## Chapter 14

Miscellaneous Commands

This chapter deals with several commands which do not fall conveniently into the discussions in other chapters. As such, it is a bit of a hodgepodge of information.

14.1 Terminal Commands

The commands in this section are all related to terminal functions in one way or another. They are not hardware commands per se, but more focused on user functionality.

14.1.1 script—Log a terminal session

The script command is used to record a log of all of the activity in a terminal session. The syntax of the command is

```
script [-a] [filename]
```

If an explicit filename is not used, the script command creates the log file in a file named typescript in the user's home directory. The -a flag may be used to append the new log information to an existing log file.

14.1.2 capture—Dump a terminal screen to a file

The capture command is used to dump the contents of a display terminal to a file. The syntax of the command is

```
capture [-a] [filename]
```

The screen is printed to the file specified by the filename parameter or the screen.out file (in the user's home directory) if no file is explicitly named.

The capture command creates a shell which emulates a VT100 type terminal through which it maintains a record of everything displayed on the screen. Ctrl-P is the default key sequence for a screen dump. This may be changed by setting the SCREENDUMP environment variable to another octal value before invoking the capture command. For instance, setting SCREENDUMP to 36 changes the screen dump key sequence to Ctrl-M. The capture shell is terminated by pressing the Ctrl-D sequence.

The only flag of the capture command is the -a flag which is used to indicate that the screen printouts should be appended to the specified file. Otherwise, each new capture session overwrites the existing file.

14.1.3   clear—Clear the screen

The clear command clears the terminal screen. It takes no other operands.

14.1.4   bell—Ring the terminal alarm

The bell command rings the terminal alarm, if it is so equipped. The command takes no other operands or flags.

14.1.5   lock—Reserve a terminal

The lock command is used to lock a terminal for a specific period of time. When the command is invoked, the user is prompted for a password. The terminal remains in an unusable state until one of the following three actions takes place:

The user enters the password again

The timeout interval expires

The command is killed by a user with appropriate permission

The default timeout value is 15 min, but this may be changed by specifying an explicit number of minutes during command invocation. For example

```
lock -45
```

sets a timeout value of 45 min.

14.1.6   logname—Display the login name

The logname command displays the login name of the current process. The command takes no optional flags or operands.

14.1.7   mesg—Enable or disable messages

The mesg command is used to control whether other users may send messages with either the write or talk commands. When used with no arguments, the mesg command displays the current value of the message-permission setting.

Entering the command

```
mesg n
```

prohibits other users from sending messages. This command is often added to a user's shell startup script as messages are enabled by default.
Entering the command

```
mesg y
```

explicitly enables (or reenables) the sending of messages.

14.2 Informational Commands

Several commands are provided which allow the user to explore information on and about the machine and AIX operating environment.

14.2.1 whatis—Find a command and its usage

The whatis command is used to display a brief, one-line description of what a command does. The syntax of the command is

```
whatis commandname
```

The whatis command database must be created by the system administrator with the catman -w command before the whatis command will work.

14.2.2 catman—Create the man pages

The catman command creates the information databases for both the man and whatis commands. When used with no operands, the command creates both databases. When the -n flag is used, only the man command database is created. Alternatively, when the -w flag is used, only the whatis database is created.

14.2.3 man—Display information about commands

The man command is used to display on-line documentation about AIX commands. When used with a specific command, man displays detailed information about it; this information includes command syntax, flags, operands, a description of the operation, and the files used.

Before this command may be used, the system administrator must have created the man pages database, as discussed in Sec. 14.2.2.

14.2.4 apropos—Locate a command by keyword

The apropos command displays information about commands based on the keyword(s) entered. The apropos command displays every man page entry related to the specified keywords; it considers each word separately. It does not perform any type of boolean searching when more than one word is entered.

14.2.5 `info`—Run the InfoExplorer program

The `info` command is used to invoke the InfoExplorer hypertext documentation system. If no operands are used with the command, the InfoExplorer program starts by displaying the navigation window and the "Welcome to InfoExplorer" article.

The flag, `-s`, is used to start InfoExplorer with a specific search string. If more than one word is entered, the string must be enclosed within quotes.

More information about this command can be displayed by using the `info` command.

Basic Problem-Solving Tools

The most important tool for problem diagnosis on AIX is the error report (errpt) command. This command formats all of the hardware and system software errors which have been logged and prints them in a human-readable format.

When errors are detected in the system, the information is sent to a system routine which writes it to the /dev/error file. The file adds a time stamp to the collected data. The errdemon process, in turn, constantly checks the /dev/error file for new entries. When a new data matches an item in the *Error Record Template Repository* the daemon collects additional information from other system components.

Normally, the errdemon is started automatically at system startup. If this has not occurred, or if the daemon has been terminated with the errstop command, it may be restarted by a user with root authority by issuing the command

```
/usr/lib/errdemon
```

The errpt command is used to generate the actual error reports. The various fields in the reports are discussed in Table A.1. Several flags are available, but some are more common than others. The command

```
errpt -a
```

generates a detailed error report, whereas

```
errpt
```

with no flags, generates a summary report: one line of information for each error.

The -s *time* flag is used to generate a report of all records logged since the given time. The format of the time parameter is *mmddhhmmyyI* (month, day, hour, minute, year). Therefore, to produce a detailed report of all records logged since November 6, 1994 at 5:00 PM, the command is

TABLE A.1 Error Report Fields

Error field	Meaning or use
ERROR LABEL	The defined name of the event
ERROR ID	The numerical identifier of the event
Date/Time	The date and time of occurrence
Sequence Number	The unique error event number
Machine ID	The identification number of the system unit
Node ID	The network name of the system
Error Class	The general type of error; these include
	H Hardware
	S Software
	O Informational messages
Error Type	The severity of the error; these can be
	PEND Loss of availability is imminent
	PERF Performance has degraded below acceptable levels
	PERM A condition which could not be recovered from
	TEMP A condition which was recovered from
	UNKN The severity of the error cannot be determined
Resource Name	The name of the failing resource
Resource Class	The general class of the failing resource (for example, TAPE)
Resource Type	The type of the failing resource (for example, a device type of 5M)
Location Code	The path to the device (drawer, slot, connector, and port)
VPD	Vital product data; this information varies widely
Error Description	A summary of the error
Probable Cause	A list of some possible error causes
User Causes	A list of possible user errors
Recommended Actions	A description of actions for correcting a user-caused error
Install Causes	A list of possible reasons due to incorrect installation or configuration
Failure Causes	A list of possible hardware or software defect
Detailed Data	Unique failure data, such as device sense data; this information varies widely

```
errpt -a -s 1106170094
```

Similarly, the -e flag is used to report on all records written before the spefied date.

The errclear command is used to clear out the error log file after
appropriate reports have been generated. The command

```
errclear 0
```

removes all entries from the files. The optional flag, -d, is used to define
particular type of records to remove. The flag -d H removes hardware e
records, -d S removes software records, and -d O removes informati
records.

A special command, `diagela`, is provided by AIX which allows for the automatic analysis of hardware errors. The root user enables this facility by issuing the command

```
/etc/lpp/diagnostics/bin/diagela ENABLE
```

Once started, the `diagela` command invokes other diagnostic applications to analyze the error logs of problem devices. When a problem is detected, a message is sent to the system console and to all members of the system group.

The automatic analysis feature can be terminated by issuing the `diagela` command with an operand of `DISABLE`.

The trace facility, which is separate from error logging, may be used to isolate system problems. The trace facility captures the flow of system events in time sequence and in the context of other system events.

Typically, the trace facility is used in background mode. That is, the trace is started, the user executes the commands to be traced, and the trace is then stopped. For example, to trace the events in the `ls -al` command, the following sequence of commands would be used.

```
trace -a
ls -al
trcstop
```

The trace report is generated with the `trcrpt` command. Typically, the output of the command is redirected to a file; otherwise, the output of the report is displayed on the user's terminal. For example, to see the report generated by the preceding sequence of commands, the user issues the

```
trcrpt >/tmp/l_trace_report
```

command.

The `-s`*time* flag is used to define the time at which reporting should begin. The `-e`*time* flag is used to stop the reporting at a specific time. The format of the time parameter in both cases is *mmddhhmmssyyI* (month, day, hour, minute, second, year).

In addition the `-o` flag may be used with several arguments which change the content or look of the generated report. These arguments include

`2line`	*On* uses two lines per event; the default is *off*.
`exec`	*On* displays the full path names of all execs; the default is *off*.
`hist`	*On* logs the number of instances each trace event type is encountered; may not be used with any other argument; the default value is *off*.
`ids`	*On* displays the trace event type in the first column of the report; the default is *off*.
`pagesize`	Sets the number of lines per page; no page breaks are performed when set to zero; the maximum is 500.
`pid`	*On* displays the process ids; the default is *off*.
`svc`	*Displays the value of the system call; the default is* off.
`timestamp`	Controls the timestamp associated with the events; valid values include
	0 Elapsed time (default).

1	Short elapsed time.
2	Microseconds.
3	No timestamp.

Therefore, to include both process ids and full path names, the previously used command is modified

```
trcrpt -0 exec=yes,pid=yes >/tmp/ls/_trace_report
```

Further information on both error reporting and trace reporting may be found in the *AIX Problem Solving Guide and Reference* (IBM Corporation, 1993).

Error Log Identifiers

The following identifiers are used in the error reporting program to identify types of errors. This listing provides the error identifier and an explanation of what the error signifies.

Error identifier	Meaning
ATE ERR1	No pacing character was received by ATE.
ATE ERR10	A sector could not be verified by ATE.
ATE ERR2	Excessive transmission errors have occurred.
ATE ERR3	No acknowledgment from the receiver has been sent to ATE.
ATE ERR4	The receiving site is not ready for transmission from ATE.
ATE ERR5	The sending site has stopped sending to ATE.
ATE ERR6	No carrier signal has been detected by ATE.
ATE ERR7	A checksum error has detected by ATE.
ATE ERR8	A sector has been received twice by ATE.
ATE ERR9	An incorrect sector has been received by ATE.
BADISK ERR1	A soft read error has been detected on a bus-attached disk.
BADISK ERR2	A hard read error has been detected on a bus-attached disk.
BADISK ERR3	A soft equipment check has been detected on a bus-attached disk.
BADISK ERR4	A hard equipment check has been detected on a bus-attached disk.
BADISK ERR5	An attachment error has occurred on a bus-attached disk.
BADISK ERR6	A seek error has occurred on a bus-attached disk.
C327 INTR	The 3270 Connection Adapter has detected an error; the control unit is not responding.
C327 START	The 3270 Connection Adapter could not start a session with the host.
CAT ERR1	The System/370 Parallel Adapter licensed internal code has stopped.

Error identifier	Meaning
CAT ERR2	The System/370 Parallel Adapter licensed internal code could not be downloaded.
CAT ERR3	The System/370 Parallel Adapter could not acquire enough buffer space to receive data.
CAT ERR4	The System/370 Parallel Adapter could not lock its internal data structures in real storage.
CAT ERR5	The System/370 Parallel Adapter could not set the adapter's parameters or download a control-unit table.
CAT ERR6	The System/370 Parallel Adapter cannot be configured.
CAT ERR7	The System/370 Parallel Adapter cannot access required memory.
CAT ERR8	The System/370 Parallel Adapter has detected an unrecoverable I/O error.
CD-ROM ERR1	Probably a defective CD; error recovery has failed after several retries.
CD-ROM ERR2	A failure occurred, but recovery was successful after several tries.
CD-ROM ERR3	Probably a defective CD drive; error recovery has failed after several retries.
CD-ROM ERR4	A CD drive error occurred, but recovery was successful after several tries.
CD-ROM ERR5	A command to the CD drive timed out.
CD-ROM ERR6	A command to the CD drive timed out but eventually succeeded after several tries.
CD-ROM ERR7	A failure occurred which was corrected by the CD-ROM drive.
CD-ROM ERR8	An undefined CD-ROM error occurred.
CHECKSTOP	A checkstop has occurred and been logged.
CMDLVM	The logical volume manager has detected a disk operation error
COM CFG ADPT	During configuration, the TTY to be configured was found to be configured already.
COM CFG BUSI	During configuration, a bad bus ID was detected by the TTY driver.
COM CFG BUSID	During configuration, an out-of-range bus ID was detected by the TTY driver.
COM CFG BUST	During configuration, a bad bus type was detected by the TTY driver.
COM CFG DEVA	During configuration, a call to the configuration manager to add a device by the TTY driver failed.
COM CFG DEVD	During configuration, a call to the configuration manager to delete a device by the TTY driver failed.
COM CFG DMA	During configuration, a DMA conflict was detected by the TTY driver.
COM CFG IFLG	During configuration, a bad interrupt flag was detected by the TTY driver.
COM CFG ILVL	During configuration, a bad interrupt level was detected by the TTY driver.
COM CFG INTR	During configuration, a bad interrupt priority was detected by the TTY driver.
COM CFG MNR	During configuration, a bad minor device number was detected by the TTY driver.

Error identifier	Meaning
COM CFG NADP	During configuration, a previously available adapter could not be found by the TTY driver.
COM CFG PIN	During configuration, an attempt to lock storage by the TTY driver failed.
COM CFG PORT	During configuration, the port to be configured was found by the TTY driver to be configured already.
COM CFG RESID	During configuration, the TTY driver detected a bad resource id.
COM CFG SLIH	During configuration, an initialization call to the second level interrupt handler (SLIH) by the TTY driver failed.
COM CFG UIO	During configuration, the TTY driver detected an incorrect I/O request.
COM CFG UNK	During configuration, the TTY driver could not determine the type of an adapter.
COM CFG UNPIN	During configuration, a call to release storage by the TTY driver failed.
COM MEM SLIH	An attempt to lock storage for the SLIH failed.
COM PERM PIO	An input or output exception has been detected by a TTY driver.
COM PERM SLIH	A permanent I/O error has been detected by the TTY driver.
COM PIN SLIH	The memory for the SLIH cannot be locked in storage.
COM TEMP PIO	A temporary I/O error has been detected by the TTY driver.
CONSOLE	An unexpected error occurred while addressing the system console.
CORE DUMP	A core dump was generated by either the system or a user program.
CORRECTED SCRUB	A physical memory error was corrected.
DCR IOCC	An I/O channel controller data storage interrupt occurred.
DISK ERR1	A media error has been detected by a SCSI driver.
DISK ERR2	A physical hardware error has been detected by a SCSI driver.
DISK ERR3	A SCSI adapter which previously had been detected can no longer be found.
DISK ERR4	A SCSI adapter detected and corrected an error.
DISK ERR5	An unknown error was detected by a SCSI adapter.
DISKETTE ERR1	A permanent diskette error has occurred.
DISKETTE ERR2	A diskette timeout has occurred.
DISKETTE ERR3	A diskette media error has occurred.
DISKETTE ERR4	An undetermined diskette error occurred.
DISKETTE ERR5	A temporary diskette I/O error occurred.
DISKETTE ERR6	A permanent diskette I/O error occurred.
DMA ERR	An undetermined direct memory access (DMA) error occurred.
DOUBLE PANIC	A second system panic occurred while the first panic was being processed.
DSI PROC	A processor data storage interrupt occurred.
DSI SCU	A storage control unit data storage interrupt occurred.
DSI SLA	A serial link adapter data storage interrupt occurred.
DUMP	The dump device could not be opened.
DUMP STATS	Status information on a system dump.
ENT ERR1	A permanent hardware error occurred on the Ethernet adapter.
ENT ERR2	A temporary hardware error occurred on the Ethernet adapter.

Error identifier	Meaning
ENT ERR3	A permanent firmware error occurred on the Ethernet adapter.
ENT ERR4	The configuration information for the Ethernet adapter is incorrect.
ENT ERR5	The Ethernet adapter has failed for lack of available storage.
ENT ERR6	The network failed.
EPOW RES	The *early power off warning* (EPOW) interrupt indicated that power had resumed.
EPOW SUS	The EPOW interrupt indicated that power was about to be lost.
ERRLOG OFF	Error logging was turned off.
ERRLOG ON	Error logging was turned on.
EU BAD ADPT	A bad adapter was detected by the Asynchronous expansion unit during configuration.
EU CFG BUSY	Configuration by the Asynchronous expansion unit failed because the device was already being used.
EU CFG GONE	Configuration by the Asynchronous expansion unit failed because the device was already unconfigured.
EU CFG HERE	Configuration by the Asynchronous expansion unit failed because the device was already configured.
EU CFG NADP	Configuration by the Asynchronous expansion unit failed because the adapter was not present.
EU CFG NPLN	Configuration by the Asynchronous expansion unit failed because the adapter could not be found.
EU DIAG ACC	The Asynchronous expansion unit driver tried to perform diagnostics while the device was in use.
EU DIAG MEM	The Asynchronous expansion unit driver could not allocate buffer space.
EXCHECK DMA	An external check occurred during a DMA.
EXCHECK SCRUB	An unrecoverable double-bit memory error occurred.
FDDI ADAP CHECK	An adapter check occurred on the FDDI interface.
FDDI BYPASS	The optical bypass switch is stuck. User intervention is not required.
FDDI DOWN	A fatal error has occurred on the FDDI device.
FDDI DWNLD	The microcode download to the FDDI device has failed.
FDDI LLC DISABLE	The logical link control (LLC- services) of the FDDI device have been disabled by a remote station.
FDDI LLC ENABLE	The LLC services for the FDDI device have been enabled remotely.
FDDI MC ERR	The FDDI device driver has detected a channel error.
FDDI PATH ERR	The FDDI adapter path test failed; recovery is attempted.
FDDI PIO	The FDDI adapter detected a physical I/O error; recovery is attempted.
FDDI PORT	A port on the FDDI device is stuck; user intervention is not required.
FDDI RCV	An FDDI packet reception error occurred; recovery is attempted.
FDDI RCVRY ENTER	The FDDI device driver has entered network recovery mode; the prior error explains the reason for entering network recovery mode.
FDDI RCVRY EXIT	The FDDI device driver successfully exited network recovery mode.
FDDI RCVRY TERM	The FDDI device driver could not recover from the prior error.

Error identifier	Meaning
FDDI RMV ADAP	The FDDI adapter received a disconnect command from a remote station.
FDDI SELF TEST	The FDDI adapter received a run self-test command from a remote station.
FDDI SELFT ERR	The FDDI self-tests have failed.
FDDI TRACE	The FDDI adapter has detected a timeout of the trace operation on the ring.
FDDI TX ERR	The FDDI adapter has detected a transmission error.
FDDI USYS	The FDDI adapter detected an unknown error.
FDDI XCARD	The self-tests of the extender adapter have failed.
FDDI NOMBUFFS	The FDDI device driver could not obtain additional buffers; the packet was discarded.
FLPT UNAVAIL	A floating-point unavailable interrupt occurred.
HFTERR	A software error occurred in the driver code for a high-function terminal.
IENT ERR1	A general error message indicating the Integrated Ethernet Adapter is failing.
IENT ERR2	The Integrated Ethernet Adapter could not be configured or customized; a resource is unavailable.
IENT ERR3	A channel error occurred for the Integrated Ethernet Adapter.
IENT ERR4	Return code 816 indicates a buffer shortage for the Integrated Ethernet Adapter.
IENT ERR4	Return code 683 indicates an invalid packet size was received.
IENT ERR4	Return code 1407 indicates that memory could not be freed.
IENT ERR4	Return code 162 indicates that memory could not be freed.
IENT ERR4	Return code 1829 indicates that a device command failed.
IENT ERR5	The Integrated Ethernet Adapter detected a transmission problem.
INTR ERR	An undetermined error occurred.
ISI PROC	An instruction storage interrupt occurred.
KERNEL PANIC	The kernel has become corrupted and cannot recover.
LION BOX DIED	Communication with the 64-port concentrator driver was lost.
LION BUFFERO	The hardware buffer in the 64-port concentrator was overrun.
LION CHUNKUMC	The number of characters transmitted does match the actual value in the buffer.
LION HRDWRE	The memory in the 64-port concentrator is not accessible.
LION MEM ADP	The 64-port concentrator cannot allocate any additional memory for the adap structure.
LION MEM LIST	The 64-port concentrator cannot allocate any additional memory for the ttyp_t list structure.
LION PIN ADAP	The 64-port concentrator cannot lock the storage for the adap structure.
LION UNKCHUNK	An unexpected error occurred in the 64-port concentrator.
LVM BBDIR90	The bad block relocation directory is over 90% full.
LVM BBDIRBAD	A bad block relocation attempt has failed; the bad block directory has been corrupted.
LVM BBDIRERR	An update operation to the bad block directory failed; no further bad block relocation will occur.
LVM BBDIRFUL	The bad block directory is full; no further bad block relocation will occur.

Error identifier	Meaning
LVM BBEPOOL	The bad block relocation pool has no free blocks left; no further bad block relocation will occur.
LVM BBFAIL	A bad block relocation failed for a reason other than a media error; no further bad block relocation will occur.
LVM BBRELMAX	An attempt at hardware relocation failed after the maximum number of software relocation attempts also failed; no further bad block relocation will occur.
LVM HWFAIL	A hardware relocation operation failed; no further bad block relocation will occur.
LVM HWREL	A hardware disk block relocation was successful after a software relocation failed.
LVM MISSPVADDED	A physical volume could not be found during varyon processing.
LVM MISSPVRET	A previously missing physical volume has become active.
LVM MWCWFAIL	A write operation to update the mirror write consistency cache failed.
LVM SA FRESHPP	A formerly stale mirror partition has been marked fresh.
LVM SA PVMISS	A physical volume was found to be missing during a consistency check of the volume status group area.
LVM SA QUORCLOSE	The quorum of a volume group has been lost; the volume group is closed.
LVM SA STALEPP	A copy of a mirrored partition has been marked stale.
LVM SA WRTERR	A write operation to update the volume group status area did not complete successfully.
LVM SWREL	A software disk block relocation was successful.
MACHINECHECK	A machine check has been logged.
MEM1	One of the memory cards in a pair is missing.
MEM2	Two or more SIMMs on a memory card have failed.
MEM3	One of the memory cards in a pair has failed.
MEMORY	An IPL ROS memory test failed during system configuration.
MISC ERR	The miscellaneous interrupt handler detected an I/O bus time-out or channel check.
MPQP ADPERR	The MPQP adapter is not functioning or is in an invalid state.
MPQP ASWCHK	A checksum error occurred on the MPQP adapter.
MPQP BFR	A buffer allocation failed for the MPQP adapter.
MPQP CTSDRP	*Clear to send* (CTS) dropped during a transmit.
MPQP CTSTO	CTS failed to come on during transmission.
MPQP DSRDRP	*Data set ready* (DSR) dropped while *data terminal ready* (DTR) was still on.
MPQP DSROFFTO	DSR was on before the call started.
MPQP DSRTO	DSR would not come on.
MPQP IPLTO	The initial program load of the MPQP adapter failed.
MPQP QUE	The MPQP device driver was unable to access a command or response queue.
MPQP RCVERR	The maximum number of receive errors has been reached.
MPQP RCVOVR	The receive queue was overrun.
MPQP X21CECLR	The network cleared a call due to an error.
MPQP X21CPS	An X.21 call progress signal was received.
MPQP X21DTCLR	An unexpected X.21 clear signal was received.
MPQP X21TO	A timeout occurred during X.21 transmission.
MPQP XFTO	A transmission did not complete.

Error identifier	Meaning
MPQP XMTUND	The driver or adapter is unable to provide communications fast enough to maintain protocol timing.
MSLA ADAPTER	An error occurred on the multisubchannel line access (MSLA) adapter.
MSLA CLOSE	An error occurred during MSLA close processing.
MSLA INTR	An error occurred during MSLA interrupt processing.
MSLA PROTOCOL	A handshaking error occurred during MSLA connection processing.
MSLA START	The MSLA connection could not be started.
MSLA WRITE	A write error occurred during MSLA processing.
NB1	NETBIOS cannot create any more program status blocks in the interrupt handler.
NB10	NETBIOS ran out of I/O buffers during an OPEN LINK STATION operation.
NB11	NETBIOS ran out of I/O buffers after the successful completion of an OPEN LINK STATION operation.
NB12	An OPEN LINK STATION IOCTL failed.
NB13	NETBIOS ran out of I/O buffers during a CONNECT LINK STATION operation.
NB14	An error occurred during a CONTACT IOCTL operation.
NB15	The maximum number of CONNECT LINK STATION retries has been reached.
NB16	A CONNECT LINK STATION operation failed.
NB17	A HALT LINK STATION IOCTL operation failed.
NB18	NETBIOS ran out of I/O buffers during an ENABLE SAP IOCTL operation.
NB19	An ENABLE SAP IOCTL operation failed.
NB2	NETBIOS has encountered an unknown router command.
NB20	A WRITE IOCTL operation failed.
NB21	An error was detected by Logical Link Control (LLC).
NB22	An unknown user-SAP correlator was received by the interrupt handler.
NB23	An unknown user-SAP correlator was received.
NB24	An invalid correlator was received from an OPEN SAP/LS (*Service Access Point / Local Service*) operation.
NB25	A NETBIOS call to devswadd failed.
NB26	A NETBIOS call to devswdel failed.
NB27	An *open* was still pending when NETBIOS was terminated.
NB28	Unknown NETBIOS configuration options were detected.
NB29	A NETBIOS call to allocate memory failed.
NB3	NETBIOS has exhausted the available input/output buffers.
NB30	A NETBIOS call to allocate fixed memory failed.
NB4	The DISABLE SAP command failed.
NB5	The Service Access Point (SAP) is already closed.
NB6	A NETBIOS buffer overflow has occurred.
NB7	NETBIOS has detected inactivity without proper termination.
NB8	A connection logged with a NB7 error has resumed.
NB9	An undefined NETBIOS result has been detected.
NLS BADMAP	The national language support map cannot interpret the received input.

Error identifier	Meaning
NLS MAP	The required national language support map cannot be found.
OPMSG	The errlogger command has been run.
PGSP KILL	A program has been abnormally terminated.
PPRINTER ERR1	An error has been logged by the printer device driver.
PROGRAM INT	A program interrupt occurred in kernel mode.
PSLA001	A hardware error was detected on the primary system/serial link adapter (PSLA).
PSLA002	A device driver or microcode error was detected on the PSLA.
PSLA003	A host link error occurred on the PSLA.
RCMERR	An unrecoverable error has been detected by the rendering context manager.
REBOOT ID	The system was shutdown by user request.
REPLACED FRU	A piece of hardware has been replaced.
RS 8 16 ARB	An invalid 8/16 port arbitration port register has been detected.
RS BAD INTER	An interrupt was received from an unknown port.
RS MEM EDGE	A call to allocate memory for a TTY edge structure failed.
RS MEM EDGEV	A call to allocate memory for a TTY edge vector failed.
RS MEM IOCC	A call to allocate memory for a TTY IOCC structure failed.
RS MEM PVT	A call to allocate memory for a TTY private structure failed.
RS PIN EDGE	A call to allocate fixed memory for a TTY edge structure failed.
RS PIN EDGEV	A call to allocate fixed memory for a TTY edge vector failed.
RS PIN IOCC	A call to allocate fixed memory for a TTY IOCC structure failed.
RS PROG IOCC	The IOCC (I/O Communications Controller) is not in a configured state.
RS PROG SLIH	The second level interrupt handler could not be found during configuration.
SCSI ERR1	A permanent hardware error on the SCSI adapter or system I/O bus has been detected.
SCSI ERR2	A nonrecoverable error occurred on the SCSI adapter or system I/O bus.
SCSI ERR3	A SCSI adapter microcode error was detected.
SCSI ERR4	An unknown and unrecoverable SCSI microcode error occurred.
SCSI ERR5	A permanent device driver logic error occurred.
SCSI ERR6	A nonrecoverable device driver logic error occurred.
SCSI ERR8	A nonrecoverable kernel service routine error has been detected.
SCSI ERR8	A permanent kernel service routine error has been detected.
SCSI ERR9	The capability level of the SCSI equipment is not equal; data loss is possible.
SDA ERR1	An unrecoverable adapter hardware error has occurred.
SDA ERR2	An unrecoverable adapter error has occurred.
SDA ERR3	An unrecoverable system-detected error has occurred.
SDA ERR4	A recoverable system-detected error has been detected.
SDC ERR1	A serial link between the controller and DASD failed.
SDC ERR2	An unrecoverable controller hardware error has occurred.
SDC ERR3	An unrecoverable controller error has occurred.
SDM ERR1	A microcode error has been detected.
SLA CRC ERR	The CRC checksum for a frame is not correct.
SLA DRIVER ERR	The optics card has detected a fault in the transmission driver.
SLA EXCEPT ERR	A physical I/O exception has occurred.

Error identifier	Meaning
SLA FRAME ERR	A response time out or send count was lost.
SLA PARITY ERR	A parity error in the TAG register or data buffer was detected.
SLA PROG ERR	A program check occurred.
SLA SIG ERR	A signal error longer than 1 s was detected.
SNA CLDF	An SNA process terminated unexpectedly.
SNA CSA1	The received XID is invalid.
SNA CSA2	The received XID has generated a protocol error.
SNA DDCF	A device configuration error occurred.
SNA IPCF	An IPC (interprocess communication) error occurred.
SNA OMDDF	The SNA device driver manager could not be opened.
SNA PRF	An error was detected in the SNA profile database.
SNA SECF	An error was detected in SNA security processing.
SNA SEMF	An error was detected in semaphore processing.
SNA SHMF	A problem was detected in a SNA shared segment.
SNA SRCF	A call to the system resource controller (SRC) failed.
SNA SRF	A SNA call module detected a system resource failure.
SRC	An abnormal condition has been detected and logged by the system resource controller (SRC).
SYS RESET	The reset button on the control panel was used to reboot the system.
SYSLOG	This error type is used to denote those messages which have been redirected from syslog to the error log
TAPE ERR1	An uncorrectable tape media error has occurred.
TAPE ERR2	A permanent hardware error has occurred on the indicated tape drive.
TAPE ERR3	A recoverable tape media or device error occurred and was corrected.
TAPE ERR4	An adapter error has been detected on the indicated tape drive.
TAPE ERR5	An unknown error occurred on the indicated tape drive.
TAPE ERR6	The indicated tape drive needs to be cleaned.
TMSCSI CMD ERR	An unrecoverable hardware error occurred on the indicated SCSI target device.
TMSCSI READ ERR	An unrecoverable hardware error occurred while reading from the indicated SCSI target device.
TMSCSI RECVRD ERR	A recoverable hardware error occurred on the indicated SCSI target device.
TSMCSI UNKN SFW ERR	A device driver has detected a software error related to the indicated SCSI target device.
TMSCSI UNRECVRD ERR	An unrecoverable error occurred while a command was being sent to the indicated SCSI target device.
TOK ADAP CHK	A token-ring adapter check has occurred.
TOK ADAP ERR	The function level of the token-ring adapter and the attached equipment do not correspond; data loss is possible.
TOK AUTO RMV	The adapter failed a self-test and has removed itself from the ring.
TOK BAD ASW	The token-ring adapter and microcode are incompatible.
TOK BEACON1	The adapter detected a beaconing condition on the ring during the insertion process.
TOK BEACON2	The ring was in a beaconing condition for longer than allowed.
TOK BEACON3	The ring was in a beaconing condition for less than 52 s and was recovered.

Error identifier	Meaning
TOK CONGEST	An adapter on the ring is experiencing excessive congestion.
TOK DOWNLOAD	The microcode downloaded to the token-ring adapter failed.
TOK DUP ADDR	The token-ring adapter detected another adapter on the ring with the same address.
TOK ERR10	The ring was in a beaconing condition but was recovered.
TOK ERR15	The token-ring device handler intercepted an unknown system error.
TOK ERR5	An unknown adapter hardware error occurred during the insertion process.
TOK ESERR	The ring error monitor has detected excessive soft errors on the ring.
TOK MC ERR	The token-ring device handler has detected a microchannel error.
TOK NOMBUFS	The token-ring device handler could not acquire a requested mbuf.
TOK PIO ERR	An input/output error has occurred on the indicated adapter.
TOK RCVRY ENTER	The token-ring device handler has entered network recovery mode.
TOK RCVRY EXIT	The token-ring device handler has exited network recovery mode successfully.
TOK RCVRY TERM	The token-ring device handler has terminated network recovery mode.
TOK RMV ADAP1	The token-ring adapter received a remove command during the insertion process.
TOK RMV ADAP2	The token-ring adapter received a remove adapter command and has left the LAN.
TOK TX ERR	The token-ring device handler has detected a transmission error.
TOK WIRE FAULT	A wire-fault condition has been detected on the ring.
TOK WRAP TST	The adapter detected a problem on its lobe during the insertion wrap-test.
TTY BADINPUT	An error occurred on the indicated TTY during an input operation.
TTY OVERRUN	The hardware buffer on the indicated TTY was overrun.
TTY PROG ERR	An addressing error occurred on the indicated TTY.
TTY TTYHOG	The indicated device is ignoring flow control.
TTYPARERR	Parity errors have occurred on the indicated TTY.
WHP0001	HCON could not allocate memory.
WHP0002	HCON encountered an Inter-Process Communication (IPC) receive error.
WHP0003	HCON encountered an IPC send error.
WHP0004	HCON could not create an IPC queue.
WHP0005	HCON encountered an IPC create queue error.
WHP0006	HCON could not retrieve IPC message queue statistics.
WHP0007	HCON encountered an IPC set message queue error.
WHP0008	HCON could not delete an IPC message queue.
WHP0009	HCON could not attach an IPC shared segment.
WHP0010	HCON could not detach an IPC shared segment.
WHP0011	HCON encountered an IPC shared segment allocation error.
WHP0012	HCON encountered an IPC shared segment start error.
WHP0013	HCON encountered an IPC shared segment set error.
WHP0014	HCON could not remove a shared segment.

LED Indicators

The table in this appendix defines the various numeric codes displayed on the system unit LED. For problem correction actions, consult the *AIX Problem Solving Guide and Reference* (IBM Corporation, 1993).

Value	Meaning
000	The kernel debugger has been entered; enter q dump at the console device to dump the system and wait for the flashing 888 code.
0c0	The user-requested dump completed successfully; the system halts.
0c2	A user-requested dump is in progress; wait for completion.
0c4	A partial user-requested dump completed; the system halts.
0c5	The user-requested dump could not be started and the system is now halted; wait for a subsequent error code.
0c6	A user-requested dump is being written to the secondary dump device; wait for completion.
0c7	A user-requested dump is being written to the remote server; wait for completion.
0c8	The system dump facilities are disabled; the system halts.
0c9	A system dump failed and the system is now halted; wait for a subsequent error code.
100	BIST (the *built-in self-test*) completed successfully.
101	BIST is running following a system reset.
102	BIST is running following a power-on reset.
103	BIST could not determine the system model number; the system halts.
104	BIST could not find the common on-chip processor bus address; the system halts.
105	BIST could not read from the on-chip sequencer EPROM; the system halts.
106	BIST detected a hardware module failure; the system halts.
111	The on-chip sequencer stopped during BIST; the system halts.
112	A checkstop occurred during BIST and could not be logged; the system halts.
113	Three successive checkstops have occurred during system restart; the system halts.
120	BIST is running the CRC (cyclical redundancy check) on the 8752 EPROM.
121	BIST detected an incorrect CRC for the on-chip sequencer EPROM; BIST continues.
122	BIST is running a CRC on the on-chip sequencer EPROM.
123	BIST detected an incorrect CRC for the on-chip sequencer NVRAM.

Value	Meaning
124	BIST is running a CRC on the on-chip sequencer NVRAM.
125	BIST detected an incorrect CRC on the time-of-day NVRAM.
126	BIST is running a CRC check on the time-of-day NVRAM.
127	BIST detected an incorrect CRC on the 8752 EPROM.
130	BIST is running the presence test (checks the reset button).
140	BIST has failed; the system is halted.
142	BIST has failed; the system is halted.
144	BIST has failed; the system is halted.
151	BIST is running the array-initialization program test.
152	BIST is running the direct-current logic self-test (DCLST).
153	BIST is running the alternating-current logic self-test (ACLST).
154	BIST is running the array self-test (AST).
160	BIST detected a missing Early Power-Off Warning (EPOW); the system halts.
164	BIST detected an error while reading from low NVRAM; the system halts.
165	BIST detected an error while writing to low NVRAM; the system halts.
166	BIST detected an error while reading from high NVRAM; the system halts.
167	BIST detected an error while writing to high NVRAM; the system halts.
168	BIST detected an error while reading the serial input/output register; the system halts.
169	BIST detected an error while writing to the serial input/output register; the system halts.
180	BIST checkstop logout in progress.
185	A checkstop has occurred during BIST; BIST continues.
187	BIST could not identify the chip release level in the checkstop logout data; the system halts.
195	BIST has completed the checkstop logout.
200	The security key is in the secure position; move it to normal or service to continue the boot process.
201	A checkstop occurred during system restart; the system halts.
203	An unexpected data storage interrupt occurred; the system halts.
204	An unexpected instruction storage interrupt occurred; the system halts.
205	An unexpected external interrupt was encountered; the system halts.
206	An unexpected alignment interrupt occurred; the system halts.
207	An unexpected program interrupt occurred; the system halts.
208	The floating-point processor is unavailable; the system halts.
209	General system fault; the system halts.
210	An unexpected switched virtual circuit interrupt occurred; the system halts.
211	A CRC in the IPL ROM failed during system restart; the system halts.
212	The processor failed the RAM power-on self-test (RPOST); the system halts.
213	No usable memory could be found by the RPOST; the system halts.
214	The power status register, the time-of-day clock, or the NVRAM has failed; the system halts.
215	The voltage level is too low to proceed with system restart; when the voltage increases to the correct level, system restart continues.
216	The IPL ROM code is being uncompressed and stored into memory.
217	The system has encountered the end of the boot devices list.
218	RPOST is testing for 1 Mbyte of available memory.
219	RPOST is generating the RPOST bitmap.

Value	Meaning
220	The IPL control block is being initialized.
221	The NVRAM failed a CRC while loading AIX; the system halts.
222	A normal-mode restart is being attempted from the standard planar-attached I/O devices in the NVRAM IPL devices list.
223	A normal-mode restart is being attempted from the SCSI-attached I/O devices in the NVRAM IPL devices list.
224	A normal-mode restart is being attempted from the 9333 disk drive subsystem specified in the NVRAM IPL devices list.
225	A normal-mode restart is being attempted from the bus-attached internal disk specified in the NVRAM IPL devices list.
226	A normal-mode restart is being attempted from the Ethernet adapter specified in the NVRAM IPL devices list.
227	A normal-mode restart is being attempted from the Token-Ring adapter specified in the NVRAM IPL devices list.
228	A normal-mode restart is being attempted from the expansion code device list in the NVRAM IPL devices list.
229	A normal-mode restart is being attempted from the devices in the NVRAM boot devices list, but none of the devices are valid; although the system continues to retry the operation, this code indicates a serious error.
230	A normal-mode restart is being attempted from the Family 2 Feature ROM in the IPL ROM devices list.
231	A normal-mode restart is being attempted from the Ethernet card specified by selection from the ROM menu.
232	A normal-mode restart is being attempted from the standard planar-attached I/O devices in the IPL ROM devices list.
233	A normal-mode restart is being attempted from the SCSI-attached I/O devices in the IPL ROM devices list.
234	A normal-mode restart is being attempted from the 9333 disk drive subsystem specified in the IPL ROM devices list.
235	A normal-mode restart is being attempted from the bus-attached internal disk specified in the IPL ROM devices list.
236	A normal-mode restart is being attempted from the Ethernet adapter specified in the IPL ROM devices list.
237	A normal-mode restart is being attempted from the Token-Ring adapter specified in the IPL ROM devices list.
238	A normal-mode restart is being attempted from the Token Ring adapter specified by selection from the ROM menu.
239	A normal-mode menu selection device failed to boot; although the system continues to retry the operation, this code indicates a serious error.
240	A service-mode restart is being attempted from the Family 2 Feature ROM in the NVRAM IPL devices list.
242	A service-mode restart is being attempted from the standard planar-attached I/O devices in the NVRAM IPL devices list.
243	A service-mode restart is being attempted from the SCSI-attached I/O devices in the NVRAM IPL devices list.
244	A service-mode restart is being attempted from the 9333 disk drive subsystem specified in the NVRAM IPL devices list.
245	A service-mode restart is being attempted from the bus-attached internal disk specified in the NVRAM IPL devices list.
246	A service-mode restart is being attempted from the Ethernet adapter specified in the NVRAM IPL devices list.

Value	Meaning
247	A service-mode restart is being attempted from the Token-Ring adapter specified in the NVRAM IPL devices list.
248	A service-mode restart is being attempted from the expansion code device list in the NVRAM IPL devices list.
249	A service-mode restart is being attempted from the devices in the NVRAM boot devices list, but none of the devices are valid; although the system continues to retry the operation; this code indicates a serious error.
250	A service-mode restart is being attempted from the Family 2 Feature ROM in the IPL ROM devices list.
252	A service-mode restart is being attempted from the standard planar-attached I/O devices in the IPL ROM devices list.
253	A service-mode restart is being attempted from the SCSI-attached I/O devices in the IPL ROM devices list.
254	A service-mode restart is being attempted from the 9333 disk drive subsystem specified in the IPL ROM devices list.
255	A service-mode restart is being attempted from the bus-attached internal disk specified in the IPL ROM devices list.
256	A service-mode restart is being attempted from the Ethernet adapter specified in the IPL ROM devices list.
257	A service-mode restart is being attempted from the Token-Ring adapter specified in the IPL ROM devices list.
258	A service-mode restart is being attempted from the Token-Ring adapter specified by selection from the ROM menu.
260	A boot menu is being displayed on the operator's console; the system is waiting for a response.
261	A display device could not be found; the system waits for an interrupt from a device on serial port 1.
262	A system keyboard could not be found; the system waits for a keyboard interrupt from the device on serial port 1.
263	A normal-mode restart is being attempted from the Family 2 Feature ROM in the NVRAM boot devices list.
271	The mouse and mouse-port POST (power-on self-test) is running.
272	The tablet port POST is running.
278	The video ROM POST is running.
281	The keyboard POST is running.
282	The parallel port POST is running.
283	The serial port POST is running.
284	The POWER Gt1 graphics adapter POST is running.
285	The POWER Gt3 graphics adapter POST is running.
286	The Token-Ring adapter POST is running.
287	The Ethernet adapter POST is running.
288	The adapter card slots are being interrogated.
289	The POWER Gt0 graphics adapter POST is running.
290	The I/O planar test is running.
291	The standard I/O planar POST is running.
292	The SCSI POST is running.
293	The bus-attached internal disk POST is running.
294	A bad single-inline-memory-module (SIMM) was detected.
295	The color graphics display POST is running.

Value	Meaning
296	The Family 2 Feature ROM POST is running.
297	The system model number could not be determined; the system halts.
298	The system is attempting a warm restart.
299	IPL ROM is passing control to code loaded in memory.
500	Interrogating the standard I/O slot.
501	Interrogating the card in slot 1.
502	Interrogating the card in slot 2.
503	Interrogating the card in slot 3.
504	Interrogating the card in slot 4.
505	Interrogating the card in slot 5.
506	Interrogating the card in slot 6.
507	Interrogating the card in slot 7.
508	Interrogating the card in slot 8.
510	Device configuration has started.
511	Device configuration is complete.
512	Device configuration files are being restored from media.
513	BOS (base operating system) files are being restored from media.
516	The network boot server is being contacted.
517	The root (/) and /usr file systems are being mounted from the network server.
518	The mount of the root (/) and /usr file systems from the network server was not successful; the system halts.
520	The bus configuration is running.
521	The /etc/inittab is corrupted or was started with incorrect options; the system halts.
522	The /etc/inittab file is corrupted or was started with conflicting options; the system halts.
523	The /etc/objrepos file is missing or inaccessible; the system halts.
524	The /etc/objrepos/Config[fru.5]Rules file is missing or inaccessible; the system halts.
525	The /etc/objrepos/CuDv file is missing or inaccessible; the system halts.
526	The /etc/objrepos/CuDvDr file is missing or inaccessible; the system halts.
527	The configuration manager was started with the boot phase 1 flag; the system halts.
528	The /etc/objrepos/Config[fru.5]Rules file is missing, inaccessible, or corrupted; the system halts.
529	The ODM database cannot be updated; either the root file system is full or the device containing the ODM is not working; the system halts.
530	The system could not save information about the base customized devices during phase 1 of the system boot; the system halts.
531	The /user/lib/objrepos/PdAt file is missing or inaccessible; the system halts.
532	The configuration manager has run out of memory; the system halts.
533	The /usr/lib/objrepos/PdDv file is missing, inaccessible, or corrupted; the system halts.
534	The configuration manager cannot lock the ODM (object data manager) database; the system halts.
535	A HIPPI diagnostics interface driver is being configured.
536	The /etc/objrepos/Config[fru.5]Rules is incorrect; the system halts.
537	The configuration manager detected an error when starting a configuration program; the system halts.
538	The configuration manager is passing control to a configuration method.
539	The configuration method is returning control back to the configuration manager.

Value	Meaning
551	The root volume group is being varied on.
552	The system was not able to varyon the root volume group; the system halts.
553	The /etc/inittab has been incorrectly modified or is corrupted; continuation is attempted.
554	The IPL device could not be opened or read; the system halts.
555	The fsck of the root file system failed; the system halts.
556	The boot logical volume is corrupted; the system halts.
557	The root file system cannot be mounted; the system halts.
558	There is not enough available memory to continue system restart; the system halts.
559	There is less than 2 Mbytes of memory left after loading the AIX kernel; the system halts.
571	The HIPPI common functions driver is being configured.
572	The HIPPI IPI-3 master-mode driver is being configured.
573	The HIPPI IPI-3 slave-mode driver is being configured.
574	The HIPPI IPI-3 user-level interface driver is being configured.
575	The 9570 disk-array driver is being configured.
576	A generic asynchronous device driver is being configured.
577	A generic SCSI device driver is being configured.
578	A generic common device driver is being configured.
579	A generic device driver is being configured.
580	A HIPPI-LE interface is being configured.
581	TCP/IP is being configured.
582	The Token-Ring data link control (DLC) is being configured.
583	The Ethernet DLC is being configured.
584	The IEEE Internet (802.3) DLC is being configured.
585	The SDLC DLC is being configured.
586	The X.25 (QLLC) DLC is being configured.
587	NETBIOS is being configured.
588	Bisynchronous read-write (BSCRW) is being configured.
589	A SCSI target mode device is being configured.
590	A diskless remote paging device is being configured.
591	A logical volume manager (LVM) device driver is being configured.
592	A high-function terminal (HFT) device driver is being configured.
593	A SNA (systems network architecture) device driver is being configured.
594	Asynchronous I/O is being defined and configured.
595	An X.31 pseudo-device is being configured.
596	A SNA DLC/LAPE pseudo-device is being configured.
597	An outboard communication server (OCS) is being configured.
598	An OCS host is being reconfigured.
599	FDDI data link control is being configured.
711	An unknown type of adapter is being identified and configured.
712	The graphic slot bus configuration is being run.
720	An unknown optical drive type is being configured.
721	An unknown type of disk or SCSI device is being identified and configured.
722	An unknown type of disk is being identified and configured.
723	An unknown type of CD-ROM or SCSI device driver is being identified and configured.

Value	Meaning
724	An unknown type of tape drive is being identified and configured.
725	An unknown type of display is being identified and configured.
726	An unknown type of input device is being identified and configured.
727	An asynchronous device is being identified and configured.
728	A parallel printer is being identified and configured.
729	An unknown type of parallel device is being identified and configured.
730	An unknown type of diskette drive is being identified and configured.
731	An unknown type of PTY (pseudo tTY device) is being identified and configured.
732	An unknown type of SCSI Initiator is being configured.
811	The processor complex is being identified and configured; the standard I/O processor is being configured.
812	System memory is being identified and configured.
813	The battery for the time-of-day, NVRAM, or system I/O control logic is being identified and configured.
814	NVRAM is being identified and configured.
815	The floating-point processor is being identified and configured.
816	The operator-panel logic is being identified and configured.
817	The time-of-day logic is being identified and configured.
819	The graphics input device adapter is being identified and configured.
821	The standard keyboard adapter is being identified and configured.
823	The standard mouse adapter is being identified and configured.
824	The standard tablet adapter is being identified and configured.
825	The standard speaker adapter is being identified and configured.
826	Serial port 1 is being identified and configured.
827	The parallel port adapter is being identified and configured.
828	The standard diskette adapter is being identified and configured.
831	Serial port 2 is being identified and configured.
834	A 64-port asynchronous controller is being identified and configured.
835	A 16-port asynchronous concentrator is being identified and configured.
836	A 128-port asynchronous controller is being identified and configured.
837	A 16-port remote asynchronous controller is being identified and configured.
841	An 8-port EIA-232 asynchronous adapter is being identified and configured.
842	An 8-port EIA-422A asynchronous adapter is being identified and configured.
843	An 8-port MIL-STD asynchronous adapter is being identified and configured.
847	A 16-port EIA-232 asynchronous adapter is being identified and configured.
848	A 16-port EIA-422 asynchronous adapter is being identified and configured.
849	An X.25 communications adapter is being identified and configured.
850	A Token-Ring network adapter is being identified and configured.
852	An Ethernet adapter is being identified and configured.
854	A 3270 connection is being identified and configured.
855	A 4-port multiprotocol adapter is being identified and configured.
857	An F-serial link adapter is being identified or configured.
858	A 508X adapter is being identified and configured.
859	An FDDI adapter is being identified and configured.
861	A serial optical channel converter is being identified and configured.
862	A 370 Parallel Channel adapter is being identified and configured.
865	An ESCON channel adapter is being identified and configured.

Value	Meaning
866	A SCSI adapter is being identified and configured.
867	An asynchronous expansion adapter is being identified and configured.
868	An integrated SCSI adapter is being identified and configured.
869	A SCSI adapter is being identified and configured.
870	A serial disk adapter is being identified and configured.
871	The graphics subsystem adapter is being identified and configured.
872	The grayscale graphics adapter is being identified and configured.
874	The color graphics adapter is being identified and configured.
876	The 8-bit color graphics processor is being identified and configured.
877	The POWER Gt3 or POWER Gt4 graphics adapter is being identified and configured.
878	The POWER Gt4 graphics process card is being identified and configured.
880	The POWER Gt1 graphics adapter is being identified and configured.
887	The integrated Ethernet adapter is being identified and configured.
888	Unexpected system halt if flashing; LED display test if steady.
889	A SCSI adapter is being identified and configured.
891	A non-IBM SCSI adapter is being identified and configured.
892	A non-IBM display adapter is being identified and configured.
893	A non-IBM LAN adapter is being identified and configured.
894	A non-IBM asynchronous adapter is being identified and configured.
895	A non-IBM IEEE 488 adapter is being identified and configured.
896	A non-IBM VME bus adapter is being identified and configured.
897	A 370 channel emulator is being identified and configured.
898	The POWER Gt1x graphics adapter is being identified and configured.
899	A 3490E tape drive is being identified and configured.
901	A non-IBM SCSI device is being identified and configured.
902	A non-IBM display device is being identified and configured.
903	A non-IBM asynchronous device is being identified and configured.
904	A non-IBM parallel device is being identified and configured.
905	A non-IBM device is being identified and configured.
906	A 2 Gbytes SCSI differential disk drive is being identified and configured.
907	A 1 Gbyte SCSI differential disk drive is being identified and configured.
908	A 56-bit 8mm differential-ended tape drive is being identified and configured.
916	A non-IBM non-SCSI tape adapter is being identified and configured.
917	A 2 Gbyte 16-bit SCSI differential disk drive is being identified and configured.
918	A 2 Gbyte 16-bit single-ended SCSI disk drive is being identified and configured.
920	A bridge box is being identified and configured.
921	A 101-key keyboard is being identified and configured.
922	A 102-key keyboard is being identified and configured.
923	A Kanji keyboard is being identified and configured.
924	A two-button mouse is being identified and configured.
925	A three-button mouse is being identified and configured.
926	A 5083-21 tablet is being identified and configured.
927	A 5083-22 tablet is being identified and configured.
928	A standard speaker is being identified and configured.
929	Tablet dials are being identified and configured.
930	A lighted programmable function keyboard is being identified and configured.
931	An Internet Protocol router is being identified and configured.

Value	Meaning
933	An asynchronous planar is being identified and configured.
934	An asynchronous expansion drawer is being identified and configured.
935	A 3.5-in diskette drive is being identified and configured.
936	A 5.25-in diskette drive is being identified and configured.
937	A HIPPI adapter is being configured.
943	A 3480/3490 control unit is being identified and configured.
948	A portable disk drive is being identified and configured.
949	An unknown type of direct bus-attached disk drive is being identified and configured.
950	Unknown SCSI options are being configured.
951	A 670 Mbytes SCSI disk drive is being identified and configured.
952	A 355 Mbytes SCSI disk drive is being identified and configured.
953	A 320 Mbytes SCSI disk drive is being identified and configured.
954	A 400 Mbytes SCSI disk drive is being identified and configured.
955	An 857 Mbytes SCSI disk drive is being identified and configured.
956	A 670 Mbytes SCSI disk drive is being identified and configured.
957	A bus-attached disk drive is being identified and configured.
958	A 160 Mbytes bus-attached disk drive is being identified and configured.
959	A 160 Mbytes SCSI disk drive is being identified and configured.
960	A 1.37 Gbytes SCSI disk drive is being identified and configured.
968	A 1 Gbytes SCSI disk drive is being identified and configured.
970	A 1/2-in 9-track tape drive is being identified and configured.
971	A 150 Mbytes, 1/4-in tape drive is being identified and configured.
972	An 8 mm SCSI tape drive is being identified and configured.
973	An unknown type of SCSI tape drive is being identified and configured.
974	A CD-ROM drive is being identified and configured.
977	An audio capture and playback adapter is being identified and configured.
981	A 540 Mbytes SCSI disk drive is being identified and configured.
985	A M-video capture adapter is being identified and configured.
986	A 1.2 Gbytes SCSI drive in a 2.4 Gbytes unit is being identified and configured.
987	A CD-ROM drive is being identified and configured.
989	A 200 Mbytes SCSI disk drive is being identified and configured.
990	A 2 Gbytes SCSI disk drive is being identified and configured.
994	An 8 mm tape drive is being identified and configured.
995	A 1/2-in, 1.2 Gbytes tape drive is being identified and configured.
996	A single-port, multiprotocol communications adapter is being identified and configured.
997	A twisted-pair FDDI adapter is being identified and configured.
998	A 4 mm tape drive is being identified and configured.
c00	AIX install / maintenance tape loaded successfully.
c01	Insert the AIX install / maintenance diskette.
c03	The wrong diskette has been inserted; insert the correct diskette.
c04	An unrecoverable error has occurred; the system halts.
c05	A diskette error occurred; the system halts.
c06	The rc.boot configuration script cannot determine the type of system boot; the system halts.
c07	Insert the next diskette.
c08	The RAM file system started incorrectly; the system halts.

Value	Meaning
c09	The system is accessing the diskette drive; wait for the action to complete.
c20	An unexpected system halt occurred; the system is configured to enter the kernel debug program instead of performing a system dump.
c21	The network could not be configured; the system halts.
c22	The tftp command could not read the clienthostname.info file; the system halts.
c24	The clienthostname.info file could not be read; the system halts.
c25	The remote miniroot file system could not be loaded; the system halts.
c26	The /usr file system was not mounted during the remote boot; the system halts.
c27	The machine is trying to perform a remote boot from a device other than a Token-Ring or Ethernet adapter.
c28	The machine cannot set the attributes of a network device.
c29	The machine is unable to configure the network device.
c31	The system is waiting for the user to choose a console; follow the instructions on the display attached to the system unit.
c32	A high-function terminal is being configured as the console.
c33	A tTY device is being configured as the console.
c34	A file is being configured as the console.
c99	The diagnostic programs have completed and a console cannot be found; the system halts.

Glossary

access control list (ACL)   Access control lists are used in AIX to extend the permissions on a file beyond the basic rights for a user, group, or others. ACLs allow for the explicit specification of permissions by user or group name.

AIX (Advanced Interactive eXecutive)   IBM's version of UNIX.

AIXwindows   The combination of X-windows and MOTIF used by AIX to provide a graphical user interface.

alias   An equivalent name; often used within a shell to rename or simplify a command.

ANSI (American National Standards Institute)   The organization responsible for coordinating United States standardization groups and committees. A constituent member of ISO.

ARP (Address Resolution Protocol)   A TCP/IP protocol that dynamically determines the physical address of a system based upon the IP address of the system.

ARPANET   The world's first packet-switching network. Sponsored by the U.S. Department of Defense, this internetworking project was the forerunner of today's Internet.

ASCII (American National Standard Code for Information Interchange)   The basic character set used by AIX.

background process   A program which runs detached from a terminal.

batch process   A group of programs which run as a unit; typically run detached from a terminal.

BIST (built-in self-test)   A test performed by the system hardware when the system is turned on.

block device   Devices, such as disk or tape drives, which store and transfer information in blocks of bytes as opposed to byte-by-byte.

BNU (Basic Networking Utilities)   IBM's name for UUCP.

boot   To initialize the system.

BOS (base operating system)   The core functionality of AIX.

Bourne shell   The original user interface (shell) of UNIX.

bridge   A device that connects two or more physical networks; the purpose being the exchange of information to be transferred between the networks.

bsd (Berkeley Software Distribution)   The name given to those versions of UNIX which are based upon the modifications made by the University of California at Berkeley.

buffer   An area of storage.

buffer pool   A group of buffers all reserved for the same purpose.

C shell   A C programming languagelike user interface for AIX.

character device   Devices, such as terminals and printers, which transfer data on a byte-by-byte basis.

child process   A process created by another process, the parent process. The child process has separate, but identically initialized data, text, and stack memory segments.

client   A requestor of some form of service from another machine, a server.

command substitution   To run a command and treat the output of the command as if it were a variable.

compiler   A program that converts the symbolic representation of another program into a machine executable form.

conditional execution   To perform one of many specific functions based upon the results of a test.

configuration   The system unit and all of the options used to make a working system.

console   The master terminal where system messages are displayed.

coprocess   A background process which is directly connected to another process via the input and output streams.

CRC (cyclical redundancy check)   A mathematical function performed upon transferred data; the values calculated before and after transmission are compared to verify that the transmission was correct.

current directory   The current location in the file system structure. All relative path names begin from the current directory.

daemon   An ongoing background process which provides a service for other processes on the system.

datagram   A unit of routed data.

DCE (distributed computing environment)   The OSF standard for performing distributed processing functions.

defunct process   Synonymous with zombie process.

demand paging   The process by which an operating system copies pages of the address space of a task to and from disk and real memory.

device driver   A program which provides the interface between the operating system and a physical device.

device handler   A low-level driver routine that controls physical functions of the applicable device.

directory   A directory manages the cataloging functions of the file system. It associates names with files and separates files into groups.

DLC (data link control)   The interface between the networking device and the networking software.

DNS (domain name server)   A set of distributed databases providing information such as IP address to system name correspondences.

dumb terminal   A character-based, display device.

EBCDIC (extended binary coded decimal interchange code) A computer code that uses eight binary positions to represent a single character, giving a possible maximum of 256 characters.

ed The original line-oriented editor of the UNIX system.

EMACS A popular public domain text editor found on UNIX systems.

ESCON (Enterprise System Connection Architecture) A fiber-optic cabling architecture used to connect computer components.

FDDI (Fiber Distributed Data Interface) A standard for high-speed data transfer.

FIFO files Special files, used as pipes, which are read and written to on a first-in-first-out basis.

file A source of input; a location to send output; a contiguous related group of bytes organized into a uniquely addressed unit.

file link A file which serves only as a reference to another file.

file system The basis of the UNIX implementation of files; that portion of a disk which supports a complete directory structure.

flag An option supplied to an AIX command.

FLIH (First-Level Interrupt Handler) The software which handles the physical messages from a device.

foreground process A program which runs connected to a terminal.

FTP (file transfer protocol) A TCP/IP protocol which enables users to manage and copy data across systems.

full pathname The name of a file starting from the root directory "/".

function Used in a shell to define an action or group of actions to occur when a specific command is entered.

gateway An IP router.

group A collection of related users.

GUI (graphical user interface) A user interface based upon graphics as opposed to the traditional character-based interface.

herald Text that is displayed with the login prompt.

HFT (High Function Terminal) A terminal which can support graphics.

history The ability to keep a record of past commands.

home directory The directory which is the current directory immediately after a user logs into the system.

host A computer system providing some type of service to another system or a user.

icon A graphical symbol which represents an object.

INed A full-screen editor specific to AIX.

InfoExplorer An on-line hypertext system for accessing documentation.

inode The first block of a file which contains the statistical information about the file.

Internet The global-network based upon TCP\IP and the former ARPANET.

internet A set of networks connected by IP routers which appears to its users as a single network.

interrupts   Well-defined interfaces which are invoked by hardware to send and receive information from the kernel.

IP (Internet Protocol)   The TCP/IP protocol responsible for transporting datagrams across an internet.

IP Address   A 32-bit address that identifies a network interface.

IPL (initial program load)   A synonym for boot or system initialization.

ISO (International Standards Organization)   An international body founded to promote trade and cooperative progress in science and technology.

JFS (journaled filed system)   The default file system in AIX which provides automatic journaling.

kernel   The central core (or nucleus) of the operating system.

Korn shell   The most modern, and default, shell supported in AIX.

logical volume   A grouping of discontiguous physical disk space which is presented to the user as if it were a contiguous, linear physical space.

LVM (Logical Volume Manager)   The system component which controls logical volumes.

metacharacter   A character with more than one meaning; the meaning of the metacharacter is determined by the position of the character within a given string.

Motif   The graphical user interface used by AIX.

mounted file system   A file system which has been made available to the operating system.

multiprocessing.   The process by which the operating system divides the processor's time among several different tasks.

name resolution   The process of converting a logical address to a physical network address.

NCS (network computing system)   A set of tools for developing applications in a distributed environment.

network   A group of independent hosts connected to shared computing resources.

NFS (network file system)   A file system used to facilitate sharing of information among hosts on a network.

NIS (network information system)   A mechanism for transparently sharing system management and information across a network.

node   Equivalent to a host.

NVRAM (nonvolatile random access memory)   Memory which can be written to, but only by special system routines.

OCS (Outboard Communications Servers)   A communications controller which is not mounted inside of the system unit.

ODM (Object Data Manager)   The ODM is used to maintain the configuration databases of AIX.

operating system   System software which enables and controls the hardware in an effort to produce useful work.

OSF (Open Systems Foundation)   A consortium which defines open standards for a portable operating environment.

paging space   An area of disk storage used for holding portions of processes' address space which are not currently being used.

parent process   The creator of a child process.

physical volume   A hard disk.

pipe   A memory buffer (represented as a special file) which is used to share data between two processes.

planar   The system board.

POSIX   A set of standards produced by the Institute of Electrical and Electronics Engineering (IEEE).

POST (power-on self-test)   A test performed when the hardware is turned on.

priority   The relative significance of a process within the group of all processes.

process   An executing program or shell.

PTY (pseudo tTY device)   A virtual terminal device.

queue   The logical name of a device or devices which perform a shared processing function.

RAM (random access memory)   Volatile memory.

redirection   The process whereby standard input, standard output, or standard error may be directed to another location within the file system.

relative pathname   The pathname of a file starting from the current directory.

RISC (reduced instruction set computing)   An architecture for processor design which uses repetitions of simple instructions to perform complex instructions.

ROM (read-only memory)   Nonvolatile memory.

root directory   The master directory of the file system; all other directories may be referenced by starting at the root directory.

router   A system used to connect separate networks into an internet and route traffic among those networks.

RPOST (RAM power-on self-test)   A test performed when the hardware is turned on which tests the validity of the installed RAM.

SCSI (small computer system interface)   An industry standard architecture for attaching removable media, such as tapes, disks, and CD-ROMs.

SDLC (Synchronous Data Link Control)   A type of DLC which relies on synchronized messages switching between the networking partners.

shell   A command interpreter.

shell script   A program written in a shell language.

signal   An interrupt sent to a process by another process or the operating system.

SIMM (Single Inline Memory Module)   The chips which contain the memory of the system.

SLIH (Second-Level Interrupt Handler)   Typically, software which handles errors for the FLIH.

SMIT (System Management Interface Tool)   A menu-based tool for managing AIX.

SNA (Systems Network Architecture)   An IBM proprietary protocol used for controlling large networks.

spool   A subsystem used to route output to printers and input to execution queues.

stanza   A group of line or more lines within a file which are related to a particular function.

string   A series of related characters.

subdirectory   A directory which is one of the files attributed to another directory.

System call   Well-defined interfaces which are invoked by user programs to send and receive information from the kernel.

TCP (Transmission Control Protocol)   The network protocol that deals with the quality of transmission of information from originating to destination machines in an internet.

TCP/IP (Transmission Control Protocol/Internet Protocol)   An abbreviation used to refer to the entire suite of network protocols used in an internet.

UUCP (UNIX-to-UNIX copy)   The original UNIX networking protocol and utilities.

vi   A full-screen text editor.

virtual memory   A technique that allows the operating system to use more real memory than is actually present on the system.

volume groups   A group of physical volumes.

VPD (vital product data)   The base information about software products installed on the system.

working directory   Synonymous with current directory.

Xstation   A graphics-capable terminal.

zombie   A process which has ceased processing but still has associated operating system resources.

Abbreviations

ACE	access control entry
ACL	access control list
ACLST	alternating correct logic self-test
AIX	Advanced Interactive eXecutive
ANSI	American National Standards Institute
APAR	Authorized Program Analysis Report
APPC	Advanced program-to-program communication
ARP	Address Resolution Protocol
ASCII	American National Standard Code for Information Interchange
BCPL	Basic Combined Programming Language
BGP	Border Gateway Protocol
BIST	built-in self-test
BNU	Basic Networking Utilities
BOS	base operating system
bsd	Berkeley Software Distribution
CD-ROM	compact disk read-only memory
CRC	cyclical redundancy check
CTS	clear to send
DARPA	Advanced Research Projects Agency of the U.S. Department of Defense
DASD	direct access storage device
DCE	distributed computing environment
DCLST	direct current logic self-test
DLC	data link control
DNS	domain name system
DOS	disk operating system
DSR	data set ready
DTR	data terminal ready

EGP	Exterior Gateway Protocol
EOF	end-of-file
EPOW	early power off warning
ESCON	Enterprise System Connection Architecture
FDDI	Fiber Distributed Data Interface
FLIH	first-level interrupt handler
FTP	File Transfer Protocol
GUI	graphical user interface
HCON	Host Connection Program
HELLO	Hello Protocol
HFT	high function terminal
IP	Internet Protocol
IPC	Inter-Process Communication
IPL	initial program load
ISO	International Standards Organization
JFS	journaled file system
LAN	local area network
LLC	logical link control
LPP	licensed program product
LV	logical volume
LVM	logical volume manager
mbufs	memory management routines
NCS	network computing system
NFS	network file system
NIC	Network Information Center
NIS	network information system
NOP	no operation
NVRAM	nonvolatile random access memory
OCS	outboard communications servers
ODM	object data manager
OSF	Open Software Foundation
PID	Process identification number
POST	power-on self-test
POWER	Performance Enhancement with Enhanced RISC
PSLA	primary system/serial link adapter
PTY	pseudo tTY device
PV	physical volume
RAM	random access memory
RCS	Revision Control System
RIP	Routing Information Protocol

RISC	reduced instruction set computing
ROM	read-only memory
rootvg	root volume group
ROS	read-only storage
RPOST	RAM power-on self-test
SAK	Secure Attention Key
SAP/LS	Service Access Point/Local Service
SCSI	small computer system interface
SDLC	synchronous data link control
SIMM	single inline memory module
SLIH	second-level interrupt handler
SLIP	Serial Line Interface Protocol
SMIT	System Management Interface Tool
SMTP	Simple Mail Transfer Protocol
SNA	Systems Network Architecture
SNMP	Simple Network Management Protocol
SRC	system resource controller
SVR4	System V Release 4
SWVPD	software vital product data
TCB	trusted computing base
TCP	Transmission Control Protocol
TCP/IP	Transmission Control Protocol/Internet Protocol
TELNET GA	Telnet Go Ahead
TELNET IP	Telnet Interrupt Process
TLB	transition look-aside buffers
TTL	Time to Live
UDP	User Datagram Protocol
UUCP	UNIX-to-UNIX copy
VGDA	volume group descriptor area
VGSA	volume group status area
vi	visual editor
VM	Virtual Machine
VPD	vital product data
VTAM	virtual telecommunications access method
XNS	Xerox Networking System

Bibliography

AIX Version 3.2 Commands Reference, vols. 1–4 (GBOF-1802), IBM Corporation, 1993.

AIX Version 3.2 Editing Concepts and Procedures (SC23-2212), IBM Corporation, 1992.

AIX Version 3.2 General Programming Concepts (SC23-2365), IBM Corporation, 1993.

AIX Version 3.2 Installation Guide (SC23-2341), IBM Corporation, 1993.

AIX Version 3.2 Kernel Extensions and Device Support Programming Concepts (SC23-2207), IBM Corporation, 1992.

AIX Version 3.2 Messages Guide and Reference (SC23-2530), IBM Corporation, 1993.

AIX Version 3.2 Performance Monitoring and Tuning Guide (SC23-2365), IBM Corporation, 1993.

AIX Version 3.2 Problem Solving Guide and Reference (SC23-2204), IBM Corporation, 1993.

AIX Version 3.2 System Management Guide: Communications and Networks (SC23-2487), IBM Corporation, 1993.

AIX Version 3.2 System Management Guide: Operating System and Devices (SC23-2486), IBM Corporation, 1993.

AIX Version 3.2 System User's Guide (SC23-2377), IBM Corporation, 1992.

AIX Version 3.2 Technical Reference, vols. 1–11 (GBOF-1539), IBM Corporation, 1993.

AIX Xstation Manager/6000 System Management Guide (SC23-2264), IBM Corporation, 1993.

Bach, M. J., *The Design of the UNIX Operating System,* Prentice Hall, Englewood Cliffs, NJ, 1986.

Chakravarty, D., *POWER RISC System/6000: Concepts, Facilities, and Architecture,* McGraw-Hill, New York, NY, 1994.

Feit, S., *TCP/IP: Architecture, Protocols, and Implementation,* McGraw-Hill, New York, NY, 1993.

Kernighan, B. W., and Pike, R., *The UNIX Programming Environment,* Prentice Hall, Englewood Cliffs, NJ, 1984.

Leininger, K. E., *UNIX Developer's Tool Kit,* McGraw-Hill, New York, NY, 1994.

Managing NFS and NIS, O'Reilly & Associates, Inc., 1993.

Printing for Fun and Profit Under AIX Version 3 (GG34-3570), IBM Corporation, 1992.

Rosenberg, B., *KornShell Programming Tutorial,* Addison-Wesley, Reading, MA, 1991.

sendmail, O'Reilly & Associates, Inc., 1993.

TCP/IP Network Administration, O'Reilly & Associates, Inc.

termcap & terminfo, O'Reilly & Associates, Inc., 1991.

Using UUCP and Usenet, O'Reilly & Associates, Inc., 1987.

Index